Symbolic Interaction

A Reader in Social Psychology

Symbolic Interaction

A Reader in Social Psychology

edited by

Jerome G. Manis

Western Michigan University

Bernard N. Meltzer

Central Michigan University

ALLYN AND BACON BOSTON

Library of Congress Catalog Number: 67-20645

Printed in the United States of America

First printing . . . . . July, 1967
Second printing . . . . November, 1967

PREFACE

This book is, we believe, the *first* attempt to bring together a sizable number of previously published contributions to symbolic interactionist theory,[1] a theory, or orientation, which has influenced most American sociologists specializing in social psychology.[2]

The historical development of symbolic interactionism has been traced by several writers.[3] Its roots are to be found in the rationalism of John Locke, the foreshadowing of the role-taking process by such "Scottish Moralists" as John Hume and Adam Smith, the idealist epistemology of Kent, and other diverse sources. Its emergence as a distinct perspective in social psychology occurred in the work of John Dewey, Charles Horton Cooley, John Mark Baldwin, William I. Thomas, Florian Znaniecki, and, most notably, George Herbert Mead. Mead, the chief architect of symbolic interactionism, lectured at the University of Chicago between 1893 and 1931, and books based upon lecture-notes taken by students in his classes were published after his death in 1931.[4]

[1] A book by Rose compiles 34 articles written from the standpoint of symbolic interactionism; however, all but nine of these were written specifically for his book. See Arnold M. Rose (editor), *Human Behavior and Social Processes* (Boston: Houghton Mifflin Company, 1962).

[2] The more widely used social psychology textbooks incorporating symbolic interaction theory have been: E. T. Krueger and Walter C. Reckless, *Social Psychology* (New York: Longmans, Green and Company, 1930); Walter Coutu, *Emergent Human Nature* (New York: Alfred A. Knopf, 1949); Alfred R. Lindesmith and Anselm L. Strauss, *Social Psychology* (New York: The Dryden Press, 1949, Revised, 1956); Robert E. L. Faris, *Social Psychology* (New York: The Ronald Press Company, 1952); Hubert Bonner, *Social Psychology* (New York: American Book Company, 1953); Hans Gerth and C. Wright Mills, *Character and Social Structure* (New York: Harcourt, Brace & World, Inc., 1953); Tamotsu Shibutani, *Society and Personality* (Englewood Cliffs, N. J.: Prentice-Hall, Inc., 1961).

[3] See, for example, Fay Berger Karpf, *American Social Psychology* (New York: McGraw-Hill Book Company, Inc., 1932), *passim;* Floyd Nelson House, *The Development of Sociology* (McGraw-Hill Book Company, Inc., 1936), Chapter XXVII; Don Martindale, *The Nature and Types of Sociological Theory* (Boston: Houghton Mifflin Company, 1960), Chapter 14.

[4] Of most relevance is *Mind, Self and Society* (Chicago: The University of

Since then, the two foremost exponents of the orientation have been Herbert G. Blumer and the late Manford H. Kuhn. At the University of Chicago and, currently, the University of California at Berkeley, Blumer has continued to lead what can properly be called "the Chicago school" of symbolic interactionism. Stressing the *processual* character of human behavior and the need for "sympathetic introspection" in the study of human behavior, the school includes most of the writers represented in this book. Kuhn's "Self Theory," based at the State University of Iowa, has sought to "operationalize" symbolic interactionism by reconceptualizing the self in structural terms, by abandoning such "nonempirical" concepts as Mead's "I," and by developing paper-and-pencil measures of the self.

The organization of the readings in this book is quite simple. Part I introduces the reader to the fundamental concepts, propositions and methods of symbolic interactionism; Parts II, III, and IV organize readings under rubrics corresponding to the words in the title of Mead's vastly influential book. Our transposition of the order of these words more accurately reflects the Meadian emphasis upon the priority of society to the rise of individual selves and minds. Part V gives attention to readings which are less concerned with the explication of concepts than with their applications in exploring a wide range of topics. Following each Part is a briefly annotated "Selected Bibliography," which suggests additional readings for the interested reader.

The introductory comments for each Part have been kept brief. By selecting material that would, largely, "speak for itself," we have reduced to a minimum the need for editorial comment.

In selecting material for this collection, we were confronted by an embarrassment of riches. Only a small portion of the works we considered worthwhile is included, because of limitations of space. Conspicuous omissions are the writings of Ernst Cassirer, Kurt Riezler, Walter Coutu, and Arnold Rose. What we present to the reader, therefore, aims at representativeness, not comprehensiveness. The criteria guiding our selection of items are several. We have sought a judicious blend of "classics" and more recent works, of speculative and research products. We have given preference to items not readily available to students in multiple copies, to items that would be readable by undergraduate students, and to items by a number of different authors rather than by a few "name" people. In addition, we have tried to avoid fragmentation of selections; articles appear in their entirety, and excerpts from books are self-sufficient units of thought.

A word of explanation is needed about our omission of readings from Mead's works. We considered such readings superfluous for the following

---

Chicago Press, 1934), edited by Charles W. Morris.

reasons: the extensive citations of his thinking in various other selections, the inclusion of a summary of his ideas, and the accessibility of his major ideas in college libraries and bookstores.[5]

This collection is designed, primarily, for use as supplementary reading in courses in social psychology, especially those in which intensive attention is given to symbolic interactionism. Our hopes for the book stress its stimulation, not of doctrinaire devotion, but of critical assessment of that perspective.

We are indebted to the various authors, journals, and publishers out of whose materials we constructed this compilation. In a very real sense, the book is the product of their labors. Both of us also acknowledge the important role played by Herbert Blumer's courses at the University of Chicago in directing our attention and interest to the subject of this book.

[5] Books summarizing Mead's position or including selections from his work abound. See, for example: Grace Chin Lee, *George Herbert Mead* (New York: King's Crown Press, 1945); Paul E. Pfuetze, *The Social Self* (New York: Bookman Associates, 1954); Anselm Strauss, editor, *George Herbert Mead on Social Psychology* (Chicago: The University of Chicago Press, 1964); Andrew J. Reck, editor, *Selected Writings: George Herbert Mead* (New York-The Bobbs-Merrill Company, Inc., 1964).

CONTENTS

PART III.
SELF, 215

PART V.
RESEARCH IMPLICATIONS AND APPLICATIONS, 369

Part I. ❧ Theory and Methods

Symbolic interactionism constitutes both a theoretical perspective within social psychology and, in the view of many of its interpreters and critics, a methodological orientation as well. Its concern with the "inner, " or phenomenological, aspects of human behavior is considered by them to have both substantive and research-technique implications. The following selections present some of the fundamental concepts and propositions held in common by symbolic interactionists. In addition, they indicate some ot the divergent views on how the validity of such theoretical materials can be tested. These views range from a demand for a special methodology that lays stress upon "feeling one's way inside the experience of the actor" to one that coincides with the traditional natural-scientific method.

The controversies over theory and method were accentuated during the latter part of the nineteenth and early part of the twentieth centuries. During this period, the natural sciences were successful in their efforts to understand, predict and control the physical world. Their achievements led scholars to examine the distinctiveness of the social world and the applicability of natural-science methods.

Perhaps, we can clarify the nature of some of the major ideas at issue by briefly contrasting the highly antithetical views of George Herbert Mead, exemplar of symbolic interactionism, and John B. Watson, founder of the school of behaviorism in psychology. Like Watsonian radical behaviorism, Mead's approach includes the observable actions of individuals; but, unlike the former, it conceives "behavior" in broad enough terms to include *covert* activity. This inclusion is deemed necessary to understanding the distinctive character of human conduct, which Mead considers a qualitatively different emergent from infrahuman behavior. Watson's behaviorism, on the other hand, reduces human behavior to the mechanisms found on the infrahuman level. Thus, while Watson insists upon a strictly "scientific" study of overt behavior, Mead allows for an intuitive, *verstehende* investigation of aspects of behavior excluded from the former's purview.

Today, among symbolic interactionists, the debate takes a less extreme form. All agree that the cognitive and affective elements of human conduct must be studied; the point of contention is the extent to which the more "subjective," non-communicable techniques of study may be used.

A related point of contention concerns the differential importance of social and psychic forces. In its earliest form, this debate centered upon "nature versus nurture"; that is, environment as compared to heredity.

This difference in perspective may be illustrated by the polar positions taken by the first two textbooks published, in 1908, under the title *Social Psychology.* Edward A. Ross, a sociologist, viewed the individual as coerced by the social processes of suggestion and imitation. In contrast, William H. MacDougall, a psychologist, traced social interaction and institutions to individual "instincts."

While these positions are now considered to be oversimplified, social psychologists still differ in their emphasis on the relative significance of the individual and society. Symbolic interactionists stress the primacy of society. Yet, they are also inclined to consider the individual as an active, creative source of behavior.

Contemporary symbolic interactionists credit Cooley, Dewey, and Mead with the converging interests and contributions responsible for the widespread influence of this perspective. During nearly four decades as a philosopher at the University of Chicago, Mead formulated and taught his developing theory. His approach, which he called "social behaviorism," is summarized in the article by Meltzer. We hope that this resumé of Mead's basic assumptions and concepts will encourage the reader to delve into its major source, *Mind, Self and Society.*

Freud's great contributions to psychiatry, psychology, and sociology permit a valuable bench-mark for assessing Mead's work. Swanson's comparison reveals some of the similarities and differences in their approaches to social behavior. Even more pertinent to our concern is the critical analysis which this comparison generates.

The article by Kuhn reviews recent major developments. The contributions of "self-defined" symbolic interactionists, as well as non-adherents, serve as the basis for his excellent integration of these contemporary achievements.

Although the first two articles focus primarily on substantive theory, the others have been selected for their methodological emphasis. The Cooley article is a classic example. In it, he distinguishes the methods he believes necessary for understanding human behavior from those appropriate for the study of other phenomena. His exposition of "sympathetic introspection" integrates closely with his discussion in a later selection (page 159) of sympathy and the related sentiments constituting "human nature." Taken together, the two selections suggest that the nature of man both requires and provides certain essential tools for the study of himself.

Although Mead has been described by John Dewey as "a seminal mind of the first order," his contributions were almost exclusively theoretical, not empirical. The impetus to research awaited Blumer's attempts to systematize and clarify the conceptual apparatus of this theory. The selection by Blumer included in Part I, an earlier article "Science Without Concepts," and the leading article in Part II offer some indication of his contribution. Blumer raises critical questions about the procedures of "variable analysis," the criteria for selecting variables, and the methods of interpretation.

In several important papers, Bolton has confronted some of the central theoretical and methodological issues in sociology and social psychology. The recent popularity of the term "behavioral science" is the starting point of the article chosen for this collection. In it, he asks whether a methodological rationale is a fruitful basis for a scientific division of labor.

The two concluding articles exemplify the research techniques of "Chicago" and "Iowa" researchers. Becker and Geer discuss the distinctive features and contributions of participant observation, while Kuhn and McPartland introduce the Twenty Statements Test. Later sections, particularly Part V, include additional illustrations of the research procedures of contemporary symbolic interactionists.

1. Mead's Social Psychology

Bernard N. Meltzer

A. Preliminary Remarks

While Mead's system of Social Psychology is given its fullest exposition in *Mind, Self and Society,* each of three other books (as well as a few articles) rounds out the complete picture.

It should be pointed out at this juncture that Mead himself published no full-length systematic statement of his theory. All four of the books bearing his authorship are posthumously collected and edited works. They comprise a loose accumulation of his lecture notes, fragmentary manuscripts, and tentative drafts of unpublished essays. Since the chief aim of his editors has been completeness — rather than organization — the books consist, in considerable part, of alternative formulations, highly repetitive materials, and sketchily developed ideas.

Nevertheless, a brief description of these volumes is in order, since they constitute the major source-materials concerning Mead's social psychology.

Philosophy of the Present (1932) contains the Paul Carus Foundation lectures delivered by Mead in 1930, a year before his death. These lectures present a philosophy of history from the pragmatist's point of view. Moreover, this volume presents his ideas on the analogous developments of social experience and of scientific hypotheses.

Mind, Self and Society (1943) is chiefly a collection of lectures delivered to his classes in Social Psychology at the University of Chicago.

Movements of Thought in the 19th Century (1936) is largely a collection of lectures delivered to his classes in the History of Ideas.

Philosophy of the Act (1938), according to Paul Schilpp, represents a fairly *systematic* statement of the philosophy of pragmatism. This "systematic" statement I found (as did G.S. Lee) to be made up of essays and miscellaneous fragments, which are technical and repetitious, obscure and difficult.

A final observation regarding the content of these books should be made: Mead's orientation is generally *philosophical.* Rather than marshall-

From *The Social Psychology of George Herbert Mead,* pp, 10-31, by Bernard N. Meltzer, 1964, Center for Sociological Research, Western Michigan University.

ing his own empirical evidence, he uses the findings of various sciences and employs frequent apt and insightful illustrations from everyday life. These illustrations usually are not used to provide points, but rather to serve as data to be analyzed in terms of his scheme.

Before launching upon a presentation of Mead's social-psychological theories, it might be wise to explain his designation of his viewpoint as that of "Social Behaviorism." By this term Mead means to refer to the description of behavior at the distinctively human level. Thus, for social behaviorism, the basic datum is the social act. As we shall later see, the study of social acts entails concern with the covert aspects of behavior. Further, the concept of the "social act" implies that human conduct and experience has a fundamental social dimension — that the social context is an inescapable element in distinctively human actions.

Like Watsonian radical behaviorism, Mead's social behaviorism starts with the observable actions of individuals; but *unlike* the former, social behaviorism conceives behavior in broad enough terms to include *covert* activity. This inclusion is deemed necessary to understanding the distinctive character of human conduct, which Mead considers a qualitatively different emergent [from] infrahuman behavior. Watson's behaviorism, on the other hand, reduces human behavior to the very same mechanisms as are found on the infrahuman level. As a corollary, Watson sees the social dimension of human behavior as merely a sort of external influence upon the individual. Mead, by contrast, views generically human behavior as *social* behavior, human acts as *social* acts. For Mead, both the content and the very existence of distinctively human behavior are accountable only on a social basis. (These distinctions should become more clear in the course of this report).

It can readily be inferred from this brief explanation of Mead's usage of the term "social behaviorism" that, before we can explore the nature and function of the mind – which Mead considers a uniquely human attribute — supporting theories of society, and of self — another uniquely human attribute — require elaboration. Hence, the natural, logical order of Mead's thinking seems to have been society, self, and mind — rather than "Mind, Self, and Society."

B. Content of Mead's Social Psychology

1. Society

According to Mead, all group life is essentially a matter of cooperative behavior. Mead makes a distinction, however, between infrahuman society and human society. Insects — whose society most closely approximates the complexity of human social life — act together in certain ways because of their biological make-up. Thus, their cooperative behavior is physiologically determined. This is shown by many facts, among which is the fact of the fixity, the stability, of the relationships of insect-society members to one another. Insects, according to the evidence, go on for countless generations without any difference in their patterns of association. This picture of infrahuman society remains essentially valid as one ascends the scale of animal life, until we arrive at the human level.

In the case of human association, the situation is fundamentally different. Human cooperation is not brought about by mere physiological factors. The very diversity of the patterns of human group life makes it quite clear that human cooperative life cannot be explained in the same terms as the cooperative life of insects and the lower animals. The fact that human patterns are not stabilized and cannot be explained in biological terms led Mead to seek another basis of explanation of human association. Such cooperation can only be brought about by some process wherein: (a) each acting individual ascertains the *intention* of the acts of others, and then (b) makes his own response on the basis of that intention. What this means is that, in order for human beings to cooperate, there must be present some sort of mechanism whereby each acting individual: (a) can come to understand the lines of action of others, and (b) can guide his own behavior to fit in with those lines of action. Human behavior is not a matter of responding directly to the activities of others. Rather, it involves responding to the *intentions* of others, *i. e.*, to the future, intended behavior of others — not merely to their present actions.

We can better understand the character of this distinctively human mode of interaction between individuals by contrasting it with the infrahuman "conversation of gestures." For example, when a mother hen clucks, her chicks will respond by running to her. This does not imply however, that the hen clucks *in order* to guide the chicks, *i.e.*, with the *intention* of guiding them. Clucking is a natural sign or signal — rather than a significant (meaningful) symbol — as it is not meaningful to the hen. That is, the hen (according to Mead) does not take the role, or viewpoint, of the chicks toward its own gesture and respond to it, in imagination, as they do. The hen does not envision the response of the chicks to her clucking. Thus, hens and chicks do not share the same experience.

Let us take another illustration by Mead: Two hostile dogs, in the pre-fight stage, may go through an elaborate conversation of gestures (snarling, growling, baring fangs, walking stiff-leggedly around one another, etc.). The dogs are adjusting themselves to one another by responding to one another's gestures. (A gesture is that portion of an act which represents the entire act; it is the initial, overt phase of the act, which epitomizes it, *e.g.*, shaking one's fist at someone.) Now, in the case of the dogs the response to a gesture is dictated by pre-established tendencies to respond in certain ways. Each gesture leads to a direct, immediate, automatic, and unreflecting response by the recipient of the gesture (the other dog). Neither dog responds to the *intention* of the gestures. Further, each dog does not make his gestures with the intent of eliciting certain responses in the other dog. Thus, animal interaction is devoid of conscious, deliberate meaning.

To summarize: Gestures, at the non-human or non-linguistic level, do not carry the connotation of conscious meaning or intent, but serve merely as cues for the appropriate responses of others. Gestural communication takes place immediately, without any interruption of the act, without the mediation of a definition of meaning. Each organism adjusts "instinctively" to the other; it does not stop and figure out which response it will give. Its behavior is, largely, a series of direct automatic responses to stimuli.

Human beings, on the other hand, respond to one another on the basis of the intentions or meanings of gestures. This renders the gestures *symbolic, i.e.,* the gesture becomes a symbol to be interpreted; it becomes something which, in the imaginations of the participants, stands for the entire act.

Thus, individual A begins to act, *i.e.,* makes a gesture: for example, he draws back an arm. Individual B (who perceives the gesture) completes, or fills in, the act in his imagination; *i.e.,* B imaginatively projects the gesture into the future: "He will strike me." In other words, B perceives what the gesture stands for, thus getting its meaning. In contrast to the direct responses of the chicks and the dogs, the human being inserts an interpretation between the gesture of another and his response to it. Human behavior involves responses to *interpreted* stimuli.[1]

We see, then, that people respond to one another on the basis of imaginative activity. In order to engage in concerted behavior, however, each participating individual must be able to attach the same meaning to the same gesture. Unless interacting individuals interpret gestures similarly, unless they fill out the imagined portion in the same way, there can be no cooperative action. This is another way of saying what has by now become a truism in sociology and social psychology: Human society rests upon a basis of *consensus, i.e.,* the sharing of meanings in the form of common understandings and expectations.

In the case of the human being, each person has the ability to respond to his own gestures; and thus, it is possible to have the same meaning for

[1] The foregoing distinctions can also be expressed in terms of the differences between "signs," or "signals," and symbols. A sign stands for something else because of the fact that it is present at approximately the same time and place with that "something else." A symbol, on the other hand, stands for something else because its users have agreed to let it stand for that "something else." Thus, signs are directly and intrinsically linked with present or proximate situations; while symbols, having arbitrary and conventional, rather than intrinsic, meanings, transcend the immediate situation. (We shall return to this important point in our discussion of "mind.") Only symbols, of course, involve interpretation, self-stimulation and shared meaning.

the gestures as other persons. (For example: As I say "chair," I present to myself the same image as to my hearer; moreover, the same image as when someone else says "chair.") This ability to stimulate oneself as one stimulates another, and to respond to oneself as another does, Mead ascribes largely to man's vocal-auditory mechanism. (The ability to hear oneself implies at least the potentiality for responding to oneself.) When a gesture has a shared, common meaning, when it is — in other words — a *linguistic* element, we can designate it as a "significant symbol." (Take the words, "Open the window": the pattern of action symbolized by these words must be in the mind of the speaker as well as the listener. Each must respond, in imagination, to the words in the same way. The speaker must have an image of the listener responding to his words by opening the window, and the listener must have an image of his opening the window.)

The imaginative completion of an act — which Mead calls "meaning" and which represents mental activity — necessarily takes place through *role-taking*. To complete imaginatively the total act which a gesture stands for, the individual must put himself in the position of the other person, must identify with him. The earliest beginnings of role-taking occur when an already established act of another individual is stopped short of completion, thereby requiring the observing individual to fill in, or complete, the activity imaginatively. (For example, a crying infant may have an image of its mother coming to stop its crying.)

As Mead points out, then, the relation of human beings to one another arises from the developed ability of the human being to respond to his own gestures. This ability enables different human beings to respond in the same way to the same gesture, thereby sharing one another's experience.

This latter point is of great importance. Behavior is viewed as "social" not simply when it is a response to others, but rather when it has incorporated in it the behavior of others. The human being responds to himself as other persons respond to him, and in so doing he imaginatively shares the conduct of others. That is, in imagining their response he shares that response.[2]

2. Self

To state that the human being can respond to his own gestures necessarily implies that he possesses a *self*. In referring to the human being as having a self, Mead simply means that such an individual may act socially toward himself, just as toward others. He may praise, blame, or encourage himself; he may become disgusted with himself, may seek to punish himself,

[2] To anyone who has taken even one course in Sociology it is probably superfluous to stress the importance of symbols, particularly language, in the acquisition of all other elements of culture. The process of socialization is essentially a process of symbolic interaction.

and so forth. Thus, the human being may become the object of his own actions. The self is formed in the same way as other objects — through the "definitions" made by others.

The mechanism whereby the individual becomes able to view himself as an object is that of role-taking, involving the process of communication, especially by vocal gestures or speech. (Such communication necessarily involves role-taking.) It is only by taking the role of others that the individual can come to see himself as an object. The standpoint of others provides a platform for getting outside oneself and thus viewing oneself. The development of the self is concurrent with the development of the ability to take roles.

The crucial importance of language in this process must be underscored. It is through language (significant symbols) that the child acquires the meanings and definitions of those around him. By learning the symbols of his groups, he comes to internalize their definitions of events or things, including their definitions of his own conduct.

It is quite evident that, rather than assuming the existence of selves and explaining society thereby, Mead starts out from the prior existence of society as the context within which selves arise. This view contrasts with the nominalistic position of the Social Contract theorists and of various individualistic psychologies.

Genesis of the Self. The relationship between role-playing and various stages in the development of the self is described below:

1) *Preparatory Stage.* (not explicitly named by Mead, but inferable from various fragmentary essays).

This stage is one of meaningless imitation by the infant (for example, "reading" the newspaper). The child does certain things that others near it do without any understanding of what he is doing. Such imitation, however, implies that the child is incipiently taking the roles of those around it, *i. e.*, is on the verge of putting itself in the position of others and acting like them.

2) *Play Stage.* In this stage the actual playing of roles occurs. The child plays mother, teacher, storekeeper, postman, streetcar conductor, Mr. Jones, etc. What is of central importance in such play-acting is that it places the child in the position where it is able to act back toward itself in such roles as "mother" or "teacher." In this stage, then, the child first begins to form a self, that is, to direct activity toward itself — and it does so by taking the roles of others. This is clearly indicated by use of the third person in referring to oneself instead of the first person: "John wants . . .," "John is a bad boy."

However, in this stage the young child's configuration of roles is unstable; the child passes from one role to another in unorganized, inconsistent fashion. He has, as yet, no unitary standpoint from which to view himself, and hence, he has no unified conception of himself. In other words, the child forms a number of separate and discrete objects of itself, depending on the roles in which it acts toward itself.

3) Game Stage. This is the "completing" stage of the self. In time, the child finds himself in situations wherein he must take a number of roles simultaneously. That is, he must respond to the expectations of several people at the same time. This sort of situation is exemplified by the game of baseball — to use Mead's own illustration. Each player must visualize the intentions and expectations of several other players. In such situations the child must take the roles of groups of individuals as over against particular roles. The child becomes enabled to do this by abstracting a "composite" role out of the concrete roles of particular persons. In the course of his association with others, then, he builds up a *generalized other,* a generalized role or standpoint from which he views himself and his behavior. This generalized other represents, then, the set of standpoints which are common to the group.

Having achieved this generalized standpoint, the individual can conduct himself in an organized, consistent manner. He can view himself from a consistent standpoint. This means, then, that the individual can transcend the local and present expectations and definitions with which he comes in contact. An illustration of this point would be the Englishman who "dresses for dinner" in the wilds of Africa. Thus, through having a generalized other, the individual becomes emancipated from the pressures of the peculiarities of the immediate situation. He can act with a certain amount of consistency in a variety of situations because he acts in accordance with a generalized set of expectations and definitions that he has internalized.

The "I" and the "Me". The self is essentially a social process within the individual involving two analytically distinguishable phases: The "I" and the "Me."

The "I" is the impulsive tendency of the individual. It is the initial, spontaneous, unorganized aspect of human experience. Thus, it represents the undirected tendencies of the individual.

The "Me" represents the incorporated other within the individual. Thus, it comprises the organized set of attitudes and definitions, understandings and expectations — or simply meanings — common to the group. In any given situation, the "Me" comprises the generalized other and, often, some particular other.

Every act begins in the form of an "I" and usually ends in the form of the "Me." For the "I" represents the initiation of the act prior to its coming under control of the definitions or expectations of others (the "Me"). The "I" thus gives *propulsion* while the "Me" gives *direction* to the act. Human behavior, then, can be viewed as a perpetual series of initiations of acts by the "I" and of acting-back-upon the act (that is, guidance of the act) by the "Me." The act is a resultant of this interplay.

The "I," being spontaneous and propulsive, offers the potentiality for new, creative activity. The "Me," being regulatory, disposes the individual to both goal-directed activity and conformity. In the operation of these aspects of the self, we have the basis for, on the one hand, social control and, on the other, novelty and innovation. We are thus provided with a basis for understanding the mutuality of the relationship between the individual and society.[3]

Implications of Selfhood. Some of the major implications of selfhood in human behavior are as follows:

1) The possession of a self makes of the individual a society in miniature. That is, he may engage in interaction with himself just as two or more different individuals might. In the course of this interaction, he can come to view himself in a new way, thereby bringing about changes in himself.

2) The ability to act toward oneself makes possible an inner experience which need not reach overt expression. That is, the individual, by virtue of having a self, is thereby endowed with the possibility of having a mental life: He can make indications to himself — which constitutes *mind*.

3) The individual with a self is thereby enabled to direct and control

[3]At first glance, Mead's "I" and "Me" may appear to bear a close affinity with Freud's concepts of Id, Ego, and Superego. The resemblance is, for the most part, more apparent than real. While the Superego is held to be harshly frustrating and repressive of the instinctual, libidinous, and aggressive Id, the "Me" is held to provide necessary direction — often of a *gratifying* nature — to the otherwise undirected impulses constituting the "I." Putting the matter in figurative terms: Freud views the Id and the Superego as locked in combat upon the battleground of the Ego; Mead sees the "I" and "Me" engaged in close collaboration. This difference in perspective may derive from different preoccupations: Freud was primarily concerned with tension, anxiety, and "abnormal" behavior; Mead was primarily concerned with behavior generically.

It is true, on the other hand, that the Id, Ego, and Superego — particularly as modified by such neo-Freudians as Karen Horney, Erich Fromm, and H. S. Sullivan — converge at a few points with the "I" and "Me." This is especially evident in the emphasis of both the Superego and "Me" concepts upon the internalization of the norms of significant others through the process of identification, or role-taking.

Incidentally, it should be noted that both sets of concepts refer to processes of behavior, *not* to concrete entities or structures. See, also, the discussion of "mind" which follows.

his behavior. Instead of being subject to all impulses and stimuli directly playing upon him, the individual can check, guide, and organize his behavior. He is, then, *not* a mere passive agent.

All three of these implications of selfhood may be summarized by the statement that the self and the mind (mental activity) are twin emergents in the social process.

3. Mind

Development of Mind. As in the instance of his consideration of the self, Mead rejects individualistic psychologies, in which the social process (society, social interaction) is viewed as presupposing, and being a product of, mind. In direct contrast is his view that mind presupposes, and is a product of, the social process. Mind is seen by Mead as developing correlatively with the self, constituting (in a very important sense) the self in action.

Mead's hypothesis regarding mind (as regarding the self) is that the mental emerges out of the organic life of man through communication. The mind is present only at certain points in human behavior, *viz.,* when significant symbols are being used by the individual. This view dispenses with the substantive notion of mind as existing as a box-like container in the head, or as some kind of fixed, ever-present entity. Mind is seen as a *process,* which manifests itself whenever the individual is interacting with himself by using significant symbols.

Mead begins his discussion of the mind with a consideration of the relation of the organism to its environment. He points out that the central principle in all organic behavior is that of continuous adjustment, or adaptation, to an environing field. We cannot regard the environment as having a fixed character for all organisms, as being the same for all organisms. All behavior involves selective attention and perception. The organism accepts certain events in its field, or vicinity, as stimuli and rejects or overlooks certain others as irrelevant to its needs. (For example, an animal battling for life ignores food.) Bombarded constantly by stimuli, the organism selects those stimuli or aspects of its field which pertain to, are functional to, the acts in which the organism is engaged. Thus, the organism has a hand in determining the nature of its environment. What this means, then, is that Mead, along with Dewey, regards all life as ongoing activity, and views stimuli — not as initiators of activity — but as elements selected by the organism in the furtherance of that activity.

Perception is thus an activity that involves selective attention to certain aspects of a situation, rather than a mere matter of something coming into the individual's nervous system and leaving an impression. Visual perception, *e.g.,* is more than a matter of just opening one's eyes and responding to what falls on the retina.

The determination of the environment by the biologic individual (infrahumans and the unsocialized infant) is not a cognitive relationship. It is selective, but does not involve consciousness, in the sense of reflective intelligence. At the distinctively human level, on the other hand, there is a hesitancy, an inhibition of overt conduct, which is *not* involved in the selective attention of animal behavior. In this period of inhibition, mind is present.

For, human behavior involves inhibiting an act and trying out the varying approaches in imagination. In contrast, as we have seen, the acts of the biologic individual are relatively immediate, direct, and made up of innate or habitual ways of reacting. In other words, the unsocialized organism lacks consciousness of meaning. This being the case, the organism has no means for the abstract analysis of its field when new situations are met, and hence no means for the reorganization of action-tendencies in the light of that analysis.[4]

Minded behavior (in Mead's sense) arises around problems. It represents, to repeat an important point, a temporary inhibition of action wherein the individual is attempting to prevision the future. It consists of presenting to oneself, tentatively and in advance of overt behavior, the different possibilities or alternatives of future action with reference to a given situation. The future is, thus, present in terms of images of prospective lines of action from which the individual can make a selection. The mental process is, then, one of delaying, organizing, and selecting a response to the stimuli of the environment. This implies that the individual *constructs* his act, rather than responding in predetermined ways. Mind makes it possible for the individual purposively to control and organize his responses. Needless to say, this view contradicts the stimulus-response conception of human behavior.

When the act of an animal is checked, it may engage in overt trial and error or random activity. In the case of blocked human acts, the trial and error may be carried on covertly, implicitly. Consequences can be imaginatively "tried out" in advance. This is what is primarily meant by "mind," "reflective thinking," or "abstract thinking."

What this involves is the ability to indicate elements of the field or situation, abstract them from the situation, and recombine them so that procedures can be considered in advance of their execution. Thus, to quote

[4] The reader should recognize here, in a new guise, our earlier distinction between signs and symbols. Signs have "intrinsic" meanings which induce direct reactions; symbols have arbitrary meanings which require interpretations by the actor prior to his response or action. The former, it will be recalled, are "tied to" the immediate situation, while the latter "transcend" the immediate situation. Thus, symbols may refer to past or future events, to hypothetical situations, to nonexistent or imaginary objects, and so forth.

a well-known example, the intelligence of the detective as over against the intelligence of the bloodhound lies in the capacity of the former to isolate and indicate (to himself and to others) what the particular characters are which will call out the response of apprehending the fugitive criminal.

The mind is social in both origin and function. It arises in the social process of communication. Through association with the members of his groups, the individual comes to internalize the definitions transmitted to him through linguistic symbols, learns to assume the perspectives of others, and thereby acquires the ability to think. When the mind has risen in this process, it operates to maintain and adjust the individual in his society; and it enables the society to persist. The persistence of a human society depends, as we have seen, upon consensus; and consensus necessarily entails minded behavior.

The mind is social in function in the sense that the individual continually indicates to himself in the role of others and controls his activity with reference to the definitions provided by others. In order to carry on though, he must have some standpoint from which to converse with himself. He gets this standpoint by importing into himself the role of others.

By "taking the role of the other," — as I earlier pointed out — we can see ourselves as others see us, and arouse in ourselves the responses that we call out in others. It is this conversation with ourselves, between the representation of the other (in the form of the"Me") and our impulses (in the form of the "I") that constitutes the mind. Thus, what the individual actually does in minded behavior is to carry on an internal conversation. By addressing himself from the standpoint of the generalized other, the individual has a universe of discourse, a system of common symbols and meanings, with which to address himself. These are presupposed as the context for minded behavior.

Mead holds, then, that mental activity is a peculiar type of activity that goes on in the experience of the person. The activity is that of the person responding to himself, of indicating things to himself.

To repeat, mind originates in the social process, in association with others. There is little doubt that human beings lived together in groups before mind ever evolved. But, there emerged, because of certain biological developments, the point where human beings were able to respond to their own acts and gestures. It was at this point that mind, or minded behavior, emerged. Similarly, mind comes into existence for the individual at the point where the individual is capable of responding to his own behavior, *i.e.,* where he can designate things to himself.

Summarizing this brief treatment of mind, mental activity, or reflective thinking, we may say that it is a matter of making indications of meanings to oneself as to others. This is another way of saying that mind is the process of using significant symbols. For, thinking goes on when an individual uses a symbol to call out in himself the responses which others would make. Mind, then is symbolic behavior.[5] As such, mind is an emergent from non-symbolic behavior and is fundamentally irreducible to the stimulus-response mechanisms which characterize the latter form of behavior.

It should be evident that Mead avoids both the behavioristic fallacy of reduction and the individualistic fallacy of taking for granted the phenomenon that is to be explained.

Objects. Returning to Mead's discussion of the organism-in-environment, we can now give more explicit attention to his treatment of *objects.* As we have seen, we cannot regard the environment as having a fixed character for all organisms. The environment is a function of the animal's own character, being greatly determined by the make-up of the animal. Each animal largely selects its own environment. It selects out the stimuli toward which it acts, its make-up and on-going activity determining the kinds of stimuli it will select. Further, the qualities which are possessed by the objects toward which the animal acts arise from the kind of experiences that the animal has with the objects. (To illustrate, grass is not the same phenomenon for a cat and for a cow.) The environment and its qualities, then, are always functional to the structure of the animal.

As one passes on to the human level, the relation of the individual to the world becomes markedly more complicated. This is so because the human being is capable of forming objects. Animals, lacking symbols, see stimuli, such as patches of color — not objects. An object has to be detached, pointed out, "imaged" to oneself. The human being's environment is constituted largely by objects.

Now, let us look at the relation of the individual to objects. An object represents a plan of action. That is, an object doesn't exist for the individual in some pre-established form. Perception of any object has telescoped in it a series of experiences which one would have if he carried out the plan of action toward that object. The object has no qualities for the individual, aside from those which would result from his carrying out a plan of action. In this respect, the object is constituted by one's activities with reference to it. (For example, chalk is the sum of qualities which are perceived as

[5]A growing number of linguists, semanticists, and students of speech disorders are becoming aware of the central role of symbols in the *content,* as well as the process, of thought. Edward Sapir and Benjamin Whorf have formulated "the principle of linguistic relativity," which holds that the structure of a language influences the manner in which the users of the language will perceive, comprehend, and act toward reality. Wendell Johnson, in the field of semantics, and Kurt Goldstein, in the study of aphasia, are representative investigators who have recognized the way in which symbols structure perception and thought. Mead's theory clearly foreshadows these developments.

a result of one's actions: a hard smooth, white writing implement.)

The objects which constitute the "effective environment," the individual's experienced environment, are established by the individual's activities. To the extent that his activity varies, his environment varies. In other words, objects change as activities toward them change. (Chalk, for instance, may become a missile.)

Objects, which are constituted by the activities of the human individual, are largely *shared* objects. They stand for common patterns of activity of individuals. This is true, Mead points out, by virtue of the fact that objects arise, and are present in experience, only in the process of being indicated to oneself (and, hence, explicitly or implicity, to others). In other words, the perspective from which one indicates an object implicates definitions by others. Needless to say, these definitions involve language, or significant symbols. The individual acquires a commonality of perspective with others by learning the symbols by which they designate aspects of the world.[6]

4. *The Act*

All human activity other than reflex and habitual action is built up in the process of its execution; *i.e.,* behavior is constructed as it goes along, for decisions must be made at several points. The significance of this fact is that people act — rather than merely reacting.

For Mead, the unit of study is "the act," which comprises both overt and covert aspects of human action. Within the act, all the separated categories of the traditional, orthodox psychologies find a place. Attention, perception, imagination, reasoning, emotion, and so forth, are seen as parts of the act — rather than as more or less extrinsic influences upon it. Human behavior presents itself in the form of acts, rather than of concatenations of minute responses.

The act, then, encompasses the total process involved in human activity. It is viewed as a complete span of action: its initial point is an impulse and its terminal point some objective which gives release to the impulse. In between, the individual is in the process of constructing, organizing his

[6] The contrast between this view of learning and the neo-behavioristic "learning theory" of Clark Hull and other psychologists should be clearly evident. Basically, learning theorists attempt to reduce human learning to the mechanisms found in infrahuman learning. This is reflected in their tendency to ignore the role of linguistic symbols in human behavior, their conceptualization of human activity in terms of stimulus-response couplets, and their view of learning as equivalent with conditioning. (For an excellent critique of learning theory from the symbolic interactionist standpoint, see: Manford H. Kuhn, "Kinsey's View of Human Behavior," *Social Problems,* 1 (April, 1954), pp. 119-125.)

behavior. It is during this period that the act undergoes its most significant phase of development. In the case of human behavior, this period is marked by the play of images of possible goals or lines of action upon the impulse, thus directing the activity to its consummation.

In pointing out that the act begins with an impulse, Mead means that organisms experience disturbances of equilibrium. In the case of the lower animals, their biological make-up channelizes the impulse toward appropriate goals. In the case of the human being, the mere presence of an impulse leads to nothing but mere random, unorganized activity. This is most clearly — but definitely not exclusively — seen in the instance of the behavior of infants. Until the defining actions of others set up goals for it, the human infant's behavior is unchannelized. It is the function of images to direct, organize and construct this activity. The presence in behavior of images implies, of course, a process of indicating to oneself, or mind.

The act may have a short span *(e.g.,* attending a particular class meeting, or starting a new page of notes) or may involve the major portion of a person's life *(e.g.,* trying to achieve a successful career). Moreover, acts are parts of an interlacing of previous acts, and are built up, one upon another. This is in contradistinction to the view that behavior is a series of discrete stimulus-response bonds. Conceiving human behavior in terms of acts, we become aware of the necessity for viewing any particular act within its psychosocial context.[7]

Using the concept of the act, Mead sets up classes of acts — the automatic act, the blocked act, the incomplete act, and the retrospective act — and analyzes them in terms of his frame of reference. Space does not permit presentation of these intriguing analyses.

[7] The reader may have noted that this discussion makes no explicit reference to the problem of motivation. Mead had little to say regarding motives. Adherents to his general orientation have tended either to regard motives as implicit in the concept of *object* ("a plan of action") or to consider them "mere" verbal labels offered in supposed explanation of the actions of oneself or of others.

In my judgment, a conception of motivation can be formulated that is both useful and consistent with Mead's theories. Motivation can refer to "a process of defining (symbolically, of course) the goal of an act." Thus, while both human and infrahuman behavior may be viewed as goal-directed, only human behavior would be considered "motivated." Just as "motive" would be restricted to the human level, "drive" might serve a comparable function on the infrahuman level.

This would not imply that motives lie back of, or "cause," human acts. Rather, human acts are in constant process of construction, and the goal-definitions by individuals undergo constant reformulation. I mean to designate by "motive," however, the definition the individual makes, *at any given time,* of the objectives of his own specific acts. Such definitions, obviously, would be socially derived.

C. Summary

At several points in this report the reader must have been aware of the extremely closely interwoven character of Mead's various concepts. In the discussions of society, of self, and of mind, certain ideas seemed to require frequent (and, perhaps, repetitous) statement. A brief summary of Mead's position may help to reveal more meaningfully the way in which his key concepts interlock and logically imply one another.

The human individual is born into a society characterized by *symbolic interaction*. The use of *significant symbols* by those around him enables him to pass from the conversation of gestures — which involves direct, unmeaningful response to the overt acts of others — to the occasional *taking of the roles* of others. This role-taking enables him to *share* the perspectives of others. Concurrent with role-taking, the *self* develops, *i.e.*, the capacity to act toward oneself. Action toward oneself comes to take the form of viewing oneself from the standpoint, or perspective, of the *generalized other* (the composite representative of others, of society, within the individual), which implies defining one's behavior in terms of the expectations of others. In the process of such viewing of oneself, the individual must carry on symbolic interaction with himself, involving an internal conversation between his impulsive aspect (the "I") and the incorporated perspectives of others (The "Me"). The *mind,* or mental activity, is present in behavior whenever such symbolic interaction goes on — whether the individual is merely "thinking" (in the everyday sense of the word) or is also interacting with another individual. (In both cases the individual must indicate things to himself.) Mental activity necessarily involves *meanings,* which usually attach to, and define, *objects.* The meaning of an object or event is simply an image of the pattern of action which defines the object or event. That is, the completion in one's imagination of an act, or the mental picture of the actions and experiences symbolized by an object, defines the act or the object. In the unit of study that Mead calls "the *act,*" all of the foregoing processes are usually entailed. The concluding point to be made in this summary is the same as the point with which I began: Mead's concepts intertwine and mutually imply one another. To drive home this important point, I must emphasize that human society (characterized by symbolic interaction) both precedes the rise of individual selves and minds, and is maintained by the rise of individual selves and minds. This means, then, that symbolic interaction is both the medium for the development of human beings and the process by which human beings associate as human beings.

Finally, it should be clearly evident by now that any distinctively human act necessarily involves: symbolic interaction, role-taking, meaning, mind, and self. Where one of these concepts is involved, the others are, also, necessarily involved. Here we see, unmistakably, the organic unity of Mead's position.

D. Critique

In criticizing Mead's social psychology, it should be borne in mind that he gave his position no extended systematic write-up; that most of the published material which forms the basis of our knowledge of that position was not originally intended for publication, at least not in the form in which it has been printed; and that the various alternative statements of that position that appear in his posthumous works sometimes carry conflicting particulars. Still, we can evaluate only on the basis of the available, published materials.

1. Many of Mead's major concepts are somewhat vague and "fuzzy," necessitating an "intuitive" grasp of their meaning. This vagueness stems, I believe, primarily from two sources: (1) the fragmentary and alternative formulations of his idea; and (2) his emergent view of human conduct, which inescapably entangles him in the necessity of striking a balance between the continuity of infrahuman and human behavior, on the one hand, and the novelty of human behavior, on the other.

(a) For example, the exact nature of "impulses" is not clearly specified. Whether impulses are biological in character, or can also be socially-derived, is not clear from Mead's exposition. However, the contexts in which the term sometimes appears suggest that the latter interpretation would be more valid and useful.

(b) Similarly, the intertwined concepts of "meaning" and of "mind" are not consistently employed. At times, these terms are used generically, applying to both infrahuman and human levels of behavior, and at times specifically, applying only at the level of self-conscious human conduct. Fortunately, the context of each usage usually provides a key to Mead's intended meanings.

(c) Coincident with Mead's varying referents of "mind" and of "meaning," we find his vacillation between a restriction of role-taking ability to the human level (in symbolic interaction) and his granting of that ability to infrahuman animals (in the conversation of gestures). Again, we are fortunate in having his distinction between self-conscious role-playing and unwitting role-playing. The reader of Mead must bear in mind that the latter type of "role-playing" is *not* what Mead usually has in mind when he employs the concept.

(d) The concept of the "I," as William Kolb indicates, represents a vaguely-defined residual category. Mead clearly specifies the nature of the "Me," but in effect, labels the "I" as simply the not-Me aspect of the self. As in the case of the very closely related concept of "impulse," Mead does not indicate the limits of the "I." From his discussion, the "I" would seem, however — and this is an inference — to include everything from biological urges to the effects of individual variations in life-history patterns. Still, as Barnes and Becker point out, the "I" serves the very useful purpose of evading a complete collective, or sociological, determinism of human conduct.

The ambiguity of the concept of the "I" also reveals itself in the various discussions in the secondary literature on Mead's treatment of habitual behavior. For some writers, habitual acts represent manifestations of the operation of the "I" alone; for others, of the "Me" alone; and for still others, a fusion of the "I" and the "Me."

(e) The concept of "self" also lacks clear, unambiguous definition in Mead's work. A certain amount of confusion enters the picture when the self is defined in terms of "the individual's viewing himself as an object." This confusion is not at all dissipated by Mead's tendency to vary between, on the one hand, synonymous usages of "self" and "self-consciousness" and on the other hand, slightly different usages of these two terms.

(f) Mead's concept of the "generalized other" needs sharpening. He oversimplifies the concept by assuming apparently, a single, universal generalized other for the members of each society — rather than a variety of generalized others (even for the same individuals), at different levels of generality.[8] The inadequacy of his concept is clearly shown in his characterization of the criminal as one who "has not taken on the attitude of the generalized other toward property, (and who therefore) lacks a completely developed self." Such a characterization overlooks, of course, the sociogenic elements in crime causation.

(g) A final case of vagueness of conceptualization that we shall consider relates to Mead's usages of "object" and "image." Both of these are described as "telescoped acts," and both are used at times interchangeably and at times slightly differently. It is probably safe to infer that images are the mental representations of objects, *i.e.,* that images are the imaginative projections of the acts which define objects.

Other sources of ambiguity lie in Mead's varying uses of the concepts of "attitude," "gesture," and "symbol"; his vacillation between, on the one hand, ascribing objects and images to the infrahuman level of behavior and, on the other hand, denying them to that level; etc. All of these ambiguities and inconsistencies reflect chiefly the confusion engendered by publication of all the alternative formulations of Mead's ideas — the early formulations along with the later. The thoughtful and assiduous reader of

[8] Current work on "reference groups" has served to remedy this deficiency. True, several competing definitions of this concept are extant. I have in mind, however, the conception of reference groups as collections of "significant others," that is, of persons with whom a given individual identifies and who, therefore, have a significant influence upon his personality.

Mead, however, should be able to abstract out some single, fairly consistent statement of Mead's position.

2. A second series of adverse criticisms centers around certain broad substantive omissions in Mead's theory.

(a) Mead's position, as Blumer states, constitutes a purely analytical scheme, which lacks content. That is, he presents an analysis of human conduct in terms of the mechanisms of development of such conduct, but indicates few ingredients of that conduct. In concerning himself wholly with process but not content, with the "how" but not the "why" of conduct, he provides no basis for explaining specific behaviors. For example, he gives no clues as to why one object rather than another will be formed by an individual or group. Thus, his scheme, as it stands, has no explanatory value with reference to such matters as the rise of particular popular heroes, or the high valuation of money, or the myth of Santa Claus.

(b) Related to this "error" of omission is Mead's virtual ignoring of the role of affective elements in the rise of the self and in social interaction generally. The importance of the sentiments and emotions manifested in personal relationships are given no recognition in Mead's position. This lack is supplied — perhaps, oversupplied — in Cooley's work.

(c) Nothing in Mead's theory enables a clear stand on the matter of the nature (or even existence) of the unconscious, or subconscious, and the related mechanisms of adjustment.

3. Mead's position can also be criticized from a third and final general standpoint, that of methodology.

(a) First of all, Mead's theory, for the most part, does not seem to be highly researchable. As yet, little truly significant research has been conducted chiefly in terms of his frame of reference. Recent efforts to measure self-conceptions may help to remedy this deficiency.

(b) Mead, himself, gives no explicit formulation as to how his analytical scheme can be used in research. He makes no specific recommendations as to the techniques appropriate to the study of human behavior.

(c) As I indicated earlier in this report, Mead presents no systematic evidence for his position. Nevertheless, many social psychologists find his theory highly congruent with the experiences of everyday life — something which cannot be as readily said for a number of competing positions.

E. Positive Contribution

The extent of Mead's contribution to social psychology can be only roughly gauged by reference to the work of other adherents of the Symbolic Interactionist approach. Among the more eminent sociologists and social psychologists influenced by his viewpoint are: Cooley, Thomas, Park, Burgess, E. Faris, and Blumer. Some of the textbooks which incorporate his position are: in Sociology, those by Park and Burgess, Dawson and Gettys, Francis

Merrill, Kingsley Davis; in Social Psychology, Lindesmith and Strauss, M. Sherif, T. Newcomb, Walter Coutu, and Hubert Bonner. In addition, the recent interests in "role theory," "reference-group theory," and "self-theory" represent, basically, derivatives of Symbolic Interactionism.

Mead's substantive contribution has converged with, or at least has found some parallels in, certain methodological positions in modern sociology and social psychology. Such positions are those in which study of the inner, subjective part of the act is deemed indispensable. Methodologies of this sort are indicated by (1) Thomas' concept of "definition of the situation," (2) Cooley's "sympathetic introspection," (3) Weber's "*Verstehen,*" (4) Znaniecki's "humanistic coefficient," (5) MacIver's "dynamic assessment," (6) Sorokin's "Logico-meaningful analysis," and other references to the covert aspects of human conduct.

Mead's more specific contributions can be only briefly listed in this report:

1. He contributed to the increasing acceptance of the view that human conduct is carried on primarily by the defining of situations in which one acts; that is, the view that distinctively human behavior is behavior in terms of what situations *symbolize.* This is the essence of the Symbolic Interactionist viewpoint.

2. Adopting a distinctly sociological perspective, he helped direct attention to the fact that mind and self are not biologically given, but are social emergents.

3. He delineated the way in which language serves as a mechanism for the appearance of mind and self.

4. His concept of the "self" explains how the development, or socialization, of the human being both enmeshes the individual in society and frees him from society. For, the individual with a self is not passive, but can employ his self in an interaction which may result in selections divergent from group definitions.

5. An extremely provocative conception of the nature of the human mind is provided by him: He views mind, or the mental, as an importation within the individual of the social process, *i.e.,* of the process of social interaction.

6. His concept of the "act" points out the tendency for individuals to construct their behavior in the course of activity and thus, to "carve out" their objects, their environments. What this means is that human beings are not passive puppets who respond mechanically to stimuli. They are, rather, active participants in a highly organized society, and what they perceive is functional in their ongoing activity. This theoretical position implies the importance of acquired predispositions (interests, values, etc.) and of the social context of behavior. It points to the influential significance of the group settings in which perceptions occur, and also places the meaning of what is perceived in the context of the ongoing activities of persons.

This leads directly into the next contribution by Mead.

7. He described how the members of a human group develop and form a common world, *i.e.,* common objects, common understandings and expectations.

8. He illuminated the character of social interaction by showing that human beings *share* one another's behavior instead of merely responding to each other's overt, external behavior as do infrahuman organisms.

As a concluding and over-all evaluation of Mead as a contributor to social psychology, I can do no better than to repeat Dewey's oft-quoted appraisal: "His was a seminal mind of the first order."

2. Mead and Freud: Their Relevance for Social Psychology [1]

Guy E. Swanson

Freud would enjoy and, doubtless, interpret the ambivalence of social psychologists toward George Mead and himself. Their ideas are viewed by many scientists with great deference and grave doubt. Mead and Freud are held to be both indispensible and incompatible. Mead's work is generally considered fundamental but without fruitful implications for research; Freud's as provocative but wrong.

It should be understood that all social psychologists are not deeply ambivalent about Mead and Freud. It is a symptom primarily of those who look to sociology as their intellectual home. The average textbook by a sociological social psychologist cites Mead and Freud more often than any of the other theorists who wrote extensively before 1935. Moreover, these books employ symbolic interactionism and psychoanalytic thinking as their major frameworks.

I want to examine the present and prospective roles of Mead and Freud in the development of a sociological social psychology. My intent is not that of offering an intellectual history. My objective is to clarify some of the potential contributions of Mead and Freud to a sociological social psychology, to locate the essential nature of the incompatibility and convergence between them, and to assess their prospective relations to empirical research. To accomplish this purpose in a limited amount of space, I deal with only some of the topics they treat. Because it seems the more fundamental, my focus is on their treatments of mind as a process rather than on their accounts of the individual's organization as a self or as a personality.

I should say at once that there are certain points which I intend to ignore. I accept as fact, but will pass over, Freud's tendencies toward instinctivism and Lamarckianism, his penchant for fictive histories of doubtful worth, and his lack of knowledge about, or understanding of, the differences between cultures. At the same time, I shall assume that it is consistent with the best evidence to say that Freud was usually correct in believing that his major conceptual distinctions represented important

From *Sociometry*, XXIV (December, 1961), pp. 319-339, by permission of the American Sociological Association and the author.

[1] Revision of a paper read at the 1960 meetings of the American Sociological Association.

empirical discriminations.[2] I have no desire to join in that variety of revisionism which removes most of Freud's empirical observations while amputating instincts and the inheritance of acquired characteristics. I shall, in short, treat Freud, not neo-Freudianism.

Further, I shall not concern myself with the important controversies about the metaphysics and social values of pragmatism, functionalism, and psychoanalysis or with their relation to public affairs.[3] My present interest is in empirical fruitfulness and technical adequacy of these theories for the problems of social psychology. What are those problems?

The Problems of Social Psychology

Social psychology is the study of the relations between human individuals and social organizations. The nature of these relations depends on one's conception of the parties involved. Because social psychologists have no consensus on this matter, the following statements represent only my personal preferences.

By "individuals" I mean, not organisms as such, but organisms engaged in selecting from, adapting to, and utilizing their surroundings. These processes are what Dewey and Mead called "mind." The organism's current potential for engaging in such a process is called its "personality."

The organism, as such, is significant for the individual on two accounts. First, its internal processes provide requirements which force it to import resources from the environment and determine the classes of environmental objects which may be so imported. Second, the organism is a self-stabilizing organization or system. This means that its internal processes operate in a manner that admits or rejects elements from the environment according to their likely effects on the system's stability. In this way, each organism's self-stabilizing processes afford a kind of unitary standard against which the environment is evaluated. Thus the sustained internal coherence of the organism provides one ground for the organization and coherence of the individual.

Social relations are the influences that individuals exert on one another. It is customary to say that one individual influences another only because he affects his associate's access to resources. Individuals have relations because they are resources for one another or because they affect the means for obtaining such resources.

Social relations are always orderly and, in that sense, organized. This does not mean, however, that they always are organizations. The term "social organization" refers to a social relation in which the individuals

[2] The evidence is surveyed in Blum (5).

[3] For a consideration of Mead's relation to these controversies, see Blau (4), Pfuetze (33), and Natanson (25). Important evaluations of Freud in relation to these controversies are found in Bartlett (3), Marcuse (21), Kaplan (19), and Rieff (34).

concerned so behave as to prevent the disruption of their mutual influences by extraneous events. (When this self-stabilizing process occurs with some awareness by the individuals of its existence and function, we speak of their relationship as a "group.")

It is usually said that organisms, individuals, and social organizations are analytically separate from one another. This analytical separation is important primarily because it represents empirical independence. I shall take it as established that organisms, individuals and social organizations are independent in three senses: They are not reducible to one another, they exercise measurable constraints on another, and, in a given population over any given period of time, the variance in the internal processes of each of these three systems or organizations may show considerable independence from variations in the other two.

This empirical independence is not equivalent to a lack of relationship. It is a potential and, occasionally, actual independence which documents the existence of three different and equally real organizations. Thus, we find that individuals provide resources required by organic systems; social organizations provide resources required by individuals. But, once each of these systems is in being, we can turn the matter around. As an organization or system, each has internal processes which operate to produce stabilization. Thus the requirements of groups for stability impose obligations and limitations on individuals who need to maintain those groups for their own purposes. In their turn, individuals, as systems, impose comparable demands and constraints on the organisms which they serve.[4]

Like the relations between individuals and social organizations, social psychology moves in two primary directions. It seeks, on the one hand, a description of individuals and of their relations to each other's resources that will explain the rise and properties of social organizations. It seeks, conversely, to define the requirements imposed on individuals by participation in social organizations and the consequences for individuals of their imposition.

Among psychological social psychologists, the greater portion have studied individuals and their relations as the source of organizations.[5] A majority of the social psychologists trained in sociology show special interest in the effects of organizations on participating individuals.

Social psychologists have sought to understand the rise of organization among individuals through the study of interpersonal influence, power, communication, symbols, and the media of communication. Their work on elementary collective behavior, as well as many laboratory investigations of small groups, illustrates the same concern.

A different set of investigations illustrates efforts to explain the

[4] Some of the evidence especially relevant to this point is reviewed by Olds (26).

[5] This variety of approach is illustrated in Floyd Allport's early work (1). Perhaps the most recent survey and synthesis appears in Thibaut and Kelley's book on groups (39).

effects of organizations on individuals and to state the conditions under which these occur. Organizations persist if individuals depend on their presence, become responsible adherents to their norms, and contribute to the solution of their problems. The social psychologist's concern with socialization, self-control, and commitment to the group reflects his interest in the effects of organizations on individuals. So also does his effort to explain how values, attitudes, and opinions are acquired and gain some degree of order and stability as indicated by the rise of individualities, identities, and selves. The explanation of individual opposition or indifference to organizational requirements has been of special interest, as has over-conformity to those requirements.

The properties of social organizations play a special role in organizing sociological work in social psychology. It is those properties which distinguish social organizations from everything else in the environment that the social psychologist pursues as conditions that shape the mind. It is those features of mind relevant for explaining these same distinctive organizational properties and their variations that are of concern as he seeks to account for the rise of groups. In short, the defining properties of social organizations, and variations on those properties and on emergents from them, afford the coherence in a sociological social psychology. Among the candidates for inclusion in a list of such properties are social norms,[6] systems of symbols, sentiments conceived after the manner of Cooley, and Bales's "system problems."

The Problems of Mead and Freud

Neither Freud nor Mead set out to develop a social psychology. The philosophical tradition which Mead sought to advance defined its task as that of clarifying the relation between knowing and being — between epistemology and ontology — between the sentient organism and its environment (24). Interest was focused on the conditions of a valid knowledge of being. Valid knowledge was conceived as rational, intelligible, and self-conscious. This conception led, in turn, to a search for the empirical connections among signs, thought, organic action, and the environment, and to a concern with the universality of ideas and the reality of relations. Mead's social behaviorism finds its major problem in accounting for rationality, or, as he liked to call it, "reflective thought." His special contribution is an explanation for the varying access which men may have to the covert parts of their own acts and the consequences of such access for the effectiveness of man's relation to the environment. Mead locates the foundations of rationality in symbolic responses which people provide for the covert aspects of each other's behavior. If those responses are absent, men cannot think reflectively.

[6] In the sense employed by Durkheim. His definition and its implications are reviewed with unusual clarity by Peristiany (32).

Like Mead, Freud wanted to account for rationality. Whereas Mead was concerned with the irrationality which appears because the environment does not respond properly to the individual's inner life, Freud sought to understand the irrationality produced by subjective conditions which prevent the individual from properly interpreting the world around him. The personalities of his patients prevented their experiencing gratification.

Because Mead finds the locus of irrationality in the absence of certain environmental events, his major focus is on the peripheral processes of behavior — on perception, the selection of stimuli, the character of the reinforcement provided by stimuli, the reformulation of instrumental acts, and the release of blocked impulse into the environment. Freud, on the other hand, wants to change the balance of forces internal to the individual with the aim of removing subjective conditions which block a correct appraisal of the environment. This leads to a conceptualization of the principal components of personality and of the distortions which their relations impose upon the individual's contacts with the environment.[7]

It is evident that Mead and Freud had quite different aspects of behavior at the center of their attention. The wide difference in their interest is a major reason why each of them retains a special claim on our attention.

Mead, Freud, and Social Psychology

We have seen that the development of a social psychology involves certain steps. Organism, mind, and social organization must be differentiated from one another and their relations identified. Minded organisms — individuals — must be so described that their relevance for organizations, whether as creators or as objects, is readily exposed.

Neither Mead nor Freud has much to offer us in the way of a description of social organization. Neither presents any detailed technical treatment of the rise of organization out of interaction. Both do something to distinguish and characterize organisms and minds. Both say a great deal about the impact of organizations on individuals. What of value does each have to offer us and how does each compare with the other? Let us begin with Mead.

Mead

From the beginning of their acquaintance with Mead's work, many sociological social psychologists valued two of its features. The first was its sophisticated presentation of a functionalist psychology. The second was

[7] There is some justice in the charge that Freud was mechanistic in his treatment of impulses, attitudes, and the like. On the other hand, this treatment does much to capture the perseverating and inflexible character of his patients' behavior. For discussions of Freud's mechanistic tendencies, see Allport (2), Bartlett (3), and Osborn (27).

its bold extension of functionalism to explain certain of the individual's inner processes, certain of the covert aspects of acts.

a. Functionalism. Since its inception, functionalism[8] has been the perennial American psychology. Many of its principles became so well accepted as to be unquestioned. Heidbreder (15) said in 1933:

> . . . functionalism does not, at present, stand out in American psychology as a distinct school and system. It did so only in its beginnings, when it had the conspicuousness of a new movement — in particular, of a movement opposed to structuralism. . . .
> . . . in functionalism, American psychology passed through a phase of its development in which it brought together and organized many tendencies already in existence, utilizing them so successfully that they passed into general practice. To treat of mental activities as well as contents, to think in terms of adaptations and adjustments, to observe psychological processes in relation to their setting, to regard man as a biological organism adapting itself to its environment — all these procedures have been so widely accepted in psychology that they no longer attract special attention.

If anything, functionalist views are even more firmly rooted in academic psychology today. Perhaps the most dramatic evidence for this is the steady revision in functionalist directions of Hullian learning theory, the closest lineal descendent of Watson's behaviorism (16,23).

Functionalism was a psychology well adapted to the requirements of sociologists and social psychologists. It fitted both their data and their theoretical tastes. More than this, it had survived the rigorous test of explaining the same phenomena treated by competing schemes while avoiding their errors.

Functionalism was not rooted in elementarist or mechanical premises. The relations among men or attitudes or particles were just as valid in ontological status as the men, attitudes, or particles themselves. Moreover, the individual element, seen from the standpoint of the organization or system in which it participated, had meaning as a part of that system — had a role in the system. This role was a condition of being, equal in validity to the element's role as one of the ingredients from which the system first arose. Here, then, was a sophisticated philosophy that agreed with the sociologist's social realism.

By granting ontological independence to relations among elements and by seeing the nature of elements as transformed by their involvement in such relations, functionalism made tenable the position that general ideas could possess empirical independence and validity. This conclusion support-

[8] Functionalism's origins are traced in Blau (4), Hook (17) and White (40).

ed those who wanted to take seriously, and treat as independently variable, the special class of general ideas designated by terms like symbols, social norms, and culture. Faris (10) and others quickly understood that here was an outlook which credited with full reality and potency "all that is noble in us as well as the ignoble" and enabled one to treat "the emergence within the actions of men of what we know as distinctly human."

The functionalists also provided conceptions of behavior itself that were congenial to sociology. Of particular importance was their description of the relation between body and mind.

Sociologists had already been impressed with the variability of behavior between cultures and between different periods in the development of given cultures. Any psychology congruent with these observations must allow for considerable malleability in behavior. Functionalism did just that.

It pictured the human organism coming out upon the world's stage equipped with a certain range of sensory capacity and with that vague impulsive quality which signalizes life. The living organism, by virtue of being alive, must have some intercourse with the environment. It is not self-sufficient and must engage in a constant interchange of energy with the environment. The organism moves ceaselessly; but only those features of the environment which it is equipped to perceive and which, additionally, impede its passage are of interest for the psychologist. Only toward these does mind arise. The psychologist's task, as Mead and other functionalists saw it, was to assume life and to explain how it comes to take one direction rather than another. Direction is movement toward or away from impediments. Life so directed is mind.

This vision of man pictures him as originally innocent of all knowledge concerning his world. It describes conditions that require sustained relations with that world, and provides the environment with a significant role in determining what those relations will be. But it does more.[9]

It describes some of those relations as instrumental. We must remember,

[9] It would probably be correct to say that the topics of special interest to sociologists in the 1920's and 1930's enhanced their enthusiasm for Mead. Their concern with urbanism as a way of life and with social marginality turned attention to the conditions under which man could be a problem to himself, to discussions of identity and individuality. Mead provided terms and principles for this discussion. The same interests in urbanism stressed the difference between ecological and normative relations — between interaction not mediated by common rules and symbols and interaction in which these media were present. Mead stressed this same distinction and provided an explanation of its consequences. Again, the twenties and thirties were years in which, like other American intellectuals, sociologists sought to find a place in scientific explanations for morality and religion, truth and honor, ideas and affect, history and aesthetics. This place had to be one which did not reduce these entities to epiphenomena. Mead, like Dewey, James, Pierce, and Cooley, sought to provide such a place.

in this connection, that the functionalists were providing an account of mind, not of behavior. An instrumental relation — mind — connects the organism and the environment. If we consider the individual seeking to establish a viable relation of this kind, he is, by definition, rational. By this I mean that he is, by definition, seeking means fitted for his ends. Means which are not fitting, in this sense, will be rejected. Mind, so conceived, is indeed a malleable affair.

This malleability is further enhanced by another feature of the functionalist's conception. Mind, as they liked to say, lies between organism and environment. Many features of the environment change regardless of the organism's stability. Therefore, whether the individual recognizes it or not, mind also changes.

It is worth remembering that this malleability granted to mind follows inexorably from the way it is defined. The functionalists were saying: If individuals seek those relations to the environment which permit the release of a given impulse, the relations chosen will be those known and available alternatives that suffice. The organism is presumed to be ready and willing. The environment determines what ends can be realized and under what conditions. The functionalists simply did not treat the problem of the intra-individual conditions that determined whether and when the individual would take the first steps to establish instrumental relations.

From this same definition of mind there follows the characteristic functionalist attitude toward the conceptualization of "reinforcement." The typical learning psychologist conceives the environment's reinforcements as rewards or deprivations, and describes them in such terms as recency, frequency, regularity, and amount. The classical functionalist did not find this description wrong. It was incomplete. These bare categories are inadequate for describing the variable relations between impulses and environment of which mind consists. They do not enable one to differentiate between love and lust, between fear and hate, between an aesthetic judgment and an ethical decision. From a functionalist view, the concepts conventional in learning psychology inform us only of the degree of fit between some impulse and the environment, and the probability that this fit will recur. Such information is necessary, but insufficient for a description or explanation, however general, of mind and its variations. It is quite clear that two instrumental relations can be identical with respect to these learning variables and very different in all other respects.

An adequate conceptualization of the dimensions of mind is still lacking. We can understand the social psychologist's flirtations with Kenneth Burke's dramaturgical vocabulary or with Lewin's properties of the life space or with Parsons' categories of action as efforts to construct appropriate conceptions.

What all of these efforts have in common is the description of the distinguishing features of an instrumental relationship — what Dewey and Mead would have called the description of the "whole meaning." The sociological social psychologist is likely to believe that humans learn about social relations, not by fitting together bits and pieces of experience, but by grasping the general character of roles and norms. If roles and norms are instances of mind, there is no need to seek in neural associations for the process by which they are constructed. Instead, the association among their elements is interpreted as instrumental, not neural, in character. Functionalism shows how this can be so.

I have said that sociologists found malleability and "whole meanings" in behavior and appreciated functionalism as a psychology which took them into account. Functionalism was suited for many other purposes as well.

Sociologists often conceived of social relations and organizations as instruments that enabled individuals to obtain what they would have lacked without sustained help from other people. Functionalism was the psychology of instrumental relations. Sociologists were impressed with the importance of the cultural inheritance in determining man's view of his environment. Functionalism, as an instrumental psychology, dictated that the environment played a part in conduct only if it was relevant for the organism's requirements, including those requirements it had gained through living with other people and learning from them.

It has sometimes been charged that functionalist social psychology advances two incompatible pictures of mind. On the one hand, it sees mind as easily changed, on the other as locked forever in its own internal functioning, prevented by its definitions from encountering the outer world.

What this criticism refers to as incompatible visions of mind actually represents earlier and later stages of action. The organism is conceived as attending only to those objects that are relevant for the release of impulse. However, once the organism constitutes some object in the environment as a stimulus, once, that is to say, it perceives some object in the framework of its impulses or motives and descries its instrumental relevance, the properties of that object play a part in conduct. They either validate or invalidate the organism's instrumental hypotheses. A line of action persists as long as it continues to be validated by the environment. It stops when the environment provides no reinforcement or negative reinforcement. Organisms that perceive the same environment in the same fashion will receive the same reinforcement from it.

Mead's account opposes the view that conduct is determined solely by the organism or by the environment. It is not opposed, in principle, to a deterministic view of behavior. Organic necessities and past experience determine the hypotheses which the organism advances in the early stages of action. Once stimuli are constituted, they write their responses to the organism's proposals in a firm, round, determining hand.

We find, then, that functionalism has multiple appeals for sociological social psychologists. It readily enables the treatment of social relations as instrumental. It affords a significant role both to a determining environment and a selecting individual. It provides a clear distinction between mind and body. It agrees with the sociological disposition to take relations as ontologically valid and to search for whole meanings in order to understand and predict.

b. Functionalism and Intra-Psychic Events. It is with functionalism's treatment of intra-psychic events — of the covert stages of action — that we come to Mead's special contributions to social psychology. Because functionalism views mind as a relation between organism and environment, all special aspects of mind are also such relationships. These include perceiving, attending, evaluating, and responding. These processes become intra-psychic events in the form of expectations about the world which are acquired from participating in it and learning about it.

When Mead took this general functionalist approach to mind and applied it to reflective thought, he was forced to locate instrumental relations between organism and environment that might provide the special instances of mind represented by self-conscious problem solving. The grounds on which he concluded that only human interaction mediated by the standardized symbols of language could provide such relations are too well known to require review. They indicate one significant method by which the *dynamics* of social relations, as well as their elements, become a part of mind. We shall return to this point in discussing Freud.

Freud

Like Dewey and Mead, Freud appreciated the importance of the mind-body problem (18). Like them, he evolved a position which provides a significant place both for human biology and for the environment in the determination of behavior. Freud, like the functionalists, pictures the adaptive behaviors of the organism flowing from motives, with stimuli being constituted, as such, by the perspective which motives afford.

There are further similarities. Both Freud and the functionalists conceive of each act as the product of a total situation, not of isolated stimuli or single impulses. Both believe that behaviors persist only because they contribute to the organism's survival. Both, though with somewhat different emphases, deny the validity of introspection as a tool for investigating conduct. Both distinguish sharply between the original nature provided by human biology and the human nature produced by man's experience with his fellows. Finally, Freud comes closer than is often appreciated to the functionalist position concerning the indeterminate character of the newborn's psychic life (5). Mead and Dewey stress the formless nature of original impulsivity. Freud separates libido as a kind of unorganized and impressionable impulsivity from those tissue states like hunger and thirst in which a periodicity of appearance is determined more by biology than experience and for which the range of suitable environmental reinforcements is quite narrow. By contrast, the organism's libido or sexuality is a generalized propensity to act, gaining structure and differentiation by virtue of its history in the environment. As Sartre (35) observes, "The libido is nothing besides its concrete fixations, save for a permanent possibility of fixing anything whatsoever upon anything whatsoever."[10]

We must turn once more to the problems of central concern for Mead and Freud to understand the essential differences between them. Mead sought the conditions of valid knowledge and defined such knowledge as the appropriate alignment of means and ends, the alignment of the act in its covert and overt aspects with the objective environment.

As we have seen, Freud's concern was with gratification. Now gratification is not a property of mind. Instead, it refers to the net balance of the organism's profits and losses resulting from his transactions with the environment. Mind is a means from which this balance emerges. Mead takes it as objectively problematic that acts and objects can be well aligned, but assumes that gratification will follow if they are. Freud assumes that such alignment is possible, but finds alignment, as such, insufficient to assure gratification.

Mead tells us how impulses, once aroused, become related to objects with which they can effect an interchange of energy. But Freud must explain why some individuals seem unable to express impulses and why others cannot modify their conduct as a result of encounters with objects. Freud would agree that, once an impulsive process is involved in becoming related instrumentally to objects, the character of the objects does much to determine the nature of the relationship that emerges and the likelihood that this impulse will arise again or in its present form.[11] Mind, as defined by Mead would be recognized by Freud as changeable. But Freud was provoked by those conditions before and after mind which prevented it from arising; which produced, not instrumental relations, but other behavioral processes. Those processes, separated from experience, are not readily changed by it.

To pursue his objectives, Freud moved in several directions. He sought, first, to characterize impulsivity prior to its shaping by contacts with the environment. He tried, second, to explain why some parts of the body were found more often than others to be centrally involved in the organism's gratification. He worked, third, to characterize the environment in terms of its potentialities for limiting the full expression of impulse. Fourth, he described certain common relations among impulse, erogenous zones, and environmental limitations. (Seen as stable patterns in a state of equilibrium, these relations are the Freudian types of character — orality, anality and the others. Considered as a self-stabilizing arrangement restoring equilibrium after its disruption by impulse or environment, these relationships

[10] McDougall (22), who welcomed Freud to the ranks of hormic psychologists, was especially critical of this indeterminate character of many Freudian "instincts."

[11] See, for example, Freud's (13) treatment of ego, the reality principle, and secondary process. A convenient review appears in Fenichel (11).

are the mechanisms of defense — projection, denial, reaction formation, and the rest.) Finally, Freud developed a theory concerning the conditions sufficient to permit the individual to experience the available gratifications — a theory of therapy.

What were Freud's conclusions from these explorations of the psychology of gratification? What is their relevance for a social psychology?

In Freud's description of impulse, we find a first condition that prevents perfect gratification. Original impulsivity knows no limits. Its source is in the internal requirements of the organism. The environment cannot provide for the full satisfaction of those limitless requirements or offer adequate compensatory satisfactions for those it denies. Given the nature of impulse, not just civilization, but any environment, is a source of discontents.

Other things being equal, such discontents are likely to become associated with the orifices of the body because these zones provide individuals with maximal pleasure. Instrumental relations with the environment have these zones as their primary foci because pleasure and pain are greatest there.

Although of lesser importance as sources of pleasure, other parts of the body have some potentialities of the same order. The eyes, ears, fingers, and limbs are relatively important. Presumably the ear lobes and the small of the back, lacking as they are in receptive sensitivity and instrumental relevance, are among the least significant sources of pleasure.

The body's zones differ not only in the degree of their erogenous potential, but in the *mode* by which each affords gratifications from contact with objects. These modes are instrumental relations shaped by the physiological properties of the several zones. Thus gratification by way of the mouth and lips involves sucking, chewing, licking, tasting, and incorporation. Gratification by way of the genitals involves insertion or reception.

Freud understood perfectly well that the organism, as a totality including its acquired skills, and not just these special zones, was the source of many gratifications. For the weight-lifter, the muscular development of the small of the back may be greatly prized; for the Kulya woman, her earlobes, grossly distended by bronze rings, are of great significance. For the intellectual, the quick mind and the apt phrase are matters of pride. But, Freud insisted, these sources of pleasure are added to those that biology originally provides, and the acquired sources become available much later in life. The socialization of the erogenous zones, coming first, establishes, as it were, a set of premises with which later socialization must contend. First, unless the individual is adequately gratified from these original sources, it is unlikely that he will have the energy available to venture a search for gratification from less immediate and less concrete sources. Second, if the mode of gratification from a later and more abstract source has features common to the mode built into some erogenous zone, some association is likely to arise between them. This association is illustrated in the famous formula (14) by which a child is proposed as the equivalent of a penis, which is shown to be equivalent to feces. It is not a matter of the individual confusing these objects with one another in perceptual or cognitive terms. Were that to occur, it would indicate grave pathology. What Freud does say is that these three objects come to be equivalent with respect to the mode through which they give pleasure to anal women.

Freud was more convinced than most of us are likely to be of the potency of the original erogenous modes for determining the nature of all later gratification. It is difficult, however, to dismiss the existence of many associations between these earlier modes and those which come later. Common figures of speech, verified interpretations of projective symbols, and clinical records provide countless illustrations of such associations (12).

In any case, one must add such associations to the inherent insatiability of impulse as sources which frustrate gratification. According to the best evidence available to Freud or to us, such associations would emerge from the phasing of neural activity. Unlike associations that arise in instrumental relations between impulse and objects, these associations between attitudes are not an aspect of mind. They are not governed by instrumental laws and utility functions, and their occurrence interferes with the operation of such laws and functions.

Consider, next, Freud's description of the environment. It is given in terms of that environment's limitations to pleasure. If those limitations make it dangerous for the individual to indicate that he has a given impulse, whether he expresses it or not, they have the quality of superego. If the limitations merely qualify the timing and means of impulse expression, they have the quality of ego. Now we are back in the realm of mind — of instrumental relations, but these relations are classified from a perspective not considered by Mead, and, what is more important, Freud's categories raise novel problems for mind's future expression.

Like Mead, Freud observed that only other people respond to our impulses as distinguished from the overt phases of our acts. Consequently, only other people will provide limitations with superego qualities.

A distinctive consequence of superego limitations is that, once they are accepted, the process we call mind vanishes, but the impulse need not. It is not merely unimplemented, it is defined in principle as unimplementable. The further associations it develops with other impulses and attitudes and the transformations it undergoes seem to owe little to instrumental associations and much to the internal self-stabilizing processes of the organisms.

Looking back over this sketch of impulse, body zones, and modes, and superego, we see that each involves considerations that fall outside the scope of a concept of mind as presented in functionalism. Yet none requires the assumption of instincts — of instrumental action established solely through biological inheritance. In a variety of ways, each of these three impediments to gratification calls our attention to non-instrumental, intra-organic events that precede, follow, or accompany mind, relating to it but having a significant degree of independent variance. We are reminded once more that Mead and Freud supplement each other's work by examining somewhat different phases of behavior. Because Freud wrote on such matters, we can be certain that he would have agreed with the functionalists concerning many of the properties of mind.[12] He would, however, have seen those properties as insufficient to account for psychopathology.

The varieties of character and the mechanisms of defense are the final result of Freud's work. Here all the ingredients previously sketched become organized in a systematic fashion. Freud, as Frenkel-Brunswik said (12):

> . . . tends to view character structure from a defensive point of view, and social influences as a series of traumata which bring to a halt or discontinue instinctual gratification and expression.
> . . . This view does not do justice to all the satisfactions gained from moving along constructive social avenues.

A number of somewhat independent observers have come to a similar view of the types of character. Erikson (9), Fromm(15), and Parsons (29,30), for example, propose that these types represent residues of the major stages of socialization.[13] Only Parsons offers a coherent account of the appearance of these particular types of character and of the order in which they arise. In essence he suggests that each type of character represents the skills required to perform adequately in one of the four major roles embodied in social systems. These roles — these organizational facts — provide the key theoretical apparatus for explaining the rise of these types of character. We may note, first, that we are now confronted by a truly social psychological account and, second, that this account pictures these particular types of character not merely as relevant for participating in some organizations but as descriptions of skills essential for participation in all organizations. One version of this approach may suffice to indicate its general character.[14]

In interactional terms, dependency is the central fact of orality as a stage of development or as a type of character. From the standpoint of its parents, the infant is functionally dependent upon adults for its survival, but is unaware of its need for social support. It gradually learns that it is dependent. If the infant does not learn to be dependent, there is no foundation for the remaining stages and they will not appear.

[12] Freud's discussion appears in (13).

[13] The interpretation that follows was developed originally in Swanson (38).

[14] For another characterization of the interactional significance of these stages, see Swanson (36).

The central interactional fact of anality is responsibility. Once the young child is committed to depend on others, they can and do make demands on him which facilitate their living together. The child must accept some responsibility for his own conduct, must exercise self-surveillance, or stable, continued interdependence is an intolerable burden to his elders. There is general agreement that most children find these responsibilities difficult to accept, and come only gradually to feel comfortable in living with them.

Observers are also in agreement in believing that the requirement for a child's assumption of stable participation with peers and others outside his family forces the generalization of dependent and responsible relations to these additional groups. Parsons has given us an especially sensitive and detailed picture of the way in which the structural demands of the family as an organization, the ultimate requirements of the total society for more mature forms of social participation, and the child's current interpersonal skills all interact to produce first the oedipal crisis and, if that is resolved successfully, the golden years of latency which take us from the fourth or fifth year to the brink of adolescence. It is plausible to regard such a sequence as common in all cultures with, perhaps some variations in timing. It is important to understand that the basic anal character, dependent and responsible, is retained throughout these stages. It is simply extended in the social relations to which it applies.

It is toward the end of childhood that another ingredient is added to this anal pattern, the ingredient of independence, or, more suggestively, of competent performance. This is the particular sign of the phallic character. We may believe that relations with peers and others outside the family are of special importance in this development.

By independence, I mean that the child is expected to be able to show sufficient self-confidence to enter easily upon new tasks and new social relations without looking to his family for constant guidance and nurturance. This is not primarily a matter of possessing appropriate intellectual and motor skills, although these are necessary. The focus of the phallic period is the demonstration that one can establish new social relations as the occasion demands and participate responsibly in them. These abilities are the fruit of latency and the foundation for the final step — the emergence of the genital character.

The genital character is dependent, responsible, and competent. In addition, he makes positive contributions to the development and maintenance of the groups to which he belongs. The description and explanation of genitality are the least developed in existing discussions of Freud's typology. Fromm catches the spirit of the matter in speaking of genitality as "the productive orientation (15)." I take this to mean that the individual feels obligated not merely to obey some limited set of rules, but to enhance and add to the lives of his fellows. He is no longer only a beneficiary of society, but one of its fully responsible operators, his welfare bound inextricably with the welfare of the whole organization.

I have been describing the normative and desirable aspects of these four types of character. Each has, of course, its deviant forms. But, in desired form or otherwise, the greet sweep of Freud's typology is from dependence to contribution, from rudimentary commitment to social relations with one's parents to commitment to ever-larger groups, from conformity to set demands to an obligation for the performance of whatever services may be necessary for social growth and survival. From the individual's perspective, these stages look somewhat different. Freud was always alert to the competition between individual needs and social demands. As sociological social psychologists, however, we may view the sequence from the organizational standpoint, seeing in it the growth of the individual's social commitments.

This social, and, we may note, functionalist, account of Freud's characterology helps us to identify its powers and limitations. It touches on only a small part of the phenomena of development and socialization. That part, however, is of central importance for sociology. Whatever else we may say of them, social roles represent positions in a pattern of influence among actors, and influence, in its turn, rests on dependence. More than this, moral, stable, and continued influence requires responsibility, competence, and contribution. Freud's typology enables us to describe significantly different readinesses with which individuals characteristically engage in such relations (36). When, as often happens, we find individuals who seek roles that are unusual in the general character of the influence which their holders exercise or receive, we can have some assurance that Freud's types will allow us to characterize those individuals in a fashion that complements our description of their roles. It was Lasswell (20) who seems first to have recognized and employed this special affinity of the psychosexual character levels for describing personality in terms compatible with essential features of all social roles.[15]

The several mechanisms of defense — turning against the self, projection, reaction formation, and the rest — are closely tied to the psychosexual stages. Each can be shown to represent an instrumental relation to one's self and others which reconciles some socially deviant desire with the particular type of dependency and obligation associated with one of the stages of socialization, I have described these connections elsewhere, and wish only to call attention to the fact that the defenses, like the types of character, are built upon the fundamental nature and basic vicissitudes of social commitments (37).

The defenses are, however, of special interest in a comparison of Mead and Freud. Each is a special instance of social control being imported as self-control. Each first exists as a relation between persons, becoming

[15] Early usage of psychoanalytic ideas by sociologists is surveyed in Burgess (6) and Eliot (7).

internalized in the course of learning to participate in such relations. In each case, the whole relationship, which includes the influences that actors exert on one another,is imported. Thus what are often called the "dynamics" of the relationship are internalized along with the actors concerned. We need not infer, as Freud often does, that these dynamics are somehow supplied by the central nervous system. The relations involved are instrumental, not neural, in character.

If we are right in saying that the defenses represent one set of fundamental varieties of self-control, they must, in Mead's theory, represent a fundamental categorization of the varieties of self-awareness. It is true that the defenses constitute only one such categorization, but it is one of special relevance for the study of social organization and social control. It provides a set of problems of description and explanation in which the joint powers of Meadian and Freudian thinking can be exploited.

Conclusion

I began this paper by observing that social psychologists often considered Mead to be theoretically fundamental but empirically unfruitful; Freud as empirically provocative but theoretically wrong. What does our survey of their work suggest concerning these judgments?

I believe there are three reasons for the current view of Mead. First, he provides a way of formulating important aspects of almost any problem we touch in social psychology, but does not suggest many problems for investigation. Second, certain of his most relevant premises are untestable. Third, many of these features of his scheme which are testable do not fall within the social psychologist's purview.

Every problem of interest in social psychology requires that we make some judgments about the relation of mind to body and social organization. Unless this relation is one that sees these three as independent but interacting, our problem is destroyed before it is answered. Mead's version of functionalist psychology provides what we require, and does so more admirably than do other available schemes.

But, as Mead left it, his functionalism does little to specify systematic relations among body, mind, and social organization and the various forms of each. In short, he left us a general approach for the formulation of our problems, but did not suggest a wealth of problems at which we should look.

Second, Mead is peculiarly unfortunate in having proposed as a major social psychological premise a dictum that seems untestable, whatever its heuristic value. I have in mind his judgment that self-awareness and reflective thought are products of social interaction mediated by language signs and products of it alone. The only relevant test of this notion would require a population of biologically normal human adults who had managed, without undue trauma, to become knowledgeable about a differentiated environment, who had learned to employ certain common vocal gestures instrumentally but not reflexively, and who lacked all human contacts from birth to maturity. I believe it is time to label as irrelevant for Mead's premise all of the materials on feral men, infra-human primates, aphasics, schizophrenics, and children. None of these provides a reasonable test of Mead's ideas. The accounts of ferals are of doubtful validity. The chimpanzees and gorillas lack human biology as well as symbols. It is as plausible to explain the aphasic's difficulty from the damage to his brain as from his conceptual disorders. Schizophrenia seems more a result of traumatic rearing than of miseducation in symbol usage. The very young child is biologically and experientially immature as well as unskilled in language.

Although I am disposed to believe that Mead's premise is sound, I am also disposed to believe that it cannot be demonstrated to be so. I would propose that whatever use we may make of Mead should not depend on the truth of this particular premise, and that we stop fruitless debate about its validity.

I suggested, third, that many of the testable features of Mead's scheme do not fall within the purview of social psychology. Such matters as the exploratory and impulsive character of the organism (41), the existence and nature of choices which are not guided self-consciously yet not distorted by repression (8), and the nature and growth of motives (26) are under intensive investigation by experimental psychologists. In each case, the evidence strongly supports a functionalist interpretation. In no case, however, are variations in social organization, as such, of crucial theoretical importance. The problems addressed are those of psychology proper, not of social psychology.

Freud's present status in social psychology is almost the exact complement of Mead's. In its original form, Freud's theory of mind was unacceptable. Once we separate out its instinctive and Lamarckian features, however, we find two remaining clusters of ideas, each of which continues to be useful, each being supported by considerable evidence (26). The first cluster is not a theory of mind, it is a theory of neural and organic functioning without consideration for the organism's instrumental relations with its environment. This theory is of the source of conditions that precede, accompany, and follow the presence of mind and provide limits to gratification.

The second cluster of ideas consists of features of instrumental relations, of mind, especially significant for understanding the way in which the social environment limits gratification. These include superego, the types of character, the methods of defense, and the process of therapy. Each has proven surprisingly easy to rationalize by means of a functionalist approach, and each fits readily into our growing social psychological treatment of socialization and social control (28, 31, 42).

Freud was wrong because he failed to distinguish clearly between mind and intra-organic functioning and because he overgeneralized the values and experiences of his patients. Freud is provocative because he provides a rich set of differentiations readily interpretable as variations in mind which, in turn, are particularly significant consequences of social organization's impact on individuals.

We should not conclude, however, that Freud and Mead have left us a psychology completely adequate for our needs. There are many current developments that extend or modify their work. Parsons' categories of action, devised to bring greater coherence to our burgeoning knowledge, represent just an elaboration of an instrumental view of mind. So also do the rapidly growing studies of identity, of socialization, of semantic principles, and of interaction process. The explanation of social change is pressing hard upon functionalism's scant treatment of reinforcement and of the processes by which images are selected to guide the release of blocked impulses. The interpretation of personality adjustment in old age is demanding a more adequate picture of the limits to the place of mind in the total pattern of behavior. Investigators have been forced to develop the causal and functional laws so scarce in psychoanalysis. Given these developments, and many others, it is unlikely that the ideas of Mead or Freud will soon be only curiosities in the museums of our discipline.

References

1. Allport, F. H., *Social Psychology,* Boston: Houghton Mifflin Co., 1924.
2. Allport, G. W., "Dewey's Individual and Social Psychology," in P. A. Schilpp (ed.), *The Philosophy of John Dewey,* Evanston: Northwestern University, 1939, 263-290.
3. Bartlett, F. H., *Sigmund Freud, A Marxian Essay,* London: Victor Gollancz, Ltd., 1938.
4. Blau, J. L., *Men and Movements in American Philosophy,* New York: Prentice-Hall, Inc., 1952.
5. Blum, G. S., *Psychoanalytic Theories of Personality,* New York: McGraw-Hill Book Co., Inc., 1953.
6. Burgess, E. W., "The Influence of Sigmund Freud upon Sociology in the United States," *The American Journal of Sociology,* 1939, 45, 356-374.
7. Eliot, T. D., "Interactions of Psychiatric and Social Theory Prior to 1940," in A. M. Rose (ed.), *Mental Health and Mental Disorder, A Sociological Approach,* New York: W. W. Norton and Co., Inc., 1955, 18-41.
8. Eriksen, C. W., "Subception: Fact or Artifact?" *The Psychological Review,* 1956, 63, 74-80.
9. Erikson, E. H., *Childhood and Society,* New York: W. W. Norton and Co., Inc., 1950.
10. Faris, E., "The Social Psychology of George Mead," *The American Journal of Sociology,* 1937, 43, 396.

11. Fenichel, O., *The Psychoanalytic Theory of Neurosis,* New York: W. W. Norton and Co., Inc., 1945.
12. Frenkel-Brunswik, E., "Psychoanalysis and the Unity of Science," *Proceedings of the American Academy of Arts and Sciences,* 1954, 80, 297-299.
13. Freud, S., *The Ego and the Id,* London: Hogarth Press, 1927.
14. Freud, S., "On the Transformation of Instincts with Special Reference to Anal Erotism," *Collected Papers,* vol. 2, London: Hogarth Press, 1948, 164-171.
15. Fromm, E., *Man for Himself, An Inquiry into the Psychology of Ethics,* New York: Rinehart and Co., Inc., 1947, 50-117.
16. Hilgard, E. R., *Theories of Learning,* New York: Appleton-Century-Crofts, Inc., 1956, Chapter 14.
17. Hook, S., *John Dewey, An Intellectual Portrait,* New York: The John Day Co., 1939.
18. Jones, E., *The Life and Work of Sigmund Freud,* vol. 1, New York: Basic Books, Inc., 1953, 367-379.
19. Kaplan, A., "Freud and Modern Philosophy," in B. Nelson (ed.), *Freud and the Twentieth Century,* New York: Meridian Books, Inc., 1957, 209-229.
20. Lasswell, H. D., *Psychopathology and Politics,* Chicago: The University of Chicago Press, 1930.
21. Marcuse, H., *Eros and Civilization,* Boston: Beacon Press, 1955
22. McDougall, W., *Psycho-Analysis and Social Psychology,* London: Methuen and Co., Ltd., 1936
23. Miller, N. E., "Liberalization of Basic S-R Concepts: Extensions to Conflict Behavior, Motivation and Social Learning," in S. Koch (ed.), *Psychology: A Study of a Science. Study I: Conceptual and Systematic,* vol. 2, New York: McGraw-Hill Book Co., Inc., 1959, 196-292
24. Morris, C., "Pierce, Mead, and Pragmatism," *The Philosophical Review,* 1938, 47, 100-127.
25. Natanson M., *The Social Dynamics of George H. Mead,* Washington D.C.: Public Affairs Press, 1956.
26. Olds, J., *The Growth and Structure of Motives,* Glencoe, Ill.: The Free Press, 1956, 60-63.
27. Osborn, R., *Freud and Marx, A Dialectical Study,* London: Victor Gollancz, Ltd., 1937.
28. Parsons, T., "An Approach to Psychological Theory in Terms of the Theory of Action," in S. Koch (ed.), *Psychology: A Study of a Science, Study I: Conceptual and Systematic,* vol. 3, New York: McGraw-Hill Book Co., Inc., 1959, 612-711
29. Parsons, T., "Family Structure and the Socialization of the Child," in T. Parsons and R. F. Bales (eds.), *Family, Socialization and Interaction Process,* Glencoe, Ill.: The Free Press, 1955, 35-131.

30. Parsons, T., "The Organization of Personality as a System of Action," in T. Parsons and R. F. Bales (eds.), *Family, Socialization and Interaction Process,* Glencoe, Ill.: The Free Press, 1955, 133-186.
31. Parsons, T., "Psychology and Sociology," in J. Gillin (ed.), *For a Science of Social Man,* New York: The Macmillan Co., 1954, 67-101.
32. Peristiany, J. G., "Introduction," in E. Durkheim, *Sociology and Philosophy,* Glencoe, Ill.: The Free Press, 1953, vii-xxxii.
33. Pfuetze, P.E., *The Social Self,* New York: Bookman Associates, 1954.
34. Rieff, P., *Freud: The Mind of the Moralist,* New York: The Viking Press, 1959.
35. Sartre, J. P., *Existential Psychoanalysis,* New York: Philosophical Library, 1953, 74.
36. Swanson, G. E., "Agitation in Face-to-Face Contacts: A Study of the Personalities of Orators," *The Public Opinion Quarterly,* 1957, 21, 288-294.
37. Swanson, G. E., "Determinants of the Individual's Defenses Against Inner Conflict: Review and Reformulation," in J. Glidewell (ed.), *Parental Attitudes and Child Behavior,* Springfield, Ill.: Charles C. Thomas, 1961, 5-41.
38. Swanson, G. E., "Individual Development as the Learning of a Sequence of Social Roles," Technical Paper P-5, Detroit Area Study of the University of Michigan, 1952.
39. Thibaut, J. W. and H. H. Kelley, *The Social Psychology of Groups,* New York: John Wiley and Sons, Inc., 1959.
40. White, M. G., *The Origin of Dewey's Instrumentalism,* New York: Columbia University Press, 1943.
41. White, R. W., "Motivation Reconsidered: The Concept of Competence," *The Psychological Review,* 1959, 66, 297-333.
42. Wilson, A. T. M., E. L. Trist, and A.Curle, "Transitional Communities and Social Reconnection . . .," in G. E. Swanson and Others (eds.), *Readings in Social Psychology,* New York: Henry Holt and Co., 1952, 561-579.

3. Major Trends in Symbolic Interaction in the Past Twenty-five Years *

Manford H. Kuhn

The year 1937 lies virtually in the middle of a four-year period which saw the publication of *Mind, Self, and Society, Movements of Thought in the Nineteenth Century,* and *The Philosophy of the Act.*[1] It would represent the greatest naiveté to suggest that thus the year 1937 represented the introduction of symbolic interactionism. We are all aware of the long development: from James, Baldwin, and Cooley to Thomas, Faris, Dewey, Blumer, and Young. Even the Tardean imitation and suggestion which underlay Ross's *Social Psychology*[2] contributed a good deal ordinarily not credited to him in the development of interaction theory. Nor is it the fact that Mead represents the fullest development of the orientation that makes so significant the posthumous publication of his works (for which we may conveniently take 1937 as an anchoring point). Mead's ideas had been known for a very long time. He had taught University of Chicago students from 1893 to 1931. His notions were bruited about in classes and seminars wherever there were professors conducting them who had studied at the University of Chicago — not least in the great heartland included in the Midwest of our society. Some of Mead's students had published their versions of his ideas or quotations from some of his philosophical papers — Kimball Young's *Source Book in Social Psychology* of a decade earlier contained a paper by Mead, and his *Social Psychology*

From *The Sociological Quarterly,* V (Winter, 1964), pp. 61-84, by permission of the journal.

*Paper read before the Midwest Sociological Society at its twenty-fifth anniversary meetings, Des Moines, Iowa, April 12-14, 1962. (The paper was prepared for oral presentation. Footnotes have been added. Where additional information is given which was not implied or suggested in the original text, this has been clearly indicated — The Editor).

[1] George H. Mead, *Mind, Self and Society,* ed. with an Introduction by Charles W. Morris (Chicago: Univ. of Chicago Press, 1934); *Movements of Thought in the Nineteenth Century,* ed. by Merritt H. Moore (Chicago: Univ. of Chicago Press, 1936); *The Philosophy of the Act,* ed. by Charles W. Morris (Chicago: Univ. of Chicago Press, 1938).

[2] Edward Alsworth Ross, *Social Psychology* (New York, 1908).

bore the strong imprint of Meadian interactionism.[3]

No, the significance of the publication of Mead's books is that it ended what must be termed the long era of the "oral tradition," the era in which most of the germinating ideas had been passed about by word of mouth. (It should be noted parenthetically that Mead had published earlier a considerable number of papers, but they were mainly in journals devoted to philosophy and ethics, journals not likely to be read by sociologists or social psychologists. His only paper in a sociological journal — of which I am aware — was his assessment of Cooley's theories.)[4]

The oral tradition, it must be noted, has some generic peculiarities which are evidenced equally by primitive myth and by unpublished intellectual orientation: there tends to be much (almost ritual) repetition; there is a strain to "get it right," that is, to be correct; there is much debate over orthodoxy, and whatever intellectual powers there may be, are more devoted to casuistry and criticism than to inquiry and creativity. The mnemic effort freed from its task of remembering "how it goes" is somehow transformed into energy for imagination on the one hand and for the drudgery of testing and justification on the other. This is what was made possible by the belated publication of the three books by Mead.

Mead had not been the only one of the symbolic interactionists who had failed to publish. The year 1937 was the one in which some of the papers of Ellsworth Faris appeared under the title, *The Nature of Human Nature.*[5] Here, too, was a belated publication which, in its sprinkling and scatter, speaks more for what Faris never published — a rounded theoretical conception of his social psychology. Thomas' *theoretical* formulations were similarly scarce, scattered and incomplete — however influential. While Dewey published voluminously, his chief formulation of symbolic interaction theory is, in my view, his *Experience and Nature* which did not appear until late and which is written in such a forbidding Germanic version of the English language that many sociologists and social psycho-

[3] George H. Mead, "Thought, Symbols, and Language," in Kimball Young (ed.), *Source Book for Social Psychology* (New York: Alfred A. Knopf, 1928), pp. 341-46, reprinted from "The Behavioristic Account of the Significant Symbol," *Journal of Philosophy,* 19: 159-63 (1922). Kimball Young, *Social Psychology: An Analysis of Social Behavior* (New York: F. S. Crofts, 1930).

[4] [Kuhn is referring to George H. Mead, "Cooley's Contribution to American Social Thought," *American Journal of Sociology,* 35:693-706 (Mar., 1930). The same journal did in fact publish two earlier papers by Mead: "The Working Hypothesis in Social Reform," *American Journal of Sociology,* 5:367-71 (Nov., 1899); "The Psychology of Primitive Justice," *ibid.,* 23:577-602 (Mar.1918). —The Editor].

[5] Ellsworth Faris, *The Nature of Human Nature and Other Essays in Social Psychology* (New York and London: McGraw-Hill, 1937).

logists have not read it even yet.[6] Blumer, the young and promising heir apparent, has published relatively little and has nowhere gathered together a rounded version of his point of view.

But even though the oral tradition has some tendency to continue in symbolic interactionism, the past twenty-five years have seen a marked increase in all kinds of activity involving the published symbol: three textbooks on "our side of the social psychological fence" — that by R.E.L. Faris, that by Lindesmith and Strauss (now in its second edition) and the very recent one by Shibutani;[7] a sizable fraction of Newcomb's text[8] and lesser amounts of others on the "other side"; a considerable number of monographs, and into the hundreds of journal articles.

Basically the past twenty-five years have constituted, in contrast to the preceding era, the *age of inquiry* in symbolic interactionism.

But while it has been an era of inquiry, the inquiry has been directed at the testing and developing of what amounts almost to a welter of sub-theories going by a variety of names other than symbolic interactionism. This spawning of smaller, less inclusive theories has been due, in my opinion, neither to the propensity of scholars to attempt to make names for themselves by renaming what has already been proposed, nor to their having modified or augmented symbolic interaction in significant measure. This development of sub- or related orientations has stemmed from the essential ambiguities and contradictions in the Meadian statement — ambiguities and contradictions which were generally interpreted to be dark, inscrutable complexities too difficult to understand as long as the orientation remained largely in the oral tradition. Much of this confusion and contradiction may be summed up — but only in a vastly oversimplifying way and for purposes limited to immediate ones I hope here to expound — as a contradiction between *determinacy* and *indeterminacy* in Mead's overall point of view.

It is apparent that Mead took the view that the individual is initially dependent on the antecedent existence of a social system, specifically as it exists in the ongoing process of a functioning language, for the means wherewith to engage in experience or to take any kind of self-conscious and self-directed action. This internalization of language and the concomitant internalization of the role of the other has, in the Meadian description, nothing

[6] John Dewey, *Experience and Nature* (Chicago: Open Court Publishing Company, 1925).

[7] Robert E. L. Faris, *Social Psychology* (New York: The Ronald Press, 1953); Alfred R. Lindesmith and Anselm L. Strauss, *Social Psychology* (New York: The Dryden Press, 1949: rev. ed., 1956); Tamotsu Shibutani, *Society and Personality: An Interactionist Approach to Social Psychology* (Englewood Cliffs, N. J.: Prentice-Hall, 1961).

[8] Theodore M. Newcomb, *Social Psychology* (New York: The Dryden Press, 1950).

in it inconsistent with strict regularity or determinism.[9] Yet, as Mead proposed the *I* and the *Me* as the internal conversationalists constituting in their conversation the self, he indicated that the *I* is impulsive and essentially unpredictable — and furthermore that the *I* is the initiating, acting aspect of the self. It is never completely clear whether he meant only that the *I* is *subjectively* unpredictable or that it is indeterminate in a scientific sense.

Furthermore, it seems apparent that there was a basic initiative attributed to the self in the whole process of role-taking, at any rate after the early learning of language and probably even during that process as well. Mead, after all, insisted that the self constitutes its own environment, its own reality. Furthermore, there is the implicit possibility of indeterminacy in the whole conversation between the *I* and the *Me*. And, finally, it is possible to see in Mead's notion of the self such an antithesis to structure, such a dynamically volatile process of shifting self-indications that, whatever the *theoretical* view of determinacy *vs.* indeterminacy in any of the attributes of the self, the whole matter is so evanescent and shifting that it is obviously a practical impossibility to obtain access to any — possibly determinate — antecedents in time to make usable or testable predictions.

We may sum up this set of ambiguities about determinism as follows: The notion that the *I* is indeterminate but the *Me's* are determinate; the notion that both the *I* and the *Me's* are indeterminate; the notion that whereas both the *I* and *Me's* are determinate results of identifiable events, the interaction (conversation) between the two is somehow itself indeterminate or emergent.

But this is a preliminary view and does not cover the varieties of ways in which symbolic interactionism may be structured and, for that matter, has been structured by those proposing inquiry under its aegis. The two most frequently complicating considerations are: (1) the question whether the self is conceived, for research purposes, as the antecedent variable with criterion events (especially behaviors) as consequent variables, or conversely whether antecedent variables (ascribed identities, affiliations, associations, or communication variables and other events) are conceived to predict — that is, to exist in regularity with — consequent self variations; and (2) the question whether the relevant antecedent variables are conceived to be *immediate* or *remote* in time with respect to the events thought of as consequent.

This set of questions and ambiguities in symbolic interaction theory has led to a variety of answers. One answer structures human behavior deterministically by conceiving antecedent, causal variables to be con-

[9] "Mead's account [of conduct] . . . is not opposed, in principle, to a deterministic view of behavior." — Guy E. Swanson, "Mead and Freud, Their Relevance for Social Psychology." *Sociometry* 24:327 (Dec., 1961).

Types of Symbolic Interaction Theory

Presupposing Determinacy	Presupposing Indeterminacy
(1) Soc A_1 ⟶ Beh C	(6) A $\overset{*}{\text{Ch}}$ Ind
(2) Soc A_1 ⟶ Self C	(7) A_2 - - - - * - - - → $\overset{*}{\text{Ch}}$ Ind
(3) Soc A_2 ⟶ Self C	(8) Self_{pr}A - - - - * - - - → $\overset{*}{\text{Self}}_{pub}$
(4) Self A ⟶ Beh C	(9) $\text{Self}_{pr}\overset{*}{\text{A}}$ - - - - * - - - → Beh C
(5) Self A ⟶ Self C	

Where Soc refers to social variable
Self refers to self variable, either holistic or elementalistic
Self_{pr} refers to "private self"
Self_{pub} refers to "public self"
A indicates antecedent variable
A_1 indicates immediately antecedent variable
A_2 indicates antecedent but temporarily distal variable
C indicates consequent variable
Beh indicates overt behavioral variable
Ch indicates internal choice-making
Ind indicates internal (self) indications
Em indicates an emergent (I or Me)
Det indicates a determinate (I or Me)
Solid arrow indicates a determinate, causal process
Broken arrow indicates an indeterminate, emergent process
Asterisk (*) indicates the locus of indeterminacy; this may lie in the nexus between antecedent and consequent variables as well as in any of the following internal aspects of the self:

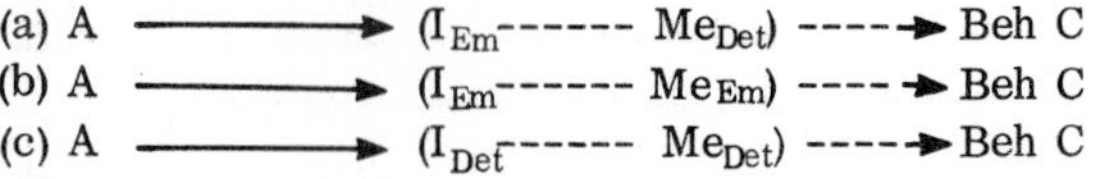

temporaneous social ones with the consequent ones having to do with the nature or structure of the self (either as a whole or of the elements seen to constitute the whole).

A second answer conceives the antecedent variables to be historical or developmental, thus possibly quite temporally remote from the consequent variables which are, as in the first answer, taken to be the nature or structure of the self, either holistically or elementally constituted.

A third answer conceives the antecedent variables to be the self, either as a whole or elementally, and the consequent variables to be those of overt behavior.

A fourth answer conceives the antecedent variables to be self variables which among themselves produce consequent, novel, but determinate self-attributes.

A similar variety of *indeterminate* answers has been given to the questions raised by ambiguities and inconsistencies in symbolic interaction orientation.

One answer appears to see virtually all significant attributes of behavior to be internal choices and other self-indications, all of which are conceived to be emergent, with no observable, regular antecedent.

Another is similar to this view but sees antecedents to these internal events in experiences lost, or partially lost, in the antiquity of the individual's early biography, and without too close a dependence on, or regularity with, such early happenings.

A third sees the significant variables as external behaviors which are either unrelated to the self, or deviously related, or only loosely related to the self. Such is often the kind of orientation held by those who see a sharp disjunction between public and private selves, where the private self is the true self with unresearchable antecedents, and where the public self is the social self, both in that it relates to observable behaviors and in that it has social antecedents.

A fourth conceives external events to be shaped more or less unpredictably by self-activities which in turn are "self-developed," *i.e.*, indeterminate in any testable way.

If one were to arrogate to oneself the privilege of deciding these issues and others raised essentially by the ambiguities in symbolic interaction orientation, one could narrow sharply the task of surveying the major trends in this theory in the past twenty-five years. This, however, I deem to be neither proper nor useful. Similarly, if symbolic interactionists had their own professional organization, their own journal or journals, their own pontifical leader or tight-knit little clique of leaders clearly assigned the role of determining the "correct" view among competing doctrinal differences, the survey of the fruits of orthodoxy might be simple. Instead, however, we have none of these things, and for the most part we wish none of them. But the consequences are that there is a welter of partial orientations which bear varying relationships to the general point of view.

There is, for example, *role theory*. Role theory has many intellectual antecedents other than those in Cooley, Dewey, Thomas, Faris, and Mead. There are debts, for instance, to Linton, to Moreno, to Parsons; there are often overtones of one or another of the learning theories. These are but a few of the strands of thought in role theory. Yet role theory is not sharply distinguishable — if at all — from symbolic interactionism. The *emphasis* in role theory is on overt role playing and on the researchable relation between role expectations and role performances; the emphasis is either less, or altogether lacking, on role-taking, on the interior processes of the self, and what Shibutani calls the sentiments are often ignored. Thus role theory tends toward what Turner wishes to call the processes of conformity.[10]

Yet I must underscore the word *emphasis,* for in Sarbin's useful chapter in the *Handbook of Social Psychology,* there is no ignoring of self nor of empathy, nor is there in his own research (of which there is a fine example indicating a positive relation between role-taking ability on the one hand and degree of malleability of self-conception on the other).[11] But on the whole, role theory has implied [determinacy] of Type I.

Among the important contributions of the quarter-century under the general aegis of role theory have been the preliminary systematization provided in the early part of Gross, Mason, and McEachern's *Explorations in Role Analysis,* and Turner's paper in Rose's *Human Behavior and Social Processes,* in which issues of determinacy *vs.* indeterminacy of the sort here proposed for all of symbolic interactionism are made with respect specifically to role theory.[12] Role theory has engendered a great deal of research; in fact, it is as much to role theory as to any other development that I point when I have designated this period under scrutiny as the era of inquiry. This is no place in which to attempt to summarize this research. By and large we can say it has underscored Thomas' dictum that "people tend to play the roles assigned to them." There is by no means any strong evidence that there is a completely determinate relation between role expectations or recipes on the one hand and role performance on the other. On the other hand, there is a growing mountain of evidence that with "known" or public role recipes in hand we can make very useful probabilistic predictions with respect to subsequent behaviors, not alone those representing the answering role performances but even those which are but logically related and ancillary behaviors.

[10] [Cp. Shibutani, *op. cit.*, pp. 323 ff., 548 ff. *et passim;* Ralph H. Turner, "Role-Taking: Process Versus Conformity," in *Human Behavior and Social Processes: An Interactionist Approach,* Arnold M. Rose, ed. (Boston: Houghton Mifflin, 1962), pp. 20-40. — The Editor].

[11] Theodore R. Sarbin, "Role Theory," in *Handbook of Social Psychology,* ed. by Gardner Lindzey (Cambridge, Mass.: Addison-Wesley Publishing Company, 1954), 1:223-58. [The example of Sarbin's own research that Kuhn probably had in mind is Theodore R. Sarbin and Norman L. Farberow, "Contributions to Role-Taking Theory: A Clinical Study of Self and Role," *Journal of Abnormal and Social Psychology,* 47:117-25 (Jan., 1952). — The Editor].

[12] Neal Gross, Ward S. Mason, and Alexander W. McEachern, *Explorations in Role Analysis: Studies of the School Superintendency Role* (New York: John Wiley, 1958); Ralph H. Turner, "Role-Taking: Process Versus Conformity," *op. cit.*

Much of the utility of role theory has been demonstrated thus far in the study of internalized role conflicts and contradictions. This study has ranged from the imaginative employment of personal documents and interviews by Mirra Komarovsky in her study of the conflicts surrounding the role of young women in college[13] to the construction of fairly precise and rigorous scales in the measure of such role conflict in the work of Stouffer and Toby. Even in such studies which imply internalization and thus the interposition of intermediate or intervening variables into our Type I determinacy pattern, such intervening variables are basically unnecessary even in the operations by Komarovsky; for although they involved reports of subjective valuations, these reports could have been replaced by direct observations of communications applying the opposing pressures — it was simply inconvenient to do so.

Another equally salient development has been that of *reference group* theory, so-named, of course, by Hyman[14] but getting much of the attention it has received from the concept of relative deprivation as employed by Stouffer in *The American Soldier* and as reworked in the well-known chapter on reference group theory by Merton and Kitt.[15] There have been a number of useful theoretical critiques as well as creative employments of reference group theory, notable among them those of Kelley, Shibutani, Turner, Newcomb, and Sherif. The notion of reference group is obviously closely related to the whole problem of the other as dealt with by Mead and Sullivan on the one hand, and to that of the primary group as described by Cooley and Faris on the other. Much of the employment of this new theory has been so far to provide *ex post* or circular explanation (explanation by naming). Controversy abounds, to be sure, over the meaning of the term *reference group* itself — whether it refers to a normative or to an evaluative function; whether it must point to groups, to categories or both; whether it may best refer to relationships, as Rose suggests, or whether we may better use it to refer to derivative orientations, as Shibutani indicates. May we use the term to refer to empirically identifiable attitudes, expectations, and norms of existent *others,* or must we limit ourselves to such matters only after they have been transmuted to the images in the imagination of the *actors* themselves, to which Cooley referred as the "solid facts" of social life?

[13] Mirra Komarovsky, *Women in the Modern World: Their Education and their Dilemmas* (Boston: Little, Brown, 1953).

[14] H. Hyman, *The Psychology of Status* (Archives of Psychology, Vol. 38, no. 269, June, 1942).

[15] Robert K. Merton and Alice S. Kitt, "Contributions to the Theory of Reference Group Behavior," in *Continuities in Social Research: Studies in the Scope and Method of "The American Soldier,"* ed. by Robert K. Merton and Paul F. Lazarsfeld (Glencoe, Illinois: The Free Press, 1950): reprinted in Robert K. Merton, *Social Theory and Social Structure,* revised and enlarged edition (Glencoe, Ill.: Free Press, 1957), pp. 225-80.

The classification of reference group theory is difficult, for in the theoretical statements of it, indeterminate model 7 fits, but in the actual application of the theory, determinate models 1 through 4 have been variously employed. The contradictions between theoretical statements and operational implications in reference group theory are one of the most unhappy aspects of symbolic interactionism today, in this author's opinion.

Next consider the related development of points of view known as *social perception* and *person perception.* If we regard the ancient dicta: "We see things not as they are but as we are," and "We do not first see and then define; we define first and then see," as intimately involved in the point of view of symbolic interactionism, we may properly claim at least a strong interest in the development of these interrelated schools. The researches contained in the volume edited by Petrullo and Tagiuri, for example, bear in many instances on hypotheses generated by symbolic interactionism.[16] On the other hand, this research movement is led by men relatively unacquainted with "our" literature. Consequently our own reaction to any one piece of research such as is contained in Petrullo and Tagiuri's volume is that it is in one or more respects naive: in its lack of sophistication about the function of language in interaction, in its failure to employ a concept equivalent to social act or social object or significant other, etc. etc.

Jerome Bruner, whose own experimental work on the differential perception of the size of coins by subjects of different income levels is a classic study in the field of social perception, has admirably stated in summary form the general position of these schools in "Social Psychology and Perception," in the third edition of *Readings in Social Psychology* edited by Maccoby, Newcomb, and Hartley.[17] His summary is such that the symbolic interactionist can easily deduce for himself the common ground this position shares with symbolic interaction theory; I am therefore spared this task by citing this article. I would only object that the Bruner paper misleads somewhat in failing to indicate the degree to which "perceptual set" as a key concept central to this school has come to serve as umbrella for Freudian rather than symbolic interaction variables, and for implying, on the other hand, that social perception treats what people are doing as central to the nature of what they perceive (for this is not borne out by their experimental designs).

The models on which social and person perception theory rests appear to be types 1 and 4. That is, they are determinate and tend to designate either immediate or temporally distal antecedent social variables and con-

[16] *Person Perception and Interpersonal Behavior,* ed. by Renato Tagiuri and Luigi Petrullo (Stanford, Calif.: Stanford University Press, 1958).

[17] Jerome Bruner, "Social Psychology and Perception," in *Readings in Social Psychology,* 3rd ed., Editorial Committee: Eleanor E. Maccoby, Theodore M. Newcomb, Eugene L. Hartley (New York: Henry Holt, 1958), pp. 85-94.

sequent behavioral variables. Had symbolic interactionists initiated the exploration of this field, they would have emphasized the ways in which the individual conceives himself as antecedent and the manner he perceives other objects including persons as consequent, with probably some attention to designs in which these types of variables are reversed in time.

So far, we have dealt with subtheories which have had very ambiguous boundaries. The same thing is certainly true of *self* theory with which I have identified my own research activities. It was my intention in 1946 or 1947 to employ a term which would not so much differentiate an emerging point of view from the more or less orthodox ideas of symbolic interaction as it would enable, on the other hand, a distinction between a body of conjectural and deductive orientation — as represented by Cooley, Dewey, and Mead — and a derivative but developing set of generalizations, tested by empirical research. I found later that, at about the same time, Carl Rogers had also termed as self theory his notions in clinical psychology having to do with the varying discrepancies between the actual or perceived self and the ideal self. Since then the term has been variously employed, often as an umbrella word, to cover several or all of the subtheories here under consideration.

The work undertaken by students of symbolic interaction at the State University of Iowa followed in several respects the programmatic proposals of the summary monograph on social psychology in the 1930's by Leonard Cottrell and Ruth Gallagher and of Cottrell's later presidential address before the American Sociological Society; that is to say, there has been considerable attention to the self itself and to role-taking.[18] McPartland[19] pioneered in his study relating differential nexi-to-social-structure to the differential characteristics of the self. Later he has studied the relations among self, social strata, and the differential syndromes of mental-emotional disturbance. Fred Waisanen[20] explored relations between self characteristics and prejudice. Stewart[21] demonstrated the often alleged

[18]Leonard S. Cottrell, Jr., and Ruth Gallagher, *Developments in Social Psychology*, 1930-1940 (New York: Beacon Press,1941); Leonard S. Cottrell, Jr., "Some Neglected Problems in Social Psychology," *American Sociological Review*, 15:705-12 (Dec., 1950).

[19]Thomas S. McPartland, "The Self and Social Structure," unpublished doctoral dissertation, State University of Iowa, 1953; "Self Conception, Social Class, and Mental Health," *Human Organization*, 17:24-29 (1958); T.S. McPartland, John H. Cumming and Wynona S. Garretson, "Self Conception and Ward Behavior in Two Psychiatric Hospitals," *Sociometry*, 24:11-24 (June, 1961).

[20]F.B. Waisanen, "The Prejudice Variable: A Social Psychological and Methodological Study," unpublished doctoral dissertation, State University of Iowa, 1954.

[21]Robert L. Stewart, "The Self and Other Objects: Their Measurement and Interrelationship," unpublished doctoral dissertation, State University of Iowa, 1955.

relation of the self to a system of objects, as did Carl Waisanen[22] and Wynona Garretson[23] in other ways. Maranell[24] studied relations between self and role-taking and began the exploration of transparency, the obverse of empathy. Rogler[25] established that there is a direct relation between role-taking and access to a communication system. The validation and extension of symbolic interaction ideas represented in these researches is for the most part preliminary and one must assess it as modest. Perhaps the most significant contribution of the Iowa research is simply that in which it joins the research of Miyamoto and Dornbusch, Deutsch and Solomon, Dick, Dinitz and Mangus, McKee and Sherriffs, Stryker, Videbeck and Bates, and many others in demonstrating to some degree at least that the key ideas of symbolic interactionism could be operationalized and utilized successfully in empirical research.[26]

Self theory of this variety has implied one or another of the five determinate models in our diagram, although this point is implicit rather than explicit, and never a salient issue. The general attempt rests on the notion that there is among the several important matters a process considered nomothetic or genotypical by the symbolic interaction orientation.

Among the subtheories that seem to imply indeterminacy — phenomenological theory, the study of careers, language, and culture of Sapir and Whorf, the interpersonal theory of H. S. Sullivan, the self-constancy and self-actualizing theories of such men as Stegner and Maslow — one seems to stand out as just a shade more radical and eye-catching than the rest: the *dramaturgical* school of Kenneth Burke, Erving Goffman, and possibly Nelson Foote and Gregory Stone. The most significant alteration made by this school is the general transmutation of the social act from what in traditional symbolic interactionism had continued to be paradoxically an individual model (triggered by organic tensions and impulses and following through the course of the action with reference to the single — almost feral — man to equilibrium, restitution of tensionlessness in the organism) to the team-of-players model which implies that social agenda rather than tissue conditions serve to initiate the act and to cue its end as well. This, of course, is but one of the extremely provocative aspects of dramaturgi-

[22] Carl E. Waisanen, "Preference Aspects of Self-Attitudes," unpublished doctoral dissertation, State University of Iowa, 1957.

[23] Wynona Smutz Garretson, "College as Social Object: A Study in Consensus," unpublished doctoral dissertation, State University of Iowa, 1961; "The Consensual Definition of Social Objects," *Sociological Quarterly,* 3:107-13 (Apr., 1962).

[24] Gary M. Maranell, "Role-Taking: Empathy and Transparency," unpublished doctoral dissertation, State University of Iowa, 1959.

[25] Lloyd H. Rogler, "An Experimental Study of the Relationship between Structured Behavior Patterns and Accuracy of Social Sensitivity," unpublished doctoral dissertation, State University of Iowa, 1957.

[26] See the appended bibliography.

cal theory, especially as initiated by Burke and developed by Goffman.

The difficulties with this subtheory are, in the main, those of deriving from it any testable generalizations. One must be tentative about this, it seems to me, for this was exactly the complaint lodged against the whole of symbolic interaction orientation in its early years. It may well be that ingenious solutions will be found to the problems of operationalizing the basic conceptions of this orientation.

Of the models we suggest diagrammatically, numbers 8 and 9 seem to be the ones most frequently implied in dramaturgical theory, although the team characteristics of Goffman's units appear to imply models indicating team rather than individual conduct.

The longitudinal study of socialization and especially of career trajectories, best indicated in the work of E. C. Hughes and Howard S. Becker, seems also to lie on the indeterminacy side. The work of these two men is virtually as imaginative and as creative as that of Burke and of Goffman, There is, in the literature, no more insightful account of the relation of the actor to a social object through the processes of communication and of self-definition, than Becker's account of becoming a marijuana user.[27] Hughes's sensitivity to lingual indicators of status is wonderfully revealed in his well-known and fundamental essay, "Work and the Self."[28] In it he presents a modern-age social psychological interpretation of "what the social classes owe to each other."

Again, the difficulties with this approach seem to lie in operationalization. It is most difficult to establish generalizations valid for human behavior without methods wherewith to make precise checks on intersubjective perceptions of events such as are involved in witnessing transitional stages in a socialization process or rites of passage in the trajectory of a career.

The indeterminate model on which this approach seems to rest is our type no. 7; that is, the antecedent variables, temporarily distal, are loosely (indeterminately) related to the processes of choice and self-indication which constitute the self.

The *interpersonal theory* of psychiatry proposed by Harry Stack Sullivan was constructed early in this quarter-century period.[29] It has been almost ubiquitously incorporated into the general body of symbolic interaction orientation, or perhaps the verb should be "reincorporated" since

[27] Howard S. Becker, "Becoming a Marihuana User," *American Journal of Sociology* 59:235-42 (Nov., 1953). (Cp. Howard S. Becker, *Outsiders: Studies in the Sociology of Deviance* (New York: Free Press of Glencoe, 1963.) — The Editor).

[28] Everett C. Hughes, "Work and the Self," in *Social Psychology at the Crossroads: The University of Oklahoma Lectures in Social Psychology,* ed. by John H. Rohrer and Muzafer Sherif (New York: Harper and Brothers, 1951), pp. 313-23.

[29] See the appended bibliography.

Sullivan had been well introduced to Meadian theory in the 1920's and had built the interpersonal theory in significant part out of elements provided by Mead on the one hand and by Freud on the other. The theory is distinctive for the unique way in which it manages a synthesis of Meadian and Freudian viewpoints without admitting any of the Freudian nonsense about phylogenetic inheritance of unconscious sense of guilt, the early Oedipus notion, the nature of man pitted against society, etc., while utilizing to the full the power of Freudian explanation of interpersonal rivalry and of distortions in communication — down to the utilization of the concept of self-derogation and self-rejection and repression (the not-me) — concepts hinging on interpersonal relations (reflected appraisals by others) rather than on thwarted instincts and biological drives as Freud had it.

Unfortunately, the Sullivan interpersonal theory is quite disjoined from ideas of culture and of formal social organization. This has led Shibutani to set up disjunctive self components: Those derived from conventional role-playing and those derived as sentiments from the kinds of interpersonal processes Sullivan described, completely divorced from culture and organized systems. It is also unfortuante that the interpersonal theory suffers from the same difficulties as the other indeterminate theories: inability to apply the usual scientific methods in order to build increasingly supported, dependable generalizations. The Sullivan model appears to rest on a combination fo models, 7, 8, and 9, thus indicating looseness between antecedent, intervening and consequent variables, plus the possibility for further emergence in the interior processes of the self. The specific, temporally distal, antecedent variables on which the theory rests are those having to do with what Sullivan calls the *parataxic* and *prototaxic* stages in what is essentially the preverbal period. In these, there is no real opportunity conceived for direct empirical observation, and thus there is further indeterminacy beyond the posited looseness between these stages and later self-attributes.

One more indeterminate subtheory is the Sapir-Worf-Cassirer *language and culture orientation.*[30] This is truly a theory behind a theory, for it tends to be presumed by symbolic interactionists as being preliminary even to a consideration of the basic assumptions of the theory under review. The language and culture point of view is surely so familiar as not to need much description. It points to the basic proposition that a language consists of a very finite and limited number of concepts out of an unlimited set of possibilities. Furthermore it underscores the fact that even the ultimate and basic concepts — which we in our society think of as those deal-

[30] [See, *e.g.* Edward Sapir, *Language: An Introduction to the Study of Speech* (New York: Harcourt, Brace, 1921): Benjamin L. Whorf, *Language, Thought and Reality: Selected Writings* edited by John B. Carroll (Technology Press of Massachusetts Institute of Technology, 1956); Ernest Cassirer, *The Philosophy of Symbolic Forms,* 2 vols. (New Haven: Yale Univ. Press, 1953-1955). — The Editor].

ing with time, motion, matter and space — are themselves lingually variable and relative. And, perhaps even more important, it takes the position that the very grammar of a language is based on an unspoken, taken-for-granted logic which determines how people in that society think about anything. Thus it must follow that the categorization of one's self and his attributes, as well as of his others, and of the significant non-human objects in his system of objects is entirely dependent on the language of his group. He cannot think of himself or his experiences, or of his relationships, except in the arbitrary conceptualizations provided him in his language.

This is an indeterminate theory in so far as the individual person's behavior is concerned, for the language only sets the basic framework for his thought and the outer limits, beyond which he cannot conceive of things. Within these limits, and around this framework, there is a looseness of connection. No determinate statements are suggested. However, attached as a preliminary set of assumptions to any of the previously examined determinate sub-theories, this point of view removes it from determinacy only in the sense that, as is pointed out posthumously in the *American Anthropologist* by the late Clyde Kluckhohn, the Whorf-Sapir-Cassirer notions are basically untestable.[31]

There are a number of other subtheories which have had their development during these past twenty-five years and which are related in one or several respects to symbolic interactionism, and which serve, if nothing else, to suggest extensions or amendments to the orientation. These include such points of view as cognitive theory, field theory, phenomenology, the developmental notions of Piaget, the current scrutiny of identity which bears strong overtones of ego psychology, the self-constancy theory of Stager and others, and the self-actualizing theory of Maslow, in addition to which there is the self theory of Carl Rogers, already mentioned. Many of those theories were developed by students in the field of psychology. Few indicate acquaintance with the intellectual stream to which symbolic interactionism belongs. The line I have drawn, excluding these from consideration but including the ones I have discussed, is highly arbitrary and may not be defensible in any other sense than that time places limitations even upon the most condensed of discussions.

Applications

So far we have considered the development of amplifications, subtheories, and operationalizations of symbolic interaction theory. We cannot conclude without considering the promising starts made in applying the orientation

[31] Clyde Kluckhohn, "Notes on Some Anthropological Aspects of Communication" *American Anthropologist* 63:895-910 (Oct., 1961).

to problem areas. There is the much neglected book by Lemert, *Social Pathology*,[32] which should have been called *A Social Psychology of Deviants*, in which the author makes the interesting proposal that a fundamental distinction exists in the behaviors of those whose deviation is accompanied by no corresponding self-definition and those whose deviation is so accompanied—he refers to the difference as secondary differentiation.

Much of the application of symbolic interaction theory has been made by students of crime and delinquency—notably Crossey, Glaser and Reckless. Of the Iowa students, Nardini in the field of the criminal,[33] Mulford in the area of the alcoholic,[34] Hurlburt in the area of family adjustment,[35] and Nass in the field of driver safety records,[36] have made application of self-dimensions as antecedent variables in promising endeavors to understand consequent variable behavior in problem fields. The new compilation edited by Rose already referred to, *Human Behavior and Social Processes*, contains as its third and final section a set of papers on the relation of interaction theory to social problem areas. Notable is Rose's own paper presenting his social-psychological theory of neurosis, which has a number of parallels with Sullivan's theory, but is distinctive in most respects for its general application of the symbolic interaction orientation.[37]

Neglected Problems

I cannot leave the consideration of the development of symbolic interactionism in the past twenty-five years without reconsidering the title of Cottrell's presidential address—the question of "neglected problems." Many of the problems which he found to be neglected are still neglected, while others—such as role-taking, on which his own student, R. F. Dy-

[32] Edwin M. Lemert, *Social Pathology: Approach to the Theory of Sociopathic Behavior* (New York: McGraw-Hill, 1951).

[33] William Nardini, "Criminal Self-Conceptions in the Penal Community: An Empirical Study," unpublished doctoral dissertation, State University of Iowa, 1959.

[34] Harold A. Mulford, Jr., "Toward an Instrument to Identify and Measure the Self, Significant Others, and Alcohol in the Symbolic Environment: An Empirical Study," unpublished doctoral dissertation, State University of Iowa, 1955.

[35] Julia Knaff Hurlburt, "Role Expectations and the Self: An Empirical Study of Their Relationship to Marital Adjustment," unpublished doctoral dissertation, State University of Iowa, 1960.

[36] Gilbert D. Nass, "A Study of the Teen-Age Driver, His Self-Definition, and Definition of the Driving Situation," unpublished Master's thesis, State University of Iowa, 1958.

[37] Arnold M. Rose, "A Systematic Summary of Symbolic Interaction Theory," in *Human Behavior and Social Processes*.

mond, made such a notable start[38]—are beginning to be studied with more and more sophistication.

There is no time here to make a thorough canvass of neglected problems, but I should like to mention two. One is the failure to make appropriate conceptualization of the varieties of functional relations that regularly occur between self and other. At present we appear to be in that rather foolish and useless situation in which we debate what a reference group really is. Most of the suggestions point to varieties of functional relations between self and groups or categories of others. The question ought not to be which of these is really a reference group, but rather, what special term shall we agree to use for each particular relation?[39] Having reached a consensus on a constructed vocabulary with which to refer to these functional relationships between self and other, we need then to consider the serious questions of operationalization. What kinds of questions must be asked to discover the nature of the particular relationship under inquiry?

A second pressing question implied in much of this paper has to do with the process by which self-conceptions change. Some theorists, notably those who lean toward the indetermintae side, discuss self-change as if it were most volatile and evanescent; the self shifts with each new indicaiton one makes to himself, and these indications are the constant accompaniments of experience. Others see in the self the more or less stable, continuous, organizing principle for the personality, offering the only constant, non-shifting anchorage for the perception of other objects. We have arrived at the point in sharpening of the tools by which we may identify self-attributes and measure them and compare them with those of others, where we may treat this issue as a researchable question. As we attempt to measure the relative stability of the self, we need to study the concomitants of self-attitude change. It may be argued that the self, like any attitude, may be usefully treated as an hypothesis which the individual holds about himself, and with respect to which he holds certain notions about testing for validity. We need to study in short what correlates of self-at-

[38](See Rosalind F. Dymond, "A Preliminary Investigation of the Relation of Insight and Empathy," *Journal of Consulting Psychology*, 12:228-33 (1948); "A Scale for the Measurement of Empathic Ability," *Journal of Consulting Psychology*, 13:127-33 (1949), reprinted in *Small Groups: Studies in Social Interaction*, ed. by A. Paul Hare, Edgar F. Borgatta, and Robert F. Bales (New York: Alfred A. Knopf, 1955), pp. 226-35. See also Rosalind F. Dymond, Anne S. Hughes, and Virginia L. Raabe, "Measurable Changes in Empathy with Age," *Journal of Consulting Psychology*, 16:202-6 (1952); Rosalind Dymond Cartwright, Julius Seeman, and Donald L. Grummon, "Patterns of Perceived Interpersonal Relations," *Sociometry* 19: 166-77 (Sept., 1956). —The Editor).

[39](Cp. Manford H. Kuhn, "The Reference Group Reconsidered" (in this issue of *The Sociological Quarterly*), which was written shortly after the present essay. —The Editor).

titude stability are phenomenal and which are non-conscious and outside self-directed control.

If I may be permitted a brief look at the crystal ball, I would see in it for the next twenty-five years of symbolic interaction theory an accelerated development of research techniques on the one hand, and a coalescing of most of the separate subtheories under consideration in this paper on the other. I have a basic confidence that symbolic interactionism will hold its own and gain against the competition of such major theories as psychoanalysis, the learning theories, and field theory. The reason I am confident is that I believe that of these major theories only symbolic interactionism is logically consistent with the basic propositions of the social sciences: the psychic unity of man (Boas); the extreme cultural variability of man; the creativity of man; the continual socializability and modifiability of man; the ability of man to feed back complex correctives to his behavior without engaging in trial and error, or conditioning, learning.

Bibliography

Apple, D. "Learning Theory and Socialization," *American Sociological Review,* 16:23-27 (Feb., 1951). Comment by J. Gillin, *American Sociological Review,* 16:384 (June, 1951).

Argyris, C. "The Fusion of an Individual with the Organization," *American Sociological Review,* 19:267-72 (June, 1954).

Becker, Ernest. "Socialization, Command of Performance, and Mental Illness," *American Journal of Sociology,* 67:484-501 (Mar., 1962).

Becker, Howard S. "Problems of Inference and Proof in Participant Observation," *American Sociological Review,* 23:652-60 (Dec., 1958).

Becker, Howard S., and Carper, James. "The Elements of Identification with an Occupation," *American Sociological Review,* 21:341-48 (June, 1956).

Becker, Howard S., and Geer, Blanche. "The Fate of Idealism in Medical School," *American Sociological Review,* 23:50-56 (Feb., 1958).

Blau, Zena Smith. "Changes in Status and Age Identification," *American Sociological Review,* 21:198-203 (Apr., 1956).

Blumer, Herbert. "Sociological Analysis and the Variable," *American Sociological Review,* 21:683-90 (Dec., 1956).

Boogs, Stephen T. "An Interactional Study of Ojibwa Socialization," *American Sociological Review,* 21:191-98 (Apr., 1956).

Bordua, David J. "Authoritarianism and Intolerance of Nonconformists," *Sociometry,* 24:198-216 (June, 1961).

Brim, Orville J., Jr. "Family Structure and Sex Role Learning by Children: A Further Analysis of Helen Koch's Data," *Sociometry,* 21:1-16 (Mar., 1958).

Brown J. C. "An Experiment in Role-taking," *American Sociological Review,* 17:587-97 (Oct., 1952).

Bucher, Rue, and Strauss, Anselm. "Professions in Process," *American Journal of Sociology,* 66:325-34 (Jan., 1961).

Burke, Kenneth. *A Grammar of Motives.* New York: Prentice-Hall, 1945.

_____. *A Rhetoric of Motives.* New York: Prentice-Hall, 1950.

Cameron, Norman. *The Psychology of Behavior Disorders.* Boston: Houghton Mifflin Co., 1947.

Cartwright, Rosalind Dymond, Seeman, Julius, and Grummon, Donald L. "Patterns of Perceived Interpersonal Relations," *Sociometry,* 19:166-77 (Sept., 1956).

Clark, John P. "Measuring Alienation Within a Social System," *American Sociological Review,* 24:849-52 (Dec., 1959).

Coates, Chas. H., and Pellegrin, Roland J. "Executives and Supervisors: Contrasting Self-Conceptions and Conceptions of Each Other," *American Sociological Review,* 22:217-20 (Apr., 1957).

Corwin, Ronald G. "A Study of Identity in Nursing," *Sociological Quarterly,* 2:69-86 (Apr., 1961).

Couch, Carl J. "Self-Attitudes and Degree of Agreement with Immediate Others," *American Journal of Sociology,* 63:491-96 (Mar., 1958).

_______. "Family Role Specialization and Self-Attitudes in Children," *Sociological Quarterly,* 3:115-21 (Apr., 1962).

Cottrell, L. A., Jr. "The Adjustment of the Individual to His Age and Sex Roles," *American Sociological Review,* 7:617-20 (Oct., 1942).

_____. "The Analysis of Situational Fields in Social Psychology," *American Sociological Review,* 7:370-82 (June, 1942).

_____. "Some Neglected Problems in Social Psychology," *American Sociological Review,* 15:705-12 (Dec., 1950).

Coutu, Walter, *Emergent Human Nature.* New York: Knopf, 1949.

_____. "Role-Playing *vs.* Role-Taking: An Appeal for Clarification," *American Sociological Review,* 16:180-87 (Apr., 1951). Comment by J. L. Moreno, *ibid.*, 16:550-51 (Aug., 1951).

Dai, B. "A Socio-Psychiatric Approach to Personality Organization," *American Sociological Review,* 17:44-49 (Feb., 1952).

_____. "Personality Problems in Chinese Culture," *American Sociological Review,* 6:688-96 (Oct., 1941).

Davis, James A. "A Formal Interpretation of the Theory of Relative Deprivation," *Sociometry,* 22:280-96 (Dec., 1959).

Deutsch, Morton, and Solomon, Leonard. "Reactions to Evaluations by Others as Influenced by Self-Evaluations," *Sociometry,* 22:93-112 (June, 1959).

Dick, Harry R. "The Office Worker: Attitudes toward Self, Labor and Management," *Sociological Quarterly,* 3:45-56 (Jan., 1962).

Dinitz, Simon, Mangus, A. R., and Passamanick, Benjamin. "Integration and Conflict in Self-Other Conceptions as Factors in Mental Illness," *Sociometry*, 22:44-55 (Mar., 1959).

Faris, R. E. L. *Social Psychology*. New York: Ronald Press, 1952.

_____ . "Sociological Causes of Genius," *American Sociological Review*, 5:689-99 (Oct., 1940).

Foote, Nelson N. "Anachronism and Synchronism in Sociology," *Sociometry*, 21:17-29 (Mar., 1958).

_____. "Identification as a Basis for a Theory of Motivation" *American Sociological Review*, 16:14-21 (Feb., 1951). Comment by R.Bendix, *ibid.*, 16:22 (Feb., 1951).

Garretson, Wynona Smutz. "The Consensual Definition of Social Objects," *Sociological Quarterly*, 3:107-13 (Apr., 1962).

Gerth, Hans, and Mills, C. Wright. *Character and Social Structure*. New York: Harcourt Brace and Co. 1953.

Getzels, J. W., and Guba, E. G. "Role, Role Conflict and Effectiveness: An Empirical Study," *American Sociological Review*, 19:164-75 (Apr., 1954).

Glaser, Daniel. "Criminality Theories and Behavioral Images," *American Journal of Sociology*, 61:433-44 (Mar., 1956).

Goffman, Erving. *The Presentation of Self in Everyday Life*. Garden City, N. Y.: Doubleday Anchor, 1959.

Goldhamer, H. "Recent Developments in Personality Studies," *American Sociological Review*, 13:555-65 (Oct., 1948).

Gough, H. G. "A New Dimension of Status: I. Development of a Personality Scale," *American Sociological Review*, 13:401-9 (Aug., 1948).

Gross, Neal, Mason, Ward S., and McEachern, Alexander W. *Explorations in Role Analysis: Studies of the School Superintendent Role*. New York: Wiley, 1958.

Halbwachs, M. "Individual Psychology and Collective Psychology," *American Sociological Review*, 3:615-23 (Oct., 1938).

Heider, Fritz. *The Psychology of Interpersonal Relations*. New York: Wiley, 1958.

Hyman, H. *The Psychology of Status* (Archives of Psychology, vol. 38. no. 269, 1942).

Ichheiser, G. "Structure and Dynamics of Interpersonal Relations," *American Sociological Review*, 8:302-5 (June, 1943).

Jackson, Jay. "Reference Group Processes in a Formal Organization," *Sociometry*, 22:307-27 (Dec., 1959).

Kohn, Melvin L. "Social Class and the Exercise of Parental Authority," *American Sociological Review*, 24:352-66 (June, 1959).

Kohn, A. Robert, and Fiedler, Fred E. "Age and Sex Differences in the Perceptions of Persons," *Sociometry*, 24:157-64 (June, 1961).

Kuenzli, Alfred E. (ed.). *The Phenomenological Problem*. New York: Harper, 1959. Papers by Combs, Snygg, McLeod, Brewster Smith, Jessor, *et al.*

Lemert, Edwin M. *Social Psychology.* New York: McGraw Hill, 1951.

Lindesmith, A.R. "The Drug Addict as a Psychopath," *American Sociological Review,* 5:914-20 (Dec., 1940).

Littman, Richard A., Moore, Robt. C.A., and Jones, John Pierce. "Social Class Differences in Child Rearing: A Third Community for Comparison with Chicago and Newton," *American Sociological Review,* 22:694-704 (Dec., 1957).

Lundy, Richard M. "Self Perceptions and Descriptions of Opposite Sex Sociometric Choices," *Sociometry,* 19:272-77 (Dec., 1956).

______. "Self Perceptions Regarding M-F and Descriptions Same and Opposite Sex Sociometric Choices," *Sociometry,* 21:238-46 (Sept. ,1958)

McKee, John P., and Sherriffs, Alex C. "Men's and Women's Beliefs, Ideals, and Self-Concepts," *American Journal of Sociology,* 64:356-63 (Jan., 1959).

McPartland, T. S., Cumming, John H., and Garretson, Wynona S. "Self-Conception and Ward Behavior in Two Psychiatric Hospitals," *Sociometry,* 24:111-24 (June, 1961).

Mead, George Herbert. *Mind, Self, and Society.* Chicago: University of Chicago Press, 1934.

______. *Movements of Thought in the Nineteenth Century.* Chicago: University of Chicago Press, 1936.

______. *The Philosophy of the Act.* Chicago: University of Chicago Press, 1938.

Merrill, Francis, "Stendhal and the Self: A Study in the Sociology of Literature," *American Journal of Sociology,* 66:446-53 (Mar., 1961).

Merton, Robert K., and Kitt, Alice S. "Contributions to the Theory of Reference Group Behavior," in R. K. Merton and P. F. Lazarsfeld (eds.), *Continuities in Social Research: Studies in the Scope and Method of "The American Soldier."* Glencoe, Ill.: Free Press, 1950.

Mills, C. Wright. "Language, Logic and Culture," *American Sociological Review,* 4:670-80 (Oct., 1939).

______. "Situated Actions and Vocabularies of Motive," *American Sociological Review,* 5:904-13 (Dec., 1940).

Miyamoto, S. Frank, and Dornbusch, Sanford M. "A Test of Interactionist Hypotheses of Self-Conception," *American Journal of Sociology,* 61: 399-403 (Mar., 1956).

Motz, A. B. "The Role Conception Inventory: A Tool for Research in Social Psychology," *American Sociological Review,* 17:465-71 (Aug., 1952).

Mullahy, Patrick. *The Contributions of Harry Stack Sullivan.* New York: Hermitage House, 1952.

Nathanson, Maurice. *The Social Dynamics of George H. Mead.* Washington, D. C.: Public Affairs Press, 1956.

Pfuetze, Paul E. *The Social Self.* New York: Bookman Associates, 1954.

Phillips, Bernard S. "A Role Theory Approach to Adjustment in Old Age," *American Sociological Review,* 22:212-17 (Apr., 1957).

Reckless, Walter C., Dinitz, Simon, and Murray, Ellen. "Self Concept as an Insulator Against Delinquency," *American Sociological Review.* 21:744-46 (Dec., 1956).

Reckless, Walter C., Dinitz, Simon, and Kay, Barbara. "The Self Component in Potential Delinquency and Potential Non-Delinquency," *American Sociological Review,* 22:566-70 (Oct., 1957).

Rose, Arnold, (ed.). *Human Behavior and Social Processes.* Boston. Houghton Mifflin Co., 1962.

Rosengren, William R. "The Self in the Emotionally Disturbed," *American Journal of Sociology,* 66:454-62 (Mar., 1961).

Sarbin, Theodore, "Role Theory," in Gardner Lindzey (ed.), *Handbook of Social Psychology* (Cambridge, Mass.: Addison-Wesley Publ. Co., 1945), vol. 1, ch. 6, pp. 223-58.

Schuessler, K. F. and Strauss, A. "A Study of Concept Learning by Scale Analysis," *American Sociological Review,* 15:752-62 (Dec., 1950).

Shibutani, Tamotsu. *Society and Personality.* Englewood Cliffs, N. J.: Prentice-Hall, 1961.

Simpson, Richard L., and Simpson, Ida Harper. "The Psychiatric Attendant: Development of an Occupational Self-Image in a Low-Status Occupation," *American Sociological Review,* 24:389-92 (June, 1959).

Slater, Philip E. "Parental Role Differentiation," *American Journal of Sociology,* 67:296-311 (Nov., 1961).

Strauss, Anselm. *Mirrors and Masks: The Search for Identity.* Glencoe, Ill.: The Free Press, 1959.

Stryker, Sheldon. "Role-Taking Accuracy and Adjustment," *Sociometry,* 20:286-96 (Dec., 1957).

Sullivan, Harry Stack. "A Note on the Implications of Psychiatry. The Study of Interpersonal Relations for Investigations in the Social Sciences," *American Journal of Sociology,* 42:846-61 (May, 1937).

_____. "Conceptions of Modern Psychiatry," *Psychiatry,* 3:1-117 (1940).

_____. *Conceptions of Modern Psychiatry.* Washington: Wm. A. White Psychiatric Foundation, 1947.

_____. *The Interpersonal Theory of Psychiatry.* New York: Norton, 1953.

Swanson, Guy E. "Mead and Freud: Their Relevance for Social Psychology," *Sociometry,* 24:319-39 (Dec., 1961).

Tagiuri, Renato, and Petrullo, Luigi (eds.), *Person Perception and Interpersonal Behavior.* Stanford, Calif.: Stanford University Press, 1958.

Tremmel, Wm. C. *The Social Concepts of George Herbert Mead.* Emporia State Research Studies, Kansas State Teachers College vol. 5, no. 4 (June, 1957).

Troyer, W. L. "Mead's Social and Functional Theory of Mind," *American Sociological Review,* 11:198-202 (Apr., 1946).

Turner, R. H. "Moral Judgment: A Study in Roles," *American Sociological Review,* 17:70-77 (Feb., 1952).

_____. "Self and Other in Moral Judgment," *American Sociological Review,* 19:249-59 (June, 1954).

Videbeck, Richard. "Self-Conception and the Reactions of Others," *Sociometry,* 23:351-59 (Dec., 1960).

Videbeck, Richard, and Bates, Alan P. "An Experimental Study of Conformity to Role Expectations," *Sociometry,* 22:1-11 (Mar., 1959).

Watson, Jeanne. "A Formal Analysis of Sociable Interaction," *Sociometry,* 21:269-80 (Dec., 1958).

White, L. A. "Culturological *vs.* Psychological Interpretations of Human Behavior," *American Sociological Review,* 12:686-98 (Dec., 1947).

Whorf, Benjamin Lee. *Language, Thought and Reality.* New York: Wiley and the Technology Press of MIT., 1956.

Wylie, Ruth. *The Self Concept: A Critical Survey of Pertinent Research Literature.* Lincoln: University of Nebraska Press, 1961.

4. The Roots of Social Knowledge [1]

Charles Horton Cooley

If we are to gain a large view of knowledge we should, it seems to me, consider it genetically by tracing it to its sources in human nature and human history. Knowledge is, after all, a phase of higher organic evolution, and has apparently been developed for the sake of its function in giving us adjustment to, and power over, the conditions under which we live. If these conditions present any fundamental division in kind we should expect that the capacities of the human mind and the knowledge based upon these capacities would show a corresponding division.

In fact, the conditions with which the mind has to deal, and has had to deal ever since life began to be human, divide themselves rather sharply into two kinds: the material, on the one hand, and the human or social, on the other. We have always needed to understand both things and persons, and the most primitive savage, though he may occasionally confuse them, is quite aware that they are different and must be understood in different ways.

This division lies as deep as anything in our experience, and it corresponds to a like division in our mental apparatus. For the external contacts we have our various senses, and also, in recent times, the extension and refinement of these through aptly named " instruments of precision" which have made the exact sciences possible. For the internal contacts we have a vast and obscure outfit of human susceptibilities, known as instincts, sentiments, emotions, drives, and the like, quite as firmly grounded in the evolutionary process as the senses, capable of extension and refinement in ways of their own, and giving rise to a kind of knowledge that we recognize as peculiarly human and social.

You will say, perhaps, that all knowledge, whether of things or of men, comes to us by the aid of the senses, and that the division I assert is therefore imaginary. It is true that all knowledge calls for sense activity of some sort or degree, but the function of this activity in material or spatial knowledge, on the one hand, and in human or social knowledge, on the other, is quite different. In dealing with things, sensation is the main

Reprinted from *The American Journal of Sociology,* XXXII (July, 1926), pp. 59-79 by permission of the University of Chicago Press.

[1] Presidential address read before the Michigan Academy of Science, Arts, and Letters, March 31, 1926.

source of the raw material which the mind works up into knowledge; in dealing with men it serves chiefly as a means of communication, as an inlet for symbols which awaken a complex inner life not primarily sensuous at all. In the one case it is our principal instrument; in the other only ancillary. When I meet a stranger and judge by his face, bearing, and voice that he is a kindly and cultured man, and by his words perceive, in a measure, the working of his mind, the sensuous images are like the starting mechanism of an automobile; they set at work processes more complicated and potent than themselves, of which, mainly, the resulting knowledge consists.

For our present purpose we may, then, distinguish two sorts of knowledge: one, the development of sense contacts into knowledge of things, including its refinement into mensurative science. This I call spatial or material knowledge. The second is developed from contact with the minds of other men, through communication, which sets going a process of thought and sentiment similar to theirs and enables us to understand them by sharing their states of mind. This I call personal or social knowledge. It might also be described as sympathetic, or, in its more active forms, as dramatic, since it is apt to consist of a visualization of behavior accompanied by imagination of corresponding mental processes.

There is nothing mysterious or unfamiliar about social knowledge, except as we may be unaccustomed to recognize and think about it. It is quite as early to appear in the child and in the race as in material knowledge, quite as useful in the everyday affairs of life, and quite as universally accepted as real by common sense. If there are men of science who do not see that it is something distinct in kind, but are inclined to regard it as spatial knowledge in an imperfect state, destined in time to be perfected by more delicate measurements, this is doubtless because they approach the matter with the a priori conceptions appropriate to physical research. In relation to social phenomena the merely spatial conception of knowledge indicates an abstract way of thinking that does not envisage the facts. It is not, in this field, in accord with common sense. All of us know that the essential things in our relation to other men are not subject to numerical measurement.

I trust it will not be supposed that I am advocating any metaphysical dualism between mind and matter. It is not necessary, for my present purpose, to take a side on that question, but I have myself no doubt that all the phenomena connected with social knowledge, including introspection, have physical concomitants in the brain and nervous system. In theory these physical facts are capable of physical measurement, but when we consider their minuteness and inaccessibility, the likelihood of their being measured in a spatial sense seems quite remote. We must get at them, in practice, through consciousness and through overt behavior.

Spatial knowledge, we know, has been extended and refined by processes of measurement, calculation, and inference, and has given rise to exact science. It is generally agreed that knowledge of this sort is verifiable and cumulative, making possible that ever growing structure of ascertained fact which is among the proudest of human achievements. It may be worth while to consider for a moment to what this peculiarly verifiable character is owing.

It is owing, I take it, to the fact that this sort of knowledge consists essentially in the measurement of one material thing in terms of another, man, with his senses and his reason, serving only as a mediator between them. If, then, a group of investigators can agree upon a technique of measurement they may go ahead, achieving results and passing them on from man to man and from generation to generation, without concerning themselves with the vagaries of human nature and social life. This technical agreement is found possible, and the accumulation of knowledge goes on. But we must, of course, discriminate between the immediate results of measurement and the body of hypothesis and theory which is constantly arising out of them. Science gives us fact out of which the intellect endeavors to build truth. And what we judge to be true, even in the spatial sciences, is largely a social matter dependent upon the general movement of thought. A group of scientific men, familiar with previous investigation in a given field and armed with a sound technique, is the best instrument we have for the pursuit of truth, and is one of the most remarkable products of our social system; yet it is, of course, far from infallible. All groups have a body of beliefs which are taken for granted merely because no one disputes them, and which often turn out to be illusions. Assent is induced by conforming influences not wholly different from those operating in religion or politics. In short, no group is a trustworthy critic of its own conclusions, and only the test of time and of exacting criticism from wholly different points of view can determine the value of its contribution. There have been many groups, made up of very intelligent men working devotedly and in full assurance of being on the right track, who are now seen to have been astray. And although scientific methods are no doubt improved, it would be fatuous to suppose that they are a guaranty against group error. Some of the teachings of science are permanent truth, but only time reveals which they are.

The practical success of spatial science in enabling us to predict, and even to control, the behavior of the material world about us has given it vast prestige and brought about a feeling that the more all our mental processes are like it the more perfect they will become. A conception of what social science ought to be has accordingly grown up and gained wide vogue which is based rather upon analogy than upon scrutiny of the conditions with which we have to deal. Let us return, then, to the sources of our knowledge of mankind, and consider for a moment the development of this sort of knowledge in a child. He comes into the human world already provided with a vast complex of innate capacity for life peculiar to the human race and embracing in its potential content those processes of social emotion, sentiment, and intelligence in which men find their chief interests and motives. All this is an outcome of evolution, highly practical, the very stuff that has made man the most puissant of animals, and it has, no doubt, the same physical reality as any other nervous or mental processes. Regarding the exact content of this inborn raw material of personal and social life there has been much discussion, into which, fortunately, we need not enter. Some say that it includes quite definitely organized mechanisms, similar to the instincts of the lower animals; others, that the inborn mechanisms of man are small and indeterminate, taking on organization only under the stimulus of a particular kind of life. However this may be, no one can doubt that we are born with an inchoate world of mental capacity, existing physically as a mass of brain and nerve complexes, which requires as the main condition of its growth an interchange of stimulation with similar complexes existing in other personal organisms.

The process by which a distinctively human or social mind and a corresponding type of knowledge grows up within us was first expounded at some length in 1895 by James Mark Baldwin, who called it "the dialectic of personal growth." It resembles a game of tennis in that no one can play it alone; you must have another on the opposite side of the net to return the ball. From earliest infancy our life is passed in eager response to incitements that reach us through the expressive behavior of other people, through facial expression, gesture, spoken words, writing, printing, sculpture, the symbols of science, and the mechanic arts. Every response we make is a step in our education, teaching us to act, to think, and to feel a little more humanly. Our brain and nerve complexes develop in the sense of our social surroundings. And at the same time our consciousness takes account of this inward experience and proceeds to ascribe it to other people in similar conditions. Thus by a single process we increase our understanding of persons, of society, and of ourselves. When you play golf you not only acquire spatial knowledge in the shape of a certain muscular skill, but also social knowledge through learning the pride one feels when he makes a long drive, or the humiliation when he tops the ball and gets into the creek. As you see another man do these things you repeat, sympathetically, your own inner response on former occasions and ascribe it to him. A new reach of human experience is opened to you and you enlarge your understanding of men. And you extend your knowledge of domestic life, of letters, arts, and sciences in much the same way. Consider scientific work in the laboratory and in the field. Does it give only material knowledge of the behavior of *things* in test tubes, of the look and feel of strata, of the habits of fishes, or does it also teach you to understand chemists, geologists, and zoölogists as *men,* to participate in a phase of human life, share its ideals, and learn its social methods? And is not the latter knowledge quite as important to the man of science as the former? Able men in every field excel, as a rule, in human as well as technical knowledge, because both are the fruit of a richly developed mind, and both must also be cultivated as instruments of success.

If the distinctive trait of spatial knowledge is that it is mensurative, that of social knowledge is, perhaps, that it is dramatic. As the former may be resolved into distinctions among our sensations, and hence among the material objects that condition those sensations, so the latter is based ultimately on perceptions of the intercommunicating behavior of men, and experience of the processes of mind that go with it. What you know about a man consists, in part, of flashes of vision as to what he would do in particular situations, how he would look, speak and move; it is by such flashes that you judge whether he is brave or a coward, hasty or deliberate, honest or false, kind or cruel, and so on. It also consists of inner sentiments which you yourself feel in some degree when you think of him in these situations, ascribing them to him. It is these latter sympathetic elements which make the difference between our knowledge of a man and our knowledge of a horse or a dog. The latter is almost wholly external or behavioristic, although those who associate intimately with them may acquire some measure of true sympathy. We know animals mostly as a peculiarly lively kind of thing. On the other hand, although our knowledge of people is likewise behavioristic, it has no penetration, no distinctively human insight, unless it is sympathetic also.

There is, no doubt, a way of knowing people with whom we do not sympathize which is essentially external or animal in character. An example of this is the practical but wholly behavioristic knowledge that men of much sexual experience sometimes have of women, or women of men — something that involves no true participation in thought and feeling. The more behavior in the other sex is instinctively sexual, the more our understanding of it is apt to be external rather than sympathetic. Or, to put it rather coarsely, a man sometimes understands a woman as he does a horse; not by sharing her psychic processes, but by watching what she does. There is, in fact, a complete series in our knowledge of persons, from the purely external, like our knowledge of babies, of idiots, of the wildly insane, up through all grades to the completely internal or sympathetic, as when, in reading a meditative writer like Marcus Aurelius, we know his consciousness and nothing else. For the most part, however, human knowledge is both behavioristic and sympathetic: the perception or imagination of the external trait is accompanied by sympathy with the feeling, sentiment, or idea that goes with it.

This is also the process by which we come to understand the meaning of a word, and through such understanding make ourselves at home in that vast realm of meanings to which words are the key. We may know words as mere behavior, as when a man speaks to us in a strange tongue, but in that case they do not admit us to the realm of meanings. To have human value the word and the inner experience that interprets it must go together.

In short, we learn to know human life outwardly and inwardly at the same time and by a single process continuous from infancy.

Adopting a convenient and popular term, I will call the individual human mind, including all these socially developed sentiments and understandings, the *mental-social complex.* I hope by the use of this colorless expression to escape from the traditional implications that obscure such terms as mind, consciousness, spirit, and soul.[2] About this, whatever we call it, the question of the nature and possibilities of social knowledge centers. It is our supreme gift; but for that very reason, because all the deep things of life are in it, it is the part of us about which we know least, and is least amenable to precise treatment. Can it be made available for science, or shall we try in some way to dodge it, or cancel it out, as the physical scientist does when he requires that the ideas about nature which come from it shall be verified by nature herself through physical measurement? The trouble with any such plan would seem to be that in human life the mental-social complex *is* nature. It is the very heart of what we seek to describe and make intelligible. It cannot be dodged without dodging life itself.

Suppose, for example, you secure, by a series of mental tests, detailed knowledge of what a certain person does in various situations. This may be of great value; I expect important results from such studies; but after all they cannot enable you to know the person as a living whole. The social man is something more than the sum of standardized acts, no matter how many or how well chosen. You can grasp him only by the understanding and synthetic power of your own mental complex, without which any knowledge you may gain from behavior tests must remain superficial and unintelligent. Is it not a somewhat equivocal use of terms when we talk of measuring intelligence or personality? What we measure is the performance of standardized operations. To pass from these to the organic whole of intelligence or personality is always a difficult and fallible work of the constructive imagination.

Many people, agreeing perhaps with what I have said about the ultimate difference in kind between spatial and social knowledge, will hold that just because of this difference anything like social science is impossible. While spatial knowledge is precise and communicable, and hence cumulative, the dramatic and intuitive perceptions that underlie social knowledge are so individual, so subjective, that we cannot expect that men will be able to agree upon them or to build them up into an increasing structure of ascertained truth.

This is, in fact, a formidable difficulty which enthusiasts for exact social science are apt to ignore. I may say at once that I do not look for

[2] In a similar way the "group mind," that is, a collective view of individual complexes communicating with, and influencing, one another, might be called the social-mental complex.

any rapid growth of science that is profound, as regards its penetration into human life, and at the same time exact and indisputable. There is a difference in kind here which it would be fatuous to overlook.

Regarding subjectivity, I may say that all knowledge is subjective in one sense: in the sense, namely, that it is mental, not the external thing, but a construct of the mind. Even the simplest perceptions of form or extent, much more the exact perceptions of science, far from being mere physical data, are the outcome of an extended process of education, interpretation, and social evolution. Your so-called physical sciences are, after all, part of the social heritage and creatures of the mental-social complex. In so far, then, spatial knowledge and social knowledge are on the same footing.

The question of more or less subjectivity, as among different kinds of knowledge, I take to be one of more or less agreement in the elementary perceptions. If the phenomena can be observed and described in such a way as to command the assent of all intelligent men, without regard to theory or to bias of any sort, then the factual basis of knowledge acquires that independence of particular minds which we call objectivity. A yardstick is objective because it provides an undisputed method of reaching agreement as to certain spatial relations. Professor Einstein has shown, I believe, that this objectivity is not absolute, but it suffices for most purposes of spatial science. Strictly speaking, there are no yardsticks in social knowledge, no elementary perceptions of distinctively social facts that are so alike in all men, and can be so precisely communicated, that they supply an unquestionable means of description and measurement. I say distinctively social facts, because there are many facts commonly regarded as social which are also material events, like marriages, and as such can be precisely observed and enumerated. But the distinctively social phenomena connected with marriage are inward and mental, such as the affection and desire of the parties, pecuniary considerations, their plans for setting up a household, and so on. These also can be known and communicated, but not with such precise agreement among observers as to make decisive measurement possible.

You may say that while it is true that the mental-social phenomena cannot be observed directly with much precision, they express themselves in behavior, which is tangible and which we may hope eventually to record and measure with great exactness. Even our inmost thoughts and feelings take form in the symbols of communication, in gesture, voice, words, and the written symbols which are preserved unchanged for ages. All this is true and much to the point: I am a behaviorist as far as I think I can be without being a fanatic. But we must not forget, as behaviorists sometimes appear to do, that the symbol is nothing in itself, but only a convenient means of developing, imparting, and recording a meaning, and that meanings are a product of the mental-social complex and known to us only through consciousness. Reliance upon symbols, therefore, in no way releases us from the difficulty arising from the unmeasurable nature of our elementary social perceptions. We can record behavior and handle the record by statistics, but I see no way of avoiding the ultimate question, What does it mean?

And how about introspection? Does not the kind of perception which I inculcate involve this disreputable practice, and if so, is it not thereby hopelessly vitiated?

The word "introspection," as commonly used, suggests a philosopher exploring his inner consciousness in more or less complete abstraction from the ordinary functions of life. While this method may have its uses it is thought to have been more relied upon in the past than it deserves. Let us observe men under more normal conditions, and preferably, it is urged, through their actions rather than through their supposed thoughts.

But just what, after all, is introspection? It is not merely the philosophic introversion I have indicated, but takes various forms, some of which, in everyday use by all of us, are indispensable to any real knowledge of the minds of other men.

That whole process of the social growth of the mind which I have mentioned involves elements introspective in character. We come to know about other people and about ourselves by watching not only the interplay of action, but also that of thought and feeling. As we perceive and remember sensuous images of gesture, voice, and facial expression, so, at the same time, we record the movements of thought and feeling in our consciousness, ascribe similar movements to others, and so gain an insight into their minds. We are not, for the most part, reflectively aware of this, but we do it and the result is social knowledge. This process is stimulated and organized by language and — indirectly, through language — by the social heritage from the past. Under the leading of words we interpret our observation, both external and introspective, according to patterns that have been found helpful by our predecessors. When we have come to use understandingly such words as "kindly," "resolute," "proud," "humble," "angry," "fearful," "lonesome," "sad," and the like, words recalling motions of the mind as well as of the body, it shows that we have not only kept a record of our inner life, but have worked up the data into definite conceptions which we can pass on to others by aid of the common symbol.

Much of our social knowledge, especially that acquired from reading, involves a process more consciously introspective. One can hardly read a play or a novel intelligently, I should say, without recalling ideas and emotions from his own past for comparison with those of the people described. The hero, as we conceive him, is fashioned out of material from our own lives. Is it not rather absurd for scientific men to repudiate introspection? Does anyone prepare a scientific report or article without first turning an inward eye upon the contents of his mind in order to see what he has to offer and how he can arrange and present it? In short, introspection, however abused by philosophers, is a normal and common process, without which we could know very little about life.

Introspection, if critical, is more objective than the usual practice of floating upon social currents without attempting to become aware of them. How can you be objective with regard to your motives unless you hold them off and look at them? I have in mind a recent book, a good book, too, in which the writer, who deprecates introspection, advances a series of opinions on social questions of the day so obviously those of his race, country, and social class that one can only smile at his naïveté. Surely a little introspection would not be out of place here: one's subjectivity needs to be understood, if only to avoid it.

It seems, then, that outside and inside in human life, consciousness and behavior mutually complement and explain each other, and that the study of external behavior as a thing by itself must, in the human field, be as barren as mere introspection, and for much the same reason, namely, that it isolates one aspect of a natural process from another. Nature has joined these things together, and I do not think that we gain anything by putting them asunder. Records of behavior without introspective interpretation are like a library of books in a strange tongue. They came from minds, and mean nothing until they find their goal in other minds.

However, I see no reason for quarreling with those extreme behaviorists who hold that we should observe men merely from the outside, as we do other animals. Let them work on this theory, if they find it helpful, and show what they can do. Even if it is wrong it may give rise to a valuable technique, as wrong theories have done in the past. It is fair to judge behaviorists by their behavior. I suspect that they will be found in practice to make use of introspection when they need it, much like the rest of us.[3]

At the opposite pole, it would seem, from behaviorism we have the method, or rather various methods, of mental analysis through the probing of consciousness and memory. These all rest in great part upon sympathetic introspection, or the understanding of another's consciousness by the aid of your own, and give full play to the mental-social complex. They may be used in sociology as well as in psychiatry, and, in fact, do not differ in principle from the personal interviews widely employed in the study of social situations. Indeed, I take it that the psychoanalytic psychology owes its vogue to its boldness in disregarding the rather narrowly spatial methods within which laboratory psychologists were confining themselves, and venturing, by the light of clinical interviews and intro-

[3] I need hardly say that the scientific study of behavior has no necessary connection with the group of men who call themselves "behaviorists." Their extreme doctrine of the rejection of consciousness is best understood as a reaction against a former extreme, in psychology, of purely introspective study. Social studies have always been mainly behavioristic.

spective interpretation, to explore the weird caverns of the human mind. Men saw that the sequent revelations resembled what they knew of their own egos. The method is quite separable from the extravagant theories associated with it and will no doubt be largely used.

I have conceded that social observation is, on the whole, less precise and verifiable, and hence less surely cumulative, than spatial observation, not only because the conditions can seldom be reproduced by experiment, but because the perceptions themselves are less alike in different persons, and so less easy to agree upon. Experience shows, however, that these difficulties are by no means sufficient to prevent objective and co-operative study of social phenomena, and a cumulation of knowledge which, though not so tangible as in experimental science, is capable in time of yielding vast results.

The basis of common social perceptions, and hence of cumulation, is in the general similarity of mental-social complexes throughout the human race, and the much closer similarity among those formed by a common language and culture. We become aware of this similarity by watching the behavior of other men, including their language, and finding that this behavior can be interpreted successfully by ascribing to them thoughts and sentiments similar to our own. The idea that they are like us is practically true; it works. It was generated in the experience of our earliest childhood, and we have gone upon it all our lives. This fundamental agreement upon meanings can be made more precise by the careful use of language and other communicative signs, something as sense-perceptions are refined by the use of instruments of precision (though probably to nothing like the same degree), and thus allows a transmission and cumulation exact enough for practical use.

All history, all news, all social investigation, is a record of what men did — of such visible acts as are thought to be significant, and also of their symbolic acts, their speech, and their works of art. But what makes the record interesting is that through our likeness to them it becomes also a record of what they were, of their meanings, of their inner life, the semblance of which is awakened in us by the acts recorded.

I open Herodotus at random and find an account of how the Carthaginians, having captured many Phoceans from disabled ships, landed them and stoned them to death. But after this the sheep, oxen, or men who passed the spot were stricken with palsy. So they consulted the Delphic Oracle, who required them to institute a custom of honoring the dead Phoceans with funeral rites. Here is a record of behavior which we interpret by sympathy. We feel the cruelty of the Carthaginians, their wonder and alarm at the strange conduct of the stricken men and animals, their anxious resort to Delphi, their awed obedience to the oracle. Of the grounds for criticizing this narrative from the standpoint of a wider study of human ideas and human behavior I need not now speak. Like all social observation that comes down from the past, it must be interpreted in view of the difference in mental complexes between the men who made the records and us who read them. We must, as we say, get their background and point of view. But men are, after all, so much alike that an imagination trained by comparative study can usually make out fairly well what the records mean. The true reason why we must, in sociology, rely mainly upon contemporary rather than historical facts is the inadequacy of the record. History does not tell what we want to know, and we must look in the world about us for answers to questions which the men of old never thought of putting.

At any rate we actually have accumulations of social knowledge. Aristotle and many other early writers collected facts which are still held to be trustworthy, and interpreted them by generalizations which still command respect. In modern times the process has gone on developing in volume, diversity, and precision, and has given rise to technical groups of specially trained men. We have many kinds of history, we have social anthropology, political science, law, economics, sociology, comparative religion, comparative literature and art, and other departments, each with its own archives of recorded fact.

Indeed, as regards cumulation the study of mankind has a great advantage in that its subject matter is uniquely self-recording. Even the records of geology and paleontology do not compare in richness with those that man hands down about himself through language and the several arts. And the more he approaches and enters a civilized state, the more extensive these records become. The dinosaur may leave his skeleton and even his (or her) eggs, but man deposits a fossil mind. We know infinitely more about him than we do about any other animal, and the difficulty of accumulating knowledge, so far as primary facts are concerned, is quite imaginary. Dispute, as in other fields, is mainly about interpretation. The selection and explanation of facts has heretofore proved provisional; it has to be done over again with every change in the general current of thought. But is not this true of all science? At this moment the whole theoretical trunk of physics has been torn up by the roots and seems likely to be thrown upon the rubbish pile. A lasting structure of knowledge is hardly to be expected, except as regards the primary facts and their simpler relations, and this much we may expect in social science as well as in spatial.

It is high time that I referred to that body of knowledge and practice known as statistics. Statistics is an exact method, and it is enabled to be such precisely because it is not in itself social but mathematical. It does not directly *perceive* social facts, or any other kind of facts, but it takes standard units of some sort, which may be perceived social facts, and compiles, arranges, manipulates, and presents them in a way intended to make them yield illumination. The statistician operates between the primary observer, on the one hand, and, on the other, the theorist who demands light on certain hypotheses. Perhaps I may without offense liken him to a cook, who neither supplies the food nor consumes it, but is a specialist upon the intervening processes.

Evidently it would not be good sense to assume any antagonism between the exact methods of statistics and the more fallible procedure of sympathetic observation and interpretation. They are complementary and do not or should not overlap. The only opposition likely to arise is one due to the bias of the practitioner. A statistician, if he lacks breadth of mind, is apt to be so fond of his exact processes that he avoids and depreciates anything else, while the sympathetic observer is apt to be impatient of statistics. This difference of tastes would not do much harm if the functions were kept separate, but when a man who is fit for only one assumes both the result is unfortunate. Much statistical work, especially that based upon questionnaires or interviews, is vitiated by a lack of dramatic insight into the states of mind of the people who supply the information. A questionnaire is an instrument of social perception, and if its use is to have any scientific character, the first duty of the user is to dramatize the play of thought and feeling that takes place between the person that puts the question and the person that answers it. What was the actual state of mind of the latter, and what the human significance of his reply? Not every investigator has the insight and the conscience to perceive and report this real fact, commonly so different from the apparent fact, upon which the value of his work depends.

And so with the questions or problems used in mental tests. If they aim only to test the power to perform standardized operations they are objective, but, socially speaking, superficial; if they go beyond this and attempt to discover social or moral attitudes they are subjective, and of no value for science without sympathetic interpretation.

It is not the case that social science is becoming exact through the substitution of statistics for social sympathy and imagination. What is taking place is, rather, that the use of sympathy and imagination is becoming more competent, while statistics is being substituted for guesswork in the manipulation of data.

Another impression which I take to be erroneous is that statistics is revealing uniformities or regularities in social phenomena which indicate that these phenomena may in time prove to be subject to exact prediction in quite the same way as those of physics. It is true that statistics is revealing sequence, order, and a remarkable degree of predictability in certain social processes. By analysis of what has taken place during the past ten years, especially in the economic field, where the facts are largely material, it may be possible to forecast what will take place in the next five; and no one can say how far we may go in this direction. The whole basis of this, however, seems to be the prevalence of inertia and the rarity and slowness of the more originative processes. The greater part of human phenomena are so far routinized as to be more or less subject to calculation. Wherever men, under the impetus of habit and suggestion, are moving ahead in a mechanical manner, or where their intelligence is merely repeating what is essentially an old synthesis of motives — as, for example, in deciding whether to marry or not — exact methods are in place. The complex of human events can, to a great extent, be resolved into currents of tendency moving on definite lines at ascertainable speeds. If we can measure these lines and speeds it may be possible to predict their combined operation, much as the motion of a comet is predicted by calculating the resultant of the gravity, tangential momentum, and other forces acting upon it. The whole basis of prediction in such fields as that of the business cycle is the belief that the underlying motivation is essentially standardized or repetitive.

Probably no exact science could have foreseen the sudden rise of the automotive industry and the genius of Henry Ford, although now that this industry is developed and institutionized we may perhaps calculate with some precision what it will bring forth in the near future.

There is no good reason to think that such statistical methods can anticipate that which, after all, chiefly distinguishes human life from physical processes, namely, originative mental synthesis, whether by outstanding individuals or by groups. The kind of mechanistic theory which would exclude the unique function of human consciousness and will is not only highly speculative and unverifiable, but seems, as a speculation, to be losing ground. Recent philosophic writers (for example, our colleague Professor Sellars[4]), in so far as they accept mechanism or determinism, interpret them in such a way as to leave intact our human power of reorganizing and redirecting life in a manner that no exact science can hope to foresee.

There is indeed one way in which physical and social science may be assimilated. We may find that atoms and electrons are not so uniform and reliable as has been believed, that the supposed physical laws are only statistical, covering diversity in the phenomena somewhat as social statistics cover the diversities of individual men. Indeed, we are told by men apparently competent that "the present state of physics lends no support whatever to the belief that there is a causality in physical nature which is founded on rigorously exact laws."[5] In some such way as this the gulf may be bridged, but never, I think, by reducing the human will to zero.

Having dealt so far with observation, either direct or mediated by technique, I come now to the interpretive use of the data, to the attempt to build a structure of social truth. This is, in all sciences, a work of the imagination, and a work which has always in the past proved to be provisional and to require renewal to meet the general advance of thought. I see no reason to expect anything else in the future.

At the present time all the sciences of life are, I suppose, controlled by the idea of organic development. Darwin gave these studies their orientation by making them studies of process rather than state, of what is going on rather than what is, of a drama rather than a picture. For many years,

[4] R. W. Sellars, *Evolutionary Naturalism, passim.*

[5] Hermann Weyl, quoted by J. W. N. Sullivan, *Aspects of Science,* p. 158.

however, evolutionary ideas were applied to social phenomena chiefly in an external and analogical way; they were imposed artificially, not allowed to grow naturally out of the social processes themselves. The result was a vast body of social theory and propaganda, all claiming to be evolutionary and scientific, but none of it the work of a technical group devoted primarily and disinterestedly to the study of social facts. Even at the present time specialists in contiguous evolutionary fields contribute profusely to social literature and by no means hide their belief that they know more about what is important to society than do the so-called "sociologists." Whether they do or not, it is a fact that some of these extraneous doctrines, like the pseudo-Darwinism of Nietzsche or the hereditary determinism of the more extreme followers of Galton, have had, and still have, a wide influence.

I shall assume, however, that, after all, social phenomena are most likely to be understood by those who make the study of them their main business, and that the application of evolutionary ideas in this sphere is the task mainly of history, anthropology, ethnology, political science, economics, social psychology, sociology, and kindred disciplines. All of these studies have, in fact, a decidedly evolutionary trend, and several of them may be said to have been created by the evolutionary movement. All of them aim at the understanding of personal and social wholes in the actual process of living. All make increasing use of social psychology. They do not aim to resolve social phenomena into elements which are not social, but rather to investigate the simpler and more general social processes and use the knowledge thus gained in synthetic interpretation of larger social wholes. This may be done by the use of well-chosen samples, as in studies of individual persons, of typical local or institutional conditions, and the like.

In general, the insights of sociology, if I may take that subject as representative, are imaginative reconstructions of life whose truth depends upon the competence of the mind that makes them to embrace the chief factors of the process studied and reproduce or anticipate their operation. This requires native ability, factual knowledge, social culture, and training in a particular technique.

It is sometimes supposed that pre-Darwinian studies in history, literature, art, and social theory were essentially unscientific and futile; in fact, mere rubbish needing to be swept aside by the advancing forces of science. On the contrary, many of these studies were based on common sense, had a sound empirical basis, and are even now of more value than hurried, dogmatical, and mostly analogical efforts to supplant them by something having the appearance of natural science. Such efforts have given rise to a variety of pseudo-sciences, some of which are flourishing at the present time, but they have not broken the real continuity of contemporary social knowledge with the solid work of earlier generations. Sociology, at least, recognizes whole-heartedly the value of pre-evolutionary research, and expects that its students shall know something of the great currents of historical, literary, and artistic tradition; shall have, indeed, as broad a culture in the humanities as possible. This culture affords the only access to great stores of facts with which we cannot dispense. It also affords a perspective of the development of social interpretation. Most of the generalizations now being defined, explored, tested, and developed into systematic knowledge were foreshadowed by penetrating minds of the past. How much of modern social psychology is implicit in the maxims of La Rochefoucauld, what insight into social processes had Gibbon! Sainte-Beuve, who saw literature as an organic human whole, observing the individual writer and the current of literary tendency with equal understanding, was a real sociologist in the field of criticism. Goethe was one in an even larger sense. An honest and competent student will be deferent to the achievements of the past and will lend no countenance to those shallow spirits who see scientific method as a sort of trick of laboratories and schedules by which they may avoid the slow approaches of actual social knowledge.

As to prediction, I have already pointed out that in the more mechanized processes of the social system it may be remarkably exact. We have no ground, however, to expect any such exactness in foretelling the multitudinous fluctuations of human life in general. Prediction, in any science, requires that the mind embrace the process, as the physicist, in his formula, embraces the process of a falling body, and so, through participation, foresee the outcome. Even in natural science this can usually be done with precision only when the process is artificially simplified, as in the laboratory. The social processes of actual life can be embraced only by a mind working at large, participating through intellect and sympathy with many currents of human force, and bringing them to an imaginative synthesis. This can hardly be done with much precision, nor done at all except by infusing technical methods with a total and creative spirit.

The human mind participates in social processes in a way that it does not in any other processes. It is itself a sample, a phase, of those processes, and is capable, under favorable circumstances, of so far identifying itself with the general movement of a group as to achieve a remarkably just anticipation of what the group will do. Prediction of this sort is largely intuitive rather than intellectual; it is like that of the man with a genius for business as contrasted with that of the statistician; it is not science, but it is the very process by which many of the great generalizations of science have first been perceived.

Predictions of any sort, however, are most likely to be sound when they are made by those who have the most precise familiarity with the observable processes, and it is the increase of this familiarity on the part of social observers, along with their greater insight into principles, that should make them better guessers of what is to happen than they have been in the past.

What, then, is there new in contemporary social science, what, if anything, that promises a more rapid and secure accumulation of knowledge than in the past? Mainly, I should say, the following:

1. Liberation from outworn theological and metaphysical assumptions and reorganization on the basis of factual study and an evolutionary outlook.
2. The rise of a technical group of adequately trained scholars, with those traditions and standards, that expert criticism and exacting group atmosphere, indispensable to all higher achievement.
3. The development, since 1860, and especially since 1900, of a network of factual theory, by which I mean theory springing from observation and capable of being verified or refuted by the closer study of fact. Such theory is to be distinguished from much of the older speculation, which was largely metaphysical, unverifiable, and for that reason of no use in stimulating research.

There is nothing startling in the present movement. It shows no break with the past, does not promise any phenomenal power of prediction, and is, in fact, chiefly occupied with the ascertainment of what is actually going on and with the development of technique. We are trying to describe and interpret human life in the same spirit that the life of animals and plants has been described and interpreted, but with due regard to the different character of the problem. The human material is peculiar not only in its enormous abundance and variety, but in requiring, to deal with it, a radically different theoretical and technical equipment.

5. Sociological Analysis and the "Variable"

Herbert Blumer

My aim in this paper is to examine critically the scheme of sociological analysis which seeks to reduce human group life to variables and their relations. I shall refer to this scheme, henceforth, as "variable analysis." This scheme is widespread and is growing in acceptance. It seems to be becoming the norm of proper sociological analysis. Its sophisticated forms are becoming the model of correct research procedure. Because of the influence which it is exercising in our discipline, I think that it is desirable to note the more serious of its shortcomings in actual use and to consider certain limits to its effective application. The first part of my paper will deal with the current shortcomings that I have in mind and the second part with the more serious question of the limits to its adequacy.

Shortcomings in Contemporary Variable Analysis

The first shortcoming I wish to note in current variable analysis in our field is the rather chaotic condition that prevails in the selection of variables. There seems to be little limit to what may be chosen or designated as a variable. One may select something as simple as a sex distribution or as complex as depression; something as specific as a birth rate or as vague as social cohesion; something as evident as residential change or as imputed as a collective unconscious; something as generally recognized as hatred or as doctrinaire as the Oedipus complex; something as immediately given as a rate of newspaper circulation to something as elaborately fabricated as an index of anomie. Variables may be selected on the basis of a specious impression of what is important, on the basis of conventional usage, on the basis of what can be secured through a given instrument or technique, on the basis of the demands of some doctrine, or on the basis of an imaginative ingenuity in devising a new term.

Obviously the study of human group life calls for a wide range of variables. However, there is a conspicuous absence of rules, guides,

Presidential address read at the annual meeting of the American Sociological Society, September, 1956.

From *American Sociological Review,* XXI (December, 1956), pp. 683-690, by permission of the American Sociological Association and the author.

limitations and prohibitions to govern the choice of variables. Relevant rules are not provided even in the thoughtful regulations that accompany sophisticated schemes of variable analysis. For example, the rule that variables should be quantitative does not help, because with ingenuity one can impart a quantitative dimension to almost any qualitative item. One can usually construct some kind of a measure or index of it or develop a rating scheme for judges. The proper insistence that a variable have a quantitative dimension does little to lessen the range or variety of items that may be set up as variables. In a comparable manner, the use of experimental design does not seemingly exercise much restriction on the number and kind of variables which may be brought within the framework of the design. Nor, finally, does careful work with variables, such as establishing tests of reliability, or inserting "test variables," exercise much restraint on what may be put into the pool of sociological variables.

In short, there is a great deal of laxity in choosing variables in our field. This laxity is due chiefly to a neglect of the careful reduction of problems that should properly precede the application of the techniques of variable analysis. This prior task requires thorough and careful reflection on the problem to make reasonably sure that one has identified its genuine parts. It requires intensive and extensive familiarity with the empirical area to which the problem refers. It requires a careful and thoughtful assessment of the theoretical schemes that might apply to the problem. Current variable analysis in our field is inclined to slight these requirements both in practice and in the training of students for that practice. The scheme of variable analysis has become for too many just a handy tool to be put to immediate use.

A second shortcoming in variable analysis in our field is the disconcerting absence of generic variables, that is, variables that stand for abstract categories. Generic variables are essential, of course, to an empirical science — they become the key points of its analytical structure. Without generic variables, variable analysis yields only separate and disconnected findings.

There are three kinds of variables in our discipline which are generally regarded as generic variables. None of them, in my judgment, is generic. The first kind is the typical and frequent variable which stands for a class of objects that is tied down to a given historical and cultural situation. Convenient examples are: attitudes toward the Supreme Court, intention to vote Republican, interest in the United Nations, a college education, army draftees and factory unemployment. Each of these variables, even though a class term, has substance only in a given historical context. The variables do not stand directly for items of abstract human group life; their application to human groups around the world, to human groups in the past, and to conceivable human groups in the future is definitely restricted. While their use may yield propositions that hold in given culture settings, they do not yield the abstract knowledge that is the core of an empirical science.

The second apparent kind of generic variable in current use in our discipline is represented by unquestionably abstract sociological categories, such as "social cohesion," "social integration," "assimilation," "authority," and "group morale." In actual use these do not turn out to be the generic variables that their labels would suggest. The difficulty is that such terms, as I sought to point out in an earlier article on sensitizing concepts,[1] have no fixed or uniform indicators. Instead, indicators are constructed to fit the particular problem on which one is working. Thus, certain features are chosen to represent the social integration of cities, but other features are used to represent the social integration of boys' gangs. The indicators chosen to represent morale in a small group of school children are very different from those used to stand for morale in a labor movement. The indicators used in studying attitudes of prejudice show a wide range of variation. It seems clear that indicators are tailored and used to meet the peculiar character of the local problem under study. In my judgment, the abstract categories used as variables in our work turn out with rare exception to be something other than generic categories. They are localized in terms of their content. Some measure of support is given to this assertion by the fact that the use of such abstract categories in variable research adds little to generic knowledge of them. The thousands of "variable" studies of attitudes, for instance, have not contributed to our knowledge of the abstract nature of an attitude; in a similar way the studies of "social cohesion," "social integration," "authority," or "group morale" have done nothing, so far as I can detect, to clarify or augment generic knowledge of these categories.

The third form of apparent generic variable in our work is represented by a special set of class terms like "sex," "age," "birth rate," and "time period." These would seem to be unquestionably generic. Each can be applied universally to human group life; each has the same clear and common meaning in its application. Yet, it appears that in their use in our field they do not function as generic variables. Each has a content that is given by its particular instance of application, e.g., the birth rate in Ceylon, or the sex distribution in the State of Nebraska, or the age distribution in the City of St. Louis. The kind of variable relations that result from their use will be found to be localized and non-generic.

These observations on these three specious kinds of generic variables point, of course, to the fact that variables in sociological research are predominantly disparate and localized in nature. Rarely do they refer satisfactorily to a dimension or property of abstract human group life. With little exception they are bound temporally, spatially, and culturally and are inadequately cast to serve as clear instances of generic sociological categories. Many would contend that this is because variable re-

[1] "What is Wrong with Social Theory?" *American Sociological Review,* 19 (February, 1954), pp. 3-10.

search and analysis are in a beginning state in our discipline. They believe that with the benefit of wider coverage, replication, and the co-ordination of separate studies disparate variable relations may be welded into generic relations. So far there has been little achievement along these lines. Although we already have appreciable accumulations of findings from variable studies, little has been done to convert the findings into generic relations. Such conversion is not an easy task. The difficulty should serve both as a challenge to the effort and an occasion to reflect on the use and limitations of variable analyses.

As a background for noting a third major shortcoming I wish to dwell on the fact that current variable analysis in our field is operating predominantly with disparate and not generic variables and yielding predominantly disparate and not generic relations. With little exception its data and its findings are "here and now," wherever the "here" be located and whenever the "now" be timed. Its analyses, accordingly, are of localized and concrete matters. Yet, as I think logicians would agree, to understand adequately a "here and now" relation it is necessary to understand the "here and now" context. This latter understanding is not provided by variable analysis. The variable relation is a single relation, necessarily stripped bare of the complex of things that sustain it in a "here and now" context. Accordingly, our understanding of it as a "here and now" matter suffers. Let me give one example. A variable relation states that reasonably staunch Erie County Republicans become confirmed in their attachment to their candidate as a result of listening to the campaign materials of the rival party. This bare and interesting finding gives us no picture of them as human beings in their particular world. We do not know the run of their experiences which induced an organization of their sentiments and views, nor do we know what this organization is; we do not know the social atmosphere or codes in their social circles; we do not know the reinforcements and rationalizations that come from their fellows; we do not know the defining process in their circles; we do not know the pressures, the incitants, and the models that came from their niches in the social structure; we do not know how their ethical sensitivities are organized and so what they would tolerate in the way of shocking behavior on the part of their candidate. In short, we do not have the picture to size up and understand what their confirmed attachment to a political candidate means in terms of their experience and their social context. This fuller picture of the "here and now" context is not given by variable relations. This, I believe, is a major shortcoming in variable analysis, insofar as variable analysis seeks to explain meaningfully the disparate and local situations with which it seems to be primarily concerned.

The three shortcomings which I have noted in current variable research in our field are serious but perhaps not crucial. With increasing experience and maturity they will probably be successfully overcome. They suggest, however, the advisability of inquiring more deeply into the interesting and important question of how well variable analysis is suited to the study of human group life in its fuller dimensions.

Limits of Variable Analysis

In my judgment, the crucial limit to the successful application of variable analysis to human group life is set by the process of interpretation or definition that goes on in human groups. This process, which I believe to be the core of human action, gives a character to human group life that seems to be at variance with the logical premises of variable analysis. I wish to explain at some length what I have in mind.

All sociologists — unless I presume too much — recognize that human group activity is carried on, in the main, through a process of interpretation or definition. As human beings we act singly, collectively, and societally on the basis of the meanings which things have for us. Our world consists of innumerable objects — home, church, job, college education, a political election, a friend, an enemy nation, a tooth brush, or what not — each of which has a meaning on the basis of which we act toward it. In our activities we wend our way by recognizing an object to be such and such, by defining the situations with which we are presented, by attaching a meaning to this or that event, and where need be, by devising a new meaning to cover something new or different. This is done by the individual in his personal action, it is done by a group of individuals acting together in concert, it is done in each of the manifold activities which together constitute an institution in operation, and it is done in each of the diversified acts which fit into and make up the patterned activity of a social structure or a society. We can and, I think, must look upon human group life as chiefly a vast interpretative process in which people, singly and collectively, guide themselves by defining the objects, events, and situations which they encounter. Regularized activity inside this process results from the application of stabilized definitions. Thus, an institution carries on its complicated activity through an articulated complex of such stabilized meanings. In the face of new situations or new experiences individuals, groups, institutions and societies find it necessary to form new definitions. These new definitions may enter into the repertoire of stable meanings. This seems to be the characteristic way in which new activities, new relations, and new social structures are formed. The process of interpretation may be viewed as a vast digestive process through which the confrontations of experience are transformed into activity. While the process of interpretation does not embrace everything that leads to the formation of human group activity and structure, it is, I think, the chief means through which human group life goes on and takes shape.

Any scheme designed to analyze human group life in its general character has to fit this process of interpretation. This is the test that I propose to apply to variable analysis. The variables which designate matters which either directly or indirectly confront people and thus enter into human group life would have to operate through this process of interpretation. The variables which designate the results or effects of the happenings which play upon the experience of people would be the outcome of the process of interpretation. Present-day variable analysis in our field is dealing predominantly with such kinds of variables.

There can be no doubt that, when current variable analysis deals with matters or areas of human group life which involve the process of interpretation, it is markedly disposed to ignore the process. The conventional procedure is to identify something which is presumed to operate on group life and treat it as an independent variable, and then to select some form of group activity as the dependent variable. The independent variable is put at the beginning part of the process of interpretation and the dependent variable at the terminal part of the process. The intervening process is ignored or, what amounts to the same thing, taken for granted as something that need not be considered. Let me cite a few typical examples: the presentation of political programs on the radio and the resulting expression of intention to vote; the entrance of Negro residents into a white neighborhood and the resulting attitudes of the white inhabitants toward Negroes; the occurrence of a business depression and the resulting rate of divorce. In such instances — so common to variable analysis in our field — one's concern is with the two variables and not with what lies between them. If one has neutralized other factors which are regarded as possibly exercising influence on the dependent variable, one is content with the conclusion that the observed change in the dependent variable is the necessary result of the independent variable.

This idea that in such areas of group life the independent variable automatically exercises its influence on the dependent variable is, it seems to me, a basic fallacy. There is a process of definition intervening between the events of experience presupposed by the independent variable and the formed behavior represented by the dependent variable. The political programs on the radio are interpreted by the listeners; the Negro invasion into the white neighborhood must be defined by the whites to have any effect on their attitudes; the many events and happenings which together constitute the business depression must be interpreted at their many points by husbands and wives to have any influence on marital relations. This intervening interpretation is essential to the outcome. It gives the meaning to the presentation that sets the response. Because of the integral position of the defining process between the two variables, it becomes necessary, it seems to me, to incorporate the process in the account of the relationship. Little effort is made in variable analysis to do this. Usually the process is completely ignored. Where the process is recognized, its study is regarded as a problem that is independent of the relation between the variables.

The indifference of variable analysis to the process of interpretation is based apparently on the tacit assumption that the independent variable predetermines its interpretation. This assumption has no foundation. The interpretation is not predetermined by the variable as if the variable emanated its own meaning. If there is anything we do know, it is that an object, event or situation in human experience does not carry its own meaning; the meaning is conferred on it.

Now, it is true that in many instances the interpretation of the object, event or situation may be fixed, since the person or people may have an already constructed meaning which is immediately applied to the item. Where such stabilized interpretation occurs and recurs, variable analysis would have no need to consider the interpretation. One could merely say that as a matter of fact under given conditions the independent variable is followed by such and such a change in the dependent variable. The only necessary precaution would be not to assume that the stated relation between the variables was necessarily intrinsic and universal. Since anything that is defined may be redefined, the relation has no intrinsic fixity.

Alongside the instances where interpretation is made by merely applying stabilized meanings there are the many instances where the interpretation has to be constructed. These instances are obviously increasing in our changing society. It is imperative in the case of such instances for variable analysis to include the act of interpretation in its analytic scheme. As far as I can see, variable analysis shuns such inclusion.

Now the question arises, how can variable analysis include the process of interpretation? Presumably the answer would be to treat the act of interpretation as an "intervening variable." But, what does this mean? If it means that interpretation is merely an intervening neutral medium through which the independent variable exercises its influence, then, of course, this would be no answer. Interpretation is a formative or creative process in its own right. It constructs meanings which, as I have said, are not predetermined or determined by the independent variable.

If one accepts this fact and proposes to treat the act of interpretation as a formative process, then the question arises how one is to characterize it as a variable. What quality is one to assign to it, what property or set of properties? One cannot, with any sense, characterize this act of interpretation in terms of the interpretation which it constructs; one cannot take the product to stand for the process. Nor can one characterize the act of interpretation in terms of what enters into it—the objects perceived, the evaluations and assessments made of them, the cues that are suggested, the possible definitions proposed by oneself or by others. These vary from one instance of interpretation to another and, further, shift from point to point in the development of the act. This varying and shifting content offers no basis for making the act of interpretation into a variable.

Nor, it seems to me, is the problem met by proposing to reduce the act of interpretation into component parts and work with these parts as variables. These parts would presumably have to be processual parts — such as perception, cognition, analysis, evaluation, and decision-making in the individual; and discussion, definition of one another's responses and other forms of social interaction in the group. The same difficulty exists in making any of the processual parts into variables that exists in the case of the complete act of interpretation.

The question of how the act of interpretation can be given the qualitative constancy that is logically required in a variable has so far not been answered. While one can devise some kind of a "more or less" dimension for it, the need is to catch it as a variable, or set of variables, in a manner which reflects its functioning in transforming experience into activity. This is the problem, indeed dilemma, which confronts variable analysis in our field. I see no answer to it inside the logical framework of variable analysis. The process of interpretation is not inconsequential or pedantic. It operates too centrally in group and individual experience to be put aside as being of incidental interest.

In addition to the by-passing of the process of interpretation there is, in my judgment, another profound deficiency in variable analysis as a scheme for analyzing human group life. The deficiency stems from the inevitable tendency to work with truncated factors and, as a result, to conceal or misrepresent the actual operations in human group life. The deficiency stems from the logical need of variable analysis to work with discrete, clean-cut and unitary variables. Let me spell this out.

As a working procedure variable analysis seeks necessarily to achieve a clean identification of the relation between two variables. Irrespective of how one may subsequently combine a number of such identified relations — in an additive manner, a clustering, a chain-like arrangement, or a "feedback" scheme — the objective of variable research is initially to isolate a simple and fixed relation between two variables. For this to be done each of the two variables must be set up as a distinct item with a unitary qualitative make-up. This is accomplished first by giving each variable, where needed, a simple quality or dimension, and second by separating the variable from its connection with other variables through their exclusion or neutralization.

A difficulty with this scheme is that the empirical reference of a true sociological variable is not unitary or distinct. When caught in its actual social character, it turns out to be an intricate and inner-moving complex. To illustrate, let me take what seems ostensibly to be a fairly clean-cut variable relation, namely between a birth control program and the birth rate of a given people. Each of these two variables — the program of birth control and the birth rate — can be given a simple discrete and unitary character. For the program of birth control one may choose merely its time period, or select some reasonable measure such as the number of people visiting birth control clinics. For the birth rate, one merely takes it as it is. Apparently, these indications are sufficient to enable the investigator to ascertain the relations between the two variables.

Yet, a scrutiny of what the two variables stand for in the life of the group gives us a different picture. Thus, viewing the program of birth control in terms of *how it enters into the lives of the people,* we need to note many things such as the literacy of the people, the clarity of the printed information, the manner and extent of its distribution, the social position of the directors of the program and of the personnel, how the personnel act, the character of their instructional talks, the way in which people define attendance at birth control clinics, the expressed views of influential personages with reference to the program, how such personages are regarded, and the nature of the discussions among people with regard to the clinics. These are only a few of the matters which relate to how the birth control program might enter into the experience of the people. The number is sufficient, however, to show the complex and inner-moving character of what otherwise might seem to be a simple variable.

A similar picture is given in the case of the other variable — the birth rate. A birth rate of a people seems to be a very simple and unitary matter. Yet, in terms of what it expresses and stands for in group activity it is exceedingly complex and diversified. We need consider only the variety of social factors that impinge on and affect the sex act, even though the sex act is only one of the activities that set the birth rate. The self-conceptions held by men and by women, the conceptions of family life, the values placed on children, accessibility of men and women to each other, physical arrangements in the home, the sanctions given by established institutions, the code of manliness, the pressures from relatives and neighbors, and ideas of what is proper, convenient and tolerable in the sex act — these are a few of the operating factors in the experience of the group that play upon the sex act. They suffice to indicate something of the complex body of actual experience and practice that is represented in and expressed by the birth rate of a human group.

I think it will be found that, when converted into the actual group activity for which it stands, a sociological variable turns out to be an intricate and inner-moving complex. There are, of course, wide ranges of difference between sociological variables in terms of the extent of such complexity. Still, I believe one will generally find that the discrete and unitary character which the labeling of the variable suggests vanishes.

The failure to recognize this is a source of trouble. In variable analysis one is likely to accept the two variables as the simple and unitary items that they seem to be, and to believe that the relation found between them is a realistic analysis of the given area of group life. Actually, in group life the relation is far more likely to be between complex, diversified and moving bodies of activity. The operation of one of these complexes on the other, or the interaction between them, is both concealed and misrepresented by the statement of the relation between the two variables.

The statement of the variable relation merely asserts a connection between abbreviated terms of reference. It leaves out the actual complexes of activity and the actual processes of interaction in which human group life has its being. We are here faced, it seems to me, by the fact that the very features which give variable analysis its high merit — the qualitative constancy of the variables, their clean-cut simplicity, their ease of manipulation as a sort of free counter, their ability to be brought into decisive relation — are the features that lead variable analysis to gloss over the character of the real operating factors in group life, and the real interaction and relations between such factors.

The two major difficulties faced by variable analysis point clearly to the need for a markedly different scheme of sociological analysis for the areas in which these difficulties arise. This is not the occasion to spell out the nature of this scheme. I shall merely mention a few of its rudiments to suggest how its character differs fundamentally from that of variable analysis. The scheme would be based on the premise that the chief means through which human group life operates and is formed is a vast, diversified process of definition. The scheme respects the empirical existence of this process. It devotes itself to the analysis of the operation and formation of human group life as these occur through this process. In doing so it seeks to trace the lines of defining experience through which ways of living, patterns of relations, and social forms are developed, rather than to relate these formations to a set of selected items. It views items of social life as articulated inside moving structures and believes that they have to be understood in terms of this articulation. Thus, it handles these items not as discrete things disengaged from their connections but instead, as signs of a supporting context which gives them their social character. In its effort to ferret out lines of definition and networks of moving relation, it relies on a distinctive form of procedure. This procedure is to approach the study of group activity through the eyes and experience of the people who have developed the activity. Hence, it necessarily requires an intimate familiarity with this experience and with the scenes of its operation. It uses broad and interlacing observations and not narrow and disjunctive observations. And, may I add, that like variable analysis, it yields empirical findings and "here-and-now" propositions, although in a different form. Finally, it is no worse off than variable analysis in developing generic knowledge out of its findings and propositions.

In closing, I express a hope that my critical remarks about variable analysis are not misinterpreted to mean that variable analysis is useless or makes no contribution to sociological analysis. The contrary is true. Variable analysis is a fit procedure for those areas of social life and formation that are not mediated by an interpretative process. Such areas exist and are important. Further, in the area of interpretative life variable analysis can be an effective means of unearthing stabilized patterns of interpretation which are not likely to be detected through the direct study of the experience of people. Knowledge of such patterns, or rather of the relations between variables which reflect such patterns, is of great value for understanding group life in its "here-and-now" character and indeed may have significant practical value. All of these appropriate uses give variable analysis a worthy status in our field.

In view, however, of the current tendency of variable analysis to become the norm and model for sociological analysis, I believe it important to recognize its shortcomings and its limitations.

6. Is Sociology a Behavioral Science?

Charles D. Bolton

Over the last ten years sociology, virtually without debate, has taken on the identity of a "Behavioral Science." Like the other social sciences, sociology has been subject to periodic seizures of intellectual fashion movements, and there seems little reason to view the behavioral science nomenclature as having a significantly different origin. However, there are certain characteristics of the behavioral science identity which make it of a more serious concern than most of the intellectual costumes sociologists have tried on in the past. No doubt there comes a time in the maturation of a science when it must settle on some identity. But serious examination should be made of the uncritically accepted assumptions implicit in the Behavioral Science identity.

The Behavioral Science identity is not merely a name but also an ideology. The Behavioral Science ideology involves the substitution of a methodological rationale for a theoretical one in identifying sociology. From the viewpoint of Behavioral Science, the unity of the various behavioral sciences lies in their common method; the differentiation among them becomes one of a division of labor, not a difference in point of view. A sociologist is defined as a person who has been trained in applying the scientific method to a particular kind of behaving system: social systems. For some years, of course, hardly any one in sociology has questioned the desirability of the field's becoming methodologically more scientific. But certain implications of the logic of the Behavioral Science ideology may prove enervating to the long run development of sociology. Let us examine the logic of this ideology.

We are told by the founders of the Unified Science group that the term "behavioral science" was chosen "primarily because its neutral character made it acceptable to both social and biological scientists."[1] Whatever the motives of its originators, the implication of "behavioral science" are by no means neutral. The clear implication to most people is that Behavioral scientists study behavior. Because of the very great importance of Behavioristic psychology in the American tradition, the study of behavior

From *Pacific Sociological Review,* VI (Spring, 1963), pp. 3-9, by permission of the journal.

[1] Editorial, "Behavioral Science, a New Journal," *Behavioral Science,* Vol. 1, 1956, p. 3.

implies the study of more or less directly observable behavior of *organisms.* This constitutes a selection of data based upon methodological considerations rather than upon the point of view of the scientist or the characteristics of the subject matter.

It would not be accurate to say that the conception of behavior has been limited in Behavioral Science to the imagery of psychological Behaviorism. Rather, the emphasis has been upon the behavior of systems. The entree of sociology into the Behavioral Science fold has come through the identification of sociology as the science which studies the "behavior" of social systems. Insofar, then, as Behavioral Science is concerned with social behavior, this behavior is seen at two levels: (1) the behavior of organisms with reference to interhuman stimuli, and (2) the behavior of social systems. However, an examination of colloquies of behavioral scientists, such as that reported in Grinker, *Toward a Unified Theory of Human Behavior,* makes clear that non-sociologists conceive of living organisms as "real" systems but think of social systems as abstract or constructed systems consisting of conceptual relations between "real" systems or the behaviors of "real" systems.[2] There is plainly implicit the reduction of social systems to forms of explanation such as the psychological and biological, which are thought to deal with "real" systems. One major devotee of the sociology-as-behavioral-science viewpoint, George Homans, has already publicly announced himself as a psychological reductionist.[3]

Does it any longer make any difference whether or not we believe that social phenomena can be reduced to psychological or biological phenomena? Should we not all sigh with relief at the passing of the acrimonious Durkheimian debates about *sui generis*? Perhaps, but the acceptance of behavior as the subject matter of sociology involves a critical change in the sociological identity. In the past, sociology has been the study of social *interaction* and social *relationships.* The sociological mode of explanation has been to take the *forms of relationship and interaction* as having *determinant* power in explaining the behavior of the individual. In the Behavioral Science ideology this approach must be abandoned in favor of an essentially descriptive approach to social systems.

In spite of some Behavioral sociologists' valiant efforts to defend the autonomy and non-reducibility of the sociological analysis of social systems,[4] three rising trends in sociological theory are indicative of the

[2] Roy R. Grinker, ed., *Toward a Unified Theory of Human Behavior,* New York: Basic Books, 1956.

[3] George Homans, "Social Behavior as Exchange," *American Journal of Sociology,* LXIII (May, 1958), p. 597.

[4] Perhaps the clearest attempt to defend the non-reducibility of the social system is Talcott Parsons' chapter, "Psychology and Sociology," in John P. Gillin, ed., *For a Science of Man: Convergences in Anthropology, Psychology, and Sociology,* New York: Macmillan, 1954, pp. 67-101.

implications of adopting the behavioral science ideology.[5]

The first is the increasing permeation of sociological thinking by terms connotative of the psychological mode of conceptualizing personality. Terms such as drive, needs, homeostasis, and tension-reduction, as well as the rich Freudian vocabulary, exemplify a mode of thinking which explains behavior in terms of predispositions brought into situations by human organisms rather than in terms of social relations and interactions specific to the episode of action.

The second trend is the increasing dependence upon the concept of the internalization of roles and norms during the socialization of the child as the explanatory mode for the functioning of the social system. That is, the orderly processes which occur in a social system are not attributed primarily to the contemporary sociological structure of the system but to the fact that the actors in the system have at some time in the *past*, usually in childhood, internalized the roles and norms of the system. For institutionalized aspects of society such a form of explanation may have a certain plausibility — though even here, Durkheim's conception of the externality and coerciveness of the collective representations is phenomenologically more acute. But for problematic and changing aspects of society, socialization cannot serve as more than a very partial explanation of the coordination of social behavior.

The third trend in contemporary theory is a drift toward an energy model of conceptualization — as illustrated not only by the equilibrium concept but also by the recent input-output mode of conceptualization.[6] The energy form of conceptualization is inevitably reductionist. Conceiving of social relationships in terms of energy is clearly a construction of the sociologist; there is no social energy. The location of energy must finally be within the organism or its technological extensions. More importantly, the energy model involves a radical abandonment of the traditional sociological form of conceptualization. Whether followers of Mead, Cooley, Simmel, Durkheim, or Weber, sociologists have emphasized the *communicational and definitional* character of social acts and social relations. This sociological form of conceptualization is a fundamentally different one from the hydraulic model employed in most psychological and biological thinking — that is, thinking centering around such concepts as homeostasis, libidinal economics, need-reduction, tension reduction, frustration-aggression, etc. From the traditional sociological viewpoint the actors' marshalling of energy is contingent upon his definition of the situation. From the viewpoint of energetics the definition of the situation

[5] The extent to which the Behavioral Science identity operates as "cause" or "reinforcing symptom" of these trends is debatable. Their consequence for sociology is the primary question.

[6] Illustrated by the article by Talcott Parsons, "General Theory in Sociology," in Robert K. Merton, Leonard Broom, and Leonard S. Cottrell, Jr., editors, *Sociology Today*, New York: Basic Books, 1959, pp. 3-38.

is essentially epiphenomenal to the balance of forces which are thought "really" to determine action. Even when input-output equations are thought of in terms of information theory, the energy model is implicit; for the function of symbols is thought of simply as that of *representing* or standing for events rather than that of *transforming* events into social objects, as is involved in Mead's conception of the function of significant symbols.[7] That is, in information theory a universally objective character is bestowed upon stimulus events, and language symbols become merely equivalent stimuli — a view entirely contrary to the evidence of cultural relativism.

To demonstrate that the Behavioral Science identity results in reductionism and the abandonment of traditional orientations does not, of course, prove that these developments are bad. There is no point here in warming over the theoretical arguments against reductionism. But some discussion of pragmatic consequences is in order. The achievement of a unified point of view for the Behavioral Sciences may be not only historically premature but plainly detrimental to the civilizing and enriching of human understanding of the social process. The sophistication and emancipation of thought from provincial bias in recent times has derived in large measure from the existence of multiple perspectives from which to analyze the social process. Mannheim has stressed the importance of relationalism in all social knowledge. Behavioral Science ideology leads away from this development, paradoxically, in two directions. One is the imposing of a single perspective or frame of reference on all the Behavioral Sciences; the other is the abandonment altogether of intellectual perspective in favor of a methodological orientation. The former stultifies the very trend which historically has produced the possibility of objective orientations toward the social process — are we yet so sure of our way that we can commit ourselves to a single orientation? The methodological perspective almost

[7] That is, Mead's conception of symbols focuses upon their function in creating objects — in the proper sense — in the field of experience during the on-going act. Words do not merely *stand* for self-constituted objects but constitute an important part of the existential character of objects. The meaning of a word is not constituted by a class of phenomenal events but by its indication of potential interactions with a class of events as experienced from a particular perspective. Perspectives may be either the goal-directedness of the on-going act or symbol structures, such as a frame of reference. Comparison of cultures makes it clear that the same class of phenomenal events may be interacted with quite differently from varying perspectives. Hence *objects* are relative to perspectives, and it cannot be said that symbols simply represent or stand for objects divorced from particular perspectives. See George Herbert Mead, *Mind, Self, and Society,* edited by Charles W. Morris, Chicago: University of Chicago Press, 1934. Sociological adherents of Behavioral Science often pay lip service to Mead's position on objects but ignore it when embracing reductionist methodologies.

certainly produces a gross oversimplification of the enormously complex character of the social process. Commitment to only a methodological orientation places the scientist in a situation analogous to the tourist who is satisfied that he has "seen" Yosemite by driving only to the floor of the valley because that is technologically the easiest point to reach.

More specific pragmatic consequences for sociology can be noted. Most crucial is the gradual abandonment by sociologists of the field of social psychology as a specific subfield of sociology. The progression has been subtle. While much is made of the conflict-filled nature of social psychology, historical analysis reveals that psychologically-oriented and sociologically-oriented social psychologists until recently had rather distinct focuses within the general field. Psychologically-oriented students focused upon the relation of the individual to the group, and hence have been concerned with personality and with cultural influences on traditional psychological variables such as motivation, perception, and emotion. The sociologically-oriented focused on social interaction as such — thus the concern of sociological social psychologists with such things as collective behavior, interpersonal interaction, primary groups, and consensus. In recent years, however, the sociological focus has gradually shifted to socialization, especially during infancy and childhood. The result is that the interaction process, as a generic problem, is nowhere in focus. Little attention is given to consensus as a process; consensus has become a majority of votes of individuals, or, at a more sophisticated level, another term for the state of social solidarity. Small group study has become a more or less autonomous activity, unintegrated with broader social psychological theory. The primary group becomes, not a distinctive process of interaction, but another variable to be "rediscovered" in the study of large-scale formal organization. Most unfortunately, the study of collective behavior, never hardy, receives only the most minimal attention from those sociologists wearing the Behavioral Science hat. Considering the concentration of sociology in the world's most extreme mass society, the pitifully small amount of attention being given to such mechanisms as fashion, fad, social movements, mass behavior, popular culture, and collective atmospheres is a most shocking failure of sociology. In the meagerness of attention given — even in theory — to collective behavior we can see most vividly the consequences of a Behavioral Science ideology which takes some organized system, organic or social, as its unit of analysis. For such an ideology, interaction is a product of the character of the system as such. There is no place for awareness that interaction is also a *constructional* process, the fulcrum of social creativity in which new convergences of human action are constantly shaped and new social forms crystalized.

The commitment to the methodological orientation in the Behavioral Science identity is probably associated with the decline of discussion about the nature of human nature. This old philosophical problem takes on new significance for a society in the process of transition from an economy of scarcity organized around a competitive work world to an economy of abundance where life must be centered around non-work activities. Does human nature condemn us to the fate that the personal concomitant of this societal transition shall be a shift from the false-fronting promoter personality of the marketplace to a dissolute TV addict, dissolving his anxieties in drugs and achieving social apathy through privatization? Or does human nature contain the potentiality that the Leisure Time Revolution can mold the bulk of men into creative, cooperative beings searching after goodness, beauty, and truth with the same intensity with which, in the past, they have pursued money, prestige, and power? Communist dogma has an answer, but Western social science has almost nothing to say on the subject. Similarly, our social science has little to tell us about what to expect of men or nations if disarmament can be achieved.

Another set of problems for sociology arises from the foundation sponsorship of the Behavioral Science ideology. In the Behavioral Science mode of thinking there is a distinct tendency to think of knowledge as having value for the control and manipulation of human behavior. I am not concerned here with the possible malevolence in the selective support of research by foundations concerned with manipulation. There is a more subtle theoretical problem. Theoretically, control is thought of as a correlary of prediction in science. But the assumption that control is simply a correlary of prediction involves a peculiar difficulty in the social sciences. If there is anything that is clear about the nature of human nature, it is the enormous flexibility and plasticity of human development. The career of any human development, individual or collective, apparently involves many turning points at which the outcome is problematic and more than one direction of movement is possible. It is also apparent that the same end may be reached by a variety of means with human beings. A major reason for this plasticity of humans is that the determinants of action may operate at any of a number of levels: chemical, physiological, unconscious, self-conscious, cultural, societal. It is crucial to recognize that at some of these levels humans are able to convert potential determinants into alternatives — that is, into cognitive, named objects which may be mentally, and often physically, manipulated: projected into the future, reflected upon, rejected, cast in new contexts, etc. However, other determinants are partially or wholly outside the linguistic-self process by which this manipulation of objects is carried on — for example, the influence of drugs and of unconscious or dissociated processes.

The aim of control in science implies, almost by definition, an effort to restrict and, ideally, to eliminate alternatives of the subjects. A social science which takes control as a major criterion for scientific success thereby has a built-in bias to focus attention upon those so-called independent variables which human subjects are least likely to be able to convert into alternatives. If evidence to date means anything, we can say that this focus leads to a concentration upon biochemical, unconscious, presocial, and nonrational influences and a studied ignoring of the processes which mark human beings as cognitive, self-conscious, creative, act-constructing creatures. Let me give a few illustrations of what I mean.

In recent years there have been a number of discoveries about the effects of various drugs upon human behavior and mentality. I am by no means questioning the desirability of studying the effects of these drugs; their value in handling certain cases of mental disorder seems established. But a science of controlling human behavior seems to be springing up around these drugs, with a concomitant ignoring on the part of their students of alternative processes by which human action may be regulated. The success of this mode of control tends to focus attention and research funds upon this physico-chemical approach to human behavior at the expense of alternative psychological and social approaches.

Within social psychology comparable trends are observable. Social psychologists concentrating upon socialization and personality have shown an extreme predilection for attention to presocial determinants — birth traumas, mothering in infancy, toilet training, etc. — with little or no attention to linguistic and cognitive factors. Doubtless the psychoanalytic influence is important here, but fascination with presocial determinants seems to go beyond the psychoanalytic influence. For example, the lengthy chapter on socialization in *The Handbook of Social Psychology* analyzes a number of variables in addition to those suggested by Freudians, but includes no mention at all of the significance of language development, of Piaget's studies of the development of the representational function, of Mead's theory of the self, nor, indeed, of a single cognitive variable.[8] The almost universal locating of the basic determinants of personality differentiation in infancy and early childhood betrays the same bias of avoiding the alternative-producing conditions of human conduct. Foote is almost a lone voice in pointing out that it is an illusion that personality development, in the sense of differentiation, slows down after childhood is passed. Yet one has only to reflect upon the shock felt at reunions with once bosom college friends to recognize the truth of Foote's statement that "ten close friends fan out far more in the individualization of their identities between, let us say, ages 30 and 40 than between 10 and 20."[9] We are constantly assured that personality is stabilized by the end of

[8] See Irving L. Child, "Socialization," in Gardner Lindzey, ed., *Handbook of Social Psychology,* Vol. II, Cambridge, Mass.: Addison-Wesley Publishing Co., 1954, pp. 655-92.

[9] Nelson N. Foote, "Concept and Method in the Study of Human Development," in Muzafer Sherif and M. O. Wilson, *Emerging Problems in Social Psychology,* Norman, Oklahoma: The University Book Exchange Duplicating Service, 1957, pp. 29-53. More recently Strauss has argued for giving more attention to changes in adult personality. See Anselm L. Strauss, *Mirrors and Masks,* Glencoe, Ill.: The Free Press, 1959.

childhood and merely unravels in adulthood. But where is the evidence for these assertions? For the most part, the point is merely assumed, and even the few studies that provide some scanty evidence for personality stability in adulthood fail to consider the fact that regularity of personal behavior may be as readily explained by regularities in the social scheduling of behavioral performances as by persistence in personality structure.

Sociologists too have distinctly favored formulations which omit consideration of the alternative-producing characteristics of the social process — stressing, for example, equilibrium maintaining systems, the determination of behavior by internalized norms and role expectations, prediction scales based upon presumed structural personality factors, and, at the extreme, motivational research emphasizing unconscious manipulation. The preference for the analysis of social interaction in terms of role interaction rather than as transactions between persons-as-selves similarly shuns the alternative-producing aspects of social action. Yet the few detailed studies of specific roles shatter the image of simple, mechanical role performance and make clear the interactional pressures toward proliferation of alternatives.[10]

I am certainly not arguing that any of the above mentioned kinds of studies should not be made. They may produce quite valid knowledge. I am only suggesting that, when not balanced by studies of the creative and alternative-producing levels of human action, such studies present a one-sided image of human nature. A more comprehensively valid scientific imagery would produce equal attention to the means of maximizing the alternative-producing conditions of human action. Consider the proportion of effort going into such areas as altruistic behavior, group factors in motivation for education, psycholinguistics, sociological factors in cognition, social contingencies of creativity, turning points in adult careers, the conditions of optimum freedom in human conduct, and human judgment. Obviously the Behavioral Science vogue is not wholly responsible for deficiencies in studying these areas. But insofar as the Behavioral Science ideology is successful in promoting the notion that success in control is the measure of scientific adequacy, it is not reasonable to expect a redress of the balance. In the social sciences there is no simple relation between prediction and control. I do not mean that we should select a particular image of the human process because it is appropriate to "good" values. Quite the contrary, I am suggesting that the present partial image has come to the fore in the Behavioral Sciences because of its appropriateness for certain values which have been accepted by scientists for essentially nonrational and nonevidential reasons — fashion, methodological convenience, foundation support, etc. What is needed is an imagery that

[10] *E.g.*, see the analysis of the role of school superintendent in Neal Gross, W. S. Mason, and A. W. McEachern, *Explorations in Role Analysis,* New York: Wiley, 1958.

at once points to all of the socially relevant levels of human phenomena and is appropriate to the particular set of problems to which the sociologist is expected to provide answers.

The Behavioral Image

The Behavioral Science usage of the word "behavior" itself creates a fundamental problem for sociology. The image involved is that behavior is a mechanical response to or expression of some other activating force — that is, a reaction to stimuli, to organic tensions, to internalized norms, to social sanctions, to dysfunctional changes, etc. In this imagery the social system becomes one of two things. For some writers the social system is a pattern of stimuli which schedule or trigger off the responses of organisms which have been socialized to react in certain ways to given stimuli. This conception is illustrated by the following quotation from two leading social scientists:

> We will look at our American system, which largely controls our behavior, much as we would a complex maze in which animals learn to behave. In such a system we must be taught to learn our way around as we grow up if we are to live normal lives and to behave normally as adults. . . . Growing up consists in learning how to behave, and learning how to behave means acquiring the proper responses to the batteries of social stimuli which compose our social order.[11]

For other writers, the social system is a supraindividual system operating in terms that can be formulated independently of the transactions between the human subjects in the system. The well-known equilibrium model used in structure-functional theory exemplifies the supraindividual system conception.

These two types of conceptualization involve three common assumptions. First, it is assumed that the basic problem of sociology, like the other Behavioral Sciences, is to explain or predict behavior. Second, it is assumed that human conduct *is* behavior, that is, responses to environmental or internalized stimuli. Third, it is assumed that social behavior is to be understood as learned behavior. I believe we must reject all three of these assumptions in sociology.

In the first place, sociology is just not concerned with "behavior," in the strict sense. In the sense appropriate to the methodological presuppositions of Behavioral Science, "behavior" is a physical movement or change of internal state of an organism — such as the movement of an

[11] W. Lloyd Warner and Robert J. Havighurst, *Who Shall Be Educated? The Challenge of Unequal Opportunities,* New York: Harper and Brothers, 1944, p. 18.

arm through space, the physiological changes we call blushing, the movement of an organism closer to or away from a stimulus. Sociology is not concerned with these things, per se. Sociology is concerned with social acts or interactions, which always involve the meaningful aspect of human phenomena that is relative to a particular symbolic context.

Furthermore, social acts are not responses to stimuli; they are interactions with objects and subjects. Stimuli are electrical or chemical or mechanical events that impinge upon a perceptor organ. Objects and subjects are products of the process of identifying the potentialities for interaction of events in the situation — identifications made not only from the viewpoint of the actor but from the roles or points of view of others involved in the episode of interaction. Interaction is more properly called inter-indication: indications of the significance of present parts of the act for future parts and indications of the significance of one person's act for the forthcoming or preceding conduct of another actor. Nor does one even, properly speaking, "respond" to social subjects and objects. One engages in interactions or transactions with them — ordinarily it is the modifying or building up of a relationship between actors which is crucial.

Most astonishing of all, social action cannot accurately be called "learned behavior." The constant and unqualified reiteration that human behavior is "learned" is a subtle evidence of the shift in sociological thinking in recent years. To be sure, the elements of organic behavior that are employed in social acts are, for the most part, learned. But this is by no means the whole story. For human beings "conduct" their actions. Social action is an organizing — in the give and take of social transactions — of the learned elements of behavior to build up a complex act that has its meaning in reference to the acts of others and to future stages of action. Social acts are constructional in character; they are *built up* rather than being simply learned responses. George Herbert Mead's conceptions of the self process and the social act are approvingly described in an early chapter of almost all major sociological works today, yet are thereafter ignored in the effort to treat the human process as reactive, learned behavior.

I wonder if any psychologist or sociologist takes seriously the "scientific" description of behavior when applied to his own conduct. Is the preparation of a lecture or a paper to be understood as "learned" behavior? The phonetics and written symbols and certain aspects of meaning, yes; the organization, the composition, basically no. The individual words and grammar and certain elements of style have been used innumerable times, but the particular ordering of words and ideas that constitutes this particular lecture or paper has never occurred before — but this is surely the aspect of the performance with which we are most concerned.

I have chosen the lecture as the example of building up of acts by interaction because in fact this apparently individual act is built up in a series of intrapersonal transactions in which the composer takes into account various audiences, possible criticisms, and a large array of behavioral elements which never appear in the finished form. In the case of the lecture one may also — and typically does — further reorganize the behavioral elements in process of delivery as a result of transactions with the actual audience. The manner in which a lecture must be understood as being built up in social transactions is often painfully brought home when one tries to use last year's lecture and cannot figure out what in the world one was trying to say. If something so individual as preparing a lecture must be understood as a constructional process, how much more so are the more typical interpersonal performances in which we are directly required to take into account the communications and acts of others. And let us be clear that this constructional process cannot profitably be broken down into a series of minute stimulus-response events. For the objective contingencies that emerge in the pattern of transactions are "real" determinants of the course of action. For example, if individuals of heterogeneous backgrounds come into interaction, the noncongruence of their definitions of the same events will produce inaccurate predictions and anticipations of one another's behavior, with varying consequences. Neither the heterogeneity nor the noncongruence of definitions are stimuli or responses; they can be dealt with only when the *process* of interaction is taken as the unit of analysis.

But if the image of man as a "behaver" fails to do justice to reality, what image can the sociologist or social psychologist use? A favorite philosophical image is that of man as an "actor." Thus Arendt, in analyzing the transition of Western Civilization from a political to a societal basis, suggests a distinction between man as behaver and actor:

> It is decisive that society, on all its levels, excludes the possibility of action, which formerly was excluded from the household. Instead, society expects from each of its members a certain kind of behavior, imposing innumerable and various rules, all of which tend to normalize its members to make them behave, to exclude spontaneous action or outstanding achievement.[12]

By "action" Arendt seems to mean some spontaneous, creative self-governance operating outside of social determinants. Clearly this is not an imagery with which a science can deal, even though it points to aspects of the human drama which we must take into account, though in different ways than the philosopher. But this image of the spontaneous actor is not the only alternative to the image of the social process as a sequence of behavioral reactions. An appropriate sociological image of the individual in the social process is neither that of 'behaver' nor 'actor' but that of

[12] Hannah Arendt, *The Human Condition,* Chicago: University of Chicago Press, 1958, p. 40.

'interactor.' By viewing the basic individual unit as 'interactor' a connection is immediately made with two crucial sociological factors, situation and transaction.

Most of the theoretical problems of sociopsychological science revolve around the intricate relationships of societal organization, personality, and situated social interaction. In most theory and research the process of situated social interaction is treated as the meeting ground of the other two. But almost invariably "meeting ground" becomes transmuted into "product of." Those of psychological bent would explain social interactions as the products of the personalities of the participants — of drives and instincts, habits and attitudes, needs and defenses. Those of sociological persuasion would explain social interaction as a product of societal organization — of roles and norms, status systems and institutional structures, ecological patterns and technological apparatus. Thus social interaction tends to be seen, not as a determining aspect of the social process, but as an end product, as a sum of the reciprocal behaviors of traited individuals in a societally structured situation.

I am suggesting that social interaction processes should be given an equalitarian position with personality and societal organization. What emerges from any episode of interaction — except the most ritualized — bears the stamp of what goes on *between* the interactors. Indeed, we may argue that the problem of sociology is to explain the manner in which human acts are fitted together in social interaction. Meaning arises in human conduct precisely because human acts are *not* behavioral reactions, but rather are constructional processes in which each individual organizes his act by taking into account — ordinarily through linguistic processes — the acts of other persons and past and future parts of the developing episode of interaction. Thus, if the sociological unit of observation and analysis is to be a unit of meaning, it cannot be a behavioral unit but must be an interactional unit.

The significance of considering the interaction process as a determinant of social action can be seen in analyzing episodes that are ordinarily described in terms of role structure. One of the fundamental errors of most role analysis is to treat each actor as occupying the same role throughout an episode, when in fact each actor ordinarily shuttles through a number of roles during an episode, some overtly expressed, some covertly. For instance, a teacher conferring with his principal about a matter of academic freedom may move through the roles of teacher, colleague, scientist, liberal, ACLU member, Jew, male, family provider, etc., not to mention the interspersing of overt and covert social type perspectives such as eager beaver, individualist, cynic, martyr, and scapegoat. Which role and social type perspectives will be occupied during an episode will depend partly on the structure of the situation and partly on which perspectives are available in the actor's personal repertoire, but also partly on the transactions that occur between the participants in the episode. The give-and-take of interaction will lead and force the individual from one position to another.

The reason that George Herbert Mead's conception of the self is central to sociological theory is that it permits us to deal with personality as an interactional unit. Many writers seem to see the importance of Mead's formulation only in his notion that the self-as-object derives its identity from the conceptions other people have of the individual. But actually more critical is Mead's conception of the self as a process of interaction, with the "me" being a role-taking activity through which the individual constantly introduces into his on-going act, in addition to the perspective of the "I," the perspective of the other or the "generalized other." As Mead shows, the self process is really internalized social communication involving two or more social perspectives, just as is the case in overt interpersonal transactions.[13] From this viewpoint, such things as motivation, attitudes, and cultural norms are seen as entering into social acts by a process of identification; that is, as being some of the steps in the defining activity by which an act is built up in an episode of interaction.[14] It is important to note that identifying in an episode what are one's own appropriate motives, attitudes, and norms is accomplished by the same kind of activity, the role-taking process of the self, by which one imputes (through taking the role of the other) the motives, attitudes, and norms of the other by which one anticipates and tries to make sense of the actions of others in the episode.

It is not my intention here to trace the process by which social interaction has lost the place of centrality it had on the sociological stage up to the 1930's. Suffice it to say that the interactionist frame of reference came to be associated with social psychology by the 1930's, and, as the broader evolution of social psychology led to the emphasis upon the relation of the individual to his groups, the concept of "socialization" gradually came to supplant "interaction" as the focus of sociological social psychologists. In time, however, thinking about the individual actor has become so infused with the imagery of psychological dynamics that the effort to connect the individual actor and the social system by the mechanism of socialization has become tenuous. With the entry of sociology into the society of behavioral sciences, the split threatens to become complete and sociology in turn to become essentially a descriptive science.

Neither functional analysis nor viewing the social system as a maze of stimuli affords the basis for making sociology a nomothetic science. Sociology cannot be a well-rounded explanatory science without the inclusion of social psychology. But it must be a social psychology which takes

[13] Mead, *op. cit.*

[14] For a statement of this view with reference to motivation see Nelson N. Foote, "Identification as the Basis for a Theory of Motivation," *American Sociological Review,* 16 (February, 1951), pp. 14-22.

interaction rather than the individual as its unit of analysis. Only when interaction is at the center of the sociological stage can the acting personality and social structure be adequately integrated in the contemporaneous situation. Similarly, only when social organization is given an interactional dimension can there be the needed recognition that collective behavior processes — social unrest, fashion, emotional contagions, social movements, ideological drifts — are not only processes out of which new social orders arise in periods of transition but are processes interwoven with institutional activities in all social organization. It is the dynamic of social interaction which ties together the other building blocks of sociological theory: sociocultural organization, the minded individual, collective behavior, and the contingencies which emerge from their interpenetration.

7. Participant Observation and Interviewing: A Comparison

Howard S. Becker and Blanche Geer

The most complete form of the sociological datum, after all, is the form in which the participant observer gathers it: an observation of some social event, the events which precede and follow it, and explanations of its meaning by participants and spectators, before, during, and after its occurrence. Such a datum gives us more information about the event under study than data gathered by any other sociological method. Participant observation can thus provide us with a yardstick against which to measure the completeness of data gathered in other ways, a model which can serve to let us know what orders of information escape us when we use other methods.[1]

By participant observation we mean that method in which the observer participates in the daily life of the people under study, either openly in the role of researcher or covertly in some disguised role, observing things that happen, listening to what is said, and questioning people, over some length of time.[2] We want, in this paper, to compare the results of such intensive field work with what might be regarded as the first step in the other direction along this continuum: the detailed and conversational interview (often referred to as the unstructured or undirected interview).[3]

From *Human Organization,* Vol. XVI, No. 3, (Fall, 1957), pp. 28-32, by permission of the Society for Applied Anthropology and the authors.

[1] We wish to thank R. Richard Wohl and Thomas S. McPartland for their critical reading of an earlier version of this paper.

[2] Cf. Florence R. Kluckhohn, "The Participant Observer Technique in Small Communities," *American Journal of Sociology,* 45 (Nov., 1940), 331-43; Arthur Vidich, "Participant Observation and the Collection and Interpretation of Data," *ibid.*, 60 (Jan., 1955), 354-60; William Foote Whyte, "Observational Field-Work Methods," in Marie Jahoda, Morton Deutsch, and Stuart W. Cook (eds.), *Research Methods in the Social Sciences* (New York: Dryden Press, 1951), II, 393-514, and *Street Corner Society* (Enlarged Edition) (Chicago: University of Chicago Press, 1955), 279-358.

[3] Two provisos are in order. In the first place, we assume in our comparison that the hypothetical interviewer and participant observer we discuss are equally skilled and sensitive. We assume further that both began their research with equally well formulated problems, so that they are indeed looking for equivalent kinds of data.

In this kind of interview, the interviewer explores many facets of his interviewee's concerns, treating subjects as they come up in conversation, pursuing interesting leads, allowing his imagination and ingenuity full rein as he tries to develop new hypotheses and test them in the course of the interview.

In the course of our current participant observation among medical students,[4] we have thought a good deal about the kinds of things we were discovering which might ordinarily be missed or misunderstood in such an interview. We have no intention of denigrating the interview or even such less precise modes of data gathering as the questionnaire, for there can always be good reasons of practicality, economy, or research design for their use. We simply wish to make explicit the difference in data gathered by one or the other method and to suggest the differing uses to which they can legitimately be put. In general, the shortcomings we attribute to the interview exist when it is used as a source of information about events that have occurred elsewhere and are described to us by informants. Our criticisms are not relevant when analysis is restricted to interpretation of the interviewee's conduct *during the interview,* in which case the researcher has in fact observed the behavior he is talking about.[5]

The differences we consider between the two methods involve two interacting factors: the kinds of words and acts of the people under study that the researcher has access to, and the kind of sensitivity to problems and data produced in him. Our comparison may prove useful by suggestive areas in which interviewing (the more widely used method at present and likely to continue so) can improve its accuracy by taking account of suggestions made from the perspective of the participant observer. We begin by considering some concrete problems: learning the native language, or the problem of the degree to which the interviewer really understands what is said to him; matters interviewees are unable or unwilling to talk about; and getting information on matters people see through distorting lenses. We then consider some more general differences between the two methods.

Learning the Native Language

Any social group, to the extent that it is a distinctive unit, will have to some degree a culture differing from that of other groups, a somewhat

[4] This study is sponsored by Community Studies, Inc., of Kansas City, Missouri, and is being carried out at the University of Kansas Medical Center, to whose dean and staff we are indebted for their wholehearted cooperation. Professor Everett C. Hughes of the University of Chicago is director of the project.

[5] For discussion of this point, see Thomas S. McPartland, *Formal Education and the Process of Professionalization: A Study of Student Nurses* (Kansas City, Missouri: Community Studies, Inc., 1957), 2-3.

different set of common understandings around which action is organized, and these differences will find expression in a language whose nuances are peculiar to that group and fully understood only by its members. Members of churches speak differently from members of informal tavern groups; more importantly, members of any particular church or tavern group have cultures, and languages in which they are expressed, which differ somewhat from those of other groups of the same general type. So, although we speak one language and share in many ways in one culture, we cannot assume that we understand precisely what another person, speaking as a member of such a group, means by any particular word. In interviewing members of groups other than our own, then, we are in somewhat the same position as the anthropologist who must learn a primitive language,[6] with the important difference that, as Icheiser has put it, we often do not understand that we do not understand and are thus likely to make errors in interpreting what is said to us. In the case of gross misunderstandings the give and take of conversation may quickly reveal our mistakes, so that the interviewee can correct us; this presumably is one of the chief mechanisms through which the anthropologist acquires a new tongue. But in speaking American English with an interviewee who is, after all, much like us, we may mistakenly assume that we have understood him and the error be small enough that it will not disrupt communication to the point where a correction will be in order.

The interview provides little opportunity of rectifying errors of this kind where they go unrecognized. In contrast, participant observation provides a situation in which the meaning of words can be learned with great precision through study of their use in context, exploration through continuous interviewing of their implications and nuances, and the use of them oneself under the scrutiny of capable speakers of the language. Beyond simply clarifying matters so that the researcher may understand better what people say to each other and to him, such a linguistic exercise may provide research hypotheses of great usefulness. The way in which one of us learned the meaning of the word "crock," as medical students use it, illustrates these points.

> I first heard the word "crock" applied to a patient shortly after I began my field work. The patient in question, a fat, middle-aged woman, complained bitterly of pains in a number of widely separated locations. When I asked the student who had so described her what the word meant, he said that it was used to refer to any patient who had psychosomatic complaints. I asked if that meant that Mr. X ——, a young man on the ward whose stomach ulcer had been discussed by a staff physician as typically psychosomatic, was a crock. The student said that that would not be correct usage, but was not able to say why.

[6] See the discussion in Bronislaw Malinowski, *Magic, Science, and Religion and Other Essays* (Glencoe: The Free Press, 1948), 232-8.

> Over a period of several weeks, through discussion of many cases seen during morning rounds with the students, I finally arrived at an understanding of the term, realizing that it referred to a patient who complained of many symptoms but had no discoverable organic pathology. I had noticed from the beginning that the term was used in a derogatory way and had also been inquiring into this, asking students why they disliked having crocks assigned to them for examination and diagnosis. At first students denied the derogatory connotations, but repeated observations of their disgust with such assignments soon made such denials unrealistic. Several students eventually explained their dislike in ways of which the following example is typical: "The true crock is a person who you do a great big workup for and who has all of these vague symptoms, and *you really can't find anything the matter with them.*"
>
> Further discussion made it clear that the students regarded patients primarily as objects from which they could learn those aspects of clinical medicine not easily acquired from textbooks and lectures; the crock took a great deal of their time, of which they felt they had little enough, and did not exhibit any interesting disease state from which something might be learned, so that the time invested was wasted. This discovery in turn suggested that I might profitably investigate the general perspective toward medical school which led to such a basis for judgment of patients, and also suggested hypotheses regarding the value system of the hospital hierarchy at whose bottom the student stood.

At the risk of being repetitious, let us point out in this example both the errors avoided and the advantages gained because of the use of participant observation. The term might never have been used by students in an ordinary interview; if it had, the interviewer might easily have assumed that the scatological term from which it in fact is descended provided a complete definition. Because the observer saw students on their daily rounds and heard them discussing everyday problems, he heard the word and was able to pursue it until he arrived at a meaningful definition. Moreover, the knowledge so gained led to further and more general discoveries about the group under study.

This is not to say that all of these things might not be discovered by a program of skillful interviewing, for this might well be possible. But we do suggest that an interviewer may misunderstand common English words when interviewees use them in some more or less esoteric way and not know that he is misunderstanding them, because there will be little chance to check his understanding against either further examples of their use in conversation or instances of the object to which they are applied. This leaves him open to errors of misinterpretation and errors of failing to see connections between items of information he has available, and may prevent him from seeing and exploring important research leads. In dealing with interview data, then, experience with participant observation indicates that both care and imagination must be used in making sure of meanings, for the cultural esoterica of a group may hide behind ordinary language used in special ways.

Matters Interviewees Are Unable or Unwilling to Talk About

Frequently, people do not tell an interviewer all the things he might want to know. This may be because they do not want to, feeling that to speak of some particular subject would be impolitic, impolite, or insensitive, because they do not think to and because the interviewer does not have enough information to inquire into the matter, or because they are not able to. The first case — the problem of "resistance" — is well known and a considerable lore has developed about how to cope with it.[7] It is more difficult to deal with the last two possibilities for the interviewee is not likely to reveal, or the interviewer to become aware, that significant omissions are being made. Many events occur in the life of a social group and the experience of an individual so regularly and uninterruptedly, or so quietly and unnoticed, that people are hardly aware of them, and do not think to comment on them to an interviewer; or they may never have become aware of them at all and be unable to answer even direct questions. Other events may be so unfamiliar that people find it difficult to put into words their vague feelings about what has happened. If an interviewee, for any of these reasons, cannot or will not discuss a certain topic, the researcher will find gaps in his information on matters about which he wants to know and will perhaps fail to become aware of other problems and areas of interest that such discussion might have opened up for him.

This is much less likely to happen when the researcher spends much time with the people he studies as they go about their daily activities, for he can see the very things which might not be reported in an interview. Further, should he desire to question people about matters they cannot or prefer not to talk about, he is able to point to specific incidents which either force them to face the issue (in the case of resistance) or make clear what he means (in the case of unfamiliarity). Finally, he can become aware of the full meaning of such hints as are given on subjects people are unwilling to speak openly about and of such inarticulate statements as people are able to make about subjects they cannot clearly formulate, because he frequently knows of these things through his observation and can connect his knowledge with these half-communications.

[7] See, for example, Arnold M. Rose, "A Research Note on Interviewing," *American Journal of Sociology,* 51 (Sept., 1945), 143-4; and Howard S. Becker, "A Note on Interviewing Tactics," *Human Organization,* 12:4 (Winter, 1954), 31-2.

Researchers working with interview materials, while they are often conscious of these problems, cannot cope with them so well. If they are to deal with matters of this kind it must be by inference. They can only make an educated guess about the things which go unspoken in the interview; it may be a very good guess, but it must be a guess. They can employ various tactics to explore for material they feel is there but unspoken, but even when these are fruitful they do not create sensitivity to those problems of which even the interviewer is not aware. The following example indicates how participant observation aids the researcher in getting material, and making the most of the little he gets, on topics lying within this range of restricted communication.

> A few months after the beginning of school, I went to dinner at one of the freshman medical fraternities. It was the night nonresident members came, married ones with their wives. An unmarried student who lived in the house looked around at the visitors and said to me, "We are so much in transition. I have never been in this situation before of meeting fellows and their wives."
>
> This was just the sort of thing we were looking for — change in student relationships arising from group interaction — but I failed in every attempt to make the student describe the "transition" more clearly.
>
> From previous observation, though, I knew there were differences (other than marriage) between the nonresidents and their hosts. The former had all been elected to the fraternity recently, after house officers had gotten to know them through working together (usually on the same cadaver in anatomy lab). They were older than the average original member; instead of coming directly from college, several had had jobs or Army experience before medical school. As a group they were somewhat lower in social position.
>
> These points indicated that the fraternity was bringing together in relative intimacy students different from each other in background and experience. They suggested a search for other instances in which dissimilar groups of students were joining forces, and pointed to a need for hypotheses as to what was behind this process of drawing together on the part of the freshman and its significance for their medical education.

An interviewer, hearing this statement about "transition," would know that the interviewee felt himself in the midst of some kind of change but might not be able to discover anything further about the nature of that change. The participant observer cannot find out, any more than the interviewer can, what the student had in mind, presumably because the student had nothing more in mind than this vague feeling of change. (Interviewees are not sociologists and we ought not to assume that their fumbling statements are attempts, crippled by their lack of technical vocabulary, to express what a sociologist might put in more formal analytic terms.) But he can search for those things in the interviewee's situation which might lead to such a feeling of transition.

While the participant observer can make immediate use of such vague statements as clues to an objective situation, the interviewer is often bothered by the question of whether an interviewee is not simply referring to quite private experiences. As a result, the interviewer will place less reliance on whatever inferences about the facts of the situation he makes, and is less likely to be sure enough of his ground to use them as a basis for further hypotheses. Immediate observation of the scene itself and data from previous observation enable the participant observer to make direct use of whatever hints the informant supplies.

Things People See Through Distorting Lenses

In many of the social relationships we observe, the parties to the relation will have differing ideas as to what ought to go on in it, and frequently as to what does in fact go on in it. These differences in perception will naturally affect what they report in an interview. A man in a subordinate position in an organization in which subordinates believe that their superiors are "out to get them" will interpret many incidents in this light, though the incidents themselves may not seem, either to the other party in the interaction or to the observer, to indicate such malevolence. Any such mythology will distort people's view of events to such a degree that they will will report as fact things which have not occurred, but which seem to them to have occurred. Students, for example, frequently invent sets of rules to govern their relations with teachers, and, although the teacher may never have heard of such rules, regard the teachers as malicious when they "disobey" them. The point is that things may be reported in an interview through such a distorting lens, and the interviewer may have no way of knowing what is fact and what is distortion of this kind; participant observation makes it possible to check such points. The following is a particularly clear example.

> Much of the daily teaching was done, and practical work of medical students supervised, in a particular department of the hospital, by the house residents. A great deal of animosity had grown up between the particular group of students I was with at the time and these residents, the students believing that the residents would, for various malicious reasons, subordinate them and embarrass them at every opportunity. Before I joined the group, several of the students told me that the residents were "mean", "nasty", "bitchy", and so on, and had backed these characterizations up with evidence of particular actions.

After I began participating daily with the students on this service, a number of incidents made it clear that the situation was not quite like this. Finally, the matter came completely into the open. I was present when one of the residents suggested a technique that might have prevented a minor relapse in a patient assigned to one of the students; he made it clear that he did not think the relapse in any way the student's fault, but rather that he was simply passing on what he felt to be a good tip. Shortly afterward, this student reported to several other students that the resident had "chewed him out" for failing to use this technique: "What the hell business has he got chewing me out about that for? No one ever told me I was supposed to do it that way." I interrupted to say, "He didn't really chew you out. I thought he was pretty decent about it." Another student said, "Any time they say anything at all to us I consider it a chewing out. Any time they say anything about how we did things, they are chewing us out, no matter how God damn nice they are about it."

In short, participant observation makes it possible to check description against fact and, noting discrepancies, become aware of systematic distortions made by the person under study; such distortions are less likely to be discovered by interviewing alone. This point, let us repeat, is only relevant when the interview is used as a source of information about situations and events the researcher himself has not seen. It is not relevant when it is the person's behavior in the interview itself that is under analysis.

Inference, Process and Context

We have seen, in the previous sections of this paper, some of the ways in which even very good interviews may go astray, at least from the perspective of the field observer. We turn now to a consideration of the more general areas of difference between the two methods, suggesting basic ways in which the gathering and handling of data in each differ.

Since we tend to talk in our analyses about much the same order of thing whether we work from interviews or from participant-observational materials, and to draw conclusions about social relations and the interaction that goes on within them whether we have actually seen these things or only been told about them, it should be clear that in working with interviews we must necessarily infer a great many things we could have observed had we only been in a position to do so. The kinds of errors we have discussed above are primarily errors of inference, errors which arise from the necessity of making assumptions about the relation of interview statements to actual events which may or may not be true; for what we have solid observable evidence on in the first case we have only secondhand reports and indices of in the second, and the gap must be bridged by inference. We must assume, when faced with an account or transcription of an interview, that we understand the meaning of the everyday words used, that the interviewee is able to talk about the things we are interested in, and that his account will be more or less accurate. The examples detailed above suggest that these assumptions do not always hold and that the process of inference involved in interpreting interviews should always be made explicit and checked, where possible, against what can be discovered through observation. Where, as is often the case, this is not possible, conclusions should be limited to those matters the data directly describe.

Let us be quite specific, and return to the earlier example of resident-student hostility. In describing this relationship from interviews with the students alone we might have assumed their description to be accurate and made the inference that the residents were in fact "mean." Observation proved that this inference would have been incorrect, but this does not destroy the analytic usefulness of the original statements made to the fieldworker in an informal interview. It does shift the area in which we can make deductions from this datum, however, for we can see that such statements, while incorrect factually, are perfectly good statements of the perspective from which these students interpreted the events in which they were involved. We could not know without observation whether their descriptions were true or false; with the aid of observation we know that the facts of the matter are sometimes quite different, and that the students' perspective is strong enough to override such variant facts. But from the interview alone we could know, not what actually happened in such cases, but what the students thought happened and how they felt about it, and this is the kind of inference we should make. We add to the accuracy of our data when we substitute observable fact for inference. More important, we open the way for the discovery of new hypotheses for the fact we observe may not be the fact we expected to observe. When this happens we face a new problem requiring new hypothetical explanations which can then be further tested in the field.

Substitution of an inference about something for an observation of that thing occurs most frequently in discussions of social process and change, an area in which the advantages of observation over an extended period of time are particularly great. Much sociological writing is concerned, openly or otherwise, with problems of process: The analysis of shifts in group structure, individual self-conception and similar matters. But studies of such phenomena in natural social contexts are typically based on data that tell only part of the story. The analysis may be made from a person's retrospective account, in a single interview, of changes that have taken place; or, more rarely, it is based on a series of interviews, the differences between successive interviews providing the bench marks of change. In either case, many crucial steps in the process and important mechanisms of change must be arrived at through inferences which can be no more than educated guesses.

The difficulties in analyzing change and process on the basis of interview material are particularly important because it is precisely in discussing changes in themselves and their surroundings that interviewees are least likely or able to give an accurate account of events. Changes in the social environment and in the self inevitably produce transformations of perspective, and it is characteristic of such transformations that the person finds it difficult or impossible to remember his former actions, outlook, or feelings. Reinterpreting things from his new perspective, he cannot give an accurate account of the past, for the concepts in which he thinks about it have changed and with them his perceptions and memories.[8] Similarly, a person in the midst of such change may find it difficult to describe what is happening, for he has not developed a perspective or concepts which would allow him to think and talk about these things coherently; the earlier discussion of changes in medical school fraternity life is a case in point.

Participant observation does not have so many difficulties of this sort. One can observe actual changes in behavior over a period of time and note the events which precede and follow them. Similarly, one can carry on a conversation running over weeks and months with the people he is studying and thus become aware of shifts in perspective as they occur. In short, attention can be focused both on what has happened and on what the person says about what has happened. Some inference as to actual steps in the process or mechanisms involved is still required, but the amount of inference necessary is considerably reduced. Again, accuracy is increased and the possibility of new discoveries being made is likewise increased, as the observer becomes aware of more phenomena requiring explanation.

The participant observer is both more aware of these problems of inference and more equipped to deal with them because he operates, when gathering data, in a social context rich in cues and information of all kinds. Because he sees and hears the people he studies in many situations of the kind that normally occur for them, rather than just in an isolated and formal interview, he builds an evergrowing fund of impressions, many of them at the subliminal level, which give him an extensive base for the interpretation and analytic use of any particular datum. This wealth of information and impression sensitizes him to subtleties which might pass unnoticed in an interview and forces him to raise continually new and different questions, which he brings to and tries to answer in succeeding observations.

The biggest difference in the two methods, then, may be not so much that participant observation provides the opportunity for avoiding the

[8]Anselm L. Strauss, "The Development and Transformation of Monetary Meanings in the Child," *American Sociological Review,* 17 (June, 1952), 275-86, and *An Essay on Identity* (unpublished manuscript), *passim.*

errors we have discussed, but that it does this by providing a rich experiential context which causes him to become aware of incongruous or unexplained facts, makes him sensitive to their possible implications and connections with other observed facts, and thus pushes him continually to revise and adapt his theoretical orientation and specific problems in the direction of greater relevance to the phenomena under study. Though this kind of context and its attendant benefits cannot be reproduced in interviewing (and the same degree of sensitivity and sense of problem produced in the interviewer), interviewers can profit from an awareness of those limitations of their method suggested by this comparison and perhaps improve their batting average by taking account of them.[9]

[9] We are aware that participant observation raises as many technical problems as it solves. (See, for instance, the discussions in Morris S. Schwartz and Charlotte Green Schwartz, "Problems in Participant Observation," *American Journal of Sociology,* 60 (Jan., 1955), 343-53, and Vidich, *op. cit.*) We feel, however, that there is considerable value in using the strong points of one method to illuminate the shortcomings of another.

8. An Empirical Investigation of Self-Attitudes *

Manford H. Kuhn and
Thomas S. McPartland

Although the self has long been the central concept in the symbolic interaction approach to social psychology, little if anything has been done to employ it directly in empirical research. There are several reasons for this, one of the most important of which is that there has been no consensus regarding the class of phenomena to which the self ought to be operationally ordered. The self has been called an image, a conception, a concept, a feeling, an internalization, a self looking at oneself, and most commonly simply the self (with perhaps the most ambiguous implications of all). One of these many designations of the self has been as *attitudes.* We do not have space here to discuss the theoretical clarification which results from the conscious conceptualization of the self as a set of attitudes[1] except to point out that this conceptualization is most consistent with Mead's view of the self as an object which is in most respects like all other objects, and with his further view that an object is a plan of action (an attitude).

If, as we suppose, human behavior is *organized* and *directed,* and if, as we further suppose, the organization and direction are supplied by the individual's *attitudes toward himself,* it ought to be of crucial significance to social psychology to be able to identify and measure self-attitudes. This paper is intended to provide an initial demonstration of the advantages to empirical research from thus treating the self as attitudes.

Problems in the Development of a Self-Attitudes Test

The obvious first step in the application of self-theory to empirical research is the construction and standardization of a test which will identify and measure self-attitudes.

From *American Sociological Review,* XIX (February, 1954), pp. 68-76, by permission of the American Sociological Association and the authors.

*The investigation on which this paper is based was made possible by a grant from the Graduate College of the State University of Iowa. The paper is a part of an extended examination of self-theory given before the social psychology section of the Midwest Sociological Society at Omaha, April 25, 1953.

[1] A paper dealing with this view is being prepared by the present authors for publication elsewhere.

The initial consideration in designing such a test is the question of accessibility. Would people give to investigators the statements which are operative in identifying themselves and therefore in organizing and directing their behavior? Or would they be inclined to hide their significant self-attitudes behind innocuous and conventional fronts? Those following symbolic interaction orientation have apparently guessed the latter to be the case for they have seldom if ever asked direct questions regarding self-attitudes, and have tended to assemble self-attitudes of those they were studying from diverse kinds of statements and behavior through the use of long and dubious chains of inference.

One of the present authors, in an earlier attempt to identify and measure self-attitudes among groups of Amish, Mennonite and Gentile school children,[2] made the assumption that self-attitudes might be studied in a fairly direct manner by collecting statements of role preference and role avoidance, role expectations, models for the self, and the like. While this investigation yielded results which corresponded to the cultural differences involved, it was clear that the self-statements which the children gave were specific to the role situations asked for and that therefore *general* self-attitudes still had to be (somewhat tenuously) inferred from them.

Subsequent pilot studies were made comparing the contents of extended autobiographies of university students with paragraphs written in answer to the question "Who are you?" These paragraphs contained virtually all the items which were yielded by rough content analyses of the self-attitudes in their corresponding autobiographies. This applied to painful and self-derogatory materials as well as to self-enhancing materials. Thus we concluded that it might be profitable to construct a test which was aimed directly at self-attitudes.[3]

[2] Manford H. Kuhn, "Family Impact upon Personality," Chapter Five of *Problems in Social Psychology: An Interdisciplinary Inquiry,* edited by J. E. Hulett, Jr. and Ross Stagner, Urbana: University of Illinois Press, 1953, esp. pp. 50-52. A more comprehensive report of this study is to be included in a symposium on culture and personality, edited by Francis L. K. Hsu, to be published in the spring of 1954.

[3] The social scientist, unlike the Freudian, assumes that most human behavior is organized and directed by internalized but consciously held role recipes. See, for example, Theodore Newcomb, *Social Psychology,* New York: Dryden, 1950, for his excellent discussion of the relation of attitudes and symbols to the *direction* of behavior (pp. 77-78, 82), and his discussion of the *directive* (versus the expressive) organization of behavior (pp. 343-344). Those absorbed in the present fashion of projective testing would seem to have the cart before the horse, for relatively few of their subjects have been studied in terms of their directive and overt attitudes. It would seem much more reasonable to run out the implications of findings from tests of such attitudes before attempting to uncover deeplying, unconscious or guarded attitudes. We have concluded that much time is wasted debating *in advance* to what extent people will hide their "true attitudes,"

The device which we then used, and upon the use of which this research report is in major part based, consisted of a single sheet of paper headed by these instructions:

> "There are twenty numbered blanks on the page below. Please write twenty answers to the simple question 'Who am I?' in the blanks. Just give twenty different answers to this question. Answer as if you were giving the answers to yourself, not to somebody else. Write the answers in the order that they occur to you. Don't worry about logic or 'importance.' Go along fairly fast, for time is limited."

Application of the "Twenty-Statements" Test

This test was given to 288 undergraduate students at the State University of Iowa. It was administered during regular class meetings of introductory courses given in the Department of Sociology and Anthropology at various times during the spring of 1952. In a few classes the instructions were presented orally rather than in writing. In every instance students were given twelve minutes in which to complete the test. The students were naïve in the sense that they had not received instruction in the area to which this research was directed.

The number of responses per respondent evoked by these instructions varied from the twenty requested to one or two (with the median being seventeen responses). The responses took the general form "I am . . . ." Frequently "I am" was omitted, the responses consisting of phrases (*e.g.*, "a student," "an athlete," "a blonde") or of single words (*e.g.*, "girl," "married," "religious.").

The responses were dealt with by a form of content analysis. They were categorized dichotomously either as *consensual* references or as *subconsensual* references.[4] These content categories distinguish between statements which refer to groups and classes whose limits and conditions of membership are matters of common knowledge, *i.e.*, *consensual;* and those which refer to groups, classes, attributes, traits, or any other matters which would require interpretation by the respondent to be precise or to place him relative to other people, *i.e.*, *subconsensual.* Examples of the consensual variety are "student," "girl," "husband," "Baptist," "from Chicago," "pre-med," "daughter," "oldest child," "studying en-

---

whether they be self-attitudes or attitudes toward other objects or states of affairs.

[4] The precise working definitions of the two categories are given in detail in Thomas S. McPartland, *The Self and Social Structure: An Empirical Approach,* Iowa City: State University of Iowa Library, 1953, p. 147, Ph.D. Dissertation, microfilm.

gineering"; that is, statements referring to consensually defined statuses and classes. Examples of the subconsensual category are "happy," "bored," "pretty good student," "too heavy," "good wife," "interesting"; that is, statements without positional reference, or with references to consensual classes obscured by ambiguous modifiers.

The assignment of responses to these dichotomous content categories was highly reliable between different analysts, differences in categorization between two judges occurring less than three times in one hundred responses.

When the content was dichotomized in this way several interesting and useful features emerged:

First, from the ordering of responses on the page it was evident that *respondents tended to exhaust all of the consensual references they would make before they made (if at all) any subconsensual ones;* that is, having once begun to make subconsensual references they tended to make no more consensual references (if indeed they had made any at all). This ordering of responses held whether a respondent made as many as nineteen consensual references or as few as one.

Second, the number of consensual references made by respondents varied from twenty to none. Similarly the number of subconsensual references made by respondents varied from twenty to none. However, the number of consensual and subconsensual references made by any given respondent did not stand in a simple arithmetic relation (such as the number of consensual references plus the number of subconsensual references equals twenty). This resulted from the fact that many respondents made fewer than twenty statements. For example, a respondent might make ten consensual statements and then leave the remaining ten spaces blank, while another might make two consensual references, twelve subconsensual references, and then leave the last six spaces blank.[5] In the analysis on which this report is based, all consensual references are on one side of the dichotomy, while "no-responses" are combined with subconsensual references on the other. An individual's "locus score" is simply the number of consensual references he makes on the 'Twenty-Statements" Test.

These characteristics of the responses to the 'Twenty-Statements" Test satisfy the definition of a Guttman scale. "The scalogram hypothesis is that the items have an order such that, ideally, *persons who answer a*

[5] The variables which result from these characteristics of responses to the "Twenty-Statements" Test are presently being utilized in further research with special reference to clinical use. There are some interesting indications that those with few if any *consensual* statements to make have symptoms of emotional disturbance, while those having few statements *of any kind* to make are of Riesman's "radar" type, taking their cues from each specific situation, and (in the phrase of John Gould) "taking their 'immediate others' to be their 'significant others.'"

given question favorably all have higher ranks on the scale than persons who answer the same question unfavorably."[6] In applying this criterion it is necessary to keep in mind that " a given question" refers in this case to a specified one (by order) of the twenty statements, and that a "favorable response" would refer to a statement with a consensual reference — one that places the individual in a social system.

"The items used in a scalogram analysis must have a special *cumulative property.*"[7] Again it must be kept in mind that "the items" must in this case be interpreted in terms of the content analysis and not in terms of the raw responses to the open-ended question. Since a person who, let us say, makes a consensual statement as his seventh has also (in more than ninety per cent of the instances) made consensual statements in his first six, and since "consensuality" or "locus" refers to anchorage or self-identification in a social system, a variable which is numerically cumulative, we may regard the criterion of cumulativeness as being satisfied in this test. Guttman states, "A third equivalent definition of a scale is the one upon which our practical scalogram analysis procedures are directly based. It requires that each person's responses should be reproducible from the rank alone. A more technical statement of the condition is that each item shall be a simple function of the persons' ranks."[8] This is true for the test under consideration.

Scores can therefore be assigned which indicate not only *how many* consensual references were made by each respondent, but *which* of his responses fell into the consensual category. The coefficient of reproducibility for this scale, based on 151 respondents, is .903. The test-retest reliability of the scale scores is approximately +.85.

Both for convenience and because consensual references are references to subjective identification by social position we have called the consensual-subconsensual variable the *locus* variable. Table I is a summary of the "scale of locus," and shows among other things the number of respondents approximating each scale type. For example, the first row in Table 1 indicates that 19 respondents most closely approximated Scale Type 20, *i. e.*, making twenty statements of the consensual reference variety. Of their 380 responses there were 41 errors (that is, randomly distributed nonconsensual statements), giving a coefficient of reproducibility of .892 for this scale type. At the other end of the scale there were three respondents who belonged in Scale Type O, which is that of making no consensual statements, thus giving a perfect coefficient of reproducibility, 1.00.

[6] S. A. Stouffer, L. Guttman, E. A. Suchman, P. F. Lazarsfeld, S. A. Star, and J. A. Clausen, *Studies in Social Psychology in World War II, Volume IV: Measurement and Prediction,* Princeton: Princeton University Press, 1950, p. 9.

[7] *Ibid.*, p. 10.

[8] *Ibid.*, p. 62.

Table 1. The Scale of Locus, Showing Scale-Types, Frequency, Total Responses[1] in Each Scale Type and the Coeficient of Reproducibility for Each Scale Type

Scale Type	Frequency	Total Response	Errors	C.R.
20	19	380	41	.892
19	5	100	13	.870
18	1	20	1	.950
17	4	80	7	.913
16	1	20	3	.850
15	6	120	24	.800
14	8	160	9	.937
13	8	160	19	.875
12	4	80	10	.875
11	13	260	21	.915
10	7	140	15	.893
9	9	180	19	.895
8	9	180	15	.912
7	7	140	9	.936
6	10	200	15	.925
5	11	220	24	.891
4	8	160	11	.932
3	12	240	24	.900
2	2	40	5	.875
1	4	80	8	.900
0	3	60	0	1.000
	151	3020	293	.903

[1]Includes failure to respond to a blank as a response.

Validity of the Test

The problem of validity of a test in a hitherto uninvestigated area is a difficult one. There are generally recognized to be two related but distinct methods of assessing validity. One is by examining the logical relatedness of the test with the body of theory on which it rests. This subsumes the test of validity by correlating test results with the criterion behavior indicated by the theory. The other method is through correlation of the results of the test with other (already standardized) tests of the problem under investigation. When — as in this case — an area has not been previously investigated by inductive research there are no other tests to use as correlational checks. We need not be held up unduly by this consideration, however, for this is apparently a very much misused method of assessing validity in the field of personality research.[9]

There are two kinds of demonstration required to deal properly with the problem of the consistency of the test with its antecedent body of orientational theory. One is that of making explicit the chains of logic which went into the designing of the test, the test operations and the manipulations of the data obtained through its application. The other is that of showing that the test results correlate in some consistent patterns with the kinds of behavior which the orientation asserts are related.

With respect to the first kind of demonstration we need indicate only that the question "Who am I?" is one which might logically be expected to elicit statements about *one's identity;* that is, his social statuses, and the attributes which are in his view relevant to these. To ask him to give these statements "as if to himself" is an endeavor to obtain from him *general* self-attitudes rather than simply ones which might be idiosyncratic to the test situation or those which might be uniquely held toward himself in his relation to the test administrator. The request in the test for as many as twenty statements of self-identity stems from a recognition by the investigators of the *complex* and *multifarious* nature of an individual's statuses, their curiosity regarding the question of whether the *ordering of responses* correlates with the individual's particular anchoring in society, and their interest in exploring the *range* of self-attitudes.

[9] There has been a considerable tendency to validate each new personality test by correlating its results with those obtained by the already existent ones, without inquiring into *their* validity. See Leonard W. Ferguson, *Personality Measurement,* New York: McGraw-Hill, 1952. Ferguson points out (p. 178) that the Bernreuter Personality Inventory was validated by correlating its scales with scores on the Allport Ascendance-Submission scale, the Bernreuter Self-Sufficiency Scale, the Laird Introversion-Extroversion Schedule and the Thurstone Personality Inventory. The correlations were high. But the Laird and Thurstone tests had been through *no validation process whatsoever,* and the other two were unsatisfactorily validated! He points out, later, that the Bell Adjustment Inventory was validated against the Allport, Thurstone and Bernreuter tests (p. 232), thus pyramiding still another validation on the original shaky base. And so it goes until people have completely forgotten all details of the construction of the earliest tests on whose validity the whole series rests as far as this variety of validation is concerned.

We should note parenthetically that we were not interested in validating this test operation of ours against any of the existent personality tests not alone for the reasons involved in the argument above, but more basically because these other tests were designed from orientations quite foreign to ours. One has only to check the items on any current personality test to see how seldom is there any logical relation to self-theory.

The manipulation of the responses by assigning them to dichotomous categories, that of consensual reference and that of subconsensual reference, rests on the self-theory view that the self is an interiorization of one's positions in social systems. One may assume from this orientation that variations in such self-identifications are equivalents of variations in the ways in which the individuals in a society such as ours have cast their lot within the range of possible reference groups.

There is an alternative hypothetical mechanism which might be advanced to explain the salience of the consensual reference statement. It is this: Our society requires such a volume of census information from its citizens that the salience of consensual references in the replies to the "Twenty-Statements" Test is according to this hypothesis, simply a superficial carry-over from other questionnaires and forms. On this view those responses which are treated in our investigation as subconsensual are "deeper" self-attitudes, and hence those which lie closer to the "authentic individual."

We do not agree with this view. It is our belief that the ordering of responses is a reflection of the make-up of the self-conception.[10] The fact that the volume of consensual responses (corresponding to social anchorings) varies greatly from respondent to respondent is taken to give indirect confirmation of our position. Another and more direct empirical confirmation is to be found in the fact that three- and four-year-old children when asked "Who are you?" give, in addition to their names, their sex and occasionally their ages; in their instances one cannot allege a carry-over from the giving of census data. Of course only the pragmatic success or failure of the technique here under consideration will give a dependable answer, and the latter part of this report is devoted to an

[10] In the ordering of responses we are dealing essentially with the dimension of *salience* of self-attitudes. Theodore Newcomb (in his *Social Psychology,* New York: Dryden, 1950, p. 151) says of salience that it "refers to a person's readiness to respond in a certain way. The more salient a person's attitude the more readily will it be expressed with a minimum of outer stimulation. It seems reasonable to assume that a very salient attitude — one expressed with great spontaneity — has more importance for the person expressing it than does an attitude which he expresses only after a good deal of prodding or questioning. The weakness of direct questions is that they provide no way of measuring the salience of an attitude; we never know whether the attitude would have been expressed at all, or in the same way, apart from the direct question." Thus when a respondent, in reply to the "Who am I?" question on the "Twenty-Statements" Test, writes "I am a man," "I am a student," "I am a football player," it is reasonable to believe that we have far more solid knowledge of the attitudes which organize and direct his behavior than if, on a checklist and among other questions, we had asked "Do you think of yourself as a man?" "Do you think of yourself as a student?" and "Do you think of yourself as an athlete?"

account of one such pragmatic test. This pragmatic test of the usefulness of the scale scores of the "locus" component of self-attitudes may serve also as the second kind of demonstration of the validity of the instrument.

Variations in Self-Attitudes by "Known Groups"

The behavior which we tested for correlation with locus scores derived from our self-attitudes test is that of differential religious affiliation. It is simply one of a multitude of possible investigations which now need to be undertaken to answer the larger question "What values of this variable (locus) are related to what kinds of behavior and to what trains of social experience?"

Our orientation indicates that the self-conception should vary with differential social anchorage in (a) large, conventional, "respectable," accepted and influential groups; (b) small, weak or different, ambivalently viewed, marginal or dissident groups; or (c) no groups at all (in institutional areas in which a large fraction of the society's membership belongs and is identified by status in one or another of the existent groups). Religious groups and corresponding affiliation by our respondents fitted this model admirably so that we might check differentials in their self-attitudes against differentials in their religious group affiliations. Some religious groups in our society are "majority groups," while others are groups whose subcultures contain norms which set their members at odds with the norms of the larger society. Then, too, a large fraction of the population either has no religious reference group or no religious group membership.

Reports of membership in religious groups in our sample were collected by means of the direct question: "What is your religious affiliation or preference?" The numbers of each variety of affiliation are given in the column under the heading "N" in Table 2. The mean locus scale scores were computed for each of these religious groups and are given in the next column. The mean scale scores ranged from 11.89 (for Catholics) to 5.75 (for "nones"). These scale scores are simply the mean number of consensual reference statements made by respondents in each of the religious groups.

Analysis of variance revealed a relation between religious affiliation and scale scores significant beyond the one per cent level. The differences between group means of Roman Catholics on the one hand and Methodists, Presbyterians, and persons reporting no affiliation on the other, were significant beyond the two per cent level. Taking the group reporting no affiliation as the base, we found significant differences between this group-mean and the group-means of Roman Catholics, "small sects," "Protestants," Congregationalists, Lutherans, Christians and Jews. Although the N's were relatively large, Methodists and Presbyterians did not differ

Table 2. Variations in Self-Attitudes by Religious Affiliation: the Significance of Observed Differences between Locus Scores of Affiliates of Various Religious Denominations

Denomination	N[1]	Denominational Mean	Significance of Difference[2]	Significance of Difference[3]
Roman Catholic	38	11.89	. .	P < .001
"Small Sects"[4]	20	11.00	not sig.	P < .01
"Protestant"	21	10.47	not sig.	P < .01
Congregationalist	13	10.30	not sig.	P < .01
Lutheran	33	10.09	not sig.	P < .01
"Christian"	11	9.81	not sig.	P < .02
Jewish	19	9.57	not sig.	P < .05
Methodist	73	8.94	P < .02	not sig.
Presbyterian	32	8.18	P < .01	not sig.
"None"	28	5.75	P < .001*	. .

[1]The total N is 288. These 288 include the 151 on whom the locus scale, reported in Table I, was established, plus 137 cases obtained subsequently.

[2]Computed from the Roman Catholic group mean as the base.

[3]Computed from the group mean of "Nones" as the base.

[4]Includes Baptists, Episcopalians, Evangelicals, Mennonites, Nazarenes, Reorganized Latter Day Saints, Unitarians.

*While this and the other measures of statistical significance of difference are such as to give great confidence that the differences are not due to chance, it will only be through repeated correlations of locus scores with other behavior with respect to representative samples that we will be able to discover the theoretical import of the *magnitude* of the difference.

significantly from "nones" at any usually accepted level of statistical significance. The results of this analysis appear in the last two columns in Table 2.

These results indicate clear differences in the relative strength of the more directly socially anchored component of the self-conception among affiliates of certain religious subcultures, but leave open the question of the antecedent correlates of these differences. If one postulates that Roman Catholics have in common with members of small Protestant denominations, Lutherans and Jews the characteristic that religious affiliation is picked out as "important" and differentiating; and that Methodists, Presbyterians, and "indifferentists" have in common the characteristic that religious affiliation is not "important" or that it is taken for granted, then the two clusters of denominations by scale scores make sense.

Table 3. Differential Self-Anchorage in Religious Groups: the Significance of Observed Differences between Mean Salience Scores of Religious References Among Affiliates of Various Religious Denominations

Denomination	Denominational Mean	Significance of Difference[1]
Roman Catholic	7.39	. .
Lutheran	7.09	not significant
"Small Sects"	7.04	not significant
Jewish	6.68	not significant
Congregationalist	5.54	not significant
Presbyterian	4.47	$P < .01$
Methodist	3.22	$P < .01$
"Christian"	1.82	$P < .01$

[1] Computed from the Roman Catholic group mean as a base.

If this postulate is sound, then Roman Catholics, Jews and members of small sects should carry religious references more saliently in the self-conception. The "Twenty-Statements" Test provides data on this point.[11]

The salience of a self-reference may be understood as the relative spontaneity with which a particular reference will be used as an orientation in the organization of behavior.[12] In this research, salience of religious reference in the self-conception was measured by the rank of religious reference (if any was made) on the page of twenty statements, mention of religious affiliation in the first place being scored 20, mention in last place scoring 1, and omission of reference to religious affiliation arbitrarily scored zero.

The mean salience of religious references on the "Twenty-Statements" Test ranged from 7.4 for Roman Catholics to 1.82 for "Christians." Analysis of variance of religious references showed salience scores to be related to religious affiliation beyond the one per cent level. The analysis of the significance of the difference between group means appears in Table 3.

A completely independent operation was conducted to test this finding of the relation between the social "importance" of group affiliation and

[11] This, obviously, is a use of data from the "Twenty-Statements" Test in an altogether different way than through the use of them to obtain locus scores. There are, in fact, almost unlimited numbers of ways in which these self-statements may be treated, but each would constitute essentially a new test.

[12] The comments and quotation in footnote 10 above apply equally here.

Table 4. Reference Group Evidence: the Dichotomous Division of 116 Respondents on the Basis of Religious Affiliation and Identification with Religious Groups

	Religious Reference Present	Religious Reference Absent	
Catholics and Jews	13 (5.5)	7 (14.5)	20
All others	19 (26.5)	77 (69.5)	96
Total	32	84	116

Chi Square: 17.03
Q: .875
P less than .0001

"importance" in the self-conception; 116 undergraduates, whose religious affiliations were known, were asked to answer one of two alternative "reference-group" questions: "With what groups do you feel most closely identified?" or "I am proudest of my membership in ———." When respondents were cross-classified (a) by religious affiliation and (b) by their giving or not giving religious affiliation references in response to these direct questions, Table 4 resulted. Since we had obtained, from the self-attitudes research done previously, an empirically derived gradient of "differentism," we used this to make a finer subdivision of these responses, which yielded Table 5.

Table 5. Reference Group Evidence on the Gradient of Differentism: the Dichotomous Division of Respondents by Religious Identification Against a Trichotomous Division by Religious Affiliation

	Religious Reference Present	Religious Reference Absent	
Catholics and Jews	13 (6.2)	7 (13.8)	20
"Small Sects"	9 (6.2)	11 (13.8)	20
"Large Denominations"	10 (19.6)	53 (43.4)	63
Total	32	71	103

Chi Square: 19.45
T: .37
P less than .0001

These independently-derived data support the hypothesized relation between salience in the self-conception and socially defined importance of group membership at high levels of statistical significance.

Conclusions

The evidence provided by the "Twenty-Statements" Self-Attitudes Test and by its application to "known groups," in this case religious groups, gives support to the following empirically grounded inferences which have, in our view, rather large theoretical implications:

(1) The consensual (more directly socially anchored) component of the self-conception is the more salient component. Stated differently, consensually supported self-attitudes are at the top of the hierarchy of self-attitudes.

(2) Persons vary over a rather wide range in the relative volume of consensual and subconsensual components in their self-conceptions. It is in this finding that our empirical investigation has given the greatest advance over the purely deductive and more or less literary formulations of George Herbert Mead. Stated in terms of the language of this test, people have locus scores which range from 0 to 20. The variable involved here is one which we can correlate with a wide variety of other attitudes and behavior.

(3) The variation indicated in (1) and (2) can be established and measured by the empirical techniques of attitude research — specifically, the Guttman scaling technique. This gives a dual advantage in that it furthers the presumption that the locus variable is a unitary one and also in that it facilitates the further manipulation of values of the variable with respect to other quantitative problems.

(4) Locus scores vary with religious affiliation, as our initial validation test shows, members of the "differentistic" religious groups having significantly higher locus scores than do members of the "conventional" religious groups (using an independent source of information to establish the fact of membership in religious groups).

(5) Religious affiliation references are significantly more salient among the self-attitudes of members of "differentistic" religious groups than among members of "majority" or conventional religious groups.

(6) Corroboratively, the religious group as a reference group appears far more frequently as an answer to a direct, reference-group type of question among those made by members of "differentistic" religious groups.

This is a first (and only partially completed) effort to build a personality test consistent with the assumptions and findings of social science.

The social science view is that people organize and direct their behavior in terms of their subjectively defined identifications. These in turn are seen as internalizations of the objective social statuses they occupy, but for prediction we need to have the *subjective* definitions of identity, in view of the looseness between the social systems and the individual occupants of statuses in them in a society such as ours, characterized by alternatives, change, and collective behavior—in short, a society toward the secular end of the scale. Our test elicits these self-definitions.

To complete a comprehensive personality test on this basis we will need to know, in addition to the subjects' subjective identifications in terms of statuses, their roles, role preferences and avoidances and role expectations, their areas of self-threat and vulnerability, their self-enhancing evaluations, their patterns of reference-group election (their "negative others" as well as their "positive others"), and probably their self-dissociated attitudes. Questions such as "What do you do?" "Who do you wish you were?" "What do you intend to do?" "What do you take the most pride in?" "As a member of what groups or categories would you like to count yourself?" are a few of the indicated types in the directions suggested of building a soundly grounded approach to a science of personality and culture.

Selected Bibliography
Part I, Theory and Methods

Blumer, Herbert, "Social Psychology," in *Man and Society,* ed. by Emerson P. Schmidt (New York: Prentice-Hall, 1938), pp. 144-198.
An early, clear statement of the "Chicago School" of symbolic interactionism, contrasting it with various other perspectives in social psychology.

Blumer, Herbert, "Sociological Implications of the Thought of George Herbert Mead," *American Journal of Sociology,* 71 (March 1966), pp. 535-44.
A recent presentation of Mead's major ideas on the self, the act, social interaction, objects, and other central concepts.

Bolton, Charles D., "Behavior, Experience and Relationships," *American Journal of Sociology,* 64 (July 1958), pp. 45-58.
A criticism of symbolic interactionism, along with an attempt to indicate remedies for its deficiencies on the basis of concepts derived from George Herbert Mead, Emile Durkheim, and Kurt Riezler.

Hickman, C. Addison and Kuhn, Manford H., *Individuals, Groups, and Economic Behavior* (New York: Dryden Press, 1956), pp. 21-45.
A comprehensive statement of self-theory, the "Iowa School" of symbolic interaction. Contrasts this approach with Freudian, field, and learning theories.

Kuhn, Manford H., "Kinsey's View of Human Nature," *Social Problems,* 1 (April 1954), pp. 119-125.
A devastating critique of the neo-behavioristic, zoomorphic assumptions underlying Kinsey's approach to human sexual behavior.

Lindesmith, Alfred R. and Strauss, Anselm L., "A Critique of Culture-Personality Writings," *American Sociological Review,* 15 (October 1950), pp. 587-600.
By the authors of an outstanding symbolic-interactionist textbook in social psychology. Indicates some significant deficiencies of an approach favored by many psychoanalytically oriented anthropologists.

McKinney, John C., "Methodological Convergence of Mead, Lundberg and Parsons," *American Journal of Sociology,* 59 (May 1954), pp. 565-574.
Indicates several points of both explicit and implicit convergence in the

methodologies of three important sociologists who are rarely considered together.

Mead, George Herbert, *Mind, Self and Society* (Chicago, University of Chicago Press, 1934),
The single most influential book, to date, on symbolic interactionism.

Rose, Arnold M. (editor), *Human Behavior and Social Processes* (Boston: Houghton Mifflin Company, 1962).
A collection of 34 articles in the symbolic interactionist tradition, most of which were prepared specifically for the book. The editor's introductory essay presents an overview of that tradition.

Schwartz, Morris S. and Schwartz, Charlotte G., "Problems in Participant Observation," *American Journal of Sociology,* 60 (January 1955), pp. 343-353.
An evaluation of one of the favorite research techniques of symbolic interactionists.

Schwirian, Kent P., "Variations in Structure of the Kuhn-McPartland Twenty Statements Test and Related Response Differences," *Sociological Quarterly,* 5 (Winter 1964), pp. 47-59.
A study of the variations in response patterns elicited by variations in the format of the Twenty Statements (or "Who Am I") Test.

Strauss, Anselm, ed., *George Herbert Mead: On Social Psychology* (Chicago: The University of Chicago Press, 1964).
A collection of important selections from Mead's major writings.

Sullivan, Harry S., *Conceptions of Modern Psychiatry* (Washington: The William Alanson White Psychiatric Foundation, 1940 and 1945).
Sullivan, outstanding exponent of a theory of interpersonal relationships, presents a theory of the formation of personality which closely parallels Mead's at several points.

Part II. ❦ *Society*

Symbolic interactionists view society as a process of ongoing activity, of varied interactions, not as a relatively static "system," "structure," or "organization." This conception of society has tended to focus attention upon interpersonal relationships, rather than upon whole societies or groups. As a consequence, some critics have questioned the applicability of the "microsociological" approach of symbolic interactionism to "macrosociological" phenomena.

In presentday American sociology, the developing emphases upon structural-functional analysis and historical and comparative studies have brought a focus upon societal systems and subsystems. Such analyses have tended to stress the role of larger social units in shaping component, smaller units. For many exponents of symbolic interactionism, this stress has been accompanied by an unacceptable collective determinism of human conduct. That is, the individual presented in such schemes of analysis is often merely a passive, pliant, taken-for-granted recipient of relatively inflexible societal influences.

On two counts, this presentation is held to be inadequate. In the first place, it overlooks the mutual, bilateral relationship between society and the individual. Most symbolic interactionists reject collective determinism almost as strongly as they reject biological determinism. In the second place, the assumption of a fixed, or durable, societal structure contradicts the symbolic interactionist's conception of a fluid, dynamic society ever in process of "becoming."

In the essay "Society as Symbolic Interaction," Blumer presents the basic premises and the methodological implications of this position. His focus is upon the distinctive character of human relationships — the learned ability of human beings to construct and share their social worlds. He links this focus with an exposition of the case for a microsociological approach to the depiction of human society.

The importance of communication in social life is stressed in the selection by Dewey. Here Dewey suggests the conception of society as existing in the process of communication. Through communication, individuals are linked together in a dynamic social process.

The excerpts from two of Cooley's books are included to clarify this relationship between individual and society. In the first, he discusses the unity of the individual and the group. The second article is his classic statement of the centrality of the family and other intimate group relationships in forming what he calls "human nature." A fairly good synoptic view of Cooley's contribution to social psychology can be gained by reading these two selections along with the selections by Cooley in Parts I and III.

Reference group theory, first formulated by Herbert Hyman, has been congruent with the ideas of symbolic interactionism. Shibutani analyzes the ways in which the concept has been used and points out its specific relevance to communication and social relationships. Kuhn's article "reconsiders" the reference group in the light of recent theory and research. The distinction between "group" and "category" leads him to propose new ways of defining the idea of "others."

The selection by Gerth and Mills concerns the ways in which institutions and roles are treated by symbolic interactionists. These are considered in the contexts of self-conceptions and interpersonal relationships.

The article by Davis is somewhat more empirical in emphasis. The author's central concern is the way in which individuals with visible physical handicaps seek to "normalize" interaction with others.

Ceremony and ritual are frequently considered in conjunction with status elevation — confirmation, graduation, marriage. The selection by Garfinkel concerns the procedures by which moral indignation is used to reduce or degrade the position of individuals. While these concluding articles do not use large samples, standardized questionnaires, or statistical techniques, their observations provide increased understanding of complex and neglected aspects of social life.

9. Society as Symbolic Interaction

Herbert Blumer

A view of human society as symbolic interaction has been followed more than it has been formulated. Partial, usually fragmentary, statements of it are to be found in the writings of a number of eminent scholars, some inside the field of sociology and some outside. Among the former we may note such scholars as Charles Horton Cooley, W. I. Thomas, Robert E. Park, E.W. Burgess, Florian Znaniecki, Ellsworth Faris, and James Mickel Williams. Among those outside the discipline we may note William James, John Dewey, and George Herbert Mead. None of these scholars, in my judgment, has presented a systematic statement of the nature of human group life from the standpoint of symbolic interaction. Mead stands out among all of them in laying bare the fundamental premises of the approach, yet he did little to develop its methodological implications for sociological study. Students who seek to depict the position of symbolic interaction may easily give different pictures of it. What I have to present should be regarded as my personal version. My aim is to present the basic premises of the point of view and to develop their methodological consequences for the study of human group life.

The term "symbolic interaction" refers, of course, to the peculiar and distinctive character of interaction as it takes place between human beings. The peculiarity consists in the fact that human beings interpret or "define" each other's actions instead of merely reacting to each other's actions. Their "response" is not made directly to the actions of one another but instead is based on the meaning which they attach to such actions. Thus, human interaction is mediated by the use of symbols, by interpretation, or by ascertaining the meaning of one another's actions. This mediation is equivalent to inserting a process of interpretation between stimulus and response in the case of human behavior.

The simple recognition that human beings interpret each other's actions as the means of acting toward one another has permeated the thought and writings of many scholars of human conduct and of human group life. Yet few of them have endeavored to analyze what such interpre-

From "Society as Symbolic Interaction," by Herbert Blumer, pp. 179-192 in *Human Behavior and Social Processes*, edited by Arnold M. Rose, copyright 1962, reprinted by permission of Houghton Mifflin Company.

tation implies about the nature of the human being or about the nature of human association. They are usually content with a mere recognition that "interpretation" should be caught by the student, or with a simple realization that symbols, such as cultural norms or values, must be introduced into their analyses. Only G. H. Mead, in my judgment, has sought to think through what the act of interpretation implies for an understanding of the human being, human action, and human association. The essentials of his analysis are so penetrating and profound and so important for an understanding of human group life that I wish to spell them out, even though briefly.

The key feature in Mead's analysis is that the human being has a self. This idea should not be cast aside as esoteric or glossed over as something that is obvious and hence not worthy of attention. In declaring that the human being has a self, Mead had in mind chiefly that the human being can be the object of his own actions. He can act toward himself as he might act toward others. Each of us is familiar with actions of this sort in which the human being gets angry with himself, rebuffs himself, takes pride in himself, argues with himself, tries to bolster his own courage, tells himself that he should "do this" or not "do that," sets goals for himself, makes compromises with himself, and plans what he is going to do. That the human being acts toward himself in these and countless other ways is a matter of easy empirical observation. To recognize that the human being can act toward himself is no mystical conjuration.

Mead regards this ability of the human being to act toward himself as the central mechanism with which the human being faces and deals with his world. This mechanism enables the human being to make indication to himself of things in his surroundings and thus to guide his actions by what he notes. Anything of which a human being is conscious is something which he is indicating to himself — the ticking of a clock, a knock at the door, the appearance of a friend, the remark made by a companion, a recognition that he has a task to perform, or the realization that he has a cold. Conversely, anything of which he is not conscious is, *ipso facto,* something which he is not indicating to himself. The conscious life of the human being, from the time that he awakens until he falls asleep, is a continual flow of self-indications — notations of the things with which he deals and takes into account. We are given, then, a picture of the human being as an organism which confronts its world with a mechanism for making indications to itself. This is the mechanism that is involved in interpreting the actions of others. To interpret the actions of another is to point out to oneself that the action has this or that meaning or character.

Now, according to Mead, the significance of making indications to oneself is of paramount importance. The importance lies along two lines. First, to indicate something is to extricate it from its setting, to hold it apart, to give it a meaning or, in Mead's language, to make it into an object. An object — that is to say, anything that an individual indicates to himself — is different from a stimulus; instead of having an intrinsic character which acts on the individual and which can be identified apart from the individual, its character or meaning is conferred on it by the individual. The object is a product of the individual's disposition to act instead of being an antecedent stimulus which evokes the act. Instead of the individual being surrounded by an environment of pre-existing objects which play upon him and call forth his behavior, the proper picture is that he constructs his objects on the basis of his on-going activity. In any of his countless acts — whether minor, like dressing himself, or major, like organizing himself for a professional career — the individual is designating different objects to himself, giving them meaning, judging their suitability to his action, and making decisions on the basis of the judgment. This is what is meant by interpretation or acting on the basis of symbols.

The second important implication of the fact that the human being makes indications to himself is that his action is constructed or built up instead of being a mere release. Whatever the action in which he is engaged, the human individual proceeds by pointing out to himself the divergent things which have to be taken into account in the course of his action. He has to note what he wants to do and how he is to do it; he has to point out to himself the various conditions which may be instrumental to his action and those which may obstruct his action; he has to take account of the demands, the expectations, the prohibitions, and the threats as they may arise in the situation in which he is acting. His action is built up step by step through a process of such self-indication. The human individual pieces together and guides his action by taking account of different things and interpreting their significance for his prospective action. There is no instance of conscious action of which this is not true.

The process of constructing action through making indications to oneself cannot be swallowed up in any of the conventional psychological categories. This process is distinct from and different from what is spoken of as the "ego" — just as it is different from any other conception which conceives of the self in terms of composition or organization. Self-indication is a moving communicative process in which the individual notes things, assesses them, gives them a meaning, and decides to act on the basis of the meaning. The human being stands over against the world, or against "alters," with such a process and not with a mere ego. Further, the process of self-indication cannot be subsumed under the forces, whether from the outside or inside, which are presumed to play upon the individual to produce his behavior. Environmental pressures, external stimuli, organic drives, wishes, attitudes, feelings, ideas, and their like do not cover or explain the process of self-indication. The process of self-indication stands over against them in that the individual points out to himself and interprets the appearance or expression of such things, noting a given social demand that is made on him, recognizing a command, observing that he is hungry, realizing that he wishes to buy something, aware that he has a given feeling, conscious that he dislikes eating with someone he despises, or aware that he is thinking of doing some given thing. By virtue of indicating such things to himself, he places himself over against them and is able to act back against them, accepting them, rejecting them, or transforming them in accordance with how he defines or interprets them. His behavior, accordingly, is not a result of such things as environmental pressures, stimuli, motives, attitudes, and ideas but arises instead from how he interprets and handles these things in the action which he is constructing. The process of self-indication by means of which human action is formed cannot be accounted for by factors which precede the act. The process of self-indication exists in its own right and must be accepted and studied as such. It is through this process that the human being constructs his conscious action.

Now Mead recognizes that the formation of action by the individual through a process of self-indication always takes place in a social context. Since this matter is so vital to an understanding of symbolic interaction it needs to be explained carefully. Fundamentally, group action takes the form of a fitting together of individual lines of action. Each individual aligns his action to the action of others by ascertaining what they are doing or what they intend to do — that is, by getting the meaning of their acts. For Mead, this is done by the individual "taking the role" of others — either the role of a specific person or the role of a group (Mead's "generalized other"). In taking such roles the individual seeks to ascertain the intention or direction of the acts of others. He forms and aligns his own action on the basis of such interpretation of the acts of others. This is the fundamental way in which group action takes place in human society.

The foregoing are the essential features, as I see them, in Mead's analysis of the bases of symbolic interaction. They presuppose the following: that human society is made up of individuals who have selves (that is, make indications to themselves); that individual action is a construction and not a release, being built up by the individual through noting and interpreting features of the situations in which he acts; that group or collective action consists of the aligning of individual actions, brought about by the individuals' interpreting or taking into account each other's actions. Since my purpose is to present and not to defend the position of symbolic interaction I shall not endeavor in this essay to advance support for the three premises which I have just indicated. I wish merely to say that the three premises can be easily verified empirically. I know of no instance of human group action to which the three premises do not apply. The reader is challenged to find or think of a single instance which they do not fit.

I wish now to point out that sociological views of human society are, in general, markedly at variance with the premises which I have indicated as underlying symbolic interaction. Indeed, the predominant number of such views, especially those in vogue at the present time, do not see or treat human society as symbolic interaction. Wedded, as they tend to be, to some form of sociological determinism, they adopt images of human society, of individuals in it, and of group action which do not square with the premises of symbolic interaction. I wish to say a few words about the major lines of variance.

Sociological thought rarely recognizes or treats human societies as composed of individuals who have selves. Instead, they assume human beings to be merely organisms with some kind of organization, responding to forces which play upon them. Generally, although not exclusively, these forces are lodged in the make-up of the society, as in the case of "social system," "social structure," "culture," "status position," "social role," "custom," "institution," "collective representation," "social situation," "social norm," and "values." The assumption is that the behavior of people as members *of a society* is an expression of the play on them of these kinds of factors or forces. This, of course, is the logical position which is necessarily taken when the scholar explains their behavior or phases of their behavior in terms of one or other of such social factors. The individuals who compose a human society are treated as the media through which such factors operate, and the social action of such individuals is regarded as an expression of such factors. This approach or point of view denies, or at least ignores, that human beings have selves — that they act by making indications to themselves. Incidentally, the "self" is not brought into the picture by introducing such items as organic drives, motives, attitudes, feelings, internalized social factors, or psychological components. Such psychological factors have the same status as the social factors mentioned: they are regarded as factors which play on the individual to produce his action. They do not constitute the process of self-indication. The process of self-indication stands over against them, just as it stands over against the social factors which play on the human being. Practically all sociological conceptions of human society fail to recognize that the individuals who compose it have selves in the sense spoken of.

Correspondingly, such sociological conceptions do not regard the social actions of individuals in human society as being constructed by them through a process of interpretation. Instead, action is treated as a product of factors which play on and through individuals. The social behavior of people is not seen as built up by them through an interpretation of objects, situations, or the actions of others. If a place is given to "interpretation," the interpretation is regarded as merely an expression of other factors (such as motives) which precede the act, and accordingly disappears as a factor in its own right. Hence, the social action of people is treated as an outward flow or expression of forces playing on them rather than as acts which are built up by people through their interpretation of the situations in which they are placed.

These remarks suggest another significant line of difference between general sociological views and the position of symbolic interaction. These two sets of views differ in where they lodge social action. Under the perspective of symbolic interaction, social action is lodged in acting individuals who fit their respective lines of action to one another through a process of interpretation; group action is the collective action of such individuals. As opposed to this view, sociological conceptions generally lodge social action in the action of society or in some unit of society. Examples of this are legion. Let me cite a few. Some conceptions, in treating societies or human groups as "social systems," regard group action as an expression of a system, either in a state of balance or seeking to achieve balance. Or group action is conceived as an expression of the "functions" of a society or of a group. Or group action is regarded as the outward expression of elements lodged in society or the group. such as cultural demands, societal purposes, social values, or institutional stresses. These typical conceptions ignore or blot out a view of group life or of group action as consisting of the collective or concerted actions of individuals seeking to meet their life situations. If recognized at all, the efforts of people to develop collective acts to meet their situations are subsumed under the play of underlying or transcending forces which are lodged in society or its parts. The individuals composing the society or the group become "carriers," or media for the expression of such forces; and the interpretative behavior by means of which people form their actions is merely a coerced link in the play of such forces.

The indication of the foregoing lines of variance should help to put the position of symbolic interaction in better perspective. In the remaining discussion I wish to sketch somewhat more fully how human society appears in terms of symbolic interaction and to point out some methodological implications.

Human society is to be seen as consisting of acting people, and the life of the society is to be seen as consisting of their actions. The acting units may be separate individuals, collectivities whose members are acting together on a common quest, or organizations acting on behalf of a constituency. Respective examples are individual purchasers in a market, a play group or missionary band, and a business corporation or a national professional association. There is no empirically observable activity in a human society that does not spring from some acting unit. This banal statement needs to be stressed in light of the common practice of sociologists of reducing human society to social units that do not act — for example, social classes in modern society. Obviously, there are ways of viewing human society other than in terms of the acting units that compose it. I merely wish to point out that in respect to concrete or empirical activity human society must necessarily be seen in terms of the acting units that form it. I would add that any scheme of human society claiming to be a realistic analysis has to respect and be congruent with the empirical recognition that a human society consists of acting units.

Corresponding respect must be shown to the conditions under which such units act. One primary condition is that action takes place in and with regard to a situation. Whatever be the acting unit — an individual, a family, a school, a church, a business firm, a labor union, a legislature, and so on — any particular action is formed in the light of the situation in which it takes place. This leads to the recognition of a second major condition, namely, that the action is formed or constructed by interpreting the situation. The acting unit necessarily has to identify the things which it has to take into account — tasks, opportunities, obstacles, means, demands, discomforts, dangers, and the like; it has to assess them in some fashion and it has to make decisions on the basis of the assessment. Such interpretative behavior may take place in the individual guiding his own action, in a collectivity of individuals acting in concert, or in "agents" acting on behalf of a group or organization. Group life consists of acting units developing acts to meet the situations in which they are placed.

Usually, most of the situations encountered by people in a given society are defined or "structured" by them in the same way. Through previous interaction they develop and acquire common understandings or definitions of how to act in this or that situation. These common definitions enable people to act alike. The common repetitive behavior of people in such situations should not mislead the student into believing that no process of interpretation is in play; on the contrary, even though fixed, the actions of the participating people are constructed by them through a process of interpretation. Since ready-made and commonly accepted definitions are at hand, little strain is placed on people in guiding and organizing their acts. However, many other situations may not be defined in a single way by the participating people. In this event, their lines of action do not fit together readily and collective action is blocked. Interpretations have to be developed and effective accommodation of the participants to one another has to be worked out. In the case of such "undefined" situations, it is necessary to trace and study the emerging process of definition which is brought into play.

Insofar as sociologists or students of human society are concerned with the behavior of acting units, the position of symbolic interaction requires the student to catch the process of interpretation through which they construct their actions. This process is not to be caught merely by turning to conditions which are antecedent to the process. Such antecedent conditions are helpful in understanding the process insofar as they enter into it, but as mentioned previously they do not constitute the process. Nor can one catch the process merely by inferring its nature from the overt action which is its product. To catch the process, the student must take the role of the acting unit whose behavior he is studying. Since the interpretation is being made by the acting unit in terms of objects designated and appraised, meanings acquired, and decisions made, the process has to be seen from the standpoint of the acting unit. It is the recognition of this fact that makes the research work of such scholars as R. E. Park and W. I. Thomas so notable. To try to catch the interpretative process by remaining aloof as a so-called "objective" observer and refusing to take the role of the acting unit is to risk the worst kind of subjectivism — the objective observer is likely to fill in the process of interpretation with his own surmises in place of catching the process as it occurs in the experience of the acting unit which uses it.

By and large, of course, sociologists do not study human society in terms of its acting units. Instead, they are disposed to view human society in terms of structure or organization and to treat social action as an expression of such structure or organization. Thus, reliance is placed on such structural categories as social system, culture, norms, values, social stratification, status positions, social roles and institutional organization. These are used both to analyze human society and to account for social action within it. Other major interests of sociological scholars center around this focal theme of organization. One line of interest is to view organization in terms of the functions it is supposed to perform. Another line of interest is to study societal organization as a system seeking equilibrium; here the scholar endeavors to detect mechanisms which are indigenous to the system. Another line of interest is to identify forces which play upon organization to bring about changes in it; here the scholar endeavors, especially through comparative study, to isolate a relation between causative factors and structural results. These various lines of sociological perspective and interest, which are so strongly entrenched today, leap over the acting units of a society and bypass the interpretative process by which such acting units build up their actions.

These respective concerns with organization on one hand and with acting units on the other hand set the essential difference between conventional views of human society and the view of it implied in symbolic interaction. The latter view recognizes the presence of organization in human society and respects its importance. However, it sees and treats organization differently. The difference is along two major lines. First, from the standpoint of symbolic interaction the organization of a human society is the framework inside of which social action takes place and is not the determinant of that action. Second, such organization and changes in it are the product of the activity of acting units and not of "forces" which leave such acting units out of account. Each of these two major lines of difference should be explained briefly in order to obtain a better understanding of how human society appears in terms of symbolic interaction.

From the standpoint of symbolic interaction, social organization is a framework inside of which acting units develop their actions. Structural features, such as "culture," "social systems," "social stratification," or "social roles," set conditions for their action but do not determine their action. People — that is, acting units — do not act toward culture, social structure or the like; they act toward situations. Social organization enters into action only to the extent to which it shapes situations in which people act, and to the extent to which it supplies fixed sets of symbols which people use in interpreting their situations. These two forms of influence of social organization are important. In the case of settled and stabilized societies, such as isolated primitive tribes and peasant communities, the influence is certain to be profound. In the case of human societies, particularly modern societies, in which streams of new situations arise and old situations become unstable, the influence of organization decreases. One should bear in mind that the most important element confronting an acting unit in situations is the actions of other acting units. In modern society, with its increasing criss-crossing of lines of action, it is common for situations to arise in which the actions of participants are not previously regularized and standardized. To this extent, existing social organization does not shape the situations. Correspondingly, the symbols or tools of interpretation used by acting units in such situations may vary and shift considerably. For these reasons, social action may go beyond, or depart from, existing organization in any of its structural dimensions. The organization of a human society is not to be identified with the process of interpretation used by its acting units; even though it affects that process, it does not embrace or cover the process.

Perhaps the most outstanding consequence of viewing human society as organization is to overlook the part played by acting units in social change. The conventional procedure of sociologists is *(a)* to identify human society (or some part of it) in terms of an established or organized form, *(b)* to identify some factor or condition of change playing upon the human society or the given part of it, and *(c)* to identify the new form assumed by the society following upon the play of the factor of change. Such observations permit the student to couch propositions to the effect that a given factor of change playing upon a given organized form results in a given new organized form. Examples ranging from crude to refined statements are legion, such as that an economic depression increases solidarity in the families of workingmen or that industrialization replaces extended families by nuclear families. My concern here is not with the validity of such propositions but with the methodological position which they presuppose. Essentially, such propositions either ignore the role of the interpretative behavior of acting units in the given instance of change, or else regard the interpretative behavior as coerced by the factor of change. I wish to point out that any line of social change, since it involves change in human action, is necessarily mediated by interpretation on the part of the people caught up in the change — the change appears in the form of new situations in which people have to construct new forms of action. Also, in line with what has been said previously, interpretations of new situations are not predetermined by conditions antecedent to the situations but depend on what is taken into account and assessed in the actual situations in which behavior is formed. Variations in interpretation may readily occur as different acting units cut out different objects in the situation, or give different weight to the objects which they note, or piece objects together in different patterns. In formulating propositions of social change, it would be wise to recognize that any given line of such change is mediated by acting units interpreting the situations with which they are confronted.

Students of human society will have to face the question of whether their preoccupation with categories of structure and organization can be squared with the interpretative process by means of which human beings, individually and collectively, act in human society. It is the discrepancy between the two which plagues such students in their efforts to attain scientific propositions of the sort achieved in the physical and biological sciences. It is this discrepancy, further, which is chiefly responsible for their difficulty in fitting hypothetical propositions to new arrays of empirical data. Efforts are made, of course, to overcome these shortcomings by devising new structural categories, by formulating new structural hypotheses, by developing more refined techniques of research, and even by formulating new methodological schemes of a structural character. These efforts continue to ignore or to explain away the interpretative process by which people act, individually and collectively, in society. The question remains whether human society or social action can be successfully analyzed by schemes which refuse to recognize human beings as they are, namely, as persons constructing individual and collective action through an interpretation of the situations which confront them.

10. Communication, Individual and Society

John Dewey

We often fancy that institutions, social custom, collective habit, have been formed by the consolidation of individual habits. In the main this supposition is false to fact. To a considerable extent customs, or widespread uniformities of habit, exist because individuals face the same situation and react in like fashion. But to a larger extent customs persist because individuals form their personal habits under conditions set by prior customs. An individual usually acquires the morality as he inherits the speech of his social group. The activities of the group are already there, and some assimilation of his own acts to their pattern is a prerequisite of a share therein, and hence of having any part in what is going on. Each person is born an infant, and every infant is subject from the first breath he draws and the first cry he utters to the attentions and demands of others. These others are not just persons in general with minds in general. They are beings with habits, and beings who upon the whole esteem the habits they have, if for no other reason than that, having them, their imagination is thereby limited. The nature of habit is to be assertive, insistent, self-perpetuating. There is no miracle in the fact that if a child learns any language he learns the language that those about him speak and teach, especially since his ability to speak that language is a pre-condition of his entering into effective connection with them, making wants known and getting them satisfied. Fond parents and relatives frequently pick up a few of the child's spontaneous modes of speech and for a time at least they are portions of the speech of the group. But the ratio which such words bear to the total vocabulary in use gives a fair measure of the part played by purely individual habit in forming custom in comparison with the part played by custom in forming individual habits. Few persons have either the energy or the wealth to build private roads to travel upon. They find it convenient, "natural," to use the roads that are already there; while unless their private roads connect at some point with the highway they cannot build them even if they would.

These simple facts seem to me to give a simple explanation of matters that are often surrounded with mystery. To talk about the priority of "society" to *the* individual is to indulge in nonsensical metaphysics. But to say that some pre-existent association of human beings is prior to every particular human being who is born into the world is to mention a commonplace. These associations are definite modes of interaction of persons with one another; that is to say they form customs, institutions. There is no problem in all history so artificial as that of how "individuals" manage to form "society." The problem is due to the pleasure taken in manipulating concepts, and discussion goes on because concepts are kept from inconvenient contact with facts. The facts of infancy and sex have only to be called to mind to see how manufactured are the conceptions which enter into this particular problem.

The problem, however, of how those established and more or less deeply grooved systems of interaction which we call social groups, big and small, modify the activities of individuals who perforce are caught up within them, and how the activities of component individuals remake and redirect previously established customs is a deeply significant one. Viewed from the standpoint of custom and its priority to the formation of habits in human beings who are born babies and gradually grow to maturity, the facts which are now usually assembled under the conceptions of collective minds, group-minds, national-minds, crowd-minds, etc., etc., lose the mysterious air they exhale when mind is thought of (as orthodox psychology teaches us to think of it) as something which precedes action. It is difficult to see that collective mind means anything more than a custom brought at some point to explicit, emphatic consciousness, emotional or intellectual.[1]

[1] Mob psychology comes under the same principles, but in a negative aspect. The crowd and mob express a disintegration of habits which releases impulse and renders persons susceptible to immediate stimuli, rather than such a functioning of habits as is found in the mind of a club or school of thought or a political party. Leaders of an organization, that is of an interaction having settled habits, may, however, in order to put over some schemes, deliberately resort to stimuli which will break through the crust of ordinary custom and release impulses on such a scale as to create a mob psychology. Since fear is a normal reaction to the unfamiliar, dread and suspicion are the forces most played upon to accomplish this result, together with vast vague contrary hopes. This is an ordinary technique in excited political campaigns, in starting war, etc. But an assimilation like that of Le Bon of the psychology of democracy to the psychology of a crowd in overriding individual judgment shows lack of psychological insight. A political democracy exhibits an overriding of thought like that seen in any convention or institution. That is, thought is submerged in habit. In the crowd and mob, it is submerged in undefined emotion. China and Japan exhibit crowd psychology more frequently than do western democratic countries. Not in my judgment because of any essentially Oriental psychology but because of a nearer background of rigid and solid customs conjoined with the phenomena of a period of transition. The introduction of many novel stimuli creates

The family into which one is born is a family in a village or city which interacts with other more or less integrated systems of activity, and which includes a diversity of groupings within itself, say, churches, political parties, clubs, cliques, partnerships, trade-unions, corporations, etc. If we start with the traditional notion of mind as something complete in itself, then we may well be perplexed by the problem of how a common mind, common ways of feeling and believing and purposing, comes into existence and then forms these groups. The case is quite otherwise if we recognize that in any case we must start with grouped action, that is, with some fairly settled system of interaction among individuals. The problem of origin and development of the various groupings, or definite customs, in existence at any particular time in any particular place is not solved by reference to psychic causes, elements, forces. It is to be solved by reference to facts of action, demand for food, for houses, for a mate, for someone to talk to and to listen to one talk, for control of others, demands which are all intensified by the fact already mentioned that each person begins a helpless, dependent creature. I do not mean of course that hunger, fear, sexual love, gregariousness, sympathy, parental love, love of bossing and of being ordered about, imitation, etc., play no part. But I do mean that these words do not express elements or forces which are psychic or mental in their first intention. They denote *ways of behavior.* These ways of behaving involve interaction, that is to say, and prior groupings. And to understand the existence of organized ways or habits we surely need to go to physics, chemistry and physiology rather than to psychology.

There is doubtless a great mystery as to why any such thing as being conscious should exist at all. But *if* consciousness exists at all, there is no mystery in its being connected with what it is connected with. That is to say, if an activity which is an interaction of various factors, or a grouped activity, comes to consciousness it seems natural that it should take the form of an emotion, belief or purpose that reflects the interaction, that it should be an 'bur" consciousness or a "my" consciousness. And by this is meant both that it will be shared by those who are implicated in the associative custom, or more or less alike in them all, and that it will be felt or thought to concern others as well as one's self. A family-custom or organized habit of action comes into contact and conflict for example with that of some other family. The emotions of ruffled pride, the belief about superiority or being "as good as other people," the intention to hold one's own are naturally *our* feeling and idea of *our* treatment and position. Substitute the Republican party or the American nation for the family and the general situation remains the same. The conditions which determine

---

occasions where habits afford no ballast. Hence great waves of emotion easily sweep through masses. Sometimes they are waves of enthusiasm for the new; sometimes of violent reaction against it — both equally undiscriminating. The war has left behind it a somewhat similar situation in western countries.

the nature and extent of the particular grouping in question are matters of supreme import. But they are not, as such, subject-matter of psychology, but of the history of politics, law, religion, economics, invention, the technology of communication and intercourse. Psychology comes in as an indispensable tool. But it enters into the matter of understanding these various special topics, not into the question of what psychic forces form a collective mind and therefore a social group. That way of stating the case puts the cart a long way before the horse, and naturally gathers obscurities and mysteries to itself. In short, the primary facts of social psychology center about collective habit, custom. In addition to the general psychology of habit — which *is* general not individual in any intelligible sense of that word — we need to find out just how different customs shape the desires, beliefs, purposes of those who are affected by them. The problem of social psychology is not how either individual or collective mind forms social groups and customs, but how different customs, established interacting arrangements, form and nurture different minds.

11. False Separation of Individual and Society

Charles Horton Cooley

If we accept the evolutionary point of view we are led to see the relation between society and the individual as an organic relation. That is, we see that the individual is not separable from the human whole, but a living member of it, deriving his life from the whole through social and hereditary transmission as truly as if men were literally one body. He cannot cut himself off; the strands of heredity and education are woven into all his being. And, on the other hand, the social whole is in some degree dependent upon each individual, because each contributes something to the common life that no one else can contribute, Thus, we have, in a broad sense of the word, an "organism" or living whole made up of differentiated members, each of which has a special function.

This is true of society in that large sense which embraces all humanity, and also of any specific social group. A university, for example, is an organic whole, made up of students, teachers, officials, and others. Every member is more or less dependent upon every other, because all contribute to the common life. And note that it is precisely his individuality, his functional difference from the rest, that gives each member his peculiar importance. The professor of Paleontology has a part that no one else can play; and so, less obviously, perhaps, has every teacher and student. The organic view stresses both the unity of the whole and the peculiar value of the individual, explaining each by the other. What is a football team without a quarterback ? Almost as useless as a quarterback without a team. A well-developed individual can exist only in and through a well-developed whole, and *vice versa.*

This seems a simple idea, and so it is, but it is so opposed to some of our most cherished habits of thought that we may well take time to look at it from various points of view.

A separate individual is an abstraction unknown to experience, and so likewise is society when regarded as something apart from individuals. The real thing is Human Life, which may be considered either in an individual aspect or in a social, that is to say a general, aspect; but is always, as a matter of fact, both individual and general. In other words, "society" and "individuals" do not denote separable phenomena, but are simply collective and distributive aspects of the same thing, the relation between them being like that between other expressions one of which denotes a group as a whole and the other the members of the group, such as the army and the soldiers, the class and the students, and so on. This holds true of any social aggregate, great or small; of a family, a city, a nation, a race; of mankind as a whole: no matter how extensive, complex, or enduring a group may be no good reason can be given for regarding it as essentially different in this respect from the smallest, simplest, or most transient.

So far, then, as there is any difference between the two, it is rather in our point of view than in the object we are looking at: when we speak of society, or use any other collective term, we fix our minds upon some general view of the people concerned, while when we speak of individuals we disregard the general aspect and think of them as if they were separate. Thus "the Cabinet" may consist of President Lincoln, Secretary Stanton, Secretary Seward, and so on; but when I say "the Cabinet" I do not suggest the same idea as when I enumerate these gentlemen separately. Society, or any complex group, may, to ordinary observation, be a very different thing from all of its members viewed one by one — as a man who beheld General Grant's army from the Missionary Ridge would have seen something other than he would by approaching every soldier in it. In the same way a picture is made up of so many square inches of painted canvas; but if you should look at these one at a time, covering the others, until you had seen them all, you would still not have seen the picture. There may, in all such cases, be a system or organization in the whole that is not apparent in the parts. In this sense, and in no other, is there a difference between society and the individuals of which it is composed; a difference not residing in the facts themselves but existing to the observer on account of the limits of his perception. A *complete* view of society would also be a complete view of all the individuals, and *vice versa;* there would be no difference between them.

And just as there is no society or group that is not a collective view of persons, so there is no individual who may not be regarded as a particular view of social groups. He has no separate existence; through both the hereditary and the social factors in his life a man is bound into the whole of which he is a member, and to consider him apart from it is quite as artificial as to consider society apart from individuals.

* * *

1. Is not society, after all, made up of individuals, and of nothing else?

I should say, Yes. It is plain, every-day humanity, not a mysterious something else.

2. Is society anything more than the sum of the individuals?

In a sense, Yes. There is an organization, a life-process, in any social whole that you cannot see in the individuals separately. To study them one by one and attempt to understand society by putting them together will lead you astray. It is "individualism" in a bad sense of the word. Whole sciences, like political economy; great institutions, like the church, have gone wrong at this point. You must see your groups, your social processes, as the living wholes that they are.

3. Is the individual a product of society?

Yes, in the sense that everything human about him has a history in the social past. If we consider the two sources from which he draws his life, heredity and communication, we see that what he gets through the germ-plasm has a social history in that it has had to adapt itself to past society in order to survive: the traits we are born with are such as have undergone a social test in the lives of our ancestors. And what he gets from communication — language, education, and the like — comes directly from society. Even physical influences, like food and climate, rarely reach us except as modified and adapted by social conditions.

4. Can we separate the individual from society?

Only in an external sense. If you go off alone into the wilderness you take with you a mind formed in society, and you continue social intercourse in your memory and imagination, or by the aid of books. This, and this only, keeps humanity alive in you, and just in so far as you lose the power of intercourse your mind decays. Long solitude, as in the case of sheep-herders on the Western plains, or prisoners in solitary confinement, often produces imbecility. This is especially likely to happen with the uneducated, whose memories are not well stored with material for imaginative intercourse.

At times in the history of Christianity, and of other religions also, hermits have gone to dwell in desert places, but they have usually kept up some communication with one another and with the world outside, certain of them, like St. Jerome, having been famous letter-writers. Each of them, in fact, belonged to a social system from which he drew ideals and moral support. We may suspect that St. Simeon Stylites, who dwelt for years on top of a pillar, was not unaware that his austerity was visible to others.

A castaway who should be unable to retain his imaginative hold upon human society might conceivably live the life of an intelligent animal, exercising his mind upon the natural conditions about him, but his distinctively human faculties would certainly be lost, or in abeyance.

12. Primary Group and Human Nature

Charles Horton Cooley

Primary groups are primary in the sense that they give the individual his earliest and completest experience of social unity, and also in the sense that they do not change in the same degree as more elaborate relations, but form a comparatively permanent source out of which the latter are ever springing. Of course they are not independent of the larger society, but to some extent reflect its spirit; as the German family and the German school bear somewhat distinctly the print of German militarism. But this, after all, is like the tide setting back into creeks, and does not commonly go very far. Among the German, and still more among the Russian, peasantry are found habits of free cooperation and discussion almost uninfluenced by the character of the state; and it is a familiar and well-supported view that the village commune, self-governing as regards local affairs and habituated to discussion, is a very widespread institution in settled communities, and the continuator of a similar autonomy previously existing in the clan. "It is man who makes monarchies and establishes republics, but the commune seems to come directly from the hand of God."[1]

In our own cities the crowded tenements and the general economic and social confusion have sorely wounded the family and the neighborhood, but it is remarkable, in view of these conditions, what vitality they show; and there is nothing upon which the conscience of the time is more determined than upon restoring them to health.

These groups, then, are springs of life, not only for the individual but for social institutions. They are only in part molded by special traditions, and, in larger degree, express a universal nature. The religion or government of other civilizations may seem alien to us, but the children or the family group wear the common life, and with them we can always make ourselves at home.

By human nature, I suppose, we may understand those sentiments and impulses that are human in being superior to those of lower animals, and also in the sense that they belong to mankind at large, and not to any particular race or time. It means, particularly, sympathy and the innumerable

[1] De Tocqueville, *Democracy in America*, vol. i, chap. 5.

sentiments into which sympathy enters, such as love, resentment, ambition, vanity, hero-worship, and the feeling of social right and wrong.[2]

Human nature in this sense is justly regarded as a comparatively permanent element in society. Always and everywhere men seek honor and dread ridicule, defer to public opinion, cherish their goods and their children, and admire courage, generosity, and success. It is always safe to assume that people are and have been human.

It is true, no doubt, that there are differences of race capacity, so great that a large part of mankind are possibly incapable of any high kind of social organization. But these differences, like those among individuals of the same race, are subtle, depending upon some obscure intellectual deficiency, some want of vigor, or slackness of moral fibre, and do not involve unlikeness in the generic impulses of human nature. In these all races are very much alike. The more insight one gets into the life of savages, even those that are reckoned the lowest, the more human, the more like ourselves, they appear. Take for instance the natives of Central Australia, as described by Spencer and Gillen,[3] tribes having no definite government or worship and scarcely able to count to five. They are generous to one another, emulous of virtue as they understand it, kind to their children and to the aged, and by no means harsh to women. Their faces as shown in the photographs are wholly human and many of them attractive.

And when we come to a comparison between different stages in the development of the same race, between ourselves, for instance, and the Teutonic tribes of the time of Caesar, the difference is neither in human nature nor in capacity, but in organization, in the range and complexity of relations, in the diverse expression of powers and passions essentially much the same.

There is no better proof of this generic likeness of human nature than in the ease and joy with which the modern man makes himself at home in literature depicting the most remote and varied phases of life — in Homer, in the Nibelung tales, in the Hebrew Scriptures, in the legends of the American Indians, in stories of frontier life, of soldiers and sailors, of criminals and tramps, and so on. The more penetratingly any phase of human life is studied the more an essential likeness to ourselves is revealed.

To return to primary groups: the view here maintained is that human nature is not something existing separately in the individual, but a *group-nature or primary phase of society,* a relatively simple and general condition of the social mind. It is something more, on the one hand, than the mere instinct that is born in us — though that enters into it — and some-

[2] These matters are expounded at some length in the writer's *Human Nature and the Social Order.*

[3] *The Native Tribes of Central Australia.* Compare also Darwin's views and examples given in chap. 7 of his *Descent of Man.*

thing less, on the other, than the more elaborate development of ideas and sentiments that makes up institutions. It is the nature which is developed and expressed in those simple, face-to-face groups that are somewhat alike in all societies; groups of the family, the playground, and the neighborhood. In the essential similarity of these is to be found the basis, in experience, for similar ideas and sentiments in the human mind. In these, everywhere, human nature comes into existence. Man does not have it at birth; he cannot acquire it except through fellowship, and it decays in isolation.

If this view does not recommend itself to common sense I do not know that elaboration will be of much avail. It simply means the application at this point of the idea that society and individuals are inseparable phases of a common whole, so that wherever we find an individual fact we may look for a social fact to go with it. If there is a universal nature in persons there must be something universal in association to correspond to it.

What else can human nature be than a trait of primary groups? Surely not an attribute of the separate individual — supposing there were any such thing — since its typical characteristics, such as affection, ambition, vanity, and resentment, are inconceivable apart from society. If it belongs, then, to man in association, what kind or degree of association is required to develop it? Evidently nothing elaborate, because elaborate phases of society are transient and diverse, while human nature is comparatively stable and universal. In short the family and neighborhood life is essential to its genesis and nothing more is.

Here as everywhere in the study of society we must learn to see mankind in psychical wholes, rather than in artificial separation. We must see and feel the communal life of family and local groups as immediate facts, not as combinations of something else. And perhaps we shall do this best by recalling our own experience and extending it through sympathetic observation. What, in our life, is the family and the fellowship; what do we know of the we-feeling? Thought of this kind may help us to get a concrete perception of that primary group-nature of which everything social is the outgrowth.

13. Reference Groups as Perspectives

Tamotsu Shibutani

Although Hyman coined the term scarcely more than a decade ago, the concept of reference group has become one of the central analytic tools in social psychology, being used in the construction of hypotheses concerning a variety of social phenomena. The inconsistency in behavior as a person moves from one social context to another is accounted for in terms of a change in reference groups; the exploits of juvenile delinquents, especially in interstitial areas, are being explained by the expectations of peer-group gangs; modifications in social attitudes are found to be related to changes in associations. The concept has been particularly useful in accounting for the choices made among apparent alternatives, particularly where the selections seem to be contrary to the "best interests" of the actor. Status problems — aspirations of social climbers, conflicts in group loyalty, the dilemmas of marginal men — have also been analyzed in terms of reference groups, as have the differential sensitivity and reaction of various segments of an audience to mass communication. It is recognized that the same generic processes are involved in these phenomenally diverse events, and the increasing popularity of the concept attests to its utility in analysis.

As might be expected during the exploratory phases in any field of inquiry, however, there is some confusion involved in the use of this concept, arising largely from vagueness of signification. The available formal definitions are inconsistent, and sometimes formal definitions are contradicted in usage. The fact that social psychologists can understand one another in spite of these ambiguities, however, implies an intuitive recognition of some central meaning, and an explicit statement of this will enhance the utility of the concept as an analytic tool. The literature reveals that all discussions of reference groups involve some identifiable grouping to which an actor is related in some manner and the norms and values shared in that group. However, the relationship between these three terms is not always clear. Our initial task, then, is to examine the conceptions of reference group implicit in actual usage, irrespective of formal definitions.

One common usage of the concept is in the designation of that group which serves as the point of reference in making comparisons or contrasts,

From the *American Journal of Sociology,* LX (May, 1955), pp. 562-569, by permission of the University of Chicago Press.

especially in forming judgments about one's self. In the original use of the concept Hyman spoke of reference groups as points of comparison in evaluating one's own status, and he found that the estimates varied according to the group with which the respondent compared himself. Merton and Kitt, in their reformulation of Stouffer's theory of relative deprivation, also use the concept in this manner; the judgments of rear-echelon soldiers overseas concerning their fate varied, depending upon whether they compared themselves to soldiers who were still at home or men in combat. They also propose concrete research operations in which respondents are to be asked to compare themselves with various groups. The study of aspiration levels by Chapman and Volkmann, frequently cited in discussions of reference-group theory, also involves variations in judgment arising from a comparison of one's own group with others.[1] In this mode of application, then, a reference group is a standard or check point which an actor uses in forming his estimate of the situation, particularly his own position within it. Logically, then, *any* group with which an actor is familiar may become a reference group.

A second referent of the concept is that group in which the actor aspires to gain or maintain acceptance: hence, a group whose claims are paramount in situations requiring choice. The reference group of the socially ambitious is said to consist of people of higher strata whose status symbols are imitated. Merton and Kitt interpret the expressions of willingness and felt readiness for combat on the part of inexperienced troops, as opposed to the humility of battle-hardened veterans, as the efforts of newcomers to identify themselves with veterans to whom they had mistakenly imputed certain values.[2] Thus, the concept is used to point to an association of human beings among whom one seeks to gain, maintain, or enhance his status; a reference group is that group in which one desires to participate.

In a third usage the concept signifies that group whose perspective constitutes the frame of reference of the actor. Thus, Sherif speaks of reference groups as groups whose norms are used as anchoring points in structuring the perceptual field,[3] and Merton and Kitt speak of a "social

[1] H. H. Hyman, "The Psychology of Status," *Archives of Psychology,* XXXVIII (1942), 15; R. K. Merton and A. Kitt, "Contributions to the Theory of Reference Group Behavior," in R. K. Merton and P. F. Lazarsfeld (eds.), *Studies in the Scope and Method of "The American Soldier"* (Glencoe, Ill.: Free Press, 1950), pp. 42-53, 69; D. W. Chapman and J. Volkmann, "A Social Determinant of the Level of Aspiration," *Journal of Abnormal and Social Psychology,* XXXIV (1939), 225-38.

[2] *Op. cit.*, pp. 75-76.

[3] M. Sherif, "The Concept of Reference Groups in Human Relations," in M. Sherif and M. O. Wilson (eds.), *Group Relations at the Crossroads* (New York: Harper & Bros., 1953), pp. 203-31.

frame of reference" for interpretations.[4] Through direct or vicarious participation in a group one comes to perceive the world from its standpoint. Yet this group need not be one in which he aspires for acceptance; a member of some minority group may despise it but still see the world largely through its eyes. When used in this manner, the concept of reference group points more to a psychological phenomenon than to an objectively existing group of men; it refers to an organization of the actor's experience. That is to say, it is a structuring of his perceptual field. In this usage a reference group becomes any collectivity, real or imagined, envied or despised, whose perspective is assumed by the actor.

Thus, an examination of current usage discloses three distinct referents for a single concept: (1) groups which serve as comparison points; (2) groups to which men aspire; and (3) groups whose perspectives are assumed by the actor. Although these terms may be related, treating together what should be clearly delineated as generically different can lead only to further confusion. It is the contention of this paper that the restriction of the concept of reference group to the third alternative — that group whose perspective constitutes the frame of reference of the actor — will increase its usefulness in research. Any group or object may be used for comparisons, and one need not assume the role of those with whom he compares his fate; hence, the first usage serves a quite different purpose and may be eliminated from further consideration. Under some circumstances, however, group loyalties and aspirations are related to perspectives assumed, and the character of this relationship calls for further exploration. Such a discussion necessitates a restatement of the familiar, but, in view of the difficulties in some of the work on reference groups, repetition may not be entirely out of order. In spite of the enthusiasm of some proponents there is actually nothing new in reference-group theory.

Culture and Personal Controls

Thomas pointed out many years ago that what a man does depends largely upon his definition of the situation. One may add that the manner in which one consistently defines a succession of situations depends upon his organized perspective. A perspective is an ordered view of one's world — what is taken for granted about the attributes of various objects, events, and human nature. It is an order of things remembered and expected as well as things actually perceived, an organized conception of what is plausible and what is possible; it constitutes the matrix through which one perceives his environment. The fact that men have such ordered perspectives enables them to conceive of their ever changing world as relatively stable, orderly, and predictable. As Riezler puts it, one's perspective is an out-

[4] *Op. cit.*, pp. 49-50.

line scheme which, running ahead of experience, defines and guides it.

There is abundant experimental evidence to show that perception is selective; that the organization of perceptual experience depends in part upon what is anticipated and what is taken for granted. Judgments rest upon perspectives, and people with different outlooks define identical situations differently, responding selectively to the environment. Thus, a prostitute and a social worker walking through a slum area notice different things; a sociologist should perceive relationships that others fail to observe. Any change of perspectives — becoming a parent for the first time, learning that one will die in a few months, or suffering the failure of well-laid plans — leads one to notice things previously overlooked and to see the familiar world in a different light. As Goethe contended, history is continually rewritten, not so much because of the discovery of new documentary evidence, but because the changing perspectives of historians lead to new selections from the data.

Culture, as the concept is used by Redfield, refers to a perspective that is shared by those in a particular group; it consists of those "conventional understandings, manifest in act and artifact, that characterize societies."[5] Since these conventional understandings are the premises of action, those who share a common culture engage in common modes of action. Culture is not a static entity but a continuing process; norms are creatively reaffirmed from day to day in social interaction. Those taking part in collective transactions approach one another with set expectations, and the realization of what is anticipated successively confirms and reinforces their perspectives. In this way, people in each cultural group are continuously supporting one another's perspectives, each by responding to the others in expected ways. In this sense culture is a product of communication.

In his discussion of endopsychic social control Mead spoke of men "taking the role of the generalized other," meaning by that that each person approaches his world from the standpoint of the culture of his group. Each perceives, thinks, forms judgments, and controls himself according to the frame of reference of the group in which he is participating. Since he defines objects, other people, the world, and himself from the perspective that he shares with others, he can visualize his proposed line of action from this generalized standpoint, anticipate the reactions of others, inhibit undesirable impulses, and thus guide his conduct. The socialized person is a society in miniature; he sets the same standards of conduct for himself as he sets for others, and he judges himself in the same terms.

[5] R. Redfield, *The Folk Culture of Yucatan* (Chicago: University of Chicago Press, 1941), p. 132. For a more explicit presentation of a behavioristic theory of culture see *The Selected Writings of Edward Sapir in Language, Culture and Personality,* ed. D. G. Mandelbaum (Berkeley: University of California Press, 1949), pp. 104-9, 308-31, 544-59.

He can define situations properly and meet his obligations, even in the absence of other people, because, as already noted, his perspective always takes into account the expectations of others. Thus, it is the ability to define situations from the same standpoint as others that makes personal controls possible.[6] When Mead spoke of assuming the role of the generalized other, he was not referring to people but to perspectives shared with others in a transaction.

The consistency in the behavior of a man in a wide variety of social contexts is to be accounted for, then, in terms of his organized perspective. Once one has incorporated a particular outlook from his group, it becomes his orientation toward the world, and he brings this frame of reference to bear on all new situations. Thus, immigrants and tourists often misinterpret the strange things they see, and a disciplined Communist would define each situation differently from the non-Communist. Although reference-group behavior is generally studied in situations where choices seem possible, the actor himself is often unaware that there are alternatives.

The proposition that men think, feel, and see things from a standpoint peculiar to the group in which they participate is an old one, repeatedly emphasized by students of anthropology and of the sociology of knowledge. Why, then, the sudden concern with reference-group theory during the past decade? The concept of reference group actually introduces a minor refinement in the long familiar theory, made necessary by the special characteristics of modern mass societies. First of all, in modern societies special problems arise from the fact that men sometimes use the standards of groups in which they are *not* recognized members, sometimes of groups in which they have never participated directly, and sometimes of groups that do not exist at all. Second, in our mass society, characterized as it is by cultural pluralism, each person internalizes several perspectives, and this occasionally gives rise to embarassing dilemmas which call for systematic study. Finally, the development of reference-group theory has been facilitated by the increasing interest in social psychology and the subjective aspects of group life, a shift from a predominant concern with objective social structures to an interest in the experiences of the participants whose regularized activities make such structures discernible.

A reference group, then, is that group whose outlook is used by the actor as the frame of reference in the organization of his perceptual field. All kinds of groupings, with great variations in size, composition, and structure, may become reference groups. Of greatest importance for most

[6] G.H. Mead, "The Genesis of the Self and Social Control," *International Journal of Ethics,* XXXV (1925), 251-77, and *Mind, Self and Society* (Chicago: University of Chicago Press, 1934), pp. 152-64. Cf. T. Parsons, "The Superego and the Theory of Social Systems," *Psychiatry,* XV (1952), 15-25.

people are those groups in which they participate directly — what have been called membership groups — especially those containing a number of persons with whom one stands in a primary relationship. But in some transactions one may assume the perspective attributed to some social category — a social class, an ethnic group, those in a given community, or those concerned with some special interest. On the other hand, reference groups may be imaginary, as in the case of artists who are "born ahead of their times," scientists who work for "humanity," or philanthropists who give for "posterity." Such persons estimate their endeavors from a postulated perspective imputed to people who have not yet been born. There are others who live for a distant past, idealizing some period in history and longing for "the good old days," criticizing current events from a standpoint imputed to people long since dead. Reference groups, then, arise through the internalization of norms; they constitute the structure of expectations imputed to some audience for whom one organizes his conduct.

The Construction of Social Worlds

As Dewey emphasized, society exists in and through communication; common perspectives — common cultures — emerge through participation in common communication channels. It is through social participation that perspectives shared in a group are internalized. Despite the frequent recitation of this proposition, its full implications, especially for the analysis of mass societies, are not often appreciated. Variations in outlook arise through differential contact and association; the maintenance of social distance — through segregation, conflict, or simply the reading of different literature — leads to the formation of distinct cultures. Thus, people in different social classes develop different modes of life and outlook, not because of anything inherent in economic position, but because similarity of occupation and limitations set by income level dispose them to certain restricted communication channels. Those in different ethnic groups form their own distinctive cultures because their identifications incline them to interact intimately with each other and to maintain reserve before outsiders. Different intellectual traditions within social psychology — psychoanalysis, scale analysis, *Gestalt*, pragmatism — will remain separated as long as those in each tradition restrict their sympathetic attention to works of their own school and view others with contempt or hostility. Some social scientists are out of touch with the masses of the American people because they eschew the mass media, especially television, or expose themselves only condescendingly. Even the outlook that the *avant-garde* regards as "cosmopolitan" is culture-bound, for it also is a product of participation in restricted communication channels — books, magazines, meetings, exhibits, and taverns which are out of bounds for most people in the middle classes. Social participation may even be vicarious, as it is in the case of a medievalist who acquires his perspective solely through books.

Even casual observation reveals the amazing variety of standards by which Americans live. The inconsistencies and contradictions which characterize modern mass societies are products of the multitude of communication channels and the ease of participation in them. Studying relatively isolated societies, anthropologists can speak meaningfully of "culture areas" in geographical terms; in such societies common cultures have a territorial base, for only those who live together can interact. In modern industrial societies, however, because of the development of rapid transportation and the media of mass communication, people who are geographically dispersed can communicate effectively. Culture areas are coterminous with communication channels; since communication networks are no longer coterminous with territorial boundaries, culture areas overlap and have lost their territorial bases. Thus, next-door neighbors may be complete strangers; even in common parlance there is an intuitive recognition of the diversity of perspectives, and we speak meaningfully of people living in different social worlds — the academic world, the world of children, the world of fashion.

Modern mass societies, indeed, are made up of a bewildering variety of social worlds. Each is an organized outlook, built up by people in their interaction with one another; hence, each communication channel gives rise to a separate world. Probably the greatest sense of identification and solidarity is to be found in the various communal structures — the underworld, ethnic minorities, the social elite. Such communities are frequently spatially segregated, which isolates them further from the outer world, while the "grapevine" and foreign-language presses provide internal contacts. Another common type of social world consists of the associational structures — the world of medicine, of organized labor, of the theater, of café society. These are held together not only by various voluntary associations within each locality but also by periodicals like *Variety,* specialized journals, and feature sections in newspapers. Finally, there are the loosely connected universes of special interest — the world of sports, of the stamp collector, of the daytime serial — serviced by mass media programs and magazines like *Field and Stream.* Each of these worlds is a unity of order, a universe of regularized mutual response. Each is an area in which there is some structure which permits reasonable anticipation of the behavior of others, hence, an area in which one may act with a sense of security and confidence.[7] Each social world, then, is a culture area, the boundaries of which are set neither by territory nor by formal group membership but by the limits of effective communication.

Since there is a variety of communication channels, differing in sta-

[7] Cf. K. Riezler, *Man: Mutable and Immutable* (Chicago: Henry Regnery Co., 1950), pp. 62-72; L. Landgrebe, "The World as a Phenomenological Problem," *Philosophy and Phenomenological Research,* I (1940), 38-58; and A. Schuetz, "The Stranger: An Essay in Social Psychology," *American Journal of Sociology,* XLIX (1944), 499-507.

bility and extent, social worlds differ in composition, size, and the territorial distribution of the participants. Some, like local cults, are small and concentrated; others, like the intellectual world, are vast and the participants dispersed. Worlds differ in the extent and clarity of their boundaries; each is confined by some kind of horizon, but this may be wide or narrow, clear or vague. The fact that social worlds are not coterminous with the universe of men is recognized; those in the underworld are well aware of the fact that outsiders do not share their values. Worlds differ in exclusiveness and in the extent to which they demand the loyalty of their participants. Most important of all, social worlds are not static entities; shared perspectives are continually being reconstituted. Worlds come into existence with the establishment of communication channels; when life conditions change, social relationships may also change, and these worlds may disappear.

Every social world has some kind of communication system — often nothing more than differential association — in which there develops a special universe of discourse, sometimes an argot. Special meanings and symbols further accentuate differences and increase social distance from outsiders. In each world there are special norms of conduct, a set of values, a special prestige ladder, characteristic career lines, and a common outlook toward life — a Weltanschauung. In the case of elites there may even arise a code of honor which holds only for those who belong, while others are dismissed as beings somewhat less than human from whom bad manners may be expected. A social world, then, is an order conceived which serves as the stage on which each participant seeks to carve out his career and to maintain and enhance his status.

One of the characteristics of life in modern mass societies is simultaneous participation in a variety of social worlds. Because of the ease with which the individual may expose himself to a number of communication channels, he may lead a segmentalized life, participating successively in a number of unrelated activities. Furthermore, the particular combination of social worlds differs from person to person; this is what led Simmel to declare that each stands at the point at which a unique combination of social circles intersects. The geometric analogy is a happy one, for it enables us to conceive the numerous possibilities of combinations and the different degrees of participation in each circle. To understand what a man does, we must get at his unique perspective — what he takes for granted and how he defines the situation — but in mass societies we must learn in addition the social world in which he is participating in a given act.

Loyalty and Selective Responsiveness

In a mass society where each person internalizes numerous perspectives there are bound to be some incongruities and conflicts. The overlapping of group affiliation and participation, however, need not lead to difficulties and is usually unnoticed. The reference groups of most persons are mutually sustaining. Thus, the soldier who volunteers for hazardous duty on the battlefield may provoke anxiety in his family but is not acting contrary to their values; both his family and his comrades admire courage and disdain cowardice. Behavior may be inconsistent, as in the case of the proverbial office tyrant who is meek before his wife, but it is not noticed if the transactions occur in dissociated contexts. Most people live more or less compartmentalized lives, shifting from one social world to another as they participate in a succession of transactions. In each world their roles are different, their relations to other participants are different, and they reveal a different facet of their personalities. Men have become so accustomed to this mode of life that they manage to conceive of themselves as reasonably consistent human beings in spite of this segmentalization and are generally not aware of the fact that their acts do not fit into a coherent pattern.

People become acutely aware of the existence of different outlooks only when they are successively caught in situations in which conflicting demands are made upon them, all of which cannot possibly be satisfied. While men generally avoid making difficult decisions, these dilemmas and contradictions of status may force a choice between two social worlds. These conflicts are essentially alternative ways of defining the same situation, arising from several possible perspectives. In the words of William James, "As a man I pity you, but as an official I must show you no mercy; as a politician I regard him as an ally, but as a moralist I loathe him." In playing roles in different social worlds, one imputes different expectations to others whose differences cannot always be compromised. The problem is that of selecting the perspective for defining the situation. In Mead's terminology, which generalized other's role is to be taken? It is only in situations where alternative definitions are possible that problems of loyalty arise.

Generally such conflicts are ephemeral; in critical situations contradictions otherwise unnoticed are brought into the open, and painful choices are forced. In poorly integrated societies, however, some people find themselves continually beset with such conflicts. The Negro intellectual, children of mixed marriages or of immigrants, the foreman in a factory, the professional woman, the military chaplain — all live in the interstices of well-organized structures and are marginal men.[8] In most instances they manage to make their way through their compartmentalized lives, although personal maladjustments are apparently frequent. In extreme cases amnesia and dissociation of personality can occur.

[8]Cf. E.C. Hughes, "Dilemmas and Contradictions of Status," *American Journal of Sociology*, L (1945), 353-59, and E.V. Stonequist, *The Marginal Man* (New York: Charles Scribner's Sons, 1937).

Much of the interest in reference groups arises out of concern with situations in which a person is confronted with the necessity of choosing between two or more organized perspectives. The hypothesis has been advanced that the choice of reference groups — conformity to the norms of the group whose perspective is assumed — is a function of one's interpersonal relations; to what extent the culture of a group serves as the matrix for the organization of perceptual experience depends upon one's relationship and personal loyalty to others who share that outlook. Thus, when personal relations to others in the group deteriorate, as sometimes happens in a military unit after continued defeat, the norms become less binding, and the unit may disintegrate in panic. Similarly, with the transformation of personal relationships between parent and child in late adolescence, the desires and standards of the parents often become less obligatory.

It has been suggested further that choice of reference groups rests upon personal loyalty to significant others of that social world. "Significant others," for Sullivan, are those persons directly responsible for the internalization of norms. Socialization is a product of a gradual accumulation of experiences with certain people, particularly those with whom we stand in primary relations, and significant others are those who are actually involved in the cultivation of abilities, values, and outlook.[9] Crucial, apparently, is the character of one's emotional ties with them. Those who think the significant others have treated them with affection and consideration have a sense of personal obligation that is binding under all circumstances, and they will be loyal even at great personal sacrifice. Since primary relations are not necessarily satisfactory, however, the reactions may be negative. A person who is well aware of the expectations of significant others may go out of his way to reject them. This may account for the bifurcation of orientation in minority groups, where some remain loyal to the parental culture while others seek desperately to become assimilated in the larger world. Some who withdraw from the uncertainties of real life may establish loyalties to perspectives acquired through vicarious relationships with characters encountered in books.[10]

Perspectives are continually subjected to the test of reality. All perception is hypothetical. Because of what is taken for granted from each standpoint, each situation is approached with a set of expectations; if transactions actually take place as anticipated, the perspective itself is reinforced. It is thus the confirming responses of other people that provide

[9] H. S. Sullivan, *Conceptions of Modern Psychiatry* (Washington, D. C. : W. H. White Psychiatric Foundation, 1947), pp. 18-22.

[10] Cf. R. R. Grinker and J. P. Spiegel, *Men under Stress* (Philadelphia: Blakiston Co., 1945), pp. 122-26; and E. A. Shils and M. Janowitz, "Cohesion and Disintegration in the Wehrmacht in World War II," *Public Opinion Quarterly*, XII (1948), 280-315.

support for perspectives.[11] But in mass societies the responses of others vary, and in the study of reference groups the problem is that of ascertaining *whose* confirming responses will sustain a given point of view.

The Study of Mass Societies

Because of the differentiated character of modern mass societies, the concept of reference group, or some suitable substitute, will always have a central place in any realistic conceptual scheme for its analysis. As is pointed out above, it will be most useful if it is used to designate that group whose perspective is assumed by the actor as the frame of reference for the organization of his perceptual experience. Organized perspectives arise in and become shared through participation in common communication channels, and the diversity of mass societies arises from the multiplicity of channels and the ease with which one may participate in them.

Mass societies are not only diversified and pluralistic but also continually changing. The successive modification of life-conditions compels changes in social relationships, and any adequate analysis requires a study of these transformational processes themselves. Here the concept of reference group can be of crucial importance. For example, all forms of social mobility, from sudden conversions to gradual assimilation, may be regarded essentially as displacements of reference groups, for they involve a loss of responsiveness to the demands of one social world and the adoption of the perspective of another. It may be hypothesized that the disaffection occurs first on the level of personal relations, followed by a weakening sense of obligation, a rejection of old claims, and the establishment of new loyalties and incorporation of a new perspective. The conflicts that characterize all persons in marginal roles are of special interest in that they provide opportunities for cross-sectional analyses of the processes of social change.

In the analysis of the behavior of men in mass societies the crucial problem is that of ascertaining how a person defines the situation, which perspective he uses in arriving at such a definition, and who constitutes the audience whose responses provide the necessary confirmation and support for his position. This calls for focusing attention upon the expectations the actor imputes to others, the communication channels in which he participates, and his relations with those with whom he identifies himself. In the study of conflict, imagery provides a fertile source of data. At moments of indecision, when in doubt and confusion, who appears in

[11] Cf. G. H. Mead, *The Philosophy of the Act* (Chicago: University of Chicago Press, 1938), pp. 107-73; and L. Postman, "Toward a General Theory of Cognition," in J. H. Rohrer and M. Sherif (eds.), *Social Psychology at the Crossroads* (New York: Harper & Bros. 1951), pp. 242-72.

imagery? In this manner the significant other can be identified.

An adequate analysis of modern mass societies requires the development of concepts and operations for the description of the manner in which each actor's orientation toward his world is successively reconstituted. Since perception is selective and perspectives differ, different items are noticed and a progressively diverse set of images arises, even among those exposed to the same media of mass communication. The concept of reference group summarizes differential associations and loyalties and thus facilitates the study of selective perception. It becomes, therefore, an indispensable tool for comprehending the diversity and dynamic character of the kind of society in which we live.

14. The Reference Group Reconsidered

Manford H. Kuhn

The Other

What I really have in mind to do is to attempt an exploration of the whole *idea of the other* in the symbolic interaction orientation as a context for the consideration of the *idea of the reference group.*

I wish to observe at the outset that while *the other* plays an incontestably crucial role in the conceptions of Cooley, Dewey, Mead, Faris, and the other writers who developed the symbolic interaction orientation, nevertheless *the other* is never attended to with the discerning and analytic interest which they give to the actor. Cooley, Dewey, and Mead all thought of the individual and society as inseparable aspects of the same reality, to use Cooley's phrase. They all shared the idea that meaning, thought, and the self arise alike in the relationships between the actor and his alters.

We are all familiar, I am sure, with Mead's conception that meaning grows out of the gesture of an actor to another, the responding gesture of the other, and the uncompleted phases of the act to which the gestures refer. Thus the omission of the other from these "relata," as Mead calls them, leaves the activity without meaning. Cooley, as we are abundantly aware, saw the self as drawn from the common life — that is, the life of the actor as immersed in a context of others. "The social self," he wrote, "is simply any idea, or system of ideas, drawn from the communicative life, that the mind cherishes as its own."[1] And his ubiquitously quoted looking-glass — self statement, "A self-idea of this sort seems to have three principal elements: the imagination of our appearance to the other person, the imagination of his judgment of that appearance, and some sort of self-feeling, such as pride or mortification," quite apparently makes the others the looking glass in which one is able to be an object to himself, and without which he would lack even self-feelings.[2] The self is indeed only an eddy of the general communicative current.

From *The Sociological Quarterly,* V (Winter, 1964), pp. 6-21, by permission of the journal and the author.

[1]Charles Horton Cooley, *Human Nature and the Social Order,* New York: Scribner's 1902, p. 179.

[2]*Ibid.*, p. 184.

Thinking, for all the symbolic interactionists, is an internal conversation among the self and internalized others. And the meaning of internalization is simply the covert segment of the general communicative process. The figures of speech differ — an internal audience, an inner forum, a covert conversation of gestures — but the meanings coincide. They all make the other crucial to the self and to meaningful action.

Cooley insisted on the reality of the internalized other. Again universally quoted is his statement that "the imaginations which people have of one another are the solid facts of society," and he went on to say that "to observe and interpret these must be a chief aim of sociology."[3] He insisted on this idea, and extended it to say that the imaginative idea is logically prior — as far as the actor is concerned — in reality to the physical organism of the other. He wrote, for example, that "I do not see how any one can hold that we know persons directly except as imaginative ideas in the mind," and "a corporeally existent person is not socially real unless he is imagined."[4] In fact he says, after rhetorically raising the question about the reality of the dead and of fictional characters: "I should say that in so far as we imagine them they are [real]."[5]

The well-known notions of Mead regarding the process by which the self arises in taking the role of the other similarly stress this internally imagined other of Cooley's. For both, "the social person is primarily *a fact of the mind.*"[6]

The elder Faris, in his not-so-well-known critique of the concept of the primary group, expresses much the same set of ideas when he disparages the notion that the quality of face-to-face existence is a necessary attribute of the primary group relation. In fact he invokes Cooley's own ideas endemic to these several quotations I have given, in suggesting that Cooley himself must have had in mind the essential characteristic of identification with the others as the basic condition for the existence of the primary group. "If there is a group consciousness, esprit-de-corps — a feeling of 'we' — then we have a primary group that will manifest attitudes appropriate and recognizable."[7]

[3] *Ibid.*, p. 121.

[4] *Ibid.*, pp. 120, 123.

[5] *Ibid.*, p. 122. It should be noted that Cooley took pains to dissociate this stance from any overtones of naive solipsism, in the following disclaimer: "In saying this I hope I do not seem to question the independent reality of persons or to confuse it with personal ideas. The man is one thing and the various ideas entertained about him are another; but the latter, the personal idea, is the immediate social reality, the thing in which men exist for one another and work directly upon one another's lives." (*Ibid.*, pp. 123-124.)

[6] *Ibid*, p. 124.

[7] Ellsworth Faris, "The Primary Group: Essence and Accident," Chapter 4 in Faris, *The Nature of Human Nature,* New York: McGraw-Hill, 1937. Quotation from p. 40.

Subsequently, Harry Stack Sullivan made similarly crucial use of the other in his formulation. His "significant other" is not basically different in its reference from Mead's other. His self, resting on "reflected appraisals of others," is very much the same self as the self of Cooley or Dewey or Mead. His analysis of communications and interpersonal relations reflect his professional focus on misunderstandings, distortions and anxiety, but otherwise his notions are very similar to those of the earlier interactionists.[8]

We might go further to explore Mead's use of the other in the constituting of *social objects* – the "things" of experience – or in the formation of the generalized other, the abstract principles of conduct. But these really but extend his general notion that the other is crucial to the rise of all meaning, all reality.[9]

Kimball Young in one of several definitions of the *social act* defined it as any act which is qualified by the act of another.[10]

Such, in brief summary, is the role of the other in the symbolic interactionist orientation. The other turns out to be the other as the actor sees him. But the actor's own view of himself is gained only through the image he imagines the other to have of him. His objects, his reality in short, derive from the same source of shared perspectives with imagined others. Even his conscience and his purposes arise in the same process. But the imagination as a process has a solid basis in communication, being in effect the very process of communication by which meaning exists in his social group. "We are able to act together because we are able to take one another's point of view." There is a singularity, unity and consensus, in this point of view, because the symbols on which it rests are significant symbols: they call out in the actor the incipient anticipations of the responses they call out in the other. In short, they have common *universal referents,* with only moderate exception and qualification.

Now there is nothing much that is incorrect in this orientation as far as we know. But by very virtue of the fact that it is only an orientation, it suffers many shortcomings as a basis for a social psychology.

To be more specific: By what process do one's others get selected? Are any features of this process accessible to observation? Is this a process characterized by regularities, and if so of what kind? Or are we to take the mechanism of identification to be essentially whimsical and capricious?

Cooley wrote that we must imagine the imaginings of the members of the groups we wish to study. This is not a very complete recipe for re-

[8] Harry Stack Sullivan, *Conceptions of Modern Psychiatry,* Washington, D. C.: W. A. White Psychiatric Foundation, 1940. See especially pp. 18-22.

[9] George Herbert Mead, *Mind, Self and Society,* Chicago: University of Chicago Press, 1934. See especially pp. 117-125, 152-164, and 375-377.

[10] Kimball Young, *Personality and Problems of Adjustment* (2nd edition), New York: Appleton-Century-Crofts, 1952, p. 154.

search, nor does its flavor suggest much that is compatible with contemporary notions of social psychological investigation. Is all social investigation to be limited to the ambiguities and imprecisions of *Einfühlung* and *Verstehen?* To speak of the inseparability of self and other, as many of these early writers did, is not very helpful except in a broadly explanatory way. We would want to have some verifiable ways of discovering just who the others are from whom the self is inseparable.

Thus, while we are led through the cogent rhetoric of the early writers to accept the crucial importance of the subjective life and of the covert features of experience, we are given by them relatively few leads on how to make this subjective life accessible to observation or systematic inquiry. Mead rightly caricatured J. B. Watson for ordering "off with their heads" respecting all problems having to do with covert events such as thought, meaning, purpose, self and the like;[11] yet in retrospect one must credit Watson for insisting on the necessity for empirical demonstrability of generalizations, i. e., the "openness of evidence."

The Reference Group Concept

In 1942 Herbert Hyman proposed the reference group concept in his monograph "The Psychology of Status."[12] The concept is a simple one. It assumes that people make fundamental judgments and self-assessments based on psychological identifications rather than on formal memberships in groups. So stated there is nothing about the idea that in any way differentiates it from the general phenomenological position of symbolic interactionists. His research use of the idea, however, was in terms of the self-assignments to *social categories* of his subjects. There was thus in the operationalization of the term a rotation of the sociological conception of the *group.* This conception has it that a *group* involves reciprocal role-playing, a common vocabulary, and a common body of values and norms. In fact, it is the nearly ubiquitous assumption of sociologists in their use of the term *group* that group membership is predicated upon some degree of group *identification.*

The reference group concept did not come immediately to the attention of sociologists. It remained for Merton and Kitt, in their widely known chapter published in 1950 on the utilization of the reference group idea by Stouffer and associates in *The American Soldier,* to introduce sociologists to the term.[13] They took the concept of "relative deprivation," used in

[11] Mead, *op. cit.*, pp. 2-3.

[12] In *Archives of Psychology,* vol. 269.

[13] Robert K. Merton and Alice S. Kitt, "Contributions to the Theory of Reference Group Behavior," in Merton and Paul F. Lazarsfeld (eds.), *Continuities in Social Research: Studies in the Scope and Method of 'The American Soldier,"* Glencoe, Ill.: Free Press, 1950, pp. 40-105.

The American Soldier, as an example of a special and effective use of Hyman's reference group concept. The "Continuities in Research" volume, *Studies in the Scope and Method of "The American Soldier,"* was — and continues to be — widely distributed and widely read. The Merton-Kitt chapter is one of the most persuasive and influential chapters in the book. Since then the chapter, together with another attempting to revise and to take into account criticisms, has appeared in the revised and enlarged edition of *Social Theory and Social Structure,* a collection of Robert Merton's papers, another influential, widely distributed book.[14]

In the meantime the idea had been having its impact on the psychological social psychologists, many of whom have a considerable audience among sociologists — men such as Sherif, Newcomb and others.[15]

With such sponsors as Robert Merton, Theodore Newcomb, Muzafer Sherif, and, by implication, the late Sam Stouffer and his associates, it is little wonder the concept enjoyed — as one observer put it— a meteoric rise in popularity. This popularity has endured.

The persistence of the popularity of this concept does not owe entirely to the prestige of its initial users. First of all, it was proposed at the time when survey research was just coming into large-scale use by sociologists and social psychologists on the sociological side. The operationalizations by Hyman and by Stouffer and associates were peculiarly adapted to use in survey research. That is to say, the operationalizations were in the form of simple questions regarding self-assignment to social categories or regarding comparisons of self with members of such categories. They were questions that were neither particularly subtle nor likely to arouse sensitivities. The demonstrations of their validity could be made through the use of other, similar questions, obviating the need for indirect, open-ended, probing or depth forms of inquiry — kinds of inquiry not at all well adapted to large-scale survey research. And while the establishment of their validity by means of this tactic of "triangulation" left necessary a certain amount of inference, this inference could easily be of the open and direct form rather than the ambiguously varied and idiosyncratic or secretive or *ad hoc* Freudian form of logically unverifiable inference. But the very fact that the inference used in these operationalizations of the reference group concept was relatively open to verification has itself tended to obscure the correlative fact that it has not, to this day, yet been concretely verified.

A second reason for the persistence in popularity of the concept (as well as for its meteoric acceptance, for that matter) was the fact that the concept represents a vast simplification and fairly sharp specification of

[14] Robert K. Merton, *Social Theory and Social Structure* (revised edition), Glencoe, Ill.: Free Press, 1957, Chapters 8 and 9.

[15] Muzafer Sherif and Carolyn W. Sherif, *An Outline of Social Psychology* (revised edition), New York: Harper and Brothers, 1956; Theodore M. Newcomb, *Social Psychology,* New York: Dryden Press, 1950.

the idea of the other. When we canvass the notion of the other as we did earlier, we can appreciate how many directions one might go with the translation of the perspective into concrete inquiry. There is always some mental relief associated with the implication in any operation that a broad and elliptical idea is "nothing but" these marks on these pieces of paper. Such relief tends to shut the mind to further logical examination of the idea involved.

This is especially true when the operation in question has even one or a few strong logical connections with the logical or orientational idea, which in this case is undeniable. It is not only undeniable, but it is called forcefully to the attention of all readers of the Merton-Kitt commentary in a section in which the reference group concept (and its use by Stouffer under the aegis of the notion of relative deprivation) is compared with the general *idea of the other* as formulated by Mead.[16] These authors suggest that the empirical use of the reference group concept and the auxiliary one of relative deprivation will enable conceptual clarification, reformulation, and useful elaboration of earlier ideas of the other. Their analysis, in their own view, yields several instances of such: e.g., (1) they find that under certain circumstances men "report . . . the objective situation rather than a socially reflected image";[17] (2) they find a sharp discrepancy between operations that inquire into "attitudes" and those which elicit "self-images";[18] and (3) they find that there are multiple reference groups which provide contexts for evaluation by individuals — some of which are conflicting and some of which are mutually sustaining.[19]

Now it may well be that sometimes a human being confronts reality directly while at other times he sees only a socially reflected image. But if this is so, there is no continuity here between the earlier formulations of Cooley, Dewey, Mead, Faris, Thomas, Blumer, *et al.*, for the whole epistemology of symbolic interaction, from Cooley to Cassirer, rests on the proposition that language is necessarily interposed between man and raw reality so that he can *never* confront it directly. If reference group theory rests on some new and different epistemology, that epistemology ought to be spelled out. It cannot rest purely on a pair of empirical findings without explanation.

But this gives one pause. The idea of the reference group is that it is a special kind of other, one with which a person feels psychologically iden-

[16]Merton, *op. cit.*, pp. 236-241. It is interesting to note that it is in this very passage that Merton and Kitt make a resounding pass at Mead and his followers by observing that Mead's theory "was not exposed to *systematic* empirical evidence" and that he, with "those of his followers who also eschew empirical research, had little occasion to move ahead to the question of conditions under which non-membership-groups may also constitute a significant frame of reference." *(Ibid.*, p. 239).

[17]*Ibid.*, p. 257. [18]*Ibid.*, p. 253. [19]*Ibid.*, pp. 241-250.

tified as opposed to one with which he is merely socially associated. Yet this was the idea central to the concept of the other (or of the group, for that matter) all along. Are we now to think in terms of two kinds of others — those whose behavior qualifies ours, and those who are merely physically real? Where does this *new* distinction differ from that in Cooley's corridor illustration?

Then, too, what shall we make of the difference between an attitude and a self-image? What is meant by the self as being an object to oneself if it is not that the self *is attitudes* — symbolic proposals for action toward or with respect to the self? And of what use is the self in any theoretical formulation unless it is the anchoring object in one's system of objects? The crucial object with respect to which the other objects have meaning? The victorious manner in which Merton and Kitt "discover" this distinction between attitude and self-image seems to imply that they are happy to be able to *dismiss all consideration* of self-image as of no significance to their research interests. If the self has no relevance to their theory of action, again what continuity is there between the symbolic interaction orientation and reference group theory? For certainly the self is central to all social acts as Mead, Dewey and Cooley saw the matter. One behaves in terms of the kind of person he thinks he is, and for the ends such a person seeks. If "reference groups," operationalized as researcher-proposed, subject-accepted reference *categories,* do not yield meaningful results having to do with the self, is it perhaps that the operationalization has netted relatively insignificant or superficial others as opposed to the ones on which the self is based?

And is not this suspicion strengthened by their third conceptual reformulation — that of multiple reference groups, sometimes conflicting, sometimes mutually reinforcing? It is indeed very plausible that one finds his own categories of self-assignation sometimes conflicting. It is even probable that groups, with which he finds himself only moderately identified or only situationally committed, present such conflicting claims. Yet one supposes the others on which his self-conception crucially rests are only rarely or occasionally such as to put him under such cross-pressures.

However, it ought to be evident that this third proposal, unlike the other two, is not a theoretical or logical discontinuity with earlier symbolic interaction notions. There has always been uncertainty in the formulations about the consistency of the others (cf. Mead's problematic others as making development of the generalized other itself problematic)[20] and the stability of the self (cf. Anselm Strauss' notion that self shifts with each episode).[21] It is only possibly — in my view probably — a quantitative overstatement of the likelihood of inconsistency and conflict among others.

[20] Mead, *op. cit,.* pp. 307-311.

[21] Anselm Strauss, *Mirrors and Masks,* Glencoe, Ill.: Free Press, 1959. See especially Chapters 3 and 4.

Group and Category in Symbolic Interactionism

Since so much is being made here of the prevalence of social categories in reference group operationalization, it is desirable to pause and examine the significance of social categories in symbolic interaction theory. In this theory they are not conceptualized as social categories but must be searched for in other guises.

The social group is paramount for the theory in that it provides both the language through which interaction takes place and the mutual others with whom interaction occurs. The group is antecedent to the individual and so is its language (from a basic standpoint this is redundant, since the group exists *in* its communication). As a new individual is inducted into the group, he takes on its objects, whose attributes derive from the group's communicative categories. That is to say, the qualities of objects which are meaningful to the group in its ongoing activity must be contained as distinctions in its vocabulary. Otherwise one could not perceive objects differentially in terms of these qualities. The most important objects to the ongoing, mutually reciprocal role activity of the group are human beings. The lexical categories that refer to them make possible differential discernment of the kinds of people there are and the differential activity that may be directed toward them or with respect to them. Universal categories, found in all groups, are age and sex. Thousands of other categories exist, many of them unique to particular groups. In fact, there is no logical limit to the number of categories that might exist. Cultural relativism as an idea may be fairly well summed up in terms of the culturally unique categories which exist in specific societies — particularly for human actors. The self of a given person is in part a set of assignments of the self to relevant categories. But these assignments reflect group assessments: in the *broad,* because there is but one vocabulary to use; in the *specific,* because one cannot behave conjointly with others without consensus on one's assignment to categories (or put another way, without consensus on one's possession of role-relevant attributes).

Thus *category membership* is in any social system a *derivative* matter. It is the *group* or groups with whom one feels identified which are the source of the very vocabulary creating the categories and their meanings. Therefore, the other with whom one has a we-feeling, that is, a self which includes him, is an altogether different kind of other than the one with whom one shares a similar age or sex or number of years of overseas service. The dynamics for the support or modification of the self and, therefore, the dynamics for the organization and redirection of action, *lie* in one's *group relationships.* They will only *refer* to his category assignments.

It is difficult to look into the vocabulary of one's own society with any likelihood of finding generic differentia among its categories which will be instructive in delineating the processes of which I have just been speaking. The vernacular yields a rich bag of terms by which we regularly differentiate among our others and with respect to the different ways we confront them. A small but completely unsystematically assembled sampling of them from my own smattering recollection gives the following: dutch uncle; wet hen; party pooper; blood brother; traitor; hypocrite; snob; underdog; lover; sissy; man; other members of the team; final oral committee; old maid (of either sex); someone in the same boat (used in *The American Soldier*); sucker; the Joneses; pig; hero; clown; cry-baby; lion; mouse; boon companion; financial angel; sidewalk superintendent; customer; having somebody as one's "property" (e. g. a movie star); operator; promoter. Words for *collectivities of others* include: audience; forum; clique; the boys; guys like me; committee; cabinet; huddle; rescue team; them bums; the officials; passersby; mob; the crew; those cave-dwellers.

How can one distill from these any generic classes of others? I do not think one can. One *can,* however, make a beginning by starting with such elementary distinctions as those based on time, continuity, physical and social space, and the like: we can differentiate present others from absent others; proximal others from distal others; contemporary others from past others; continuous others from intermittent others; in-category from out-category others; immediate, impulsive, passing others from considered others. Behind these proffered distinctions lie testable hypotheses of considerable importance for the extension of symbolic interaction theory. It is simple to see what these might be, so I will not burden you with specific formulations of them. One cannot help acknowledging the debt symbolic interaction theory has to reference group theory, if only in the demonstration that the problem of the other may be approached systematically and empirically. But the examination of regularities with respect to the implicit hypotheses in the distinctions I suggested may not necessarily be best approached through survey research. It is especially important — given the assumptions of symbolic interactionism — to note what amounts to an aside made by Merton and Kitt to the effect that it is important to find out *what others the subject himself will give most saliently* — that is, presumably in answers to open-ended questions.[22] Although this kind of question may be used in survey research, it is the kind of question which evidently requires other forms of inquiry for the validation of its answers and to provide a broad base of understanding for their meaning.

It may be that some kind of orderliness lies in a possible hierarchy with which an actor holds — and invokes — his others. This kind of notion best fits the mechanistic models of Parsons and Homans and learning theory of several varieties. It tends to be incompatible with the all-or-none types of others envisaged in symbolic interactionism — others whose im-

[22] Merton, *op. cit.* pp., 249-250.

portance to one's self-conception rests on inclusion in groups with which one's self is coextensive and inclusive.

The dramatistic model of Burke, Goffman, Duncan and others suggests a process of casting acquaintances in various roles of others, depending on the kind of act to be presented and the circumstances and audience involved.[23] Such a casting process presents complexity which baffles imaginative attempts to categorize aspects and procedures for the purposes of finding regularities about which one might form useful generalizations. Much introspective experience supports the use of this model. We ought to be reminded that sociological inquiry must be directed toward events as they occur rather than toward fictions that please or seem to represent efficiencies or economies of investigation. It would be an error to create models of processes from a consideration of the tools we have readily available for research rather than from a consideration of the evidences of the processes we already have available for examination. If there is further evidence that we cast our others on the basis, not of conditioned or habitual experience, but at least partially on the basis of anticipated self-fulfillment by or in others of traits, qualities and potentialities for enactment, then the notions of hierarchy may not be at all relevant.

One of the claimed advantages of the reference group concept, as far as it was employed in such a study as *The American Soldier,* is that it enables us to examine the regularities with which social structure influences the creation and invocation of others, particularly in the process of self-evaluation and in the development of attitudes of relative deprivation. This is a cogent argument, deserving serious examination. It would seem, however, that if the major regularities of individual behavior hang on categorical memberships in social systems, there is little need for a social psychology in general or for the concept of the other in particular. The intervening factors between system regularity and individual regularity are in the nature of constants rather than of variables. One need not pry open the lid of the little black box or even worry about what's in it. It is when systems crosscut, or when personality processes and structures deriving from the diversity of past statuses and roles in other systems make difficult the discovery of regular relation between present social system and individual behavior, that we need to understand how the self and self-appraisal work and from whence they derive.

But in our kind of society, cross-cutting memberships are the rule rather than the exception — and so is diversity of past role-playing and past others. Furthermore, the situations in which most people find themselves are seldom so close to the nature of total institutions as those in

[23] Kenneth Burke, *A Grammar of Motives,* New York: Prentice-Hall, 1945; Erving Goffman, *The Presentation of Self in Everyday Life,* Garden City, N.Y.: Doubleday, 1959; and Hugh Dalziel Duncan, *Communication and Social Order,* New York: Bedminister Press, 1962.

which the subjects of *The American Soldier* found *themselves.* In such tight circumstances, others presumably are often nearly prefabricated, certainly predesignated, by the norms of the system itself. Independence of judgment and autonomy of conduct are rather uncommon in the services in wartime. It is not such regularized and routinized, subservient and ordered behavior which an understanding of self-conception assists us in understanding. Even the attitudinal reactions to these regularities and routines are to some large degree contained within the controlling framework of the total institution itself rather than being, as they normally are, inclusive of possible elections and choices that would get one to "leave the field," in Lewin's term.

Thus, if a study of the other is to assist us in the general study of social psychology, it has considerably larger tasks to perform in the area of the *lack* of regularity of relation between present social system and individual acts. In my view we have far more use for concepts of self and other, say, in studying the family than in the study of the prison. This is not to say that the concept of other has *no* utility in the study of behavior in the total institution, but that its use is more or less one which inverts that to which it is put by Merton and Kitt.

The Orientational Other

If what I have just suggested makes sense, I should like to advance the implicit idea in it by proposing a new concept — a new category of the other, which I shall call, for want of a better name, *the orientational other.* (It is singular by language convention only. It refers to a social object which may be a single other or a group). I should have preferred to call it by the name of *significant other,* but since that term has become so solidly entrenched in our usage as meaning something not basically different from simply "the other," in Mead's terms, I will suggest the rather less desirable name "orientational other." The orientational other has, in my proposal, four defining attributes: (1) The term refers to the others to whom the individual is most fully, broadly and basically committed, emotionally and psychologically; (2) it refers to the others who have provided him with his general vocabulary, including his most basic and crucial concepts and categories; (3) it refers to the others who have provided and continue to provide him with his categories of self and other and with the meaningful roles to which such assignments refer; (4) it refers to the others in communication with whom his self-conception is basically sustained and/or changed.

This orientational other has some kinship with the concept of the primary self advanced some years ago by Bingham Dai, but Dai's notion begged the essential question of sequence and assumed that the primary self — and presumably the primary others — are necessarily primary in the life trajectory — that is, they are events and objects of infancy and childhood only.[24]

The study of the orientational other would be one which would lie quite at the opposite end of the scale of significance from the study of the reference group. It would attempt, that is, to study the processes by which the self is formed and sustained and to discover if there are regularities in the relation between orientational other and the self which can account *for the discrepancies* between regularities of social system and the phenomena of individual behavior. It would afford the opportunity for inquiry regarding the possible relation between absence or diversity of orientational others and disoriented behavior.

It might be pointed out in conclusion that one has a *history* in his relations with his orientational others, but he has *only spent abstract time* in his social categories. When his reference categories have "come alive" for him, they have done so in terms of vivid role events vis-à-vis his orientational others, not in tilting windmills vis-à-vis all green recruits.

Summary

I know from several oblique comments that Professor Merton believes symbolic interactionists have an orientational aversion to empirical research — and from my own earlier-voiced doubts about Professor Blumer, you can guess that I at least have once *entertained thoughts* that *some* of them do. (Notice my perfidious shift from *us* to *them!*) But I want to remind myself and also Professor Merton that Professor Cooley's early study of the uses of personal pronouns by his children as a clue to the development of the self was one of the earliest empirical studies in social psychology.[25] And Professor Bain's replication of it was one of the earliest replication studies.[26] Now, in these days of survey research and of IBM 7070's, such studies of one's own children are to be looked upon, I suppose, as in the same genre as analysis by introspection! But I digress.

It had never occurred to me until the other day that one might study the other in much the same way that Cooley studied the self — through the use of pronouns by children. My ten-year-old daughter Abigail reported at dinner table the other day that "when she was *very* young and her older brother came home from school to report what 'they' did — she thought 'they' meant little people dressed in white clothes — people about six inches

[24] Bingham Dai, "A Socio-Psychiatric Approach to Personality Organization," *American Sociological Review,* 1952, 17:44-49.

[25] Charles Horton Cooley, "A Study of the Early Use of the Self-Words by a Child," *Psychological Review,* 1908, 15:339-357.

[26] Read Bain, "The Self-and-Other Words of a Child," *American Journal of Sociology,* 1936, 41:767-775.

tall who lived under the furniture." Suddenly it occurred to me that questions like "Compared with the chances of promotion for *raw recruits,* what do you think of your chances?" might have something in common with the notion that "they" refers to people under the furniture who wear little white coats. I think perhaps we are in the infancy of our study of the other.

I hope that this — or for that matter, my previous remarks — will not be taken as an indication that I wish to scrap the reference group concept altogether. I do think it should be amended to be the "reference *category*" concept. But I have no intention of suggesting that those who are persuaded by the cogency of the arguments behind it cease their research efforts. My proposal of the concept of *orientational other* was in no sense intended as a proposal of an *alternative* to the reference category concept.

The burden of what I have been attempting to say is that there are serious *discontinuities* between the symbolic interaction orientation and the reference-group concept of the other as it has generally been employed, and that whatever empirical successes have been achieved in its employment are not very large or persuasive when one considers the context of the research — a war, for example, is extraordinarily framed off from the rest of life, both in time and space. It is important to consider and to explore how far reference categories are coextensive with significant others. I have suggested that they may not even be of the same order. I am inclined to think that, if one is to demonstrate that they *are* of the same order, one must demonstrate that reference categories have major importance in the development and maintenance of the self as an object to the person. Ordinarily one keeps himself together and headed in the right direction by remembering who he is. If he remembers saliently that he is a second lieutenant, it is not, dynamically, because all second looies clutch him to their bosoms and think of him as one of them, but because the people with whom he is in a continual interchange of communicative symbols think of him saliently, and in respects significant to themselves and their mutual interaction, as a second lieutenant. If members of the faculty of the University of Wisconsin are asked, "Compared with those who got their B. A.'s at the University of Wisconsin, how good do you think your chances for promotion at the University of Wisconsin are?" regularities in their responses do not carry proof to me that faculty members there regularly and saliently divide in their self-conceptions between those who think of themselves as University of Wisconsin B. A.'s and "elsewhere B. A.'s."

Yet symbolic interactionism owes a considerable debt to this new development, for it has demonstrated that the other can probably be empirically researched and that it is very likely to be quite important to do so.

If these remarks have seemed excessively concerned with terminological distinctions, it might remind us of Stephen Leacock's wonderful characterization of our whole enterprise: "Ignorance, in its wooden shoes, shuffles around the portico of the temple of learning, stumbling among the litter of terminology. The broad field of human wisdom has been cut into a multitude of little professional rabbit warrens. In each of these a specialist burrows deep, scratching a shower of terminology, head down in an unlovely attitude which places an interlocutor at a grotesque conversational disadvantage."

15. Institutions and Persons

Hans Gerth and C. Wright Mills

If we shift our view from the external behavior of individual organisms and from explanations of such behavior in terms of physiological elements and mechanisms, and view man as a person who acts with and against other persons, we may then (1) examine the patterns of conduct which men enact together, and (2) avail ourselves of the direct experiences which persons have of one another and of themselves. At its minimum, social conduct consists of the actions of one person oriented to another, and most of the actions of men are of this sort. Man's action is interpersonal. It is often informed by awareness of other actors and directly oriented to their expectations and to anticipations of their behavior.

Out of the metaphors of poets and philosophers, who have likened man's conduct to that of the stage actor, sociologists have fashioned analytical tools. Long-used phrases readily come to mind: "playing a role" in the "great theater of public life," to move "in the limelight," the "theater of War," the "stage is all set." More technically, the concept "role" refers to (1) units of conduct which by their recurrence stand out as regularities and (2) which are oriented to the conduct of other actors. These recurrent interactions form patterns of mutually oriented conduct.

By definition, roles are interpersonal, that is, oriented to the conduct and expectations of others. These others, who expect things of us, are also playing roles: we expect them to do things in certain ways and to refrain from doing and feeling things in other ways. Interpersonal situations are thus built up and sets of roles held in line by mutual expectation, approbation, and disfavor.

Much of our social conduct, as we know from direct experience, is enacted in order to meet the expectations of others. In this sense, our enemies often control us as much as our friends. The father of a patriarchal family is expected by his wife and children to act in certain ways when confronted with given situations, and he in turn expects them to act in certain regular ways. Being acquainted with these simple facts about patriarchal families we expect regularities of conduct from each of their members, and having experienced family situations, we expect, with some

From *Character and Social Structure*, pp. 10-14, by Hans Gerth and C. Wright Mills, copyright 1953, by Harcourt, Brace & World, Inc., and reprinted with their permission.

degree of probability, that each of these members will experience his place and his self in a certain way.

Man as a person is an historical creation, and can most readily be understood in terms of the roles which he enacts and incorporates. These roles are limited by the kind of social institutions in which he happens to be born and in which he matures into an adult. His memory, his sense of time and space, his perception, his motives, his conception of his self... his psychological functions are shaped and steered by the specific configuration of roles which he incorporates from his society.

Perhaps the most important of these features of man is his image of his self, his idea of what kind of person he is. This experience of self is a crucially interpersonal one. Its basic organization is reflected from surrounding persons to whose approbation and criticism one pays attention.

What we think of ourselves is decisively influenced by what others think of us. Their attitudes of approval and of disapproval guide us in learning to play the roles we are assigned or which we assume. By internalizing these attitudes of others toward us and our conduct we not only gain new roles, but in time an image of our selves. Of course, man's "looking-glass self" may be a true or a distorted reflection of his actual self. Yet those from whom a man continually seeks approval are important determinants of what kind of man he is becoming. If a young lawyer begins to feel satisfaction from the approval of the boss of the local political machine, if the labels which this boss uses to describe his behavior matter a lot to the lawyer, he is being steered into new roles and into a new image of his self by the party machine and its boss. Their values may in time become his own and he will apply them not only to other men but to his own actions as well.[1] The self, Harry Stack Sullivan once said, is made up of the reflected appraisals of others.[2]

The concept of role does not of course imply a one person — one role equation. One person may play many different roles, and each of these

[1] The mechanism by which persons thus internalize roles and the attitudes of others is language. Language is composed of gestures, normally verbal, which call forth similar responses in two individuals. Without such gestures man could not incorporate the attitudes of others, and could not so easily make these attitudes a condition of his own learning and enactment of roles of his own image of self.

These conceptions will be discussed in greater detail in Chapters III: Organism and Psychic Structure and IV: The Person. Here we are only concerned with setting forth in the most general way the sociological model of explanation. [Ed. Note: reference is to chapters in *Character and Social Structure.*]

[2] "Conceptions of Modern Psychiatry," *Psychiatry,* Vol. III, No. 1 (February 1949), pp. 10-11. Compare also C.H. Cooley's *Human Nature and the Social Order* (rev. ed.; New York: Scribner's, 1922). The tradition is well documented by Fay B. Karpf, *American Social Psychology* (New York: McGraw-Hill, 1932).

roles may be a segment of the different institutions and interpersonal situations in which the person moves. A corporation executive acts differently in his office than in his child's nursery. An adolescent girl enacts a different role when she is at a party composed of members of her own clique than when she is at her family's breakfast table. Moreover, the luxury of a certain image of self implied in the party role is not often possible in her family circle. In the family circle the party role might be amusing, as a charming attempt at sophistication "beyond her age and experience," but at the party it might bring prestige and even the adulation of young males. She cannot, usually, act out the self-conception of a long-suffering lover before her grandfather, but she can when she is alone with her young man.

The chance to display emotional gestures, and even to feel them, varies with one's status and class position. For emotional gestures, expected by others and by one's self, form important features of many social roles. The Victorian lady could dramatize certain emotions in a way that today would be considered silly, if not hysterical. Yet the working girl who was her contemporary was not as likely to faint as was the lady; there would probably not have been anyone to catch the working girl. During the nineties in America it was expected that women who were also ladies, that is, members of an upper status group, would faint upon very exciting occasions. The role of the delicate and fainting lady was involved in the very being of a lady.[3] But the "same" occasions would not elicit fainting on the part of the ladies' maid, who did not conceive of her "place," and of her self, as a fainting lady; fainting requires a certain amount of leisure and gentlemanly attention, and accordingly offers opportunities to the gentleman to demonstrate that chivalry is not dead.

The roles allowed and expected, the self-images which they entail, and the consequences of these roles and images on the persons we are with are firmly embedded in a social context. Inner psychological changes and the institutional controls of a society are thus interlinked.

An institution is an organization of roles, which means that the roles carry different degrees of authority, so that one of the roles — we may call it the "head" role — is understood and accepted by the members of the other roles as guaranteeing the relative permanence of the total conduct pattern. An *institution* is thus (1) an organization of roles, (2) one or more of which is understood to serve the maintenance of the total set of roles.

The "head role" of an institution is very important in the psychic life of the other members of the institution. What "the head" thinks of them in their respective roles, or what they conceive him to think, is internalized, that is, taken over, by them. In a strictly patriarchal family, the head, the father, is looked up to; his is that most important attitude toward the

[3] Cf. Ralph Linton, *The Study of Man* (New York: Appleton-Century, 1936).

child that may determine the child's attitude toward his, the child's, own conduct and perhaps toward his self: in taking over this attitude the child builds up an "other" within his self, and the attitude he conceives this other to have toward him is a condition for his attitude toward his own self. Other persons in other roles also have attitudes toward him and each of these may be internalized, and eventually form segments of his self-conception. But the attitude of the head of the major institution in which we play a role is a decisive one in our own maturation. If "he says it is all right," we feel secure in what we are doing and how we are conceiving our self. When his attitudes are taken over into the self, this head constitutes in a concrete form, a "particular other." But he is not seen merely as a particular person; he is the symbol and the "mouth piece" of the entire institution. In him is focused the "final" attitudes toward our major roles and our self within this institution; he sums them up, and when we take over these attitudes and expectations we control our institutional conduct in terms of them. It is by means of such internalized others that our conduct, our playing of roles within institutions, is "self-controlled."

By choosing the social role as a major concept we are able to reconstruct the inner experience of the person as well as the institutions which make up an historical social structure. For man as a *person* (from the Latin *persona,* meaning "mask") is composed of the specific roles which he enacts and of the effects of enacting these roles upon his self. And society as a *social structure* is composed of roles as segments variously combined in its total circle of institutions. The organization of roles is important in building up a particular social structure; it also has psychological implications for the persons who act out the social structure.

Most of the various interpersonal situations in which we are involved exist within institutions, which make up a social structure; and changes of social structure make up the main course of human history. In order to understand men's conduct and experience we must reconstruct the historical social structures in which they play roles and acquire selves. For such regularity of conduct, and of the motives for this conduct, as we may find will rest upon the historical regularities of these social structures, rather than upon any suprahistorical, biological elements assumed to be innate and constant within the organism. From the sociological point of view, man as a person is a social-historical creation. If his view of his self and of his motives is intimately connected with the roles which are available to him and which he incorporates, then we may not expect to learn much that is very concrete about individual men unless we investigate a number of his specific roles in a number of varied social-historical settings.

Rather than constant elements within a physiological organism, the sociologist rests his primary model of explanation upon the interpersonal situations, and in the last analysis, the social structures within which persons live out their lives.

16. Deviance Disavowal: The Management of Strained Interaction by the Visibly Handicapped

Fred Davis

A recurring issue in social relations is the refusal of those who are viewed as deviant[1] to concur in the verdict. Or, if in some sense it can be said that they do concur, they usually place a very different interpretation on the fact or allegation than do their judges. In our society this is especially true of deviance which results from ascription (e.g., the Negro) as against that which partakes to some significant degree of election (e.g., the homosexual). And, while it may be conjectured that ultimately neither the Negro nor the homosexual would be cast in a deviant role were it not for society's devaluation of these attributes in the first place, barring such a hypothetical contingency it remains the more persuasive argument in a democracy to be able to claim that the social injury from which one suffers was in no way self-inflicted.

In these pages I wish to discuss another kind of non self-inflicted social injury, the visible physical handicap. My aim though is not to survey and

From *Social Problems* IX (Fall, 1961), pp. 120-132, by permission of the journal and the author.

The study from which this paper derives was supported by a grant from the Association for the Aid of Crippled Children. I am indebted to Stephen A. Richardson and David Klein of the Association for their help and advice. I also wish to thank Frances C. Macgregor, Cornell Medical Center, New York, for having so generously made available to me case materials from her research files on persons with facial disfigurements. See Frances C. Macgregor et. al., *Facial Deformities and Plastic Surgery: A Psychosocial Study,* Springfield, Ill.: Charles C. Thomas, 1953.

[1] Following Lemert, as used here the term deviant (or deviance) refers 1) to a person's deviation from prevalent or valued norms, 2) to which the community-at-large reacts negatively or punitively, 3) so as to then lead the person to define his situation largely in terms of this reaction. All three conditions must be fulfilled for it to be said that deviance exists (secondary deviation, in Lemert's definition). In this sense the Negro, the career woman, the criminal, the Communist, the physically handicapped, the mentally ill, the homosexual, to mention but a few, are all deviants, albeit in different ways and with markedly different consequences for their life careers. Edwin M. Lemert, *Social Pathology,* New York: McGraw-Hill, 1951, 75-77.

describe the many hardships of the visibly handicapped,[2] but to analyze certain facets of their coping behavior as it relates to the generalized imputations of deviance they elicit from society, imputations which many of them feel it necessary to resist and reject.

There are, of course, many areas in which such imputations bear heavily upon them: employment, friendship, courtship, sex, travel, recreation, residence, education. But the area I treat here is enmeshed to some extent in all of these without being as categorically specific as any. I refer to situations of sociability, and more specifically to that genre of everyday intercourse which has the characteristics of being: 1) face-to-face, 2) prolonged enough to permit more than a fleeting glimpse or exchange, but not so prolonged that close familiarity immediately ensues, 3) intimate to the extent that the parties must pay more that perfunctory attention to one another, but not so intimate that the customary social graces can be dispensed with, and 4) ritualized to the extent that all know in general what to expect, but not so ritualized as to preclude spontaneity and the slightly novel turn of events. A party or other social affair, a business introduction, getting to know a person at work, meeting neighbors, dealing with a salesman, conversing with a fellow passenger, staying at a resort hotel — these are but a few of the everyday social situations which fall within this portion of the spectrum of sociability, a range of involvement which can also be thought of as the zone of first impressions.

In interviews I conducted with a small number of very articulate and socially skilled informants who were visibly handicapped[3] I inquired into their handling of the imputation that they were not "normal, like everyone else." This imputation usually expresses itself in a pronounced stickiness of interactional flow and in the embarrassment of the normal by which he conveys the all too obvious message that he is having difficulty in relating to the handicapped person[4] as he would to "just an ordinary man

[2] Comprehensive and excellent reviews are to be found in R. G. Barker et al., *Adjustment to Physical Handicap and Illness: A Survey of the Social Psychology of Physique and Disability,* New York: Soc. Sci. Res. Council, 1953, Bulletin 55, 2nd ed. and Beatrice A Wright, *Physical Disability, A Psychological Approach,* New York: Harper, 1960.

[3] Six were orthopedically handicapped, three blind and two facially disfigured. Additional detailed biographical and clinical materials were secured on one blind and four facially disfigured persons, making for a total of sixteen records.

[4] Throughout this paper, whether or not the term 'handicap' or 'handicapped' is joined by the qualifier 'visible,' it should be read in this way. Unfortunately, it will not be possible to discuss here that which sociologically distinguishes the situation of the visibly handicapped from that of persons whose physical handicaps are not visible or readily apparent, and how both differ from what is termed the 'sick role.' These are, though, important distinctions whose analysis might illuminate key questions in the study of deviance.

or woman." Frequently he will make *faux pas,* slips of the tongue, revealing gestures and inadvertent remarks which overtly betray this attitude and place the handicapped person in an even more delicate situation.[5] The triggering of such a chain of interpersonal incidents is more likely with new persons than with those with whom the handicapped have well-established and continuing relations. Hence, the focus here on more or less sociable occasions, it being these in which interactional discomfort is felt most acutely and coping behavior is brought into relief most sharply.

Because the visibly handicapped do not comprise a distinct minority group or subculture, the imputations of generalized deviance that they elicit from many normals are more nearly genuine interactional emergents than conventionalized sequelae to intergroup stereotyping as, for example, might obtain between a Negro and white. A sociable encounter between a visibly handicapped person and a normal is usually more subject to ambiguity and experimentation in role postures than would be the case were the parties perceived by each other primarily in terms of member group characteristics. The visibly handicapped person must with each new acquaintance explore the *possibilities* of a relationship. As a rule there is no ready-made symbolic shorthand (e.g., "a Southerner can't treat a Negro as a social equal," "the Irish are anti-Semitic," "working class people think intellectuals are effeminate") for anticipating the quality and degree of acceptance to be accorded him. The exchange must be struck before its dangers and potentialities can be seen and before appropriate corrective maneuvers can be fed into the interaction.[6]

The Handicap as Threat to Sociable Interaction

Before discussing how the visibly handicapped cope with difficult interaction, it is appropriate to first consider the general nature of the threat posed to the interactional situation *per se* as a result of their being perceived routinely (if not necessarily according to some prevalent stereotype) as "different," "odd," "estranged from the common run of humanity," etc.; in short, other than normal. (Achieving ease and naturalness of interaction with normals serves naturally as an important index to the handicapped person of the extent to which his preferred definition

[5] In the sections that follow the discussion draws heavily on the framework of dramaturgic analysis developed by Erving Goffman. See especially his "Alienation from Interaction," *Human Relations,* 10 (1957), 47-60; "Embarrassment and Social Organization," *American Journal of Sociology,* 62 (November, 1956), 264-71; *Presentation of Self in Everyday Life,* New York: Doubleday and Co., Inc., 1959.

[6] Cf. Anselm Strauss, *Mirrors and Masks,* Glencoe, Ill.: Free Press, 1959, 31-43.

of self — i.e., that of someone who is merely different physically but not socially deviant — has been accepted. Symbolically, as long as the interaction remains stiff, strained or otherwise mired in inhibition, he has good reason to believe that he is in effect being denied the status of social normalcy he aspires to or regards as his due.) The threat posed by the handicap to sociability is, at minimum, fourfold: its tendency to become an exclusive focal point of the interaction, its potential for inundating expressive boundaries, its discordance with other attributes of the person and, finally, its ambiguity as a predicator of joint activity. These are not discrete entities in themselves as much as varying contextual emergents which, depending on the particular situation, serve singly or in combination to strain the framework of normative rules and assumptions in which sociability develops. Let us briefly consider each in turn.

A Focal Point of Interaction

The rules of sociable interaction stipulate a certain generality and diffuseness in the attentions that parties are expected to direct to each other. Even if only superficially, one is expected to remain oriented to the whole person and to avoid the expression of a precipitous or fixed concern with any single attribute of his, however noteworthy or laudable it may be.[7] When meeting someone with a visible handicap, a number of perceptual and interpretative responses occur which make adherence to this rule tenuous for many. First, there is the matter of visibility as such. By definition, the visibly handicapped person cannot control his appearance sufficiently so that its striking particularity will not call a certain amount of concentrated attention to itself.[8] Second, the normal, while having his attention so narrowly channeled, is immediately constrained by the requirements of sociability to act as if he were oriented to the totality of the other rather than to that which is uppermost in his awareness, i.e., the handicap. Although the art of sociability may be said to thrive on a certain playful discrepancy between felt and expressed interests, it is perhaps equally true that when these are too discrepant strain and tension begin to undermine the interaction. (Conversely, when not discrepant enough, flatness and boredom frequently ensue.)[9] Whether the handicap is overtly and tactlessly responded to as such or, as is more

[7] Kurt H. Wolff, ed., *The Sociology of Georg Simmel,* Glencoe, Ill.: Free Press, 1950, 45-46.

[8] Cf. R. K. White, B. A. Wright and T. Dembo, "Studies in Adjustment to Visible Injuries," *Journal of Abnormal and Social Psychology,* 43 (1948), 13-28.

[9] In a forthcoming paper, "Fun in Games: An Analysis of the Dynamics of Social Interaction," Goffman discusses the relationship between spontaneous involvement in interaction and the manner in which "external attributes" — those which in a formal sense are not situationally relevant — are permitted to penetrate the situation's boundaries.

commonly the case, no explicit reference is made to it, the underlying condition of heightened, narrowed, awareness causes the interaction to be articulated too exclusively in terms of it. This, as my informants described it, is usually accompanied by one or more of the familiar signs of discomfort and stickiness: the guarded references, the common everyday words suddenly made taboo, the fixed stare elsewhere, the artificial levity, the compulsive loquaciousness, the awkward solemnity.[10]

Second-order interactional elaborations of the underlying impedance are also not uncommon. Thus, for example, the normal may take great pains to disguise his awareness, an exertion that is usually so effortful and transparent that the handicapped person is then enjoined to disguise his awareness of the normal's disguise. In turn, the normal sensing the disguise erected in response to his disguise . . . and so forth. But unlike the infinitely multiplying reflections of an object located between opposing mirrors, this process cannot sustain itself for long without the pretense of unawareness collapsing, as witness the following report by a young woman:

> I get suspicious when somebody says, "Let's go for a uh, ah [imitates confused and halting speech] push with me down the hall," or something like that. This to me is suspicious because it means that they're aware, really aware, that there's a wheelchair here, and that this is probably uppermost with them. . . . A lot of people in trying to show you that they don't care that you're in a chair will do crazy things. Oh, there's one person I know who constantly kicks my chair, as if to say "I don't care that you're in a wheelchair. I don't even know that it's there." But that is just an indication that he *really* knows it's there.

Inundating Potential

The expressive requirements of sociability are such that rather strict limits obtain with respect to the types and amount of emotional display that are deemed appropriate. Even such fitting expressions as gaiety and laughter can, we know, reach excess and lessen satisfaction with the occasion. For many normals, the problem of sustaining sociable relations with someone who is visibly handicapped is not wholly that of the discrepancy of the inner feeling evoked, e.g., pity, fear, repugnance, avoidance. As with much else in sociability, a mere discrepancy of the actor's inner state with the social expectation need not result in a disturbance of interaction. In this instance it is specifically the marked dissonance of such emotions with those outward expressions deemed *most* salient for the occasion (e.g., pleasure, identification, warm interest) that seems to result frequently in an inundation and enfeeblement of the expressive controls of the individual. With some persons, the felt intrusion, of this kind of

[10] Cf. Goffman on "other-consciousness" as a type of faulty interaction. "Alienation from Interaction," *op. cit.*

situationally inappropriate emotion is so swift and overwhelming as to approximate a state of shock, leaving them expressively naked, so to speak. A pointed incident is told by a young blind girl:

> One night when I was going to visit a friend two of the people from my office put me into a taxi. I could tell that at first the taxi driver didn't know I was blind because for a while there he was quite a conversationalist. Then he asked me what these sticks were for [a collapsible cane]. I told him it was a cane, and then he got so different. . . . He didn't talk about the same things that he did at first. Before this happened he joked and said, "Oh, you're a very quiet person. I don't like quiet people, they think too much." And he probably wouldn't have said that to me had he known I was blind because he'd be afraid of hurting my feelings. He didn't say anything like that afterwards.

The visibly handicapped are of course aware of this potential for inundating the expressive boundaries of situations and many take precautions to minimize such occurrences as much as possible. Thus, an interior decorator with a facial deformity would when admitted to a client's house by the maid station himself whenever he could so that the client's entrance would find him in a distantly direct line of vision from her. This, he stated, gave the client an opportunity to compose herself, as she might not be able to were she to come upon him at short range.

Contradiction of Attributes

Even when the inundating potential is well contained by the parties and the normal proves fully capable of responding in a more differentiated fashion to the variety of attributes presented by the handicapped person (e.g., his occupational identity, clothes, speech, intelligence, interests, etc.), there is frequently felt to be an unsettling discordance between these and the handicap. Sociable interaction is made more difficult as a result because many normals can only resolve the seeming incongruence by assimilating or subsuming (often in a patronizing or condescending way) the other attributes to that of the handicap, a phenomenon which in analogous connections has been well described by Hughes.[11] Thus, one informant, a strikingly attractive girl, reports that she frequently elicits from new acquaintances the comment, "How strange that someone so pretty should be in a wheelchair." Another informant, a professional worker for a government agency, tells of the fashionable female client who after having inquired on how long the informant had been in her job remarked, "How nice that you have something to do." Because the art of

[11] Everett C. Hughes, *Men and their work,* Glencoe, Ill.: Free Press, 1958, 102-06.

sociability deigns this kind of reductionism of the person, expressions of this type, even when much less blatant, almost invariably cast a pall on the interaction and embarrass the recovery of smooth social posture. The general threat inherent in the perceived discordance of personal attributes is given pointed expression by still another informant, a paraplegic of upper middle class background who comments on the attitude of many persons in his class:

> Now, where this affects them, where this brace and a crutch would affect them, is if they are going someplace or if they are doing something, they feel that, first, you would call attention and, second — you wouldn't believe this but it's true; I'll use the cruelest words I can — no cripple could possibly be in their social stratum.

Ambiguous Predicator

Finally, to the extent to which sociability is furthered by the free and spontaneous initiation of joint activity (e.g., dancing, games, going out to eat; in short, "doing things") there is frequently considerable ambiguity as regards the ability of the handicapped person to so participate and as regards the propriety of efforts which seek to ascertain whether he wants to. For the normal who has had limited experience with the handicapped it is by no means always clear whether, for example, a blind person can be included in a theater party or a crippled person in a bowling game. Even if not able to engage in the projected activity as such, will he want to come along mainly for the sake of company? How may his preferences be gauged without, on the one hand, appearing to "make a thing" out of the proposal or, on the other, conveying the impression that his needs and limitations are not being sufficiently considered? Should he refuse, is it genuine or is he merely offering his hosts a polite, though half-hearted, out? And, for each enigma thus posed for the normal, a counter-enigma is posed for the handicapped person. Do they really want him? Are they merely being polite? In spite of the open invitation, will his acceptance and presence lessen somehow their enjoyment of the activity? It is easy to see how a profusion of anticipatory ambiguities of this kind can strain the operative assumptions underlying sociable relations.

Process of Deviance Disavowal and Normalization

The above features then, may be said to comprise the threat that a visible handicap poses to the framework of rules and assumptions that guide sociability. We may now ask how socially adept handicapped persons cope with it so as to either keep it at bay, dissipate it or lessen its impact upon the interaction. In answering this question we will not consider those broad personality adjustments of the person (e.g., aggression, denial, compensation, dissociation, etc.) which at a level once removed, so to speak, can be thought of as adaptive or maladaptive for, among other things, sociability. Nor, at the other extreme, is it possible in the allotted space to review the tremendous variety of specific approaches, ploys and stratagems that the visibly handicapped employ in social situations. Instead, the analysis will attempt to delineate in transactional terms the stages through which a sociable relationship with a normal typically passes, assuming, of course, that the confrontation takes place and that both parties possess sufficient social skill to sustain a more than momentary engagement.

For present purposes we shall designate these stages as: 1) fictional acceptance, 2) the facilitation of reciprocal role-taking around a normalized projection of self and 3) the institutionalization in the relationship of a definition of self that is normal in its moral dimension, however qualified it may be with respect to its situational contexts. As we shall indicate, the unfolding of these stages comprises what may be thought of as a process of deviance disavowal or normalization,[12] depending on whether one views the process from the vantage point of the "deviant" actor or his alters.[13]

Fictional Acceptance

In Western society the overture phases of a sociable encounter are to a pronounced degree regulated by highly elastic fictions of equality and normalcy. In meeting those with whom we are neither close nor familiar, manners dictate that we refrain from remarking on or otherwise reacting too obviously to those aspects of their persons which in the privacy of our thoughts betoken important differences between ourselves. In America at least, these fictions tend to encompass sometimes marked divergencies in social status as well as a great variety of expressive styles; and, it is perhaps the extreme flexibility of such fictions in our culture rather than, as is mistakenly assumed by many foreign observers, their absence

[12] As used here the term 'normalization' denotes a process whereby alter for whatever reason comes to view as normal and morally acceptable that which initially strikes him as odd, unnatural, "crazy," deviant, etc., irrespective of whether his perception was in the first instance reasonable, accurate or justifiable. Cf. Charlotte G. Schwartz, "Perspectives on Deviance — Wives' Definitions of their Husbands' Mental Illness," *Psychiatry,* 20 (August, 1957), 275-91.

[13] Because of the paper's focus on the visibly handicapped person, in what follows his interactional work is highlighted to the relative glossing over of that of the normal. Actually, the work of normalization calls for perhaps as much empathic expenditure as that of deviance disavowal and is, obviously, fully as essential for repairing the interactional breach occasioned by the encounter.

that accounts for the seeming lack of punctiliousness in American manners. The point is nicely illustrated in the following news item:

> NUDE TAKES A STROLL IN MIAMI
>
> MIAMI, Fla., Nov.13, (UPI) — A shapely brunette slowed traffic to a snail's pace here yesterday with a 20-minute nude stroll through downtown Miami. . . .
>
> "The first thing I knew something was wrong," said Biscayne Bay bridgetender E. E. Currey, who was working at his post about one block away, "was when I saw traffic was going unusually slow."
>
> Currey said he looked out and called police. They told him to stop the woman, he said.
>
> Currey said he walked out of his little bridge house, approached the woman nervously, and asked, "Say, girl, are you lost?"
>
> "Yes," she replied. "I'm looking for my hotel."
>
> Currey offered help and asked, "Say, did you lose your clothes?"
>
> "No," he said the woman replied, "Why?'
>
> Currey said that he had to step away for a moment to raise the bridge for a ship and the woman walked away. . . .[14]

Unlike earlier societies and some present day ones in which a visible handicap automatically relegates the person to a caste-like, inferior, status like that of mendicant, clown or thief — or more rarely to an elevated one like that of oracle or healer — in our society the visibly handicapped are customarily accorded, save by children,[15] the surface acceptance that democratic manners guarantee to nearly all. But, as regards sociability, this proves a mixed blessing for many. Although the polite fictions do afford certain entree rights, as fictions they can too easily come to serve as substitutes for "the real thing" in the minds of their perpetrators. The interaction is kept starved at a bare subsistence level of sociability. As with the poor relation at the wedding party, so the reception given the handicapped person in many social situations: sufficient that he is here, he should not expect to dance with the bride.

At this stage of the encounter, the interactional problem confronting the visibly handicapped person is the delicate one of not permitting his

[14] *San Francisco Chronicle,* November 14, 1960.

[15] The blunt questions and stares of small children are typically of the 'Emperor's Clothes' variety. "Mister, why is your face like that?" "Lady, what are you riding around in that for? Can't you walk?" Nearly all my informants spoke of how unnerving such incidents were for them, particularly when other adults were present. None the less, some claimed to value the child's forthrightness a good deal more than they did the genteel hypocrisy of many adults.

identity to be circumscribed by the fiction while at the same time playing along with it and showing appropriate regard for its social legitimacy. For, as transparent and confining as the fiction is, it frequently is the only basis upon which the contact can develop into something more genuinely sociable. In those instances in which the normal fails or refuses to render even so small a gesture toward normalizing the situation, there exists almost no basis for the handicapped person to successfully disavow his deviance.[16] The following occurrence related by a young female informant is an apt, if somewhat extreme, illustration:

> I was visiting my girl friend's house and I was sitting in the lobby waiting for her when this woman comes out of her apartment and starts asking me questions. She just walked right up. I didn't know her from Adam, I never saw her before in my life. "Gee, what do you have? How long have you been that way? Oh gee, that's terrible." And so I answered her questions, but I got very annoyed and wanted to say, "Lady, mind your own business."

"Breaking Through" — Facilitating Normalized Role-Taking

In moving beyond fictional acceptance what takes place essentially is a redefinitional process in which the handicapped person projects images, attitudes and concepts of self which encourage the normal to identify with him (i.e., "take his role") in terms other than those associated with imputations of deviance.[17] Coincidentally, in broadening the area of minor verbal involvements, this also functions to drain away some of the stifling burden of unspoken awareness that, as we have seen, so taxes ease of

[16] On the other side of the coin there are of course some handicapped persons who are equally given to undermining sociable relations by intentionally flaunting the handicap so that the fiction becomes extremely difficult to sustain, An equivalent of the "bad nigger" type described by Strong, such persons were (as in Strong's study) regarded with a mixture of admiration and censure by a number of my informants. Admiration, because the cruel stripping away of pretenses and forcing of issues was thought morally refreshing, especially since, as the informants themselves recognized, many normals refuse to grant anything more than fictional acceptance while at the same time imagining themselves ennobled for having made the small sacrifice. Censure, because of the conviction that such behavior could hardly improve matters in the long run and would make acceptance even more difficult for other handicapped persons who later came into contact with a normal who had received such treatment. Cf. Samuel M. Strong, "Negro-White Relations as Reflected in Social Types," *American Journal of Sociology,* 52 (July, 1946), p. 24.

[17] George H. Mead, *Mind, Self and Society,* Chicago: University of Chicago Press, 1934. See also the discussion on interaction in Strauss, *op. cit.,* 44-88.

interaction. The normal is cued into a larger repertoire of appropriate responses, and even when making what he, perhaps mistakenly, regards as an inappropriate response (for example, catching himself in the use of such a word as cripple or blind) the handicapped person can by his response relieve him of his embarrassment. One young informant insightfully termed the process "breaking through":

> The first reaction a normal individual or good-legger has is, "Oh gee, there's a fellow in a wheelchair," or "there's a fellow with a brace." And they don't say, "Oh gee, there is so-and-so, he's handsome" or "he's intelligent," or "he's a boor," or what have you. And then as the relationship develops they don't see the handicap. It doesn't exist any more. And that's the point that you as a handicapped individual become sensitive to. You know after talking with someone for awhile when they don't see the handicap any more. That's when you've broken through.

What this process signifies from a social psychological standpoint is that as the handicapped person expands the interactional nexus he simultaneously disavows the deviancy latent in his status; concurrently, to the degree to which the normal is led to reciprocally assume the redefining (and perhaps unanticipated) self-attitudes proffered by the handicapped person, he comes to normalize (i.e., view as more like himself) those aspects of the other which at first connoted deviance for him. (Sometimes, as we shall see, the normal's normalizing is so complete that it is unwittingly applied to situations in which the handicapped person cannot possibly function "normally" due to sheer physical limitations.) These dynamics might also be termed a process of identification. The term is immaterial, except that in "identifying" or "taking the role of the other" much more is implicated sociologically than a mere subjective congruence of responses. The fashioning of shared perspectives also implies a progressively more binding legitimation of the altered self-representations enacted in the encounter; that is, having once normalized his perception of the handicapped person, it becomes increasingly more compromising — self-discrediting, as it were — for the normal to revert to treating him as a deviant again.

The ways in which the visibly handicapped person can go about disavowing deviance are, as we have stated, many and varied. These range from relatively straightforward conversational offerings in which he alludes in passing to his involvement in a normal round of activities, to such forms of indirection as interjecting taboo or privatized references by way of letting the normal know that he does not take offense at the latter's uneasiness or regard it as a fixed obstacle toward achieving rapport. In the above quote, for example, the informant speaks of "good-leggers," an in-group term from his rehabilitation hospital days, which along with "dirty normals" he sometimes uses with new acquaintances "because it has a humorous connotation . . . and lots of times it puts people at their ease."[18]

Still other approaches to disavowing deviance and bridging fictional acceptance include: an especially attentive and sympathetic stance with respect to topics introduced by the normal, showing oneself to be a comic, wit or other kind of gifted participant, and, for some, utilizing the normalization potential inherent in being seen in the company of a highly presentable normal companion.[19] These, and others too numerous to mention, are not of course invariably or equally successful in all cases; neither are such resources equally available to all handicapped persons, nor are the handicapped equally adept at exploiting them. As a class of corrective strategies however, they have the common aim of overcoming the interactional barrier that lies between narrow fictional acceptance and more spontaneous forms of relatedness.

Inextricably tied in with the matter of approach are considerations of setting, activity and social category of participants, certain constellations of which are generally regarded as favorable for successful deviance disavowal and normalization while others are thought unfavorable. Again, the ruling contingencies appear to be the extent to which the situation is seen as containing elements in it which: 1) contextually reduce the threat posed by the visible handicap to the rules and assumptions of the particular sociable occasion, and 2) afford the handicapped person opportunities for "breaking through" beyond fictional acceptance.

The relevance of one or both of these is apparent in the following social situations and settings about which my informants expressed considerable agreement as regards their preferences, aversions and inner reactions. To begin with, mention might again be made of the interactional rule violations frequently experienced at the hands of small children. Many of the informants were quite open in stating that a small child at a social occasion caused them much uneasiness and cramped their style because they were concerned with how, with other adults present, they would handle some barefaced question from the child. Another category of persons with whom many claimed to have difficulty is the elderly. Here the problem was felt to be the tendency of old people to indulge in patronizing sympathy, an attitude which peculiarly resists

[18] Parallel instances can easily be cited from minority group relations as, for example, when a Jew in conversation with a non-Jew might introduce a Yiddish phrase by way of suggesting that the other's covert identification of him as a Jew need not inhibit the interaction unduly. In some situations this serves as a subtle means of declaring, "O.K., I know what's bothering you. Now that I've said it, let's forget about it and move on to something else."

[19] Alan G. Gowman, "Blindness and the Role of the Companion," *Social Problems,* 4 (July, 1956).

re-definition because of the fulsome virtue it attributes to itself. In another context several of the informants laid great stress on the importance of maintaining a calm exterior whenever the physical setting unavoidably exposed them to considerable bodily awkwardness. (At the same time, of course, they spoke of the wisdom of avoiding, whenever possible, such occasions altogether.) Their attitude was that to expressively reflect gracelessness and a loss of control would result in further interactional obstacles toward assimilating the handicapped person to a normal status.

> It makes me uncomfortable to watch anyone struggling, so I try to do what I must as inconspicuously as possible. In new situations or in strange places, even though I may be very anxious, I will maintain a deadly calm. For example, if people have to lift the chair and I'm scared that they are going to do it wrong, I remain perfectly calm and am very direct in the instructions I give.

As a final example, there is the unanimity with which the informants expressed a strong preference for the small, as against the large or semipublic social gathering. Not only do they believe that, as one handicapped person among the non-handicapped, they stand out more at large social gatherings, but also that in the anonymity which numbers further there resides a heightened structural tendency for normals to practice avoidance relations with them. The easy assumption on such occasions is that "some other good soul" will take responsibility for socializing with the handicapped person. Even in the case of the handicapped person who is forward and quite prepared to take the initiative in talking to others, the organization and ecology of the large social gathering is usually such as to frustrate his attempts to achieve a natural, non-deviant, place for himself in the group. As one young man, a paraplegic, explained:

> The large social gathering presents a special problem. It's a matter of repetition. When you're in a very large group of people whom you don't know, you don't have an opportunity of talking to three, four or five at a time. Maybe you'll talk to one or two usually. After you've gone through a whole basic breakdown in making a relationship with one — after all, it's only a cocktail party — to do it again, and again, it's wearing and it's no good. You don't get the opportunity to really develop something.

Institutionalization of the Normalized Relationship

In "breaking through" many of the handicapped are confronted by a delicate paradox, particularly in those of their relationships which continue beyond the immediate occasion. Having disavowed deviance and induced the other to respond to him as he would to a normal, the problem then becomes one of sustaining the normalized definition in the face of the many small amendments and qualifications that must frequently be made to it. The person confined to a wheelchair, for example, must brief a new acquaintance on what to do and how to help when they come to stairs, doorways, vehicle entrances, etc. Further briefings and rehearsals may be required for social obstructions as well: for example, how to act in an encounter with — to cite some typical situations at random — an overly helpful person, a waitress who communicates to the handicapped person only through his companion, a person who stares in morbid fascination.[20]

Generally, such amendments and special considerations are as much as possible underplayed in the early stages of the relationship because, as in the case of much minority group protest, the fundamental demand of the handicapped is that they first be granted an irreducibly equal and normal status, it being only then regarded as fitting and safe to admit to certain incidental incapacities, limitations and needs. At some point however, the latter must be broached if the relationship to the normal is to endure in viable form. But to integrate effectively a major claim to "normalcy" with numerous minor waivers of the same claim is a tricky feat and one which exposes the relationship to the many situational and psychic hazards of apparent duplicity: the tension of transferring the special arrangements and understandings worked out between the two to situations and settings in which everyone else is "behaving normally"; the sometimes lurking suspicion of the one that it is only guilt or pity that cements the relationship, of the other that the infirmity is being used exploitatively, and of on-lookers that there is something "neurotic" and "unhealthy" about it all.[21]

From my informants' descriptions it appears that this third, "normal, but . . ." stage of the relationship, if it endures, is institutionalized mainly in either one of two ways. In the first, the normal normalizes his perceptions to such an extent as to suppress his effective awareness of many of the areas in which the handicapped person's behavior unavoidably deviates from the normal standard. In this connection several of the informants complained that a recurring problem they have with close friends is that the latter frequently overlook the fact of the handicap and the restrictions it imposes on them. The friends thoughtlessly make arrangements and involve them in activities in which they, the handicapped, cannot participate conveniently or comfortably.

[20] *Ibid.*

[21] The rhetoric of race relations reflects almost identical rationalizations and "insights" which are meant among other things to serve as cautions for would-be transgressors. "Personally I have nothing against Negroes [the handicapped], but it would be bad for my reputation if I were seen socializing with them." "She acts nice now, but with the first argument she'll call you a dirty Jew [good-for-nothing cripple]." "Regardless of how sympathetic you are toward Negroes [the disabled], the way society feels about them you'd have to be a masochist to marry one."

The other major direction in which the relationship is sometimes institutionalized is for the normal to surrender some of his normalcy by joining the handicapped person in a marginal, half-alienated, half-tolerant, outsider's orientation to "the Philistine world of normals."[22] Gowman[23] nicely describes the tenor and style of this relationship and its possibilities for sharply disabusing normals of their stereotyped approaches to the handicapped. *Épater le bourgeois* behavior is often prominently associated with it, as is a certain strictly in-group license to lampoon and mock the handicap in a way which would be regarded as highly offensive were it to come from an uninitiated normal. Thus, a blind girl relates how a sighted friend sometimes chides her by calling her "a silly blink." A paraplegic tells of the old friend who tries to revive his flagging spirits by telling him not to act "like a helpless cripple." Unlike that based on over-normalization, the peculiar strength of this relationship is perhaps its very capacity to give expressive scope to the negative reality of the larger world of which it is inescapably a part while simultaneously removing itself from a primary identification with it.

Implications

Two, more general, implications seem worth drawing from this analysis.[24]

First, in studies which trace the process wherein an actor who deviates comes to be increasingly defined as a deviant (e.g., the pre-mental patient, the pre-alcoholic, the pre-juvenile delinquent), unusual prominence is given to the normalizing behavior of those close to him (spouse, parents, friends, etc.). The picture that emerges is one of these persons assuming nearly the whole burden — by rationalizing, denying and overlooking his offensive acts — of attempting to re-establish a socially acceptable relationship with him. He is depicted typically as compulsively wedded to his deviance and incapable or uninterested in making restitutive efforts of his own. Finally, following some critical act of his, normalization fails *in toto* and community agencies are called in to relieve the primary group of its unmanageable burden.

There is much about this picture that is doubtlessly true and consonant with the ascertainable facts as we later come to learn of them from family, friends, police, courts and social agencies. We may question, however, whether it is a wholly balanced picture and whether, given the situational biases of these informational sources, all of the relevant facts have had an

[22] Students of race relations will recognize in this a phenomenon closely akin to "inverse passing" as when a white becomes closely identified with Negroes and passes into a Negro subculture.

[23] Gowman, *op. cit.*

[24] I am indebted to Sheldon Messinger for his valuable comments in these connections.

equal chance to surface. The perspective developed here suggests that it may be useful to consider whether, and to what extent, the deviator himself is not also engaged, albeit ineffectively, in somehow trying to sustain a normal definition of his person. Were research to indicate that such is the case, we might then ask what it is about his reparative efforts and the situations in which they occur that, as contrasted with the subjects of this study, so often lead to failure and an exacerbation of the troublesome behavior. (We probably will never know, except inferentially by gross extrapolation, of the possibly many cases in which some such interactive process succeeds in favorably resolving the deviating behavior.) In other words, as against the simplistic model of a compulsive deviant and a futile normalizer we would propose one in which it is postulated that both are likely to become engaged in making corrective interactional efforts toward healing the breach. And, when such efforts fail, as they frequently do, it is as important in accounting for the failure to weigh the interactional dynamics and situational contexts of these efforts as it is the nature of the deviant acts and the actor.

Second, we would note that the interactional problems of the visibly handicapped are not so dissimilar from those which all of us confront, if only now and then and to a lesser degree. We too on occasion find ourselves in situations in which some uncamouflageable attribute of ours jars the activity and the expectations of our company. We too, if we wish to sustain — and, as is typically the case, our company wishes us to sustain — a fitting and valued representation of ourselves, will tacitly begin to explore with them ways of redressing, insulating and separating the discrepant attribute from ourselves.[25] Our predicament though is much less charged with awareness, more easily set to rights, than that of the visibly handicapped person and his company. But it is precisely this exaggeration of a common interactional predicament that affords us an added insight into the prerequisites and unwitting assumptions of sociable behavior in general. Put differently, it can be said that our understanding of a mechanism is often crude and incomplete until it breaks down and we try to repair it. Breakdown and repair of interaction is what many of the visibly handicapped experience constantly in their lives. In studying this with them we are also studying much about ourselves of which we were heretofore unaware.

[25] Goffman, "Embarrassment and Social Organization," *op. cit.*

17. Conditions of Successful Degradation Ceremonies

Harold Garfinkel [1]

Any communicative work between persons, whereby the public identity of an actor is transformed into something looked on as lower in the local scheme of social types, will be called a "status degradation ceremony." Some restrictions on this definition may increase its usefulness. The identities referred to must be "total" identities. That is, these identities must refer to persons as "motivational" types rather than as "behavioral" types,[2] not to what a person may be expected to have done or to do (in Parsons' term,[3] to his "performances") but to what the group holds to be the ultimate "grounds" or "reasons" for his performance.[4]

The grounds on which a participant achieves what for him is adequate understanding of why he or another acted as he did are not treated by him in a utilitarian manner. Rather, the correctness of an imputation is decided by the participant in accordance with socially valid and institutionally recommended standards of "preference." With reference to these standards, he makes the crucial distinctions between appearances and reality, truth and falsity, triviality and importance, accident and essence, coincidence and cause. Taken together, the grounds, as well as the behavior that the grounds make explicable as the other person's conduct, constitute a person's identity. Together, they constitute the other as a social object. Persons identified by means of the ultimate "reasons" for

Reprinted from *The American Journal of Sociology,* LXI (March, 1956), pp. 420–424, by permission of the University of Chicago Press. Copyright 1956 by the University of Chicago.

[1] Acknowledgment is gratefully made to Erving Goffman, National Institute of Mental Health, Bethesda, Maryland, and to Sheldon Messinger, Social Science Research Council pre-doctoral fellow, University of California, Los Angeles, for criticisms and editorial suggestions.

[2] These terms are borrowed from Alfred Schutz, "Common Sense and Scientific Interpretation of Human Action," *Philosophy and Phenomenological Research,* Vol. XIV, No. 1 (September, 1953).

[3] Talcott Parsons and Edward Shils, "Values, Motives, and Systems of Action," in Parsons and Shils (eds.), *Toward a General Theory of Action* (Cambridge: Harvard University Press, 1951).

[4] Cf. the writings of Kenneth Burke, particularly *Permanence and Change* (Los Altos, Calif.: Hermes Publication, 1954), and *A Grammar of Motives* (New York: Prentice-Hall, Inc., 1945).

their socially categorized and socially understood behavior will be said to be "totally" identified. The degradation ceremonies here discussed are those that are concerned with the alteration of total identities.

It is proposed that only in societies that are completely demoralized, will an observer be unable to find such ceremonies, since only in total anomie are the conditions of degradation ceremonies lacking. Max Scheler[5] argued that there is no society that does not provide in the very features of its organization the conditions sufficient for inducing shame. It will be treated here as axiomatic that there is no society whose social structure does not provide, in its routine features, the conditions of identity degradation. Just as the structural conditions of shame are universal to all societies by the very fact of their being organized, so the structural conditions of status degradation are universal to all societies. In this framework the critical question is not whether status degradation occurs or can occur within any given society. Instead, the question is: Starting from any state of a society's organization, what program of communicative tactics will get the work of status degradation done?

First of all, two questions will have to be decided, at least tentatively: *What are we referring to behaviorally when we propose the product of successful degradation work to be a changed total identity?* And *what are we to conceive the work of status degradation to have itself accomplished or to have assumed as the conditions of its success?*

I

Degradation ceremonies fall within the scope of the sociology of moral indignation. Moral indignation is a social affect. Roughly speaking, it is an instance of a class of feelings particular to the more or less organized ways that human beings develop as they live out their lives in one another's company. Shame, guilt, and boredom are further important instances of such affects.

Any affect has its behavioral paradigm. That of shame is found in the withdrawal and covering of the portion of the body that socially defines one's public appearance — prominently, in our society, the eyes and face. The paradigm of shame is found in the phrases that denote removal of the self from public view, i. e., removal from the regard of the publicly identified other: "I could have sunk through the floor; I wanted to run away and hide; I wanted the earth to open up and swallow me." The feeling of guilt finds its paradigm in the behavior of self-abnegation — disgust, the rejection of further contact with or withdrawal from, and the bodily and symbolic expulsion of the foreign body, as when we cough, blow, gag, vomit, spit, etc.

[5] Richard Hays Williams, "Scheler's Contributions to the Sociology of Affective Action, with Special Attention to the Problem of Shame," *Philosophy and Phenomenological Research*, Vol. II, No. 3 (March, 1942).

The paradigm of moral indignation is *public* denunciation. We publicly deliver the curse: "I call upon all men to bear witness that he is not as he appears but is otherwise and *in essence*[6] of a lower species."

The social affects serve various functions both for the person as well as for the collectivity. A prominent function of shame for the person is that of preserving the ego from further onslaughts by withdrawing entirely its contact with the outside. For the collectivity, shame is an "individuator." One experiences shame in his own time.

Moral indignation serves to effect the ritual destruction of the person denounced. Unlike shame, which does not bind persons together, moral indignation may reinforce group solidarity. In the market and in politics, a degradation ceremony must be counted as a secular form of communion. Structurally, a degradation ceremony bears close resemblance to ceremonies of investiture and elevation. How such a ceremony may bind persons to the collectivity we shall see when we take up the conditions of a successful denunciation. Our immediate question concerns the meaning of ritual destruction.

In the statement that moral indignation brings about the ritual destruction of the person being denounced, destruction is intended literally. The transformation of identities is the destruction of one social object and the constitution of another. The transformation does not involve the substitution of one identity for another, with the terms of the old one loitering about like the overlooked parts of a fresh assembly, any more than the woman we see in the department store window that turns out to be a dummy carries with it the possibilities of a woman. It is not that the old object has been overhauled; rather it is replaced by another. One declares, *"Now,* it was otherwise in the first place."

The work of the denunciation effects the recasting of the objective character of the perceived other: The other person becomes in the eyes of his condemners literally a different and *new* person. It is not that the new attributes are added to the old "nucleus." He is not changed, he is reconstituted. The former identity, at best, receives the accent of mere appearance. In the social calculus of reality representations and test, the former identity stands as accidental; the new identity is the "basic reality." What he is now is what, "after all," he was all along.[7]

The public denunciation effects such a transformation of essence by

[6] The man at whose hands a neighbor suffered death becomes a "murderer." The person who passes on information to enemies is really, i.e., "in essence," "in the first place," "all along," "in the final analysis," "originally," an informer.

[7] Two themes commonly stand out in the rhetoric of denunciation: (1) the irony between what the denounced appeared to be and what he is seen now really to be where the new motivational scheme is taken as the standard and (2) a re-examination and redefinition of origins of the denounced. For the sociological relevance of the relationship between concerns for essence and concerns for origins see particularly Kenneth Burke, *A Grammar of Motives.*

substituting another socially validated motivational scheme for that previously used to name and order the performances of the denounced. It is with reference to this substituted, socially validated motivational scheme as the essential grounds, i.e., *the first principles,* that his performances, past, present, and prospective, according to the witnesses, are to be properly and necessarily understood.[8] Through the interpretive work that respects this rule, the denounced person becomes in the eyes of the witnesses a different person.

II

How can one make a good denunciation?[9]

To be successful, the denunciation must redefine the situations of those that are witnesses to the denunciation work. The denouncer, the party to be denounced (let us call him the "perpetrator"), and the thing that is being blamed on the perpetrator (let us call it the "event") must be transformed as follows:[10]

1. Both event and perpetrator must be removed from the realm of their everyday character and be made to stand as "out of the ordinary."

[8] While constructions like "substantially a something" or "essentially a something" have been banished from the domain of scientific discourse, such constructions have prominent and honored places in the theories of motives, persons, and conduct that are employed in handling the affairs of daily life. Reasons can be given to justify the hypothesis that such constructions may be lost to a group's "terminology of motives" only if the relevance of socially sanctioned theories to practical problems is suspended. This can occur where interpersonal relations are trivial (such as during play) or, more interestingly, under severe demoralization of a system of activities. In such organizational states the frequency of status degradation is low.

[9] Because the paper is short, the risk must be run that, as a result of excluding certain considerations, the treated topics may appear exaggerated. It would be desirable, for example, to take account of the multitude of hedges that will be found against false denunciations; of the rights to denounce; of the differential apportionment of these rights, as well as the ways in which a claim, once staked out, may become a vested interest and may tie into the contests for economic and political advantage. Further, there are questions centering around the appropriate arenas of denunciation. For example, in our society the tribal council has fallen into secondary importance; among lay persons the denunciation has given way to the complaint to the authorities.

[10] These are the effects that the communicative tactics of the denouncer must be designed to accomplish. Put otherwise, in so far as the denouncer's tactics accomplish the reordering of the definitions of the stituation of the witnesses to

2. Both event and perpetrator must be placed within a scheme of preferences that shows the following properties:

A. The preferences must not be for event A over event B, but for event of *type A* over event of *type B.* The same typing must be accomplished for the perpetrator. Event and perpetrator must be defined as instances of a uniformity and must be treated as a uniformity throughout the work of the denunciation. The unique, never recurring character of the event or perpetrator should be lost. Similarly, any sense of accident, coincidence, indeterminism, chance, or monetary occurrence must not merely be minimized. Ideally, such measures should be inconceivable; at least they should be made false.

B. The witnesses must appreciate the characteristics of the typed person and event by referring the type to a dialectical counterpart. Ideally, the witnesses should not be able to contemplate the features of the denounced person without reference to the counterconception, as the profanity of an occurrence or a desire or a character trait, for example, is clarified by the references it bears to its opposite, the sacred. The features of the mad-dog murderer reverse the features of the peaceful citizen. The confessions of the Red can be read to teach the meanings of patriotism. There are many contrasts available, and any aggregate of witnesses this side of a complete war of each against all will have a plethora of such schemata for effecting a "familiar," "natural," "proper," ordering of motives, qualities, and other events.

From such contrasts, the following is to be learned. If the denunciation is to take effect, the scheme must not be one in which the witness is allowed to elect the preferred. Rather, the alternatives must be such that the preferred is morally required. Matters must be so arranged that the validity of his choice, its justification, is maintained by the fact that he makes it.[11] The scheme of alternatives must be such as to place constraints upon his making a selection "for a purpose." Nor will the denunciation succeed if the witness is free to look beyond the fact that he makes the selection for evidence that the correct alternative has been chosen, as, for example, by the test of empirical consequences of the choice. The alternatives must be such that, in "choosing," he takes it for granted and beyond any motive for doubt that not choosing can mean only preference for its opposite.

3. The denouncer must so identify himself to the witnesses that during the denunciation they regard him not as a private but as a publicly known

---

the denunciatory performances, the denouncer will have succeeded in effecting the transformation of the public identity of his victim. The list of conditions of this degrading effect are the determinants of the effect. Viewed in the scheme of a project to be rationally pursued, they are the adequate means. One would have to choose one's tactics for their efficiency in accomplishing these effects.

[11] Cf. Gregory Bateson and Jurgen Ruesch, *Communication: The Social Matrix of Psychiatry* (New York: W W Norton & Co., 1951), pp. 212-27.

person. He must not portray himself as acting according to his personal, unique experiences. He must rather be regarded as acting in his capacity as a public figure, drawing upon communally entertained and verified experience. He must act as a bona fide participant in the tribal relationships to which the witnesses subscribe. What he says must not be regarded as true for him alone, not even in the sense that it can be regarded by denouncer and witnesses as matters upon which they can become agreed. In no case, except in a most ironical sense, can the convention of true-for-reasonable-men be invoked. What the denouncer says must be regarded by the witnesses as true on the grounds of a socially employed metaphysics whereby witnesses assume that witnesses and denouncer are alike in essence.[12]

4. The denouncer must make the dignity of the supra-personal values of the tribe salient and accessible to view, and his denunciation must be delivered in their name.

5. The denouncer must arrange to be invested with the right to speak in the name of these ultimate values. The success of the denunciation will be undermined if, for his authority to denounce, the denouncer invokes the personal interests that he may have acquired by virtue of the wrong done to him or someone else. He must rather use the wrong he has suffered as a tribal member to invoke the authority to speak in the name of these ultimate values.

6. The denouncer must get himself so defined by the witnesses that they locate him as a supporter of these values.

7. Not only must the denouncer fix his distance from the person being denounced, but the witnesses must be made to experience their distance from him also.

8. Finally, the denounced person must be ritually separated from a place in the legitimate order, i.e., he must be defined as standing at a place opposed to it. He must be placed "outside," he must be made "strange."

These are the conditions that must be fulfilled for a successful denunciation. If they are absent, the denunciation will fail. Regardless of the situation when the denouncer enters, if he is to succeed in degrading the other man, it is necessary to introduce these features.[13]

[12] For bona fide members it is not that these are the grounds upon which we are agreed but upon which we are *alike*, consubstantial, in origin the same.

[13] Neither of the problems of possible communicative or organizational conditions of their effectiveness have been treated here in systematic fashion. However, the problem of communicative tactics in degradation ceremonies is set in the light of systematically related conceptions. These conceptions may be listed in the following statements:

1. The definition of the situation of the witnesses (for ease of discourse we shall use the letter *S*) always bears a time qualification.

2. The S at t_2 is a function of the S at t_1. This function is described as an operator that transforms the S at t_1.

Not all degradation ceremonies are carried on in accordance with publicly prescribed and publicly validated measures. Quarrels which seek the humiliation of the opponent through personal invective may achieve degrading on a limited scale. Comparatively few persons at a time enter into this form of communion, few benefit from it, and the fact of participation does not give the witness a definition of the other that is standardized beyond the particular group or scene of its occurrence.

The devices for effecting degradation vary in the feature and effectiveness according to the organization and operation of the system of action in which they occur. In our society the arena of degradation—whose product, the redefined person, enjoys the widest transferability between groups—has been rationalized, at least as to the institutional measures for carrying it out. The court and its officers have something like a fair monopoly over such ceremonies, and there they have become an occupational routine. This is to be contrasted with degradation undertaken as an immediate kinship and tribal obligation and carried out by those who, unlike our professional degraders in the law courts, acquire both right and obligation to engage in it through being themselves the injured parties or kin to the injured parties.

Factors conditioning the effectiveness of degradation tactics are provided in the organization and operation of the system of action within which the degradation occurs. For example, timing rules that provide for serial or reciprocal "conversations" would have much to do with the kinds of tactics that one might be best advised to use. The tactics advisable for an accused who can answer the charge as soon as it is made are in contrast with those recommended for one who had to wait out the denunciation before

3. The operator is conceived as communicative work.

4. For a successful denunciation, it is required that the S at t_2 show specific properties. These have been specified previously.

5. The task of the denouncer is to alter the *S's* of the witnesses so that these *S's* will show the specified properties.

6. The "rationality" of the denouncer's tactics, i.e., their adequacy as a means for effecting the set of transformations necessary for effecting the identity transformation, is decided by the rule that the organizational and operational properties of the communicative net (the social system) are determinative of the size of the discrepancy between an intended and an actual effect of the communicative work. Put otherwise, the question is not that of the temporal origin of the situation but always and only how it is altered over time. The view is recommended that the definition of the situation at time 2 is a function of the definition at time 1 where this function consists of the communicative work conceived as a set of operations whereby the altered situation at time 1 is the situation at time 2. In strategy terms the function consists of the program of procedures that a denouncer should follow to effect the change of state S_{t1} to S_{t2}. In this paper S_{t1} is treated as an unspecified state.

replying. Face-to-face contact is a different situation from that wherein the denunciation and reply are conducted by radio and newspaper. Whether the denunciation must be accomplished on a single occasion or is to be carried out over a sequence of "tries," factors like the territorial arrangements and movements of persons at the scene of the denunciation, the numbers of persons involved as accused, degraders, and witnesses, status claims of the contenders, prestige and power allocations among participants, all should influence the outcome.

In short, the factors that condition the success of the work of degradation are those that we point to when we conceive the actions of a number of persons as group-governed. Only some of the more obvious structural variables that may be expected to serve as predicters of the characteristics of denunciatory communicative tactics have been mentioned. They tell us not only how to construct an effective denunciation but also how to render denunciation useless.

Selected Bibliography
Part II, Society

Coutu, Walter, "Role-playing *vs.* Role Taking: An Appeal for Clarification," *American Sociological Review,* 16 (April 1951), pp. 180-187.
Precursor of Turner's paper, listed below. Shows the need for a clearer distinction between two useful and closely related concepts.

Davis, Fred, "The Cab Driver and His Fare: Facets of a Fleeting Relationship," *American Journal of Sociology,* 65 (September 1959), pp. 158-165.
Participant-observation study of a special kind of human encounter.

Garfinkel, Harold, "Studies of the Routine Grounds of Everyday Activities," *Social Problems,* 11 (Winter 1964), pp. 225-250.
Inspired by Alfred Schuetz's phenomenology. An insightful delineation of taken-for-granted elements in everyday human relationships.

Goffman, Erving, *Asylums* (Garden City: Doubleday and Company, 1961), pp. 3-24.
Description of "total institutions" (prisons, mental hospitals, convents, orphanages, and other societies-in-miniature) and the kinds of interaction typifying them.

Goffman, Erving, "On Face-Work: An Analysis of Ritual Elements in Social Interaction," *Psychiatry,* 18 (August 1955), pp. 213-231.
Discusses the elaborate social rituals that function primarily to reduce the likelihood of invalidation of self-image, particularly in casual contacts.

Gross, Edward and Stone, Gregory P., "Embarrassment and the Analysis of Role Requirements," *American Journal of Sociology,* 60 (July 1964), pp. 1-15.
Study of 1,000 instances of recalled embarrassment, revealing some of the major sociological functions of deliberate embarrassment.

Mead, George Herbert, *Mind, Self, and Society* (Chicago: University of Chicago Press, 1934), pp. 260-328.
Mead here explores the complex relationship between society and the individual.

Riezler, Kurt, "Comment on the Social Psychology of Shame," *American Journal of Sociology,* 48 (January 1943), pp. 457-465.
Insightful speculations about a common human sentiment. A precursor of articles by Goffman and by Gross and Stone on embarrassment.

Schatzman, Leonard and Strauss, Anselm, "Social Class and Modes of Communication," *American Journal of Sociology,* 60 (January 1955), pp. 329-338.
Observed differences in role-taking and standpoints revealed by interviews with lower-class and middle-class persons.

Stryker, Sheldon, "Relationships of Married Offspring and Parent: A Test of Mead's Theory," *American Journal of Sociology,* 62 (November 1956), pp. 308-319.
Empirical tests of hypotheses on role-taking drawn from propositions of Mead.

Swanson, Guy E., "On Explanations of Social Interaction," *Sociometry,* 28 (June 1965), pp. 101-123.
A lengthy and difficult but rewarding analysis of the assumptions underlying various conceptions of the nature of human interaction.

Turner, Ralph H., "Role-Taking, Role Standpoint, and Reference-Group Behavior," *American Journal of Sociology,* 61 (January 1956), pp. 316-328.
Clarification of certain important social psychological concepts.

Part III. ❧ Self

During the latter part of the nineteenth century, the concept of the self received considerable attention by philosophers and psychologists. To William James, Josiah Royce, James Mark Baldwin, and others, the development and the functioning of the self were central concerns in the study of social life. With the rise of Watsonian behaviorism, however, the concept was rejected as subjective and unscientific. In turn, behaviorism has been criticized for neglecting important, though covert, aspects of human behavior.

Mead's "social behaviorism" stressed the processes by which the individual becomes aware of, and learns to guide, his own behavior. The article by Meltzer summarizing Mead's approach has discussed the major contributions and problems of his usage of the concept of self. The ambiguity in Mead's work has been paralleled by recent divergences in definitions and methods of empirical study of the concept.

Among current symbolic interactionists, those who see the self as a dynamic process of viewing and responding to one's own behavior emphasize participant-observation, interviews, and Cooley's "sympathetic introspection" in their studies. Those who see the self as a structure of internalized roles stress the use of such devices as the "Who Am I Test." Finally, some investigators, conceiving of the self as a set of attitudes or evaluations, have used self-rating scales in their research.

The first two selections in this section deal with two distinct facets of the self — object and actor. The selection from Cooley's work describes how the individual comes to experience himself as an object. Through the eyes and the attitudes of others, each person learns to "see" and to evaluate his own appearance, attitudes, and behavior. It is in this sense, that the self is sometimes defined as "the individual as known to the individual." Cooley's depiction of the "looking-glass self" is in close accordance with his suggested method for the acquisition of social knowledge (see number 4, Part I).

The Goffman article is concerned with the individual as subject rather than object. Here the self is considered in its active aspect. The individual is capable not only of viewing his own behavior but also of directing and guiding this behavior, and of shaping the images of him available to others. In explaining his view of the self, Goffman draws upon the drama, literature, and observation. His perspective is dramaturgical, interpreting the individual as an actor presenting a theatrical type of performance.

Kinch seeks to clarify self theory by formal or axiomatic logic. He states the basic postulates of the theory, then deduces their logical consequences. Because it is a recent formulation, its heuristic value cannot be certain at this time. However, some of its deductions correspond to the findings of prior researches.

The theoretical distinction between the "I" and the "Me" receives critical scrutiny in the article by Kolb. Although these concepts have been analytically useful, Kolb points out their lack of clarity. The absence of empirical research using these concepts may stem from their ambiguity.

Bain explores the relationship of society and the self through the medium of language. His article replicates Cooley's earlier research and findings, which support the claim that the child learns to "know" others before himself. Since the author has been a life-long advocate of scientific objectivity and his present study is based upon careful observation and recording of data, his findings are especially noteworthy.

Research findings based upon the Twenty Statements Test are described in the next two articles. Couch, trained at Iowa, presents empirical confirmation of the influence of family relationships. He uses the Twenty Statements Test to explore the relationship between family roles and individual self-images. His study is an example of the kinds of research suggested by the first of the selections by Stryker in Part V.

Mulford and Salisbury, former students of Kuhn, report the findings of a state-wide sample survey of adult self-conceptions. Their data point up the importance of work and family roles in the process of self-identification.

Experimental techniques are used by Videbeck to test three hypotheses concerning self-conceptions. By varying the reactions of others ("experts") under controlled conditions, he has been able to assess their influence.

The concluding article, by Merrill, represents the interpretative, humanistic mode of inquiry. From the perspective of the sociology of literature, Merrill considers the interactionist conception of the self in Stendhal's novel *The Red and The Black.* Although he notes that literary insights are not empirical verification, they are a datum of scientific study and a source of ideas and understanding.

18. Looking-Glass Self

Charles Horton Cooley

In a very large and interesting class of cases the social reference takes the form of a somewhat definite imagination of how one's self — that is any idea he appropriates — appears in a particular mind, and the kind of self-feeling one has is determined by the attitude toward this attributed to that other mind. A social self of this sort might be called the reflected or looking-glass self:

"Each to each a looking-glass
Reflects the other that doth pass."

As we see our face, figure, and dress in the glass, and are interested in them because they are ours, and pleased or otherwise with them according as they do or do not answer to what we should like them to be; so in imagination we perceive in another's mind some thought of our appearance, manners, aims, deeds, character, friends, and so on, and are variously affected by it.

A self-idea of this sort seems to have three principal elements: the imagination of our appearance to the other person; the imagination of his judgment of that appearance, and some sort of self-feeling, such as pride or mortification. The comparison with a looking-glass hardly suggests the second element, the imagined judgment, which is quite essential. The thing that moves us to pride or shame is not the mere mechanical reflection of ourselves, but an imputed sentiment, the imagined effect of this reflection upon another's mind. This is evident from the fact that the character and weight of that other, in whose mind we see ourselves, makes all the difference with our feeling. We are ashamed to seem evasive in the presence of a straightforward man, cowardly in the presence of a brave one, gross in the eyes of a refined one, and so on. We always imagine, and in imagining share, the judgments of the other mind. A man will boast to one person of an action — say some sharp transaction in trade — which he would be ashamed to own to another.

. . .

The process by which self-feeling of the looking-glass sort develops in children may be followed without much difficulty. Studying the movements of others as closely as they do they soon see a connection between their own acts and changes in those movements; that is, they perceive their own influence or power over persons. The child appropriates the visible actions of his parent or nurse, over which he finds he has some control, in quite the same way as he appropriates one of his own members or a plaything, and he will try to do things with this new possession, just as he will with his hand or his rattle. A girl six months old will attempt in the most evident and deliberate manner to attract attention to herself, to set going by her actions some of those movements of other persons that she has appropriated. She has tasted the joy of being a cause, of exerting social power, and wishes more of it. She will tug at her mother's skirts, wriggle, gurgle, stretch out her arms, etc., all the time watching for the hoped-for effect. These performances often give the child, even at this age, an appearance of what is called affectation, that is, she seems to be unduly preoccupied with what other people think of her. Affectation, at any age, exists when the passion to influence others seems to overbalance the established character and give it an obvious twist or pose. It is instructive to find that even Darwin was, in his childhood, capable of departing from truth for the sake of making an impression. "For instance," he says in his autobiography, "I once gathered much valuable fruit from my father's trees and hid it in the shrubbery, and then ran in breathless haste to spread the news that I had discovered a hoard of stolen fruit."[1]

The young performer soon learns to be different things to different people, showing that he begins to apprehend personality and to foresee its operation. If the mother or nurse is more tender than just, she will almost certainly be "worked" by systematic weeping. It is a matter of common observation that children often behave worse with their mother than with other and less sympathetic people. Of the new persons that a child sees, it is evident that some make a strong impression and awaken a desire to interest and please them, while others are indifferent or repugnant. Sometimes the reason can be perceived or guessed, sometimes not; but the fact of selective interest, admiration, prestige, is obvious before the end of the second year. By that time a child already cares much for the reflection of himself upon one personality and little for that upon another. Moreover, he soon claims intimate and tractable persons as *mine,* classes them among his other possessions, and maintains his ownership against all comers. M., at three years of age, vigorously resented R.'s claim upon their mother. The latter was "*my* mamma," whenever the point was raised.

Strong joy and grief depend upon the treatment this rudimentary social self receives. In the case of M. I noticed as early as the fourth month a "hurt" way of crying which seemed to indicate a sense of personal slight.

[1] *Life and Letters of Charles Darwin,* by F. Darwin, p. 27.

It was quite different from the cry of pain or that of anger, but seemed about the same as the cry of fright. The slightest tone of reproof would produce it. On the other hand, if people took notice and laughed and encouraged, she was hilarious. At about fifteen months old she had become "a perfect little actress," seeming to live largely in imaginations of her effect upon other people. She constantly and obviously laid traps for attention, and looked abashed or wept at any signs of disapproval or indifference. At times it would seem as if she could not get over these repulses, but would cry long in a grieved way, refusing to be comforted. If she hit upon any little trick that made people laugh she would be sure to repeat it, laughing loudly and affectedly in imitation. She had quite a repertory of these small performances, which she would display to a sympathetic audience, or even try upon strangers. I have seen her at sixteen months, when R. refused to give her the scissors, sit down and make-believe cry, putting up her under lip and snuffling, meanwhile looking up now and then to see what effect she was producing.[2]

In such phenomena we have plainly enough, it seems to me, the germ of personal ambition of every sort. Imagination co-operating with instinctive self-feeling has already created a social "I," and this has become a principal object of interest and endeavor.

Progress from this point is chiefly in the way of a greater definiteness, fulness, and inwardness in the imagination of the other's state of mind. A little child thinks of and tries to elicit certain visible or audible phenomena, and does not go back of them; but what a grown-up person desires to produce in others is an internal, invisible condition which his own richer experience enables him to imagine, and of which expression is only the sign. Even adults, however, make no separation between what other people think and the visible expression of that thought. They imagine the whole thing at once, and their idea differs from that of a child chiefly in the comparative richness and complexity of the elements that accompany and interpret the visible or audible sign. There is also a progress from the naive to the subtle in socially self-assertive action. A child obviously and simply, at first, does things for effect. Later there is an endeavor to suppress the appearance of doing so; affection, indifference, contempt, etc., are simulated to hide the real wish to affect the self-image. It is perceived that an obvious seeking after good opinion is weak and disagreeable.

[2] This sort of thing is very familiar to observers of children. See, for instance, Miss Shinn's Notes on the Development of a Child, p. 153.

19. Presentation of Self to Others

Erving Goffman

When an individual enters the presence of others, they commonly seek to acquire information about him or to bring into play information about him already possessed. They will be interested in his general socio-economic status, his conception of self, his attitude toward them, his competence, his trustworthiness, etc. Although some of this information seems to be sought almost as an end in itself, there are usually quite practical reasons for acquiring it. Information about the individual helps to define the situation, enabling others to know in advance what he will expect of them and what they may expect of him. Informed in these ways, the others will know how best to act in order to call forth a desired response from him.

For those present, many sources of information become accessible and many carriers (or "sign-vehicles") become available for conveying this information. If unacquainted with the individual, observers can glean clues from his conduct and appearance which allow them to apply their previous experience with individuals roughly similar to the one before them or, more important, to apply untested stereotypes to him. They can also assume from past experience that only individuals of a particular kind are likely to be found in a given social setting. They can rely on what the individual says about himself or on documentary evidence he provides as to who and what he is. If they know, or know of, the individual by virtue of experience prior to the interaction, the can rely on assumptions as to the persistence and generality of psychological traits as a means of predicting his present and future behavior.

However, during the period in which the individual is in the immediate presence of the others, few events may occur which directly provide the others with the conclusive information they will need if they are to direct wisely their own activity. Many crucial facts lie beyond the time and place of interaction or lie concealed within it. For example, the "true" or "real" attitudes, beliefs, and emotions of the individual can be ascertained only indirectly, through his avowals or through what appears to be involuntary expressive behavior. Similarly, if the individual offers the others a product or service, they will often find that during the interaction there will be no time and place immediately available for eating the pudding that the proof can be found in. They will be forced to accept some events as conventional or natural signs of something not directly available to the senses. In Ichheiser's terms,[1] the individual will have to act so that he intentionally or unintentionally *expresses* himself, and the others will in turn have to be *impressed* in some way by him.

The expressiveness of the individual (and therefore his capacity to give impressions) appears to involve two radically different kinds of sign activity: the expression that he *gives,* and the expression that he *gives off.* The first involves verbal symbols or their substitutes which he uses admittedly and solely to convey the information that he and the others are known to attach to these symbols. This is communication in the traditional and narrow sense. The second involves a wide range of action that others can treat as symptomatic of the actor, the expectation being that the action was performed for reasons other than the information conveyed in this way. As we shall have to see, this distinction has an only initial validity. The individual does of course intentionally convey misinformation by means of both of these types of communication, the first involving deceit, the second feigning.

Taking communication in both its narrow and broad sense, one finds that when the individual is in the immediate presence of others, his activity will have a promissory character. The others are likely to find that they must accept the individual on faith, offering him a just return while he is present before them in exchange for something whose true value will not be established until after he has left their presence. (Of course, the others also live by inference in their dealings with the physical world, but it is only in the world of social interaction that the objects about which they make inferences will purposely facilitate and hinder this inferential process.) The security that they justifiably feel in making inferences about the individual will vary, of course, depending on such factors as the amount of information they already possess about him, but no amount of such past evidence can entirely obviate the necessity of acting on the basis of inferences. As William I. Thomas suggested:

> It is also highly important for us to realize that we do not as a matter of fact lead our lives, make our decisions, and reach our goals in everyday life either statistically or scientifically. We live by inference. I am, let us say, your guest. You do not know, you cannot determine scientifically, that I will not steal your money or your spoons. But inferentially I will not, and inferentially you have me as a guest.[2]

[1] Gustav Ichheiser, "Misunderstandings in Human Relations," Supplement to *The American Journal of Sociology.* LV (September, 1949), pp. 6-7.

[2] Quoted in E. H. Volkart, editor, *Social Behavior and Personality.* Contributions of W. I. Thomas to Theory and Social Research (New York: Social Science Research Council, 1951), p. 5.

Let us now turn from the others to the point of view of the individual who presents himself before them. He may wish them to think highly of him, or to think that he thinks highly of them, or to perceive how in fact he feels toward them, or to obtain no clear-cut impression; he may wish to ensure sufficient harmony so that the interaction can be sustained, or to defraud, get rid of, confuse, mislead, antagonize, or insult them. Regardless of the particular objective which the individual has in mind and of his motive for having this objective, it will be in his interests to control the conduct of the others, especially their responsive treatment of him.[3] This control is achieved largely by influencing the definition of the situation which the others come to formulate, and he can influence this definition by expressing himself in such a way as to give them the kind of impression that will lead them to act voluntarily in accordance with his own plan. Thus, when an individual appears in the presence of others, there will usually be some reason for him to mobilize his activity so that it will convey an impression to others which it is in his interests to convey. Since a girl's dormitory mates will glean evidence of her popularity from the calls she receives on the phone, we can suspect that some girls will arrange for calls to be made, and Willard Waller's finding can be anticipated:

> It has been reported by many observers that a girl who is called to the telephone in the dormitories will often allow herself to be called several times, in order to give all the other girls ample opportunity to hear her paged.[4]

Of the two kinds of communication — expressions given and expressions given off — this report will be primarily concerned with the latter, with the more theatrical and contextual kind, the non-verbal, presumably unintentional kind, whether this communication be purposely engineered or not. As an example of what we must try to examine, I would like to cite at length a novelistic incident in which Preedy, a vacationing Englishman, makes his first appearance on the beach of his summer hotel in Spain:

> But in any case he took care to avoid catching anyone's eye. First of all, he had to make it clear to those potential companions of his holiday

[3] Here I owe much to an unpublished paper by Tom Burns of the University of Edinburgh. He presents the argument that in all interaction a basic underlying theme is the desire of each participant to guide and control the responses made by the others present. A similar argument has been advanced by Jay Haley in a recent unpublished paper, but in regard to a special kind of control, that having to do with defining the nature of the relationship of those involved in the interaction.

[4] Willard Waller, "The Rating and Dating Complex," *American Sociological Review,* II, p. 730.

> that they were of no concern to him whatsoever. He stared through them, round them, over them — eyes lost in space. The beach might have been empty. If by chance a ball was thrown his way, he looked surprised; then let a smile of amusement lighten his face (Kindly Preedy), looked round dazed to see that there *were* people on the beach, tossed it back with a smile to himself and not a smile *at* the people, and then resumed carelessly his nonchalant survey of space.
>
> But it was time to institute a little parade, the parade of the Ideal Preedy. By devious handlings he gave any who wanted to look a chance to see the title of his book — a Spanish translation of Homer, classic thus, but not daring, cosmopolitan too — and then gathered together his beach-wrap and bag into a neat sand-resistant pile (Methodical and Sensible Preedy), rose slowly to stretch at ease his huge frame (Big-Cat Preedy), and tossed aside his sandals (Carefree Preedy, after all).
>
> The marriage of Preedy and the sea! There were alternative rituals. The first involved the stroll that turns into a run and a dive straight into the water, thereafter smoothing into a strong splashless crawl towards the horizon. But of course not really to the horizon. Quite suddenly he would turn on to his back and thrash great white splashes with his legs, somehow thus showing that he could have swum further had he wanted to, and then would stand up a quarter out of water for all to see who it was.
>
> The alternative course was simpler, it avoided the cold-water shock and it avoided the risk of appearing too high-spirited. The point was to appear to be so used to the sea, the Mediterranean, and this particular beach, that one might as well be in the sea as out of it. It involved a slow stroll down and into the edge of the water-not even noticing his toes were wet, land and water all the same to *him!*-with his eyes up at the sky gravely surveying portents, invisible to others, of the weather (Local Fisherman Preedy).[5]

The novelist means us to see that Preedy is improperly concerned with the extensive impressions he feels his sheer bodily action is giving off to those around him. We can malign Preedy further by assuming that he has acted merely in order to give a particular impression, that this is a false impression, and that the others present receive either no impression at all, or worse still, the impression that Preedy is affectedly trying to cause them to receive this particular impression. But the important point for us here is that the kind of impression Preedy thinks he is making is in fact the kind of impression that others correctly and incorrectly glean from someone in their midst.

I have said that when an individual appears before others his actions will influence the definition of the situation which they come to have. Some-

[5] William Sansom, *A Contest of Ladies* (London: Hogarth, 1956), pp. 230-32.

times the individual will act in a thoroughly calculating manner, expressing himself in a given way solely in order to give the kind of impression to others that is likely to evoke from them a specific response he is concerned to obtain. Sometimes the individual will be calculating in his activity but be relatively unaware that this is the case. Sometimes he will intentionally and consciously express himself in a particular way, but chiefly because the tradition of his group or social status require this kind of expression and not because of any particular response (other than vague acceptance or approval) that is likely to be evoked from those impressed by the expression. Sometimes the traditions of an individual's role will lead him to give a well-designed impression of a particular kind and yet he may be neither consciously nor unconsciously disposed to create such an impression. The others, in their turn, may be suitably impressed by the individual's efforts to convey something, or may misunderstand the situation and come to conclusions that are warranted neither by the individual's intent nor by the facts. In any case, in so far as the others act *as if* the individual had conveyed a particular impression, we may take a functional or pragmatic view and say that the individual has "effectively" projected a given definition of the situation and "effectively" fostered the understanding that a given state of affairs obtains.

There is one aspect of the others' response that bears special comment here. Knowing that the individual is likely to present himself in a light that is favorable to him, the others may divide what they witness into two parts; a part that is relatively easy for the individual to manipulate at will, being chiefly his verbal assertions, and a part in regard to which he seems to have little concern or control, being chiefly derived from the expressions he gives off. The others may then use what are considered to be the ungovernable aspects of his expressive behavior as a check upon the validity of what is conveyed by the governable aspects. In this a fundamental asymmetry is demonstrated in the communication process, the individual presumably being aware of only one stream of his communication, the witnesses of this stream and one other. For example, in Shetland Isle one crofter's wife, in serving native dishes to a visitor from the mainland of Britain, would listen with a polite smile to his polite claims of liking what he was eating; at the same time she would take note of the rapidity with which the visitor lifted his fork or spoon to his mouth, the eagerness with which he passed food into his mouth, and the gusto expressed in chewing the food, using these signs as a check on the stated feelings of the eater. The same woman, in order to discover what one acquaintance (A) "actually" thought of another acquaintance (B), would wait until B was in the presence of A but engaged in conversation with still another person (C). She would then covertly examine the facial expressions of A as he regarded B in conversation with C. Not being in conversation with B, and not being directly observed by him, A would sometimes relax usual constraints and tactful deceptions, and freely express what he was "actually" feeling about B. This

Shetlander, in short, would observe the unobserved observer.

Now given the fact that others are likely to check up on the more controllable aspects of behavior by means of the less controllable, one can expect that sometimes the individual will try to exploit this very possibility, guiding the impression he makes through behavior felt to be reliably informing.[6] For example, in gaining admission to a tight social circle, the participant observer may not only wear an accepting look while listening to an informant, but may also be careful to wear the same look when observing the informant talking to others, observers of the observer will then not as easily discover where he actually stands. A specific illustration may be cited from Shetland Isle. When a neighbor dropped in to have a cup of tea, he would ordinarily wear at least a hint of an expectant warm smile as he passed through the door into the cottage. Since lack of physical obstructions outside the cottage and lack of light within it usually made it possible to observe the visitor unobserved as he approached the house, islanders sometimes took pleasure in watching the visitor drop whatever expression he was manifesting and replace it with a sociable one just before reaching the door. However, some visitors, in appreciating that this examination was occurring, would blindly adopt a social face a long distance from the house, thus ensuring the projection of a constant image.

This kind of control upon the part of the individual reinstates the symmetry of the communication process, and sets the stage for a kind of information game — a potentially infinite cycle of concealment, discovery, false revelation, and rediscovery. It should be added that since the others are likely to be relatively unsuspicious of the presumably unguided aspect of the individual's conduct, he can gain much by controlling it. The others of course may sense that the individual is manipulating the presumably spontaneous aspects of his behavior, and seek in this very act of manipulation some shading of conduct that the individual has not managed to control. This again provides a check upon the individual's behavior, this time his presumably uncalculated behavior, thus re-establishing the asymmetry of the communication process. Here I would like only to add the suggestion that the arts of piercing an individual's effort at calculated unintentionality seem better developed than our capacity to manipulate our own behavior, so that regardless of how many steps have occurred in the information game, the witness is likely to have the advantage over the actor, and the initial asymmetry of the communication process is likely to be retained.

When we allow that the individual projects a definition of the situation when he appears before others, we must also see that the others, however passive their role may seem to be, will themselves effectively project a

[6] The widely read and rather sound writings of Stephen Potter are concerned in part with signs that can be engineered to give a shrewd observer the apparently incidental cues he needs to discover concealed virtues the gamesman does not in fact possess.

definition of the situation by virtue of their response to the individual and by virtue of any lines of action they initiate to him. Ordinarily the definitions of the situation projected by the several different participants are sufficiently attuned to one another so that open contradiction will not occur. I do not mean that there will be the kind of consensus that arises when each individual present candidly expresses what he really feels and honestly agrees with the expressed feelings of the others present. This kind of harmony is an optimistic ideal and in any case not necessary for the smooth working of society. Rather, each participant is expected to suppress his immediate heartfelt feelings, conveying a view of the situation which he feels the others will be able to find at least temporarily acceptable. The maintenance of this surface of agreement, this veneer of consensus, is facilitated by each participant concealing his own wants behind statements which assert values to which everyone present feels obliged to give lip service. Further, there is usually a kind of division of definitional labor. Each participant is allowed to establish the tentative official ruling regarding matters which are vital to him but not immediately important to others, e.g., the rationalizations and justifications by which he accounts for his past activity. In exchange for this courtesy he remains silent or non-committal on matters important to others but not immediately important to him. We have then a kind of interactional *modus vivendi*. Together the participants contribute to a single over-all definition of the situation which involves not so much a real agreement as to what exists but rather a real agreement as to whose claims concerning what issues will be temporarily honored. Real agreement will also exist concerning the desirability of avoiding an open conflict of definitions of the situation.[7] I will refer to this level of agreement as a "working consensus." It is to be understood that the working consensus established in one interaction setting will be quite different in content from the working consensus established in a different type of setting. Thus, between two friends at lunch, a reciprocal show of affection, respect, and concern for the other is maintained. In service occupations, on the other hand, the specialist often maintains an image of disinterested involvement in the problem of the client, while the client responds with a show of respect for the competence and integrity of the specialist. Regardless of such differences in content, how-

[7] An interaction can be purposely set up as a time and place for voicing differences in opinion, but in such cases participants must be careful to agree not to disagree on the proper tone of voice, vocabulary, and degree of seriousness in which all arguments are to be phrased, and upon the mutual respect which disagreeing participants must carefully continue to express toward one another. This debaters' or academic definition of the situation may also be invoked suddenly and judiciously as a way of translating a serious conflict of views into one that can be handled within a framework acceptable to all present.

working consensus

ever, the general form of these working arrangements is the same.

In noting the tendency for a participant to accept the definitional claims made by the others present, we can appreciate the crucial importance of the information that the individual *initially* possesses or acquires concerning his fellow participants, for it is on the basis of this initial information that the individual starts to define the situation and starts to build up lines of responsive action. The individual's initial projection commits him to what he is proposing to be and requires him to drop all pretenses of being other things. As the interaction among the participants progresses, additions and modifications in this initial informational state will of course occur, but it is essential that these later developments be related without contradiction to, and even built up from, the initial positions taken by the several participants. It would seem that an individual can more easily make a choice as to what line of treatment to demand from and extend to the others present at the beginning of an encounter than he can alter the line of treatment that is being pursued once the interaction is underway.

In everyday life, of course, there is a clear understanding that first impressions are important. Thus, the work adjustment of those in service occupations will often hinge upon a capacity to seize and hold the initiative in the service relation, a capacity that will require subtle agressiveness on the part of the server when he is of lower socio-economic status than his client. W. F. Whyte suggests the waitress as an example:

> The first point that stands out is that the waitress who bears up under pressure does not simply respond to her customers. She acts with some skill to control their behavior. The first question to ask when we look at the customer relationship is, "Does the waitress get the jump on the customer, or does the customer get the jump on the waitress?" The skilled waitress realizes the crucial nature of this question...
>
> The skilled waitress tackles the customer with confidence and without hesitation. For example, she may find that a new customer has seated himself before she could clear off the dirty dishes and change the cloth. He is now leaning on the table studying the menu. She greets him, says, "May I change the cover, please?" and, without waiting for an answer, takes his menu away from him so that he moves back from the table, and she goes about her work. The relationship is handled politely but firmly, and there is never any question as to who is in charge.[8]

When the interaction that is initiated by "first impressions" is itself merely the initial interaction in an extended series of interactions involving the

[8] W. F. Whyte, "When Workers and Customers Meet", Chap. VII, *Industry and Society,* ed. W. F. Whyte (New York: McGraw-Hill, 1946), pp. 132-33.

same participants, we speak of "getting off on the right foot" and feel that it is crucial that we do so. Thus, one learns that some teachers take the following view:

> You can't ever let them get the upper hand on you or you're through. So I start out tough. The first day I get a new class in, I let them know who's boss... You've got to start off tough, then you can ease up as you go along. If you start out easy-going, when you try to get tough, they'll just look at you and laugh.[9]

Similarly, attendants in mental institutions may feel that if the new patient is sharply put in his place the first day on the ward and made to see who is boss, much future difficulty will be prevented.[10]

Given the fact that the individual effectively projects a definition of the situation when he enters the presence of others, we can assume that events may occur within the interaction which contradict, discredit, or otherwise throw doubt upon this projection. When these disruptive events occur, the interaction itself may come to a confused and embarrassed halt. Some of the assumptions upon which the responses of the participants had been predicated become untenable, and the participants find themselves lodged in an interaction for which the situation has been wrongly defined and is now no longer defined. At such moments the individual whose presentation has been discredited may feel ashamed while the others present may feel hostile, and all the participants may come to feel ill at ease, nonplussed, out of countenance, embarrassed, experiencing the kind of anomy that is generated when the minute social system of face-to-face interaction breaks down.

In stressing the fact that the initial definition of the situation projected by an individual tends to provide a plan for the co-operative activity that follows — in stressing this action point of view — we must not overlook the crucial fact that any projected definition of the situation also has a distinctive moral character. It is this moral character of projections that will chiefly concern us in this report. Society is organized on the principle that any individual who possesses certain social characteristics has a moral right to expect that others will value and treat him in an appropriate way. Connected with this principle is a second, namely that an individual who implicitly or explicitly signifies that he has certain social characteristics ought in fact to be what he claims he is. In consequence, when an individual projects a definition of the situation and thereby makes an implicit or ex-

[9] Teacher interview quoted by Howard S. Becker, "Social Class Variations in the Teacher- Pupil Relationship," *Journal of Educational Sociology,* XXV, p. 459.

[10] Harold Taxel, "Authority Structure in a Mental Hospital Ward" (unpublished Master's thesis, Department of Sociology, University of Chicago, 1953).

plicit claim to be a person of a particular kind, he automatically exerts a moral demand upon the others, obliging them to value and treat him in the manner that persons of his kind have a right to expect. He also implicitly forgoes all claims to be things he does not appear to be[11] and hence forgoes the treatment that would be appropriate for such individuals. The others find, then, that the individual has informed them as to what is and as to what they *ought* to see as the "is."

One cannot judge the importance of definitional disruptions by the frequency with which they occur, for apparently they would occur more frequently were not constant precautions taken. We find that preventive practices are constantly employed to avoid these embarrassments and that corrective practices are constantly employed to compensate for discrediting occurrences that have not been successfully avoided. When the individual employs these strategies and tactics to protect his own projections, we may refer to them as "defensive practices"; when a participant employs them to save the definition of the situation projected by another, we speak of "protective practices" or "tact". Together, defensive and protective practices comprise the techniques employed to safeguard the impression fostered by an individual during his presence before others. It should be added that while we may be ready to see that no fostered impression would survive if defensive practices were not employed, we are less ready perhaps to see that few impressions could survive if those who received the impression did not exert tact in their reception of it.

In addition to the fact that precautions are taken to prevent disruption of projected definitions, we may also note that an intense interest in these disruptions comes to play a significant role in the social life of the group. Practical jokes and social games are played in which embarrassments which are to be taken unseriously are purposely engineered.[12] Fantasies are created in which devastating exposures occur. Anecdotes from the past—real, embroidered, or fictitious—are told and retold, detailing disruptions which occurred, almost occurred, or occurred and were admirably resolved. There seems to be no grouping which does not have a ready supply of these games, reveries, and cautionary tales, to be used as a source of humor, a catharsis for anxieties, and a sanction for inducing individuals to be modest in their claims and reasonable in their projected expectations. The individual may tell himself through dreams of getting into impossible positions. Families tell of the time a guest got his dates mixed and arrived when neither the house nor anyone in it was ready for him. Journalists tell of times when an all-too-meaningful misprint occurred, and the paper's

[11] This role of the witness in limiting what it is the individual can be has been stressed by Existentialists, who see it as a basic threat to individual freedom. See Jean-Paul Sartre, *Being and Nothingness,* trans. by Hazel E. Barnes (New York: Philosophical Library, 1956), p. 365 ff.

[12] Goffman, *op. cit.*, pp. 319-27.

assumption of objectivity or decorum was humorously discredited. Public servants tell of times a client ridiculously misunderstood form instructions, giving answers which implied an unanticipated and bizarre definition of the situation.[13] Seamen, whose home away from home is rigorously he-man, tell stories of coming back home and inadvertently asking mother to "pass the fucking butter."[14] Diplomats tell of the time a near-sighted queen asked a republican ambassador about the health of his king.[15]

To summarize, then, I assume that when an individual appears before others he will have many motives for trying to control the impression they receive of the situation. This report is concerned with some of the common techniques that persons employ to sustain such impressions and with some of the common contingencies associated with the employment of these techniques. The specific content of any activity presented by the individual participant, or the role it plays in the interdependent activities of an ongoing social system, will not be at issue; I shall be concerned only with the participant's dramaturgical problems of presenting the activity before others. The issues dealt with by stagecraft and stage management are sometimes trivial but they are quite general; they seem to occur everywhere in social life, providing a clear-cut dimension for formal sociological analysis.

It will be convenient to end this introduction with some definitions that are implied in what has gone before and required for what is to follow. For the purpose of this report, interaction (that is, face-to-face interaction) may be roughly defined as the reciprocal influence of individuals upon one another's actions when in one another's immediate physical presence. *An* interaction may be defined as all the interaction which occurs throughout any one occasion when a given set of individuals are in one another's continuous presence; the term "an encounter" would do as well. A "performance" may be defined as all the activity of a given participant on a given occasion which serves to influence in any way any of the other participants. Taking a particular participant and his performance as a basic point of reference, we may refer to those who contribute the other performances as the audience, observers, or co-participants. The pre-established pattern of action which is unfolded during a performance and which may be presented or played through on other occasions may be called a "part" or "routine".[16] These

[13] Peter Blau, "Dynamics of Bureaucracy" (Ph. D. dissertation, Department of Sociology, Columbia University, forthcoming, University of Chicago Press), pp. 127-29.

[14] Walter M. Beattie, Jr., "The Merchant Seaman" (unpublished M. A. Report, Department of Sociology, University of Chicago, 1950), p. 35.

[15] Sir Frederick Ponsonby, *Recollections of Three Reigns* (New York: Dutton 1952), p. 46.

[16] For comments on the importance of distinguishing between a routine of interaction and any particular instance when this routine is played through,

situational terms can easily be related to conventional structural ones. When an individual or performer plays the same part to the same audience on different occasions, a social relationship is likely to arise. Defining social role as the enactment of rights and duties attached to a given status, we can say that a social role will involve one or more parts and that each of these different parts may be presented by the performer on a series of occasions to the same kinds of audience or to an audience of the same persons.

---

see John von Neumann and Oskar Morgenstern, *The Theory of Games and Economic Behavior* (2nd ed.; Princeton: Princeton University Press, 1947), p. 49.

20. A Formalized Theory of the Self-Concept

John W. Kinch

In recent years many sociologists have become concerned with the relation between the research process and existing theory. The use of formal mathematical models to enhance this relationship has not proved completely satisfactory. In this note we discuss the use of a type of formalization[1] which has many of the advantages of the mathematical model, yet at the same time maintains some of the values of the more subjective theoretical approach with which we are familiar in sociology. The interactionist notions about the self-concept will be used to exemplify what is involved in this type of formalization. The strategy is very simple: First, we scrutinize the theory to search out what seem to be its basic propositions and make these postulates explicit; second, the variables or concepts are identified and carefully defined; third, all interrelationships between the variables that can be derived from the basic postulates are considered. We will use those rules of logic which are part of ordinary language rather than the rules of mathematics. Finally, after the formalized theory has been explicated, we can consider the conditions under which each of the basic postulates will be expected to hold. Let us now proceed by stating the formalized theory of the self-concept, considering an example of its application, and finally evaluating this approach as a method of handling theory.

[1] Terminology is always a problem in this area. Some have talked about axiomatic theories, some about formal theories. We prefer the term "formalized theory" because it connotes a process of dealing with existing theory which is our concern. Also, one finds several words used in the literature to refer to the statements of a theory; words like postulates, propositions, axioms, theorems, and hypotheses. Here we will use the word "proposition" to refer to any statement which involves an empirical claim. Those propositions which the theory starts with we have called basic "postulates." Statements which are used to define a concept will be referred to simply as "definitions."

Reprinted from *The American Journal of Sociology,* LXVIII (January, 1963) pp. 481-486, by permission of the University of Chicago Press.

The Self-Concept

The interactionist notions about the self-concept, based on the writings of G. Mead, Cooley, and several others, are well known to social psychologists. The theory attempts to explain the conception that the individual has of himself in terms of his interaction with those about him.

Although there have been a variety of words used in describing what is meant by an individual's conception of himself, it appears that general agreement could be reached on the following definition: *The self-concept is that organization of qualities that the individual attributes to himself.* It should be understood that the word "qualities" is used in a broad sense to include both *attributes* that the individual might express in terms of adjectives (ambitious, intelligent) and also the *roles* he sees himself in (father, doctor, etc.).[2]

The general theory. — In very general terms the basic notions of the theory can be stated in one sentence: *The individual's conception of himself emerges from social interaction and, in turn, guides or influences the behavior of that individual.*

Basic Propositions of Formalized Theory of Self-Concept

The following statements are at least implicit in most treatments of the self-concept using this tradition and will be used as the basic postulates of our formalized theory.

1. The individual's self-concept is based on his perception of the way others are responding to him.
2. The individual's self-concept functions to direct his behavior.
3. The individual's perception of the responses of others toward him reflects the actual responses of others toward him.

(These postulates are not expected to hold under all conditions: The formalization procedure described below allows us to consider under what conditions they will hold.)
These three statements make up the postulates of the theory. The reason for this selection will become apparent later. Within these propositions there are four basic concepts or variables:

[2] The language used in this definition comes mainly from Theodore R. Sarbin, "Role Theory," in Gardner Lindzey (ed.), *Handbook of Social Psychology* (Cambridge, Mass.: Addison-Wesley Publishing Co., 1954), 223-58.

1. The individual's self-concept (S). (Defined above.)
2. His perception of the responses of others toward him (P). (The response of the individual to those behaviors of others that he perceives as directed toward him.)
3. The actual responses of others toward him (A). (The actual behavior of the others, that is, in response to the individual.)
4. His behavior (B). (The activity of the individual relevant to the social situation.)

At this point it is possible to see the first advantage from our formalized theory. By the use of simple logic we may take the three basic propositions and deduce from them three more. For example, from postulates 1 and 2 we can conclude that the way an individual perceives the response of others toward him will influence his behavior, for if his perception determines his self-concept and his self-concept guides his behavior, then his perception will determine his behavior. In symbolic form,

if $P \rightarrow S$	postulate 1
and $S \rightarrow B$	postulate 2
then $P \rightarrow B$	proposition 4

Therefore, the fourth proposition of the theory (call it a derived proposition) is:

5. The way the individual perceives the responses of others toward him will influence his behavior.

In like manner from postulates 1 and 3 we deduce a fifth proposition:

6. The actual responses of others to the individual will determine the way he sees himself (his self-concept).

And, finally, by combining either propositions 5 and 2, or 3 and 4 we get the sixth proposition:

7. The actual responses of others toward the individual will [a]ffect the behavior of the individual.

Our theory so far can be summarized in the following statement: The actual responses of others to the individual will be important in determining how the individual will perceive himself; this perception will influence his self-conception which, in turn, will guide his behavior. Symbolically,

$$A \rightarrow P \rightarrow S \rightarrow B \qquad \rightarrow = \text{"leads to"}$$

Before proceeding further into the analysis of the theory let us consider a short anecdote to clarify what we have said so far. The following story is alleged by some to be true; however, the present author has no confirmation of this and the story is presented only as a helpful device to make a point.

> A group of graduate students in a seminar in social psychology became interested in the notions implied in the interactionist approach. One evening after the seminar five of the male members of the group were discussing some of the implications of the theory and came to the realization that it might be possible to invent a situation where the "others" systematically manipulated their responses to another person, thereby changing that person's self-concept and in turn his behavior. They thought of an experiment to test the notions they were dealing with. They chose as their subject (victim) the one girl in the seminar. The subject can be described as, at best, a very plain girl who seemed to fit the stereotype (usually erroneous) that many have of graduate student females. The boys' plan was to begin in concert to respond to the girl as if she were the best-looking girl on campus. They agreed to work into it naturally so that she would not be aware of what they were up to. They drew lots to see who would be the first to date her. The loser, under the pressure of the others, asked her to go out. Although he found the situation quite unpleasant, he was a good actor and by continually saying to himself "she's beautiful, she's beautiful. . ." he got through the evening. According to the agreement it was now the second man's turn and so it went. The dates were reinforced by the similar responses in all contacts the men had with the girl. In a matter of a few short weeks the results began to show. At first it was simply a matter of more care in her appearance; her hair was combed more often and her dresses were more neatly pressed, but before long she had been to the beauty parlor to have her hair styled, and was spending her hard-earned money on the latest fashions in women's campus wear. By the time the fourth man was taking his turn dating the young lady, the job that had once been undesirable was now quite a pleasant task. And when the last man in the conspiracy asked her out, he was informed that she was pretty well booked up for some time in the future. It seems there were more desirable males around than those "plain" graduate students.

Our story suggests that the girl perceived the actual response of others (the men) in such a way as to require a change in her self-concept which in turn eventually changed her behavior. So their behavior influenced hers. However, the story brings to light another proposition that has so far been overlooked. At the end of the experiment we saw that the men's responses to the girl's behavior had changed, and they were now reacting to her as a desirable young lady. A new postulate then would be:

7. The behavior that the individual manifests influences the actual responses of others toward that individual.

We are not dealing with any new variables but rather with a new combination of the old ones. The theory at this point becomes circular:

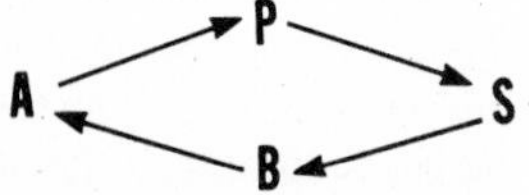

It will be noted that with the addition of this new postulate a whole new set of derived propositions emerge. There are now sixteen interrelated propositions in our simple theory which has only four variables. Rather than laboriously listing these propositions, let us now consider some of the factors which modify one of the propositions.

It is apparent that as the theory now stands it has not gone far enough in explaining the phenomena under consideration, and it might prove misleading if left as is. The major problem lies in the fact that the propositions are presented as if there was a one-to-one relationship between the variables dealt with. It is obvious that in reality these propositions hold only in varying degrees under certain conditions. To illustrate the type of thing that might be done, we will briefly consider the conditions under which we would expect proposition 3 to hold.

This postulate states that the individual's perception of the responses of others toward him reflects the actual responses of others. We have a rather generous supply of evidence relating to the accuracy of this postulate: Studies of role-taking ability have, almost without exception, operationally defined role-taking ability in terms of the relationship between the individual's perception of the responses of others and the actual responses. *The evidence seems to suggest that the accuracy of postulate 3 varies with (1) the individual's familiarity with the others, (2) his familiarity with the situation, (3) the social visibility*[3] *of the situation, (4) the individual's past experience in interpersonal situations, and (5) other factors which relate to all types of perception (conditions of body, immediate past,*

[3] Here we are using Merton's definition of "visibility": "the extent to which the structure of a social organization provides occasion to those variously located in that structure to perceive the norms obtaining in the organization and the character of role-performance by those manning the organization. In reference to an attribute of social structure, not to the perceptions which individuals happen to have" see Robert K. Merton, *Social Theory and Social Structure* (rev. ed.; Glencoe, Ill.: Free Press, 1957), p. 350.

etc.). Briefly, what this proposition says is that the more familiar the individual is with the situation and the others in the situation, the more socially visible the situation is, the more experience the individual has had in interpersonal situations and the less interference there is from irrelevant conditions, the more likely it is that postulate 3 will hold.

Evaluation

With the formalized statement of the basic postulates and derived propositions of the theory and an example of how the postulates must be conditioned, it is now possible to evaluate, at least to some extent, the usefulness of this method of dealing with theory in the social sciences. The following evaluation will be concerned primarily with the advantages and disadvantages of this approach over the informal, unsystematic approaches usually used in sociology. The advantages seen in this approach are listed below. No rank order is implied.

1. *The formalized theory offers the most parsimonious summary of anticipated or actual research findings.*[4] By designing our research so that we test four postulates of our theory and by the use of logical deductions we obtain support for sixteen propositions by testing only the four. Although this is an obvious virtue of the formalized theory, our modifying propositions make it clear that it must be taken with a certain degree of caution. Hypothesis-testing in sociology is such that the confirmation of propositions 1 and 2 at a certain level will not necessarily mean that proposition 4 can be stated at the same level of significance. Zetterberg cautions, "it is at present desirable that we in sociological research do not claim too much from the transfer of probability since our deductions are not too precise so long as our concepts are defined in normal prose and the deduction rules of ordinary language are used."[5] Even with some awareness of the factors which modify the postulates, words like "guides," "directs," and "influences" cannot be translated into rigorous mathematical operations.

   Zetterberg also points out another type of parsimony seen by comparing the results of sixteen isolated hypotheses (say, sixteen different investigators testing each of our propositions) with sixteen interrelated hypotheses (say, the same investigator does all

[4] Here we borrow extensively from Hans Zetterberg's discussions of axiomatic theory *(On Theory and Verification in Sociology* [New York: Tressler Press, 1954], pp. 16-28).

[5] *Ibid.*, p. 22.

the research using our theory).[6] It is obvious that the same data will provide more confirmation with the systematic theory than with the isolated hypotheses.

2. *The formalized theory will make the present knowledge on the subject accumulative and point to gaps if they exist.* The theory provides a way of bringing together the evidence that has emerged on the subject of the self. For example, we find that there is a good bit of evidence accumulating on the relationship between perception and the self-concept, and there is some evidence on the actual responses of others as these responses relate to perception and self-concepts.[7] However, very little has been done in relating the self-concept of a person to his behavior.[8]
3. *The formalized theory requires a clear distinction between statements that define the concepts of the theory and statements that are empirical propositions.* Careless writers on the topic of the self have often used a definition such as: "The self is defined as that organization of qualities *originating in social interaction...*" Then the author goes on to attempt to convince his readers that that self is a social phenomena and not something innate or individualistic. Of course, he turns out to be right *by definition.* If he wishes to consider the social origin of the self as an empirical hypothesis (such as our postulate 1) then he is required to define his concept "self" independently of the concept of social interaction. The formalized theory should eliminate errors of this type by clearly differentiating those statements that are definitions and those statements that are empirical claims (postulates or propositions).[9]
4. *The formalized theory allows for careful consideration of the condi-*

[6] *Ibid.*, p. 21.

[7] There are a great number of articles on this topic. The following is only a sample: Leo G. Reeder, George Donohoe, and Arturo Biblarz, "Conception of Self and Others," *American Journal of Sociology,* LXVI, No. 2 (September, 1956), 153-59; S. Frank Miyamoto and Sanford Dornbusch, "A Test of the Symbolic Interactionist Hypothesis of Self-Conception," *American Journal of Sociology,* LXI, No. 5 (March, 1956), 339-403; William R. Rosengren, "The Self in the Emotionally Disturbed," *American Journal of Sociology,* LXVI, No. 5 (March, 1961), 454-62; Carl J. Couch, "Self-Attitudes and Degree of Agreement with Immediate Others" *American Journal of Sociology,* LXIII (1958), 491-96.

[8] For an example of the type of thing that might be done see Thomas S. McPartland, John H. Cumming, and Wynona S. Garretson, "Self-Conception and Ward Behavior," *Sociometry,* XXIV, No. 2 (June, 1961), 111-24.

[9] For an excellent statement of this point see Clarence C. Schrag, review of Talcott Parsons and Edward Shils (eds.), *Toward a General Theory of Action in American Sociological Review,* XVII (1952), 247-49.

tions under which the theory is expected to hold. In our discussion of postulate 3 we attempted to show how a proposition could be scrutinized to find the conditions under which it would hold. This procedure requires empirical evidences outside the theory itself, since the limitations are in no way implicit in the propositions.

5. *The formalized theory provides a systematic procedure for scrutinizing the theory in terms of hidden implications and conceptual problems.* The requirement that all the propositions which are derived from the basic postulates be considered individually should reveal any hidden implications within the theory itself. The requirement for clear definitions of major concepts should go a long way in eliminating, or at least clarifying, conceptual problems.
6. *The formalized theory enables the investigator to bridge gaps in his data.* Often in empirical research there are situations in which it is impossible to gather data on one or more of the variables of the theory. In these situations a formalized theory may make it possible to bridge the gap between the data available by providing a conceptual link between these data. Suppose we have a situation where the only source of data is through direct observation (say participant-observation technique). If we wish to test our notions about the self, it is obvious that only two of our four variables can be measured. We can observe the variable we called "the actual responses of others," and we can observe the individual's behavior. However, we know of no way of directly observing the individual's perception or his self-concept. Our data then consist of observations of the actual responses of other persons toward the subject and the subject's actual behavior. Our theory allows us to "make sense" of these observations by suggesting that the relationship might be explained in terms of the two intervening variables of perception and self-concept. This was the case in the anecdotal example we used earlier. The girl's perceptions and self-concept were never observed, but we inferred something about them by applying the theory to the observations that were available. The theory stated in a formalized manner enabled us to bridge the gap in our data.
7. *The formalized theory facilitates communication.* A major problem that the sociologist faces today is understanding what his colleagues are talking about. We read passage after passage only to wonder what in the world the author is trying to say. If the theorist was required to formalize his notions as we have suggested in this paper, many of the misunderstandings would disappear. Many of us would find ourselves exclaiming. "Was that what he was saying?" The author cannot help but feel that some theorists, if required to handle their theories in this manner, might themselves end up saying, "Was that what I've been saying?"

The one disadvantage to this approach is that the formalized theory must not be treated as a set of logically and conceptually tight statements complete within themselves. Throughout this paper we tried to make it clear that the formal statements of the theory must be limited by statements of conditions. Our present state of development in sociology requires that we temper our statements even more with some "common-sense" notions we have about the subject with which we are concerned. We are suggesting here that, since the formalized theory may look like a mathematical model, some may assume that the conclusions can be treated with the rigor of a mathematical derivation. This could prove disastrous. The careful investigator can reap the benefits of the advantages mentioned in this paper and avoid the disadvantages if he does not expect the theory to do more than it is capable of doing.

The purpose of this note has been to suggest the possibility of developing models that are not so restrictive as the conventional mathematical models, yet are formal and systematic enough to be a considerable improvement over the general run of theory in sociology. The hope is that this paper might stimulate other attempts at formalizing existing sociological and social psychological theories. The results of a trend in this direction may prove extremely valuable in unscrambling the present state of theory.

21. A Critical Evaluation of Mead's "I" and "Me" Concepts

William L. Kolb

Social scientists have finally come to the realization that the task of a specific systematic science is not the exhaustive explanation of the empirical reality from which it draws its data, but rather the verifying of a series of abstract hypotheses which can then be used in conjunction with the concepts of other sciences to explain a specific situation in reality.[1] The infinite divisibility of reality makes any other approach impossible; any empirical situation is made up of a multiplicity of systems, physical, biological and social. These variables combine in determining the structure of the situation, and any attempt to explain this tangled web of phenomena within the frame of reference offered by any one science can only end in disaster. Conversely, any attempt to construct a systematic science on the basis of all these variables can only result in the crudest form of eclecticism and inconsistent systematization. The social psychologist has been one of the most persistent offenders of this unalterable canon of science. This inability or disinclination to deal only with that which falls properly within the sphere of social psychology is reflected in the unsystematic character of textbooks that are purported to be systematic analyses of personality or of other social psychological phenomena.[2]

William L. Kolb, "A Critical Evaluation of Mead's 'I' and 'Me,' " *Social Forces* 22 (March 1944), pp. 291-296, by permission of the Publisher, The University of North Carolina Press.

[1]Cf. Talcott Parsons, *The Structure of Social Action* (New York, 1937), pp. 3-42. Here the emphasis is on the relation between a given body of theory and empirical fact. See also Florian Znaniecki, *The Method of Sociology* (New York, 1934), passim. Both of these works are concerned with the necessity of abstraction in what might be called sociology proper, but their strictures are applicable to any systematic body of knowledge.

[2]Since the writer is unfamiliar with any social psychology text which has not been conceived in too grandiose a fashion, it is unfair to single out any particular offender, but for a somewhat similar criticism pointed at a specific text see H. H. Gerth's review of Steuart Henderson Britt, *Social Psychology of Modern Life* (New York, 1941), in *American Sociological Review*, 6 (December 1941), 915-916.

Of all social psychologists the one that would seem least guilty of this desire to explain everything about personality is G. H. Mead.[3] Yet, even here, it is possible to discover the results of an attempt to explain aspects of personality and self that more properly belong to other sciences. In his logical development of a systematic theory of the social nature of the growth of the self and of the personality through social interaction and role-taking, Mead gives no explicit explanation of the facts of social change or of the fact that the actions of individuals never exactly correspond to the rôles which they are expected to play, prior to the introduction of the "I" and "me" concepts. If he had closed his system without taking these phenomena into consideration, the personality and social structures formed by the processes delineated in his analysis would have been constant, i.e., personality would not vary from the various rôles defined by the culture of the society. This is not an a priori impossibility, since as we have seen, a systematic science may not explain everything concerning a particular phenomenon, and thus all differences in personality not accounted for by differentiated rôles might conceivably be due to differences generated by other than social factors. Nevertheless, Mead was perfectly justified in attempting to discover whether or not some of these differences could be explained within his frame of reference. In so doing, however, he erred in attempting to explain these residual phenomena under one concept, the "I", and in attempting to close his system by enclosing within it heterogeneous phenomena. The "I" becomes accountable for everything that cannot be explained by the organized set of rôles which the individual takes over in the processes of social interaction.[4] This conceptualizing of a resi-

[3] G. H. Mead, *Mind, Self, and Society* (Chicago 1934). See also his "The Social Self," *Journal of Philosophy, Pyschology and Scientific Method,* X (1913), 374-380; "The Mechanism of Social Consciousness," *Journal of Philosophy, Psychology and Scientific Method,* IX (1912), 401-406; "What Social Objects Must Psychology Presuppose," *Journal of Philosophy, Psychology and Scientific Method,* VII (1910), 174-180; "A Behavioristic Account of the Significant Symbol," *Journal of Philosophy,* XIX (1922), 157-163; and "Genesis of the Self and Social Control," *International Journal of Ethics,* XXXV (1924-1925), 251-277.

[4] For Mead's basic discussion of the "I" see *Mind, Self and Society,* pp. 173-178 and 192-199. It should be noted that the chronological development of Mead's thinking is not involved here. It may well be that Mead first made the distinction between the "I" and "me" long before other elements of his system had been chronologically developed; but the fact remains, the reader of *Mind, Self, and Society* is more interested in the logic of Mead's discussion as it is developed in this book; and in the logical argument social change and personal uniquenesses are only accounted for after the "I" and "me" have been introduced on p. 173. After the "I" is introduced it is then used as an explanation of the emergence of the novel, pp. 196-200.

dual category of phenomena as being homogeneous has been a source of confusion for both Mead and his interpreters; the nature of this confusion can be demonstrated by an analysis of the characteristics which have been attributed to the "I" as opposed to the "me."

The first characteristic of the "I," that we do not experience it until it passes into memory, fails to distinguish it from the "me," if we define the latter behavioristically. Since this point of view involves defining attitude as an early stage of an act, the "me," which consists of organized internalized attitudes of others, can and must be regarded, unless one is willing to disregard the behavioristic aspects of Mead's work, as realizing itself only in responses. In other words, unless one regards the aspects of the active "me" as existing in various responses called out by various stimuli, including earlier actions of the individual, the "me" becomes merely a fictional concept, useful, perhaps, but unrelated to a behavioristic psychology.[5] If then we are unconscious of what we are doing until we respond to our doing it, as Mead assumed when he speaks of our consciousness of the "I", we are unconscious of any specific active aspect of the "me" until we have responded to it. This being true, the first criterion by means of which we can distinguish the "I" from the "me" becomes meaningless: the assumption that we become conscious of the "I" only when it has passed into experience and become part of the "me." If we use a behavioristic definition of the "me" as outlined above, the "me" and the "I" become hopelessly confused because we are conscious of neither of them until they have passed into experience, i.e., until we respond to them.

Another criterion used to identify the "I" can, if properly developed, be used to differentiate between sectors of the self, but can hardly be used to account for the uniqueness of response which it is supposed to explain. We are told that one of the distinguishing characteristics of the "I" is that around it persists "...the sense of individuality of our own movements in relation to outer objects or persons, and of our activity in regard to these internalized "me's."[6] If we use this conception of the "I" it becomes differentiated from the "me" only in that it is that segment of attitudes which will issue in overt action unless modified by the responses of other segments of attitudes. What is one time the "I" may next time be the "me."

[5] *Ibid.*, pp. 1-41. In a social psychology devoted purely to the content of personality structures, i.e., those devoted to such phenomena as value hierarchies and their effect on action, little attention need be paid to this technical psychological point, for this relation between psychology and social action can be assumed; but it forms the center of a systematic analysis which is directed toward an explanation of the dynamics of personality and self-development.

[6] Kimball Young, *Personality and Problems of Adjustment* (New York, 1940), p. 175. *Cf.* Mead, *op. cit.*, pp. 177-178.

If, for example, a man sees someone beating a woman, his definition of the situation may be of such a nature that his immediate impulse is to strike the woman-beater; but this impulse calls out in him an attitude of discretion,[7] which may lead to inaction. In that case the "I" would be the anti-woman beating attitude, and the "me" would be the attitude of caution which nullified the active impulse. If, however, his wife does something of which he disapproves there may be called out in him a wife-beating response, which in turn may call out an anti-woman beating response of the nature described above. In that event, the "I" would consist of the wife-beating impulse, and the "me" of the anti-woman beating response. Thus this differentiation is merely a convenient method of distinguishing the original impulse from the modifying attitudes which prevent its fruition in overt action. Both attitudes are part of the generalized pattern of attitudes or generalized other which make up the personality of the individual, and offer no explanation of uniqueness of overt action.[8]

The third distinguishing feature of the "I" is that it is unpredictable. Thus we are given the illustration of the baseball player whose "me" calls for a throw to first base when a ground ball is hit in his direction, but who actually may either succeed in throwing the ball directly to his man or ten feet over his head.[9] It is in this example that we must take care not to fall into an erroneous conception of the relations of the various segments of the action: it is not the action of throwing the ball and throwing it ten feet over the first baseman's head which are related socially, but rather the attitude of throwing the ball to first base and the actual throwing of the ball that are bound together. If the "I" concept is meaningful at all in this case it

[7] No social action is as simple as this example might lead one to believe, but there still remains a convenient distinction to be drawn between the initial impulse to act and the various "me's" which are drawn out by it; it is the function of this example to illustrate this distinction in its simplest form.

[8] In this analysis the sense of individuality would grow out of the set of attitudes which one took toward one's self as distinct from other objects in the environment, and not out of some mystical concept of "being." Thus this approach is in line with Mead's analysis of how the individual becomes self-conscious, but refutes any attempt to account for later self-consciousness in terms of the "I." Another somewhat related, although not identical, conception of the "I" is that it is that attitude which is issuing into response at any instant of time. In this case the conception of the "I" would be compatible with the "I" as not directly experienced, but would be undistinguishable from the "me" except as the latter concept is used to refer to attitudes in their *latent* state. This conception may be useful for some purposes, but cannot be used to explain the residual category of phenomena which it is intended to explain.

[9] Mead, *op. cit.*, pp. 175-176.

must consist of the attitude which is called forth by the internalized attitudes of others, and its relation to the subsequent action. If we accept this as sound, there may or may not be a relation between the attitudes involved and the fact that the ball was thrown wild. If there is such a relation it can be explained only in terms of the uniqueness of the organized set of attitudes in terms of which the player was acting.[10] Any other explanation involves the appeal to another system of causation. Thus if the player in throwing had slipped on a banana peel, there would have been no relationship between the wild throw and the attitude which we have designated as the "I." To force the banana peel or an organic rheumatic twinge in the thrower's arm into a social frame of reference would of course be sheer nonsense.[11] There is then no significance to the concept of the "I" as the unpredictable unless we regard the "I" as that attitude, located in the generalized system of attitudes, which was called out by the situation and by the attitudes of the other players internalized in the same system. If this is so, then the problem becomes one of the analysis of the determinants of the uniqueness of the attitude configuration or of a specific attitude which renders unnecessary any division of the self into the "I" and the "me" unless it is used in the manner exemplified above, i.e., as a means of distinguishing between that attitude which is called out in any specific situation and all those others which respond to it and perhaps modify it.

This still leaves us, however, with the problem of the definite residual category that Mead introduced when he had practically finished his analysis. It is necessary to carve out of that category those sectors which contain factors related to the unpredictability of human behavior which can be analyzed within Mead's scheme and to separate them from those sectors which can only be handled within a different frame of reference. This is not an easy task to perform and the following schematization must be regarded as preliminary and provisional in nature.

Physical factors, of course, can be most easily eliminated, since the social psychologist has never insisted on including phenomena in his research that can only be explained on the basis of physical laws. Thus human behavior which is rendered deviant from expectations by changes in the physical environment must merely be regarded as something that complicates the task of prediction within the empirical sphere and about which nothing can be done within the framework of a systematic social psychology.

[10] Again we see that the concept of the "I" becomes functionally useless, since it is either part of the generalized other, or is part of another system of relations that has no place within a social frame of reference.

[11] If the banana peel and the rheumatic twinge become defined within the system of attitudes which constitutes the generalized other of the player, then they may be interpreted within a sociological theory of personality, but not until that time.

Our ball player who slipped on a banana peel must be regarded as a phenomenon unexplainable in terms of our frame of reference, and we must recognize that the "I" has nothing to do with the outcome of a situation in which a man is kept from reaching his goal by reason of the fact that he is bound by iron chains.

When we come to the realm of biological phenomena, however, the problem becomes somewhat more complicated, since the relationship prevailing between biological and social phenomena is much more complex and subtle, and the effect of the biological is discernible even on that fundamentally social phenomenon, the pattern of integrated attitudes which Mead calls the "generalized other." While Mead himself attached no explicit biological significance to the "I," others have attempted to explain the "I" as being composed of basically biological elements. Young, for example, finds the roots of the "I" partly located in the biological or constitutional foundations of action.[12] While there is some validity in this conception of the "I," the issue is still basically confused. We cannot think of the "I" as being a biological response to the "generalized other" which is social in nature, since we know that the actual response is made up of an attitude called out from this generalized system of attitudes, and hence if they are social it too must be regarded as social. The solution to this dilemma is to be found in analyzing the "generalized other" as the product of social interaction in which an individual with certain biological characteristics has engaged. Thus the "me" or the "generalized other" of a given individual is unique in that as a biological specimen he is unique.

The question then arises as to the possibility of explaining this uniqueness within a social frame of reference. It is the writer's position that this is an impossibility if we intend to develop a systematic social psychology of personality. Since the set of attitudes is the product of both biological and social factors which present almost infinite possibilities of combining with one another, attempts to explain the importance of shifting biological conditions while at the same time analyzing the effect of socialization can only result in the conclusion that each personality is incapable of being compared with any other. This does not mean, however, that we should ignore the biological, but rather that we should assess it as a constant.[13] We must take the typical biological characteristics of man as man and consider them as dynamic factors in the development of personality, not merely as the preconditions of social development. In doing this we forego the urge to explain differences of behavior arising within the same social group as a product of biological differences be-

[12] Young, *op. cit.*, p. 178.

[13] Mead treats the biologic individual as a constant, but tends to emphasize the non-dynamic aspects of the constant . See *Mind, Self, and Society,* p. 139, 347-353, and *passim.*

tween the members, but we are enabled to open up a new realm of research to Mead's frame of reference: the phenomenon which Kardiner calls basic personality structure.[14]

Thus we find a connective link between the work of a cultural psychoanalyst and Mead, which will make Mead's work more dynamic and the research of Kardiner more relevant for the sociologist and the social psychologist. If Mead's theory is used as an explanation of the process of socialization and Kardiner's work used as a means of delineating the dynamic relationship between the socially incorporated attitudes and the constant biological drives of men, there is some possibility of the two theories merging into one.[15] Even if this is not accomplished, there is still some benefit to be derived from the addition of a dynamic biologic element to Mead's theory; and the work of tracing the relation between socially derived attitudes, the basic personality structure, and the secondary institutions, which are the product of the dynamic interaction of basic drives and social attitudes, will not suffer because of an increased knowledge of how the incorporation of social attitudes into the personality actually takes place. Attempts to reconcile different bodies of theory that stem from such divergent origins as do these two is obviously dangerous, but since the psychoanalysts are gradually approaching a social point of view the gap

[14]Abram Kardiner, *The Individual and His Society* (New York, 1939). Basic personality structure is defined by Linton in the foreword of Kardiner's study as "the constellation of personality characteristics which would appear to be congenial with the total range of institutions comprised within a given culture." p. vi. The importance of this concept is that with it Kardiner emphasizes the dynamic relationships existing between the demands of the Society and the basic biological characteristics of man. This is not a reversion to instinct theory, since it is recognized that the drives are generalized and that all that is necessary is that they be satisfied some way, not in any specific way. Thus: "If, in a particular culture, the biological need for sexual gratification is systematically interfered with, from infancy on, from our knowledge of human nature we can expect that this will give rise to a series of reactions, and that these reactions may eventually become petrified in institutions which offer some expression for the effects created by the frustrations concerned." p. 11. Since any institution is the result of human action we have here a situation in which the internalization of attitudes interfering with a basic drive result in something new: a culture complex which was not present before, and which is due to just this dynamic interaction between internalized attitude and biological drives.

[15]It must be remembered that this convergence becomes possible only after we have reopened Mead's system by throwing out the concept of the "I" and re-examining the residual category of phenomena which Mead cloaked with this concept.

between the two bodies of theory is much more apparent than real.[16]

The application of this point of view which considers biological factors as dynamic elements in the formation of the personality also makes it possible to explain widely divergent overt behavior where the difference between the social attitudes involved seems very slight. If one family adds just a slightly higher degree of emphasis on anti-masturbation attitudes than does another, with the result that the sexual behavior of the offspring of the two families varies widely, it might be possible to explain this difference on the basis of the relation between the sex drive and the two sets of attitudes.

In all the above analysis of the relation of biological factors to social factors in the formation of unique attitudes and behavior, we have approached the central problem which faces us, but have not quite come to grips with it. That problem is, of course, whether there is any source of uniqueness of attitudes and behavior that is definitively social in nature, and that does not involve extra-social considerations. The generic answer to this question is probably in the negative. Given absolutely the same biological makeup, the identical geographic environment, a constancy in the time element, and identical physical conditions, there seems no reason to believe that there is anything in the process of socialization that would lead to divergent attitudes and hence to divergent behavior. This, however, is scarcely a relevant answer. Once a process of attitude differentiation sets in, for whatever reason, it should be obvious that the operation of purely social factors will increase that differentiation. This is most apparent in the social interaction that takes place between people who have divergent backgrounds. The personality structures of both are modified, usually in an unpredictable direction, and in a direction which perhaps has never been manifested before in either of the social groups from which the individuals originated. If either of these individuals returns to his group the result is the differentiation of attitudes within the group, provided the individual is not removed in order to remove the danger of change. The literature which we have accumulated concerning culture contact, acculturation, and social change within a society bears witness to this analysis. Thus a unique set of attitudes is the product of the social interaction in which one engages with an individual who has a different set of attitudes, and at least part of this

[16] The dangers inherent in the reconciling of divergent bodies of theory grow primarily from two sources: premature reconciliation and crude eclecticism. This attempt to bring together the work of Kardiner and Mead may be somewhat premature since the cultural psychoanalysts are still hazy in their ideas concerning the influence and nature of social factors, and since such convergence also depends on the validity of the writer's arguments concerning the "I"; but it certainly does not suffer from eclecticism since there is no picking and choosing involved, but rather a conjunction of the theories in their totality has been suggested.

change can be viewed as brought about by purely social factors.

The result of continued differentiation of this sort is a growing discrepancy between the various basic attitudes which are the common property of the group, and a child born into this type of society is likely to inherit a set of attitudes which are not consistently related to one another. The analysis of this situation is best carried out in terms of Mead's theory of internal conversation.[17] When a situation arises which is governed by conflicting attitudes, unless the self of the individual is compartmentalized, a conversation between various aspects of the self ensues and the resultant attitude is likely to diverge significantly from both of the previously existing ones, so that the overt action may be greatly different from what anyone expected.

Finally, there are shifts in attitudes which occur as a result of success or failure in reaching the goals or values defined by the attitudes so that the behavior becomes unpredictable. Success is almost certain to result in the reinforcement of the attitude, but prolonged and persistent failure may result in shifts in attitudes in at least two basic fashions. The first is simply that if the defined value is important enough, the ethically enjoined attitudes toward the means will gradually lose their strength so that the goal may be sought by a new pattern of activity.[18] The second involves an evaluation of failure. If, for example, the culture places a high premium on success, prolonged failure is likely to result in self-condemnation which in turn violates basic security attitudes. In turn the interaction of these attitudes may result in what Horney has called neurotic trends, set up to protect the individual.[19] The nature of this trend is likely to depend on other techniques for gaining security which are approved by the society.

[17]Mead, *op cit.*, pp. 61-75.

[18]An analysis of this type of attitude shift is to be found in Robert K. Merton's article, "Social Structure and Anomie," *American Sociological Review,* III (1938) 672-682.

[19]While the cultural psychoanalysis of Kardiner is oriented about the interplay of biological and social factors, Karen Horney's studies are concerned with the nature of conflict between social attitudes within the individual. If we disregard her undue emphasis on security, her research delineates quite clearly certain types of personality conflict based on the presence of conflicting attitudes, or of attitudes conflicting with actual performance, and traces the conflicts back to their origin in the culture pattern of our society. The same things may be said of the possible convergence of Horney's theory with that of Mead as were said in the case of Kardiner and Mead, except that in this case Horney offers a technique for unraveling the relations existing between conflicting attitudes within Mead's frame of reference. See Karen Horney, *New Ways in Psychoanalysis* (New York, 1939); *The Neurotic Personality of Our Time* (New York, 1937); and "Culture and Neurosis, "*American Sociological Review,* I (1936), pp. 221-230.

It is manifestly impossible to present all the various forms of attitude differentiation which arise out of the dynamic interplay between differing social attitudes and the situation in which they are expressed, but we have succeeded, perhaps, in pointing out the scientific benefits to be derived from the breaking down of the residual category which Mead called the "I" into some of its various components. We have discovered that some uniquenesses in behavior are unexplainable in terms of a social frame of reference; that others can be explained only in terms of the dynamic interaction of a constant biological factor and various social factors; and finally, that there does exist a realm of attitude differentiation which analytically belongs wholly within the field of social interaction. We must remember that these various forms are intermixed in the real world, but nevertheless, they are analytically separable.

One more result of this breakdown of the residual category should now be apparent: Within the framework of Mead's theory certain aspects of behavior which were unexplainable except by the use of the ambiguous concepts of the "I" and the "me" are now not only explainable but have been processed so that they may to some extent even become predictable. If we recognize the basic social factors at work in attitude differentiation, it should be possible to discover predictable features in their recurrence. The way has already been opened by the cultural psychoanalysts, and with the reopening of Mead's system to include the basic findings of these researchers, it seems plausible to expect that future research will discover that variation from the dominant sets of attitudes of any society are not random but follow a pattern that can be discovered, provided one stays within the limits of the social frame of reference. That there always will be unexplainable differences in attitude and action is obvious, but that the area not only of theoretical unpredictability but of empirical unpredictability will be cut down can certainly be anticipated. In that case the extremely high probabilities that of necessity accompany all theoretical prediction will be of more significance, in that they will serve to increase the somewhat low probabilities which attend our present efforts at empirical prediction. We shall never know all about reality, but if we recognize the nature of systematic science and its limitations, we can approach closer and closer to the goal.

22. The Self-and-Other Words of a Child

Read Bain

The organic relation between self and others is one of the basic ideas of social psychology and sociology. J. Mark Baldwin was one of the first to make this theory explicit in his dictum, "The Ego and the Alter are thus born together."[1] He discussed the "conversation of gestures" later elaborated by G. H. Mead and also stressed in the "internal speech" which is now frequently attributed to J. B. Watson, but his work was largely dialectic and did not stimulate much scientific research.

Somewhat later Charles Horton Cooley studied the development of the self-words of his third child, his general theory having been formulated from "scanty observations" of the first two. He thought such study would throw some light upon the genesis of personality. Although this work was done nearly thirty years ago, it has not been repeated.[2]

Cooley's method is so simple that fairly exact repetition is possible. It consists merely of daily observation and record of the child's speech. Greatest attention is paid to the period during which the child is learning to talk, but some earlier observations are given "as being possibly suggestive of the growth of the self-idea before it becomes articulate."[3] Care was taken not to stimulate responses in accord with his theories. The "method" was merely careful observation of the self-and-other language habits of a normal child in a normal family situation.

We followed this procedure with S, born May 24, 1930. The record begins on the twenty-first day and continues until the self-and-other words were practically mastered, but only such data as refer rather directly to self and others, and especially to their pronominal symbols, are included

Reprinted from *The American Journal of Sociology,* XLI (May, 1936), pp. 767-775, by permission of the University of Chicago Press.

[1] *Mental Development in the Child and the Race* (New York, 1915 rev.; first published, 1895), p. 321.

[2] First published in the *Psychological Review,* XV (1908), 339-57: "A Study of the Early Use of the Self-Words by a Child"; reprinted in *Sociological Theory and Social Research* (New York, 1930), pp. 229-47. References herein are to the latter source.

[3] *Sociological Theory and Social Research,* p. 230.

in this report. Because of the general interest in infant vocabularies, I have departed from the foregoing principle to the extent of including vocabulary counts at fourteen and twenty-four months.

The general social situation of the two little girls was somewhat similar although S was an only child while B had an older brother and sister. This may account for S's rather large vocabulary at two years and for her earlier mastery of the self-and-other words with a minimum of confusion.[4] After S had learned to talk fairly well, we noticed that play sessions with children of her own age frequently were followed by reversion to more infantile language habits. S has never shown any signs of precocity, but her language habits have always been (and still are) somewhat advanced for her age. This is probably due to the fact that she has associated with adults more than most children do.

Preyer, Shinn and Cooley,[5] and this study (3-23[?], 6-26, 7-9, 8-1, 10-6, 13-0) agree that infants learn the names of others before they learn their own. This study (9-21, 10-20, 11-3) also confirms Shinn (p. 150) and Cooley (p. 230) that inarticulate but pronounced self-feeling, self-assertion, or "will," occurs at an early age, perhaps before there is much responsiveness to other persons, or at least reciprocally with it. Cooley says the "I" refers to the self-as-social-interactor, not to the bodily self (p. 231). We agree that the meaning of self-words is essentially social (9-21, 14-8, 15-19, 16-0, 16-12, 17-18 for the social reference of preverbal self-behavior; 19-14, 19-20, 20-0, 22-15, 22-28, 24-7, 25-9, 25-19, 26-18, 27-7 for social reference of self-words). S paid some attention to parts of her body but always treated them as aspects of the "I" as social interactor. The bodily self as object appears to have only the vaguest meaning for an infant. This may seem inconsistent with the child's early interest in his mirror image, but it seems clear in Cooley's record (14-26, 15-8) and in this (7-9, 8-1) that attention to the mirror image is not connected with the self-sense at all; rather, it is similar to interest in other babies and their pictures. S's attention to F's mirror image, on the other hand, was plainly associated with F out of the mirror, as a social object.

Cooley (pp. 231, 236) and Shinn (p. 137) agree with this study (11-0, 11-3, 12-0, 14-8) on the importance of explosive words. This may suggest the interjection theory of language, but babbling and vocal play are also very important. However, the self-sense seems peculiarly fraught with this explosive emphasis. This emotionally toned, subjective "I" sense is well-developed long before any verbal symbols are attached to it. This is perhaps the cue to all language development. Words as stereotyped sounds

[4] See Otto Jespersen, *Language: Its Nature, Development and Origin* (New York, 1922), p. 123, for pronoun-shifting (confusion), and Cooley, *op. cit.*, pp. 233, 236, 240, 242, *passim.*

[5] M. W. Shinn, *The Biography of a Baby,* pp. 124, 133, and Cooley, p. 232. Except where the context is obvious, numbers in parentheses refer to months and days in the appended record.

are quite different from words with meanings. The latter are always emotionally toned like the self-words of a child. True words are these emotional, subjective experiences symbolized by objective (social) sounds (and gestures). The objectification of the subjective, i.e., the process by which private experience becomes public, is the basis of all communication. Perhaps Cooley's theory of how the self-words are acquired (p. 231), if generalized for all word acquisition, is as good an explanation of communication as we have at present.

Cooley (pp. 235-36), Shinn (pp. 171, 236), and this study (9-16, 9-21, 10-0, 10-6, 10-20, 14-0, 15-19) agree that babies "understand" rather complicated word patterns before they have acquired many verbal symbols. Shinn reports little or no "memory" at one year (p. 244) although her observations belie her statement. Cooley's record also implies the existence of preverbal memory. Certainly it was pronounced in the case of S. While memory probably has the same organic basis as language habits and is at first inarticulate, it is doubtless an important factor in the development of the personality of a child under two years of age, and especially so in the distinction he makes between himself and others.

The record follows.

Third month, twenty-third day. S distinguishes between F and R and others. Cried loudly when left with a strange girl. Stopped at once when F took her up.

6-26. Dawdles at food, although perfectly healthy. (Attention-getting?) Seems to respond to her name by turning toward the speaker more quickly than for other sounds. It may be the tone of F and R rather than the name.

7-9. Definite bids for attention; waves "bye-bye." S is much interested by her mirror image and her baby pictures.

8-1. Waves "bye-bye" to herself in the mirror and to R; formerly did it to everyone. (A vague distinction between herself and others?) Pays more attention to S in mirror than to F. When F says "Hello, Mother!" S looks at F in the mirror and then at F out of the mirror and grins.

9-16. F says S reaches for her shoe, doll, etc., when F says "Where's Sheila's shoe?" etc.

9-21. S makes definite responses to about fifteen verbal stimuli. When one says "Where's mama's shoe, foot?" etc., S reaches for the object. Some of these responses are self-references. In response to "Where's the baby, where's Sheila?" S covers her face with paper or shawl and then uncovers it with laughter and grinning. In response to "Where's the baby?" (when shown her own or other baby picture), S runs her hand over it and laughs. In response to "Where's your foot, hand, dress?" etc., S reaches for her foot, holds up hand, reaches for her dress, etc. Protests at being left alone and bids for attention.

Was greatly excited by a baby of her own age and seemed to interact with it more actively than with adults (cf. 7-9, 8-1, above).

10-0. Winks both eyes in response to "Wink your eyes." F is sure S knows "Read" and "Då-Då" for R. When F says "Where's Read?" or "Where's Daddy?" S turns directly toward R, smiles, and says "Då-Dá." F says S says "She-e! She-e!" when she sees her mirror image or her picture.

10-6. When R returned after five days' absence, S recognized him at once. There is no doubt but that S "knows" words. She makes differential, specific responses to "Where's S, F, R, Mama, Daddy?" and also for objects and parts of her body. Her responses to person-words seem to give her greater emotional satisfaction that her responses to thing-words do. She stimulates ("imitates"?) herself much more than others stimulate her.

10-20. S invariably turns toward F and R and smiles when asked "Where's F, where's R?" To "Where's Sheila?" she responds "She-e! She-e-e!" and looks toward her picture on the mantle. It has been clear for some time that S "understands" sentences long before she can say even single words. It is out of this rudimentary prespeech "memory" that consciousness of self and others arises.

11-0. Much repetitive babbling and imitating, both of herself and of others. F said "Ouch!" and S repeated it, explosively, several times. Two of her favorite "words" are "she-she" and "lă-lă." A combination would form her name. She makes practically all the phonetic sounds.

11-3. "Ow-itch!" and "la!" are still doing constant, explosive duty. When asked "Where's your hair? Let's see your hand?" etc., S frequently refuses to respond, although she knows all these things well. The "your" plainly has no self-reference, but is just part of the total verbal stimulus. She quite consistently takes her hand out of her mouth in response to the verbal command. She "understands" a number of simple sentences.

12-0. No evidence of any self-words (nor any other kind) except "Mama," "Dá-Dá," and "Bye"--which are definitely associated with persons and acts. She teases, i.e., does things she knows are forbidden, and enjoys it. Has begun to "talk" in a new way—sharp, staccato, explosive "Blă! Blop! Blă! (Cf. Cooley's remark about the emotional-release nature of words.) Points at things and looks at things we point to; increasing interest in parts of her body. Responds to "Sing, Sheila!" by "singing."

13-0. During the last two or three days S has learned the names and faces of twelve relatives whom she has never seen before. When one says "Where's __ ? Go to __," she points or goes to the right person. This may be a response to the speaker's gestures rather than to his words.

13-13. Language habits greatly improved in accuracy and number, but no clear consciousness of self except marked self-assertion and "teasing."

14-0. Discovered her saying words to herself: "Howdy-do, Mama, Då-då, Bobo [the little dog], Biddy," etc. F says this has been going on for some time. Her single-word speaking vocabulary consists of about 21 words: 10 names of persons; 6 actions, viz., "bye-bye," "how-do," "peek," "beautiful," "all gone," "da"; 5 objects. In addition, she "recognizes" by appropriate actions 29 objects and 31 acts. Her working vocabulary is probably close to 100 words.

14-8. S distinguishes "daddy's ear" from "your ear," but the "your" probably does not mean any definite S-sense-of-self. Make-believe play is common now — drinking from empty cup, giving herself a bath, etc. All successful action is accompanied by an explosive "dă!"

14-15. Makes blundering attempts at word combinations, with great vocal stress: "How-de-do, Bill!"; "Bye-bye, Dȧddȧ!" Shy of strangers, although she hides for fun from F and R.

15-0. Last night in the car S suddenly began to say "See-lah!" and repeated it all the way home. Today she has been saying "See-lah says Mama, Bobo, Dȧddȧ," etc.; pats F and R and says, "See's Mama"; "See's Dȧddȧ." This seems to be the first true self-word.

15-8. S shouted the names of all the family who saw us off on the train. All the way across, whenever the train stopped, she would go to the window and shout "bye-bye!" to the whole family, each by name.

15-19. Has almost stopped saying "See says. . . . ," except "See says doon!" — which she shouts until put down; resents having her hand held while walking. Said "I see" the other day — imitatively, I judge. The "I" has not been heard since. She does not seem confused by her explosive "See" [look] and "See" [her name]. Uses "baby" a great deal but never applies it to herself. She knows her own toys, but allows other children to snatch them with no protest.

16-0. When told to say "Sheila Bain" she says "Baby!" This is another true self-word. In response to "Where's Sheila?" she pats her chest and points to herself.

16-12. S says "baby" when told to say her own name and also whenever she sees another baby, doll, child, or picture of any of them. So this "baby" is both a self-and-other word, or it is neither.

17-0. Many three- and four-word sentences containing everybody's name except her own. "Baby" still used as in 16-12. When S "pats" R she insists on patting F, and vice versa.

17-18. Possessives are quite well established: "See's dȧddȧ, See's Mama, Dȧddȧ's bä [bath]," etc. Said "I do" several times after hearing an explosive "I do!" from R to F--mere sound imitation, I think. Still refers to herself as "baby" but also uses a rough approximation of her name.

18-0. Rough approximation of R's name, but when told to say "F______," she says "Mama!" Seldom tries her own name.

19-14. S says "I eat, I sit, I peek," etc., and performs the proper actions. There appears to be no definite bodily-self reference in her use of "I." When told to say Sheila Bain she says "Baby Baim."

19-20. Coming home from a drive, F said "Sheila's house." S said "*My* house!" and repeated it several times. "I" is much in use with no confusion.

20-0. S says "Seebee Baim, Baby Seebee Baim, Seebee's buch," etc., a great deal. Also, "I do, Seebee eat, my buch, my hair, my eyes," etc., are very common and so far no single case of pronoun-shifting has been noted.

20-4. Great increase of words. "My" and "I" in constant use with no confusion.

20-7. Likes to "argue," e.g., shouts "mon" when you say a picture is a baby, and vice versa. Strongly insists that F and R be treated equally, e.g., when R takes a cigarette, S says "Dȧddȧ, get Mama cig-a-mätch!" All her *a's* are broad or Italian although both F and R use the western *a.*

20-14. "Seebee" has become "Sheebee." "I see *you"* appears to be repetitive but is used properly. No confusion in self-and-other words noted so far.

20-17. Used "my" for "I" — "My see you."

20-20. F says S used "me" — "Bye-bye, Dȧddȧ, Mama, me!"

20-21. First clear case of a preposition — "Go back to Mama!" Noticed another "my" for "I."

21-0. "My' for "your" or "the" is apparently a fixed confusion, though it occurs infrequently: "Dȧddȧ, take my baby"; "My baby go bye-bye."

21-12. "I," "my," "you," "your," and possibly "me" are used correctly.

21-14. In response to "What's your name?" S sings "My name, my name is Sheebee Baim!" Goes around singing *"My* name, *my* Dȧddȧ, *my* Mama" with a definite, explosive sense of possession.

21-18. S whispers to herself and to F and R.

21-22. F reports S said "Baby bumps herself."

21-25. S has invented a telephone game with the curtain pull. She speaks only her own part, making proper pauses for the other person. (Cf. Cooley's "personal ideas" and "imagined other.")

21-28. Said "Dȧddȧ bumps me."

22-0. Said "I bump myself." (F's report.)

22-3. Calls her toy cabinet "my office" — "I go work in my office." Shows everybody her six months' baby picture — "See Sheebee? See that baby?"

22-8. After a child of her own age had snatched several toys from her, S suddenly objected. She said nothing, although she knows the words. This is the first instance of possessiveness for *her* things. She does a great deal of helping: "I help Dȧddȧ, I help Mama!"

22-13. She takes her fingers out of her mouth when told, but usually says, "I bite my wrist, elbow, or arm," and does it.

22-15. "What's your name?" "Sheebee." "What else?" "Baim." "What's Daddy's name?" "Eed." "What else?" "Baim." All the people she knows are "Baim."

22-18. "I," "my," "me," "mine," "you," "your," are correctly used with occasional confusion between "I" and "my." Have not noticed "myself" or "herself" since the two doubtful cases mentioned. Never says "I tickle you," but "I giggle your nose, or Dȧddȧ's nose"; not "I bump myself," but "I bump my head, foot," etc.

22-26. Says "I love Mama's Sheebee" for "Sheebee's Mama." This inverted possessive is common, but the correct form is also used.

22-28. "Mama, see! Baby's hair is yellow, like mine!" (pointing to a picture).

23-8. When S is upstairs and hears someone come in, she calls "Is it *Do?* Is it *Ray?*—through eight or ten names, when she knows all the time it is Jean.

24-0. Started vocabulary count today: 406 words. Most of these can be readily understood by strangers; all are stereotyped sounds referring to specific things or actions. Some are mere verbalisms, of course, as "Oxford is my town," "Ohio is my state." Plurals and forms of the same verb are not counted as separate words.

24-4. Much doll-play. S does and says to dolls what F does and says to S.

24-7. R to S, "Careful, or you will hurt yourself." S says, "Careful, I hurt myself—Sheila." For some time S has changed "you" and "your" to the first person with no confusion. Uses second person pronouns some but third person very little. Has said "we" repetitively but with no clear we-reference.

24-9. Vocabulary count completed. The list is probably not complete but a considerable number has been acquired since May 24, so this is approximately correct for S's two-year-old vocabulary. The "recognition" vocabulary is considerably greater.

Classification

1.	Common nouns	336
2.	Proper nouns (places, Oxford, etc.)	9
3.	Proper nouns (persons)	71
4.	Pronouns (I, me, my, mine, myself, we, us, you, your, something, it, both, any, none)	14
5.	Conjunctions (and)	1
6.	Prepositions (in, on, down, to, up, of, like, around, over, from, after, before, under	13
7.	Adjectives and adverbs	76
8.	Verbs and actions	125
	Total	645

24-16. S says "I bring Mama my shoes," meaning F's shoes. Seldom uses "your" although "you" is common.

24-24. Said "I's" for "I'm." Only time I've noted this.

24-30. Said "We go uptown; we go upstairs." First use of "we" showing clear intent to include self with another.

25-6. Says "my" for "your" quite regularly although she uses "my" correctly for her own things.

25-9. When R says "I'll take you upstairs," S protests loudly, "No! No!

I go upstairs by *myself*." This *myself* insistence applies to everything. Cats, dogs, dolls, etc., are all called "Bain" with deep emotion. (She learned the *n*- sound a couple of months ago.)

25-13. "Mine" and "my" are used frequently and with great self-feeling. "Mine" is often used for "my" — "I want mine *own* cup!"

25-19. R scolds S for wetting on the floor. S says "No! Not Sheebee — Dåddå!" and spanks R's cheek: "Not do it any more, Dådda!" S calls others by their last names; heretofore all persons have been "Bain."

25-21. S says "Janet goes to see my mama, no, *her* mama." First use of third personal pronoun and also first verbal self-criticism. At a friend's house S says "This is *mine* house," but her laugh shows she knows it is not.

25-26. "Alan goes to see *his* mama!" S is also using "your" correctly.

26-6. Out driving, everything S saw elicited "That's *my* house, pig, etc. When F said "No, that's not your house," S laughed and said "No, it's a game!"

26-11. S said "That's ouah cah!" R said "What do you mean by 'our'? S said "Daddy's and Mama's and mine."

26-14. "Daddy, get your coat, we're going uptown."

26-18. Tonight S said "*I* want to! *I* want to!" R said "Who is I?" S said "I is *me!*"

26-24. Great sympathy for F, who bumped herself.

26-27. "We," "us," "our," "you," "your," "his," "her," commonly and correctly used.

26-30. Calls up the "groceryman" and orders ten or twelve different articles (toy-telephone), says "goodbye," and reports with great satisfaction: "There! I told the groceryman to bring *all* the groceries!"

27-7. S said "See those people? They are my friends. *All* the people are my friends." "These" and "them" are also used occasionally.

The record ends here. Most of the self and other words seem to be learned and used correctly most of the time. This study confirms Cooley's observations on most points. The child "knows" other selves before he knows his own. It is out of his responses to others that his "consciousness of self" arises, together with appropriate verbal symbols for naming it. The "I" is a social concept. It is quite different from the concept of self as object which arises much later. Pronoun confusion, like other awkward verbal habits, probably comes from confused response relations between the infant and other children and adults. Baby-talk, "talking down" to the infant, and talking about him rather than to him undoubtedly contribute to his confusion, if such practices do not cause it entirely.

The "I"-sense is closely connected with the self-assertive responses of self-active infants to other persons who are also self-active and self-assertive. This does not mean the writer thinks infants have any "self" at birth. They have neuromuscular activity, sensitivity to internal and external stimuli, but no self-activity. Self is wholly social. It is that integration of responses to other objects, both personal and non-personal, which appears very early in a vague, undifferentiated way, develops rapidly and observably from five months on, and begins to be verbalized after about one year. It is explosive, aggressive, and strongly emotional in its linguistic as well as in its muscular manifestations. Becoming adult and "well adjusted" consists largely of disciplining, or modifying, the modes and intensity of this ego-assertion and learning to express it in ways that are acceptable to others with whom the person must interact. This is what we mean by "acquiring the culture" or becoming a "socialized person."

Read Bain

23. Family Role Specialization and Self-Attitudes in Children *

Carl J. Couch

For those social psychologists subscribing to self-role theory, the proposition that the self arises through interaction is a crucial one. In the past few years there have been several procedures developed to put into operational form the concepts "self" and "role," thereby rendering them useful in the formulation of empirical propositions. One of these, the Twenty Statements Test (TST),[1] has been validated by the demonstration that dimensions of the self, abstracted from responses to the TST, are related to other aspects of behavior.[2] In addition, Kuhn has found professional training, age, and sex to be related to the nature of the self as measured by the TST,[3] while McPartland and Cumming report a relationship between social class and self-conception.[4]

The research reported here is a limited attempt to investigate a relationship between the role structure of a group and the way members of the group define themselves. Specifically, this research attempts to discern relationships between the role structure within families and the self-identi-

From *The Sociological Quarterly,* III (April, 1962), pp. 115-121, by permission of the journal.

*The author wishes to thank Bernard Meltzer for his critical reading of the manuscript.

[1] The TST consists of a single sheet of paper with the following instructions: "In the twenty blank spaces provided below please make 20 different statements in response to the question, "Who am I?" Give these answers as if you were giving them to yourself, not to somebody else. Write fairly rapidly, for the time is limited."

The TST was originally discussed in Manford H. Kuhn and Thomas S. McPartland, An Empirical Investigation of Self-Attitudes," *American Sociological Review* 19:68-78 (1954).

[2] Carl J. Couch, "Self-Attitudes and Degree of Agreement with Immediate Others," *The American Journal of Sociology,* 63:491-96 (1958). Thomas S. McPartland, John H. Cumming, and Wynona S. Garretson. "Self-Conception and Ward Behavior in Two Psychiatric Hospitals," *Sociometry,* 24:111-24 (1961).

[3] Manford H. Kuhn, "Self Attitudes by Age, Sex, and Professional Training," *The Sociological Quarterly,* 1:39-55 (1960).

[4] Thomas S. McPartland and John H. Cumming, "Self-conception, Social Class, and Mental Health," *Human Organization,* 17:24-29.

fications of children of the families. That such relationships should prevail derives from our awareness that the family is a pervasive group in our society, and that the development and maintenance of the self for most individuals depends in large part upon the interaction that occurs within the family group. As families differ in structure this difference should be reflected in the ways children define themselves.

The subjects for the research were college students, the majority of them freshmen, enrolled in introductory sociology classes. In an ideal research design, the structure of the families would be delineated by a direct study of the families of the subjects. The practical difficulties of this procedure forced an indirect approach. The students were asked to complete a questionnaire which was designed to measure the degree of role specialization within their families. The instructions took the following form:

> This questionnaire is to determine what tasks various members of your family perform. There are no right or wrong answers. In order for this research to be successful it is necessary that you attempt to be as accurate as possible in describing your family. In the spaces provided below write in one of the following words: "Usually," "sometimes," "seldom," or "never."

Below these instructions, on the left-hand side of the questionnaire, were seventeen items. Sample items are: "Shops for groceries," "Earns money for family," "Helps children with school work," "Shows affection for children in presence of others," etc. To the right of these items were four columns with the headings: mother, father, female teenager, and male teenager.

On the basis of the responses, role-specialization scores for "father-mother" and for "male-female teenagers" were computed. "usually" was scored as four, "sometimes" as three, "seldom" as two, and"never" as one. On the item "Drives family car," for example, if the respondent indicated "usually" for the father and "never" for the mother, the difference would be three points. As there were seventeen items on the questionnaire, a score of 51 was possible for each measure. The highest observed role-specialization score for the parents was 30, and the lowest was four. For the teenagers the highest role-specialization score observed was 24 and the lowest 2.

To standardize family background in some respects other than degree of role specialization, all respondents with any of the following characteristics were discarded: (1) those who were married, (2) those who reported step-children in the family, (3) those who reported they were living with only one parent or with neither parent, and (4) those who did not have a sibling of the opposite sex within five years of their age. Of approximately 200 who completed the questionnaire, only 64 met all qualifications, leaving a rather small sample. Moreover, of these 64, only 60 had completed the TST, so that the total sample of this study was 60, composed of 22 males and 38 females. The average age of the males was 19.3, ranging from 17 to 23 with only two over 21 years old. For the females the average age was

Table 1. Mean Role-Specialization Scores of Males And Females By Identification Or Non-Identification Of Self by Sex

	Females			*Males*		
	Mean Score of Parental Role-Specialization	*N*	*Mean Score of Teenager Role-Specialization*	*Mean Score of Parental Role-Specialization*	*N*	*Mean Score of Teenager Role-Specialization*
Self-identification by sex	13.83*	30	11.97	18.14	14	11.00
No self-identification by sex	17.88*	8	13.25	14.37	8	10.13

*Difference significant at the .06 level.

18.3, ranging from 17 to 21 years of age. With the above controls and with all subjects being students at a specific college, the sample is quite homogeneous.

Fundamental to George Herbert Mead's orientation is the proposition that humans perceive and define themselves as they believe others perceive and define them.[5] It appears logical to assume that families with a high degree of role specialization would be more likely to define their members in terms of sex statuses than would families marked by a low degree of role specialization. Therefore, the empirical hypothesis tested is: The greater the reported role specialization is between sexes within a family, the more frequently will the children use their sex status as a means of self-identification in responding to the TST.

As a test of the hypothesis, it was noted whether or not respondents had identified themselves on the TST as male or female, boy or girl, or man or woman. Self-identifications as son or daughter or reference to interest in activities that are traditionally male or female, were not considered in this test. Reported role specialization of neither parents nor... teenagers appeared to be associated with identification or nonidentification of self on the TST by sex. A parallel analysis was performed for associations between self-identification as son or daughter and role-specialization scores. No associations were noted. In short, the data completely failed to support the hypothesis.

The data were then reanalyzed for each sex separately, and an interesting pattern emerged. As Table 1 indicates, while an *inverse* association obtains between degree of reported role specialization and identification of self by sex for female respondents, a *positive* association is present for male respondents.

The TST protocols were also examined for mentioning or failing to mention son or daughter status. The mean parental role-specialization scores of those girls who identified themselves as daughters was slightly higher than was the mean of those who did not, a direct association (see Table 2). This difference, while slight, is in the opposite direction from the general pattern observed. For males, the mean parental role-specialization score of those who identified themselves as sons was significantly higher than the mean for those who did not.

A consideration of the relationship between children's role specialization and self-identification as son or daughter indicates that role specialization is inversely associated with self-identification as daughter, while there is a slight positive association of role specialization with self-identification as son (see Table 2).

Table 3 presents the results when it is noted whether the respondent identifies himself by both sex and son or daughter statuses, by one or the

[5] G. H. Mead, *Mind, Self and Society* (Chicago: Univ. of Chicago Press, 1934).

Table 2. Mean Role-Specialization Scores of Males and Females by Identification or Non-Identification Of Self As Son Or Daughter

	Females			*Males*		
	Mean Score of Parental Role-Specialization	*N*	*Mean Score of Teenager Role-Specialization*	*Mean Score of Parental Role-Specialization*	*N*	*Mean Score of Teenager Role-Specialization*
Self-identification as son or daughter	15.08	24	10.92†	19.17*	12	11.25
No self-identification as son or daughter	14.00	14	14.50†	13.90*	10	10.00

*Difference significant at the .05 level.
†Difference significant at the .02 level.

Table 3. Mean Role-Specialization Scores of Males and Females by Self-Identification by Sex and Son or Daughter, by Sex or Son or Daughter, And Neither

	Females			Males		
	Mean Score of Parental Role-Specialization	*N*	*Mean Score of Teenager Role-Specialization*	*Mean Score of Parental Role-Specialization*	*N*	*Mean Score of Teenager Role-Specialization*
Identified self by sex and as son or daughter	14.42	19	10.89	19.75	8	10.37
Identified self by sex or as son or daughter	14.31	16	12.94	16.80	10	12.30
Failed to identify self by sex or as son or daughter	18.33	3	17.00	10.75	4	7.25

other, or fails to make either type of self-identification. The number who failed to make either type of self-identification is small, but there is consistency in the results obtained. Females with neither form of self-identification tend to have high scores on both measures of role specialization. In contrast, males with neither form of self-identification tend to have low role-specialization scores on both measures.

In summary, despite some minor exceptions, the data rather consistently display (1) a direct association between degree of role specialization within the family and self-identification as son or by sex status for male respondents and (2) an inverse association between degree of role specialization within the family and self-identification as daughter or by sex status for female respondents.

Any interpretation of the findings of this research must take into account other common findings relevant to self-identification by sex and family statuses. It has been rather consistently observed that females of college age use their sex status and family status as means for self-identification more frequently than do males in responding to the TST.[6] In this sample 30 of 38 females (79 per cent) made a sex reference, compared to 14 of 22 males (64 per cent). Also 24 of 38 females (63 per cent) indentified themselves as daughters compared to 12 of 22 males (56 per cent) identifying themselves as sons. Kuhn has reported that members of minority groups commonly identify themselves by reference to their ethnic background. In conjunction with the use by females of their sex and family statuses more frequently than by males, he offers: "One. . . hypothesis is that the salience of defining oneself as a woman is related to the status of women as a minority group (sociologically speaking) in our society."[7] Members of a minority group are rather continually made aware of their status by restrictions placed upon their behavior and, therefore, tend to utilize this status as a means of self-identification.

While this could account for the difference in frequency between the sexes in defining themselves by sex, this interpretation makes it difficult to understand the finding that females from families with the highest degree of role specialization are the very ones who fail to identify themselves by reference to sex. It would seem that these persons would be most saliently aware of their "minority" status and, therefore, if awareness is the crucial variable, would identify themselves by sex.

It has been frequently observed that people do not always think of themselves as they are consensually defined by others. Self-conceptions are not a mere replication of the definitions applied to the person by others. Perhaps the findings of this study and the observation that self-conceptions are not a direct reflection of definitions furnished by others can be interpreted as follows. The acquisition of a self involves, in nearly all

[6] Kuhn, *op. cit.*, pp. 46-49; Couch, *op. cit.*, p. 496.

[7] Kuhn, *op. cit.*, p. 48.

cases, learning to place positive value upon the self as a general object.[8] Humans also learn techniques or means for the maintenance of positive self-conceptions. One way humans learn to acquire and maintain a positive self-conception is to acquire those statuses that are positively valued within their groups and to avoid acquiring those statuses that are negatively valued.

It seems highly probable that those families with a high degree of role specializations are patriarchal families, in which high role specialization is associated with high evaluation of male and son statuses. This leads to self-identification as male or son by the males, for the value assigned to both statuses is consistent with the value placed upon the self as a general object. In contrast, females with a family background of high role specialization learn that the statuses of female and daughter are somewhat negatively evaluated. This is in conflict with the positive value placed upon the self as a general object. As a consequence, they think of themselves less frequently as daughters and as females than do females from families with low role specialization.

The above interpretation assumes a level of awareness by females of their sex and daughter statuses that is of sufficient intensity that variation in role specialization within the family has no appreciable effect upon it. An alternative interpretation may be that in the case of those females with a family background of high role specialization the negative evaluation of these statuses is of such intensity as to override the effect of greater awareness.

[8] Although this proposition needs intensive investigation, it is tentatively accepted.

24. Self-Conceptions in a General Population *

Harold A. Mulford and
Winfield W. Salisbury II

One of the most promising efforts to operationalize the concept of the "self" has been that of the late Professor Manford H. Kuhn and his students. This approach has employed the "Twenty-Statements Test," or TST, an open-ended instrument which is designed to elicit the respondent's "spontaneous" self-definitions in their order of salience. Since its first publication in 1954, the TST has been used in a variety of studies.[1] However, previous

From the *Sociological Quarterly,* V (Winter, 1964), pp. 35-46, by permission of the journal.

*This article is part of a larger study mainly designed to replicate an earlier survey of the behavior patterns and attitudes regarding the use of alcoholic beverage by adult Iowans. Analysis and evaluation of the sampling and interviewing procedures as well as some of the replication results have been published elsewhere. See Harold Mulford and Donald Miller, "The Prevalence and Extent of Drinking in Iowa," 1961: A Replication and Evaluation of Methods," *Quarterly Journal of Studies on Alcohol,* 24:39-53 (Mar. 1963). The study was supported by the Department of Psychiatry and the State Psychopathic Hospital, College of Medicine, University of Iowa. The data were collected with the kind assistance of the Iowa Poll organization of the *Des Moines Register and Tribune.*

[1] Kuhn's research interest in spontaneous self-concepts reaches back to his comparative study of the self-concepts of Amish and "gentile" children in 1948. See Manford H. Kuhn, "Factors in Personality, Socio-Cultural Determinants as Seen through the Amish," in *Aspects of Culture and Personality,* ed. by Francis L.J. Hsu (New York: Abelard-Schuman, 1954), pp. 43-65, where self-definitions were elicited by thirteen questions directed at specific status-role areas of self-identification. The Twenty-Statements Test was constructed by Professor Kuhn in 1952 and was first described in Manford H. Kuhn and T.S. McPartland, "An Investigation of Self-Attitudes," *American Sociological Review,* 19:68-76 (Feb., 1954).

Since that time, the following studies using the TST have been published: T.S. McPartland and John H. Cumming, "Self-Conception, Social Class and Mental Health," *Human Organization,* vol. 17, no. 3, pp. 24-29 (1958); M.H. Kuhn, "Self Attitudes by Age, Sex, and Professional Training," *Sociological Quarterly,* 1:39-55 (Jan., 1960); T.S. McPartland, John H. Cumming, and Wynona S. Garretson, "Self-Conception and Ward Behavior in Two Psychiatric Hospitals," *Sociometry,* 24:111-24 (June, 1961); Wynona studies of the "self" have been conducted on restricted population samples, and little is known about the self-definitions held by a general population.

The present paper describes the TST responses of a representative sample of the general adult population of Iowa.[2]

Procedure

Forty-three interviewers administered the TST to 1,213 respondents chosen by quota sampling procedures to represent the adult population of Iowa (21 years of age and older).

Analysis of the methods, including comparisons between the observed sample and the "known" population on a number of check factors, confirmed the sample's representativeness and provided added confidence in the interviewers' performance.[3]

The TST was placed near the beginning of the interview to avoid the possibility of contamination by other questions. The interviewer handed the respondent a sheet of paper containing the question. "Who Am I?" and some brief instructions. The sheet was otherwise blank, and the respondent was asked to record his own answers. The instructions were designed to encourage the subject to respond as spontaneously and unreflectively as possible, and they were repeated verbally by the interviewer.[4] Interviewers were instructed to give the respondent as much time as he needed, but to proceed with the remainder of the interview after two or three minutes if the respondent seemed unable to give further answers to the question.

These procedures differ from those followed in past studies in that previous investigators numbered the lines and gave the respondent six minutes to answer. They also urged the respondents to write twenty statements, or at least as many as possible in the allotted time. While the effects of these procedural differences are unknown, we were of the opinion that omitting the line numbers and not insisting upon the completion of a specific number of statements would reduce the danger of antagonizing the respondent. However, the new procedure may also account for the relatively

---

S. Garretson, "The Consensual Definition of Social Objects," *Sociological Quarterly,* 3:107-13 (Apr. 1962); Carl J. Couch, "Family Role Specialization and Self-Attitudes in Children," *Sociological Quarterly,* 3:115-21 (Apr., 1962); Glenn M. Vernon, "Religious Self-Identification," *Pacific Sociological Review,* 5:40-43 (Spring, 1962); Fred B. Waisanen, "Self-Attitudes and Performance Expectations," *Sociological Quarterly,* 3:208-19 (July, 1962).

[2] A survey of a similar nature has been reported by Kuhn, but his population was restricted to school children and college students: "Self-Attitudes by Age, Sex, and Professional Training," *op. cit.*

[3] Mulford and Miller, *op. cit.*

[4] For a description of the TST see Kuhn and McPartland, *op. cit.*

small number of statements obtained in the present study. The median number of statements was 4 and the mean number was 4.4. Only eighteen respondents failed to give any response, and fifty-nine gave ten or more.[5] In spite of the low mean number of statements, those which were obtained are judged to provide a minimally adequate sample of the most salient and spontaneous self-definitions held by a general population.

Mode of Analysis

The responses were analyzed for content. In developing the classification scheme, consideration was given to those content categories which (a) have most commonly appeared in "self-concept" studies and (b) which offer the most promise for explanatory research. The response categories reported here are some of the sociocultural categories (age, sex, etc.) most frequently found in sociological research.[6]

This paper, then, will primarily be concerned with how Iowa adults define themselves on the TST in terms of their statuses and roles. This includes the following content categories. The numbering corresponds to that in Table 1.

1. *Specific sex identity.* This includes direct references to sex status, such as "I am a man, woman, boy, girl," etc., as well as modified sex mention, such as "I am a young woman," or "I am a family man." However, terms from which sex could be inferred (such as sportsman, wife) but which were seemingly not intended to denote sex status were excluded.

[5] See Kent P. Schwirian, "Variations in Structure of the Kuhn-McPartland Twenty-Statements Test and Related Response Differences," *The Sociological Quarterly,* V (Winter, 1964), pp. 47-59.

[6] The responses have also been analyzed in terms of more abstract categories, such as "social anchorage" and "self-disturbance." These results will be the subject of a later report. Several classification schemes have been employed in earlier investigations to explore specific dimensions of the self-concept. "Locus score" has been used by Kuhn and McPartland *(op. cit.)* and by Garretson, *(op. cit.),* as well as in numerous unpublished dissertations at the University of Iowa. Kuhn has proposed a content analysis scheme consisting of five categories: see C.A. Hickman and M.H. Kuhn, *Individuals, Groups, and Economic Behavior* (New York: Dryden Press, 1956), p. 245. Kuhn's categories are (1) social groups and classifications, (2) ideological beliefs, (3) interests and aversions, (4) ambitions, and (5) self-evaluations. McPartland and Cumming have proposed still another scheme consisting of four categories based upon the level of abstraction of the response. This scheme was used to predict the ward behavior of institutionalized mental patients: see McPartland and Cumming, *op. cit.*

2. *Age.* Both exact statements of age in years and general categorical references to age status (I am young, middle-aged, old) were included as mention of age status.
3. *Marital status and role.* This included both direct mention of marital status (I am a wife, a husband, married, etc.) and also statements in which the respondent indicated involvement in his marital role (I have a lovely wife; I help my husband at work).
4. *Nuclear family status and role.* This includes category 3, above, as well as any mention of parental status and any mention of involvement in parental roles; for single persons it also includes any mention of status or involvement in family of orientation.
5. *Extended family relationships.* This includes all mention of family status and roles outside the nuclear family, including references

Table 1. Classification of TST Responses by Total Sample*
(In percentages)

Types of Self-Identity	One or More Mentions		
	Total N= 1208	Men N= 572	Women N= 631
1 Specific sex identity	17	25	10 †
2 Age, specific and categorical	11	12	9
3 Marital status and role	34	27	39 †
4 All types of nuclear family status and role	60	43	74 †
5 Extended family relationships	10	6	13 †
6 Primary group identities	10	6	14 †
7 Secondary group identities	14	12	16 †
8 Religion			
a) Specific denomination	5	5	5
b) All types of religions self-identity	25	19	30 †
9 Occupation			
a) specific occupational identity	62	60	64
b) all types of work role identity	68	69	67
10 Ethnic group			
a) Identity as an American	6	9	4 †
b) Other ethnic groups	1	1	..
11 Education	3	3	3
12 Social class identity ‡	..	..	..
13 Racial identity	1	1	1

*In a test of interjudge reliability there was 87.2 per cent agreement on a sample of 256 responses.

† Significant sex differences at the .05 level.

‡ Only one person gave a self-concept indicating class identity.

to being a grandparent, grandchild, aunt, uncle, nephew, etc., and to related roles.

6. *Primary groups.* The statements of membership status or role-playing in non-family primary groups are included, such as being or playing the role of friend, neighbor, liking one's fellow workers, etc.
7. *Secondary groups.* These are references to being a member of or playing a role in a specific secondary group—a church, club, secondary association, or work or school institution.
8. *Religion*
   a) *Specific denomination.* Mention of membership in a specific religious denomination, such as "I am a Methodist, Catholic, Mennonite," etc.
   b) *Religious self-identity.* This category includes category *a,* above, and adds to it all definitions of the self as a religious person, such as "I am religious," "I believe in God," "I try to live by the Ten Commandments."
9. *Occupation*
   a) *Specific occupational identity.* All statements which refer to a specific type of job that could be classified in the usual U.S. Census occupational categories are included.
   b) *Work role identities.* These include category *a,* above, as well as any general statement in which the respondent indicates involvement in a "work" status, role, or task, such as "I enjoy my work," "I help my husband with the crops," "I do a lot of housework."
10. *Ethnic group*
   a) *Identity as an American.* This includes any close variant of the simple statement, "I am an American."
   b) *Mention of other ethnic groups.* Any statement was counted in which the respondent indicated that he saw himself as belonging to any ethnic or national minority group, such as "I am Scots-Irish," "I came from German stock."
11. *Education.* Any mention of a former or present educational status (level of attainment) or experience, such as, "I graduated from high school," "I went to high school in Mason City," "I graduated from college."
12. *Social class identity.* Here three simple categories were used: references to being (1) working class, poor, etc.; (2) middle, average class, etc.; (3) upper-class, well-to-do, etc.
13. *Mention of racial identity.* This includes any mention of racial status.

While our major aim was to present a descriptive atlas of self-definitions, attention will be given to certain differences that are statistically significant as tested by the standard test of significance of difference between proportions. In the interest of space, some of the finer breakdowns employed in the original analysis will be combined for tabular presentation here.[7]

Selected Findings

Total Sample

Table 1 shows that of the thirteen categories of self-definitions examined only four have relatively high rates of mention by the total population (25 per cent to 68 per cent). These are (3) marital status and role, (4) all types of nuclear family status and role—includes (3), (8b) religious identity, and (9) occupation.

Only moderate rates of mention (10 per cent to 17 per cent) are found for (1) sex and (2) age identities as well as for (5) extended family relationships and for (6) all types of identification with non-family primary groups and (7) secondary groups. Although general religious self-identity (8b) was common, identification with a specific denomination (8a) was rare. Virtually no one defined himself in terms of education, race, class, or ethnic groups of origin, except that 9 per cent of the men and 4 per cent of the women mentioned that they were "American."

Sex Differences

There are eight cases where the rates for the sexes are significantly different. Women seem more concerned than men with family-oriented self-definitions (categories 3, 4, and 5, Table 1) and with anchoring themselves in non-family groups (categories 6 and 7). They also more often conceive of themselves as being religious—(category 8b). Men mention their sex and ethnic identity more often than women. The greater frequency of mention of most of the categories by women probably reflects the greater number of statements made by them. The mean number of responses for women was 4.7 as compared to 4.1 for the men. In effect, about half of the women made an extra statement as compared to the men, and it most frequently referred to family, religion, friends, or a club, in that order. This difference in number of responses raises a question about the meaning of the statistical comparison of sex rates. However, we will assume that the fact that men did not feel compelled to make another statement, when they had the same opportunity to do so as women, reflects their lesser concern with the particular identity in question.

Age

Analysis of age mention by the age of the respondent revealed that the rates of mention of age are virtually identical for the decades 30 through 60. How-

[7] Detailed data and results are available from the authors on request.

ever, mention of age by persons aged 20 to 30 and by those over 70 were significantly higher. Perhaps it is not surprising that age is a more salient identity for persons in their twenties in our youth-centered culture. Age mention by those in their seventies and eighties may be higher because many other significant status anchorages have been lost. However, it is somewhat surprising that the increase in later years does not begin in the sixties, when the usual age of retirement occurs.

Sex Identity by Sex and Age

Table 2 reveals that men mention their sex two to three times as often as women do. Although the difference remains, it appears to be smaller beyond

Table 2. Mention of Sex Identity By Age and Sex

Age	Number in Sample			Sex Identity Mention (percentage)		
	Total	Men	Women	Total	Men	Women
20-29	201	93	108	*19*	*29*	*11*
30-39	256	117	139	*16*	*27*	*6*
40-49	254	123	131	*19*	*26*	*11*
50-59	199	100	99	*16*	*25*	*7*
60-69	160	73	87	*16*	*19*	*13*
70 +	137	69	68	*19*	*22*	*16*
Total	1207	575	632	*17*	*25*	*10*

the age of sixty. These findings contrast with Kuhn's evidence that among college students women more often make direct mention of their sex than do males.[8] The greater mention of sex roles by college women may be linked to their concern over courtship. On the other hand, women in the general population appear to be satisfied to express their sex identity more indirectly by mentioning sex-linked family roles.

There appears to be no age difference in sex mention until we look at the sexes separately. The rate of mention of sex by women appears to increase slightly with age, being highest in the two oldest age categories, whereas for men the rate of mention is lowest in the two oldest age groups.

Family Status and Roles

Table 1 indicates that women more often than men define themselves in terms of their family status and roles. However, a more accurate notion of the sex differences can be obtained by controlling for marital status and the number of children.

[8] Kuhn, *op. cit.*; see Table 3, p. 47. For a discussion of sex differences in sex mention, see pages 46 and 48.

Considering only those persons who are married, we find in Table 3 that 29 per cent of the men and 41 per cent of the women either refer to

Table 3. Sex Differences in Mentions of Family Statuses And Roles (Married Subjects)

Type of Self-Identity	Total N= 1012		Men N= 499		Women N= 513	
	N	pct.	N	pct.	N	pct.
1 Husband or Wife Status or Role	355	*35*	143	*29*	212	*41*
2 Specific Mention of "Mother" or "Father" Identity	375	*37*	97	*19*	278	*54*
3 All Types of Nuclear Family Status or Role	657	*65*	244	*49*	413	*81*
4 Extended Family Status or Role	88	*9*	27	*5*	61	*12*

their status as "husband" or "wife," or refer to the performance of the role involved. The rate of mention for women is about 40 per cent greater than the rate for men. When all types of mention of nuclear family status and roles are considered, half of the men, but 81 per cent of the women, make one or more mentions. Here, the rate for women is two-thirds greater than that for men. It is likely that this greater difference is due to the inclusion of "mother" and "father" identities in the more general Nuclear Family category.

However, rates of mention of parental status are more meaningfully compared if only those with children living at home are used as a base. Such analysis revealed that 30 per cent of the men define themselves as "father", but 78 per cent of the women or proportionately two and one-half times as many, define themselves as "mother." This rate for fathers is virtually identical with the proportion of husbands (29 per cent) who define themselves in terms of the husband role. By contrast, the proportion of mothers who define themselves as "mother" is double the proportion of wives who mention the "wife" role (40 per cent). This suggests that the status of "mother" is far more crucial to women than the status of "father" is to men, at least in terms of anchoring their identity in social space.

This difference between men and women with regard to their involvement in the family role is revealed even more clearly when these rates are broken down by the number of children living at home, as in Table 4. The

Table 4. Mention of Nuclear Family Roles By Sex And Number of Children (Married Subjects)

Number Of Children	Number in Sample: Total	Men	Women	Percentage Mention: Total	Men	Women
None	171	98	73	*44*	*36*	*55*
1-3	522	252	270	*72*	*55*	*89*
4 +	152	67	85	*88*	*75*	*98*

broad category of nuclear family status and roles shows a sufficient frequency to permit this kind of analysis. When there are no children in the family, approximately one-third of the married men (36 per cent) but more than half of the women (55 per cent) make some kind of nuclear family statement. For respondents with one to three children, the rate for men increases to 55 per cent, whereas the rate for women increases to 89 per cent. Given the original differences, the effect of a small family on men and women seems to be nearly equal. However, when there are four or more children, the rate of "nuclear family" statements increases 36 per cent for men to 75 per cent, and 10 per cent for women to 98 per cent. In other words, nearly all of the women define themselves in terms of nuclear family roles as soon as a minimal family appears.[9] However, the rate for men does not approach its maximum until there are four or more children.

The examination of extent of mention of nuclear family roles also reveals the delayed impact of the family on men as compared to women. When those who made two or more statements of nuclear family identity are considered, the rates for husbands and wives without children is almost identical (20 per cent and 25 per cent, respectively). With one child, the rate for women increases to 56 per cent, whereas the rate for men remains virtually unchanged. With more than one child, the rate of two or more statements does not change at all for women, but for men it increases until those with four or more children have a rate (51 per cent) equal to that for women.

If one considers the specific mention of "father" or "mother" to be a more accurate indicator of the degree to which identity is affected by the number of children, the evidence again points to the same conclusion. While the rate of "father" mention is generally low, it increases from 11 per cent to 37 per cent as we proceed from one to four or more children. Of course, the time order assumed in this interpretation cannot be established from

Table 5. Mentions of Nuclear Family Roles By Length of Marriage

		Percentage Mentioning		
Years Married	N	Spouse Role	Parental Role	All Nuclear Family Roles
0-4	100	50	25	70
5-9	141	37	48	76
10-14	166	41	48	71
15-19	111	39	39	72
20-29	222	28	33	59
30-39	93	25	33	55
40+	123	29	27	46
Total	956	35	37	64

[9] For women with one child, the rate of mention was 93 per cent.

these data, and it is possible that self-definitions may influence family size.

Evidence was also gathered regarding changes in self-definitions of family role through the course of marital life. Since the sample is composed of adults, and we are interested in kinship identities, years of marriage rather than age was chosen as the appropriate time measure.

Both sexes show a high level of family identification for the first twenty years of marriage. More than one-half of the men and nearly 90 per cent of the women married not more than twenty years made some mention of nuclear family roles. However, the rates of family mention drop markedly after twenty years of marriage, and there is a further significant drop for those married more than forty years.

When we examined the two major subcategories of nuclear family identity, viz., definition of self as "spouse" and as "parent" (see Table 5), this apparent lack of change in mention of family roles during the early years of marriage is seen to be the outcome of opposite trends in mention of marital status as compared with mention of parental status. For both sexes the salience of parental identity increases after five years of marriage, whereas identity with "spouse" status and roles, fairly high at first, declines at about the same time. In the next fifteen years of marriage, there is no change in either set of rates. After the twenty-year mark is reached, the rate for both categories drops as previously pointed out.

Occupation

It will be recalled from Table 1 that 62 per cent of the sample defined them-

Table 6. Mentions of Occupation and Work Roles By Occupation and Sex

Occupation	Number in Sample			Percentage Mention		
	Total	Men	Women	Total	Men	Women
Professional, technical	46	36	10	74	69	90
Business	72	64	8	60	61	50
Clerical sales	93	56	37	66	63	70
Skilled	63	61	2	59	59	..
Semiskilled	54	45	9	52	49	..
Service	63	28	35	67	64	69
Farmer	137	137	..	89	89	..
Unskilled	29	27	2	62	59	..
Housewife	506	..	506	68	..	68
Retired, student, unemployed	95	77	18	61	66	39
Blank (N.R.)	55	44	11	60	66	36
Total	1213	575	638	68	68	67

selves in terms of specific occupational statuses and a total of 68 per cent made some mention of work role.

Table 6 analyzes mentions of occupational status and work role in terms of the subjects' stated occupations. The table reveals very high rates of occupational and work role identities for both sexes and for all occupations. The reason for the similarity in rates between the sexes noted in Table 1 becomes apparent in Table 6. It is due to the frequency with which women identify themselves as "housewife," and to the fact that this response was coded as an occupational identity. Of the 506 women who claimed the occupation of housewife, more than two-thirds (68 per cent) also defined themselves as housewives or referred to housework roles on the TST.

These findings have been presented in the hope of providing the beginnings, at least, of a base line to guide future research using the self-concept as measured by the minimally structured TST. However, the fact should be considered, as the late Professor Kuhn has pointed out to the authors, that the responses used for this analysis contained an average of only 4.5 statements. Whether the forced acquisition of the full twenty statements would lead to different results is, of course, a moot question.

25. Self-Conception and the Reactions of Others

Richard Videbeck *

The view that one's self-conception is learned from the reactions of other individuals to him has achieved wide acceptance in social psychology today, but its implications have not been much exploited empirically. Helper (3), Manis (4), and Miyamoto and Dornbusch (6) report findings which show that an individual's self-ratings are significantly correlated with the ratings of him made by his associates. Their work on the social origins of the self is lodged in Cooley's formulation of the "looking glass self" (1), and in Mead's conception of the self as an organization of socially derived and symbolically represented self-identification (5). Helper, Manis, and other investigators make inferences from their findings about the tenability of this general view, but they do not demonstrate that "other's reactions" are necessary antecedent conditions to self-ratings. It is the purpose of the study reported in this paper to test the hypothesis in a more direct fashion, by experimentally varying the reactions of others and observing subsequent changes in self-ratings.

Self-conception is a term used to refer to a person's organization of his self attitudes. Operationally, it is frequently defined as a set of interrelated self-ratings, usually upon bipolar scales using some personal or behavioral quality as the referent of the scale. It is possible to distinguish between *ideal-self* ratings, i.e., the degree of the attribute implied in the scale which the person would like to possess, and *actual-self* ratings, i.e., the extent to which, in the person's own opinion, he currently possesses the specified scale attribute. This report is concerned only with changes in the latter self-ratings. As used here, actual-self rating are defined as *reinforced* scale responses. It is assumed that the person's choice of one scale point over the alternative points on the scale reflects the fact that informational cues have been supplied to the individual which "verify or validate" the selected scale point as being correct. According to the hypothesis, the principal source of such cues lies in the reactions of other people to the individual. Commonly, in the course of social interaction, other persons

From *Sociometry*, XXIII (December, 1960), pp. 351-359, by permission of the American Sociological Association and the author.

*The writer is indebted to Drs. Alan P. Bates, Harry Shelley, and John C. Loehlin for suggestions and criticisms. The project grew out of the writer's joint work with Alan Bates in the area of role analysis.

will express some degree of approval or disapproval of the individual or his behavior. The expressed degree of approval or disapproval is such a cue. Insofar as these expressions represent reward or punishment for the individual, the other's reactions reinforce a particular self-rating response. The response which is reinforced by such reaction is the choice of that point on the rating scale which corresponds to the degree of approval or disapproval inferred from the reaction. In simple outline, if a person is told that he is doing something very well, he will be *more likely* to rate himself as being more capable of doing that something or possessing the qualities related to doing it, than if he had been told he was doing it poorly.

The extent to which another can effectively reinforce an individual's self-rating response on a specific scale will depend on a number of factors, of which only four are considered here. First it will depend upon the *number of times* the other consistently approves or disapproves of the individual with reference to the specific qualities of the scale referent. Secondly it will depend upon *how appropriate or qualified the other is,* in the opinion of the individual, to show approval or disapproval. Thirdly it will depend upon how *strongly motivated* the individual is with reference to the attribute of the scale, i.e., how strongly he strives to attain some ideal-self point on the scale. Fourth, the effectiveness of another's reaction in reinforcing the individual's self-rating response will vary with the *intensity* with which the approval or disapproval is expressed, i.e., the other's apparent confidence and conviction of his expression. If these four conditions are held constant at a level sufficient to insure reinforcement of an individual's self-ratings, two hypotheses about the effects of another's reaction can be stated: (a) If another person reacts approvingly toward the individual with reference to some specified attribute, then the subject will change his actual-self rating, re that attribute, to a point closer to his ideal-self rating; but if the other reacts disapprovingly, then the subject will change his actual-self rating to a point farther away from his ideal-self rating. (b) If disapproving reactions do not substantively differ from approving reactions except for the element of negation, then there will be no difference in absolute amounts of change in self-ratings between subjects reacted to approvingly and disapprovingly, with reference to a given attribute.

Defining self-conceptions as organizations of interrelated sets of self-ratings may be interpreted to mean that in some way changes in one scale, measuring self-ratings, will lead to changes in the self-ratings upon other scales. If the attribute of a scale is viewed as a stimulus pattern, then by the principle of stimulus generalization it can be hypothesized that: (c) If another person reacts approvingly or disapprovingly to the qualities of an individual referred to in one scale, and if as a result the individual changes his self-rating on that scale, he will also change his self-ratings on other scales to the extent that the attributes of these other scales are functionally similar to the evaluated attribute.

Method

To test the hypotheses, a 2 by 3 design was employed, with two variations in the evaluative reactions of another, and three variations of similarity between rating-scale attributes. The three dependent variables, corresponding to the three hypotheses, are (a) the direction of change, (b) the amount of change, and (c) the spread of change of self-rating responses.

Thirty subjects, who had been rated superior by their instructors, were chosen from introductory speech classes. They were told that they would participate in an experiment to determine whether men or women were better in certain forms of oral communication. In the experimental session each read six poems. After the subject had read each poem, a person, who had been introduced as a visiting speech expert, evaluated the subject's reading performance. The subjects had been randomly assigned to one of the two "evaluative treatments." Regardless of the objective quality of their performance, half the subjects received approving reactions and half received disapproving reactions. The evaluative reactions were standardized, prepared statements which the "experts" read as if they were their own comments.

Before and after the experimental session, each subject rated himself on 24 items, each of which began with the prefatory phrase: "If you were required to, how adequately could you..." A nine-point scale was used with "extremely adequate" and "extremely inadequate" defining the poles of the scale. Sixteen of the items dealt with aspects of oral intepretive reading in which all of the subjects had had equal and extensive training in their speech course. Eight of these items specifically dealt with (a) conveying meaning and emotional tone and (b) voice control in oral reading. These items constituted the *Criticized Scale,* since the reactions of the "expert" were exclusively confined to the referents of these eight items. The other eight items constituted a scale which is called the *Related Scale,* because they are substantively similar to the items of the Criticized Scale, but were not reacted to by the expert. The remaining eight items dealt with oral communication in general social situations, such as leading a discussion group, engaging a stranger in conversation, etc. This scale is called the *Unrelated Scale,* to indicate that it is substantively less similar to the Criticized Scale than is the Related Scale.

After the second administration of the scales, the subjects were given a full explanation of what had transpired and the purposes of the study. The experiment lasted somewhat less than an hour for each subject.

In the above design the four factors relating to effectiveness for reinforcing an individual's self-rating were held constant. To illustrate, each subject entered the experiment with approximately the same level of rated competence and training and each subject received six reactions, hence the first factor (number of consistent reactions) was constant for all subjects.

With regard to the second factor (qualification of other to evaluate) all subjects reported in the post-experimental interview that they thought their critic was an expert. According to the estimates of their speech instructors, all subjects were above the average of their classes in interest in the subject matter and in their aspirations for quality of oral reading performance, thus all subjects were similar in general motivational level. As for the fourth factor, the assistants who served as "experts" had been trained to read both the approving and disapproving evaluations with the same intensity of expression. The standardized reactions were identical in wording for all subjects, except for evaluative terms, such as good-poor, succeeded in-failed to, etc. Thus, in terms of scale values, it was assumed that the approving reaction conveyed approval to the same degree as the disapproving reaction conveyed disapproval.

Findings

The initial differences between the approval and disapproval treatments for each scale are small and could have occurred more than nine times out of ten by chance (Table 1, Row B, Cols. 7-9). Therefore, any observed difference between the experimental groups in their after-ratings cannot be attributed to initial differences. Furthermore, the consistently high correlation between before and after ratings for all scales (Table 1, Row F) suggest that the rating scales are reliable as used in this experiment, and thus any significant differences in means between the two ratings can be attributed to the experimental conditions.

Hypothesis 1—Direction of Change

Considering only changes in the Criticized Scale scores, the mean change for subjects under the approval treatment are positive, and negative for disapproval subjects (Table 1, Row D, Cols. 1 and 4). An analysis of each subject's change reveals that 13 of the 15 approval subjects and 14 of the 15 disapproval subjects changed in the predicted direction. On the basis of these findings, the hypothesis that a person will rate himself closer to his ideal-self rating if he receives approval and farther away from it if he receives disapproval is considered tenable.

Hypothesis 2—Absolute Amounts of Change

If this hypothesis is acceptable, then differences between treatments in mean absolute amounts of change will not be significant at the .01 level for Criticized Scale scores. The results (Table 1, Row D, Cols. 1, 4, and 7) reveal that, disregarding signs, the difference is significant and the disapproval mean is two and a half times greater than the approval mean. This difference may be due to one of several factors. First, the degrees of approval and disapproval implied in the reactions of the other may not have

Table 1

Changes in Self-Rating, after Approval or Disapproval, by Relation of Rating Scale to Content of Criticism

	1			2			3		
	Approval Treatment			Disapproval Treatment			Significance of Difference between Treatment Means (One Tailed "t" Test for Uncorrelated Means)		
	(1) Criticized Scale	(2) Related Scale	(3) Unrelated Scale	(4) Criticized Scale	(5) Related Scale	(6) Unrelated Scale	(7) Criticized Scale	(8) Related Scale	(9) Unrelated Scale
A. Ideal-Self Rating	2.16	2.21	2.32	2.09	2.26	2.22	ns	ns	ns
B. Actual-Self Rating: "Before" Mean Score	3.99	3.78	3.66	3.86	3.95	3.70	>.90	>.90	>.90
C. Actual-Self Rating: "After" Mean Score	3.50	3.53	3.54	5.16	4.47	3.79	<.01	<.01	ns
D. Change: Difference between "Before" and "After" Mean Scores (in scale units)	+.49	+.25	+.12	-1.30	-.52	-.09	<.01	<.05	ns
E. Level of significance of difference between "Before" and "After" Mean Scores (one tailed, "t" test for correlated means)	ns	ns	ns	<.01	ns	ns			
F. Correlation between "Before" and "After" Scale Scores (Pearson product-moment correlation coefficients)	.873*	.927*	.742*	.807*	.828*	.597**			

*Significant at .01 level.

**Significant at .05 level.

been equal, as was initially assumed. Secondly, the observed difference may be an artifact of limitations imposed on the self-rating response by the scale. Thirdly, it is possible that approving and disapproving reactions lead to differential psychological effects, thereby producing differences in rating responses.

The assumption of equality of degrees of approval and disapproval was tested after the experiment by asking nine speech students to rate the reactions *qua* reactions for the amount of approval and disapproval implicit in them. These students, not used as experimental subjects, were asked first to read the approving reactions and then indicate how adequately they felt the person who received the reaction had performed. This was then repeated for the disapproval reactions. The mean rating assigned to the approval reactions was 1.89 or 3.11 scale units from the scale mid-point "5," and for disapproving reactions the mean rating was 7.91 or 2.91 scale units from the mid-point. By "t" test, the difference between the mean distances from the midpoint was not significant at the .01 level for 8 degrees of freedom. On the basis of this post-experimental evidence, the assumption of "objective" equality of degrees of approval and disapproval would appear to be tenable and not likely to account for the observed differences in absolute amounts of change between treatments.

A second factor which might account for the observed difference may be the relatively greater maximum amount of change possible for disapproval subjects. The maximum amount possible for subjects receiving approving reactions was 2.99 scale units, i.e., the scale distance from their initial mean to the "approval" extreme of the scale. For disapproval subjects, the maximum amount possible was 5.14 scale units. When the observed amounts of change are expressed in terms of their appropriate maximums, the disapproval subjects still changed relatively more than did the approval subjects: .253 vs. .167 of their respective maximum. All evidence considered, the hypothesis is not acceptable.

Since the correlation between the before and after ratings for both treatments is significant, the observed amounts of change must be seen as a product of the experimental conditions. In like manner, the observed differences between treatments must also be seen as the result of some systematic variation between the treatments. In part, the reaction of the other serves as an informational cue, i.e., tells the subject where the other judges him to be on the rating scale. For example, according to the ratings given the reactions by the nine speech subjects, the subjects receiving the approval treatment were in effect "told" by the other that they had performed in a "decidedly adequate" fashion, and the disapproval subjects that they had performed "decidedly inadequately." For the approval subjects, the "expert's" reactions tend generally to confirm the self-ratings derived from their experiences in the speech class and hence changed their self-rating only slightly. However, the disapproval subjects were confronted with an appraisal of their performance which was at variance with what they had become accustomed to receiving from their speech instructor, necessitating a revision of their self-estimates. According to the "adaptation level" principle, each subject enters the experimental situation with a self-estimate which reflects past-experiences tempered by the unfamiliar experimental setting. Successive self-ratings will in turn be joint products of the initial self-ratings and the subsequent stimuli, i.e., the reactions of the "expert." Following the adaptation level interpretation, shifts between before and after ratings should be proportional to the *interval* between the initially anchored scale point (i.e., the before rating) and the "objective" scale point of the intervening stimuli. Since the "objective" scale point of the other's reactions is constant within treatments, the "adaptation level" interpretation of the observed changes of self ratings can be tested by correlating the initial self-ratings with the absolute amount of change between self-ratings. For approval subjects, the correlation coefficient is .018 and for disapproval subjects it is .863. The latter coefficient tends to support this interpretation; the higher the initial self rating the greater the amount of change resulting from disapproving reactions. The nearly zero coefficient associated with the approval treatment is not surprising, in view of the fact that the difference between the before and after mean ratings was quantitatively small and statistically not significant.

Hypothesis 3 —Spread of Change between Scales

This hypothesis will be deemed acceptable if, within treatments, the amount of change for the Related Scale is *less* than the amount of change for the Criticized Scale but *more* than the change associated with the Unrelated Scale. The evidence (Table 1, Row D; Figure 1) tends to support the hypothesis.

The findings suggest that the reactions of others tend to have generalized effects upon self-ratings, but the degree of generalization diminishes as the scales become functionally dissimilar. When the data are presented in graphic form, as in Figure 1, it can be seen that the gradient of change for the disapproval treatment is steeper than the gradient for the approval treatment. No doubt this difference in steepness is due in part to marked differences in change in Criticized Scale scores; however, it does not explain why both gradients converge at the Unrelated Scale. Heider's concept "cognitive balance" (2) offers a possible explanation. When a subject is confronted with information which contradicts previously acquired information, and the information cannot readily be ignored or refuted, then the individual will incorporate the new information into his existing cognitive organization in such a way as to produce the least amount of change. Since the reactions of the other presented confirming information to the approval subjects, there is no need of isolating the other's evaluation within their total conception of themselves. The effects of negative reactions, on the other hand, seem to lead to greater discrimination between attributes of one's self-conception.

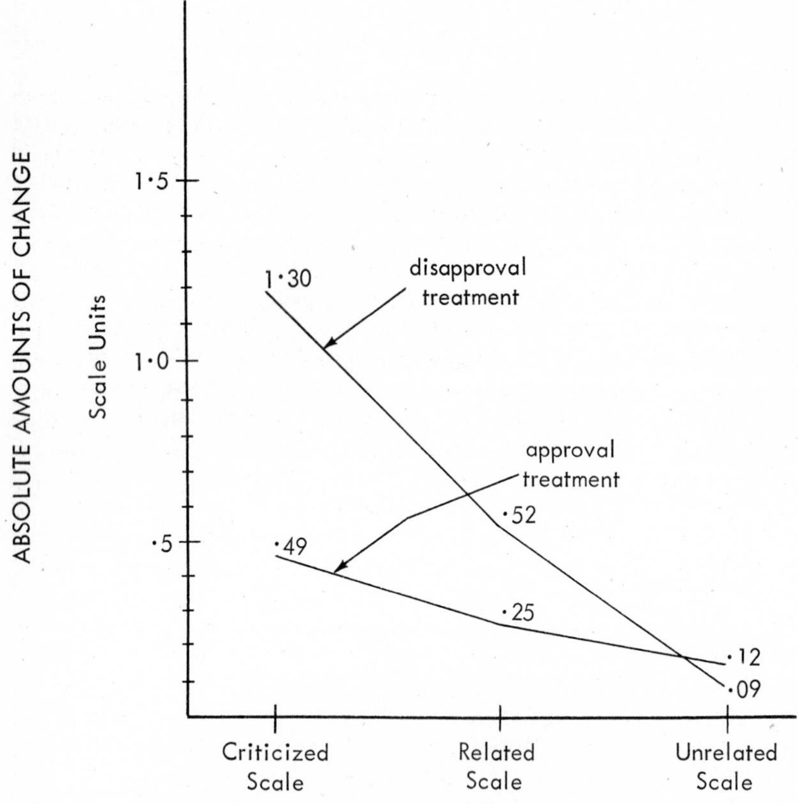

Figure 1

Furthermore, it is interesting to note that the relative rates of change between adjacent scales is almost identical for both treatments. For example, when the difference between the amount of change associated with the Criticized Scale and for the Related Scale is expressed as a proportion of the total amount of change between the Criticized and Unrelated Scales, there is no difference between treatments, the percentages being 64 per cent for the approval treatment and 65 per cent for the disapproval treatment. This constant, relative rate of change suggests that the adaptation level concept applies not only to the criticized scale but equally well to functionally similar scales.

Summary

The findings of this study tend to support the general view that self-conceptions are learned, and that the evaluative reactions of others play a significant part in the learning process. Observed differential effects of approval and disapproval treatments were interpreted to be a function of an interaction between the subject's initially anchored self-rating and the objective scale value of the approval or disapproval implied in the other's reaction. The findings also tend to support the hypothesis that one's self conception is an organization of discrete self-ratings which are unitized by the principle of stimulus generalization. These findings and interpretations are qualified by the fact that the number of reactions of others, the consistency of reactions within treatments, the qualifications of the other to evaluate, and the subjects' motivation were held constant.

References

1. Cooley, C. H., *Human Nature and the Social Order,* New York: Scribners, 1902.
2. Heider, F., "Attitudes and Cognitive Organization," *Journal of Psychology,* 1946, 21, 107-112.
3. Helper, M., "Learning Theory and the Self Concept," *Journal of Abnormal and Social Psychology,* 1955, 51, 184-194.
4. Manis, M., "Social Interaction and the Self Concept," *Journal of Abnormal and Social Psychology,* 1955, 51, 362-370.
5. Mead, G. H., *Mind, Self, and Society,* Charles W. Morris, (ed.), Chicago, University of Chicago Press, 1934.
6. Miyamoto, S. F., and S. M. Dornbusch, "A Test of Interactionist Hypotheses of Self Conception," *American Journal of Sociology,* 1956, 399-403.

26. Stendhal and the Self: A Study in the Sociology of Literature

Francis E. Merrill

Literature And Social Interaction

"A novel," said Stendhal, "is like a bow; the violin which makes the sounds is the reader's soul." The novelist tries to communicate an emotional and imaginative experience to the reader, to which the latter reacts. From this interaction comes the "meaning" of the novel. The characters have no objective existence outside the pattern of words that comprises the novel. The important consideration is the impact of this pattern upon the "soul" of the reader. In a basic sense, therefore, reading is a form of symbolic interaction between writer and reader, in which the latter reacts like the violin to the bow.[1] Reading and writing are reciprocal forms of social interaction and hence constitute a subject for the sociologist.[2]

The most intensely "human" of all qualities, the ability to take the role of other persons and regard one's self as an object, has been intuitively grasped by a long line of psychologists and social psychologists from William James (not forgetting his brother Henry), through Cooley and Dewey, to Mead. In more recent decades the insights of these and other seminal thinkers have been subjected to experimental verification by persons using more refined research techniques.[3] This is not the place to review these investigations; the point is that literature, essentially "great" literature, is a major source of knowledge of the social self. "Artists," in short, "have. . .

Reprinted from *The American Journal of Sociology,* LXVI (March, 1961), pp. 446–453, by permission of the University of Chicago Press.

[1] Martin Turnell, *The Novel in France* (New York: Vintage Books, 1958), pp. 6–7.

[2] Milton C. Albrecht, "The Relationship of Literature and Society," *American Journal of Sociology,* LIX (November, 1954), 425–36.

[3] Martin H. Kuhn and Thomas S. McPartland, "An Empirical Investigation of Self-attitudes," *American Sociological Review,* XIX (February, 1954), 68–76; Carl J. Couch, "Self-attitudes and Degree of Agreement with Immediate Others," *American Journal of Sociology,* LXIII (March, 1958), 491–96; Ralph H. Turner, "Self and Other in Moral Judgment," *American Sociological Review,* XIX (June, 1954), 249–59.

provided us with the richest mine of material in existence for the study of self-perception."[4]

Allport makes this relationship clear in his study of personality. "Through the ages," he remarks, ". . . this phenomenon of personal individuality has been depicted and explored by the humanities. The more aesthetic philosophers and the more philosophical artists have always made it their special province of interest."[5] A novel is a picture of personality in depth, with the continuity that marks this dynamic entity and distinguishes one from another. In all too many cases the psychologist, in his study of personality, fails to realize or, more often, to measure this continuity. Hence he depicts personality as a series of virtually unrelated actions like — to use Allport's expressive phrase — those of a water-skate darting about one a pond. "Good literature," continues Allport, "never makes the mistake of confusing the personality of man with that of a water-skate." Hence personality is a theme for both the novelist and the scientist. Only by this collaboration can its full richness and depth be grasped.

Science is based upon the gathering of facts, their classification, and the recognition of their sequences and relationships. Literature involves the insights into human behavior of a man of genius. The two activities are of different orders, but they involve the same phenomena. Merely because literary insights do not ordinarily lend themselves to empirical verification is no reason to reject or ignore them. Literature is an important aspect of culture, which is clearly a legitimate object of scientific exploration. Literature uses language, which is the most social of all activities, employing the symbols of human communication. Man is uniquely a symbol-using and rational animal. "Man," said Pascal, "is only a reed. But he is a *thinking* reed."

There are, as Redfield has well said, several ways of making order of experience: among them are religion, philosophy, science, and art.[6] They are not mutually exclusive, even though their methods differ. The humanities add to our knowledge of behavior, especially that of a past society where men lived and died without benefit of attitude scales and research teams. "Literature," therefore, "is a paramount source of insight for the scientist who attempts to formulate the core values of a culture, to characterize its guiding tenets in brief compass."[7] The situation does not call for polemics — either pro-literature or pro-science. Each has its contribution to human (and humane) learning.[8] This essay is a modest plea for tolerance of the human-

[4] Robert N. Wilson, *Man Made Plain* (Cleveland, Ohio: Howard Allen, Inc. 1958), p. 5.

[5] Gordon W. Allport, *Personality* (New York: Henry Holt & Co., 1937), quoted in Wilson, *op. cit.*, p. 7.

[6] Robert Redfield, "Social Science in Our Society," *Phylon,* XI (1950), 32.

[7] Wilson, *op. cit.*, p. 12

[8] Robert Bierstedt, "Sociology and Humane Learning," *American Sociological Review,* XXV (February, 1960), 3-9.

istic position, together with some notes on the insights of one author on the social self.

Stendhal and the Self

Stendhal, whose real name was Henri Beyle, is sometimes called the first of the "modern" novelists. He is unquestionably one of the greatest. In France his life and works have become the object of a cult whose fervor is surpassed only by the admirers of Balzac.[9] Stendhal was born in 1783 and took an active part in Napoleon's Italian and Russian campaigns in his youth. His military and political career came to an end with the fall of Napoleon, and he spent most of his adult years in "retirement" in Milan or Paris, writing continually. In his last years he held a minor consular post in Italy, from which he returned to Paris to die in 1842. He thus lived in a period of transition, social change, and intellectual ferment that has many of the characteristics of our own time. Perhaps this is why this writer, who predicted that he would hardly be read at all for fifty years and not widely for a hundred, is so enthusiastically accepted in France today. In an era of passion, humiliation, and self-doubt, he has a great deal to say to modern Frenchmen and, perhaps, to Americans.

Some years ago, the late André Gide was asked to name his favorite French novel.[10] The moralist and critic found himself in a difficult position. There was no question of his favorite novelist; Stendhal held that place beyond any question. A more difficult choice was that of his favorite novel: either *Le Rouge et le noir* or *La Chartreuse de Parme* deserved that honor. After considerable soul-searching, Gide chose *La Chartreuse.* For reasons that will soon appear, I choose *Le Rouge.* This novel is a study of the social self, perhaps the most subtle ever written. It is, as we have said, a "modern" novel, by which we mean, I suppose, a novel in which the self is constantly changing as the protagonist interacts with different persons and ideologies. The central character continually takes the role of the other toward himself and reacts accordingly.

Stendhal's intense preoccupation with his own self-image is apparent throughout his writings, both those which were frankly autobiographical and those in which the hero is a fictional projection of the person Stendhal would like to be. The most revealing of his autobiographical works is *La Vie de Henry Brulard,* in which he tells the story of his early years in Grenoble. In this amazing document he anticipated, among other things, the Oedipus complex. As a child, little Henry was passionately in love with his mother and, in later years, indicates that this affection was far from being merely

[9] The leading Stendhal scholar is the late Henri Martineau; see his *L'Œuvre de Stendhal* (Paris: Albin Michel, 1951); also his *Le Cœur de Stendhal* (2 vols.; Paris: Albin Michel, 1952-53).

[10] This incident is recounted by Martin Turnell *(op. cit.,* p., vii).

platonic. He reports candidly that he wanted to cover his mother with kisses and wished her to have no clothes on. Madame Beyle loved her precocious son "passionately" and gave him kisses which the little fellow returned with such ardor that his mother was often obliged to leave him. He wished, he said, especially to kiss his mother on the bosom. It need hardly be added that, to complete the classic pattern, Beyle hated his father.[11]

But it was his clinical interest in himself that marks Stendhal as an unusual novelist, even in a nation that has produced such masters of self-analysis as Montaigne and Pascal. As he broods over his life at the age of fifty, he returns again and again to the crucial question of his own identity: "What have I been?" he asks himself; "What am I?" He sees himself as the product of his family milieu, his ancestors, and his times. He also sees himself as the object of his own self-attitudes, which he intuitively realizes are the result of a continuous process of role-taking. The heroes of his novels are likewise concerned with their own self-images, which might or might not be exact renditions of the judgments of others toward them. It is no accident that Stendhal, the most self-conscious of men, should produce the most self-conscious of heroes.

The Red and the Black

The central interest in this essay is *Le Rouge et le noir.* The time is 1830, the place France. Julien Sorel is the son of a peasant in the Franche-Comté, a province in the mountains of east-central France. At the tender age of nineteen Julien secures a position as tutor to the children of M. de Rênal, mayor of the little town of Verrières. Julien is planning to enter the Church ("the Black") because he believes that this is the only way a poor boy can rise to the top of his society. The days of revolutionary and military glory ("the Red") have passed with the fall of Napoleon, and the Church remains the chief vehicle of vertical mobility for him, even though he has no true vocation for it. During his stay with M. Rênal, Julien falls in love with the beautiful, tender, and motherly wife of the mayor, and she with him. When their relationship becomes widely suspected, he leaves Verrières to study for the priesthood in nearby Besançon.

By a fortunate combination of circumstances, Julien is soon rescued from this distasteful existence and is received as private secretary to the liberal and witty Marquis de la Mole, a great Parisian nobleman and thus enters, at one bound, into the highest society of his day, although his position there is equivocal because of his peasant origin and his poverty. He is still an outsider, even though physically received into the upper nobility. At the same time, he falls in love with the brilliant, beautiful, and high-spirited Mathilde, the daughter of the Marquis. Julien regards this relationship as

[11] Stendhal, *La Vie de Henry Brulard,* ed. Henri Martineau (Paris: Editions Emile-Paul Frères, n.d.).

another challenge to him, and he seduces Mathilde (and she him) in a series of confrontations that among the most subtle in all fiction.

Mathilde becomes pregnant, and her father is naturally furious. Despite his chagrin, the Marquis decides to make the best of it, buys Julien a commission in a smart regiment, and settles some property on him and his daughter. At this point, a letter arrives from Madame de Rênal, written at the command of her holy confessor. The letter denounces Julien to the Marquis as a cold-blooded seducer and libertine. Beside himself with rage and frustrated ambition, Julien hurries back to Verrières. He finds Madame de Rênal in church and shoots, but does not kill, her. In his subsequent trial Julien refuses to defend himself, despite the entreaties of both Madame de Rênal and Mathilde. By so refusing he virtually commits suicide, and he is guillotined for premeditated attempted murder. Mathilde carries off his severed head and erects a chapel to his memory. Madame de Rênal dies of chagrin.

The story, baldly summarized above, has many facets. It is, first of all, a striking account of vertical mobility. The tragic saga of Julien Sorel is an account of the rise of a young man in Restoration France through a combination of good looks, exceptional intelligence, and the patronage of the rich and well born. The novels of Balzac, written at approximately the same period, also tell of poor boys from the provinces who storm the heights of the high society of the Faubourg Saint-Germain. *Le Rouge* is also a study of social institutions and their relationships, especially those of church and state in a reactionary society. For a while Julien cynically attaches himself to this venerable religious institution which, in conjunction with the nobility and the rising bourgeoisie, dominated the society of his day. The decade of the 1820's and 1830's saw the consolidation of the power of these institutions after the heady decades of the Napoleonic adventures.

Le Rouge is, above all, a love story, albeit one of the least "romantic" of all such stories. Love was a subject in which Stendhal maintained both a theoretical and a practical interest. His book on the subject *(De l'Amour)* is one of the most original and penetrating analyses of this tender sentiment that has ever been written. Love between the sexes is a direct and dramatic form of self-other relationship. The dialectic of love is the interaction of two persons, who are continually taking the other into account and responding in imagination to the resulting judgments. During this process the self-attitudes of the lover reflect his opinion of the attitudes of the other toward himself.[12] In a succession of subtle dialogues between Julien and Mathilde this self-other pattern is made abundantly clear.

"True" love is a matter of treating the other as an end in himself rather than as a means to an end. In this sense love is "that relationship between one person and another which is most conducive to the optimal development

[12] Francis E. Merrill, "The Self and the Other: An Emerging Field of Social Problems," *Social Problems,* IV (January, 1957), 200-207.

of both."[13] In the initial phases of his love affair with Madame de Rênal she was merely a means to Julien's ambition (self-feeling) and his fantastic pride. This ambivalence of affection and ambition was even more apparent in his relationship with Mathilde. His conception of himself was enhanced by his ability to bring this high-born beauty, literally, to his feet. He was never able to escape his ambivalent attitude throughout his affair with Mathilde, which is equivalent to saying that he never "really" loved her. After his attempted assassination of Madame de Rênal in the little church at Verrières, Julien realized that his love for her was truly unselfish. She ceased to be a means to his ambition and became an end in herself. He did not discover this fact until he lay in the grim shadow of the guillotine and it was too late.

The Dialectic of the Self

The dialectic of the self in *Le Rouge* has many aspects of the conception advanced a century later by George Herbert Mead. The latter saw the development of the self as a progression in which the person first takes the role of other individuals (mother, father, siblings, friends) toward himself. Later on he begins to take the role of the "generalized other" (i.e., that of society as a whole) toward himself and view himself in the light of these general precepts and behavior patterns. The generalized other is, in essence, sometimes the culture of the society and sometimes a segment thereof. In Mead's words, "the self reached its full development by organizing these individual attitudes of others into the organized social or group attitudes, and by thus becoming an individual reflection of the general systematic pattern of social or group behavior in which it and others are all involved."[14]

In *Le Rouge* Stendhal intuitively anticipated many of these ideas of the dialectical quality of the self. He was not, as he would have been the first to admit, a systematic thinker in the sense of evolving an organized system, much less of setting down a conceptual scheme such as the social self. Nevertheless, his insights were so acute that they foreshadowed many of the systematic ideas later developed by James, Cooley, Dewey, and Mead and subsequently verified empirically by others. I shall expand somewhat on Mead's dialectic by adding here a third interactive process, namely, that between the self and the "intermediate" other. The self of Julien Sorel will, therefore, be examined in terms of the direct other, the intermediate other, and the ideological (generalized) other.

[13] Nelson N. Foote, "Love," *Psychiatry,* XVI (August, 1953), 247.

[14] Anselm Strauss (ed.), *The Social Psychology of George Herbert Mead* (Chicago: University of Chicago Press, 1956), p. 235. The words are Mead's.

The Self and the Direct Other

The most important contribution of the pragmatic school to our knowledge of the self is its insistence upon its objective quality. The self is seen as the object, rather than the subject, of self-attitudes. In this sense, Julien Sorel is continually regarding himself through the eyes of a variety of others — from Madame de Rênal and Mathilde de la Mole, who are very near and "direct"; through such intermediate individuals and groups as the people of Verrières, the young men in the seminary, and the aristocracy of the Faubourg Saint-Germain; to the abstract ideological elements of pride, ambition, and honor. His extreme self-consciousness is at once his glory and his undoing. His personality is marked by an extraordinary sensibility to the real or supposed judgments of others. "He was," comments Stendhal, "sick to death of all his own good qualities, of all the things he had once enthusiastically loved, and in this state of *inverted imagination* he attempted, in the light of his imagination, to interpret life. "This," concludes Stendhal gloomily, "is the error of a man of superior quality."[15]

Julien was, first of all, always taking the role of the other toward himself. Depending upon the circumstances, this other might be Madame de Rênal, Mathilde, the Marquis de la Mole, or his old friend and confessor, the good Abbé Pirard. In this dialectical interchange the author indicates how often Julien was mistaken in his self-judgments — thus emphasizing an important element in the analysis of the self that is not always sufficiently stressed. Many of his judgments of the attitudes of others are wholly or partially incorrect. Because of his inexperience, Julien was unaware of his good looks — although he was very much aware of his superior intelligence and, he hoped, his character. He therefore failed to realize how much his handsome appearance appealed to women; on the contrary, he usually regarded himself as a bungler. "It was," remarks Stendhal in this connection, "a fatal trait in his character to be acutely conscious of his mistakes"(p. 341).

In his confrontations with others Julien was, therefore, tremendously self-conscious. Even in his amorous transports he is aware that he is playing a role. "I'm playing an undignified part here" (p. 375), he thought unhappily. This feeling is first apparent in his liaison with Madame de Rênal, and it becomes even more evident in his affair with Mathilde, who is just as self-conscious as he. In this reflexive fashion Julien loves himself (not very often), is pleased with himself (sometimes), and more often despises himself. "He was frightfully contemptuous of himself" (p. 61). Whether trying to play the role of Don Juan in the boudoir of Madame de Rênal or

[15] Stendhal, *Scarlet and Black,* trans. Margaret R. B. Shaw (London: Penguin Books, 1959), pp. 368-69. The English translate the *rouge* in the title as "scarlet," rather than as "red." Subsequent page references refer to this edition. The italics above are Stendhal's.

Mathilde, to shine as a worldly courtier in the salons of the Faubourg Saint-Germain, or to act the dandy in the Bois de Boulogne, Julien constantly views himself through the eyes of others. In most cases he finds himself wanting, a quality that is often, to use Stendhal's phrase, the basic error of a person of "superior quality."

The Self and the Intermediate Other

By the "intermediate other" I mean persons or groups with whom one is not actually communicating (interacting) at the moment but whose real or supposed judgments nevertheless influence one's self-judgments. This concept is somewhat similar to the reference group, defined as "that group whose outlook is used by the actor as the frame of reference in the organization of his perceptual field."[16] The two concepts differ, however, in that the intermediate other or others are not necessarily united in groups, either cohesive or otherwise. The intermediate others, indeed, may be disparate, and they may consist of isolated individuals with no sense of group unity. The person, furthermore, may or may not be conscious of his identification with the intermediate others. He may, indeed, be ambivalent toward this aspect of his environment and profess acute loathing for persons whose imputed judgments, nevertheless, play an important part in his self-feeling.

In the development of Julien's self there were a number of intermediate others whose attitudes he took into account. He was aware, for example, of the people of Verrières when he was considering his entry into the Mayor's home. When Julien's father raised this possibility, the boy's immediate concern was the figure he would cut in the community. He was not primarily concerned with his wages, living conditions, or work. His first question was about his *status.* "But whom," he demanded impatiently, "should I have my meals with?" (p. 39). In other words, what will be my role in the household of this leading figure? Will I be a servant and eat with the other servants in the kitchen? Or will I be treated as a member of the family and eat my meals with them? For, "rather than let myself be reduced to eating with the servants, I'd rather die" (p. 40).

When Julien goes to Paris and enters the town house of the Marquis de la Mole, he stands gaping in the courtyard of the great mansion. His sponsor, the good Abbé Pirard, admonishes him to look "sensible" if he does not want the Marquis' lackeys to make fun of him. "I defy them to do it," replied Julien, his self-possession rudely shattered (p. 253). When he begins to

[16] Tamotsu Shibutani, "Reference Groups as Perspectives," *American Journal of Sociology,* LX (May, 1955), 565; see also Robert K. Merton and Alice S. Kitt, "Contributions to the Theory of Reference Group Behavior," in Robert K. Merton and Paul F. Lazarsfeld (eds.), *Continuities in Social Research* (Glencoe, Ill.,: Free Press, 1950), pp. 53-59.

meet the men and women of the smart world, he becomes aware of his own shortcomings — his poverty, gaucherie, and peasant background. He constantly measures himself in the eyes of these intermediate others, and his self-attitudes waver between pride of his superior intellect and (later) his mastery over Mathilde, on the one hand, and a miserable self-deprecation, on the other. He was afraid of being shamed by these intermediate others, and his behavior was marked by an exaggerated arrogance to compensate for his galling self-judgments.

The Self and the Ideological Other

The ideological other in this context is similar to, but not identical with, the generalized other of Mead. The ideological other is the spirit of the times, the general patterns of belief that characterize a particular society at a given time. In Julien's case the ideological other was the *Zeitgeist* of France in the first three decades of the nineteenth century. This ideological imperative contained elements of the grandeur of Napoleon, the heroism of his revolutionary armies, the political adroitness of Talleyrand, and the seductiveness of Don Juan.

Julien was buffeted by these intellectual currents and saw himself first as one of these characters and then as another. Napoleon was dead, but his glory haunted the young man, even as it continued to haunt the aging Stendhal. As a young dragoon, the latter had served the Corsican in his Italian and Russian campaigns. Talleyrand was another cultural force whose talents for dissimulation, intrigue, and diplomacy comprised a different aspect of Julien's ideological other. The latter also aspired to be a great seducer of women, like Don Juan, a role in which he succeeded beyond his wildest dreams — in quality, if not in quantity. Two beautiful, well-born, and amorous women were his mistresses. As the book ends, they were both at his feet, as he languished in prison awaiting the guillotine.

In his affairs with women, Julien saw his love as a battle and himself as the hero. He tried to be a cynical man of the world, but his true goodness and sensibility did not allow him to play this role for very long. He feels that he "ought" to respond to Madame de Renal's affection with some positive action. "This woman cannot despise me any longer," he mused, "in that case, I ought to respond to her beauty. I owe it to myself to become her lover" (p. 96). During his first rapturous night, his pride kept him from enjoying his experience, for he still regarded himself as a Don Juan, accustomed to subduing any woman at his whim. As a result, Julien "made incredibly determined efforts to spoil what was lovable in himself" (p. 103). As he left Madame de Rênal's room in the dawn, he reflected: "Is being happy, is being loved no more than that?" (p. 104). Like one of Napoleon's troopers returning from the field of Marengo, Julien could think of nothing but his role. "Have I," he thought, "been wanting in anything I owe to myself? Have I played my part well?" (p. 104).

After his abortive attempt to assassinate Madame de Rênal, Julien spent several weeks in prison. During this time he thought of the different roles he had played during his life. He had never been able to lose the acute self-consciousness that so corroded his character. On the other hand, his self-pride was his chief sustaining force in his hour of adversity. "And what shall I have left," he reflected, "if I despise myself? I have been ambitious; I am not going to blame myself for that; *I acted then in accordance with the demands of the time*" (p. 509; italics mine). This self-conception led him to the prison cell; under other conditions, it might have led to a marshal's baton. In his own way Julien was a genius, or at least an exceptional man. In a corrupt society he was thwarted and struck down.

The ideological other was instrumental in forming Julien's ego-ideal — that is, his conception of himself as he would like to be. This self-conception is a composite portrait, derived from taking the roles of a variety of others toward ourselves. Julien identified himself, first of all, with Napoleon, whose *Memoires* constituted virtually his sole reading matter during his most impressionable years. His ego-ideal also embodied certain elements of probity which he saw in his early friend, the old parish priest, Father Chélan. As he grew older and came in contact with the smart world of Paris society, he hoped to be a dandy, a duelist, and a drawing-room diplomat. Added to these elements was the driving force of ambition, whereby he hoped to be a "success" in his own eyes and those of the world. It was another measure of his innocence that the various elements in this ego-ideal were incompatible and could never be reconciled. Indeed, the cream of the tragic jest was that his basic goodness and integrity made it impossible for him to realize the mundane ambitions of his ego-ideal.

This essay has explored some of the relationships between literature and society in a single novel and a single facet of personality. The social self has been depicted as the object of different self-attitudes, derived from taking the role of the direct other, the intermediate other, and the ideological other; Julien Sorel is one of the characters in fiction that illustrates most clearly this interactionist conception of the self. The genius of Stendhal is distilled into this portrait of a young man who is both ambitious and sensitive. Julien was unable to realize the baser aspects of his ego-ideal, and he died because he could not reconcile the conflicting elements in his self-conception. The social self as seen by modern social psychologists is the product of the real or assumed judgments of others, and in several ways Stendhal anticipated this formulation. *The Red and the Black* is an account of the interaction between one man and the incompatible elements of his psychological world.

Selected Bibliography
Part III, Self

Abu-Laban, Bahu, "Self-Conception and Appraisal by Others: A study of Community Leaders," *Sociology and Social Research,* 48 (October 1963), pp. 32-37.
How 25 "leaders" view themselves and are viewed by others.

Cooley, Charles Horton, "A Study of the Early Use of Self-Words by a Child," *Psychological Review,* 15 (November 1908), pp. 339-357.
Forerunner of the study described in Bain's article (page 251).

Couch, Carl, "Self-Attitudes and Degree of Agreement with Immediate Others," *American Journal of Sociology,* 63 (March 1958), pp. 491-496.
Reveals the extent to which identification of oneself in terms of group membership affects agreement with estimated evaluations of others in a small-group situation.

Kuhn, Manford H., "Self-Attitudes by Age, Sex, and Professional Training," *The Sociological Quarterly,* I (January, 1960), pp. 39-55.
Research comparing self-identifications of individuals in different social roles.

Mead, George Herbert, *Mind, Self and Society,* (Chicago: University of Chicago Press, 1934), pp. 144-178.
Mead's exposition of the genesis of the self.

Miyamoto, S. Frank, and Dornbusch, Sanford M., "A Test of Interactionist Hypotheses of Self-Conception," *American Journal of Sociology,* 61 (March 1956), pp. 399-403.

Pfuetze, Paul E., *The Social Self* (New York: Bookman Associates, 1954).
A comparison and synthesis of Mead's ideas on the self with those of the eminent theologian Martin Buber.

Plog, Stanley C., "The Disclosure of Self in the United States and Germany," *The Journal of Social Psychology,* 65 (April 1965), pp. 193-203.
Example of an approach to study of the self that does *not* derive directly from the symbolic interaction perspective.

Reckless, Walter C., Dinitz, Simon, and Murray, Ellen, "Self-Concept as an Insulator Against Delinquency," *American Sociological Review,* 21 (December, 1958), pp. 744-748.

Research study of non-delinquents living in a high delinquency area.

Reeder, Leo G., Donahue, George A., Biblarz, Arturo, "Conceptions of Self and Others," *American Journal of Sociology,* 66 (September 1960), pp. 153-159.

Research among military personnel, comparing self-concepts with ratings by others in the group.

Sherwood, J.J., "Self-Identity and Referent Others," *Sociometry,* 28 (March 1965), pp. 66-81.

Tests the proposition that "the individual's self-identity (and his self-evaluation) is dependent upon his subjectively held version of the peer group's actual ratings of him."

Wylie, Ruth C., *The Self Concept: A Critical Survey of Pertinent Research Literature* (Lincoln: University of Nebraska Press, 1961).

A fairly comprehensive summary of researches on the self, including studies based on symbolic interactionism.

Part IV. ❦ *Mind*

For symbolic interactionists, "mind" refers to the processes of behavior through which the human being carries on his "transactions" with his environment. The processes, consisting of designations to oneself by means of symbols, enable the individual to construct his acts as he executes them and to "carve out" the objects constituting his environment.

The concept of mind refers to a mental process or activity, not a physical entity such as the brain. Although the activity is covert, it is behavior — behavior which closely resembles the overt communication between individuals. The inner processes of thought rely on the same symbols used on observable behavior. Thinking can be viewed as a process of internal conversation — of symbolic interaction between the individual and himself.

As Read Bain's research on self-and-other words has demonstrated, the learning of language is the basis of interaction both with others and with oneself. To that extent, his research is pertinent to our consideration of mind. Yet, while mind was one of Mead's central concepts, it has generated little empirical research. Most of the readings in Part IV, therefore, are theoretical orientations to the subject.

Troyer's brief article presents Mead's major ideas on mind, stressing its social genesis and its adaptive, processual character. The crucial role of significant symbols in "minded behavior" emerges clearly in this summary.

The selection by Dewey further underscores the functional view of mind. This pragmatic, instrumental conception stands in sharp contrast to the conception of mind in substantive terms. While this article focusses on the relationship of mind to behavior, Dewey has also stressed the importance of society and communication on page 153.

The excerpt from Thomas' book discusses the indications to oneself that are entailed in thought-processes. That human beings act on the basis of their "definitions of the situation" is, of course, axiomatic for the symbolic-interactionist perspective. Strauss carries the analysis further by showing some of the relationships between the symbols, labels, or definitions we apply to persons or other objects and our "plans of action" toward the objects. It is in the light of Thomas' and Strauss's ideas that we can best understand the excerpt from Goldstein's book on aphasia. Here is found empirical information demonstrating the importance of language (symbols) in cognition and action.

One of the few researches on Mead's "social objects" concept is that by Garretson. Her report presents some ingeniously derived relationships between the labels individuals apply to themselves and those they apply to certain other objects.

The selections by Foote and Mills grapple with "motive," a concept that has proved troublesome to students of human behavior. Both authors indicate the usefulness of treating motives as labels, or definitions, human beings apply to their own conduct and to the conduct of others. It is important to contrast this view with the more prevalent view of motives as internal stimuli which move the individual to behave in given ways.

27. Mead's Social and Functional Theory of Mind

William Lewis Troyer

The development of an adequate theory of mind in relation to nature was a central interest of the late George Herbert Mead's philosophical career. His general position is best designated with the term "social behaviorism." The basic datum from this point of view is the social act. But this datum is by no means an obvious and simple element for observation. Before it can be used to explore and understand the nature and function of mind, supporting theories of society and of self require elaboration. Hence, the natural order of Mead's own thinking seems to have been that of society-self-mind, instead of the reverse as suggested by the title of the edited volume of his famous lectures in social psychology.[1] A well-proportioned and discerning outline of Mead's position should culminate rather than begin with his understanding of mind.

The Internal Organization of the Act

Mead, like John Dewey, was very critical of that form of behaviorism set forth by John Watson and his followers. These latter, he believed, had played a positive role in the development of a science of psychology but had, nevertheless, greatly oversimplified the concept and, consequently, the analysis of the act. They failed to take full account of the social character of the act, and what was worse yet, they limited analysis to fragmentary portions of the act. A thoroughgoing behaviorism would include within its purview the *complete* act, and particularly that portion of it which goes on "in the central nervous system as the beginning of the individual's act and as the organization of the act."[2] This larger inclusiveness would necessarily take the investigator beyond the field of direct observation, Watson's stopping point. An earlier retort that such procedure goes beyond science loses force in the light of a modern subatomic physics and a biochemistry of colloids and viruses.

From *American Sociological Review,* XI (April, 1946), pp. 198-202, by permission of the American Sociological Association and the author.

[1] G. H. Mead, *Mind, Self and Society* (Chicago: University of Chicago Press, 1934).

[2] *Ibid.*, p. 11.

Mead's criticism and his constructive development both begin with the concept of the reflex, or so-called stimulus-response arc. His position is essentially the same as that advanced by Dewey in his well-known article of 1896.[3] Both Mead and Dewey insisted that action is present in the living organism from the very outset. What has to be accounted for is not action but the direction which action takes. The process of responding is present in the entire act determining the very entertainment of stimuli. The living organism, in other words,

> . . . is not a sensitive protoplasm that is simply receiving these stimuli from without and then responding to them. It is primarily *seeking* for certain stimuli. . . . Whatever we are doing determines the sort of a stimulus which will set free certain responses which are merely ready for expression, and it is the *attitude* of action which determines for us what the stimulus will be.[4]

The use of the term "attitude" in this connection is highly important. Mead recognized that the functioning of the nervous system is as yet only partially explored, but he regarded the results already obtained as substantial enough to indicate an organization of the act in terms of social attitudes. Thus, he declared:

> There is an organization of the various parts of the nervous system that are going to be responsible for acts, an organization which represents not only that which is immediately taking place, but also the later stages that are to take place. If one approaches a distant object, he approaches it with reference to what he is going to do when he arrives there. If one is approaching a hammer, he is muscularly all ready to seize the handle of the hammer. *The later stages of the act are present in the early stages*—not simply in the sense that they are ready to go off, but in the sense that *they serve to control the process itself.* They determine how we are going to approach the object, and the steps in our early manipulation of it.[5]

Whatever may be found by biological research to be the actual physiological pattern of functioning in the nervous system, the important point emphasized by Mead probably will not be gainsaid; that is, that the complete act is present as a determining factor in the beginning of the overt phase of the act. The attitude, as Mead uses the term, stands simply for this internal organization of the act.

[3] John Dewey, "The Reflex Arc Concept in Psychology," *Psychological Review,* III (July, 1896), 357-370.

[4] G. H. Mead, *Movements of Thought in the Nineteenth Century* (Chicago: University of Chicago Press, 1936), pp. 389-390 (italics not in the original).

[5] Mead, *Mind, Self and Society,* p. 11 (italics not in the original).

A closely associated fact, brought to emphasis in Mead's outlook, is that the central nervous system, among human beings at least, provides a mechanism of *implicit* response. Not only does the human organism select its stimuli on the basis of attitudes, but it may also test out implicitly the various possible completions of an already initiated act in advance of the actual completion of that act. This it does through the employment of significant symbols. There is thus interposed between stimulus and response a process of selection. Mead referred to this phenomenon as "delayed reaction." To him this seemed to be the basis upon which it is legitimate to speak of choice and conscious control of behavior. It is this process, when considered in conjunction with the development of social attitudes, which constitutes intelligence or mind.[6] Obviously, this is far removed from the behaviorism of Watson; yet it is thoroughly behavioristic. It imports nothing from outside the act itself. It simply refuses to conceive the act narrowly as a mechanistic and individualistic reaction to external pressures.

Biological and Social Bases of Mind

Now, it should be clear from the foregoing that Mead emphasized the indispensability of the physiological organism in his account of mind. Individual experience and behavior was, in his thought, "physiologically basic" to social experience and behavior, and the processes and mechanisms essential to the origin and continued existence of society, self, and mind were dependent upon the social functioning of that which is physiologically individual.[7]

> The individual members of even the most advanced invertebrate societies do not possess sufficient physiological capacities for developing minds or selves, consciousness or intelligence, out of their social relations and interactions with one another; and hence these societies cannot attain either the degree of complexity which would be presupposed by the emergence of minds and selves within them, or the further degree of complexity which would be possible only if minds and selves had emerged or arisen within them. Only the individual members of human societies possess the required physiological capacities for such development of minds and selves, and hence only human societies are able to reach the level of complexity, in their structure and organization, which becomes possible as the result of the emergence of minds and selves in their individual members.[8]

[6] *Ibid.*, pp. 99-100; 117-118.

[7] *Ibid.*, pp. 1-2.

[8] *Ibid.*, p. 236 (footnote).

For Mead the central nervous system, and particularly the cortex, furnished the physiological mechanism by means of which the "genesis of minds and selves out of the human social processes of experience and behavior — out of the human matrix of social relations and interactions — is made biologically possible in human individuals." Minds do not occur without brains. Looked at from the physiological angle, therefore, mind is an extraordinarily complex adjustment mechanism; an extension of distance receptors and motor effectors, a refined type of antennae, so to speak, by which more efficient adaptation of organism and environment is achieved.

Important as this grounding of mind and self-hood in physiology is, however, the repeated reference in the above quotations to *social relations and interactions* must be fully appreciated if Mead's notion of mind is not to be gravely misunderstood. Brains are necessary to the emergence of mind, but brains, *per se,* do not make mind. It is society — social interaction — using brains, which makes mind. Intelligent human behavior is "essentially and fundamentally social";

> . . . it involves and presupposes an ever on-going social life-process; and . . . the unity of that on-going social process — or any one of its component acts — is irreducible, and in particular cannot be adequately analyzed simply into a number of discrete nerve elements.[9]

If this be true, it follows that the psychologist should study social relations and social behavior primarily, rather than physiology, if he would know what mind is and how it functions.

In pursuing this line of approach, Mead took his students over ground dealing with the emergence of human society and the self. He focused attention on the gesture, particularly the *vocal gesture,* and especially upon the vocal gesture at the point where it becomes a *significant symbol.* He declared that mentality "resides in the ability of the organism to indicate that in the environment which answers to his responses, so that he can control these responses in various ways."[10]

In his discussion of society and the self this indicating process is designated as "taking the role of the other" or participation in the "conversation of attitudes." As a self can arise only in a society where there is communication, so mind can arise only in a self or personality within which this conversation of attitudes or social participation is taking place. It is this conversation, this symbolic interaction, interposed as an integral part of the act, which constitutes mind.[11] Looked at from one standpoint, it is mind; from another, it is communication. Function-

[9] *Ibid.,* p. 118 (footnote).

[10] *Ibid.,* p. 132.

[11] Mead, *Movements of Thought,* pp. 384-385.

ing within the organismic processes and social activities of the specific individual, communication is mind. It is symbolic social interaction, the process which makes human life distinctive.

The concrete import of such a theory of mind cannot be better summarized than in Mead's own words.

> In defending a social theory of mind we are defending a functional, as opposed to any form of substantive or entitative, view as to its nature. And in particular, we are opposing all intracranial or intra-epidermal views as to its character and locus. For it follows from our social theory of mind that the field of mind must be co-extensive with, and include all the components of, the field of the social process or experience and behavior: i. e., the matrix of social relations and interactions among individuals, which is presupposed by it, and out of which it arises or comes into being. If mind is socially constituted, then the field or locus of any given individual mind must extend as far as the social activity or apparatus of social relations which constitutes it extends; and hence that field cannot be bounded by the skin of the individual organism to which it belongs.[12]

The advantage of this view of mind resides in its plausibility as an account and explanation of the genesis and development of mind without postulation of supernatural endowment or special Being.[13] It thoroughly naturalizes mind in such a way as to give the concept of mind heuristic value in any full-fledged science of human nature. In so far as originality can be assigned to Mead, this achievement in understanding, if sustained by later criticism, may well rank with those of Newton and Darwin in its importance to mankind.

The Object as a Collapsed Act

Mead's discussion of the self as an object to itself and also of the possibility of social responses toward inanimate objects raises a question as to the nature of objects and how they are known. While the ramifications of this phase of his thought are too varied for appropriate summary here, the matter does involve the concept of meaning and, therefore, warrants some consideration in the presentation of any rounded understanding of Mead's theory of mind.

In Mead's way of thinking, meaning arises only through communication. The significance of a gesture (symbol), for instance, is found in

[12] Mead, *Mind, Self and Society,* p. 223 (footnote).

[13] *Ibid.*, pp. 223-225

the response of others to it as a part of a social act. The various acts of individuals presuppose the social process, and

> . . . the gesture arises as a separable element in the social act, by virtue of the fact that it is selected out by the sensitivities of other organisms to it; it does not exist as a gesture merely in the experience of the single individual. The meaning of a gesture by one organism . . . is found in the response of another organism to what would be the completion of the act of the first organism which that gesture initiates and indicates.[14]

The relationship, in other words, between a stimulus as a gesture and the later phases of the social act constitutes the field within which meaning originates and exists.

What is particularly of significance in such a statement is that meaning, as thus considered, is a development *objectively there* as a relation between certain phases of the social act. It is not to be thought of as a "psychical addition" to the act. It is no mere "idea" in the traditional sense.[15] Meaning is implicit wherever there is present a certain "triadic relation of a gesture of one individual, a response to that gesture by a second individual, and completion of the given social act initiated by the gesture of the first individual."[16] Meaning is, therefore, thoroughly social in origin and nature.

According to Mead gestures may be either significant or non-significant. Below the human level of life the conversation of gestures is largely, if not completely, non-significant, non-meaningful, because it is not *self*-conscious. A lower organism acts, but its activity, from its own standpoint, or from that of any other non-human organism, is meaningless. There is gesture and response, as in the dog-fight, and things happen, but there is no self and no other; that is, no designation of objects. Any such designation would imply symbolic interaction. Meaning, as the object-matter of such symbolic interaction, or thought,

> . . . arises in experience through the individual stimulating himself to take the attitude of the other in his reaction toward the object. *Meaning is that which can be indicated to others while it is by the same process indicated to the indicating individual.*[17]

This point of view may be put in other terms. Mead laid emphasis, for example, upon the selective quality of organic activity. The living

[14] *Ibid.*, pp. 145-146.

[15] *Ibid.*, pp. 75-76.

[16] *Ibid.*, p. 81.

[17] *Ibid.*, p. 89 (italics not in the original).

organism, within limits, but nevertheless definitely, selects or carves out its own environment. Among human beings this environment is distinctive in that it is composed of objects. At first the environment, or the world, is one of social objects, but as self and social other are acquired, physical objects and relationships may also be constructed by a process of abstraction. In this latter process the human hand, in conjunction with the eye, plays a major role.

Mead did not question that nature — or the extra-human world — is objectively there regardless of our experience of it. He was a pragmatist, not an idealist, in philosophy. He consequently held, however, that all objects are defined as such in and through human experience. Objective nature thereby comes to possess certain characteristics by virtue of its relationship to human experiencing or mind which it would not possess otherwise, or apart from this relationship. These characteristics, Mead held, constitute the meanings of objects to us, and to all intents and purposes, give definition and functional reality to the objects themselves.[18] An object is always in this sense a "construct," a resultant, the kind of response which will ensue after a certain type of activity. A blackboard, for example, is what it is for us, has certain properties associated with writing in black and white, because that is the way it responds to our activity. As a symbol, an object, it stands for certain consequences in activity. Certain qualities are there, but as parts of an act, and not of some independently existing "essence" or "extension." From this standpoint, an object may be defined as a "collapsed act"; the sign of what would happen if the act were carried to completion.[19]

Following this point to its conclusion, Mead declared:

> . . . The earliest objects are social objects, and all objects are social objects. Later experience differentiates the social from the physical objects, but the mechanism of the experience of things over against self as an object is the social mechanism. The identification of the individual with physical objects which appear in the effective occupation of space is a derivative of this.[20]

An object, thus, becomes a meaningful reality to a human being because of his ability to make indications, either imaginatively to himself, or directly to others. All objects, all symbols with semantic reference, represent telescoped acts. By means of the conversation of attitudes and the use of significant symbols — essentially a social process — the world (both social and physical) of each individual comes into being. Viewed,

[18] *Ibid.*, p. 131.

[19] G. H. Mead, *The Philosophy of the Act* (Chicago: University of Chicago Press, 1938), pp. 368-370.

[20] *Ibid.*, pp. 428-430.

indeed, as consisting of objects and their relationships, the world is an out-and-out social world, as self and mind are also social, that is emergent within the human social process of activity itself. As Charles W. Morris, to whose labors we owe much for the possession of Mead's thought in print, declares in the introduction to the latest of the posthumous volumes,

> . . . Mind, as involving the symbolic internalization of the complete or social act, and the self, as an object that has itself for an object, are on this view seen as social emergents made possible through the process of linguistic communication within the social act. . . . In man, animal impulse becomes enormously elaborated and intelligently guided, sensitivity to stimuli becomes the perception of enduring objects, manipulation is elaborated into the physical world of science, and communication shares in the elaboration of impulse and its illumination through reason. Animals live in a world of events; man lives in a world of common meanings—and meaning for Mead is socially generated and sustained.[21]

[21] *Ibid.*, pp. ix-x.

28. Mind, Experience, and Behavior

John Dewey

Let us begin with the technical side — the change in psychology. We are only just now commencing to appreciate how completely exploded is the psychology that dominated philosophy throughout the eighteenth and nineteenth centuries. According to this theory, mental life originated in sensations which are separately and passively received, and which are formed, through laws of retention and association, into a mosaic of images, perceptions and conceptions. The senses were regarded as gateways or avenues of knowledge. Except in combining atomic sensations, the mind was wholly passive and acquiescent in knowing. Volition, action, emotion, and desire follow in the wake of sensations and images. The intellectual or cognitive factor comes first and emotional and volitional life is only a consequent conjunction of ideas with sensations of pleasure and pain.

The effect of the development of biology has been to reverse the picture. Wherever there is life, there is behavior, activity. In order that life may persist, this activity has to be both continuous and adapted to the environment. This adaptive adjustment, moreover, is not wholly passive; is not a mere matter of the moulding of the organism by the environment. Even a clam acts upon the environment and modifies it to some extent. It selects materials for food and for the shell that protects it. It does something to the environment as well as has something done to itself. There is no such thing in a living creature as mere conformity to conditions, though parasitic forms may approach this limit. In the interests of the maintenance of life there is transformation of some elements in the surrounding medium. The higher the form of life, the more important is the active reconstruction of the medium. This increased control may be illustrated by the contrast of savage with civilized man. Suppose the two are living in a wilderness. With the savage there is the maximum of accommodation to given conditions; the minimum of what we may call hitting back. The savage takes things "as they are," and by using caves and roots and occasional pools leads a meagre and precarious existence. The civilized man goes to distant mountains and dams streams. He

From *Reconstruction in Philosophy*, pp. 84-87, 90-92, by John Dewey, copyright 1920 by Henry Holt and Company, 1942 by John Dewey. Reprinted by permission of Holt, Rinehart and Winston, Inc.

builds reservoirs, digs channels, and conducts the water to what had been a desert. He searches the world to find plants and animals that will thrive. He takes native plants and by selection and cross-fertilization improves them. He introduces machinery to till the soil and care for the harvest. By such means he may succeed in making the wilderness blossom like the rose.

Such transformation scenes are so familiar that we overlook their meaning. We forget that the inherent power of life is illustrated in them. Note what a change this point of view entails in the traditional notions of experience. Experience becomes an affair primarily of doing. The organism does not stand about, Micawberlike, waiting for something to turn up. It does not wait passive and inert for something to impress itself upon it from without. The organism acts in accordance with its own structure, simple or complex, upon its surroundings. As a consequence the changes produced in the environment react upon the organism and its activities. The living creature undergoes, suffers, the consequences of its own behavior. This close connection between doing and suffering or undergoing forms what we call experience. Disconnected doing and disconnected suffering are neither of them experiences. Suppose fire encroaches upon a man when he is asleep. Part of his body is burned away. The burn does not perceptibly result from what he has done. There is nothing which in any instructive way can be named experience. Or again there is a series of mere activities, like twitchings of muscles in a spasm. The movements amount to nothing; they have no consequences for life. Or, if they have, these consequences are not connected with prior doing. There is no experience, no learning, no cumulative process. But suppose a busy infant puts his finger in the fire; the doing is random, aimless, without intention or reflection. But something happens in consequence. The child undergoes heat, he suffers pain. The doing and undergoing, the reaching and the burn, are connected. One comes to suggest and mean the other. Then there is experience in a vital and significant sense.

Certain important implications for philosophy follow. In the first place, the interaction of organism and environment, resulting in some adaptation which secures utilization of the latter, is the primary fact, the basic category. Knowledge is relegated to a derived position, secondary in origin, even if its importance, when once it is established, is overshadowing. Knowledge is not something separate and self-sufficing, but is involved in the process by which life is sustained and evolved. The senses lose their place as gateways of knowing to take their rightful place as stimuli to action. To an animal an affection of the eye or ear is not an idle piece of information about something indifferently going on in the world. It is an invitation and inducement to act in a needed way. It is a clue in behavior, a directive factor in adaptation of life in its surroundings. It is urgent not cognitive in quality. The whole controversy between empiricism and rationalism as to the intellectual worth of sensations is rendered strangely obsolete. The discussion of sensations belongs under the head of immediate stimulus and response, not under the head of knowledge.

* * *

When experience is aligned with the life-process and sensations are seen to be points of readjustment, the alleged atomism of sensations totally disappears. With this disappearance is abolished the need for a synthetic faculty of super-empirical reason to connect them. Philosophy is not any longer confronted with the hopeless problem of finding a way in which separate grains of sand may be woven into a strong and coherent rope — or into the illusion and pretence of one. When the isolated and simple existences of Locke and Hume are seen not to be truly empirical at all but to answer to certain demands of their theory of mind, the necessity ceases for the elaborate Kantian and Post-Kantian machinery of *a priori* concepts and categories to synthesize the alleged stuff of experience. The true "stuff" of experience is recognized to be adaptive courses of action, habits, active functions, connections of doing and undergoing; sensori-motor co-ordinations. Experience carries principles of connection and organization within itself. These principles are none the worse because they are vital and practical rather than epistemological. Some degree of organization is indispensable to even the lowest grade of life. Even an amoeba must have some continuity in time in its activity and some adaptation to its environment in space. Its life and experience cannot possibly consist in momentary, atomic, and self-enclosed sensations. Its activity has reference to its surroundings and to what goes before and what comes after. This organization intrinsic to life renders unnecessary a super-natural and super-empirical synthesis. It affords the basis and material for a positive evolution of intelligence as an organizing factor within experience.

Nor is it entirely aside from the subject to point out the extent in which social as well as biological organization enters into the formation of human experience. Probably one thing that strengthened the idea that the mind is passive and receptive in knowing was the observation of the helplessness of the human infant. But the observation points in quite another direction. Because of his physical dependence and impotency, the contacts of the little child with nature are mediated by other persons. Mother and nurse, father and older children, determine what experiences the child shall have; they constantly instruct him as to the meaning of what he does and undergoes. The conceptions that are socially current and important become the child's principles of interpretation and estimation long before he attains to personal and deliberate control of conduct. Things come to him clothed in language, not in physical nakedness, and this garb of communication makes him a sharer in the beliefs of those about him. These beliefs coming to him as so many facts form his mind; they furnish the centres about which his own personal expeditions and perceptions are ordered. Here we have "categories" of connection and unification as important as those of Kant, but empirical not mythological.

29. The Definition of the Situation

William I. Thomas

One of the most important powers gained during the evolution of animal life is the ability to make decisions from within instead of having them imposed from without. Very low forms of life do not make decisions, as we understand this term, but are pushed and pulled by chemical substances, heat, light, etc., much as iron filings are attracted or repelled by a magnet. They do tend to behave properly in given conditions — a group of small crustaceans will flee as in a panic if a bit of strychnia is placed in the basin containing them and will rush toward a drop of beef juice like hogs crowding around swill — but they do this as an expression of organic affinity for the one substance and repugnance for the other, and not as an expression of choice or "free will." There are, so to speak, rules of behavior but these represent a sort of fortunate mechanistic adjustment of the organism to typically recurring situations, and the organism cannot change the rule.

On the other hand, the higher animals, and above all man, have the power of refusing to obey a stimulation which they followed at an earlier time. Response to the earlier stimulation may have had painful consequences and so the rule or habit in this situation is changed. We call this ability the power of inhibition, and it is dependent on the fact that the nervous system carries memories or records of past experiences. At this point the determination of action no longer comes exclusively from outside sources but is located within the organism itself.

Preliminary to any self-determined act of behavior there is always a stage of examination and deliberation which we may call *the definition of the situation.* And actually not only concrete acts are dependent on the definition of the situation, but gradually a whole life-policy and the personality of the individual himself follow from a series of such definitions.

But the child is always born into a group of people among whom all the general types of situation which may arise have already been defined and corresponding rules of conduct developed, and where he has not the slightest chance of making his definitions and following his wishes with-

From *The Unadjusted Girl,* pp. 41-50, by William I. Thomas (Boston: Little, Brown and Company, 1931), reprinted by permission of Social Science Research Council.

out interference. Men have always lived together in groups. Whether mankind has a true herd instinct or whether groups are held together because this has worked out to advantage is of no importance. Certainly the wishes in general are such that they can be satisfied only in a society. But we have only to refer to the criminal code to appreciate the variety of ways in which the wishes of the individual may conflict with the wishes of society. And the criminal code takes no account of the many unsanctioned expressions of the wishes which society attempts to regulate by persuasion and gossip.

There is therefore always a rivalry between the spontaneous definitions of the situation made by the member of an organized society and the definitions which his society has provided for him. The individual tends to a hedonistic selection of activity, pleasure first; and society to a utilitarian selection, safety first. Society wishes its member to be laborious, dependable, regular, sober, orderly, self-sacrificing; while the individual wishes less of this and more of new experience. And organized society seeks also to regulate the conflict and competition inevitable between its members in the pursuit of their wishes. The desire to have wealth, for example, or any other socially sanctioned wish, may not be accomplished at the expense of another member of the society,—by murder, theft, lying, swindling, blackmail, etc.

It is in this connection that a moral code arises, which is a set of rules or behavior norms, regulating the expression of the wishes, and which is built up by successive definitions of the situation. In practice the abuse arises first and the rule is made to prevent its recurrence. Morality is thus the generally accepted definition of the situation, whether expressed in public opinion and the unwritten law, in a formal legal code, or in religious commandments and prohibitions.

The family is the smallest social unit and the primary defining agency. As soon as the child has free motion and begins to pull, tear, pry, meddle, and prowl, the parents begin to define the situation through speech and other signs and pressures: "Be quiet", "Sit up straight", "Blow your nose", "Wash your face", "Mind your mother", "Be kind to sister", etc. This is the real significance of Wordsworth's phrase, "Shades of the prison house begin to close upon the growing child." His wishes and activities begin to be inhibited, and gradually, by definitions within the family, by playmates, in the school, in the Sunday school, in the community, through reading, by formal instruction, by informal signs of approval and disapproval, the growing member learns the code of his society.

In addition to the family we have the community as a defining agency. At present the community is so weak and vague that it gives us no idea of the former power of the local group in regulating behavior. Originally the community was practically the whole world of its members. It was composed of families related by blood and marriage and was not so large that all the members could not come together; it was a face-to-face group. I asked a Polish peasant what was the extent of an "okolica" or neighborhood—how far it reached. "It reaches," he said, "as far as the report of a man reaches—as far as a man is talked about." And it was in communities of this kind that the moral code which we now recognize as valid originated. The customs of the community are "folkways", and both state and church have in their more formal codes mainly recognized and incorporated these folkways.

The typical community is vanishing and it would be neither possible nor desirable to restore it in its old form. It does not correspond with the present direction of social evolution and it would now be a distressing condition in which to live. But in the immediacy of relationships and the participation of everybody in everything, it represents an element which we have lost and which we shall probably have to restore in some form of cooperation in order to secure a balanced and normal society,—some arrangement corresponding with human nature.

Very elemental examples of the definition of the situation by the community as a whole, corresponding to mob action as we know it and to our trial by jury, are found among European peasants. The three documents following, all relating to the Russian community or *mir* give some idea of the conditions under which a whole community, a public, formerly defined a situation.

> 25. We who are unacquainted with peasant speech, manners and method of expressing thought—mimicry—if we should be present at a division of land or some settlement among the peasants, would never understand anything. Hearing fragmentary, disconnected exclamations, endless quarreling, with repetition of some single word; hearing this racket of a seemingly senseless, noisy crowd that counts up or measures off something, we should conclude that they would not get together, or arrive at any result in an age. . . .Yet wait until the end and you will see that the division has been made with mathematical accuracy—that the measure, the quality of the soil, the slope of the field, the distance from the village—everything in short has been taken into account, that the reckoning has been correctly done and, what is most important, that every one of those present who were interested in the division is certain of the correctness of the division or settlement. The cry, the noise, the racket do not subside until every one is satisfied and no doubter is left.
>
> The same thing is true concerning the discussion of some question by the *mir.* There are no speeches, no debates, no votes. They shout, they abuse each other, they seem on the point of coming to blows. Apparently they riot in the most senseless manner. Some one preserves silence, silence, and then suddenly puts in a word, one word, or an ejaculation, and by this word, this ejaculation, he

turns the whole thing upside down. In the end, you look into it and find that an admirable decision has been formed and, what is most important, a unanimous decision.[1]

26. As I approached the village, there hung over it such a mixed, varied violent shouting, that no well brought-up parliament would agree to recognize itself, even in the abstract, as analogous to this gathering of peasant deputies. It was clearly a full meeting today. . . . At other more quiet village meetings I had been able to make out very little, but this was a real lesson to me. I felt only a continuous, indistinguishable roaring in my ears, sometimes pierced by a particularly violent phrase that broke out from the general roar. I saw in front of me the "immediate" man, in all his beauty. What struck me first of all was his remarkable frankness; the more "immediate" he is, the less able is he to mask his thoughts and feelings; once he is stirred up the emotion seizes him quickly and he flares up then and there, and does not quiet down till he has poured out before you all the substance of his soul. He does not feel embarrassment before anybody; there are no indications here of diplomacy. Further, he opens up his whole soul, and he will tell everything that he may ever have known about you, and not only about you, but about your father, grandfather, and great-grandfather. Here everything is clear water, as the peasants say, and everything stands out plainly. If any one, out of smallness of soul, or for some ulterior motive, thinks to get out of something by keeping silent, they force him out into clear water without pity. And there are very few such small-souled persons at important village meetings. I have seen the most peaceable, irresponsible peasants, who at other times would not have thought of saying a word against any one, absolutely changed at these meetings, at these moments of general excitement. They believed in the saying, "On people even death is beautiful", and they got up so much courage that they were able to answer back the peasants commonly recognized as audacious. At the moment of its height the meeting becomes simply an open mutual confessional and mutual disclosure, the display of the widest publicity. At these moments when, it would seem, the private interests of each reach the highest tension, public interests and justice in turn reach the highest degree of control.[2]

27. In front of the volost administration building there stands a

[1] A. N. Engelgardt: "Iz Derevni: 12 Pisem" ("From the Country; 12 Letters"), p. 315.

[2] N. N. Zlatovratsky: "Ocherki Krestyanskoy Obshchiny" ("Sketches of the Peasant Commune"), p. 127.

crowd of some one hundred and fifty men. This means that a volost meeting has been called to consider the verdict of the Kusmin rural commune "regarding the handing over to the [state] authorities of the peasant Gregori Siedov, caught red-handed and convicted of horse-stealing." Siedov had already been held for judicial inquiry; the evidence against him was irrefutable and he would undoubtedly be sentenced to the penitentiary. In view of this I endeavor to explain that the verdict in regard to his exile is wholly superfluous and will only cause a deal of trouble; and that at the termination of the sentence of imprisonment of Siedov the commune will unfailingly be asked whether it wants him back or prefers that he be exiled. Then, I said, in any event it would be necessary to formulate a verdict in regard to the "non-reception" of Siedov, while at this stage all the trouble was premature and could lead to nothing. But the meeting did not believe my words, did not trust the court and wanted to settle the matter right then and there; the general hatred of horse-thieves was too keen. . . .

The decisive moment has arrived; the head-man "drives" all the judges-elect to one side; the crowd stands with a gloomy air, trying not to look at Siedov and his wife, who are crawling before the *mir* on their knees. "Old men, whoever pities Gregori, will remain in his place, and whoever does not forgive him will step to the right," cries the head man. The crowd wavered and rocked, but remained dead still on the spot; no one dared to be first to take the fatal step. Gregori feverishly ran over the faces of his judges with his eyes, trying to read in these faces pity for him. His wife wept bitterly, her face close to the ground; beside her, finger in mouth and on the point of screaming, stood a three-year-old youngster (at home Gregori had four more children). . . . But straightway one peasant steps out of the crowd; two years before some one had stolen a horse from him. "Why should we pity him? Did he pity us?" says the old man, and stooping goes over to the right side. "That is true; bad grass must be torn from the field," says another one from the crowd, and follows the old man. The beginning had been made; at first individually and then in whole groups the judge-elect proceeded to go over to the right. The man condemned by public opinion ran his head into the ground, beat his breast with his fists, seized those who passed him by their coat-tails, crying: "Ivan Timofeich! Uncle Leksander! Vasinka, dear kinsman! Wait, kinsmen, let me say a word. . . . Petrushenka." But, without stopping and with stern faces, the members of the *mir* dodged the unfortunates, who were crawling at their feet. . . . At last the wailing of Gregori stopped; around him for the space of three *sazen* the place was empty; there was no one to implore. All the judges-elect, with the exception of one, an uncle of the man to be exiled, had gone over to the right.

The woman cried sorrowfully, while Gregori stood motionless on his knees, his head lowered, stupidly looking at the ground.[3]

The essential point in reaching a communal decision, just as in the case of our jury system, is unanimity. In some cases the whole community mobilizes around a stubborn individual to conform him to the general wish.

28. It sometimes happens that all except one may agree but the motion is never carried if that one refuses to agree to it. In such cases all endeavor to talk over and persuade the stiff-necked one. Often they even call to their aid his wife, his children, his relatives, his father-in-law, and his mother, that they may prevail upon him to say yes. Then all assail him, and say to him from time to time: "Come now, God help you, agree with us too, that this may take place as we wish it, that the house may not be cast into disorder, that we may not be talked about by the people, that the neighbors may not hear of it, that the world may not make sport of us!" It seldom occurs in such cases that unanimity is not attained.[4]

A less formal but not less powerful means of defining the situation employed by the community is gossip. The Polish peasant's statement that a community reaches as far as a man is talked about was significant, for the community regulates the behavior of its members largely by talking about them. Gossip has a bad name because it is sometimes malicious and false and designed to improve the status of the gossiper and degrade its object, but gossip is in the main true and is an organizing force. It is a mode of defining the situation in a given case and of attaching praise or blame. It is one of the means by which the status of the individual and of his family is fixed.

The community also, particularly in connection with gossip, knows how to attach opprobrium to persons and actions by using epithets which are at the same time brief and emotional definitions of the situation. "Bastard", "whore", "traitor", "coward", "skunk", "scab", "snob", "kike", etc., are such epithets. In "Faust" the community said of Margaret, "She stinks." The people are here employing a device known in psychology as the "conditioned reflex." If, for example, you place before a child (say six months old) an agreeable object, a kitten, and at the same time pinch the child, and if this is repeated several times, the child will immediately cry at the sight of the kitten without being pinched; or if a dead rat were always served beside a man's plate of soup he would eventually have a disgust for soup when served separately. If the word "stinks" is

[3] "V. Volostnikh Pisaryakh" ("A Village Secretary"), p. 283.

[4] F. S. Krauss: "Sitte und Brauch der Südslaven", p. 103.

associated on people's tongues with Margaret, Margaret will never again smell sweet. Many evil consequences, as the psychoanalysts claim, have resulted from making the whole of sex life a "dirty" subject, but the device has worked in a powerful, sometimes a paralyzing way on the sexual behavior of women.

Winks, shrugs, nudges, laughter, sneers, haughtiness, coldness, "giving the once over" are also language defining the situation and painfully felt as unfavorable recognition. The sneer, for example, is incipient vomiting, meaning, "you make me sick."

And eventually the violation of the code even in an act of no intrinsic importance, as in carrying food to the mouth with the knife, provokes condemnation and disgust. The fork is not a better instrument for conveying food than the knife, at least it has no moral superiority, but the situation has been defined in favor of the fork. To smack with the lips in eating is bad manners with us, but the Indian has more logically defined the situation in the opposite way; with him smacking is a compliment to the host.

In this whole connection fear is used by the group to produce the desired attitudes in its member. Praise is used also but more sparingly. And the whole body of habits and emotions is so much a community and family product that disapproval or separation is almost unbearable.

30. Language and Identity

Anselm L. Strauss

Central to any discussion of identity is language. The word "central" is used advisedly. Language is ofttimes construed as just one more kind of behavior — encompassing speaking, reading, writing, and hearing — within a long listing of other kinds of behavior. An important and recurring theme of this essay is that a proper theoretical account of men's identities and action must put men's linguistics into the heart of the discussion.

Names

Consider, as a beginning, that *distinctive appelation by which a person is known:* his name. A name can be very revealing, both of its donor and its owner; if we are observant we shall find it speaks volumes. First generation Jewish immigrants to this country were called by old-fashioned names resounding with rich historical overtones, names like Isaac, Benjamin, Abraham, Hannah, and Ruth; but the children of their children are hardly ever named after such Biblical models, since as their styles of life change, so have their ideals and aspirations. The children's names represent this change if not as precisely, at least as surely, as pink litmus signifies acid. Any name is a container; poured into it are the conscious or unwitting evaluations of the namer. Sometimes this is obvious, as when post-civil war Negroes named their children after the Great Emancipator; sometimes the position of the namer has to be sought and one's inference buttressed by other evidence.

If the name reveals the judgments of the namer, what of the person who receives it? How does he react to this attempt to fix his identity in some way, beforehand? There is a range here running from relative indifference to violent rejection or prideful acceptance. There is the name that announces its bearer to be the third of a line of famous personages, destined not to be the last to do it honor. Probably more common in this country are those names over which children have blushed and been ashamed as their teachers stuttered over pronunciation, these names often later to be shortened, discarded, or relegated to alphabetized shorthand. The point is not whether or not a man can be wholly indifferent to his name but that an extensive range of reaction can be evoked by his imaginings of what he must look like to certain audiences if he bears the name that he does.

The names that are adopted voluntarily reveal even more tellingly the indissoluble tie between name and self-image. The changing of names marks a rite of passage. It means such things as that the person wants to have the kind of name he thinks represents him as a person, does not want any longer to be the kind of person that his previous name signified. The commonest and perhaps least emotionally charged instance of name-changing occurs when a bride takes over her husband's last name and so signifies her changed status. Suppose the wife of an American male were to insist that he change his last name to hers! The phenomenon of "passing" is often marked by name-changing: you disguise who you were or are in order to appear what you wish to be. Benny Ginsburgh may become Basil Gainsborough to express — not necessarily passing and secrecy — but only mobility aspirations. Secrecy sometimes gets mingled with personality transition, as when revolutionists adopt new names and thus seek to bury publicly their pasts; but the new names also mark passage to new self-images. Conversion, religious or otherwise, is often marked by a complete change of name, that act signifying the person's new status in the eyes of God, the world, and himself — marking status and setting a seal upon it.

Less complete changes of status are commonly marked by the partial qualifications of name through the addition of a title, as if to say "this man is now a member of the Senate, so let us accord him his due and address him as Senator." There are some names, like titles, that have to be earned; having earned them, one tells himself that this is what he is and that other people think so too or they would not so address him. Some Indian tribes, for instance, recognized a warrior's major achievement in battle by sanctioning an entire change of name. Americans use a similar device in applying nicknames to express earned status, and by them, can denote a change in status.

* * *

Naming as an Act of Placement

The philosophers, John Dewey and Arthur Bentley, in *Knowing and the Known,* have argued that to name is to know, and that the extent of knowing is dependent upon the extent of the naming. By this they do not mean to suggest anything magical about the act of naming, but to make that act central to any human's cognition of his world. This view informs much of the discussion that will follow.

Suppose a mother wishes her very young child to pay attention to an object. She moves his body so that his eyes focus somewhere near the object and then she points toward it. But when he is at an age when he can respond to a word, she will hope to attract his attention more efficiently to some thing by naming it. This is what is called "ostensive definition," meaning an indication of an object without any description whatever; it is the simplest kind of identification. The first identifications are singular; they indicate particular objects. But the child soon learns that certain objects can be called by the same word, albeit his groupings are frequently amusing and seem incorrect to his elders. At first parents often bow to the child's peculiar classification of objects, in order to keep peace in the family, but in the end they win the game, for the youngster must eventually conform to more conventional, if less colorful, lexicology.

To name, then, is not only to indicate; it is to identify an object as some kind of object. An act of identification requires that the thing referred to be placed within a category. Borrowing from the language of logic, we may say that any particular object that is referred to is a member of a general class, a representative of that class. An orange is a member of a class called oranges; but note that this class itself receives its placement, or definition, only by virtue of its relationships with other classes. These relationships are of quite a systematic sort. Thus oranges may be defined in relation to such classes as fruits, foods, tropical growths, tree products, and moderately priced objects. Defining any class, then, means relating it to systematically associated classes. "To tell what a thing is, you place it in terms of something else. This idea of locating, or placing, is implicit in our very word for definition itself: to *define*, or *determine* a thing, is to mark its boundaries.[1]

It should be noted, however, that any particular object can be named, and thus located, in countless ways. The naming sets it within a context of quite differently related classes. The nature or essence of an object does not reside mysteriously within an object itself but is dependent upon how it is defined by the namer. An object which looks so much like an orange — in fact which really is an orange — can also be a member of an infinite number of other classes. If it is in its nature to be an orange, it is also in its nature to be other things. In the case of an orange, we may choose to view it within different contexts for other equally legitimate purposes. It may thus be viewed as a spherical object, with rough, warm-colored skin, suitable for catching and casting lights, hence eminently definable as a model for a beginning art student. Essentially it is just that. This is only to repeat a point made earlier that to name or designate is always to do this from some point of view. From a single

[1] Kenneth Burke, *A Grammar of Motives* (New York: Prentice-Hall, 1945), p. 24.

identical perspective, otherwise seemingly different things can be classed together. Justification lies in the perspective, not in the things. If you do not agree with your neighbor's classification, this may only signify that you have a somewhat or wholly different basis for drawing symbolic circles around things.

The way in which things are classed together reveals, graphically as well as symbolically, the perspectives of the classifier. For instance, an anthropologist (Robert Pehrson) studying the Laplanders recently discovered that a single word is used to encompass both "people" and reindeer." The life of the Laplander revolves around activities having to do with reindeer. Is a reindeer a human or is a human a reindeer? The question is senseless; the people and reindeer are identified, they go together, and the very fact of their identification in terminology gives the anthropologist one of his best clues to the Laplander's ordering of the world and its objects.

Any group of people that has any permanence develops a "special language," a lingo or jargon, which represents its way of identifying those objects important for group action. Waitresses classify types of customers and other workers in the restaurant, give shorthand names to foods, and have special signs and gestures standing for important activities. So do criminals; and even ministers are not immune from the necessity of classifying their clientele and colleagues, otherwise how could they organize activity in an orderly and sensible manner?

The propensity for certain categories invented by any group to be slanderous, to partake of epithet, derogation and innuendo, has been bemoaned by liberals, debunkers, teachers, and all others who have wished to set other's classifications straight. Since groups inevitably are in conflict over issues — otherwise they would not be different groups — and since events inevitably come to be viewed differently by those who are looking up or down opposite ends of the gun, it is useless to talk of trying to eradicate from the human mind the tendency to stereotype, to designate nastily, and to oversimplify. This is not to say that humans are brutish, but that they are thoroughly human. Animals do not name-call, neither do they possess or assign identities in the elaborate sense in which we are discussing identity.

Classification and the Direction of Action

This necessity for any group to develop a common or shared terminology leads to an important consideration: the direction of activity depends upon the particular ways that objects are classified. This can be simply illustrated. Not so long ago, children used to be fed large quantities of spinach according to the syllogism that spinach contained iron and that iron was needed for building bones. Now it appears that excessive consumption of spinach reduces body calcium and therefore is bad for the bones. Spinach is thus reclassified and only if you wish to reduce calcium content should you overindulge. The renaming of any object, then, amounts to a reassessment of your relation to it, and *ipso facto* your behavior becomes changed along the line of your reassessment. In any event it is the definition of what the object "is" that allows action to occur with reference to what it is taken to be. Mark Twain tells how as an apprentice pilot he mistook a wind reef (not dangerous) for a bluff reef (deadly dangerous) and, to the hilarity of his boss who "properly" read the signs, performed miraculous feats of foolishness to avoid the murderous pseudo-bluff.

The naming of an object provides a directive for action, as if the object were forthrightly to announce, "You say I am this, then act in the appropriate way toward me." Conversely, if the actor feels he does not know what the object is, then with regard to it his action is blocked. Suppose that in the dark one reached for a glass of milk, raised it to his lips, recoiled at the strange taste, and stood immobilized until he was able to label the taste as tomato juice. Energy for action was there, but was temporarily unharnessed, immobilized, until naming occurred. Of course, in this example the moment of immobilization would be fleeting, since as soon as one set about to discover what the taste was he would be acting toward something belonging to the category of "unidentified liquid, whose nature is to be discovered." A person need not be certain that he knows what an object is in order to organize a line of action toward it — he merely has to be willing to take a chance on his judgment.

Classification and Evaluation

An act of classification not only directs overt action, but arouses a set of expectations toward the object thus classified. A chair ought to hold anyone who sits on it, not turn into a piano or a cat, and a buzzing housefly should not piteously ask us not to swat her, saying she is a fairy in disguise. We are surprised only if our expectations are unfulfilled, as when a presumed salesman in a department store assures us that he is just an ordinary shopper like ourselves, or when milk turns out to be strongly spiked with rum. When we classify, our expectations necessarily face both past and future. Expectations have to do with consequential relations between ourselves and the object. However expectations rest also upon remembrances of past experiences with objects resembling — we believe — the one currently before us.

Since this is so, classifications not only carry our anticipations but also those values that were experienced when we encountered the things, persons, or events now classified. For example, the Japanese have a food called "tofu" which is a soy-bean product. Let us imagine that the first time we meet tofu it is served cold with soy sauce over it and that it strikes us as unpalatable. Tofu is for us an indifferent food, and if at some future time we should see tofu or hear the word our images would likely be of the indifferent experience we had with a whitish jellied object covered with brown sauce. But suppose that some time later we are treated to a delicious soup in which there are pieces of a mushy substance. "What is that good stuff in the soup?" we ask, and are surprised to find it is cooked tofu. Now we revise our evaluation: tofu in soup, good; tofu uncooked, not so good. This substance, as used by the Japanese, appears in several guises, so yet more surprises may be in store for us. The range of our experience with tofu is both what we know of it and how we value it. The wider grows this range, the better we know the object — what it can do and what can be done with it — and likewise the more extensive become our judgments of its capacities and qualities. It would appear that classification, knowledge and value are inseparable.

There are several more lessons suggested by the illustration. One is that values attributed to any object — like "good" or "hateful" — really are not "in" the object. In having an experience one does not put value into it like water into a kettle. Value is not an element; it has to do with a relation between the object and the person who has experiences with the object. This is just another way of stating that the "essence" or "nature" of the object resides not in the object but in the relation between it and the namer. Value as a relation is easily seen in conjunction with such an adjective as "useful" — useful for whom, under what conditions, for which of his purposes? Precisely the same is true whether the object is a thing or an event, and whether the value is "useful" or, say, "sinful." Sinfulness is not fixed in the event, a quality of it within the eye of God. An act is sinful to particular definers when perceived as committed under certain circumstances by persons of specified identities.

Since values are not in objects but are evaluations of objects, it follows that persons must do their own experiencing in order to do their own evaluating. This does not mean that I cannot teach you the meaning of something prior to your direct experience of it. I can say that the dust rises off the city streets in a certain country and constantly hangs so heavy in the air that it is hard to breath. You have experienced similar conditions, so readily understand. But when you are introduced to a new terminology, the best you can do is draw upon possibly analogous experiences, and these may or may not lead to accurate conceptions. To experience, hence to evaluate, a Balinese trance as do the Balinese probably cannot even be approximated by an American. Everyone has at some time been introduced to new terms representing new ways of looking at objects, as when entering upon a new job. Such occupational terms cannot be fully grasped, the objects and events be perceived as others perceive them, until we have undergone similar experiences ouselves. Of course an articulate informant drawing colorfully and accurately upon whatever is similar in his and your experiences can bring you to closer comprehension and appreciation; hence the great usefulness of some novels and biographies. But no amount of description in advance, if the shift in perspective called for is radical, will teach you how you yourself will finally evaluate. You yourself must do, suffer, and undergo — to use John Dewey's terms.[2]

As people "undergo," their evaluations change. Values are not eternal. Expectations cannot always be fulfilled. Things change; so do we. "Good things change and vanish not only with changes in the environing medium but with changes in ourselves."[3] Even without direct new experience something novel may be learned about an object — such as one might learn something new about life in prison, or as when a college student studies about geological strata and rainfall and so comes into somewhat different relationships with rocks, rain, and water. As long as learning continues, revision of concepts continues; and as long as revision takes place, reorganization of behavior takes place.

The naming or identifying of things is, then, a continual problem, never really over and done with. By "continual" I do not mean "continuous" — one can lie in a hammock contentedly watching the moon rise and raising no questions about it, the world, or oneself. Nevertheless, some portion of one's classificatory terminology, the symbolic screen through which the world is ordered and organized, is constantly under strain — or just has been — or will be. George H. Mead (who asserted that classifications are really hypotheses) would say it necessarily must be, from the very nature of action which brings in its train the reconstruction of past experience and the arising of new objects.[4]

[2] John Dewey, *Reconstruction in Philosophy* (New York: Henry Holt, 1920), p. 86.

[3] John Dewey, *Experience and Nature* (Chicago: Open Court, 1925), p. 399.

[4] George H. Mead, *Mind, Self and Society* (Chicago: University of Chicago Press, 1934).

31. Speech and Thinking

Kurt Goldstein

The impairment of the abstract attitude is clearly revealed in characteristic changes in the speech of patients with brain lesions. We know various forms of speech defects in such patients and usually class them together as aphasia.[1] No other pathological material can teach us so much about the organization of the human being. Since we cannot deal with all the various types of aphasia, I shall confine the discussion to a special form, known as amnesic aphasia,[2] which in my opinion is particularly well suited to give us an insight into the nature of man.

If one examines a patient with this type of aphasia one observes as a striking symptom that he is totally or partially unable to find names for concrete things. This is especially noticeable in cases where he has the task of naming presented objects, but it is also apparent in his spontaneous language, which is conspicuously lacking in nouns and verbs. Usually this symptom is considered as the characteristic change, but closer examination shows that other changes also occur. Many circumlocutions are used where we would use single words. A patient shown a cup, for example, may respond with, "This is for drinking," or say, on seeing a penholder, "That is for writing," etc. In another case, a patient of mine said, "That is something for the rain," in a situation in which we should merely say, "That is an umbrella." Or she said: "I must have it for the rain," or, "I have three umbrellas at home." In the last sentence she used the right word in her periphrasis, yet she was unable to repeat it in reply to a repeated question, "What is that?" soon afterward. Evidently such a patient has not lost the word itself but for

From *Human Nature in the Light of Psychopathology*, pp. 69-84, by Kurt Goldstein, copyright 1940, reprinted by permission of Harvard University Press.

[1] See Henry Head, *Aphasia and Kindred Disorders of Speech* (New York, 1926); Theodore Weisenburg and Katherine McBride, *Aphasia* (New York, 1935); Kurt Goldstein, *Uber Aphasie* (Zurich, 1927).

[2] See Kurt Goldstein and Adhemar Gelb, *Psychologische Analysen hirnpathologischer Falle* (Leipsig, 1920); Kurt Goldstein, "The Problem of the Meaning of Words Based upon Observation of Aphasic Patients," *Journal of Psychology,* vol. II, 1936; Ernst Cassirer, *Philosophie der symbolischen Formen,* vol. II (Berlin, 1928).

some reason is unable to use it in naming an object. Further, his entire behavior shows peculiarities. All his acting and thinking seems to center, to an unusual degree, around his own personality and its relation to the world. He is acting in the world rather than thinking or speaking about it. His speech is accompanied to a marked degree by expressive movements. Very often we observe that he seems unable to express his meaning by words but can do so quite well by movements.

The change involving the whole behavior appears still more strikingly in special examinations. I shall begin by presenting the results of one examination with a sorting test because the results seem particularly well suited to carry us into the core of our problem, namely, the basic change in patients with amnesic aphasia.

We place before the patient a heap of colored woolen skeins — Holmgren's well-known samples used for testing color efficiency. We ask him to pick out all the red skeins and put them together. (There are, of course, many different shades of red.) Or we pick out one particular skein — for example, a dark red one — and ask him to choose strands of the same and similar colors.

In the first task a normal person with good color efficiency usually selects a great number of different shades of the same ground color — that is, for example, different reds, without regard to intensity, purity, lightness, etc. In the same task patients with amnesic aphasia behave quite differently, and exhibit varying types of behavior. For example, when he is told to choose all the skeins that are similar to a given skein, one patient chooses only skeins of the very same or of a closely similar shade. Though urged to go on he chooses a small number because there are only a few very similar ones in the heap. Another patient matches a given bright shade of red with a blue skein of similar brightness. At first such a patient may seem to be color-blind, but it can be demonstrated beyond doubt that his color efficiency is normal and that he is able to differentiate very distinctly between colors that are much alike. More precise observations disclose that in this case the choice is determined by a particular color attribute of the given skein, its brightness. We observe, further, that the choice may be decided by a number of different attributes — at one time by brightness, at another by softness, or coldness, warmth, etc. However — and this is a very amazing thing — a patient who seems to be choosing according to a certain attribute is not able to follow this procedure voluntarily if it is demanded of him — that is, if he is asked to choose only bright skeins, etc. Further, we observe that he does not seem to be able to hold to a certain procedure. He has chosen, for instance, some bright skeins. Suddenly he begins selecting on the basis of another attribute — the coldness of the color or some other factor. In another case, the patient arranges the skeins as if guided by a scale of brightness. He begins with a very bright red, then adds one less bright, and so on to a dull one. But if we ask him to place the skeins in a succession according to their brightness he shows himself incapable of the performance, even if it is demonstrated to him.

To understand the behavior of our patients, it is necessary to examine the procedure of normal persons in such tasks. If we normal persons want to choose a color, we select various nuances, even though we see that they have various attributes not equal to one another, because we recognize that they belong together in respect to their *basic* quality. The several shades are merely examples of this quality, and we treat the skeins not as different individual things but as representatives of that one basic color. For the moment we ignore all differences in shade and disregard all singular attributes. We are able to do this because we can abstract and because we can hold fast to a procedure once initiated.

There is another approach, however, which is open to the normal person. We can start with one particular skein and move it about over the heap, *passively* surrendering ourselves to the impressions that emerge. Then either of two things will take place. If we find skeins resembling our sample in *all* attributes, all these immediately cohere in a unitary sensory experience with the sample. If we find skeins which match our sample in some respects, we experience a characteristic unrest concerning the heap, and an alternating sense of relationship between skeins in the heap and the sample, according to different attributes. No matter whether we experience rivalry or matching, the coherence we feel results directly from sense data and takes place passively; we do not experience a definite attitude toward any attribute.

There is an essential difference between the more passive kind of approach and the former, in which we definitely choose a particular color. In the one, a definite ordering principle determines our actions; in the other, there is no such principle, and our actions are passively determined by outer impressions. These two kinds of behavior correspond to what we have called abstract and concrete behavior and what we may now call categorical and concrete behavior.

A particular kind of language belongs to each of these types of behavior. Our behavior is abstract when we give a name to an object. When we speak of "table" we do not mean a special given table with all its accidental properties; we mean table in general. The word is used as a representative of the category "table" even when naming a particular table. Thus, if we are asked to group together all reds, upon hearing the word "red" we are immediately prepared to select colors in a categorical fashion. In this approach language plays a great role, and the particular form it takes here may be designated by Karl Buehler's term, *darstellende Sprache,* which may be translated as "representative speech."

In the second form of behavior language does not play much of a role at all. Our words merely accompany our acts and express a property of the object itself, like other properties, such as color, size, etc. This fact is shown in the particular kind of words we use in such situations.

The words are especially adapted to the individuality of the given object. We use words like "rose-red," "violet"; we do not say "red," but "pink," "dark red," "strawberry-red," "sky-blue"; not green but "grass-green," etc. Often we have no word for naming a given object, and then we do it in a roundabout way. Words are used here less as representative of categories than as individual properties which, like other properties, belong to the object in question. We call such words "individual" words.

Now when we consider the behavior of the patient in the light of these elucidations we may say that it is similar to the second approach of normal persons. He is able to assume only the more concrete, the more realistic, attitude. Therefore he chooses identical skeins or skeins which are similar in an outstanding property, such as brightness. This interpretation finds confirmation in the greater concreteness of the patient's general behavior, in the predominance of acting over thinking, in the accompaniment of speech by expressive movements.

Our assumption is finally substantiated by the results of another type of sorting test. If a normal person tries to arrange a number of objects lying before him — say, on the writing table of a very busy man — he may do it in various ways, according to various attitudes. He may arrange them by size, by color, by function, by the importance of their situation, in terms of activity, of thought, etc. Further, he is able both to shift from one attitude and one kind of order to another as the situation demands it, and to effect a particular arrangement on demand. A patient with amnesic aphasia, confronted with miscellaneous objects with the instruction to group them, will exhibit the same behavior as in the color test. He is capable of proceeding only in a manner that indicates that he is guided by *concrete* promptings.

A particularly instructive example is the following. Among a number of different objects there were placed on a table before a patient a corkscrew and a bottle with a cork loosely set in its neck. The patient, asked to arrange these, did not put the bottle and the corkscrew together. Asked if these two objects did not belong together, he said, "No," very positively, backing his answer up with the explanation, "The bottle is already opened." Under these circumstances most normal people would pay no attention to the fact that the cork was not fast. For the immediate task — the grouping together of objects that belong together — it is quite incidental and unimportant whether the cork is loose or fast. With the abstract attitude, in a form of sorting which involves grouping objects according to categories, we assume that bottle and corkscrew belong together, independently of their occurence in any particular situation. But for the patient who is able to take the objects only as they are given in sense experience, the corkscrew does not belong to the bottle and the cork if the cork is already loose. From this and similar cases it is plain that he takes the concrete attitude toward objects as well — we may say toward all objects, toward the world in its entirety.

Our conclusion is that the patient's inability to name objects is a consequence of his inability to assume the abstract attitude, for this is a prerequisite for the naming of objects. As we have shown in the example of the umbrella, he has not lost the words themselves, but he is unable to use them in situations which demand their use as categories. Often a patient, asked to name a color presented to him, calls out over and over various color names: red, blue, yellow, etc. He may even utter the appropriate name, but in spite of this he is still unable to connect it with the color itself. Furthermore, it does not help him when we say the different color names for him to repeat after us.

But what makes these words unsuitable for use in connection with objects in the normal way—that is, as names? Why can they not be used as symbols for objects? This may be disclosed in observations of patients who utter appropriate words in connection with some objects but, as closer analysis shows, do not use them in a normal categorical fashion. Here we learn that the patients have the same *concrete* attitude toward the words that they have toward objects they are asked to sort.

Asked to mention the names of several different kinds of animals, the patient may be at first unable to do so. In one case it was not until we had given a patient such examples as dog, cat, mouse, that she replied to the question at all. Then suddenly she said: "A polar bear; a brown bear; a lion; a tiger." Asked why she named these particular animals, she said, "If we enter the zoological gardens, we come at first to the polar bear and then to the other animals."[3] Obviously she had recalled the animals as they were situated in the zoological gardens, and had used the words only as belonging to the concrete situation, not as names for objects. It was very characteristic that she did not simply say "bear," a word which represents the category of all bears, and which we would use when asked to name animals, but that instead she selected the words "polar bear," "brown bear." The same fact appeared when the patient was asked to recite different female first names. She said: "Grete, Paula, Clara, Martha," and, asked why she had mentioned these particular names, answered, "These are all G——s" (G—— was her family name), and went on, "one sister died of a heart neurosis." The last sentence demonstrates very clearly that the patient did not recite names but only uttered words which belonged to a particular concrete situation, namely, to her family situation.

How very concretely such words are apprehended may be demonstrated by the following example. When, to such a patient of ours, a knife was offered with a pencil, she called the knife a "pencil sharpener"; when the knife was offered with an apple, it was to her an "apple parer";

[3] Eva Rothmann, "Untersuchung eines Falles von umschriebener Hirnschadigung mit Storungen auf verschiedenen Leistungsgebieten," *Schweizer Archiv fur Neurologie und Psychiatrie,* vol. XXXIII, 1933.

when offered with a potato, it was a "potato peeler"; in company with a piece of bread, it became a "bread knife"; and with a fork it was "knife and fork." The word "knife" alone she never uttered spontaneously, and when she was asked, "Could we not always call it simply 'knife?' " she replied promptly, "No."

With different mental sets the same word may mean for the normal person different things. For example, in German the word *Anhänger* is used for a lavalier which hangs on a chain around a girl's neck, or for a follower of a personage, or for the second car which is customarily attached to a street-car in Germany. Our patient was unable to use the word in more than one sense or in connection with more than one object. If she understood the word in a particular sense she could not understand that it could be used in another sense. This observation shows clearly that the words themselves are qualitatively different for such patients as compared with normal people, by whom the same word can be used for various totally different objects. By patients with amnesic aphasia they can be used only in a concrete way, for they seem to have lost the characteristic that is necessary if they are to be used in a categorical sense — that is, as symbols. They may be useful as properties belonging to a definite object, but they have become unfit to serve as symbols for ideas. *They have lost their meaning.*

It has usually been assumed, even by those authors who recognize that these patients have lost the categorical attitude toward objects, that the cause of this lack is the loss of words, or a difficulty in evoking words. This cannot be the case. There is no doubt that words provide a very important means of helping us to assume the categorical attitude and of stabilizing concepts, but, as we have explained, our patients have not really lost the words. Instead, the words have lost their character of being usable in the abstract, and this change in language is only one expression of the basic change in our patients, *the lack of the capacity to create any sort of abstraction.*

These observations are important for understanding the character of the capacity for naming objects. This apparently simple performance does not represent a superficial connection between a thing and a word; naming objects presupposes the abstract attitude and is an expression of a very high mental function. But these observations reveal another point still more important for our discussion. They show that speech is one of the essential characteristics of human nature, inasmuch as it is tied to man's highest capacity, the capacity for abstract behavior.

Another significant point appears. The patients we have been discussing have not lost the capacity to use words in a concrete way, and from the advantage this type of speech gives them we can infer what role it may play in normal life.

A patient of mine could name pure colors with their respective color names — red, blue, and so on — but she declined to extend the same word to the several shades of a given color. The words were at her disposal only as individual, concrete things belonging to definite objects. In the course of time, after repeated examinations, she came to call various shades by the same name; for instance, she would use the word "red" for all shades of red. Superficially she seemed to behave like a normal person. One might have thought that she had improved, that she had regained the *meaning* of the words. But it was not so. Asked why she now called all these different shades by the same word, she answered, "The doctors have told me that all these colors are named red. Therefore I call them all red." Asked if this was not correct, she laughed and said, "Not one of these colors is red, but I am told to call them by this word." It is clear that she had not used the words as symbols but had learned to build a quite external connection between one word and a diversity of things, a quite meaningless connection, which, however, because she had a good memory, helped her to carry out a task, if only in a very external way.

Thus we must distinguish very definitely between two ways of using words in connection with objects: real naming, which is an expression of the categorical attitude toward the world in general, and pseudo-naming of objects, which is simply a use of words held in memory. The incidence of this pseudo-naming depends on the extent of the individual's verbal possessions. In it words are used as properties of objects just as other properties — color, size, hue — are used; they belong to concrete behavior. To this type of words belong the speech automatisms of ordinary people — the alphabet, numbers in series, the days of the week, and many other longer or shorter speech expressions of everyday life. This use of words plays a great role in ordinary speech. In learning a foreign language, for example, as long as we have no real conception of it as a language, we possess its words only by such superficial connections with the words of our own language. If we understand their meaning within the realm of the foreign language itself, then the words achieve an absolutely different character; then they become representative of a category.

Important as these speech possessions are for our everyday language, they obtain their significance only from their position against a background of representational, meaningful speech. This may be gathered from the fact that to a certain extent speech automatisms are developed only if a human being possesses the function of meaning. Certainly a child acquires many automatisms by repeated imitation of his own speech and that of others. If he is not able to use them later in connection with meaningful speech, however, his learning of these words is limited, and he forgets many that he has learned. We know that children with an inborn deficiency in the attitude toward the abstract are not able to develop speech automatisms to any extent, and that they forget them, in spite of a good memory, if the words are not practiced constantly. In the same way, patients with a loss of categorical behavior may lose their speech automatisms if they are not continuously kept in use by the demands of concrete situations. Thus, for example, if the meaning of numbers is lost, these patients lose the ability to count and the knowledge of the simple multiplication table, which are usually regarded as well-established possessions of memory.

Speech automatisms may be designated as "tools," but it is false to consider language in general as a mere tool. Even speech automatisms are dependent upon the categorical attitude both in their building and in their use. This point is most important. The use of speech automatisms alone is not real language. Our patients, despite their lack of the categorical attitude, may be able to use speech automatisms which they acquired at a time when they were capable of the categorical attitude, but the fact that their speech lacks the spontaneity and fluidity which characterizes normal language, and that they are not able to use the words as symbols, demonstrates very clearly that language without a categorical background is not real language. Whenever human beings use language to establish natural connections between themselves and the world, particularly with their fellow men, language is not merely a tool. It is not merely a superficial means of communication, not a simple naming of objects through words; it represents a particular way of building up the world — namely, by means of abstractions. "Language," said Wilhelm von Humboldt, "never represents objects themselves but the concepts which the mind has formed of them in the autonomous activity by which it creates language." It is this that makes language so important, so essential to the development of a culture. It becomes a manifestation both of all that is human, the human being at his deepest, and of man's psychic bond with his fellows; in none of his cultural creations does man reveal himself so fully as in the creation of language itself. It would be impossible for animals to create a language, because they do not have this conceptual approach toward the world. If they had, they would be not animals but human beings. Nothing brings this home to us more strikingly than observing in patients with amnesic aphasia the parallelism between the changes which occur in personality and the loss of the meaning of words.

32. The Consensual Definition of Social Objects

Wynona Smutz Garretson

The general theory of symbolic interaction, specifically self theory, is focused upon the importance of language as an instrument of definition and communication. People are seen as responding not directly to a resistant outer reality but to meanings of objects which are defined within a cultural system and social organization.

G. H. Mead, in his discussion of the way persons develop self-concepts and the accompanying ability to take roles effectively, speaks of the degree to which persons develop a "general other."[1] This general other is an organized structure of attitudes believed to be common to all and is defined in terms of a universe of discourse growing out of the symbolic interaction of a community of individuals.

Replies to the Twenty Statements Test, described by Kuhn and McPartland, display this quality.[2] Self-identifying statements which people make fall along a rough spectrum of reference which can be broken up in various ways. The distinction which Kuhn and McPartland have reported is between what they call consensual and nonconsensual statements. Consensual statements are defined as those statements which would be generally understood by persons in the larger society without explanation. Nonconsensual statements are defined as those requiring interpretation before their social relevance can be assessed. The consensual statement is language behavior directed to the general other, while the nonconsensual statement is language directed to a more limited audience. H. S. Sullivan's contribution in developing the notion of the "significant other" consists in accounting for the fact that persons often do not seem to internalize standards and norms from the whole society but from segments of it on some selective basis.[3]

In this paper, the number of consensual statements made in response

From *The Sociological Quarterly,* III (April, 1962), pp. 107-113, by permission of the journal.

[1] G. H. Mead, *Mind, Self and Society* (Chicago: Univ. of Chicago Press, 1934), pp. 135-78.

[2] M. H. Kuhn and T. S McPartland, "An Empirical Investigation of Self-Attitudes," *American Sociological Review,* 19:68-76 (Feb., 1954).

[3] H. S. Sullivan, *Conceptions of Modern Psychiatry* (Washington, D.C.: The William Alanson White Psychiatric Foundation, 1947), pp. 95-96.

to the Twenty Statements Test will be called the locus score. Respondents are assigned to "high" and "low" locus categories as they make more or less than the median number of consensual statements.

Expanding upon this frame of reference, it seems reasonable to propose that the locus quality found in self-conceptions of a given person is also characteristic of his conceptions of other objects. This hypothesis is based on the assumption that the self is the core of a set of inter-related attitudes, and that the level of reference employed by the respondent in his attitudes toward the self would therefore be applicable to other attitudes as well.

In order to test this hypothesis, a schedule was administered to the entire student and faculty populations of four liberal arts colleges. The schedule contained the twenty statements problem, a further object problem (directed at a definition of their college), and a face data sheet.[4] It was expected that respondents who wrote highly consensual answers to "Who am I?" would also write highly consensual answers to "What is ——?" and that respondents who wrote relatively nonconsensual answers to the self question would write relatively nonconsensual answers to the question which directed their attention to another object.

The cross classification for all four colleges is presented in Table 1A. The range of the locus scores on each problem was zero to twenty. The median number of consensual statements made in answer to the twenty statements problem in this case was nine, and for the object problem the median was four. The contingency coefficient and the chi square indicate that while the size of the association is not large, it is statistically significant. The association is in the expected form — high locus score in the self-conception is associated with high locus score in the conception of the college, and vice versa. Some 60 per cent of our population behaved as expected.

Further tests showed that locus score was not associated with sex or socioeconomic status in our population on either test. We did find, when controlling for the college of origin, that the contingency coefficients varied for the partial associations. Medians were reconstructed for each college population, and the tables constructed for each college in this way resulted in statistically significant coefficients of .90-.97. In other words, while there is a locus-score relationship in the data as a whole, limiting the investigation to one campus tends to sharpen that connection. This indicates, in our opinion, that real groups or collectivities are the more appropriate units of analysis, since they may

[4] We followed exactly the procedure of Kuhn and McPartland, except to replace the question, "Who am I?" with "What is ——?" in constructing the object problem and developing the coding for consensual and nonconsensual statements.

reasonably be expected to share a communicative system to a greater degree than a population constructed of students and faculty from four different colleges.

Once we had established a tentative connection between self and object locus scores among these college people, we sought further tests of the locus relationship to examine its generality. Two possible variations occurred to us: to ask the college-oriented object question, but dealing with people who were not students or faculty at that college; and to ask the question about other objects. Some of these possibilities have been tested.

The college study was replicated by an independent investigator who used a service club in a community where one of the colleges was located.[5] Table 1B presents the result of the analysis for locus scores. The range of the locus scores in this case was 1 to 20 for the self-conceptions and 0 to 9 for the college conceptions. The median number

Table I.
Distribution of Locus Scores in Self-conception
and in the Conception of Selected Objects

Population and Selected Objects	*Self Score*	*Object Score*			*Q*	*Chi square*	*p*
		High	*Low*	*Total*			
A. College Population — College	High	555(478)*	404(481)	959	.31	52.34	< .05
	Low	356(433)	506(429)	862			
	Total	911	910	1821			
B. Service Club Members — College	High	14(10)	5(9)	19	.71	6.76	< .05
	Low	6(10)	13(9)	19			
	Total	20	18	38			
C. High School Students — S.U.I.	High	14(7)	1(8)	15	.98	26.35	< .05
	Low	1(8)	16(9)	17			
	Total	15	17	32			
D. Grade School Teachers— City	High	6(4)	2(4)	8	.76		.059
	Low	2(4)	5(3)	7			
	Total	8	7	15			

*Numbers in parentheses are expected frequencies assuming that there is no association between the variables.

[5] Karen M. Neff, "Object Conceptions in a Service Club," unpublished study, Iowa Wesleyan College, 1960.

of consensual statements made in answer to "Who am I?" was 7.5. The median number of consensual statements made about the college was 3. In spite of these relatively small samples of statements our association appears to be strong in the service club. The contingency coefficient is large and statistically significant. Again, the association is of the type we would logically expect, according to our hypothesis. In this case, some 70 per cent of our population behaved as expected, a fact which lends strength to our opinion that what we have reported here is a reliable (replicable) finding.

A further test of the generality of the locus-score relation was made in the course of an experimental study with high school students in a speech workshop at the State University of Iowa. These students were enrolled in the workshop upon the recommendation of their high school teachers. The "Who am I?" question and "What is S.U.I.?" were administered in the experimental situation. Conditions were generally comparable with those of the other groups mentioned above. The same coding was used. Table 1C presents the results of the analysis for locus. The range of the locus scores for self-concepts in this case is 0 to 18, and 0 to 8 for the conceptions of S.U.I. The median number of consensual statements on the "Who am I?" question was 7, and 3 for the answers to "What is S.U.I.?" The contingency coefficient and the chi square indicate a large and statistically significant association between the levels of reference employed in answering the two questions. Only two of the thirty-two respondents failed to behave as we would predict.

Finally, a group of grade school teachers, enrolled for an adult education course in social psychology, were given the "Who am I?" problem and the "What is ——?" In this situation the city was used as the object to be defined. Administration and coding were comparable with the other inquiries. Table 1D presents the analysis for similarity of locus scores.

The range of the locus scores is 5 to 17 for "Who am I?" and 0 to 14 for the statements about the city. Median numbers of consensual statements are 7.5 and 2.5 for the two questions. The coefficient of association again indicates a large connection in the expected form. However, in this case, statistical significance (at the .05 level) was not achieved, probably because of the very small sample used.

One may also note throughout a consistent relationship between the medians for the two questions: the median number of consensual statements in answer to "Who am I?" is regularly at least twice as large as that for "What is ——?" in all four studies.

In summary, the association between locus scores of self-conception and locus scores of conceptions of other objects holds in the populations tested. "Q" value suggests that this association is a relatively strong one. It is true that some of the N's are small. There is, on the other hand, a representation of several age groups, both sexes, socio-economic and status differences, and a variety of objects. Consistent results obtained.

Discussion

Mead suggests that "in an experience within which the individual and the environment mutually determine each other, the unity of the environment and of its constituent objects, as well as that of the individual, arises out of the activity of the individual." [6]

One aspect of this unity, arising out of the perceptual activity of the individual, has been demonstrated in this paper. In part, we have presented evidence that the individual experiences himself as such, and other objects as objects in a consistent way, either from the standpoint of the other individual members of a limited social group (low locus score), or from the generalized standpoint of the social group as a whole (high locus score). In the light of this evidence, some clarification of the interpretation of locus scores, and of the statement made by Kuhn and McPartland that the locus score "reflects social anchorage,"[7] may be in order.

The high locus score is by definition a function of a respondent making a large number of consensual statements. These statements are reasonably specific and indicate widely known social statuses. Earlier research suggests that this may be regarded as an indication that the respondent will behave in generally acceptable ways in standard social situations where those statuses are relevant.[8] In this sense he is "anchored" in the over-all pattern of social life as most people understand it — in terms of Mead's view of the general other.

A low locus score is a function of a respondent making relatively few of these standard, socially relevant statements. We may then expect him to behave in less standardized ways as far as the larger society is concerned. He may of course be firmly anchored in particular

[6] *The Social Psychology of G. H. Mead,* ed. by Anselm Strauss (New York: Phoenix, 1956), pp. 86-87.

[7] Kuhn and McPartland, *op. cit.*

[8] T. S. McPartland, "Self Conception, Social Class and Mental Health," *Human Organization,* vol. 17 (1958), No. 3, pp. 24-29; Kay Clifton, "Convergence in Self-Attitudes in Social Groups at Iowa Wesleyan College," unpublished study, State University of Iowa, 1960. The Wesleyan study particularly clarifies the point made by McPartland that persons who exhibit different modes on the TST behave in predictably different ways. Further investigation of this point appears in T. S. McPartland, J. H. Cumming, and W. S. Garretson, "Self-Conception and Ward Behavior in Two Psychiatric Hospitals," *Sociometry,* 24: 111-24 (June, 1961).

groups and statuses where definition is normally made in terms other than those of general reference. Significant others may at this point indicate special identifications and objects which transcend ordinary social norms.

The social anchorage reflected by the locus score refers then to relative anchorage in the general other of the mass society. Persons whose self-statements result in low locus scores may have intense social investments, emphasizing special or individual characteristics.

We have shown that the individual who sees himself from the standpoint of the general other will also see other objects from that standpoint. Previous studies have shown strong connections between the locus of self-conception and behavior. If there is a strong connection also between locus of self-conception and locus of conception of other objects, the connections between locus and behavior may be tentatively extended, pending empirical investigation, to those other objects. This extension would permit reasoned guesses about behavior from knowledge of the degree of consensuality evidenced in a respondent's descriptions of relevant objects. Attention to the literal content of these descriptions would of course enable finer distinctions and more specific predictions.

But the crucial point for this research is that there is a unity in the conceptions that a person has of objects, and that this unity stems, at least in part, from a fairly consistent generality of the audience to which these conceptions are addressed.

Another important point is suggested by the fact that the locus scores for self-conceptions tend to be considerably larger than locus scores obtained for conceptions of other objects. As was noted earlier, median locus scores are generally twice as large for the question, "Who am I?" in this study as they are for "What is ——?" In our opinion this fact supports the assumption that the self-conception is the core conception in the person's organization of objects into a coherent whole or total view of himself and the world around him. The conceptions of other objects become then the secondary level in the pattern of organization of a person's attitudes. As such, they may reasonably be more easily changed, open to discussion and constant revision than the more stable and basic conception of self.

33. Identification as the Basis for a Theory of Motivation

Nelson N. Foote

Role theory has suffered since inception from lack of a satisfactory account of motivation. It is all very well as far as it goes to state that a person learns to recognize standard situations and to play expected roles in them according to the status defined for him in each. But this is not enough when the person encounters alternatives and must resolve conflicting definitions of his appropriate behavior.[1] Nor is it enough to account for the emergence of new roles in his conduct, nor for his more or less unique variations upon conventional roles. A striking revelation of the need for some theory of motivation to back up situational analysis [2] is disclosed by apathy in the performance of conventional roles, when these are on the verge of abandonment or are accepted only under duress. Roles as such do not provide their own motives.

Most of the recent writers on role theory [3] have recognized this deficiency and have endeavored to make it up through the expedient of eclecticism. Like a Ford car with a Chevrolet motor, each of these "integrators" puts on the road his own model of role theory, one powered by psychic energy, another by a system of tensions or a drive-reduction apparatus, a third by some hierarchy of innate and derived needs. Also, a number of models on the road are said to run through some tendency-to-run established through experiences of the early years, these early years being made to do the work of instincts. Despite the unscientific effort of each writer to achieve uniqueness, their theories all share the postulation of motives as predispositions, purportedly inferred from behavior. As many critics have contended, this either pushes the problem

From *American Sociological Review,* XVI (February, 1951), pp. 14-21, by permission of the American Sociological Association and the author.

[1] Leonard S. Cottrell, Jr., "The Adjustment of the Individual to His Age and Sex Roles," *American Sociological Review,* 7 (Dec., 1942).

[2] Leonard S. Cottrell, Jr., "The Analysis of Situational Fields in Social Psychology," *American Sociological Review,* 7 (June, 1942).

[3] Walter Coutu, *Emergent Human Nature,* New York: Knopf, 1949; Gardner Murphy, *Personality,* New York: Harper, 1947; Theodore M. Newcomb, *Social Psychology,* New York: Dryden, 1950; S. S. Sargent, *Social Psychology,* New York: Ronald, 1950.

back into an infinite regress or leads circularly to the pseudo-explanation of behavior by inferences from itself.

Only two or three writers, such as Sherif and Cantril[4] or Lindesmith and Strauss[5] come close to dispensing with the effort to sustain a system of predispositions. After much stretching of "frames of reference," however, Sherif and Cantril emerge with an ego consisting of "ego-attitudes," which unlike some other attitudes are not traceable to basic drives, and they promise another work on motivation. Lindesmith and Strauss are far more daring in describing motives, like Mills,[6] as rationalizations of acts, whereby one relates his acts to previous experience and to the values of the groups to which one feels he must justify his behavior. Their analysis correctly calls attention to the function of language in motivation, but leaves the reader with the uncomfortable feeling of an unanalyzed hiatus between words and acts, of mystery as to just how language does in fact motivate. It is this hiatus which the concept of identification seems adequate to fill.

So that we may ignore non-motivated behavior, motivation or motivated behavior has to be defined. We are inclined to scoff at those medieval souls who ascribed purpose to the shape of stones, the falling of water or the absence of beards among women, although remnants of such thinking are common. It is likewise easy to make jokes about Lundberg's assertion that there is no more justification scientifically to seek out the motives of a man who runs down the street than those of a piece of paper which blows down the street, although Lundberg brings strong arguments to support his extreme position. It is far less easy to specify where between these extremes a line can be drawn to differentiate motivated from non-motivated human behavior.

The growing of whiskers we take to be non-motivated; the shaving of them off, motivated. Going to bed is motivated, sleeping is not. Physiological functions like growth, digestion, circulation, metabolism, are clearly non-motivated, but there are marginal activities of the organism, like elimination, over which conscious control is only slowly won and may be lost under stress. While we may not gain similar direct control over the former functions, there are almost none which cannot be disrupted by psychic stress or modified by manipulation of their physical conditions.

To approach the dividing line from the opposite side, we go from conscious, rational actions involving choice among alternatives to those

[4] M. Sherif, and H. Cantril, *The Psychology of Ego-Involvements,* New York: Wiley, 1947, pp. 4-8.

[5] A. R. Lindesmith and A. Strauss, *Social Psychology,* New York: Dryden, 1949.

[6] C. W. Mills, "Situated Actions and Vocabularies of Motive," *American Sociological Review,* 5 (December, 1940).

which seem compulsive or "unconsciously" motivated, but are not universally so, and thence again to those which seem to be physiologically autonomous.

To generalize, motivated behavior is distinguished by its prospective reference to ends in view, by being more or less subject to conscious control through choice among alternative ends and means. All kinds of human behavior are characterized by direction (or form), intensity, frequency and duration; all literally require expenditure of energy. But only motivated behavior exhibits the fluidity of organization, the paradoxical combinations of phenomenally-experienced choice and compulsion ("I don't want to but I have to because . . ."), the dependence upon learning and the content of previous experience, and, above all, the symbolic structuring which must be taken into account even to begin to understand, for example, the prodigies of effort and self-sacrifice put forth by our representatives in Korea. In a sentence, we take motivation to refer to the degree to which a human being, as a participant in the ongoing social process in which he necessarily finds himself, defines a problematic situation as calling for performance of a particular act, with more or less anticipated consummations and consequences, and *thereby* his organism releases the energy appropriate to performing it. Even the behavior consequent to an irritating organic condition, e.g., heat or hunger, has to be defined according to its meaning in the situation and is so defined, often fallibly. Organic *irritations,* which may or may not be anterior to definition of an act, contrary to some predispositionalists have no direct and uniform connection with organic *mobilizations,* which are always posterior to definition of an act.

To the extent that we find the term *attitude* useful, it is as a synonym for these mobilizations. Definitions of the situation account for attitudes, not the reverse. And to avoid predispositionalist connotations, we prefer not to speak of particular motives, but only of motivated acts. If we were to speak of motives, it would be as rationalizations of acts, in the sense of Mills and Lindesmith — that is, as symbolic constructs which not only organize these acts in particular situations but make them recognizably recurrent in the life-history of any person or group. This pattern of recurrence constitutes what is often reified as "personality" or "culture." But what is it that makes culture and personality in action different from culture and personality in abstraction? We are back where we began.

Consider the game. For brevity's sake, we must assume reader familiarity with Mead's analysis of play, the game and the generalized "other." Let eighteen strangers, familiar with the rules of baseball and having nothing to do, be told to choose up sides and play a game. At the moment the choosing begins, it makes not the slightest difference to any potential player which side he is on — or which side wins, though if competitively indoctrinated, he might want to be on the winning side. The groups, if such they may be called — the two teams — have no identity.

If they could go ahead and play under such conditions — of no identity — the game would be almost pointless. True, people would play the roles appropriate to their positions on the teams, when at bat or in the field, and any physiological needs defined by them as satisfied through exercise might be met. Here would be role theory in action, as Mead left off in describing it[7] — a sort of empty bottle of behavior and formal relations, without motive or incentive save the undifferentiated physiological necessity to dispense energy and kill time. There would be no more reason to obey the rules than to cheat, but the game might proceed by unimaginative observance of them. Since its progress would offer no more interest or involvement to the players than to a spectator ignorant of the rules, it is inconceivable how the observer could ever get them to play it, unless by offering them a reward, such as money, whose value was extraneous to the game itself. Some jobs are like that, but we do not call them games.

Now by contrast consider a ball game like last year's World Series, when the Dodgers came up against the Yankees. The roles and the statuses are the same, as are the rules of the game. But what a difference! And what is the nature of the difference? It is in the fact that the empty bottle of role and status suddenly has a content. That content is not drives, tensions, energy or needs; it is *identity.* Yet remember that it is still a game; for all the frenzied involvement of players and spectators, of winners and losers, the gain and loss are purely symbolic. Except for the special identity which gives value to their ensuing activity, the behavior of the players would be mere rote — a perfect example of anomie.

As Mead has shown, one learns many more roles than he ever plays overtly. To interact intelligently with another, he must learn correctly to anticipate the responses of that other — that is, to empathize. But implicit role-taking is no metaphysical transmigration of consciousness. It requires playing sub-overtly the role appropriate to the identity of the other in the situation, as accurately as one can read off that identity. In play or in role-playing experiments, a person may disclose the great range of his latent repertoire. The reason he limits his real or realistic behavior to a selected few of all the roles he has learned is that he knows and defines only these certain ones as *his own.* And he can only ascertain which role is his in each situation by knowing *who* he is. Moreover, he must know who he is with considerable conviction and clarity, if his behavior is to exhibit definiteness and force, which is to say, degree of motivation.

All of which thus far may seem so patent as to preclude the raising of more analytical questions about the nature of identity and identification. Is it not altogether obvious that the chairman of this meeting, for instance, is Edward Rose, the one who exists at such and such a time and place and

[7] G. H. Mead, *Mind, Self and Society,* University of Chicago Press, 1934.

performs largely as others hereabout expect him to? Yet it is just this simple and obvious fact that has to be broken down analytically, like the atom, into its various constituents. And as the analogy suggests, the process of analyzing the self into its parts may go on indefinitely.

Intrusion of the concept of *self* here, however, permits mention of what we take to be the misplaced abstractness of much use of it by social psychologists. Just this wrapping of all the particular constituents of a person's identity into one round bundle and labelling it "the self" have long delayed the analysis of the self and of identity. Too-ready generalization of the identities of any given self into indefinitely extensible statuses has led many social psychologists to feel that they must look "behind" the self for the "underlying" motives of the particular kinds of behavior which spring out of it — even to perpetrate such super-generalities as a "drive for self-actualization."

We mean by *identification* appropriation of and commitment to a particular identity or series of identities. As a process, it proceeds by *naming;* its products are ever-evolving self-conceptions — with the emphasis on the *con-*, that is, upon ratification by significant others. If space permitted, it would be valuable to show in detail how much this concept of identification owes to Freud[8] — where it differs from his concept, and where it supplements. Being more psychologist than sociologist, Freud tends to ignore the functions of language; for all his discussion of identification, he never speaks of identity or common identity. We are not concerned here to kick the dead horse of Freudian instinct theory, nor to appreciate the leads he gave to the study of empathy, but only to affirm that his concept of identification is inadequate as a basis for a situational theory of motivation. Neither is it the missing link of social psychology — a description of the specific tie which unites individuals with their fellows. Yet expansion and reinterpretation in interactional terms of his concept of identification provides both.

In surveying the multitude of predispositional theories of motivation which have been set forth, one is struck not only by their regular failure. Equally striking and suggestive is the seductive — not to say sinister, as Burke[9] charges — appeal which is exerted by the hope of reducing human behavior to some permanently definitive order through finding certain elemental imperatives to underly its bewildering variety. Criticism has negated every specific naming of "the mainsprings of human action." If we now boldly draw the indicated conclusion and deny wholesale the *scientific* validity of all such attempts, it remains illuminating to ask why their great continuing appeal in the face of repeated collapse or suppression.

[8] Sigmund Freud, *Group Psychology and the Analysis of the Ego,* London: Hogarth, 1922; *The Ego and the Id,* London: Hogarth, 1927.

[9] Kenneth Burke, *A Grammar of Motives,* New York: Prentice-Hall, 1945.

Upon close examination it seems predictable that such attempts will continue, for what is involved is the necessary activity of every social being, and not merely of social psychologists. Every man must categorize his fellows in order to interact with them. We never approach another person purely as a human being or purely as an individual. If a being is human, it shares characteristics with a class of human beings which distinguish them from the non-human. If we ever encountered a creature not identifiable in any other respect than its human-ness, we would be non-plussed. Dewey[10] puts it succinctly:

> We come to know or note not merely this particular which as a particular cannot strictly be known at all (for not being classed it cannot be characterized and identified) but to recognize it as man, tree, stone, leather — an individual of a certain kind, marked by a certain universal form characteristic of a whole species of thing. Along with the development of this common-sense knowledge, there grows up a certain regularity of conduct. The particular incidents fuse, and a *way* of acting which is general, as far as it goes, builds up. . . . This regularity signifies, of course, that the particular case is not treated as an isolated particular, but as one of a kind, which therefore demands a *kind* of action.

Where Dewey's tree, stone or leather is inert and its properties unchanging throughout the known past, his man, however, is not. A rose by any other name may smell as sweet, but a person by another name will act according to that other name. The regularities in our behavior toward him are necessarily based upon our expectation of regularities in his behavior. The regularities in his behavior toward us are in turn based in the same way upon his sharing our conception of his identity and his expectation that we share his conception of our identity. Naturally there is many a slip!

The common man is always classifying thus. And to make things harder for the social psychologist, his classifications vary with time and place, as identities are elaborated and re-determined. Moreover, the common man assumes that categories applied to his fellows immediately indicate the motives to be imputed to them. "I dislike Communists because I am a Catholic and they are atheistic" is an example of such common-sense explanation (rationalization) of behavior. It is enough for him when imputation suffices for investigation, and extrapolation for prediction — enough, that is, to make possible a more or less orderly social life. Likewise, his identities give common meaning, stability and predictability to his own behavior as long as he clings to them. Possibly

[10] John Dewey, *Reconstruction in Philosophy,* New York: Holt, 1920, pp.79-80.

the predictions of social scientists will never excel their apprehension of the categories of identity and motive employed among the groups they study; but predictive power is certainly lost when, in place of these, psychologists substitute simpler and less relevant categories of their own— their lists of predispositions.

If the regularities in human behavior are organized responses to situations which have been classified more or less in common by the actors in them, then names motivate behavior. It is by analysis of the function of language, and especially of names ascribed to categories of people, that we can dispense with predispositions and yet maintain a theory of motivation subject to empirical testing — not throwing out baby with bath, as the positivists do.[11]

Establishment of one's own identity to oneself is as important in interaction as to establish it for the other. One's own identity in a situation is not absolutely given but is more or less problematic. Many expositions of interpersonal behavior omit this point, and describe only the process of ascertaining the position of the other, as if that could be read off like a set of labels. Labels are there, to be sure, but the important fact is what these labels mean in a unified definition of the situation embracing both parties. In abstraction one can consider statuses analytically, as the anthropologists do, but in action it is the unique concatenation of relevant statuses at this one time and place — in this *situation* — which constitutes identity.

Social situations always contain standard elements, and always some unique elements, if only a different position in time and space. When one enters a new situation, he attempts to relate it to old ones by familiar signs, and his response may be automatic. Or the preponderance of new elements may make the situation too problematic for a habitual response to be appropriate. For its definition, nonetheless, he must approach it from some fixed point of reference. He must start from what is most definite, find some *given* elements in it. His capacities are given, but they constitute only inert *limits* to his potential behavior, so they are not definitive enough. Although some pressing organic irritation may be quite definite, again his physical condition helps create the situation he confronts, but does not alone dictate what his response will be. The identity of the others involved is dependent upon his own in the familiar reciprocal manner. So inevitably the elements which have to be "taken as given" are his identities or, more exactly, his special pattern of identity.

In most situations our identity is so completely habitual and taken for granted that we virtually ignore its presence or relevance in our reactions, concentrating only upon the stimulating environment. Re-

[11] C. L. Stevenson, *Ethics and Language,* New Haven: Yale University Press, 1944.

search-wise, it is strategic to focus observations upon those situations where identity itself is acutely problematic in order to observe its determining effect upon behavior (although study of the opposite type of situation — the teacher who insists she was cut out only for fifth-grade math, the fifth-grader who insists he was never cut out for it — is also illuminating).[12] When doubt of identity creeps in, action is paralyzed. Only full commitment to one's identity permits a full picture of motivation. Faith in one's conception of one's self is the key which unlocks the physiological resources of the human organism, releases the energy (or capacity, as Dewey would say) to perform the indicated act. Doubt of identity, or confusion, where it does not cause complete disorientation, certainly drains action of its meaning, and thus limits mobilization of the organic correlates of emotion, drive and energy which constitute the introspectively-sensed "push" of motivated action. We are reminded of James Michener's[13] heroes in the South Pacific who were plagued by the question, "What am I doing here?" Also, of William James's contention that only he who has played seriously with the idea of suicide has plumbed the phenomenon of self.

At this moment we can only speculate on how one acquires and gets committed to particular identities. Unless we assume a heaven of unborn souls, the process is obviously a matter of experience. We are limited to the experience available to us from birth, although these limitations become more flexible as we gain in variety of experience. That is, the richer our experience, the more possible it becomes to exercise conscious direction over its further accumulation. Nevertheless, limitations continue, and few persons ever reach the point of considering such a deliberate and drastic shift of identity as to change their names or pass the color line. Primarily then the compulsive effect of identification upon behavior must arise from absence of alternatives, from unquestioned acceptance of the identities cast upon one by circumstances beyond his control (or thought to be). From the point of view of the experiencing individual, however, the process is bound to seem much less like a process of limitation to a few among infinite possibilities than a process of discovery. His accruing conceptions of who he is are usually taken as something verging upon ultimate reality rather than as ultimately arbitrary ascriptions by others. Of course as soon as he encounters alternatives, he is released from such pre-conscious bondage to any particular conception of himself. Thenceforth his identities accrue from more conscious choice and pursuit of the values he has discovered in his experience.

Value, we would insist, is discovered in experience, not conferred

[12] Prescott Lecky, *Self-Consistency,* New York: Island Press, 1945.

[13] James Michener, *Tales of the South Pacific,* New York: Pocketbooks, 1948.

upon it from without. The concepts by which we may name our various ends-in-view, and through manipulation of which we are enabled to judge among alternatives, should not — in value theory or motivation theory — be allowed to obscure the concrete consummations to which they refer. Once experienced, these appear permanently registered in the organism. If the concepts have no concrete reference for a person, or if through faulty communication the connection between the abstract values and the actual experience is not made, the abstractions are not motivating to *him,* as every parent finds out daily. Our learning is immensely expedited through being directed by means of these names for experienceable values to undergo and acquire them. Also, if through identification with more experienced mentors upon whose judgment we depend, we hold to the expectation of realizing recommended values eventually, experiential confirmation may remain lacking indefinitely. Nevertheless, all signals pointing to where value may be found in experience probably must be corroborated by its actual discovery, at least by some members of any group which shares them, or these signals become empty shibboleths and lingering memorials of an extinct value community.

If we insist that prior experience is necessary to motivation, however, have we not fallen back once more into predispositional thinking? Not if we are correct in assuming that a predisposition denotes more than a mere statistical tendency, some active thrust which constantly presses like a coiled spring to set off a particular line of action. Metaphorically put, the operation of values in the formulation of responses to situations is advisory, not executive. While we can only mobilize for our next act when it or its elements can be construed as similar to acts which have gone before, the determination of the appropriate act is made in the situation, not prior to it. Experience is continually being recombined in new patterns; and even the most habitual act must be defined as appropriate to its immediate context to be launched overtly. In place of predisposition, therefore, it is necessary and sufficient to put memory (memory plus mobilization equals motivation), by virtue of which we can call up in the present, images of past consummations of acts.[14] We set these before us as ideal futures, to be achieved again when we have reconstructed the present situations so as to put us — if this is possible to one of our identity — into an imagined new position where that remembered good will be actually re-experienced. Because we have the capacity through language for conceptualizing these remembered goods as values, and the ingenuity to devise new schemes of relations under which they may be revived in the same or fuller measure, we can invent new roles or deviate from conventional ones. Also, we simultaneously inherit thereby the constant possibility of conflict — both internal

[14] G. H. Mead, *The Philosophy of the Act,* University of Chicago Press, 1938, pp. 23-25.

and external — which characterizes members of human society.

Because our learning has more often than not been perfected to the point where cognitive judgments in standardized situations are made instantaneously, and the energy for performing the appropriate behavior is released immediately, it has been an easy mistake for many observers to suppose that the organic correlates came first and even account for the definition of the situation, rather than the reverse. Also, it has often led them to ignore or depreciate the long, historical accumulation of experience, organized by our shared conceptual apparatus, which brings our whole past to bear upon our behavior in the momentary present. Yet if past and future did not figure in the determination of the present, would we logically have a phenomenon of motivation or valuation to ponder?

Without the binding thread of identity, one could not evaluate the succession of situations. Literally, one could say there would be no value in living, since value only exists or occurs relative to particular identities — at least value as experienced by organisms which do not live in the mere present, as animals presumably do, devoid of self and unaware of impending death. Moreover, it is only through identification as the sharing of identity that individual motives become social values and social values, individual motives.

Fuller recognition of these functions of identity should increase the scope, power and precision of situational analysis in social research, while in turn research oriented to identification should contribute to the elaboration and clarification of its working. It is only because one conceives of himself, via a certain identity, as a member of a class which includes certain others, that he can enjoy or suffer the successes and failures of a group. It is only commitment to his identity which makes him subject without physical compulsion to the control of the groups to which he belongs, or arouses his antagonism to members of a category construed as inimical to his category. In fact, we will carry this so far as to say that only full commitment to identities shared with others makes possible the grand human phenomena of love and grief. This is not tautological, because it calls attention to language in general and names in particular as the mediating links among individuals. It enables us to rephrase such imponderable speculations as "What are the psychological functions of love?" into definitely researchable form, such as "How did this person acquire his identity?" or "How does he get committed to particular identities which tie him constitutionally as a self to other persons?" Also, in reverse, "What kinds of new experience are sufficient to free him from the compulsion of certain old identities?"

This paper must end where it ought to begin. Originally it described some proposals for research on various types of acutely problematic identity, and some suggestions for experimentation with the methods every propagandist — which includes each of us part of the time — uses to motivate others. Space permits only mention of studies of identification among adopted and illegitimate children, the effects of ambiguous identity upon the motivation of "marginal men," the psychological consequences of name-changing, and problems of self-conception among women who keep their husbands' names. Much understanding is already coming from observation of marked effects upon behavior from identification with Alcoholics Anonymous and other therapeutic groups. Regarding the techniques by which the propagandist succeeds in invoking identification of listener with speaker, Kenneth Burke gives the experimenter many leads in his valuable recent book, *A Rhetoric of Motives.*[15] Would practical successes as a recipe for motivating others be too stringent a test of the validity of a theory of motivation?

We have set forth that (1) role theory needs to be supplemented with an account of motivation consistent with its main premises, (2) a proper definition of motivated and non-motivated behavior makes clear how to avoid both dissolution of the concept of motivation and unchecked imputation of motives, (3) identification is the process whereby individuals are effectively linked with their fellows in groups, (4) predispositional theories, being oblivious to the function of language in motivated behavior, ascribe metaphysical reality to what are actually only the verbal categories whereby human beings regularize their doings, (5) these categorizations of experience motivate behavior through the necessary commitment of individuals to particular concatenations of identity in all situations, (6) commitment to particular identities arises through a limiting and discovering process of acquiring conceptions of self, which are confirmed, revised or elaborated partly by instruction from significant others and partly through direct experience, and (7) the compelling or inhibiting effect of identifications upon the release of varying kinds of behavior can be studied empirically.

In conclusion, let it be emphasized that the title of this paper offered expansion of the concept of identification only as the *basis* for a situational theory of motivation, not as a full theory itself, even though it helps dispel certain false theories. By its use are avoided the fallacies of both biological determinism — the person impelled from within — and of cultural determinism — the person driven from without. It also avoids the ingenious pretensions by which some theorists, through the invention of such terms as "bio-social," have resolved a putative opposition between biology and culture which never existed to begin with. When theorists can do no better in explaining conflict and change than to make the environment the enemy of the organism, or give no better explanation of personality organization than as a meeting of protoplasm and society, it is puzzling to note that Cooley was insisting as early as 1902 that individual and social are two sides of the same phenomena.[16] They do not have to be joined together by integration in textbooks. In the concept

[15] Kenneth Burke, *A Rhetoric of Motives,* New York: Prentice-Hall, 1950.

[16] C. H. Cooley, *Human Nature and the Social Order,* Scribners, 1902.

of identity we can see this clearly: One has no identity apart from society; one has no individuality apart from identity.[17] Only by making use of this concept can we account for motivation in terms consistent with the only social psychology that truly deserves the name "social."

[17] Kenneth Burke, *A Grammar of Motives,* New York: Prentice-Hall, 1945, pp. 469-470. A searching criticism of the organism-environment framework.

34. Situated Actions and Vocabularies of Motive*

C. Wright Mills

The major reorientation of recent theory and observation in sociology of language emerged with the overthrow of the Wundtian notion that language has as its function the "expression" of prior elements within the individual. The postulate underlying modern study of language is the simple one that we must approach linguistic behavior, not by referring it to private states in individuals, but by observing its social function of coordinating diverse actions. Rather than expressing something which is prior and in the person, language is taken by other persons as an indicator of future actions.[1]

Within this perspective there are suggestions concerning problems of motivation. It is the purpose of this paper to outline an analytic model for the explanation of motives which is based on a sociological theory of language and a sociological psychology.[2]

As over against the inferential conception of motives as subjective "springs" of action, motives may be considered as typical vocabularies having ascertainable functions in delimited societal situations. Human actors do vocalize and impute motives to themselves and to others. To explain behavior by referring it to an inferred and abstract "motive" is one thing. To analyze the observable lingual mechanisms of motive imputation and avowal as they function in conduct is quite another. Rather than fixed elements "in" an individual, motives are the terms with which interpretation of conduct *by social actors* proceeds. This imputation

From *American Sociological Review,* V. (December, 1940), pp. 904-913, by permission of the American Sociological Association.

*Revision of a paper read to The Society for Social Research, University of Chicago, August 16-17, 1940.

[1] See C. Wright Mills, "Bibliographical Appendices," Section I, 4: "Sociology of Language" in *Contemporary Social Theory,* Ed. by Barnes, Becker & Becker, New York, 1940.

[2] See G. H. Mead, "Social Psychology as Counterpart of Physiological Psychology," *Psychol. Bul.,* VI: 401-408, 1909; Karl Mannheim, *Man and Society in an Age of Reconstruction,* New York, 1940; L. V. Wiese-Howard Becker, *Systematic Sociology,* part I, New York, 1932; J. Dewey, "All psychology is either biological or social psychology," *Psychol. Rev.,* vol. 24: 276.

and avowal of motives by actors are social phenomena to be explained. The differing reasons men give for their actions are not themselves without reasons.

First, we must demarcate the general conditions under which such motive imputation and avowal seem to occur.[3] Next, we must give a characterization of motive in denotable terms and an explanatory paradigm of why certain motives are verbalized rather than others. Then, we must indicate mechanisms of the linkage of vocabularies of motive to systems of action. What we want is an analysis of the integrating, controlling, and specifying function a certain type of speech fulfils in socially situated actions.

The generic situation in which imputation and avowal of motives arise, involves, first, the *social* conduct or the (stated) programs of languaged creatures, i.e., programs and actions oriented with reference to the actions and talk of others; second, the avowal and imputation of motives is concomitant with the speech form known as the "question." Situations back of questions typically involve *alternative* or *unexpected* programs or actions which phases analytically denote "crises."[4] The question is distinguished in that it usually elicits another *verbal* action, not a motor response. The question is an element in *conversation*. Conversation may be concerned with the factual features of a situation as they are seen or believed to be or it may seek to integrate and promote a set of diverse social actions with reference to the situation and its normative pattern of expectations. It is in this latter assent and dissent phase of conversation that persuasive and dissuasive speech and vocabulary arise. For men live in immediate acts of experience and their attentions are directed outside themselves until acts are in some way frustrated. It is then that awareness of self and of motive occur. The "question" is a lingual index of such conditions. The avowal and imputation of motives are features of such conversations as arise in "question" situations.

Motives are imputed or avowed as answers to questions interrupting acts or programs. Motives are words. Generically, to what do they refer? They do not denote any elements "in" individuals. They stand for anticipated situational consequences of questioned conduct. Intention or purpose (stated as a "program") *is* awareness of anticipated consequence;

[3] The importance of this initial task for research is clear. Most researches on the verbal level merely ask abstract questions of individuals, but if we can tentatively delimit the situations in which certain motives *may* be verbalized, we can use that delimitation in the construction of *situational* questions, and we shall be *testing* deductions from our theory.

[4] On the "question" and "conversation," see G. A. DeLaguna, *Speech: Its function and Development,* 37 (and index), New Haven, 1927. For motives in crises, see J. M. Williams, *The Foundations of Social Science,* 435 ff, New York, 1920.

motives are names for consequential situations, and surrogates for actions leading to them. Behind questions are possible alternative actions with their terminal consequences. "Our introspective words for motives are rough, shorthand descriptions for certain typical patterns of discrepant and conflicting stimuli."[5]

The model of purposive conduct associated with Dewey's name may briefly be stated. Individuals confronted with "alternative acts" perform one or the other of them on the basis of the differential consequences which they anticipate. This nakedly utilitarian schema is inadequate because: (a) the "alternative acts" of *social* conduct "appear" most often in lingual form, as a question, stated by one's self or by another; (b) it is more adequate to say that individuals act in terms of anticipation of *named* consequences.

Among such names and in some technologically oriented lines of action there may appear such terms as "useful," "practical," "serviceable," etc., terms so "ultimate" to the pragmatists, and also to certain sectors of the American population in these delimited situations. However, there are other areas of population with different vocabularies of motives. The choice of lines of action is accompanied by representations, and selection among them, of their situational termini. Men discern situations with particular vocabularies, and it is in terms of some delimited vocabulary that they anticipate consequences of conduct.[6] Stable vocabularies of motives link anticipated consequences and specific actions. There is no need to invoke "psychological" terms like "desire" or "wish" as explanatory, since they themselves must be explained socially.[7] Anticipation is a subvocal or overt naming of terminal phases and/or social consequences of conduct. When an individual names consequences, he elicits the behaviors for which the name is a redintegrative cue. In a *societal* situation, implicit in the names for consequences is the social dimension of motives. Through such vocabularies, types of societal controls operate. Also, the terms in which the question is asked often will contain both alternatives: "Love or Duty?" "Business or Pleasure?" Institutionally different situations have different *vocabularies of motive* appropriate to their respective behaviors.

This sociological conception of motives as relatively stable lingual phases of delimited situations is quite consistent with Mead's program to approach conduct socially and from the outside. It keeps clearly in mind that "both motives and actions very often originate not from within

[5] K. Burke, *Permanence and Change,* 45, New York, 1936. I am indebted to this book for several leads which are systematized into the present statement.

[6] See such experiments as C. N. Rexroad's "Verbalization in Multiple Choice Reactions," *Psychol. Rev.,* Vol. 33: 458, 1926.

[7] Cf. J. Dewey, "Theory of Valuation," *Int. Ency. of Unified Science,* New York, 1939.

but from the situation in which individuals find themselves. . . ."[8] It translates the question of "why"[9] into a "how" that is answerable in terms of a situation and its typical vocabulary of motives, i.e., those which conventionally accompany that type situation and function as cues and justifications for normative actions in it.

It has been indicated that the question is usually an index to the avowal and imputation of motives. Max Weber defines motive as a complex of meaning, which appears to the actor himself or to the observer to be an adequate ground for his conduct.[10] The aspect of motive which this conception grasps is its intrinsically social character. A satisfactory or adequate motive is one that satisfies the questioners of an act or program, whether it be the other's or the actor's. As a word, *a motive tends to be one which is to the actor and to the other members of a situation an unquestioned answer to questions concerning social and lingual conduct.* A stable motive is an ultimate in justificatory conversation. The words which in a type situation will fulfil this function are circumscribed by the vocabulary of motives acceptable for such situations. Motives are accepted justifications for present, future, or past programs or acts.

To term them justification is *not* to deny their efficacy. Often anticipations of acceptable justification will control conduct. ("If I did this, what could I say? What would they say?") Decisions may be, wholly or in part, delimited by answers to such queries.

A man may begin an act for one motive. In the course of it, he may adopt an ancillary motive. This does not mean that the second apologetic motive is inefficacious. The vocalized expectation of an act, its "reason," is not only a mediating condition of the act but it is a proximate and controlling condition for which the term "cause" is not inappropriate. It may strengthen the act of the actor. It may win new allies for his act.

When they appeal to others involved in one's act, motives are strategies of action. In many social actions, others must agree, tacitly or explicitly. Thus, acts often will be abandoned if no reason can be found that others will accept. Diplomacy in choice of motive often controls the diplomat. Diplomatic choice of motive is part of the attempt to motivate

[8] K. Mannheim, *Man and Society*, 249, London, 1940.

[9] Conventionally answerable by reference to "subjective factors" within individuals. R. M. MacIver, "The Modes of the Question Why," *J. of Soc. Phil.*, April, 1940. Cf. also his "The Imputation of Motives," *Amer. J. Sociol.*, July, 1940.

[10] *Wirtschaft und Gesellschaft*, 5, Tubingen, 1922, "'Motiv' heisst ein Sinnzusammenhang, Welcher dem Handelnden selbst oder dem Beobachtenden als sinnhafter 'Grund' eines Verhaltens in dem Grade heissen, als die Beziehung seiner Bestandteile von uns nach den durchschnittlichen Denk-und Gefühlsgewohnheiten als typischer (wir pflegen in sagen: 'richtiger') Sinnzusammenhang bejaht Wird."

acts for other members in a situation. Such pronounced motives undo snarls and integrate social actions. Such diplomacy does not necessarily imply intentional lies. It merely indicates that an appropriate vocabulary of motives will be utilized — that they are conditions for certain lines of conduct.[11]

When an agent vocalizes or imputes motives, he is not trying to *describe* his experienced social action. He is not merely stating "reasons." He is influencing others — and himself. Often he is finding new "reasons" which will mediate action. Thus, we need not treat an action as discrepant from "its" verbalization, for in many cases, the verbalization is a new act. In such cases, there is not a discrepancy between an act and "its" verbalization, but a difference between two disparate actions, motor-social and verbal.[12] This additional (or *"ex post facto")* lingualization may involve appeal to a vocabulary of motives associated with a norm with which both members of the situation are in agreement. As such, it is an integrative factor in *future* phases of the original social action or in other acts. By resolving conflicts, motives are efficacious. Often, if "reasons" were not given, an act would not occur, nor would diverse actions be integrated. Motives are common grounds for mediated behaviors.

Perry summarily states the Freudian view of motives "as the view that the real motives of conduct are those which we are ashamed to admit either to ourselves or to others."[13] One can cover the facts by merely saying that scruples (i.e., *moral* vocabularies of motive) are often efficacious and that men will alter and deter their acts in terms of such motives. One of the components of a "generalized other," as a mechanism of societal control, is vocabularies of acceptable motives. For example, a business man joins the Rotary Club and proclaims its public-spirited vocabulary.[14] If this man cannot act out business conduct without so doing, it follows that this vocabulary of motives is an important factor in his behavior.[15] The long acting out of a role, with its appropriate

[11] Of course, since motives are communicated, they may be lies; but this must be proved. Verbalizations are not lies merely because they are socially efficacious. I am here concerned more with the social function of pronounced motives, than with the sincerity of those pronouncing them.

[12] See F. Znaniecki, *Social Actions,* 30, New York, 1936.

[13] *General Theory of Value,* 292-293, New York, 1936.

[14] *Ibid.*, 392.

[15] The "profits motive" of classical economics may be treated as an ideal-typical vocabulary of motives for delimited economic situations and behaviors. For late phases of monopolistic and regulated capitalism, this type requires modification; the profit and commercial vocabularies have acquired other ingredients. See N. R. Danielian's *AT&T,* New York, 1940, for a suggestive account of the *noneconomic* behavior and motives of business bureaucrats.

motives, will often induce a man to become what at first he merely sought to appear. Shifts in the vocabularies of motive that are utilized later by an individual disclose an important aspect of various integrations of his actions with concomitantly various groups.

The motives actually used in justifying or criticizing an act definitely link it to situations, integrate one man's action with another's, and line up conduct with norms. The societally sustained motive-surrogates of situations are both constraints and inducements. It is a hypothesis worthy and capable of test that typal vocabularies of motives for different situations are significant determinants of conduct. As lingual segments of social action, motives orient actions by enabling discrimination between their objects. Adjectives such as "good," "pleasant," and "bad" promote action or deter it. When they constitute components of a vocabulary of motives, i.e., are typical and relatively unquestioned accompaniments of typal situations, such words often function as directives and incentives by virtue of their being the judgments of others as anticipated by the actor. In this sense motives are "social instruments, i.e., data by modifying which the agent will be able to influence [himself or others]." [16] The "control" of others is not usually direct but rather through manipulation of a field of objects. We influence a man by naming his acts or imputing motives to them — or to "him." The motives accompanying institutions of war, e.g., are not "the causes" of war, but they do promote continued integrated participation, and they vary from one war to the next. Working vocabularies of motive have careers that are woven through changing institutional fabrics.

Genetically, motives are imputed by others before they are avowed by self. The mother controls the child: "Do not do that, it is greedy." Not only does the child learn what to do, what not to do, but he is given standardized motives which promote prescribed actions and dissuade those proscribed. Along with rules and norms of action for various situations, we learn vocabularies of motives appropriate to them. These are the motives we shall use, since they are a part of our language and components of our behavior.

The quest for "real motives" supposititiously set over against "mere rationalization" is often informed by a metaphysical view that the "real" motives are in some way biological. Accompanying such quests for something more real and back of rationalization is the view held by many sociologists that language is an external manifestation or concomitant of something prior, more genuine, and "deep" in the individual. "Real attitudes" versus "mere verbalization" or "opinion" implies that at best we only infer from his language what "really" is the individual's attitude or motive.

Now what *could we possibly* so infer? Of precisely *what* is verbaliz-

[16] *Social Actions,* 73.

ation symptomatic? We cannot *infer* physiological processes from lingual phenomena. All we can infer and empirically check[17] is another verbalization of the agent's which we believe was orienting and controlling behavior at the time the act was performed. The only social items that can "lie deeper" are other lingual forms.[18] The "Real Attitude or Motive" is not something different in kind from the verbalization or the "opinion." They turn out to be only relatively and temporally different.

The phrase "unconscious motive" is also unfortunate. All it can mean is that a motive is not explicitly vocalized, but there is no need to infer unconscious motives from such situations and then posit them in individuals as elements. The phrase is informed by persistence of the unnecessary and unsubstantiated notion that "all action has a motive," and it is promoted by the observation of gaps in the relatively frequent verbalization in everyday situations. The facts to which this phrase is supposedly addressed are covered by the statements that men do not always explicitly articulate motives, and that *all* actions do not pivot around language. I have already indicated the conditions under which motives are typically avowed and imputed.

Within the perspective under consideration, the verbalized motive is not used as an index of something in the individual but *as a basis of inference for a typal vocabulary of motives of a situated action.* When we ask for the "real attitude" rather than the "opinion," for the "real motive" rather than the "rationalization," all we can meaningfully be asking for is the controlling speech form which was incipiently or overtly presented in the performed act or series of acts. There is no way to plumb behind verbalization into an individual and directly check our motive-mongering, but there is an empirical way in which we can guide and limit, in given historical situations, investigations of motives. That is by the construction of typal vocabularies of motives that are extant in types of situations and actions. Imputation of motives may be controlled by reference to the typical constellation of motives which are observed to be societally linked with classes of situated actions. Some of the "real" motives that have been imputed to actors were not even known to them. As I see it, motives are circumscribed by the vocabulary of the actor. The only source for a terminology of motives is the vocabularies of motives actually and usually verbalized by actors in specific situations.

Individualistic, sexual, hedonistic, and pecuniary vocabularies of motives are apparently now dominant in many sectors of twentieth-

[17] Of course, we could infer or interpret constructs posited in the individual, but these are not easily checked and they are not explanatory.

[18] Which is not to say that, physiologically, there may not be cramps in the stomach wall or adrenalin in the blood, etc., but the character of the "relation" of such items to social action is quite moot.

century urban America. Under such an ethos, verbalization of alternative conduct in these terms is least likely to be challenged among dominant groups. In this milieu, individuals are skeptical of Rockefeller's avowed religious motives for his business conduct because such motives are not *now* terms of the vocabulary conventionally and prominently accompanying situations of business enterprise. A medieval monk writes that he gave food to a poor but pretty woman because it was "for the glory of God and the eternal salvation of his soul." Why do we tend to question him and impute sexual motives? Because sex is an influential and widespread motive in our society and time. Religious vocabularies of explanation and of motives are now on the wane. In a society in which religious motives have been debunked on rather wide scale, certain thinkers are skeptical of those who ubiquitously proclaim them. Religious motives have lapsed from selected portions of modern populations and other motives have become "ultimate" and operative. But from the monasteries of medieval Europe we have no evidence that religious vocabularies were not operative in many situations.

A labor leader says he performs a certain act because he wants to get higher standards of living for the workers. A business man says that this is rationalization, or a lie; that it is really because he wants more money for himself from the workers. A radical says a college professor will not engage in radical movements because he is afraid for his job, and besides, is a "reactionary." The college professor says it is because he just likes to find out how things work. What is reason for one man is rationalization for another. The variable is the accepted vocabulary of motives, the ultimates of discourse, of each man's dominant group about whose opinion he cares. *Determination of such groups, their location and character, would enable delimitation and methodological control of assignment of motives for specific acts.*

Stress on this idea will lead us to investigations of the compartmentalization of operative motives in personalities according to situation and the general types and conditions of vocabularies of motives in various types of societies. The motivational structures of individuals and the patterns of their purposes are relative to societal frames. We might, e.g., study motives along stratified or occupational lines. Max Weber has observed:

> . . . that in a free society the motives which induce people to work vary with . . . different social classes. . . . There is normally a graduated scale of motives by which men from different social classes are driven to work. When a man changes ranks, he switches from one set of motives to another. [19]

The lingual ties which hold them together react on persons to constitute

[19] Paraphrased by K. Mannheim, *op. cit.*, 316-317.

frameworks of disposition and motive. Recently, Talcott Parsons has indicated, by reference to differences in actions in the professions and in business, that one cannot leap from "economic analysis to ultimate motivations; the institutional patterns *always* constitute one crucial element of the problem."[20] It is my suggestion that we may analyze, index, and gauge this element by focusing upon those specific verbal appendages of variant institutionalized actions which have been referred to as vocabularies of motive.

In folk societies, the constellations of motives connected with various sectors of behavior would tend to be typically stable and remain associated only with their sector. In typically primary, sacred, and rural societies, the motives of persons would be regularly compartmentalized. Vocabularies of motives ordered to different situations stabilize and guide behavior and expectation of the reactions of others. In their appropriate situations, verbalized motives are not typically questioned.[21] In secondary, secular, and urban structures, varying and competing vocabularies of motives operate coterminously and the situations to which they are appropriate are not clearly demarcated. Motives once unquestioned for defined situations are now questioned. Various motives can release similar acts in a given situation. Hence, variously situated persons are confused and guess which motive "activated" the person. Such questioning has resulted intellectually in such movements as psychoanalysis with its dogma of rationalization and its systematic motive-mongering. Such intellectual phenomena are underlaid by split and conflicting sections of an individuated society which is characterized by the existence of competing vocabularies of motive. Intricate constellations of motives, for example, are components of business enterprise in America. Such patterns have encroached on the old style vocabulary

[20] "The Motivation of Economic Activities," 67, in C. W. M. Hart, *Essays in Sociology,* Toronto, 1940.

[21] Among the ethnologists, Ruth Benedict has come up to the edge of a genuinely sociological view of motivation. Her view remains vague because she has not seen clearly the identity of differing "motivations" in differing cultures with the varied extant and approved vocabularies of motive. "The intelligent understanding of the relation of the individual to his society . . . involves always the understanding of the types of human motivations and capacities capitalized in his society . . ." "Configurations of Culture in North America," *Amer. Anthrop.,* 25, Jan. - Mar. 1932; see also: *Patterns of Culture,* 242-243, Boston, 1935. She turns this observation into a quest for the unique "genius" of each culture and stops her research by words like "Apollonian." If she would attempt constructively to observe the vocabularies of motives which precipitate acts to perform, implement programs, and furnish approved motives for them in circumscribed situations, she would be better able to state precise problems and to answer them by further observation.

of the virtuous relation of men and women: duty, love, kindness. Among certain classes, the romantic, virtuous, and pecuniary motives are confused. The asking of the question: "Marriage for love or money?" is significant, for the pecuniary is now a constant and almost ubiquitous motive, a common denominator of many others.[22]

Back of "mixed motives" and "motivational conflicts" are competing or discrepant situational patterns and their respective vocabularies of motive. With shifting and interstitial situations, each of several alternatives may belong to disparate systems of action which have differing vocabularies of motives appropriate to them. Such conflicts manifest vocabulary patterns that have overlapped in a marginal individual and are not easily compartmentalized in clear-cut situations.

Besides giving promise of explaining an area of lingual and societal fact, a further advantage of this view of motives is that with it we should be able to give sociological accounts of other theories (terminologies) of motivation. This is a task for sociology of knowledge. Here I can refer only to a few theories. I have already referred to the Freudian terminology of motives. It is apparent that these motives are those of an upper bourgeois patriarchal group with strong sexual and individualistic orientation. When introspecting on the couches of Freud, patients used the only vocabulary of motives they knew; Freud got his hunch and guided further talk. Mittenzwey has dealt with similar points at length.[23] Widely diffused in a postwar epoch, psychoanalysis was never popular in France where control of sexual behavior is not puritanical.[24] To converted individuals who have become accustomed to the psychoanalytic terminology of motives, all others seem self-deceptive.[25]

In like manner, to many believers in Marxism's terminology of power, struggle, and economic motives, all others, including Freud's, are due to hypocricy or ignorance. An individual who has assimilated thoroughly only business congeries of motives will attempt to apply these motives to all situations, home and wife included. It should be noted that the business terminology of motives has its intellectual articulation, even as psychoanalysis and Marxism have.

It is significant that since the Socratic period many "theories of

[22] Also motives acceptably imputed and avowed for one system of action may be diffused into other domains and gradually come to be accepted by some as a comprehensive portrait of *the* motive of men. This happened in the case of the economic man and his motives.

[23] Kuno Mittenzwey, "Zur Sociologie der psychoanalystischer Erkenntnis," in Max Scheler, ed. *Versuche zu einer Sociologie des Wissens,* 365-375, Munich, 1924.

[24] This fact is interpreted by some as supporting Freudian theories. Nevertheless, it can be just as adequately grasped in the scheme here outlined.

[25] See K. Burke's acute discussion of Freud, *op. cit.,* Part I.

motivation" have been linked with ethical and religious terminologies. Motive is that in man which leads him to do good or evil. Under the aegis of religious institutions, men use vocabularies of moral motives: they call acts and programs "good" and "bad," and impute these qualities to the soul. Such lingual behavior is part of the process of social control. Institutional practices and their vocabularies of motives exercise control over delimited ranges of possible situations. One could make a typal catalog of religious motives from widely read religious texts, and test its explanatory power in various denominations and sects.[26]

In many situations of contemporary America, conduct is controlled and integrated by *hedonistic* language. For large population sectors in certain situations, pleasure and pain are now unquestioned motives. For given periods and societies, the situations should be empirically determined. Pleasure and pain should not be reified and imputed to human nature as underlying principles of all action. Note that hedonism as a psychological and an ethical doctrine gained impetus in the modern world at about the time when older moral-religious motives were being debunked and simply discarded by "middle class" thinkers. Back of the hedonistic terminology lay an emergent social pattern and a new vocabulary of motives. The shift of unchallenged motives which gripped the communities of Europe was climaxed when, in reconciliation, the older religious and the hedonistic terminologies were identified: the "good" is the "pleasant." The conditioning situation was similar in the Hellenistic world with the hedonism of the Cyrenaics and Epicureans.

What is needed is to take all these *terminologies* of motive and locate them as *vocabularies* of motive in historic epochs and specified situations. Motives are of no value apart from the delimited societal situations for which they are the appropriate vocabularies. They must be situated. At best, socially unlocated *terminologies* of motives represent unfinished attempts to block out social areas of motive imputation and avowal. Motives vary in content and character with historical epochs and societal structures.

Rather than interpreting actions and language as external manifestations of subjective and deeper lying elements in individuals, the research task is the locating of particular types of action within typal frames of normative actions and socially situated clusters of motive. There is no explanatory value in subsuming various vocabularies of motives under some terminology or list. Such procedure merely confuses the task of explaining specific cases. The languages of situations as given must be considered a valuable portion of the data to be interpreted and related to their conditions. To simplify these vocabularies of motive into a

[26] Moral vocabularies deserve a special statement. Within the viewpoint herein outlined many snarls concerning "value-judgments," etc., can be cleared up.

socially abstracted terminology is to destroy the legitimate use of motive in the explanation of social actions.

Selected Bibliography
Part IV, Mind

Blumer, Herbert, "Attitudes and the Social Act," *Social Problems,* 3 (October 1955), pp. 59-65.

A critique of "attitude," one of the most widely used concepts in social psychology.

Burke, Kenneth, *Permanence and Change* (New York: New Republic, 1963), pp. 30-53.

An early statement on the relationship between language and motives. Burke is also the author of the more recent *The Grammar of Motives* (New York: Prentice-Hall, 1945) and *The Rhetoric of Motives* (New York: Prentice-Hall, 1950), which present this relationship in much greater detail.

Carroll, John B. and Casagrande, Joseph B., "The Function of Language Classifications in Behavior," in Eleanor E. Maccoby, Theodore M. Newcomb, and Eugene L. Hartley (editors), *Readings in Social Psychology,* 3rd edition (New York: Henry Holt and Company, 1958), pp. 18-31.

An empirical test of Whorf's linguistic relativity hypothesis, using two experiments with Hopi, Navaho, and Anglo subjects.

Cassirer, Ernst, *An Essay on Man* (New Haven: Yale University Press, 1944), pp. 27-56.

Expounds the nature and function of symbols, which account for the evolution "from animal responses to human responses."

Langer, Suzanne, *Philosophy in a New Key* (New York: Penguin Books, 1942), pp. 42-63.

On the logic of signs and symbols.

Levy, David M , "The Act as a Unit," *Psychiatry,* 25 (November 1962), pp.295-309.

A psychiatrist adapts Mead's concept of "the act" to the analysis of mental disorder.

Mead, George Herbert, *Mind, Self and Society* (Chicago: University of Chicago Press, 1934), pp. 67-74 and 94-125.

Descriptions of the development of significant symbols and the process of minded behavior.

Strong, Samuel W., "A Note on George H. Mead's 'The Philosophy of the Act,' " *American Journal of Sociology,* 45 (July 1939), pp. 71-76.

A good, but difficult, summary of the concept, "the act."

Vigotsky, L. S., "Thought and Speech," *Psychiatry,* 2 (February 1939), pp. 29-52.

Argues for the identity of thought and speech, as opposed to the conception of speech as merely the means for expressing and communicating thought.

White, Leslie A., "Mind is Minding," *Scientific Monthly,* 48 (1939), pp. 169-171.

An eminent anthropologist views mind as behavior, paralleling the functionalist views of Dewey and Mead.

White, Leslie A., "The Symbol: The Origin and Basis of Human Behavior," *Philosophy of Science,* 7 (1940), pp. 451-463.

Presents a set of ideas that is entirely consistent with those of symbolic interaction.

Whorf, Benjamin L., *Language, Thought and Reality,* edited by J B. Carroll (New York: Wylie and the M.I.T. Press, 1956).

Includes articles on the role of language in shaping perception and thought.

Part V. ❧ Research Implications and Applications

The preceding sections of this volume have analyzed the concepts and propositions constituting the perspective of symbolic interactionism upon human behavior. In this concluding section, the readings present heuristic implications and illustrative researches documenting the broad use that perspective has in research.

The first three articles deal with research implications in the study of the family, education, and crime. Stryker does much to refute the widely held view that symbolic interactionism does not generate researchable hypotheses. In the first of his two articles, he indicates the kinds of answers this theory can give to certain persistent questions on the family. Further, he describes some research suggestions that emerge from the theory.

Ellsworth Faris, Mead's contemporary at the University of Chicago, provides us with the next selection. He analyzes some educational implications of a common form of human behavior, that involved in viewing one's own past behavior.

In an influential article, Glaser shows the images of human behavior underlying various theories of criminality. His "differential identification" theory, entirely consistent with symbolic interactionism, stresses the role of reference groups in criminal behavior. The theory is a modification of Edwin H. Sutherland's clearly social-psychological "differential association" explanation of crime.

The next seven readings report researches in such diverse areas as marihuana use, occupations, terminal illness, mental illness, political behavior, and adaptation to other persons. Becker's widely cited article describes how individuals learn to define the use of marihuana in terms favoring the continuation of such use. The compatibility of these findings with differential identification theory should be noted.

A study of the self-conceptions and conceptions of each other held by top-level executives and first-line supervisors is the subject of the selection by Coates and Pellegrin. The findings reported here should be compared with those of Videbeck in Part III.

Glaser and Strauss direct attention to an important aspect of all human interaction — the identities actors assign themselves and their co-actors. The complexities of this topic are explored in the authors' impressionistic accounts of terminally ill patients in hospitals. Such cases illustrate how interaction is shaped by the identity each actor assigns himself, the identities he assigns others, the identity he believes others assign him, and the identity others actually assign him.

The relationship between self-conceptions of psychiatric patients and their ward behavior is reported in the article by McPartland, Cumming, and Garretson. Categorizing responses to the Twenty Statements Test (see page 445) in an unusual way, McPartland and his associates find support for certain basic propositions of symbolic interactionism. Further support for such propositions is found in Rosengren's study, which reveals that changes in self-conception tend to be associated with changes in the overt behavior of a small sample of emotionally disturbed boys.

Brooks introduces the reader to a "significant others test" and demonstrates the usefulness of symbolic interactionism in accounting for the political party preferences of college students.

The final selection, by Stryker, centers upon the hypothesis that "the adjustment of the individual is a function of the accuracy with which he can take the role of the other(s) implicated with him in some social situation." The fact that this hypothesis is not fully supported by Stryker's data argues against a "sectarian" total commitment to symbolic interactionism and urges upon us, rather, a critically open-minded orientation.

35. Symbolic Interaction as an Approach to Family Research *

Sheldon Stryker

Various commentators have stated that the ideas covered by the label symbolic interaction are part of the intellectual baggage of almost all who concern themselves with human behavior. On the other hand, persons identifying themselves as symbolic interactionists commonly hold that this theory suffers from general, albeit certainly undeserved, neglect. There is a good deal of validity in both views. Many social psychologists have made at least some of the ideas of symbolic interaction part of their theoretical equipment, whether or not they are aware of their debt. Yet the implications of this theoretical scheme are not always perceived and appreciated even by men calling themselves symbolic interactionists. The problem seems to be that at least some of the once-novel ideas of the theory have become, for many, simple commonplaces or platitudes, and like most platitudes, more likely to defeat thought than to stimulate it.

This paper is above all an attempt at a straightforward review of symbolic interaction theory. Its aim is to stimulate renewed interest in a simple, but relatively powerful, set of ideas which remain largely unexploited. It is perhaps particularly in the family field that these are open to exploitation.

The theory being dealt with has a venerable tradition, beginning at least as far back as Hegel. Modern formulations have their roots in American pragmatism, in the writings of Peirce and James. Suggestions contained here were elaborated and systematized by James Mark Baldwin, John Dewey, Charles Horton Cooley and, most important of all, George Herbert Mead. Specifically in the family field, Waller, Burgess, Hill, and Foote represent persons whose work, to important degree, stems from this framework.

There is no single orthodoxy which is symbolic interaction theory. There is certainly a hard core of agreement, and there are certainly important differences, among representatives of the position. Some see it as no more than a set of concepts serving to sensitize one to aspects of social

From *Marriage and Family Living,* XXI (May, 1959), pp. 111-119, by permission of the journal and the author.

*A slightly amended version of a paper presented to the 21st Groves Conference on Marriage and the Family, Washington, D.C., April 15, 1958.

life, some as a general theory of human behavior. The present discussion proceeds on another view, which sees the theory as addressing itself to a relatively modest series of questions.

Theory can be taken to mean a set of assumptions or postulates with which one approaches some part of the empirical world, a set of concepts in terms of which this part of the world is described, and a set of propositions, emerging from the assumptions and relating the concepts, about the way this part of the world "works" which are checked against observations of that world. This presentation begins by noting briefly the general questions to which symbolic interaction theory is addressed, and turns successively to the assumptions underlying the theory, the concepts provided by the theory, and illustrative instances of the propositions which are the answers to its questions. It concludes by considering some of the implications of the theory for family research.

The Problems to Which the Theory Is Addressed

As a social psychological theory, symbolic interaction addresses a set of interrelated questions, most of which take their place in the context of two major problems. The first is that of socialization: how the human organism acquires the ways of behaving, the values, norms and attitudes of the social units of which he is a part. The focus here is on development — that which happens over time to the human neophyte: the infant, the recruit entering the army, the student entering the university, the bride entering a new set of family relationships.

The twin of the problem of socialization is that of personality: the organization of persistent behavior patterns. Such organization cannot be assumed but must be demonstrated and accounted for. The task of a social psychology is to account for such organization insofar as it depends upon social relationships. It should be added that symbolic interaction addresses itself largely to the normal person — in the sense of the person without gross physical, physiological, or psychological defect.

To say that this position is oriented to the normal person is not to say that it is concerned only with personal organization, for the theory seeks to explore personal disorganization as well. As a matter of fact, one of the strengths of this position is that it treats personal organization and personal disorganization as facets of the same problem, rather than different problems, and that it can provide answers to both without invoking principles lying outside its theoretical scheme.

These are the major problems which symbolic interaction theory seeks to resolve. They have been stated in general form, for more specific formulation depends on the assumptions and concepts with which the theory approaches the parts of the world in which it has interest.

Assumptions

The initial assumption is that, insofar as interests are social psychological, man must be studied on his own level. The position of symbolic interactionism is anti-reductionist; it argues that valid principles of human social psychological behavior cannot be derived from, or inferred from, the study of non-human forms. This assertion rests on the principle of emergence. Emergence suggests the existence of qualitative differences as well as quantitative continuities among the precipitates of the evolutionary process. If man is qualitatively different in some respects from other animal forms, it follows that principles derived from other forms cannot completely account for his behavior. The task of at least some social psychologists is to focus on that which is different in man.

A second assumption is that the most fruitful approach to man's social behavior is through an analysis of society. This assumption involves no assertion of some metaphysical priority of society over the individual. Social psychologists of one stripe have argued that society is *the* ultimate reality; social psychologists of another variety give ontological precedence to the individual, denying the reality of society. Either position leads to confusion and contradiction. Symbolic interaction has not resolved the argument; but it has bypassed it. It has done so by beginning its analyses with the social act. Its basic unit of observation is interaction, and from interaction both society and individual derive. It is worth noting that this formulation permits an articulation between sociology and social psychology which alternative frameworks can forge, if at all, only with great difficulty. Both begin with the same "building bricks": social actions. Sociology builds in one direction to the behavior of collectivities. Social psychology builds in another direction to the behavior of individuals. Those whose problems bridge the two fields, as is true of many students of the family, are provided with a framework facilitating movement from one level to the other, allowing systematic transactions between the two levels.

A third assumption concerns the equipment with which the newborn enters life. The human infant is, from this point of view, neither social nor anti-social, but rather asocial. It has the potentialities for social development. It is an active organism, it has "impulses," but these impulses are not channelized or directed toward any specific ends. Original nature is amorphous and plastic; it lacks organization.

A last assumption is that the human being is actor as well as reactor. The human being does not simply respond to stimuli occurring outside himself. In fact, what is a stimulus depends on the activity in which the organism is engaged: objects become stimuli when they serve to link impulses with satisfactions. The environment of the organism is a selected segment of the "real" world, the selection occurring in the interests of behavior which the human being himself has initiated. It is this assumption which leads to the fundamental methodological principle of symbolic interaction: the demand that the investigator see the world from the point of view of the subject of his investigation.

These seem to be the assumptions underlying symbolic interaction theory. Not an assumption, but closely related to those discussed, is a predilection on the part of adherents of this theory to stay close to the world of everyday experience. The viewpoint develops out of such experience, and it is with such experience that it seeks to deal.

Major Concepts

An assumption of this theory, again, is emergence. The principle emergent on the human level is language behavior. The initial concern in this review of concepts thus must be with language and its correlatives.

The starting point is with the *act:* behavior by an organism stemming from an impulse requiring some adjustment to appropriate objects in the external world. A *social act* is one in which the appropriate object is another individual. But another individual does not "stand still"; he, too, acts with reference to the first actor. Thus every social act implicates at least two individuals, each of whom takes the other into account in the processes of satisfying impulses. Since such acts occur over time, they have a history. This makes possible the appearance of *gestures,* defined as any part of the act which stands for, or comes to be a sign of, those parts of the act yet to occur. Thus, in responding to one another, individuals may be involved in what Mead called a "conversation of gestures": they may come to use early stages of one anothers' acts as indicators of later stages. Such gestures have meaning. Vocal sounds can serve as gestures, and they too may have meaning. The meaning of a gesture (an early stage of an act) is the behavior which follows it (the later stages of the act): meaning is, by definition, behavior. Some gestures have an additional property. They may mean the same thing, imply the same set of subsequent behaviors, to the organism which produces the gesture and that which perceives it. When this occurs, the gesture becomes a *significant symbol.* To illustrate: the cry of the infant may serve as a sign of hunger to the mother, and she responds by feeding the infant. The cry is a gesture whose meaning lies in the parental response. At a later stage, the child may call out "milk!" and, unless the appropriate parental response is made, protest vigorously. The word "milk" is here a significant symbol. Language, basically, is a system of significant symbols. This is equivalent to asserting that language is a system of shared meanings, and this in turn implies that language is a system of shared behavior. Communication between human beings presupposes these characteristics of language symbols.

Retreat is necessary before going forward. Symbols arise in the context of social acts, and they function in completing acts: they reflect the interests from which the acts stem. We respond to symbols as predicters of further behavior, our own as well as that of others. Since these symbols predict later behavior, they provide a basis for adjusting our activity before that later behavior has occurred. Thus symbols may be said to function in the context of the act in place of that which they symbolize, and may further be said to organize behavior with reference to that which is symbolized. Symbols entail a plan of action. To illustrate and summarize:

> Thus if one hunter shouts to another, "A duck!" the second hunter immediately looks into the air and makes appropriate preparations for shooting at a bird on the wing. If the first hunter shouts, "Rabbit!" his partner responds in a different manner. Language symbols do not merely stand for something else. They also indicate the significance of things for human behavior, and they organize behavior toward the thing symbolized.[1]

Some symbols represent generalizations of behavior toward objects; these are *categories.* To categorize is to apply a class term to a number of objects, to signify that a number of different things are, for certain purposes, to be treated as the same kind of thing. Classification or categorization is essential to activity, for life would be impossible if one were forced to respond to every object in the world as unique. Class terms, or categories, are of course symbols, and as such they share the characteristics of symbols. They have meaning, they are cues to behavior, and they organize behavior.

Humans respond to a classified world, one whose salient features are named and placed into categories indicating their significance for behavior. In short, humans do not respond to the environment as physically given, but to an environment as it is mediated through symbols — to a *symbolic environment.* Persons frequently enter situations in which their behavior is problematic. Before they can act, they must define the situation, that is, represent it to themselves in symbolic terms. The products of this defining behavior are termed "definitions of the situations."

A particularly important kind of category is that called "position."[2] Positions are socially recognized categories of actors, any general category serving to classify persons: father, sergeant, teacher are positions

[1]Alfred R. Lindesmith and Anselm L. Strauss, *Social Psychology,* New York: Dryden Press, 1956, p. 63.

[2]Others have used the term "status" here. I prefer "position" in order to avoid the hierarchical implications of status. Positions may certainly be hierarchized, but hierarchy and position are conceptually distinct and it is important to distinguish between them.

by this usage, as are playboy, intellectual, blacksheep.

The significance of such categories is that they serve to organize behavior toward persons so categorized. An equivalent assertion is that in attaching one of these position designations to a person we are led to expect certain behaviors from him and we behave toward him on the basis of these expectancies. To the expectations with regard to behavior attached to a position the term "role" is given. These expectations are social in the same sense symbolic behavior is always social: the ultimate meaning of the positions to which these expectations apply is shared behavior. They are social in another and most important sense, namely, that it is impossible to talk about *a* position without reference to some context of *other* positions: one cannot talk about the behavior of father except with reference to the positions of mother, child, and so on. Thus every position assumes some counter-position, and every role presumes some counter-role. To use the term "role" is necessarily to refer to an interpersonal relation.

The discussion of categories has been couched in terms of an actor responding to objects in the external world, including people, by classifying them in functionally relevant ways. Under certain circumstances, an actor may apply such categories to himself: he may respond to himself as he responds to other people, by naming, defining, classifying himself. To engage in this kind of behavior is to have a *self.* Self can be defined in various ways, each calling attention to slightly different aspects of the same activity. Mead defined the self as that which is an object to itself. Others have discussed the self as a set of responses of an organism serving to organize other responses of the same organism. It is useful in the present context to define the self in terms of categories one applies to himself, as a set of self-identifications.

However defined, self refers to activity, to reflexive activity, and not to an object, thing, or essence. It is a necessary concept, from the standpoint of the symbolic interactionist, but it is one fraught with the dangers of reification. As Robert W. White notes:[3]

> The necessity of using the concept of self does not confer the privilege of misusing it. As we use concepts in our thinking, they tend to get firmer and harder. Thought about fluid events tends to curdle and form solid clots. Before long we begin to think of the self as if it were a lump in the personality. It becomes a region, an institution, an entity. . . . In the end the self is standing like a solid boulder of granite in the midst of personality, and one's thinking about it is as flexible as granite.

[3] Robert W. White, *The Abnormal Personality,* New York: Ronald Press, 1948, p. 140.

The self is defined in terms of socially recognized categories and their corresponding roles. Since these roles necessarily imply relationships to others, the self necessarily implies such relations. One's self is the way one describes to himself his relationships to others in a social process.

The discussion thus far has presumed but not made explicit the concept of "role-taking," or alternatively, "taking the role of the other." Role-taking refers to anticipating the responses of others implicated with one in some social act. The meaning of the concept can best be elucidated through illustration. Consider the classroom instructor who presents to his students an especially difficult conception. He perhaps finds that the words ordinarily used to cover the topic do not allow the discussion to proceed beyond the immediate issue. He then casts about for words which will allow him to clarify the conception, and so allow him to move beyond it to further materials. How shall he select such words? Presumably he will do so in terms of what he knows or guesses about the backgrounds or experiences of the students before him. He will, in other words, attempt to put himself in the place of the students; he will attempt to anticipate their responses to the words he will use. He takes the role of the other.

Role-taking may involve the anticipation of responses of some particular other. More frequently, it involves the anticipation of responses of what Mead called the "generalized other." To revert to the class-room illustration, the instructor must deal with the class not as discrete individuals but as an organized unit, the members of which can be expected to behave in differentiated yet related ways. To take the role of the generalized other is to see one's behavior as taking place in the context of a defined system of related roles. The concept of reference group, as it is currently used, represents partially a restatement and partially an extension of the generalized other concept.

In comparatively recent work, the concept of "significant other" has come into use. This concept represents the recognition that, in a fragmented and differentiated world, not all the persons with whom one interacts have identical or even compatible perspectives; and that, therefore, in order for action to proceed, the individual must give greater weight or priority to the perspectives of certain others. To speak, then, of significant others is to say that given others occupy high rank on an "importance" continuum for a given individual.

One last set of concepts must be mentioned. Symbolic interaction makes unashamed use of "mental" concepts such as thinking, volition, and self-consciousness. The case can be put in stronger fashion; its judgment is that any scheme which rules out such concepts distorts the facts of human experience. However, its usage of these terms is not traditional. Where frequently these concepts are defined in such way as to place them outside the bounds of scientific discourse, symbolic interaction defines these terms behavioristically and, in so doing, permits their treatment within the conventions of scientific procedure. Thus, thinking is defined as the internalized manipulation of language symbols. Volition becomes the process of selecting among alternatives symbolically present in the experience of the individual. And self-consciousness is the activity of viewing oneself from the standpoint of others.

The Answers Provided by the Theory: Illustrative Cases

It will be impossible, given limitations of space, to do full justice to the complexities of the problems raised or the explanations provided by symbolic interaction theory; all that can be done is to review these in barest outline.

The problem of socialization has a number of interrelated facets, among them questions of how meanings are obtained by the human infant, how the self develops and is structured, and how thinking and objectivity arises in the course of experience.

The human infant, active but unorganized, is born into an ongoing set of social relationships. Such relationships are premised upon a set of shared meanings. The infant acts, but randomly: he thrashes his arms, he exercises his vocal cords. The adult responds to these actions, say the crying of the infant, by doing something to the infant — he feeds it, or changes it, or turns it over on its stomach. He will eventually find that response which will complete the act in a desired way, that is, stop the crying. There is in this situation an "impulsive" act which is, incipiently, a gesture, and there is incipient meaning as well. The incipient meaning is that part of the act supplied by the adult. In time, both the cry of the infant and the response of the adult become specialized; when this occurs, the cry is a gesture in the previously-defined sense. The significant point is that, since it is the adult who completes the act, it is he who supplies the meaning of the gesture. What kinds of completions will he supply? He is, of course, limited by the repertory of meanings available in the social unit of which he is a part. Further, the adult will have defined the situation, including his positional relationship to the infant, for example, that of father to son, and this definition will invoke the set of expected behaviors we call the role of the father. If the father is a middle class American, and if he takes the cry of the infant to mean that the infant is thirsty, his response will be to supply milk or water — but not wine or whiskey. The meanings attached to the gestures of the infant are social meanings, and they are supplied through his relationships with already socialized participants in an ongoing society.

The early activity of the child will include random vocalization. Eventually, too, he will imitate sounds others make. Others respond to the initially random vocalization by selecting out particular sounds and responding to these. They respond to the imitated sounds as well by acts which contain the adult meanings of these sounds. For the child, the correspondence between sound and meaning will be initially vague, but in the process of interaction over time the correspondence will become more pronounced. So, for example, the child may use the sound "ba" to refer to any approximately round object and, having played this game with daddy, may be led to roll any such object — ball, orange, egg — around the floor. The response of parent to the rolling of an egg — especially an uncooked one — will soon make clear that an egg is not a "ba" and thus is not to be rolled on the floor. In the course of time, child and parent will come to agree on what is and is not a ball, and thus a significant symbol will have come into existence. A sound, initially meaningless to the child, comes to mean for the child what it already means for the adult.

The "self" comes into existence in the same way. Just as the sound "ba" took on meaning through the responses of others, so too the human organism as an object takes on meaning through the behavior of those who respond to that organism. We come to know what we are through others' responses to us. Others supply us with a name, and they provide the meaning attached to that symbol. They categorize us in particular ways — as an infant, as a boy, et cetera. On the basis of such categorization, they expect particular behaviors from us; on the basis of these expectations, they act toward us. The manner in which they act towards us defines our "self," we come to categorize ourselves as they categorize us, and we act in ways appropriate to their expectations.

The evolution of the self is, of course, gradual; moreover, it is continual. This development is one of increasing complexity, in a sense, for as the child moves into the social world he comes into contact with a variety of persons in a variety of self-relevant situations. He comes, or may come, into contact with differing expectations concerning his behavior, and differing identities on which these expectations are based. Thus he has, through the role-taking process, a variety of perspectives from which to view and evaluate his own behavior, and he can act with reference to self as well as with reference to others. In short, the socialization process as described makes possible the appearance of objectivity. Furthermore, since these processes may be internalized through the use of language symbols, it also makes possible the appearance of self-control.

The individual, at the same time and through time as well, occupies a variety of positions in sets of social relationships. If he responded in each of these in terms of unique sets of role-expectations and self-definitions, his behavior would be discontinuous. Usually, however, there is a continuity and organization among the behaviors of a given individual. The question is how such personal organization can be accounted for. The basic answer provided by symbolic interaction theory uses the concepts of self, role, and definition of the situation. On entering an ongoing social situation, one responds to that situation by defining it. This definition includes the assignment of positions to others, and thus the setting up of expectations concerning their behavior. It, further, includes an assessment of self, that is, the assignment of positional identities to oneself. Others in the situation are, of course, engaged in the same kind of activity. The behavior that ensues is a function of such definitions. A crucial question thus becomes one of the congruence of definitions, situation, role and self, of the interacting persons. Congruence permits efficient, organized behavior. Expanding this, again noting that the individual moves through a variety of interpersonal situations, the congruence of definitions, and so the behavioral expectations these imply, is fundamental to continuity of behavior. Personal organization is thus seen as a function, not simply of that which the individual carries around with him, but of the relationship between that which he carries with him — in the form of self-concepts — and the situations in which he interacts with others as these are mediated symbolically.

When one asks what kinds of social conditions foster or permit such congruence, the generalized answer is that when meanings are widely shared in a society, or among those persons within a society with whom one actually interacts, congruence is likely.

What happens when meanings are diverse among the others with whom one interacts? Reversing the above process, but maintaining the same explanatory principle, it may be said that incongruities in definition and so incongruities in expectations will result, and that personal disorganization is the outcome. A number of possible types of incongruity may be suggested: conflicts or lack of coordination between self concepts and the expectations of others; conflicts among aspects of self called into play in the same situation; the temporal succession of expectations which do not articulate, and so on.

It may be worthwhile to take one type of incongruity, say lack of coordination between self concepts and expectations of others, and note more closely its relevance to personal disorganization. At the same time, the question can be raised: under what circumstances do identities change? Suppose one enters a situation with a set of self identifications which include the name "professor," and suppose he defines the situation — for example, as a classroom — in such a way that this identity is appropriate. He will then presumably conduct himself in ways indicated by that identity. He speaks in judicious, measured tones, he adopts a knowledgeable air, and so on. He can behave this way only so long as his audience accepts this definition of himself and so responds in such ways as validate his behavior, by taking notes, by concentrating attention upon him, by directing questions at him. Suppose, however, the audience fails to accept this definition; they think him a fool rather than a professor (although perhaps the two are not completely incompatible). They disregard what he is saying, they challenge his competency, they pay more attention to friends in class than they do to him. In short, they fail to validate his self identification. How will he behave? It is highly probable that behaviors ordinarily inappropriate to the classroom will ensue. He will likely lose his judicious tones and become emotional. He is likely to act confused, uncertain, embarrassed, ambivalent. At the same time, since persons typically have considerable investment in identities, he very probably will attempt to defend himself. He may do so by redoubling his efforts to act the complete professor, by dismissing the incident as a joke, by regarding the audience as consisting of morons. But if, persistently, his identity as professor fails to be validated by others, he cannot retain that identity. Others validate identities by behaving in appropriate ways, ways which provide cues on the basis of which further performance in terms of the identity is possible. If these cues are not provided, then such performance is no longer possible, and the identity will fade.

Implications for Family Research

Rather than attempt to detail implications of symbolic interaction for family research, a few brief indications of researchable questions stimulated by this theory will be presented.

One question, or set of questions, has to do with differential commitment to family identities. It is obvious, for example, that not all persons who are objectively fathers are equally committed to such an identity. What accounts for such differentials, for the fact that for one man identity as father supersedes all other ways in which he sees himself, while for another the father identity is relatively low on the self totem pole? The theory suggests that this will be a function of the extent to which one is defined by significant others as a father. It also suggests that the degree of congruence of definitions by significant others will be of import. Borrowing a phrase from studies of political behavior, could the presence or absence of "cross-pressures" deriving from others with whom one interacts account for this differential commitment, at least in some degree?

Perhaps of greater significance to students of the family is the question of the consequences of differential commitment to familial identities. Foote[4] has contended that differences in motivation of role performances may fruitfully be seen in these terms. Political apathy seems to be in good part a consequence of lack of commitment to a clear-cut political identity; it seems reasonable to suspect that apathetic familial behavior has a similar source. It is also quite possible that, for example, the prediction of divorce would be on sounder ground when questions dealing with

[4] Nelson N. Foote, "Identification as the Basis for a Theory of Motivation," *American Sociological Review,* 16 (February, 1951), pp. 14-21.

commitment to family identities are included in batteries of predictive items.

Closely related to these questions is another set. Are there extra-familial identities which are in varying degree compatible with familial identities? What are the effects of identities deriving from diverse spheres of activity on one another, and on behavior in these diverse spheres? Someone has suggested that the deviant behavior of a man in a work situation which appears to be idiosyncratic when viewed in this limited context, may rather be a consequence of his position and role within his family. That is, for example, the rate-buster on the job may not be acting "selfishly," but may simply be acting in accord with his conception of self as family breadwinner. It is certain that one's extra-familial identities operate within the family situation. Which identities so operate, their specific mode of articulation with family identities, and their consequences for family relationships are questions of obvious importance.

Another set of questions can be phrased around the relationship of crises to identity. Crises will always threaten identifications, for the latter depend on stable activities of others with reference to oneself; and crises are likely to be important in the process by which identities change. It may be that adaptation in crisis situations is a function of the ease with which identities alter; adaptation to the death of a spouse, for example, might profitably be approached in these terms. Yet that ease with which identities are altered is not always functional is suggested by Hill's[5] research on war separation and return; in such multi-phased crises it may be that, at least for some, easy alteration of identity at one point creates problems at still another point. Such questions, too, are worth the research energies of students of the family.

A different kind of question suggested by the theory may be prefaced by relating an overheard conversation. A young lady was speaking of her relationships with her boy friend. The two were, apparently, sufficiently involved to talk about marriage and their future. But, it seems, they argued when they engaged in such talk. The basis for the argument was this: she labelled such talks "plans," he called them "dreams," and each bridled at the other's conception of their conversations. Nonsense? Arguing over mere words? Not when one has in mind the significance of defining behavior and the consequences of classification. Plan implies a greater stake in a projected course of action than does dream. Dreams suggest freedom of action, plans a commitment. Suggested here is the potential fertility of studying the courtship process, marital role relationships, parent-child relationships, and so on, in terms of role-linked symbolic behavior: for example, the investigation of possible sex-linked differences in defining family situations, and the consequences of such differential definitions as may exist.

[5]Reuben Hill, *Families Under Stress,* New York: Harpers, 1949.

Finally, the theory suggests that studies focusing on the role-taking process may be rewarding. Role-taking is a variable; anticipation of the responses of others is not always correct. Foote[6] and his associates have conducted an impressive series of studies designed to uncover means by which role-taking ability can be improved, on the assumption that role-taking ability, or empathy in their language, is one aspect of interpersonal competence. While this may well be justified, some research[7] indicates that if one expects that interpersonal adjustment will always result from accurate role-taking, he is likely to be disappointed. But this still leaves open questions of the specific consequences, under varying conditions, of role-taking accuracy. Are the consequences the same, for example, when husband and wife share the same value framework and when they do not? Might it not be that accurate role-taking differs in its consequences as role relationships change, when a couple moves through the sequential stages of courtship, early marital experience, and later family experience? These, too, are questions worth raising and answering.

One final remark: symbolic interaction is not a general theory of human behavior. That is, it does not incorporate all the variables presumably important in accounting for human behavior, but rather selects from these a few for concentrated attention. Thus it would not do to deny the contributions of alternative theoretical views from which human behavior can be approached. It is contended, however, that alternative views can be enriched by taking into account the set of ideas which have been developed.

[6]Nelson N. Foote, Editor, *Developing Interpersonal Competence: A Manual of Procedures for Family Life Educators,* unpublished manuscript.

[7]See, for example, Sheldon Stryker, "Role-Taking Accuracy and Adjustment," *Sociometry,* 20 (December, 1957). pp. 286-296.

36. The Retrospective Act and Education

Ellsworth Faris

I

The teacher in the school is concerned with what the children do. Their work and play, their relations with each other, and the performance of their school tasks are all held to be of importance. Some of the acts of the children involve violent and strenuous exertion, other actions are made with a more moderate use of energy as they move around or handle things, while still other acts consist of writing or talking or thinking. We must include thinking in the class of actions, for what people think is very important and it is clear that when people think they are doing something. Some of the actions of children are, therefore, visible and audible, some are visible but silent, others are audible but not visible, while the acts we call thinking and reflection are neither visible nor audible. Yet all are actions and are the concern of educators.

Acts may, of course, be classified in an indefinite number of ways and any classification may be useful if it serves to clarify human conduct. With respect to the ease of performance, we may suggest briefly another classification in addition to the one above.

1. Immediate acts. To see a pin and pick it up does not usually call for planning or thought. The attitude represented by an interest in pins is aroused by the sight of one and with no check or difficulty the little object is retrieved. Oft-repeated habitual actions tend to fall into this class. Such an act may be said to have a beginning and an end, but no middle, or mediating, phase. It is an immediate act.

2. The delayed act. As defined here, this class of actions may be said to have a beginning, a middle, and an end. It has a middle because there is delay in reaching the end, a delay that requires some adjustment, foresight, or reasoning. The delayed act, as here defined, presents a problem or difficulty and the delay is occasioned by the necessity of resolving the problem or overcoming the difficulty so that the act can proceed and the end be reached or achieved. For when there is obscurity or uncertainty or difficulty the matter must be thought out. Life is full

From *Journal of Educational Sociology,* XIV (October, 1940), pp. 79-91, by permission of Kraus Reprint Corporation.

of these and every one can recall instances. If a traveler finds himself off the road and realizes that he has lost his way, it is necessary to consult maps, recall directions, or seek advice. His conduct cannot immediately go on for he does not know how to go on. This act is also called the reasoned act or the rational act. There are many of these in school and the office of the teacher includes the presenting of problems that the pupils can reason out, care being had that the tasks are within the power of the developing child.

3. A third category is the frustrated act. This is the act that has failed or has been so long delayed that its lateness is equivalent to failure — as a man who arrives at the station but too late for the train. Acts which begin with a purpose in mind or an end in view are finished when the purpose is realized or the end achieved. The frustrated act does not reach the goal. We may say that the frustrated act has a beginning and a middle but no end. This class of actions is very important since in the wake of frustration follow many disorganizing possibilities. The competent teacher will be on the alert to offer wise and prudent help when needed in order that the sense of failure may be avoided and, when this outcome cannot be prevented, to redirect the energies into compensating and ameliorative activities. Unless this is done, results of the most serious nature may be the outcome.

One of these unfavorable results is daydreaming. Of course, a certain amount of anticipatory fantasy is universal and pleasant and may lead to fortunate outcomes and to high and worthy ambitions. But daydreaming may become a habit and the child may dwell on the pleasant emotion of imagined success so persistently that the result is an ineffective personality. Frustration can be shown to be antecedent to this sort of avowed imagining.

Not all frustrations result in daydreaming. Often the child turns to something else, substituting what can be obtained for that which is beyond his reach. When this substituted end is more highly esteemed, it is sometimes called sublimation, but often the substitution is of a lower level. Like Omar, we take the cash and let the credit go. It is indeed necessary to accept the inevitable but in the process a child needs guidance. Substitution as the result of frustration and failure calls for vigilance on the part of teachers.

Aggression may be the result of frustration if the frustration is due to the opposition or interference of another person. And this aggression can be turned against the teacher as an object, as every one knows. And, as every one also knows, this aggressive feeling may not be obvious. It does have its serious aspects, however, and should receive attention, and preventive methods are called for.

There are many other possible outcomes of frustration but one more may be mentioned here. Sometimes there is a confusion of wish and fulfillment with the result that a delusion appears. The wish is father to the thought and what the deluded soul wanted to be and could not, he imagines he is, in spite of the way others treat him. In the institutions for mental disorders can be seen the extreme cases, pathetic patients who imagine that they are presidents or kings or great heroes, because they have failed so miserably in life and have not been able to face the world in which men live. Another and even more serious delusion is called the delusion of persecution which results from a tendency to find excuses for one's own failure in the imagined opposition or hostility of some one else. Extreme cases of dementia in the asylums may be seen, some of them cowed in terror over the plots of imaginary enemies while other cases involve hostility and aggressive rage against those who never did anything against the patient but who are thought, in the delusion, to have been the cause of all the difficulties and lack of success. For every one who is confined to an institution there are perhaps hundreds who have such delusions in a form so mild that serious disorganization does not result. The effect is very unfavorable to the personality, however, and they could be nipped in the bud if teachers and parents were possessed of adequate skill and insight. In the mental hygiene of children this matter is of obvious importance.

II

The discussion thus far is introductory to the topic of this article, which is the retrospective act. Other actions have ends or goals to be attained; the retrospective act has for its end the consideration of a former act. We may assume that there is a tendency for every action that is interesting or emotional to return to consciousness in retrospect, to be lived over again in enjoyment, or to be better understood if it is puzzling or annoying or disturbing. It is not the mere frustration of an act which produces any of the results which have been enumerated above. It is only if there is subsequent recall, reflection, and definition of the disturbing event that any final result is to be expected in the developing personality.

While this paper was in preparation the writer and another trained observer recorded careful observations over a period of three weeks of the behavior of a healthy normal infant of eight months. B. could sit alone and could pull himself up into a standing position. His toys would often roll out of the bars of his pen beyond his reach, especially a celluloid ball which was his favorite plaything. Attempts to stand up would often be frustrated when his legs were tangled up the wrong way. Active interference with his actions frequently occurred when he got hold of objects outside, particularly the grass and weeds when his pen was set up on the lawn. Numerous frustrations took place in connection with his feeding and experimental annoyances were introduced in the interest of science. It is to be recorded that the frustrations produced a brief protest, followed promptly by a period of equilibrium and the initiation of another act. B. gave every evidence of a complete lack of hostility, aggression, or resentment. It is the assumption of this paper that the explanation is to be found in the fact that infants of this age have not acquired a conception of self and that retrospection and recall could not take place.

Whether this interpretation be accepted or not, it is certain that when personality is achieved there is the retrospective tendency. When we are in the presence of our fellows and companions the retrospection takes place in the form of "talking it over" as long as it continues to be interesting or until a solution is arrived at, if the matter has been disturbing. After an exciting ball game or prize fight or drama, friends can be heard discussing the interesting phases and reliving, if only very briefly, what has been enjoyed. It there has been a serious disturbance to the life of the group then there are councils, conferences, and discussions in the effort to make clear what was not clear.

It would doubtless be desirable from the standpoint of mental hygiene if all our retrospective acts took the form of conversation and discussion with our friends and companions. But whether this be true or not, many and perhaps the greater number of these actions are performed alone and in silent thought. In the absence of others to listen, we go over the matter in our own minds. Because those at hand might not understand or might be unsympathetic, we recall the disturbing event without letting any one know what we are doing. Having no one to talk to, we talk to ourselves, and having no one to answer, we answer ourselves, and then find a response to that response and so go on and on, the act recurring over and over if no good way out is found.

It is to George Mead that we are indebted for an understanding of the manner and importance of this solitary activity. In recalling a past unpleasantness, for example, we begin by thinking of what was said to us, recalling the words of the other and our own reply, then the response of the other to what we said, and so on to the end. But sometimes there is no end. There may be left a feeling of injury which should have its proper satisfaction but no way is in sight to even the matter up. And so the whole process is gone over again and yet again. This we call brooding, and to brood over one's self and the wrongs that have been suffered is to prepare the way for disorganization, sometimes of the most extreme character. To brood over one's self and one's wrongs is sometimes to ripen for the committing of murder or suicide or less tragic deeds.

The "mechanism" of the retrospect lies importantly in the fact that we take the role of the other and it is by taking the role of the other and only by this method that a conception of the self is formed and the attitudes of a personality and character are organized.

For the self, as experienced, is defined by the actions and responses of others, although the actions and reactions, the responses and gestures of the others are not sufficient in and of themselves to produce the result.

In order that the actions and responses of others shall affect the personality it is necessary for the self to assume them on his part. The function of the retrospective act lies just here. It is in the rehearsal of the past event that one takes the attitude of another, because he is repeating what the other has said. This is seemingly the reason the infant in the prelinguistic stage does not feel resentment or hold a grudge. Because there is no language, the past cannot be recalled in symbolic ways. When, however, one can talk to one's self and answer his own talk, he necessarily takes the role of the other for no one can talk without being talked to beforehand. The mother tongue is acquired from the mother and all language is a social product. It is only after some one has spoken to me that I can speak to myself. And when I have learned to speak to myself, I have a self and not till then. A self is best defined as a subject which is its own object. One takes an attitude toward one's self. The "me" appears in experience. The very formation of the self is dependent on the retrospective act.

For it is an act. To recall what some one did to you, to rehearse what was said, to decide what it meant and how it is to be regarded, all this, though it may take place when an observer could not detect the twitching of a muscle nor any one hear the slightest sound, is to be regarded as action just as literally as knocking a home run or spinning a top.

It is in the retrospective act, then, that objects are defined, attitudes formed, personality determined, and character organized. And since many if not most of the retrospective actions of children are performed in silence and relative immobility, the act and its outcome are often inaccessible to the teacher and the parent. But since the importance of this form of activity is so great, it would seem that those who have to do with children should consider seriously its importance.

There is an apparent paradox that appears in the cases of delusion and negativism. Although the self is defined by the actions of others and the self is normally a "looking glass self" as Cooley has called it, yet from the insane asylums clear down to the schoolroom there are those who have a conception of themselves at variance with the way in which they are regarded or ever have been regarded. It is suggested here that the explanation may be found in isolation and solitude, when, for any reason, there is a lack of adequate sympathetic social contacts. We all know that it is possible to be very lonely in the midst of many people, if they do not know us or do not like us. Many a child in a large school is very completely isolated. There is no one whom he is "close to." Such an isolated personality will be less likely to discuss his troubles with others than if he had many friends and intimate companions. But he must discuss his troubles and so he discusses them with himself.

Suppose a child has been affronted or insulted and nothing more has been done about it. The solitary one will not talk it over with his friends, thus getting comfort and consolation and, often, a modification of his notion of what has happened. On the contrary, the isolated child will recall the insult and, in all likelihood, rehearse what he might have said and done. This may leave the hurt unhealed and so the matter recurs once more and he again recalls the insult. And every time he recalls the insult he is taking the role of the insulter and is being hurt afresh. And so it may come to pass that, instead of being insulted once, he has, in the role of the other, insulted himself twenty times, and to be insulted twenty times is far more painful than to be hurt once.

If he has been belittled and an attack made on his self-respect he will normally seek, in the retrospective act, some defense and justification of what he has done or of what he is. If this self-defense and self-justification is rehearsed again and again, the original social definition gives place to the definition he has made of and for himself in the solitude of his too frequent retrospection.

A graduate student who found it difficult to do the work in the keen competition at the university came up for his examinations and failed to pass them. He was profoundly shocked and disappointed and his isolation was marked. He was able to convince himself that the faculty had not been able to understand his excellent presentation of his material and that they were unfair to him for various reasons. He came to consider himself a distinctly superior person intellectually, and, though he had difficulty in holding any one of the several positions which he managed to secure, the result was always due to the incompetence of the administration who did not know how to appreciate an exceptionally gifted man. This pathetic effort to salvage one's self-respect and high opinion of one's self resulted, as often, in a paranoid type of personality. His definition of himself was different from the social definition, the difference being the result of his repeated retrospections in which he came to his own defense against his detractors again and again till he became convinced that he was right and all the world was wrong.

Attitudes are sustained and strengthened by successful repetitions, as a boy keeps alive and growing his interest in baseball or swimming. But in situations that are new, attitudes may be altered or reversed. Unexpected or surprising or puzzling events make objects uncertain that were formerly well understood, and force a reexamination. This revision and redefinition is the function of the retrospective act. Retrospection is the workshop where the new attitudes are fabricated and the old ones made over. One's whole conception of one's self may be completely revised after such an occasion. A graduate student was invited by a college president to accept an appointment in a college. He had in mind the salary he would ask for, in case the position should be acceptable. The president did not ask him to name a figure but proceeded to offer twice the amount that the student had decided upon. Difficulties arose in the arrangements and the appointment did not go through, but the student revised his estimate of his worth and never thought of himself again as deserving anything less than the surprising stipend which had been offered to him. We get our conception of ourselves from the way others treat us and talk to us.

It would not, perhaps, be necessary to write insistently about the importance of the retrospective act but for the confusion that has been produced by the school of behaviorist psychologists. Although there have been modifications of the extreme statements with which their very vigorous writings formerly abounded, yet even to this day the emphasis on behavior tends to obscure the importance of that which cannot be observed or photographed or recorded. Retrospection of the solitary kind can neither be seen, heard, nor measured. Some writers would consider that, since this is so, we must confine attention to the accessible behavior. But behavior is only part of life. In addition to behavior there is conduct, and conduct is not the same as behavior. We may speak of the behavior of a storm or the behavior of a wild rhinoceros. Men also exhibit mere behavior, as when a man steps on your foot or slips on the ice. But conduct involves behavior with the addition of a judgment on the movements, and this goes deeper than cameras can record.

The importance of the secret springs of action has always been recognized, but the older writers made a sharp distinction between thought and action. Thought and reasoning were in the soul or in the mind, while action was assumed to be a function of the larger muscles. It is the position of this paper that thought is quite literally a part of action and that retrospection is, in every way, deserving of this classification. It is true that thinking is often the preparation for action but so is the buying of a railway ticket. It is true that thought precedes action and may be said, in some sense, to be the cause of action, but it is also true that action precedes thought and that action may be the cause of thought. It is far better to consider our thinking as one form of action, sometimes indulged in for its own sake, just as we may at times look at a picture or listen to a symphony with no utilitarian purpose. But whether we think for a purpose or merely indulge in a pleasant reverie, the thinking is what we are doing. The thinking is a form of action. And the thinking we do in retrospection is a very important form of action.

Teachers are able to control with approximate success the behavior of children. Where they may go and when, what they say and how they may say it (at least in the classroom) are not too difficult for a skillful teacher to manage. But the retrospective acts are performed in silence and with a closed mouth. Their control must be indirect but such control is very important.

In autobiographies and life histories are to be found in abundance instances of the undesirable and sometimes disastrous results of the silent and unaided misinterpretation which the children make of the actions of their teachers. One adult reported an incident that occurred when he was in the sixth grade. The bell for the ending of the recess period had rung and most of the children had gone in. He, an overgrown and sensitive lad, ran noisily down the hall only to be stopped by a teacher and ordered sternly to go back outside and then to enter in a proper manner. What the teacher had in mind was the desirability of good habits and the proper form of behavior. What the teacher produced, as the incident was recalled again and again, was an attitude of lasting resentment. In the schoolroom the teacher thought he was studying but what he was really doing was living over the event, growing more and more resentful. The teacher was continually disliked during the two years he remained in the community. When the incident was reported, still further mature retrospection had again altered the attitude and all resentment had long since disappeared. But all will agree that the teacher acted unwisely under the circumstances, either in speaking as he did or in not following it up so that the retrospection might not have such undesired consequences.

Analogous instances are by no means rare and the importance of the effort of the teacher in influencing the behavior after the child recalls it in retrospect should not be minimized. One of the sources of confusion and error is the failure to distinguish accurately between habit as a form of behavior which may be controlled and attitude as a tendency toward a generalized mode of conduct. The habit can often be controlled directly if the child is under observation, but the attitude is formed in the retrospective act and may be the very opposite of what it is desired to inculcate.

It seems quite clear that the most favorable condition for the direct transfer of an attitude from one person to another is what sociologists call the primary group relation, by which is meant a situation in which there is face-to-face association and cooperation and in which the "we feeling" is present. In such a situation the chances of a negative attitude developing from retrospection are at a minimum. This type of relation may be seen in any good kindergarten but is often absent in the later years of the school. The traditional practices involve a whole complex of methods of control which include the assertion of authority, the promulgation of formal orders and rigid rules which in their turn imply commands. And there can be no effective commands without explicit or implied threats, and threats necessitate punishment and penalties. That these do operate to secure order and external conformity cannot be denied but that the results are often disappointing is universally admitted. What the child will think and feel about it, when he brings to mind in retrospection the whole incident, is as important as the subsequent observable behavior — some of us think it is much more important.

To place the entire burden of caring for the mental health of children on the school is at once unjust and ineffective. A child has lived several years before the school has seen him. Some of the basic foundation stones of his personality have been already laid down. Moreover the hours spent in the school are hardly one eighth of the total hours in a year, so that outside influences have ample time to undo the best of school influences.

Nevertheless, the influence of the school is very great and the opportunity of the teacher is everywhere appreciated. Children may have warped and twisted souls at times in spite of all that the school can do. And yet experience has abundantly shown the possibilities of wise and skillful handling of these problems. Notwithstanding the fact that the school only has a fraction of the day, the children are thinking of school activities much of the time they are at home and in their going and coming. The keen sense of competition which is often so unwisely encouraged by well-meaning teachers has been the cause of much suffering on the part of children and not a little disorganization. A sense of failure on the part of a child is not only a bitter experience for him, it is also a reproach to our knowledge of life and human nature. It is the growing conviction of many specialists that every child, with the exception of the feeble-minded, has some gift or talent which marks him off as slightly superior to others in that one way. Slavish dependence on the ability to manipulate figures and to play with words, which ability is measured by the so-called intelligence tests, will in time, let us hope, be replaced by an appreciation of the unique gifts of each of our children.

The sense of failure eliminated, there remains the problem of isolation. The origin of this may be and usually is quite outside the school but it can receive needed attention by teachers. The greater number of the children will not be in need of any special attention in this regard but for those who do need it there should come wise and understanding help. The child who suffers from a feeling of isolation may be hard to reach, but he will usually respond with eagerness to the well-considered approach. If the isolation is overcome, the retrospective act is not prevented, for retrospection is universal and normal. But when wrongs or hurts or failures or frustrations are talked over instead of brooded over, a great gain is had.

And it hardly need be insisted that a wise teacher will not be guilty of a rude command or an ironical retort or a sarcastic affront to any child, whether a lonely sufferer from isolation or a highly socialized and friendly pupil. To do so, as already pointed out, may not produce any immediately visible results but in retrospection the teacher may be defined in terms of the bitterest hostility. More probable is the outcome in which the teacher comes to be regarded as a necessary evil, to be watched and "worked" but whose views and opinions have little or no influence. The retrospective act has, in extreme cases, resulted in a determination to run away from the school and never to return. In still rarer cases, the end of the retrospective act has been the determination to attack the teacher. In not a few cases the end is suicide. But usually the worst result is the loss of influence of the teacher at a time when such influence is in the highest degree important and when it should be at its maximum of strength.

The object of this discussion has been to call attention to the unseen and unheard actions of children which follow every interesting and emotional experience and which are determinative of attitudes and of the organization of personality. Those who deal with children may well pay heed to the possible effects of disciplinary treatment which, though they occur in silence and unobserved, represent the actions in which the structure of the character is erected. Not that this is new, however much neglected in recent years. It is with the thought that retrospective actions are deserving of renewed emphasis that these words have been written.

37. Criminality Theories and Behavioral Images [1]

Daniel Glaser

This article attempts to appraise the scientific utility of alternative theories proposed for the explanation of that individual behavior which is most uniformly designated "crime" in our society. All such theories are derived, explicitly or implicitly, from more general psychological or social-psychological theories applicable to the larger class of behavior of which crime is considered an instance.

Theories and Imagery

The language which explains a human act evokes imagery by which certain aspects of the act are abstractly conceived and are related to other phenomena. For example, an act may be explained as the rational pursuit of a purpose, as the expression of inner drives, as a conditioned neural response, or as a mechanical resultant of external pressures. Each type of explanatory language evokes a somewhat different image of how human beings behave — as rational, as driven from within, as internally mechanical, or as atoms in fields of external forces. Each set of terms for explaining behavior and the associated imagery constitutes a psychological frame of reference. When made explicit, they are called "models" or "paradigms."

"Language is by its very nature and essence, metaphorical," Cassirer observed.[2] For example, such psychological concepts as "force," "stimulus," and "response" were imported from physics and physiology, where they were first developed to deal with phenomena other than those to which they are applied by psychologists. These concepts evoke images which give meaning to our observations by interrelating them. But since con-

Reprinted from *The American Journal of Sociology,* LXI (March, 1956), pp. 433-444, by permission of the University of Chicago Press.

[1] Acknowledgment is made of useful comments, leading to revisions of this article, which were received from Drs. J. E. Hulett, Jr., Alvin W. Gouldner, Bernard Farber, and others, all of the University of Illinois, and from Martin U. Martel, now of the University of Washington.

[2] Ernst Cassirer, *An Essay on Man* (Garden City, N. Y.: Doubleday, 1953), p. 142.

siderable compression, deletion, or extension of available observations of behavior are usually necessary to fit our observations into our frame of reference, these conceptual frameworks determine both what we look for and what we overlook.[3]

As a theory is more rigorously tested, it becomes increasingly formalized. Ultimately, it may be expressed as mathematical relations between quantitative variables which are operationally defined by objectively specified rules of observational procedure. It then evokes little in the way of concrete images. While any theory may be formalized, more or less adequately, the imagery evoked when the theory is first formulated limits what later testing seeks. As testing proceeds, the theory may be delimited on the basis of negative findings. But additions to scientific theory have always depended upon the introduction of new imagery, from the theory of evolution to time-space relativity to any hypothesis which is clearly new to a particular research situation (though probably metaphorically drawn from another situation). If we focus on explaining an empirical phenomenon, a theory may be sufficiently tested to provoke extensive revision before it is highly formalized. That is a justification for this article. If we focus on developing and applying techniques for formalizing theory, we are likely to select theories on the basis of their amenability to the techniques of formalization rather than by their relevance to the phenomenon which we initially sought to explain.[4]

Crime, like most topics in social psychology, refers to a class of behavior the separate instances of which have many and diverse subjective and objective aspects.[5] Our theoretical conceptions of criminal or other

[3] Cf. Herbert Blumer, "Science without Concepts," *American Journal of Sociology,* XXXVI (January, 1931), 515-33; Kenneth Burke, *Permanence and Change* (New York: New Republic, 1936); Susanne K. Langer, *Philosophy in a New Key* (Cambridge: Harvard University Press, 1942), esp. chap. iv.

[4] Cf. A.H. Maslow, "Problem Centering versus Means Centering in Science," *Philosophy of Science,* XIII (October, 1946), 326-31; Gordon W. Allport, "The Psychologist's Frame of Reference," *Psychological Bulletin,* XXXVII (January, 1940), 1-28; Paul H. Furfey, "The Formalization of Sociology," *American Sociological Review,* XIX (October, 1954), 525-28.

[5] The term "crime" is here confined primarily to felonies, as felonies are defined by criminal courts in their prosecution and adjudication of cases, to which we add misdemeanors, such as petty larceny and assault, which are identified by lesser forms of the same attributes which identify felonies. This usage, which we believe corresponds to the usual connotation of "crime," excludes those misdemeanors which do not become felonies when "exaggerated," such as most disorderly conduct, vagrancy, and indecent exposure. It also excludes those "white-color crimes" not commonly prosecuted as felonies. We also include as crime any act legally called "delinquency" if the only attribute which is the basis for its being considered delinquency rather than crime is the fact that the doer is below a particular age.

behavior necessarily simplify this complexity, and in our effort to comprehend such behavior we may distort it. Nevertheless, we strive for the most valid theoretical image of actual behavior, assuming thereby that this effort will ultimately produce the most fruitful basis for prediction or control of behavior.

In distinguishing the images which various criminality theories evoke, a somewhat imperfect distinction will be made between (1) "monistic" theories, which are based upon a single type of simple behavioral image; (2) "pluralistic" theories, which involve two or more distinct behavioral images; and (3) "integrative" theories, which attempt to subsume the aspects of behavior dealt with in pluralistic theories under a single relatively complex behavioral image. These theories will be appraised with respect to the interconnectedness of their explanatory imagery,[6] their comprehensiveness (the types or aspects of crime to which they apply), and their implications for the continuity and validity of empirical research.

Monistic Theories

Underlying prevailing monistic criminality theories, the following types of imagery may be distinguished: spontaneity, possession, rationality, external forces, internal mechanism, and role.

An image of behavior as spontaneous underlies that "pure" free-will criminality theory which is still voiced in lay discussions of crimes and is implicit in the judicial notion of "choosing" between right and wrong. Such an explanation is the epitome of disconnectedness, since it indicates in-

---

We believe that there is a predominantly stable and uniform content to this reference of "crime" in Western society, despite some variation in its limits under different legal jurisdictions. Indicative of the complexity of crime as a topic for social-psychological study are the facts that crimes (a) occur in diverse situations; (b) must be identified by the symbolic interpretation given the behavior by the actors in the situation (e.g., identifying the victim's property as "owned" or his compliance as "involuntary"); (c) can be experienced or imputed subjectively as symbolic processes (ideation) and feelings (reflected in such legal language as "willfully," "maliciously," etc.).

[6] The significance of interconnectedness in theory was indicated when, in a lecture at the University of Chicago in 1939, Bertrand Russell distinguished mysticism from science by saying that mysticism accepts the possibility of distance between cause and effect, while "science cannot accept action at a distance." As Hume suggested, this distinction is relative rather than absolute, since the connection is conceived rather than directly observed. In terms of that philosophy of science which eschews the language of "causality," disconnectedness refers to the failure to specify intervening variables between a dependent and an independent variable.

ability or unwillingness to relate the behavior to anything else. Actually, "pure" free-will theory is seldom maintained continuously, for, when practical problems are considered, it must be modified to reflect other types of imagery.[7]

Possession imagery, which involves an image of a prepotent force resident in the person and determining his behavior, has been evoked by biological determinism theories of criminality, from Lombroso to Sheldon. While criminal behavior is asserted to be caused by malformed biological structures, no direct connection between the specific actions involved in crime and the defective structure is indicated, at least not in terms of specific known functions of organic structures. Much use of the term "psychopath," especially when explicitly or implicitly modified by the adjective "constitutional," still conveys this image of determination by an ill-defined condition. Another such disconnected explanation is that implied in the assertions that criminality is correlated with hypoglycemia or with organic brain damage. These hypotheses have never been tested on representative samples of persons with these ailments. However, if such correlation were established, there would be pressure to focus theory and research on establishing a conceptual connection between the correlated data. As an explanation for crime, it would still be "disconnected," as we use this adjective, because of the large conceptual gaps between organic phenomena and complex behavior.[8]

[7] We are implying that the free-will position in most debate on free-will versus determinism in criminology involves simultaneous employment of several definitions of "free will." No one endeavors to educate or to persuade without assuming that an individual's behavior is influenced by the experience to which he is exposed and that when this experience brings alternative choices to an individual's attention, he has the experience of choosing between alternative courses of action. Neither of these assumptions contradicts the notion of universal determinism in nature on which all science rests, nor has either the remotest relationship to the question of the [indeterminacy] of quantum particles, to which the free-will issue is often referred (cf. C. H. Cooley, *Social Organization* [New York: Charles Scribner's Sons, 1929], pp. 20-21; and *Human Nature and the Social Order* [rev. ed.; New York: Charles Scribner's Sons, 1922], pp. 38-43 and 55, n.).

[8] When comparing delinquents and non-delinquents from high-delinquency areas, the Gluecks found the delinquents to be stronger and more athletic (mesomorphic) anatomically than the non-delinquents, as well as more aggressive and extroverted in what they call "temperament." An example of conceptual connection between such "biological" data and criminality is the following earlier statement by Sutherland (which is amenable to empirical validation): "In an area where the delinquency rate is high a boy who is sociable, gregarious, active and athletic is very likely to come in contact with the other boys in the neighborhood, learn delinquent behavior from them, and become a gangster. . . . In another situation

Freudian criminologists have ascribed criminality to instinct.[9] This conception also involves possession imagery. However, in psychoanalysis, controls by the rational mind (ego) and society (superego) are seen as repressing or redirecting the instinctive criminal force (id), latent and manifest criminality being ascribed to the failure of the controls. Like other possession images, this conception fails to explain any aspect of criminality in which learning can be observed (such as complex criminal techniques, pride in conception of self as criminal, and pious loyalty to a criminal group). In the purely Freudian conception, we are possessed of criminal impulses, and we learn or fail to learn to control them; there is no learning of distinctively new criminality.

The frustration-equals-aggression formula, an amalgamation of behavioristic and psychoanalytic theory, provides another variation of possession imagery. A sum of vaguely defined emotional energy is seen as fixed in an individual. If the steady and relatively moderate expression of this energy is blocked, one of two alternative results is predicted: either there is an immediate outburst of unusually violent and reckless behavior, or there is a slow accumulation of "blocked energy" which must ultimately be expressed. The immediate outburst may explain some "crimes of passion" which seem unplanned, but it is inapplicable where blockage does not lead to immediate aggression. The "blockage-leads-to-ultimate-expression-in-some-other-manner" formulation provides a disconnected explanation for any emotional behavior; early frustration, perhaps in infancy or even prenatal, can always be demonstrated or assumed and can then be cited as the cause of later behavior without a clearly connecting causal mechanism.

Observations of aggression following frustration are explained in less disconnected imagery by certain older theories of emotional behavior which also account more adequately for observations contradicting the frustration-equals-aggression formula. We may develop the habit of reacting to frustration by violence, growing more set in the habit with each occasion of

---

the sociable, athletic, aggressive boy may become a member of a scout troop and not become involved in delinquent behavior" (E. H. Sutherland, *Principles of Criminology* [4th ed.; Chicago: J. B. Lippincott Co., 1947], p. 8; cf. also S. and E. Glueck, *Unravelling Juvenile Delinquency* [New York: Commonwealth Fund, 1950]).

[9] E. g., "The ideal criminal has not structured his personality in accordance with any value system. . . . Instinctual forces drive him on without any opposition from a restraining conscience" (K. R. Eissler, "General Problems of Delinquency," in K. R. Eissler, [ed.], *Searchlights on Delinquency* [New York: International Universities Press, 1949], p. 7). Similar quotations from several other psychoanalytic writers are presented in Albert K. Cohen, *Delinquent Boys* (Glencoe, Ill.: Free Press, 1955), pp. 181-82.

it. The current reaction against extreme permissiveness in child-rearing, which had been advocated as preventing children from accumulating aggression, is based on the newer tenet that tolerance of their aggression develops aggressive children. The James-Lange theory of emotions, that "we are afraid because we run," can be restated as: When habitual behavior is frustrated, we mobilize attention and energy for initiating a new course of behavior. Emotions are sense-experiences of bodily changes concomitant with such mobilization. We experience anger when we react by mobilizing to strike, and fear when we mobilize to flee. Mobilization may be inhibited before completion; we may only raise our voice rather than strike. Different experience leads to different habits of mobilization for given types of frustrating situation: one person mobilizes to fight, another flees, another deliberates. Different emotional experience accompanies each of these behavioral patterns.

The "classical" theory of criminality, identified with utilitarian philosophy and expressed in most criminal law, implies free will but immediately modifies it with the notion that man's behavior is determined by the nearness and efficacy of the choosable means for obtaining happiness. (Crime is to be prevented by making it produce unhappiness.) This is really a pluralistic theory, since the image of man shifts from a purely spontaneous actor to a rational calculator and, finally, to an atom moved by its external field of pleasant and painful forces.

Economic determinism in criminology is simply classical theory which assumes that economic ends are the primary means to the ultimate end of happiness. Crime is viewed as an alternative means to such ends when other means fail. The behavioral image of rational man in classical theory provides an insufficiently comprehensive explanation of irrational habits, predilections, and prejudices in specific cases of criminality; it also does not explain the absence of criminality in people whose economic need is equal to, or greater than, that of criminals. The imagery of external forces does not connect economic, geographic, and other abstract forces to specific criminal techniques and loyalties. Extreme cultural determinism theories may also arouse an imagery of external forces. They have been criticized for implying greater homogeneity of criminal subcultures than can be established empirically.

An image of internal mechanism (personality) developing through conditioning underlies many psychological explanations of crime which dispense with the concept of instinct. Its adequacy depends in part on the answer to the question of whether conditioning explains the acquisition of new responses rather than the association of new stimuli with old responses. Indicative of the issue of disconnectedness is the current debate on reductionism in the behavioral sciences: whether "voluntary" human behavior, in which images and symbolic evaluations of completed acts continuously enter into the initiation of new acts, can usefully be reduced to the conditioned-reflex model which physiologists verify from the study of isolated muscles or glands.[10] The discovery of the extreme diversity of personality in criminals and of the frequency of allegedly criminal categories of personality among non-criminals supports the view that ascribing criminality to the habitual modes of behavior which psychologists usually connote by the term "personality" is based on an invalid image of criminal behavior.[11]

The image of behavior as role-playing, borrowed from the theater, presents people as directing their actions on the basis of their conceptions of how others see them. The choice of another, from whose perspective we view our own behavior, is the process of identification. It may be with the immediate others or with distant and perhaps abstractly generalized others of our reference groups. (The "amateur" criminal may identify himself with the highly professional "master"-criminal whom he has never met.) Rationalization is seen as a necessary concomitant of voluntary behavior, particularly when role conflicts exist. Acceptance by the group with which one identifies one's self and conceptions of persecution by other groups are among the most common and least intellectual bases for rationalization by criminals. Role imagery provides the most comprehensive

[10] Still highly relevant are the questions raised in John Dewey, "The Reflex-Arc Concept in Psychology," *Psychological Review*, III (July, 1896), 357-70. New response learning seems accounted for by the concept of operants as response components which are "emitted rather than elicited" and which are continuously shaped into even the most complex behavior through reinforcement of those components yielding favorable consequences and extinction of the remainder (cf. B. F. Skinner, *Science and Human Behavior* [New York: Macmillan Co., 1953]). While mechanistic data on animal learning may support this theory, such data are related only by gross analogy to human learning of complex "voluntary" behavior like crime, since we have negligible evidence of animal ability to learn complex behavior through symbolic communication (hence accumulation of learning from one generation to the next) or of animals reinforcing their acts by verbal rationalization. Apart from the need to learn those gross principles applicable to both human and animal learning, further "control" of such human learning as that involved in crime requires more discriminating analysis and more reliable data on human verbal processes, feelings, and relationships.

[11] Where the measure of personality is a measure of the extent of criminal behavior (psychopathy scales), the empirical correlation discovered is that between criminality and itself. This has no explanatory value and does not compare with the fruitful logical reduction of complex theories to quasi-tautological relations between distinct conceptual frameworks (cf. Karl F. Schuessler, review of Hathaway and Monachesi, "Analyzing and Predicting Juvenile Delinquency with the MMPI," *American Journal of Sociology*, LX [November, 1954], 321-22; Donald R. Cressey and Karl F. Schuessler, "Personality Characteristics of Criminals," *American Journal of Sociology*, LV [March, 1950], 476-84).

and interconnected theoretical framework for explaining the phenomena of criminality.[12] We shall take up the problem of articulating the specific relationship of role theory with criminality in discussing "integrative" criminality theories.

Pluralistic and Integrative Theories

Serendipity — the influence of "unanticipated, anomalous and strategic"[13] observations — in causing us to revise theory, has usually resulted in patchwork eclecticism rather than the systematic revision of criminality theory. Where one behavioral image does not fit, we skip to another. Most textbooks in criminology present a cluster of disparate monistic theories as "the theory of multiple causation." These should be regarded as temporary expedients in the course of revising theory. Instead, since the nineteenth-century writings of Enrico Ferri, they have been repeatedly extolled as the ultimate most satisfactory formulations.

Pluralistic theories evoke a mixed metaphorical image — the criminal is possessed, pushed, rationally chooses, or interpretively interacts. The major practical objection is that no rules are provided for interrelating component theories and for shifting from one to another. Starting an analysis from the standpoint of one theory, one is likely to persevere in that theory in analyzing behavior and thus may be blinded to observations which might be revealed, were one to start with another theory. For example, even sociologists repeatedly find themselves neglecting social relationships through the natural tendency to look only at individual traits when trying to explain an individual's criminality. Both the defects and the merits of the component theories thereby remain in the multiple-causation mixtures.

There are precedents in the physical sciences for the simultaneous acceptance of alternative theoretical images of phenomena, such as the wave and the corpuscular conceptions of light, each being employed to explain different types of observation. This is considered a temporary and unsatisfactory state of affairs pending the appearance of a more general integrative theory which will account for all the observations. The old theories often become special cases of the more general theory (e.g., as Newtonian physics is a special case of Einsteinian physics).

[12] Cf. Nelson N. Foote, "Identification as the Basis for a Theory of Motivation," *American Sociological Review,* XVI (February, 1951), 14-22; C. Wright Mills, "Situated Actions and Vocabularies of Motive," *American Sociological Review,* V (December, 1940), 904-13; Tamotsu Shibutani, "Reference Groups as Perspectives," *American Journal of Sociology,* LX (May, 1955), 562-69.

[13] Robert K. Merton, *Social Theory and Social Structure* (Glencoe, Ill.: Free Press, 1949), p. 98.

The outstanding attempt to formulate an integrative theory of criminality is the "differential association" theory, proposed by the late Edwin H. Sutherland, who summarized his theory in the statement: "A person becomes delinquent because of an excess of definitions favorable to violation of law."[14] Personality, economic conditions, and other elements of monistic criminality theories are related to crime by this theory only to the extent that they lead to the procurement of an excess of definitions favorable to violation of law. Unlike the pluralistic approaches, such theory interrelates the separate monistic factors in each case. Differential association theory channels research by knitting diverse data together, whereas multiple-factor conceptions lead to the collection of disparate observations.

Sutherland's formal statement of this theory actually conveys a rather mechanistic image of criminality, which differs from the multiple-factor conception in one major respect. While the multiple-factor imagery presents the criminal as an atom in a multidimensional field, the differential association conception involves imagery of the criminal on a unidimensional continuum. Criminality is at one extreme of this continuum and non-criminality at the other, with the individual's associations pushing him toward one extreme or the other. This imagery is not altered essentially when Sutherland observes that criminal and non-criminal associations may vary in "frequency, duration, priority and intensity." The phrase "excess of definitions" itself lacks clear denotation in human experience.

Probably, the failure of Sutherland's language to evoke a clearly recognizable behavioral image is responsible for the limited acceptance of his theory. The criticisms have been of two principal types. First, there have been assertions that the differential learning of crime is more complex than the critics assume Sutherland's conception of differential association to be. Some critics have interpreted "association" in Sutherland's writings as synonymous with "contact."[15] Sutherland seems to have been dismayed by an assumption that "association" is distinct from "identifica-

[14] E. H. Sutherland, *Principles of Criminology,* prepared by Donald R. Cressey (5th ed.; Chicago: J. B. Lippincott Co., 1955), p. 78 (p. 6 in 4th ed.).

[15] E. g.: "While this theory of crime explains the delinquent behavior of many juveniles, it does not adequately explain why some individuals who have extensive contacts with criminal norms and with persons who engage in criminal behavior do not themselves commit delinquencies" (Martin H. Neumeyer, *Juvenile Delinquency in Modern Society* [New York: D. Van Nostrand Co., 1949], p. 226); "[Sutherland's theory]. . . does not adequately explain why two or more children in the same home often respond differently to the situation of delinquent and criminal members of the family" (Milton L. Barron, *The Juvenile in Delinquent Society* [New York: A. A. Knopf, 1954], p. 147). We might also note the recurrent question by students: Why doesn't the prison guard become a criminal, since his association is primarily with criminals?

tion."[16] Donald R. Cressey has suggested modification of differential association theory by:

> the substitution of a different conception of the process by which criminality is learned for the conception of a differential in the quantity and quality of contacts with the two varieties of behavior problems. For example . . . a search for the differences in the typical vocabularies used by criminals and non-criminals in specific situations might reveal that it is the presence or absence of a specific, learned verbal label in a specific situation which determines the criminality or non-criminality of a particular person.[17]

These diverse comments suggest the need for a restatement of Sutherland's theory so as to make its behavioral referent less ambiguous.

A second criticism of Sutherland's theory consists of arguments for certain pluralistic criminality theories on the grounds that Sutherland's theory accounts for only one of several distinct types of criminality. The most common of these views evokes a dualistic image of criminality as manifesting either differential association or personality, or both.[18] It frequently ignores Sutherland's reference to personality as one of several factors determining patterns of differential association and therefore related to crime indirectly (cf. our n. 7). Usually it also involves the assumption that the major aspects of personality determining crime are relatively fixed from childhood on. A conception of personality reconcilable with Sutherland's theory would be as the sum total of a person's regular role patterns in a given period. This includes, as personality, aspects of roles which develop only in adulthood, such as class and occupational roles. Criminality itself would then be considered a component of personality,

[16] Cf. "The opposition to 'differential association' as an explanation seems to be based on a misconception of a meaning of that process, as indicated by the sentence, 'Identification with a group of boys who stole was as important as contact with the differential association' " (Sutherland, *op. cit.*, n. 25, pp. 157-58; p. 138 in 4th ed.). In his posthumous revision of Sutherland, Cressey added to the above: "Differential identification is a clearly implied and congruous aspect of the differential association theory." The reformulation of "differential identification" set forth below supports everything in this added sentence except the word "clearly." Sutherland's theory has been very diversely interpreted.

[17] Donald R. Cressey, "Application and Verification of the Differential Association Theory," *Journal of Criminal Law, Criminology, and Police Science,* XLIII (May-June, 1952), 43-52.

[18] Cf. Paul W. Tappan, *Juvenile Delinquency* (New York: McGraw-Hill Book Co., Inc., 1949), pp. 82 ff.; S. Kirson Weinberg, "Theories of Criminality and Problems of Prediction," *Journal of Criminal Law, Criminology, and Police Science,* XLV (November-December, 1954), 412-24.

and the theory for explaining criminality presumably would be analogous with the theory for explaining other components of personality; it would go beyond descriptive designation of criminality as a component of the referent for the term "personality."

Some critics of Sutherland augment the dualism of personality and association by also calling for recognition of accidental and transitory situational causes of crime.[19] Such criticism, prompted by the premises of pluralistic theory, implies that Sutherland's theory either should be radically revised or should be applied to a much more limited range of criminality than he and his students believed. But neither of these changes is necessary if we reconceptualize Sutherland's theory in terms which we call "differential identification."

Differential Identification As An Integrative Criminality Theory

We describe identification somewhat unconventionally as "the choice of another, from whose perspective we view our own behavior." What we have called "differential identification" reconceptualizes Sutherland's theory in role-taking imagery, drawing heavily on Mead as well as on later refinements of role theory.[20] Most persons in our society are believed to identify themselves with both criminal and non-criminal persons in the course of their lives. Criminal identification may occur, for example, during direct experience in delinquent membership groups, through positive reference to criminal roles portrayed in mass media, or as a negative reaction to forces opposed to crime. The family probably is the principal non-criminal reference group, even for criminals. It is supplemented by many other groups of anti-criminal "generalized others."

The theory of differential identification, in essence, is that *a person pursues criminal behavior to the extent that he identifies himself with real or imaginary persons from whose perspective his criminal behavior seems acceptable.* Such a theory focuses attention on the interaction in which choice of models occurs, including the individual's interaction with himself in rationalizing his conduct. This focus makes differential identification theory

[19] Cf. "The theory of differential association does not explain the incidental, the highly emotional, or the accidental crimes, but applies only to the confirmed types of criminality in which the offender accepts anti-social behavior as a suitable way of life" (Mabel A. Elliott, *Crime in Modern Society,* [New York: Harper & Bros. 1952], p. 402).

[20] Cf. D. Glaser, "A Reconsideration of Some Parole Prediction Factors," *American Sociological Review,* XIX (June, 1954), 335-41; G.H. Mead, *Mind, Self, and Society* (Chicago: University of Chicago Press, 1934), Foote, *op. cit.*; Mills, *op. cit.*; Shibutani, *op. cit.*

integrative, in that it provides a criterion of the relevance, for each individual case of criminality, of economic conditions, prior frustrations, learned moral creeds, group participation, or other features of an individual's life. These features are relevant to the extent that they can be shown to affect the choice of the other from whose perspective the individual views his own behavior. The explanation of criminal behavior on the basis of its imperfect correlation with any single variable of life-situations, if presented without specifying the intervening identification, evokes only a disconnected image of the relationship between the life-situation and the criminal behavior.

Sutherland supported the differential association theory by evidence that a major portion of criminality is learned through participation in criminal groups. Differential identification is a less disconnected explanation for such learning, and it also does not seem vulnerable to most of the objections to differential association. Because opposing and divisive roles frequently develop within groups, because our identification may be with remote reference groups or with imaginary or highly generalized others, and because identifications may shift rapidly with dialectical processes of role change and rationalization during social interaction, differential association, as ordinarily conceived, is insufficient to account for all differential identification.

In practice, the use of differential identification to explain lone crimes the source of learning which is not readily apparent (such as extremes of brutality or other abnormality in sex crimes) gives rise to speculation as to the "others" involved in the identification. The use of this theory to explain a gang member's participation in a professional crime against property presents fewer difficulties. In so far as the former types of offense are explained by psychiatrists without invoking instincts or other mystical forces, they usually are interpreted, on a necessarily speculative basis, in terms of the self-conception which the offender develops in supporting his behavior and the sources of that self-conception. Such differential identification, in the case of most unusual and compulsive crimes, offers a less disconnected explanation than explanations derived from the alternative theories.[21]

The one objection to the theory of differential association which cannot be met by differential identification is that it does not account for "accidental" crimes. Differential identification treats crime as a form of voluntary (i. e., anticipatory) behavior, rather than as an accident. Indeed, both legal and popular conceptions of "crime" exclude acts which are purely

[21] For an outstanding illustration of what becomes differential identification rather than the usual conception of differential association, applied to compulsive crimes, see Donald R. Cressey, "Differential Association and Compulsive Crimes, " *Journal of Criminal Law, Criminology, and Police Science,* XLV (May-June, 1954), 29-40.

accidental, except for some legislation on felonious negligence, to which our discussion of criminality must be considered inapplicable. Even for the latter offenses, however, it is noteworthy that the consequences of accidentally committing a crime may be such as to foster identification with criminal-role models (whether one is apprehended for the accidental crime or not).

During any period, *prior identifications* and *present circumstances* dictate the selection of the persons with whom we identify ourselves. Prior identifications which have been pleasing tend to persist, but at any time the immediate circumstances affect the relative ease (or salience) of alternative identifications. That is why membership groups so frequently are the reference groups, although they need not be. That, too, is why those inclined to crime usually refrain from it in situations where they play satisfying conventional roles in which crime would threaten their acceptance. From the latter situations their identification with non-criminal others may eventually make them anticriminal. This is the essence of rehabilitation.[22]

There is evidence that, with the spread of urban secularism, social situations are becoming more and more deliberately rather than traditionally organized. Concurrently, roles are increasingly adjusted on the basis of the apparent authority or social pressure in each situation.[23] Our culture is said to give a common level of aspiration but different capacities of attainment according to socioeconomic class. At the same time, it is suggested, economic sources of status are becoming stronger while non-economic sources are becoming weaker. Therefore, when conventional occupational avenues of upward mobility are denied, people are more and more willing to seek the economic gains anticipated in crime, even at the risk of losing such non-economic sources of status as acceptance by non-criminal groups.[24]

[22] Cf. Donald R. Cressey, "Contradictory Theories in Correctional Group Therapy Programs," *Federal Probation,* XVIII (June, 1954), 20-26.

[23] This evidence has come most dramatically from recent studies of race relations. Cf. Joseph D. Lohman and Dietrich C. Reitzes, "Note on Race Relations in Mass Society," *American Journal of Sociology,* LVIII (November 1952), 240-46; Dietrich C. Reitzes, "The Role of Organizational Structures" *Journal of Social Issues,* IX, No. 1 (1953), 37-44; William C. Bradbury, "Evaluation of Research in Race Relations," *Inventory of Research in Racial and Cultural Relations,* V (winter-spring, 1953), 99-133.

[24] Cf. Merton, *op. cit.*, chap. iv. It may be noteworthy here that classification of Illinois parolees by status ratings of the jobs to which they were going was more predictive than classification by the status of their father's occupation or by whether their job was of higher, lower, or equal status than their father's occupation. Regardless of their class background, the parolee's infractions seemed primarily to be a function of their failure to approach middle-class status (cf. Daniel Glaser, "A Reformulation and Testing of Parole Prediction Factors" [unpublished Ph. D. dissertation, University of Chicago, 1954,] pp. 253-59).

All these alleged features of urbanism suggest a considerable applicability of differential identification to "situational" and "incidental" crimes; focus on differential identification with alternative reference groups may reveal "situational imperatives" in individual life-histories.

Differential identification may be considered tautological, in that it may seem merely to make "crime" synonymous with "criminal identification." It is more than a tautology, however, if it directs one to observations beyond those necessary merely for the classification of behavior as criminal or non-criminal. It is a fruitful empirical theory leading one to proceed from the legalistic classification to the analysis of behavior as identification and role-playing.[25]

Implications

Three general hypotheses are derived from the assumption that the image of criminal behavior evoked by the theory of differential identification is more valid than those evoked by alternative formulations.

The first hypothesis is that the imagery invoked by the theory of differential identification is the most adequate and parsimonious theoretical framework with which to account for the findings of criminology. We have shown the more disconnected imagery and the failure to comprehend major aspects of criminality inherent in theories which do not evoke an image of criminality as role-expressive activity. Parsimony of preconception is indicated by (1) its "integrative" function in interrelating the diverse phenomena which may be associated with crime through specifying intervening behavior; (2) its relating of criminal behavior to other behavior rather than to conceptually more distant phenomena; (3) its capacity to comprehend a tremendous diversity of criminal behavior. The theory of differential identification, by indicating the relevance of phenomena grossly correlated with crime, promotes continuity in research and theoretically should direct attention to phenomena having higher correlations with crime. Even more than differential association, as that theory is ordinarily conceived, differential identification should facilitate the recognition of "behavior systems" in crime.[26]

The second hypothesis is that differential identification orients one to evaluate soundly the rehabilitative effects of correctional techniques. Tests of this hypothesis will require more extensive and sophisticated research than that now applied to the appraisal of rehabilitative

[25] A number of examples of useful tautologies in social science are presented in Arnold Rose, *Theory and Method in the Social Sciences* (Minneapolis: University of Minnesota Press, 1954), pp. 328-38. In so far as a proposition is of heuristic use, however, one may question whether it is appropriately designated a "tautology."

[26] Cf. Sutherland, *op. cit.*, chap. xiii.

efforts.[27] However, some suggestive clues are available, for example, from studies of inmate social systems. These systems are seen as coercing each prison inmate into identification with fellow-inmates, and hampering, if not preventing, his identification with non-criminal persons. Many prison policies sometimes considered "progressive," such as housing men in large dormitories, facilitating freedom of contact between inmates, assigning prison social workers to cope with prisoners grievance claims, and keeping relations between inmates and the rest of the institution staff highly formal, may be criticized from the standpoint of their effects upon identifications.[28]

The third hypothesis is that research workers of diverse background are converging on a differential identification type of theory. While the proposition can be tested only be time, illustrations of the trend can be provided from several areas.

1. Psychoanalysts are supplied by adult neurotic patients with a wealth of volunteered verbal data on which to speculate freely. When juvenile delinquents are referred to analysts, however, such cooperation is not always forthcoming. Milieu therapy, which developed in part to meet this contingency, requires that the analyst (a) live intimately with small groups of delinquents, (b) capture his data when manifested in their interaction, and (c) exert a therapeutic influence by counseling and manipulating the environment when strategic moments arise. It is interesting that milieu therapists increasingly seem to be forced by their data to interpret their observations and justify their treatment techniques by analysis of simple role expression. Their efforts to fit their data into traditional psychoanalytic frameworks then seem superfluous and the strain obvious. Aichhorn's pioneer discussion of the ego ideal in milieu therapy provides considerable analysis of differential identification in both group and individual delinquency. Redl and Wineman, who drop Aichhorn's postulation of instincts, are even more dependent on role analysis to interpret behavior and to justify therapeutic techniques. When superimposing Freudian conceptions on role analysis, they are forced to contradictory portrayals of the delinquent's reified ego as both weak and strong, depending on which chapter one reads. It is quite easy to reconceptualize their data as illustrating ambivalent and undefined roles in the case of the weak ego, highly

[27] Cf. Daniel Glaser, "Testing Correctional Decisions," *Journal of Criminal Law, Criminology, and Police Science,* XLV (March-April, 1955), 679-84.

[28] A sophisticated analysis of the impact of inmate social systems on correctional programs is presented in Lloyd W. McCorkle and Richard Korn, "Resocialization within Walls," *Annals,* CXCIII (May, 1954), 88-98; see also Donald Clemmer, *The Prison Community* (Boston: Chistopher Publishing House, 1940); Richard McCleary, "The Strange Journey," *University of North Carolina Extension Bulletin,* Vol. XXXII (March, 1953).

organized learned delinquent roles in the case of delinquent egos and super-egos, and therapy as a shift of identification from delinquent to non-delinquent persons.[29]

2. The Gluecks once wrote: "It is the presence or absence of certain traits and characteristics in the constitution and early environment of the different offenders which determines...what such offenders will ultimately become and what will become of them."[30] This preconception is reflected in their choice of alternative possible explanations of their findings. For example, they have been criticized for dismissing their datum that gang membership was the feature most differentiating delinquents from non-delinquents.[31] It is interesting that, of three of the Gleuck's delinquency prediction scales, two based on personality traits and one on early parent-child relationships ("Social Background Scale"), only the latter has been validated.[32] Warm and consistent relationships with parents are the basis for predicting non-delinquency by this scale, for, say the Gluecks, such relationships create personalities free of criminal tendencies. Yet there is no evidence that early personality classifications are as predictive of delinquency as classifications of the social relationships themselves. A more adequate explanation for the predictive value of the data on social relationships may be that warm relationships inside the family strengthen the identifications with it. These latter, which are predominantly non-criminal, compete with the identifications developing from delinquent and criminal contacts.

[29] As another psychoanalytic milieu therapist has put it: "The basic requirement in all education [of delinquents] is that the adult place himself in relation to the child whereby the child accepts him and therefore accepts his social concepts and community values" (S. R. Slavson, *Re-educating the Delinquent through Group and Community Participation* [New York: Harper & Bros., 1954], p. 242, Cf. August Aichhorn, *Wayward Youth* [New York: Viking Press, 1935]; F. Redl and D. Wineman, *Children Who Hate* [Glencoe, Ill.: Free Press, 1951]; and Redl and Wineman, *Controls from Within* [Glencoe, Ill.: Free Press, 1952]).

[30] S. and E. Glueck, *Criminal Careers in Retrospect* (New York: Commonwealth Fund, 1943, p. 285 (original italicized).

[31] Cf. E.W. Burgess, review of Gluecks' *Unravelling Juvenile Delinquency,* in *Federal Probation,* XV (March, 1951), 53-54; A.J. Reiss, Jr., "*Unravelling Juvenile Delinquency.* II. An Appraisal of the Research Methods," *American Journal of Sociology,* LVII (September, 1951). 115-20.

[32] Cf. Richard E. Thompson, "A Validation of the Glueck Social Prediction Scale for Proneness to Delinquency," *Journal of Criminal Law, Criminology, and Police Science,* XLIII (November-December, 1952), 451-70; S. Axelrad and S. J. Glick, "Application of the Glueck Social Prediction Table to 100 Jewish Delinquent Boys," *Jewish Social Service Quarterly,* XXX (winter, 1953), 127-36.

3. Psychologists studying delinquency have increasingly been forced by their data to focus on peer-group relations rather than on personality traits. Harris, in summarizing research findings, stated:

> It is interesting to note that Hart's factor analysis of 25 traits in 300 delinquent boys yielded six factors, at least four of which have a distinct group reference....
> There is ample evidence that the delinquent is quite conversant with the wide social code, yet there are suggestions that on an absolute basis as well as on a relative basis his values are scaled somewhat differently than are similar values in the experience of non-delinquents. Much more research is needed, not only on the values that are accepted, but also on the process by which they become "interiorized."[33]

The differential identification theory, we suggest, offers a fruitful theoretical orientation for the fulfillment of the above-mentioned need.

Editors from diverse backgrounds in behavioral science have asserted: "The role concept provides the principal theoretical point of articulation between analyses of the behavior of groups by anthropologists and sociologists and analyses of individual motivation by psychologists and psychiatrists."[34] We have submitted differential identification as a frame of reference for fruitfully integrating criminality theory by giving that theory an image of behavior as role-playing.

[33] Dale B. Harris, "The Socialization of the Delinquent," *Child Development,* XIX (September, 1948), 1943-53.

[34] H.A. Murray, Clyde Kluckhohn, and D.M. Schneider, *Personality in Nature, Society, and Culture* (New York: A.A. Knopf, 1953), p. 361.

38. Becoming a Marihuana User *

Howard S. Becker

The use of marihuana is and has been the focus of a good deal of attention on the part of both scientists and laymen. One of the major problems students of the practice have addressed themselves to has been the identification of those individual psychological traits which differentiate marihuana users from nonusers and which are assumed to account for the use of the drug. That approach, common in the study of behavior categorized as deviant, is based on the premise that the presence of a given kind of behavior in an individual can best be explained as the result of some trait which predisposes or motivates him to engage in the behavior.[1]

This study is likewise concerned with accounting for the presence or absence of marihuana use in an individual's behavior. It starts, however, from a different premise: that the presence of a given kind of behavior is the result of a sequence of social experiences during which the person acquires a conception of the meaning of the behavior, and perceptions and judgments of objects and situations, all of which make the activity possible and desirable. Thus, the motivation or disposition to engage in the activity is built up in the course of learning to engage in it and does not antedate this learning process. For such a view it is not necessary to identify those

Reprinted from *The American Journal of Sociology,* LIX (November, 1953), pp. 235-242, by permission of the University of Chicago Press.

*Paper read at the meetings of the Midwest Sociological Society in Omaha, Nebraska, April, 25, 1953. The research on which this paper is based was done while I was a member of the staff of the Chicago Narcotics Survey, a study done by the Chicago Area Project, Inc., under a grant from the National Mental Health Institute. My thanks to Solomon Kobrin, Harold Finestone, Henry McKay, and Anselm Strauss, who read and discussed with me earlier versions of this paper.

[1] See, as examples of this approach, the following: Eli Marcovitz and Henry J. Meyers, "The Marihuana Addict in the Army," *War Medicine,* VI (December, 1944), 382-91; Herbert S. Gaskill, "Marihuana, an Intoxicant," *American Journal of Psychiatry,* CII (September, 1945), 202-4; Sol Charen and Luis Perelman, "Personality Studies of Marihuana Addicts," *American Journal of Psychiatry,* CII (March, 1946), 674-82.

"traits" which "cause" the behavior. Instead, the problem becomes one of describing the set of changes in the person's conception of the activity and of the experience it provides for him.[2]

This paper seeks to describe the sequence of changes in attitude and experience which lead to *the use of marihuana for pleasure.* Marihuana does not produce addiction, as do alcohol and the opiate drugs; there is no withdrawal sickness and no ineradicable craving for the drug.[3] The most frequent pattern of use might be termed "recreational." The drug is used occasionally for the pleasure the user finds in it, a relatively casual kind of behavior in comparison with that connected with the use of addicting drugs. The term "use for pleasure" is meant to emphasize the noncompulsive and casual character of the behavior. It is also meant to eliminate from consideration here those few cases in which marihuana is used for its prestige value only, as a symbol that one is a certain kind of person, with no pleasure at all being derived from its use.

The analysis presented here is conceived of as demonstrating the greater explanatory usefulness of the kind of theory outlined above as opposed to the predispositional theories now current. This may be seen in two ways: (1) predispositional theories cannot account for that group of users (whose existence is admitted)[4] who do not exhibit the trait or traits considered to cause the behavior and (2) such theories cannot account for the great variability over time of a given individual's behavior with reference to the drug. The same person will at one stage be unable to use the drug for pleasure, at a later stage be able and willing to do so, and still later, again be unable to use it in this way. These changes, difficult to explain from a predispositional or motivational theory, are readily understandable in terms of changes in the individual's conception of the drug as is the existence of "normal" users.

The study attempted to arrive at a general statement of the sequence of changes in individual attitude and experience which have always occurred when the individual has become willing and able to use marihuana for pleasure and which have not occurred or not been permanently maintained when this is not the case. This generalization is stated in universal terms in order that negative cases may be discovered and used to revise the explanatory hypothesis.[5]

[2] This approach stems from George Herbert Mead's discussion of objects in *Mind, Self, and Society* (Chicago: University of Chicago Press, 1934), pp. 277-80.

[3] Cf. Roger Adams, "Marihuana," *Bulletin of the New York Academy of Medicine,* XVIII (November, 1942), 705-30.

[4] Cf. Lawrence Kolb, "Marihuana," *Federal Probation,* II (July, 1938), 22-25; and Walter Bromberg, "Marihuana: A Psychiatric Study," *Journal of the American Medical Association,* CXIII (July 1, 1939), 11.

[5] The method used is that described by Alfred R. Lindesmith in his *Opiate Addiction* (Bloomington: Principia Press, 1947), chap. i. I would like also

Fifty interview with marihuana users from a variety of social backgrounds and present positions in society constitute the data from which the generalization was constructed and against which it was tested.[6] The interviews focused on the history of the person's experience with the drug, seeking major changes in his attitude toward it and in his actual use of it, and the reasons for these changes. The final generalization is a statement of that sequence of changes in attitude which occurred in every case known to me in which the person came to use marihuana for pleasure. Until a negative case is found, it may be considered as an explanation of all cases of marihuana use for pleasure. In addition, changes from use to nonuse are shown to be related to similar changes in conception, and in each case it is possible to explain variations in the individual's behavior in these terms.

This paper covers only a portion of the natural history of an individual's use of marihuana,[7] starting with the person having arrived at the point of willingness to try marihuana. He knows that others use it to "get high," but he does not know what this means in concrete terms. He is curious about the experience, ignorant of what it may turn out to be, and afraid that it may be more than he has bargained for. The steps outlined below, if he undergoes them all and maintains the attitudes developed in them, leave him willing and able to use the drug for pleasure when the opportunity presents itself.

I

The novice does not ordinarily get high the first time he smokes marihuana, and several attempts are usually necessary to induce this state. One explanation of this may be that the drug is not smoked "properly," that is, in a way that insures sufficient dosage to produce real symptoms of intoxication. Most users agree that it cannot be smoked like tobacco if one is to get high:

> Take in a lot of air, you know, and...I don't know how to describe it, you don't smoke it like a cigarette, you draw in a lot of air and get it deep down in your system and then keep it there. Keep it there as long as you can.

---

to acknowledge the important role Lindesmith's work played in shaping my thinking about the genesis of marihuana use.

[6] Most of the interviews were done by the author. I am grateful to Solomon Kobrin and Harold Finestone for allowing me to make use of interviews done by them.

[7] I hope to discuss elsewhere other stages in this natural history.

Without the use of some such technique[8] the drug will produce no effects, and the user will be unable to get high:

> The trouble with people like that [who are not able to get high] is that they're just not smoking it right, that's all there is to it. Either they're not holding it down long enough, or they're getting too much air and not enough smoke, or the other way around or something like that. A lot of people just don't smoke it right, so naturally nothing's gonna happen.

If nothing happens, it is manifestly impossible for the user to develop a conception of the drug as an object which can be used for pleasure, and use will therefore not continue. The first step in the sequence of events that must occur if the person is to become a user is that he must learn to use the proper smoking technique in order that his use of the drug will produce some effects in terms of which his conception of it can change.

Such a change is, as might be expected, a result of the individual's participation in groups in which marihuana is used. In them the individual learns the proper way to smoke the drug. This may occur through direct teaching:

> I was smoking like I did an ordinary cigarette. He said, "No, don't do it like that." He said, "Suck it, you know, draw in and hold it in your lungs till you... for a period of time."
> I said, "Is there any limit of time to hold it?"
> He said, "No, just till you feel that you want to let it out, let it out."
> So I did that three or four times.

Many new users are ashamed to admit ignorance and, pretending to know already, must learn through the more indirect means of observation and imitation:

> I came on like I had turned on [smoked marihuana] many times before you know. I didn't want to seem like a punk to this cat. See, like I didn't know the first thing about it—how to smoke it, or what was going to happen, or what. I just watched him like a hawk—I didn't take my eyes off him for a second, because I wanted to do everything just as he did it. I watched how he held it, how he smoked it, and everything. Then when he gave it to me I just came on cool, as though I knew exactly what the score was. I held it like he did and took a poke just the way he did.

[8] A pharmacologist notes that this ritual is in fact an extremely efficient way of getting the drug into the blood stream (R. P. Walton, *Marihuana: America's New Drug Problem* [Philadelphia: J. B. Lippincott, 1938], p. 48).

No person continued marihuana use for pleasure without learning a technique that supplied sufficient dosage for the effects of the drug to appear. Only when this was learned was it possible for a conception of the drug as an object which could be used for pleasure to emerge. Without such a conception marihuana use was considered meaningless and did not continue.

II

Even after he learns the proper smoking technique, the new user may not get high and thus not form a conception of the drug as something which can be used for pleasure. A remark made by a user suggested the reason for this difficulty in getting high and pointed to the next necessary step on the road to being a user:

> I was told during an interview, "As a matter of fact, I've seen a guy who was high out of his mind and didn't know it."
> I expressed disbelief: "How can that be, man?"
> The interviewee said, "Well, it's pretty strange, I'll grant you that, but I've seen it. This guy got on with me, claiming that he'd never got high, one of those guys, and he got completely stoned. And he kept insisting that he wasn't high. So I had to prove to him that he was."

What does this mean? It suggests that being high consists of two elements: the presence of symptoms caused by marihuana use and the recognition of these symptoms and their connection by the user with his use of the drug. It is not enough, that is, that the effects be present; they alone do not automatically provide the experience of being high. The user must be able to point them out to himself and consciously connect them with his having smoked marihuana before he can have this experience. Otherwise, regardless of the actual effects produced, he considers that the drug has had no effect on him: "I figured it either had no effect on me or other people were exaggerating its effect on them, you know. I thought it was probably psychological, see." Such persons believe that the whole thing is an illusion and that the wish to be high leads the user to deceive himself into believing that something is happening when, in fact, nothing is. They do not continue marihuana use, feeling that "it does nothing" for them.

Typically, however, the novice has faith (developed from his observation of users who do get high) that the drug actually will produce some new experience and continues to experiment with it until it does. His failure to get high worries him, and he is likely to ask more experienced users or provoke comments from them about it. In such conversations he is made aware of specific details of his experience which he may not have noticed or may have noticed but failed to identify as symptoms of being high:

> I didn't get high the first time...I don't think I held it in long enough. I probably let it out, you know, you're a little afraid. The second time I wasn't sure, and he [smoking companion] told me, like I asked him for some of the symptoms or something, how would I know, you know....So he told me to sit on a stool. I sat on—I think I sat on a bar stool—and he said, "Let your feet hang," and then when I got down my feet were real cold, you know.
> And I started feeling it, you know. That was the first time. And then about a week after that, sometime pretty close to it, I really got on. That was the first time I got on a big laughing kick, you know. Then I really knew I was on.

One symptom of being high is an intense hunger. In the next case the novice becomes aware of this and gets high for the first time:

> They were just laughing the hell out of me because like I was eating so much. I just scoffed [ate] so much food, and they were just laughing at me, you know. Sometimes I'd be looking at them, you know, wondering why they're laughing, you know, not knowing what I was doing. [Well, did they tell you why they were laughing eventually?] Yeah, yeah, I come back, "Hey, man, what's happening?" Like, you know, like I'd ask, "What's happening?" and all of a sudden I feel weird, you know. "Man, you're on you know. You're on pot [high on marihuana]." I said, "No, am I?" Like I don't know what's happening.

The learning may occur in more indirect ways:

> I heard little remarks that were made by other people. Somebody said, "My legs are rubbery," and I can't remember all the remarks that were made because I was very attentively listening for all these cues for what I was supposed to feel like.

The novice, then, eager to have this feeling, picks up from other users some concrete referents of the term "high" and applies these notions to his own experience. The new concepts make it possible for him to locate these symptoms among his own sensations and to point out to himself a "something different" in his experience that he connects with drug use. It is only when he can do this that he is high. In the next case, the contrast between two successive experiences of a user makes clear the crucial importance of the awareness of the symptoms in being high and re-emphasizes the important role of interaction with other users in acquiring the concepts that make this awareness possible:

> [Did you get high the first time you turned on?] Yeah, sure. Although, come to think of it, I guess I really didn't. I mean, like that first time it was more or less of a mild drunk. I was happy, I guess, you know

> what I mean. But I didn't really know I was high, you know what I mean. It was only after the second time I got high that I realized I was high the first time. Then I knew that something different was happening.
> [How did you know that?] How did I know? If what happened to me that night would of happened to you, you would've known, believe me. We played the first tune for almost two hours—one tune! Imagine, man! We got on the stand and played this one tune, we started at nine o'clock. When we got finished I looked at my watch, it's a quarter to eleven. Almost two hours on one tune. And it didn't seem like anything. I mean, you know, it does that to you. It's like you have much more time or something. Anyway, when I saw that, man, it was too much. I knew I must really be high or something if anything like that could happen. See, and then they explained to me that that's what it did to you, you had a different sense of time and everything. So I realized that that's what it was. I knew then. Like the first time, I probably felt that way, you know, but I didn't know what's happening.

It is only when the novice becomes able to get high in this sense that he will continue to use marihuana for pleasure. In every case in which use continued, the user had acquired the necessary concepts with which to express to himself the fact that he was experiencing new sensations caused by the drug. That is, for use to continue, it is necessary not only to use the drug so as to produce effects but also to learn to perceive these effects when they occur. In this way marihuana acquires meaning for the user as an object which can be used for pleasure.

With increasing experience the user develops a greater appreciation of the drug's effects; he continues to learn to get high. He examines succeeding experiences closely, looking for new effects, making sure the old ones are still there. Out of this there grows a stable set of categories for experiencing the drug's effects whose presence enables the user to get high with ease.

The ability to perceive the drug's effects must be maintained if use is to continue; if it is lost, marihuana use ceases. Two kinds of evidence support this statement. First, people who become heavy users of alcohol, barbiturates, or opiates do not continue to smoke marihuana, largely because they lose the ability to distinguish between its effects and those of the other drugs.[9] They no longer know whether the marihuana gets them high. Second, in those few cases in which an individual uses mari-

[9] "Smokers have repeatedly stated that the consumption of whiskey while smoking negates the potency of the drug. They find it very difficult to get 'high' while drinking whiskey and because of that smokers will not drink while using the 'weed' " (cf. New York City Mayor's Committee on Marihuana *The Marihuana Problem in the City of New York* [Lancaster, Pa.: Jacques Cattel Press, 1944], p. 13.)

huana in such quantities that he is always high, he is apt to get this same feeling that the drug has no effect on him, since the essential element of a noticeable difference between feeling high and feeling normal is missing. In such a situation, use is likely to be given up completely, but temporarily, in order that the user may once again be able to perceive the difference.

III

One more step is necessary if the user who has now learned to get high is to continue use. He must learn to enjoy the effects he has just learned to experience. Marihuana-produced sensations are not automatically or necessarily pleasurable. The taste for such experience is a socially acquired one, not different in kind from acquired tastes for oysters or dry martinis. The user feels dizzy, thirsty; his scalp tingles; he misjudges time and distances; and so on. Are these things pleasurable? He isn't sure. If he is to continue marihuana use, he must decide that they are. Otherwise, getting high, while a real enough experience, will be an unpleasant one he would rather avoid.

The effects of the drug, when first perceived, may be physically unpleasant or at least ambiguous:

> It started taking effect, and I didn't know what was happening, you know, what it was, and I was very sick. I walked around the room, walking around the room trying to get off, you know; it just scared me at first, you know. I wasn't used to that kind of feeling.

In addition, the novice's naive interpretation of what is happening to him may further confuse and frighten him, particularly if he decides, as many do, that he is going insane:

> I felt I was insane, you know. Everything people done to me just wigged me. I couldn't hold a conversation, and my mind would be wandering, and I was always thinking, oh, I don't know, weird things, like hearing music different. . . . I get the feeling that I can't talk to anyone. I'll goof completely.

Given these typically frightening and unpleasant first experiences, the beginner will not continue use unless he learns to redefine the sensations as pleasurable:

> It was offered to me, and I tried it. I'll tell you one thing. I never did enjoy it at all. I mean it was just nothing that I could enjoy. [Well, did you get high when you turned on?] Oh, yeah, I got definite feelings from it. But I didn't enjoy them. I mean I got plenty of reactions, but they were mostly reactions of fear. [You were frightened?] Yes, I

didn't enjoy it. I couldn't seem to relax with it, you know. If you can't relax with a thing, you can't enjoy it, I don't think.

In other cases the first experiences were also definitely unpleasant, but the person did become a marihuana user. This occurred, however, only after a later experience enabled him to redefine the sensations as pleasurable:

> [This man's first experience was extremely unpleasant, involving distortion of spatial relationships and sounds, violent thirst, and panic produced by these symptoms.] After the first time I didn't turn on for about, I'd say, ten months to a year.... It wasn't a moral thing; it was because I'd gotten so frightened, bein' so high. An' I didn't want to go through that again, I mean, my reaction was, "Well, if this is what they call bein' high, I don't dig [like] it." ... So I didn't turn on for a year almost, accounta that....
>
> Well, my friends started, an' consequently I started again. But I didn't have any more, I didn't have that same initial reaction, after I started turning on again.
>
> [In interaction with his friends he became able to find pleasure in the effects of the drug and eventually became a regular user.]

In no case will use continue without such a redefinition of the effects as enjoyable.

This redefinition occurs, typically, in interaction with more experienced users who, in a number of ways, teach the novice to find pleasure in this experience which is at first so frightening.[10] They may reassure him as to the temporary character of the unpleasant sensations and minimize their seriousness, at the same time calling attention to the more enjoyable aspects. An experienced user describes how he handles newcomers to marihuana use:

> Well, they get pretty high sometimes. The average person isn't ready for that, and it is a little frightening to them sometimes. I mean, they've been high on lush [alcohol], and they get higher that way than they've ever been before, and they don't know what's happening to them. Because they think they're going to keep going up, up, up till they lose their minds or begin doing weird things or something. You have to like reassure them, explain to them that they're not really flipping or anything, that they're gonna be all right. You have to just talk them out of being afraid. Keep talking to them, reassuring, telling them it's all right. And come on with your own story, you know: "The same thing happened to me. You'll get to like that after awhile." Keep coming on like that; pretty soon you talk them out of being scared. And

[10] Charen and Perelman, *op. cit.*, p. 679.

> besides they see you doing it and nothing horrible is happening to you, so that gives them more confidence.

The more experienced user may also teach the novice to regulate the amount he smokes more carefully, so as to avoid any severely uncomfortable symptoms while retaining the pleasant ones. Finally, he teaches the new user that he can "get to like it after awhile." He teaches him to regard those ambiguous experiences formerly defined as unpleasant as enjoyable. The older user in the following incident is a person whose tastes have shifted in this way, and his remarks have the effect of helping others to make a similar redefinition:

> A new user had her first experience of the effects of marihuana and became frightened and hysterical. She "felt like she was half in and half out of the room" and experienced a number of alarming physical symptoms. One of the more experienced users present said, "She's dragged because she's high like that. I'd give anything to get that high myself. I haven't been that high in years."

In short, what was once frightening and distasteful becomes, after a taste for it is built up, pleasant, desired, and sought after. Enjoyment is introduced by the favorable definition of the experience that one acquires from others. Without this, use will not continue, for marihuana will not be for the user an object he can use for pleasure.

In addition to being a necessary step in becoming a user, the represents an important condition for continued use. It is quite common for experienced users suddenly to have an unpleasant or frightening experience, which they cannot define as pleasurable, either because they have used a larger amount of marihuana than usual or because it turns out to be a higher-quality marihuana than they expected. The user has sensations which go beyond any conception he has of what being high is and is in much the same situation as the novice, uncomfortable and frightened. He may blame it on an overdose and simply be more careful in the future. But he may make this the occasion for a rethinking of his attitude toward the drug and decide that it no longer can give him pleasure. When this occurs and is not followed by a redefinition of the drug as capable of producing pleasure, use will cease.

The likelihood of such a redefinition occurring depends on the degree of the individual's participation with other users. Where this participation is intensive, the individual is quickly talked out of his feeling against marihuana use. In the next case, on the other hand, the experience was very disturbing, and the aftermath of the incident cut the person's participation with other users to almost zero. Use stopped for three years and began again only when a combination of circumstances, important among which was a resumption of ties with users, made possible a redefinition of the nature of the drug:

> It was too much, like I only made about four pokes, and I couldn't even get it out of my mouth, I was so high, and I got real flipped. In the basement, you know, I just couldn't stay in there anymore. My heart was pounding real hard, you know, and I was going out of my mind; I thought I was losing my mind completely. So I cut out of this basement, and this other guy, he's out of his mind, told me, "Don't, don't leave me, man. Stay here." And I couldn't.
>
> I walked outside, and it was five below zero, and I thought I was dying, and I had my coat open; I was sweating. I was perspiring. My whole insides were all..., and I walked about two blocks away, and I fainted behind a bush. I don't know how long I laid there. I woke up, and I was feeling the worst, I can't describe it at all, so I made it to a bowling alley, man, and I was trying to act normal, I was trying to shoot pool, you know, trying to act real normal, and I couldn't lay and I couldn't stand up and I couldn't sit down, and I went up and laid down where some guys that spot pins lay down, and that didn't help me, and I went down to a doctor's office. I was going to go in there and tell the doctor to put me out of my misery...because my heart was pounding so hard, you know.... So then all week end I started flipping, seeing things there and going through hell, you know, all kinds of abnormal things....I just quit for a long time then.
>
> [He went to a doctor who defined the symptoms for him as those of a nervous breakdown caused by "nerves" and "worries." Although he was no longer using marihuana, he had some recurrences of the symptoms which led him to suspect that "it was all his nerves."] So I just stopped worrying, you know; so it was about thirty-six months later I started making it again. I'd just take a few pokes, you know. [He first resumed use in the company of the same user-friend with whom he had been involved in the original incident.]

A person, then, cannot begin to use marihuana for pleasure, or continue its use for pleasure, unless he learns to define its effects as enjoyable, unless it becomes and remains an object which he conceived of as capable of producing pleasure.

IV

In summary, an individual will be able to use marihuana for pleasure only when he goes through a process of learning to conceive of it as an object which can be used in this way. No one becomes a user without (1) learning to smoke the drug in a way which will produce real effects; (2) learning to recognize the effects and connect them with drug use (learning, in other words, to get high); and (3) learning to enjoy the sensations he perceives. In the course of this process he develops a disposition or motivation to use marihuana which was not and could not have been present when he began use, for it involves and depends on conceptions of the drug which could only grow out of the kind of actual experience detailed above. On completion of this process he is willing and able to use marihuana for pleasure.

He has learned, in short, to answer "Yes" to the question: "Is it fun?" The direction his further use of the drug takes depends on his being able to continue to answer "Yes" to this question and, in addition, on his being able to answer "Yes" to other questions which arise as he becomes aware of the implications of the fact that the society as a whole disapproves of the practice: "Is it expedient?" "Is it moral?" Once he has acquired the ability to get enjoyment out of the drug, use will continue to be possible for him. Considerations of morality and expediency, occasioned by the reactions of society, may interfere and inhibit use, but use continues to be a possibility in terms of his conception of the drug. The act becomes impossible only when the ability to enjoy the experience of being high is lost, through a change in the user's conception of the drug occasioned by certain kinds of experience with it.

In comparing this theory with those which ascribe marihuana use to motives or predispositions rooted deep in individual behavior, the evidence makes it clear that marihuana use for pleasure can occur only when the process described above is undergone and cannot occur without it. This is apparently so without reference to the nature of the individual's personal makeup, or psychic problems. Such theories assume that people have stable modes of response which predetermine the way they will act in relation to any particular situation or object and that, when they come in contact with the given object or situation, they act in the way in which their makeup predisposes them.

This analysis of the genesis of marihuana use shows that the individuals who come in contact with a given object may respond to it at first in a great variety of ways. If a stable form of new behavior toward the object is to emerge, a transformation of meanings must occur, in which the person develops a new conception of the nature of the object.[11] This happens in a series of communicative acts in which others point out new aspects of his experience to him, present him with new interpretations of events, and help him achieve a new conceptual organization of his world, without which the new behavior is not possible. Persons who do not achieve the proper kind of conceptualization are unable to engage in the given behavior and turn off in the direction of some other relationship to the object or activity.

This suggests that behavior of any kind might fruitfully be studied developmentally, in terms of changes in meanings and concepts, their organization and reorganization, and the way they channel behavior, making some acts possible while excluding others.

[11] Cf. Anselm Strauss, "The Development and Transformation of Monetary Meanings in the Child," *American Sociological Review,* XVII (June, 1952), 275-86.

39. Executives and Supervisors: Contrasting Self-Conceptions of Each Other *

Charles H. Coates and
Roland J. Pellegrin

Cooley's "looking-glass self" and Mead's "taking the role of the generalized other" rank among the foremost concepts in sociology.[1] In spite of their utility and significance, however, these concepts have rarely been exploited in the investigation of why some individuals achieve more vertical occupational mobility and career success than others in the same or similar occupational environments.

Successful executives in business and industry have often been and are continually being studied through self-appraisals obtained by personal interviews and questionnaires.[2] Their success stories are widely publicized, and the top-level business and industrial executive has been popularized as an ideal type of successful American. From such self-appraisals by outstanding executives, so many generalizations have been made about "how to become successful" that it is often erroneously assumed that the means of achieving executive success have universal applicability. What is usually overlooked is that executive success, like leadership and success in other occupational fields, is subject to situational and environmental variability. It would therefore seem logical to study differential executive success situationally by asking top-level executives to appraise their "looking-glass selves," and to take the roles of "generalized others" on the top and bottom rungs of the executive ladder by appraising retrospectively their own personal attributes in contrast with those of subordinates in their own or similar occupational environments. It would also seem logical to compare these top-level appraisals oriented downward with similar lower-level appraisals oriented upward.

Essentially, this was the approach employed in a comparative study made in 1954 and 1955 of 50 top-level executives in 30 large and bureau-

From the *American Sociological Review,* XXII (April, 1957), pp. 217-220, by permission of the American Sociological Association and the authors.

* Revised version of paper read at the annual meeting of the American Sociological Society, September, 1956.

[1] Charles H. Cooley, *Human Nature and the Social Order,* New York: Scribner's, 1902; and George H. Mead, *Mind, Self and Society* (Charles W. Morris, ed.), Chicago: University of Chicago Press, 1934.

[2] A recent example of such research is found in W. Lloyd Warner and James C. Abegglen, *Big Business Leaders in America,* New York: Harper and Brothers, 1955.

cratically structured business, industrial, governmental, and educational organizations, and 50 first line supervisors in the same or similar occupational environments.[3] The setting of the study was a dynamic Southern community, fictitiously called "Bigtown," which had experienced within a span of 30 years a growth to a population of 200,000 as a result of industrial and business expansion. The confidential personal interview was used in studying the comparative samples of top- and low-level individuals in management, all of whom had long occupational histories. Because of the effective matching of the samples on the basis of age and long occupational histories, the retrospective appraisals had a unique quality of depth in time. The confidential nature of the study made possible considerable interviewer-interviewee rapport, which brought forth a wealth of subjective data. Since standardized interview schedules were utilized, comparative analysis of the data was facilitated.

The following analysis is limited to the executives' and the supervisors' self-conceptions and conceptions of each other. In eliciting these self- and other-conceptions, open-ended questions were utilized on the interview schedule, and no pre-conceived list of desirable or undesirable attributes was employed. The attributes presented below are derived from a content analysis of equivalent terms most frequently mentioned by interviewees. There was virtually no disagreement concerning the attributes of executives and supervisors, although some respondents listed more attributes than others. Each attribute was mentioned independently by at least 15 of the 50 persons involved in each self- or other-rating.

Results

Most executives conceived of themselves as possessing several of the dynamic personal attributes revealed in Henry's well-known study of 100 executives in the Chicago business community.[4] Among these were: strong achievement desire, high mobility drive, sympathetic conception of authority, considerable ability to organize, firm decisiveness, strong self-

[3] Further information on the scope, method, and content of the study is presented in the following papers by the authors: "Absentee-Owned Corporations and Community Power Structure," *American Journal of Sociology,* 61 (March, 1956), pp. 413-419; "Executives and Supervisors: A Situational Theory of Differential Occupational Mobility," *Social Forces* 31 (December 1956), pp. 121-126; and "Executives and Supervisors: Contrasting Definitions of Career Success," *Administrative Science Quarterly,* 1 (March 1957) pp. 506-517.

[4] William E. Henry, "The Business Executive: The Psychodynamics of a Social Role," *The American Journal of Sociology,* 54 (January, 1949), pp. 286-291.

structure, much aggressive activity, and direct orientation toward reality. Mention of these executive attributes was to be expected, but of more interest were the main distinctions that executives made between themselves, their associates, and first-line supervisors they had known through the years.

These comparative self- and other-appraisals usually began with a statement of qualities that executives possess and that supervisors either lack or possess to a lesser degree. Among the distinctions most frequently made by executives between themselves and supervisors were: more energy, alertness, and initiative; aggressive as opposed to submissive attitudes; more understanding of and ability to get along with and manipulate people; greater willingness to assume responsibilities and make decisions; greater ability to deal with and impress superiors; better judgment and foresight; more magnetic, well-rounded, projective personalities; more tact and poise; better problem-solving ability; more adaptability to changing situations; more determination and strength of personal character; different definitions of the meaning of success; greater ability to sell themselves and their ideas, and to get things done through group effort; more education and training; different occupational and social contacts and opportunities; different loyalties and job interests. Illustrative of the self- and other-conceptions of the executives are the following:

> *Executive A:* Successful executives are not "born," or "made" in college, but are products of their social environments. Compared to low level supervisors they have much more ability, personality, human understanding, and motivation. They have different attitudes and values and different definitions of organizational and personal success. Low level men simply lack the inner determination to climb further up the executive ladder.
>
> *Executive B:* The main distinctions are: "spark" or lack of it, willingness to accept responsibility and make decisions or the lack of it, ability to handle people or the lack of it. I can't define "spark," but you know it when you see it. Maybe it is a combination of personality and drive.
>
> *Executive C:* The big difference in the two levels is in the ability to analyze the motives of others and to foresee their reactions. Low level men are unable to realize why people react as they do. Because of this they lack the ability to plant ideas in others and get them to do things.

Like the executives whom Henry studied, these executives placed high values on achievement and self-directedness, but they may also pay a high price for holding these values.[5] The executives were asked to give their conceptions of the penalties and sacrifices associated with the achievement of

[5] *Ibid,* p. 291.

top level executive success. Among those most frequently mentioned were: adverse effect of a pressure environment on personal health; considerably more worry than the average professional person; lack of time for recreation and leisure; insufficient opportunity for normal family life; a certain amount of loneliness associated with an isolated position; feeling that hard work would lead to even harder work; recurring invasions of personal privacy; forced suppression of personal desires; continuous disruption of personal plans; constant fear of making wrong decisions. One executive stated:

> *Executive D:* This corporation has been reorganized just so I could turn over the presidency to a younger man. I wanted to get rid of all of these responsibilities, worries, and pressures. The ups and downs in the competitive business world are terrific. You're always on the 'phone, days and nights and holidays. I've got to get more time with my family and more time for recreation before it is too late. I haven't had a vacation in four years, and the only way to get one is to just pack up and leave town.

In order to compare the self- and other-conceptions of the executives oriented downward, the supervisors were invited to give similar self- and other-conceptions oriented upward.[6] When asked to make the main distinctions between themselves, their supervisory associates, and executives they had known through the years, the great majority rather surprisingly tended to concede to executives greater amounts of the same personal attributes in which executives had tended to claim superiority. What was of more interest, however, were their reasons for conceding to executives this superiority. Their concessions seemed to have resulted not only from their conceptions of their own personal limitations and those of their associates, but also from their conceptions of the differential role expectations of executives and supervisors. Supervisors tended to be acutely aware of the handicaps of their socio-cultural backgrounds, education and training, and occupational opportunities.[7] As derivatives of these self-conceived personal limitations, they tended to concede to executives: better social and educational backgrounds; more ambition and motivation; higher level attitudes, values and life goals; more energy, alertness, and initiative; better understanding of human nature; better rounded, more magnetic personalities; more ability to handle large numbers of people; more ability to solve problems and make long-range plans; more willingness to dele-

[6] See Robert Dubin, "Upward Orientation Toward Superiors" in his *Human Relations in Administration,* New York: Prentice-Hall, 1951, pp. 272-273.

[7] The effects of these factors upon career patterns are analyzed in the authors' "Executives and Supervisors: A Situational Theory of Differential Occupational Mobility," *op. cit.*

gate authority, accept responsibility, and make decisions. Illustrative self- and other-conceptions of the supervisors follow:

> *Supervisor A:* Top men are totally different from supervisors. Top men have better social backgrounds and education and thus have different abilities and goals. Most supervisors want to get so high and no higher because they don't want big responsibilities. They just want to carry out instructions without having to make decisions.
> *Supervisor B:* Top level men are like Army Generals. They sit down, make the plans, and issue the orders, though in doing so they are thoughtful, courteous, understanding, and helpful. Supervisors carry out the orders like Army Sergeants. Some are hard-boiled, and some are soft-boiled. Some are drivers, and some are leaders. It all depends on how they think the boss wants them to behave.
> *Supervisor C:* The top level is better at getting jobs done through group effort because they have more flexible, more magnetic personalities. They are the better planners, organizers, coordinators, decision-makers, and administrators. That's what top men are for, anyway.

To throw further light upon their conceptions of the roles of top level executives, the supervisors were asked the question, "If you could start all over again, would you like to become a top level executive?" The great majority of the supervisors stated emphatically that they would *not.* Usually they gave as their reasons, "too many worries, headaches, and responsibilities." As one veteran supervisor expressed it:

> *Supervisor D:* Who, me? Hell no! Not way up top. Look at our head man. He has a wonderful education, makes a lot of money, and has a big reputation. But that kind of a job commands a man's whole being, day and night, and almost commands his soul. He's always contending with worries, responsibilities, and decisions. The directors hound him to death. With the power and the glory go the headaches and the ulcers. One of my top level friends died the other day of "industrial suicide." As for me, I'd rather have a happy, pleasant life. What's the use of killing yourself?

Thus, there appeared in the self- and other-conceptions of supervisors an acute awareness, not only of their own personal limitations, but also of the penalties and sacrifices associated with top level executive roles.

Implications

1. Superiors tend to judge their subordinates in terms of their own self-images, and to appraise low-level role performance by comparing

it with their own high-level role performance.
2. Subordinates tend to judge their superiors in terms of their own images of high-level role expectations, and to account for their own personal limitations in terms of socio-cultural backgrounds and conceptions of low-level expectations.
3. Both superiors and subordinates tend to be aware of the rewards, penalties, and sacrifices associated with high-level roles. Such an awareness differentially influences achievement desires on the two levels.
4. Such self-conceived achievement desires positively or negatively affect role performance and therefore differentially influence life-span career success. [8]

Further study of comparative samples of individuals at different levels in various occupational hierarchies may be helpful in increasing understanding of such factors as differential motivation, role performance, and status striving.

[8] On this point, see the discussion in *ibid.* and in our "Executives and Supervisors: Contrasting Definitions of Career Success," *op. cit.*

40. Awareness Contexts and Social Interaction *

Barney G. Glaser and
Anselm L. Strauss

When men confront each other, each cannot always be certain — even when given seemingly trustworthy guarantees — that he knows either the other's identity or his own identity in the eyes of the other. An honest citizen may be taken in by a confidence man, a government official by a foreign spy passing as his secretary, or a dying patient by his doctor. But the confidence man's mark may actually be from the local detective squad; the official, suspecting undercover play, may be pretending innocence while slipping the secretary false documents; and the dying patient may suspect his true condition but not reveal his suspicion to the physician. Thus, who is really being "taken in" is a matter of the awareness of both parties to the situation.

The phenomenon of awareness — which is central to the study of interaction — can be quite complex for at least two reasons. First, interaction may involve not merely two persons, but a third or quite a few more. For instance, when a homosexual flashes cues to another homosexual in the presence of many straight people, some may not notice and others may misread the cues, while others might be aware of their intended meaning. The identity of the homosexual is, therefore, unknown or suspect to some straights and known to still others. Conversely, a homosexual cannot always be certain who suspects or who is or is not aware of his true identity. Second, each person involved may be the representative of a system with specific requirements for, and perhaps a high stake in, how the person manages his own and the

From *American Sociological Review,* XXIX (October, 1964), pp. 669-679, by permission of the American Sociological Association and the authors.

*Many of the examples used in this paper are taken from the author's study of Hospital Personnel, Nursing Care and Dying Patients, supported by National Institutes of Health, Grant GN9077. For a full discussion of awareness contexts related to social interaction in the hospital dying situation, see our . . . book, *Awareness of Dying: A Study of Social Interaction.* Jeanne Quint, a member of our project team, has worked closely with us on these data. We are indebted to Howard S. Becker, Fred Davis, Erving Goffman, Sheldon Messinger, and Melvin Sabshin for their helpful comments on this paper.

other's identity. Spies and counterspies are linked to such systems as often as are doctors and nurses.

These considerations highlight important features of the relation between interaction and awareness. To establish our basic notions, however, we shall content ourselves in this paper with the least complex situation: two interactants (whether persons or groups) who face the dual problem of being certain about both their identity in the other's eyes and the other's identity.

Contexts of Awareness

By the term *awareness context* we mean the total combination of what each interactant in a situation knows about the identity of the other and his own identity in the eyes of the other.[1] This total awareness is the context within which are guided successive interactions between the two persons over periods of time — long or short. Empirically the question of true identity may focus only on that of one of the two persons (the dying patient) or on that of both persons (spy and counterspy).

We have singled out four types of awareness context for special consideration since they have proved useful in accounting for different types of interaction. An *open* awareness context obtains when each interactant is aware of the other's true identity and his own identity in the eyes of the other. A *closed* awareness context obtains when one interactant does not know either the other's identity or the other's view of his identity. A *suspicion* awareness context is a modification of the closed one: one interactant suspects the true identity of the other or the other's view of his own identity, or both. A *pretense* awareness context is a modification of the open one: both interactants are fully aware but pretend not to be.

[1] The concept of awareness context is a structural unit, not a property of one of the standard structural units such as group, organization, community, role, position, etc. By "context" we mean it is a structural unit of an encompassing order larger than the other unit under focus: interaction. Thus, an awareness context surrounds and affects the interaction. Much as one might say that the interaction of staff with dying patients occurs within the context of a cancer ward or a veteran's hospital, one can also say that this interaction occurs within a type of awareness context. Note that ward or hospital are concrete, conventional social units, while awareness context is an analytic social unit, constructed to account for similarities in interaction in many diverse conventional units.

A more general definition of awareness context is the total combination of what specific people, groups, organizations, communities or nations know what about a specific issue. Thus, this structural concept can be used for the study of virtually any problem entailing awareness at any structural level of analysis.

These types illustrate how the sociologist's total picture may differ from that held by each interactant, no matter how well informed or expert. For example, a doctor may state that a patient does not yet know that he is dying (his identity in the eyes of the doctor) while the patient may very well suspect the physician's definition. Thus, the doctor believes that closed awareness obtains when actually there is a suspicion context within which the patient is testing his suspicions. If the doctor recognizes those suspicions he may attempt to parry them. If the doctor believes himself successful, he may only report to the sociologist that as yet the patient is unaware, neglecting to mention the patient's suspicions. Therefore, delimiting an awareness context requires always that the sociologist ascertain independently the awareness of each interactant. The safest method is to obtain data, through observation or interview, from each interactant on his own state of awareness. To accept the word of only one informant is risky, even perhaps for the open awareness context.

The successive interactions occurring within each type of context tend to transform the context. As yet it is an empirical question as to the direction in which a change in one context will lead, or what are some patterns of successive transformations. Thus, a closed context can be shattered by arousing suspicions; but if suspicions are quelled, the closed context is reinstituted. If suspicions are validated, the context may change to either pretense or open awareness. With a change in identity of one interactant in the eyes of the other, an open context can easily become either closed or pretense. For instance, the government official who suspects that his secretary is a spy must now check his suspicions. If he discovers that she is a spy but does not reveal his knowledge, then she in turn misreads his view of her identity. Thus, a closed context now obtains! If she in turn surreptitiously learns of his new view of her but says nothing, the context is again closed. But if he unmasks her spying, then the context now becomes open, since each now fully acknowledges the other's true identity.

How long each context will last before it is transformed is also an empirical question. In the abstract none is inherently less stable than another; although within a given substantive area, differential degrees of stability may become apparent. For dying patients, a suspicion context is probably the least stable, becoming resolved by successive interactions with staff which confirm the patient's suspicions.

A Paradigm for the Study of Awareness Contexts

To organize a study of interaction within different awareness contexts, we have developed a paradigm or set of directives. These directives focus on the study of developmental interaction process — interaction that changes as it continues—as distinct from the relatively static study of the rules that govern interaction.[2]

The component parts of the paradigm are as follows: (1) a description of the given type of awareness context; (2) the structural conditions under which the awareness context exists;[3] (3) the consequent interaction; (4) changes of interaction that occasion transformations of context, along with the structural conditions for the transformations; (5) the tactics of various interactants as they attempt to manage changes of awareness context; and (6) some consequences of the initial awareness context, its transformation and associated interactions—for interactants and for the organizations or institutions notably affected.

To illustrate the use of this paradigm, we briefly sketch the closed awareness context surrounding dying patients.

(1) Hospitalized patients frequently do not recognize their impending death while staff does.[4] Thus interaction between staff and patient occurs within a closed awareness context about the patient's true identity.

(2) At least four major structural conditions determine this closed awareness context. First, most patients are not especially experienced at recognizing the signs of impending death. Second, the hospital is magnificently organized, both by accident and design, for hiding the medical truth from the patient. Records are kept out of reach. Staff is skilled at withholding information from him. Medical talk about him occurs generally in far-removed places. Also, the staff is trained or accustomed to act collusively around patients so as not to disclose medical secrets. Third, physicians are supported in their withholding of information by professional rationales: "Why deny them all hope by telling them they are dying?" Fourth, ordinarily the patient has no allies who can help him discover the staff's secret: even his family or other patients will withhold such information if privy to it.

[2] Cf. Erving Goffman, *Behavior in Public Places,* New York: Free Press of Glencoe, 1963.

[3] We use the phrase "structural conditions" to emphasize that the conditions are conceived of as properties of social structural units. These units may vary from the smallest (such as role, status, or relationship) to the largest (such as organization, community, nation or society) and may be either larger or smaller than the unit of discussion. Usually they are larger contextual units. Structural conditions tend to have a determining or guiding effect on the unit of discussion. Since structural conditions are the tools-in-trade of most sociologists, this footnote is not meant for them. The structural conditions under which interaction takes place, however, are not typically included in the work of social psychologists, especially those trained in departments of psychology.

[4] We shall assume that the staff members all share the same awareness and the staff's definition of a patient's identity (dying) is correct.

(3) To prevent the patient's comprehension of the truth, the personnel utilize a number of "situation as normal" interaction tactics. They seek to act in his presence as if he were not dying but only ill. They talk to him as if he were going to live. They converse about his future, thus enhancing his belief that he will regain his health. They tell him stories about others (including themselves) who have recovered from similar or worse illnesses. By such indirect signaling they offer him a false biography. Of course, they may directly assure him that he will live, lying with a clear purpose.

To supplement these tactics the staff members use additional ones to guard against disclosure. They carefully guard against the patient's overhearing any conversation about his real condition. They engage also in careful management of expressions, controlling their facial and other gestures so as not to give the show away:[5] they must control the expression of any sadness they experience over the patient's approaching death. Almost inevitably they attempt, not always consciously, to reduce the number of potentially disclosing cues by reducing time spent with the patient or by restricting their conversations with him.

(4) In such collusive games, the teamwork can be phenomenal but the dangers of disclosure to the patient are very great. Unless the patient dies quickly or becomes permanently comatose, the patient tends to suspect or even clearly understand how others identify him. Patients do overhear occasional conversations about themselves. Personnel unwittingly may flash cues or make conversational errors, which arouse the patient's suspicions. Day and night staff may give him contradictory information or divergent clues. The frequent practice of rotating personnel through the hospital services, or adding new personnel, may add to the danger of disclosure. The patient himself may become more knowledgeable about what is going on around him after some days in the hospital, or after repeated hospitalizations. Eventually he may also understand that the hospital is organized not to give him all the information about his condition but rather to withhold most information. He therefore takes what is told him with a grain of salt and some distrust of its accuracy. In short, the original structural conditions that sustain closed awareness begin to disappear, or are counteracted by new structural conditions that make for suspicion or open awareness. This is true even when the patient's symptoms do not badly worsen, but when he does turn worse this may cause him to ask new questions about his illness, which staff members need to handle cannily to keep from him their knowledge that he is dying.

(5) Some interactants may wish to move him along into other types

[5] Erving Goffman, *The Presentation of Self in Everyday Life,* Edinburgh, Scotland: University of Edinburgh, 1956; see also the Anchor edition.

of awareness context. If so, they can employ certain interactional tactics which are, for the most part, merely the opposites of the non-disclosure tactics. Intentionally, a staff member may give the show away wholly or partly, by improper management of face, by carefully oblique phrasing of words, by merely failing to reassure the patient sufficiently about a hopeful prognosis, by changing all talk about the future into concentration upon the present, or by increasing avoidance both of conversation and the patient himself. Of course, personnel occasionally may just plain tell him that he is dying.

(6) The closed awareness that "surrounds" the dying patient has many significant consequences for patient and staff. The patient, unaware of the other's view of his identity, cannot act as if he were aware of dying. Thus, he cannot talk to close kin about his fate. He cannot assuage their grief. Nor can he act toward himself as if he were dying, by facing his expected death gracefully — or with panic and hysteria.

The kinsmen and hospital personnel are saved from certain stressful scenes that accompany open awareness about death, but they are also blocked from participating in various satisfying rituals of passage to death. Wives cannot openly take farewells of husbands; personnel cannot share the patient's sometimes ennobling acceptance of death. A profound consequence for the hospital itself, as well as for staff, of the closed awareness context is an interesting division of labor wherein nurses carry the brunt of stressful verbal interaction during which dying and death talk must be avoided. The physicians escape much of this stress since only brief visits are required for patients seemingly on the mend, hence talk is held to a minimum. Moreover, the climate of certain hospital services would be quite different (usually less oppressive) if closed awareness contexts were completely absent — as they are on certain special types of hospital wards.[6]

Previous Analyses of Interaction

The notion of awareness context is useful for understanding other theoretical approaches to awareness as it relates to social interaction. Our paradigm for the study of interaction within awareness contexts may be used to locate, in a single scheme, the diverse aspects of awareness and social interaction attended to in sociological writings. To illustrate this application of both concept and paradigm, we shall discuss the theoretical work of George H. Mead and Erving Goffman as well as the researches of Donald Roy and Fred Davis. Rather than assess their work *per se*, we shall discuss the writings of these men

[6] Cf. Renée Fox, *Experiment Perilous*, Glencoe, Ill.: The Free Press 1959.

as good examples of the current state of theory and research about social interaction.

George H. Mead:

Mead's concern with social interaction was secondary to a lifetime preoccupation with the problems of social order and its orderly change. We interpret his analysis of interaction — also his writing about communication and thought — as bearing principally on an open awareness context. In a well known passage he wrote that: "In short, the conscious or significant conversation of gestures is a much more adequate and effective mechanism of mutual adjustment within the social act — involving, as it does, the taking, by each of the individuals carrying it on, the attitudes of the others toward himself — than is the unconscious or non-significant conversation of gestures." [7] For Mead, "awareness" was essentially an *accurate* awareness of how one's own gesture (vocal or otherwise) was being defined by others, followed by further action based on that awareness. Thus: "That process . . . of responding to one's self as another responds to it, taking part in one's own conversations with others, being aware of what one is saying and using that awareness of what one is saying to determine what one is going to say thereafter — that is a process with which we are all familiar" (p. 217). This perceptive social philosopher gave his readers a rich but highly generalized analysis of that universal situation in which men genuinely and openly communicate.

Mead was not always consistently concerned with shared communication but — as the preceding quotations suggest — also with how one guesses the other's perception of his behavior so as further to direct that behavior oneself. Whether on the basis of these guesses one then misleads the other or plays the game honestly is left ambiguous. Presumably Mead meant the ensuing interaction to be genuinely open and cooperative.[8] The full force of our commentary on this aspect of his work is best demonstrated by an unusual passage wherein Mead raises and dismisses those aspects of interaction that do not involve shared symbolization. He remarks:

> There is, of course, a great deal in one's conversation with others that does not arouse in one's self the same response it arouses in others. That is particularly true in the case of emotional attitudes.

[7] Anselm Strauss (ed.), *The Social Psychology of George Herbert Mead,* Chicago: University of Chicago Press, 1956, p. 173. All references are to this volume.

[8] Herbert Blumer, in pointing to the great value of Mead's approach, has also emphasized concerted action, whether accomplished or developed. See Blumer's "Society as Symbolic Interaction" in Arnold Rose (ed.), *Human Behavior and Social Processes,* Boston: Houghton Mifflin, 1962, esp. pp. 187-188.

> One tries to bully somebody else; he is not trying to bully himself. . . . . We do at times act and consider just what the effect of our attitude is going to be, and we may deliberately use a certain tone of voice to bring about a certain result. Such a tone arouses the same response in ourselves that we want to arouse in somebody else. But a very large part of what goes on in speech has not this . . . status.
>
> It is the task not only of the actor but of the artist as well to find the sort of expression that will arouse in others what is going on in himself. . . the stimulus calls out in the artist that which it calls out on the other, but this is not the natural function of language. . . ." (pp. 224-226).

And what is the natural function of language? "What is essential to communication is that the symbol should arouse in one's self what it arouses in the other individual." Mead seems here to touch on interaction based on something different from open awareness and genuine communication. In deliberate bullying, for example, one's activity may frighten the other but does not frighten oneself. In writing poetry, one finds the means to arouse responses in others [to] what one finds in himself (and Mead remarks that Wordsworth took some years to turn those immediate responses into poetry). And in this same passage, Mead notes that "we do not assume that the person who is angry is calling out the fear in himself that he is calling out in someone else;" that is, in this spontaneous expression of feeling, actor and audience do not respond identically. We should not be surprised to find, sandwiched within this passage, Mead's laconic comment that though we can act — quite like the actor does — "It is not a natural situation; one is not an actor all of the time." Of course no one is! But what about the times when we do act?

Mead's analysis is especially pertinent to this paper because it emphasizes a property of interaction so often absent in other men's work: the developmental properties of interaction. In Mead's writing the concept of significant symbol not only underscores the consensual character of social order but also shows how social order is changed — how social objects are formed and transformed during the course of constructed acts. In current reading of Mead, this developmental aspect tends to be overlooked; so does his processual, rather than substantial, treatment of the self. The self as process insures that interaction is usually not static or merely repetitive. In Mead's world, acts are open-ended, frequently surprising to the actors themselves. And in some of his finest writings Mead emphasizes how even past events are reconstructed, powerfully influencing the directions taken by present events. In short, interaction always tends to go somewhere, but exactly where is not always known for certain by the interactants.

Erving Goffman:

Erving Goffman's work is probably the most influential among current theoretical analyses of interaction. If he does not stand at an opposite pole from Mead, he surely stands far removed—in style, temperament, theoretical perspective, and above all in his focus on the interplay of people. In his first book, *The Presentation of Self in Everyday Life,*[9] one can easily follow his detailed central analysis of interaction.

From the beginning, Goffman emphasizes an audience's need to define an individual's identity. "When an individual enters the presence of others, they commonly seek to acquire information about him or to bring into play information about him already possessed" (p. 2). Whether or not an actor wishes, his actions yield impressions of him to his audiences. Therefore, people most frequently "devote their efforts to the creation of desired impressions" rather than act completely without guile or contrivance. "Engineering a convincing impression" is an inescapable fact (p. 162). It is a way for each interactant "to control the conduct of others" (p. 2).

Because of such impression management, "events may occur within the interaction which contradict, discredit, or otherwise throw doubt upon the actor's projection of himself." Much of Goffman's book turns around the confusion or embarrassment that occurs when interaction is thus disrupted. He analyzes extensively the "preventive practices" consequent upon disruptions: "defensively by the actor himself, and protectively when the audience strives to save the definition of the situation projected by another" (p. 7).

In all of this, Goffman focuses on closed awareness. He has a section on "team collusion" (pp. 112-120), and another on the maint[en]ance of expressive control" (pp. 33-37). Second, he explicitly treats pretense awareness contexts. For instance, "each team tends to suppress its candid view of itself and of the other team, projecting a conception of self and a conception of other that is relatively acceptable to the other. And to insure that communication will follow established, narrow channels, each team is prepared to assist the other team, tacitly and tactfully, in maintaining the impression it is attempting to foster" (page 107).[10] In general, Goffman, at least in this volume, is uninterested in open awareness contexts; and though he touches on contexts where audiences are suspicious of the actor's projected definition, he does not go into the ways in which the suspicion gradually grows and then is validated.

But whether pretense or closed awareness is at issue, Goffman's

[9] All references are to the original Edinburgh edition.

[10] This passage is a pretty fair description of the situation in which a dying patient and his nurses both engage in pretense by delicately avoiding talk about the patient's impending death.

principal focus is on how the interaction is kept going, or if disrupted, how interactants manage to get it going again. He has little interest in awareness contexts that are transformed through the deliberate operations of the interactants or through the continued course of the interaction itself. Indeed, his analysis is geared to episodic or repeated interactions rather than to sustained interplay. Consistently with this non-developmental focus, his dramaturgical model refers to the *team* of stage actors who night after night seek to create an acceptable illusion, rather than to the *drama* itself, with its plot line and evolving, relatively unpredictable, sequence of transactions.[11] Particularly it is worth underscoring that the identity of Goffman's actor is rarely problematical to himself, but only and always to his audience.[12]

In this book Goffman tends to leave implicit the structural conditions imposed by the larger social unit. Rather, he focuses mainly on situational conditions such as setting and front and back regions. Of course, most interaction in *The Presentation of Self* occurs in establishments containing service personnel and clients, insiders and outsiders; that is, persons who are either relatively unknown to each other or respectively withhold significant aspects of their private lives from each other. Goffman leaves to his readers the task of considering what kinds of structural conditions might lead to interactions quite different from those described. For example, his discussions of impression management might have been very different had he studied neighborhood blocks, small towns, or families, where participants are relatively well known to each other. Similarly, he is not much concerned with systematically tracing various consequences of the interaction (especially for larger social units); although for interactants, of course, consequences are noted in terms of specific linkages with the disruption or smooth continuance of encounters.

Aside from its restricted range of awareness contexts, Goffman's world of interaction is non-developmental and rather static. In other writings, he is concerned with interaction of considerable duration, but characteristically his interest is in the rules that govern that interaction. Often interaction proceeds to its termination almost as inexorably as a Greek tragedy.[13] For these aspects, however, his analysis is a considerable advance beyond those of his predecessors.

Next we re-examine two useful papers, our aim being first, to

[11] Many readers seemed to have missed this point. Cf. a similar comment in Sheldon Messinger, Harold Sampson and Robert Towne, "Life as Theater: Some Notes on the Dramaturgic Approach to Social Reality," *Sociometry*, 25 (March, 1962), p. 108.

[12] To Goffman, surprise means potential disruption of interaction—as compared with Mead's notion of the creative and surprising impulsivity of the "I."

[13] Cf. Messinger, *et al.*, *op. cit.*

locate the reported research within our awareness paradigm; second, to assess its contribution to interactional analysis; and third, to suggest what might be added to that analysis if one were now to undertake such research.

Donald Roy:

In his "Efficiency and 'The Fix': Informal Intergroup Relations in a Piecework Machine Shop,"[14] Roy is interested in demonstrating "that the interaction of two groups in an industrial organization takes place within and is conditioned by a larger intergroup network of reciprocal influences." The interaction is a contest between management and the workers. The latter adroitly scheme, connive and invent methods for attaining quotas set by management; while management attempts to minimize the success of these "black arts of 'making out.'" These arts "were not only responses to challenge from management but also stimulations, in circular interaction, to the development of more effective countermagic in the timing process" established by management's timecheckers. An important segment of Roy's discussion deals with "intergroup collusion" among workers from other departments, who become allies in this unending contest with management.

Where shall we locate Roy's research in our awareness context paradigm? From Roy's description, the awareness contexts are not entirely clear since we do not always know the extent to which management was aware of what was going on among the workers. But in general, workers' attempts to keep closed awareness about their specific collusive games seem to have alternated with management's periodic awareness of such games. Whether this periodic awareness of management transformed the closed context temporarily into pretense or open awareness is difficult to determine. Roy does, however, clearly give the structural conditions that permit both the closed awareness context and its periodic, temporary transformation to pretense or open before the workers reinstitute the closed context with a new collusive game.

Roy describes in great detail the interactional tactics of both sets of players which maintain, transform and reinstitute closed awareness. Teamwork on the worker's side is exceptionally well sketched. Managerial tactics, however, are described principally from "below," for two reasons. First, Roy was doing field work as an industrial worker, and could scarcely be privy to management's specific perspectives and decisions. Second, he did not need to scrutinize management's views because his research was designed to explore how workers organized their work.

In spite of the fact that Roy describes the phases through which

[14] *American Journal of Sociology*, 60 (November, 1954), pp. 255-266.

the contest, and hence the awareness context, oscillates, true temporal development is lacking. This is because he conceives of the interaction as unendingly the same. Apparently the limits of the interaction were set by the time period devoted to the research itself. As Roy himself notes in passing: "How far the beginning of the series [of new rules] antedated the writer's arrival is not known. Oldtimers spoke of a 'Golden Age' enjoyed before the installation of the 'Booth System' of production control." An interest in interaction process must raise these questions: from what situation did the interaction phases develop, where did they end, and what happened if someone attempted to bring the collusive interaction out into the open?

The consequences of the interaction are noted sporadically — mainly in terms of work blockages and cumulative inefficiency — but again we might wish to know much more, especially about diverse consequences for the functioning of the organization at large.

Fred Davis:

A very different presentation of interaction is Fred Davis' "Deviance Disavowal: The Management of Strained Interaction by the Visibly Handicapped."[15] The sub-title accurately describes what this paper is all about. The visible stigma of the handicapped person presents a threat to sociability which "is, at minimum, fourfold: its tendency to become an exclusive focal point of the interaction, its potential for inundating expressive boundaries, its discordance with other attributes of the person and, finally, its ambiguity as a predicator of joint activity." These are "contextual emergents which, depending on the particular situation, serve singly or in combination to strain the framework of normative rules and assumptions in which sociability develops."

After a discussion of these various emergents, which constitute a grave threat to interaction, we are shown "how socially adept handicapped persons cope with it so as to either keep it at bay, dissipate it or lessen its impact upon the interaction." The analysis is aimed at delineating "in transactional terms the stages through which a social relationship with a normal typically passes." The stages are: (1) fictional acceptance, (2) "breaking through" or facilitating normalized role-taking, and (3) institutionalization of the normalized relationship. From the viewpoint of the handicapped person, the "unfolding" of the stages represents deviance disavowal; from that of the normal person it is normalization. For each stage in the process, a certain number of interactional tactics are noted, though Davis is more interested in interactional stages than in the "tremendous variety of specific approaches, ploys and strategems that the visibly handicapped employ in social situations."

[15] *Social Problems*, 9 (Winter, 1961), pp. 120-132.

This research deals with the transformation of pretense awareness ("fictional acceptance") to open awareness ("institutionalization of the normalized relationship"), chiefly but not solely under the control of transforming operations by the handicapped. As Davis describes it, the handicapped person attempts first to keep interaction in the fictional mode (both interactants mutually aware of his stigma but neither acting as though it existed); then, gradually, the handicapped person engineers matters to a final phase where it is openly "fitting and safe to admit to certain incidental capacities, limits, and needs" — that is, where both parties may openly refer to the stigma of the handicapped person.

Davis' discussion is additionally rich because he makes some very explicit remarks about how difficult the open awareness (normalization) phase is for either party to maintain. For instance: "to integrate effectively a major claim to 'normalcy' with numerous minor waivers of the same claim is a tricky feat and one which exposes the relationship to the many situational and psychic hazards of apparent duplicity. . . ." By implication, this relationship between the two parties has a future: because it is difficult to maintain, it cannot remain at a standstill. We say "by implication" because Davis is content to carry the story only to where something like normal sociability can take place. Said another way, Davis actually is analyzing a developmental — not merely an engineered — interaction situation. "As against the simplistic model of a compulsive deviant and a futile normalizer we would propose one in which it is postulated that both are likely to become engaged in making corrective interactional efforts toward healing the breach." Precisely because *both* are likely to make those correctional efforts, this is a developmental relationship. Our paradigm helps raise the question of where the relationship is going and what further transformations, under what conditions, may occur.

Our paradigm also suggests focusing on both parties to the interplay even when it is relatively adeptly controlled by one, since our understanding of the relationship's developmental aspects necessarily requires knowledge of the actions and awareness of both parties. Thus, how does the normal interactant see the handicapped, and the interaction, at various phases of the interaction — and what is he doing, or deciding to do, about it? What will his tactics be, whether occasional or continual? Davis also assumes that the handicapped person has often been through this type of interaction — hence has evolved tactics for handling it — while the normal person is a novice. This may be so, but in actual life both players may have had similar experiences.

Lastly, Davis attempts to specify one class of structural conditions that permit the handicapped person to manage strained interaction. He begins his paper by referring to "that genre of everday intercourse" which is characteristically face-to-face, not too prolonged but not too fleeting either, with a certain degree of intimacy, and "ritualized to the extent that all know in general what to expect but not so ritualized as to preclude spontaneity and the slightly novel turn of events." This explicit detailing is not a mere backdrop but an intrinsic part of the analysis of interaction in the presence of physical stigma. The consequences of interaction (e. g., the satisfaction of both parties and the possibility of a continuing relationship) are left mainly implicit.

General Implications of Paradigm

Our examination of these four writers indicates that future research and theory on interactional problems should encompass a far broader range of phenomena than heretofore. Of course, one need not do everything demanded by the paradigm. But it guides the researcher in exploring and perhaps extending the limits of his data, and in stating clearly what was done and left undone, perhaps adding why and why not. The paradigm helps the theorist achieve greater clarity, integration, and depth of analysis by encouraging reflection upon what he has chosen *not* to make explicit. It also raises questions about development and structure that a straight factor approach to the study of interaction typically does not:[16] How does one type of context lead to another; what are the structural conditions — including rules — in the relevant institutions that facilitate or impede existence of a context, and changes in it; what are the effects of a changing awareness context on the identity of a participant; why does one party wish to change a context while another wishes to maintain it or reinstate it; what are the various interactional tactics used to maintain or reinstate change; and what are the consequences for each party, as well as for sustaining institutional conditions?

This developmental focus helps to eliminate the static quality and restricted boundaries for analysis that are characteristic of the factor approach. The factor approach is useful only when the analyst is conscious of the location of his conceptual boundaries within a larger developmental, substantive scheme, and can thereby explain their relevance to his readers, rather than implicitly declaring all other substantive factors out of bounds. Only then is it sensible to leave out so

[16] The factor approach is a standard one in sociology: it is legitimated by the notion that one can only consider so much at one time with precision and clarity, and therefore boundaries must be chosen, usually according to one's interests, provided they are theoretically relevant. For a discussion of "simultaneous *versus* sequential" factor models, see Howard S. Becker, *Outsiders,* New York: The Free Press, 1963, pp. 22-25.

much that other sociologists, in the light of present theory and knowledge, recognize as relevant to the area under consideration.

The focus on structural conditions increases the likelihood that the microscopic analysis of interaction will take into account the nature of the larger social structure within which it occurs. The usual structural approach in sociology tends to neglect microscopic analysis of interaction and also inhibits attention to its developmental character. Our paradigm encompasses in one developmental scheme the twin, but often divorced, sociological concerns with social structure and social interaction. Neither need be slighted, or forgotten, for a focus on the other.

Our discussion has touched on only four possible types of awareness contexts: open, closed, pretense and suspicion. These four types are generated by the substantively relevant combinations of four variables found in our study of the literature and in our data on awareness of identity and interaction. We have considered two variables as dichotomous — *two interactants; acknowledgment of awareness* (pretense or no pretense) — and two as trichotomous — *degree of awareness* (aware, suspicious and unaware); and *identity* (other's identity, own identity, and own identity in the eyes of the other). Logical combination of these variables would yield 36 possible types, but to start research with all the logical combinations of these variables would be an unnecessarily complex task, considering that many or most types are empirically non-existent. Therefore, the procedure used to develop awareness context types related to interaction was first, to search data for relevant types; second, to logically substruct the variables involved; and third, on the basis of these variables to judge whether other possible types would be useful or necessary for handling the data.

Presumably, more empirically relevant types can be found by scrutinizing the sociological literature, one's own data, and one's own life.[17] Another implication of the present analysis is that increasingly complex types of awareness contexts and their distinctive consequences should be systematically sought. We recommend our procedure for evolving types, as opposed to starting out with the full set of logical combinations, each of which must then be screened for empirical relevance.

We suggested, at the beginning of the paper, two factors that further complicate awareness contexts: additional people, and people

[17] We are working with the "unawareness" context, in which neither party knows the identity of the other or his identity in the other's eyes. This is illustrated by strangers meeting or passing each other on a dark street. If they stop to talk, the first task they are likely to engage in is to transform the "unawareness" context to facilitate interaction.

representing organized systems with a stake in certain types of awareness context. Certain types of social phenomena are probably strategic for extending our knowledge of awareness contexts: for example, research discoveries in science and in industry, spy systems, deviant communities whose actions may be visible to "square," types of bargaining before audiences, such as occurs in diplomatic negotiations, and unofficial reward systems like those depicted by Melville Dalton and Alvin Gouldner.[18]

[18] *Men Who Manage,* New York: Wiley, 1959; and *Patterns of Industrial Bureaucracy,* Glencoe, Ill.: The Free Press, 1954, respectively.

41. Self-Conception and Ward Behavior in Two Psychiatric Hospitals

Thomas S. McPartland, John H. Cumming, and Wynona S. Garretson

This paper reports the results of two separate studies which test the usefulness of certain social psychological notions in describing, explaining and predicting the behavior of psychiatric patients in the ward setting. The first study was done on the wards of a small (72 beds) municipally supported hospital which emphasizes active and intensive treatment of acute disorders;[1] the second study, a replication of the design and procedures of the first, was done in a State Mental Hospital with 1,420 beds.[2] Both researches were done with newly admitted patients. The two studies are reported together because they used the same design and practically the same procedures, because they are based on and therefore test the same underlying assumptions, and because their results support and illuminate each other.

We set out in both studies to examine the usefulness of a direct approach to the self-conception in explaining the variations in behavior observed among recently admitted psychiatric patients. We used patients' responses to the question, "Who am I?" to derive descriptions of patients' conceptions of self (1, 2, 3), and the reports of ward personnel to make determinations about the characteristic behavior of patients. We found that certain formal differences in self-identification are reliably related to differences in the ward behavior of patients. We further found that the observed relationships between attitudes toward the self and behavior were consonant with inferences made from social psychological propositions about the dynamics of human social behavior.

From *Sociometry,* XXIV (June, 1961), pp. 111-124, by permission of the American Sociological Association and the authors.

[1] This research was supported by a grant (M-1882) from the National Institute of Mental Health and conducted, under the auspices of the Greater Kansas City Mental Health Foundation, by John H. Cumming and Thomas S. McPartland.

[2] This research, a deliberate replication of the first, was directed by Wynona S. Garretson and carried out by members of the Sociology Research Club at Iowa Wesleyan College.

Procedures and Relevant Assumptions

The Twenty Statements Problem is the device we used to characterize the different self-conceptions of patients.[3] This problem asks the respondent to write 20 different answers (or as near 20 as he can) to the question, "Who am I?" and provides no further structure to guide him in answering this rather challenging question. In both studies we gathered groups of patients and described our objectives in very general terms. Then the problem was distributed. At the top of a single sheet of paper were a set of instructions. Numbers from 1 to 20 ran down the left-hand margin. The instructions were read aloud from a copy of the form. They were: "There are twenty numbered spaces on this sheet. Just write twenty different things about yourself in the spaces. Don't worry about how important they are or in what order you put them. Just write the first twenty answers you think of to the question: 'Who am I?' " Some patients inquired whether a particular response was "right"; the answer was always given, "Yes, write whatever you think answers the question." After about 15 minutes the sheets were collected. A small number of respondents wrote only five or six responses and then gave signs that they regarded the task finished. These were quietly informed that they might leave if they wished. Others wrote a half dozen statements, or even fewer, and continued to sit in a thoughtful attitude until the end of the period. It should be pointed out that the same kinds of behavior in the test situation have been observed in many groups of non-patients.

The device involves certain assumptions which need examination, particularly when it is used with psychiatric patients, people who have long been supposed to have disturbed conceptions of themselves. Indeed, it was a moot question, at the outset, whether psychiatric patients would be able or willing to respond to the "Who am I?" problem at all. (The answer to this question is "yes"; more than 95 per cent of psychiatric patients wrote codable responses to the Twenty Statements Problem.)

The crucial operational assumption which underlies the Twenty Statements Problem is that scientifically important parts of the self-conception are available to awareness and can be put into words. We are primarily concerned, therefore, with that very important block of "intended" behavior which is carried out in socially defined, normatively governed situations. This choice of focus does not deny the importance of behavior which is "unconsciously determined." Neither does this emphasis dismiss as unimportant those unquestioned patterns of action which are so deeply imbedded in cultural expectations that they rarely come to awareness.

[3] This device was originally presented and discussed in reference (1).

Nevertheless, it is of scientific interest to develop and to test hypotheses which deal primarily with the conscious control of behavior when the population studied is psychiatrically ill and is characterized by disturbed behavior. We assume that the behavioral deviations which define various functional illnesses are special cases of events and processes which are observable in all human social behavior and that the dynamics of pathological behavior, apart from organic and toxic syndromes, are not different in kind from the dynamics of other, "normal" behavior, although they obviously differ in detail. In addition, we make the assumption that ongoing social and cultural events have major consequences in the behavior of normal and psychiatrically ill persons alike; the logic of our research, and of psychiatric treatment as well, rules out the assumption that basic patterns of personality organization and social behavior are immutably set by either bio-physical determinants or past experiences.

We assume, more generally, that one's self-conception is an internalization and organization of identities which significant others have attributed, or currently attribute to one, combined in some way with the results of interactions based on these identities. We also assume, on symbolic interactionist premises, that the person sees himself involved in social action and that he organizes his behavior symbolically to fit his conceptions of himself, of the other actors in the situation, and of the situation in which action takes place. If these assumptions hold for psychiatric patients, then differences in conception of self will co-occur with differences in behavior, while similarities of self-conception will be associated with similarities in behavior. The key questions then become: (a) Are there socially relevant behavioral differences which correspond to different self-conceptions? (b) If there are, what dimensions of the self-conception are relevant to predictions about particular kinds of behavior? (c) Are there operations which will permit empirically useful statements to be made about similarities and differences in patients' self-conceptions? For the purpose of this paper, these three questions may be stated as one: Can responses to the Twenty Statements Problem distinguish among self-conceptions in ways which are relevant to observable differences in the behavior of acutely ill psychiatric patients? By dealing with this compound question, this paper proposes a partial answer to the three more general questions.

The hypothesis implicit in the above question is that the responses which psychiatric patients give to the Twenty Statements Problem can be separated into meaningfully and reliably different kinds of self-conceptions and that these different kinds of self-conceptions are related to differences in behavior in the hospital ward setting. Also implicit in the question is the expectation that the characteristic ward behavior of patients can be reliably differentiated. The discussion of the categorization of self-conceptions will precede the discussion of behavioral characterizations of patients.

It is obvious that an adult might make many hundreds, or indeed, thousands of statements which identify or describe himself. Twenty statements represent a very small fraction of all possible statements that a respondent might make. The median number of responses actually given by different groups of patients to the Twenty Statements Problem varied from ten to fourteen. This compares with a median of about seventeen statements in the replies which have been collected from "normal" adults. The evidence at hand indicates that these very small samples of statements about the self are nevertheless useful samples, since they permit differentiation among persons and reliable predictions about certain aspects of their behavior.

In view of the unstructured problem which is set before respondents, it is noteworthy that responses to the Twenty Statements Problem do not vary greatly in form and can be reliably categorized into four rather discrete groupings along a spectrum of self-identifying references, at different levels of abstraction from social experience. The categories are described in another publication (3) from a different point of view, and more fully in a manual which is available on application to the authors.

The most concrete level of reference which we distinguish presents the self as a physical entity (I am six feet tall, I weigh 170 pounds) or as an identity card does (age, sex, home address, eye color, hair color, and the like). We designate this class of self-identifications "A" and relate it theoretically to experiences of self as a concrete organism with at best indirect reference to interpersonal transactions. Of course, the capacity to write a statement in English, reporting this kind of experience of the self, requires a fairly high degree of socialization, and the terms of self-identification are certainly consensual and commonly used, but the notion of self reported in the concrete class of "A" statements is a physical organism moving in space and time, without reference to, or involvement in, social relations or socially consequential action. To write the statement, "I am 28 years old," requires knowledge of a written language, a scheme of counting, an established calendar, and a way of relating personal existence to the passage of time; it does not require a relationship with other human beings and social institutions in the way that the statement, "I am a student," does. In the frame of reference proposed by G. H. Mead (4), "A" self-identifications imply no *others*, although they certainly present the self as a social object.

We use the letter "B" to designate statements which abstract institutionalized statuses or roles as self-identifying references and therefore imply a "generalized other" on an institutional pattern. Examples are: "I am a student" (related to some educational organization and through it to others in their various statuses in that organization),

"I am a Catholic," "I am a father," "I am a taxpayer." We also use this category to include statements which give a status-like form to less clearly institutionalized self-references, e.g., "I am a music lover," "I am a newspaper reader," "I am a whiskey drinker." "B" statements generally support inference to experience of the self as involved in structured interpersonal relations, as governed by a web of rights and duties, as related to others through the mediation of internalized norms.

The "C" category includes statements which abstract characteristic ways of acting, feeling, or responding in social interaction. "I am moody sometimes," "I like to be with people," "I am afraid of new things," "I enjoy good music," "I love my husband," are examples. The *others* implicit in this kind of statement are not generalized into institutional patterns or abstract rules of conduct; rather, other people and other objects appear as individual preferences or dislikes or as sources of particularized approval, support, agreement, enjoyment, or antagonism. The identities presented in "C" statements are not bound by institutional contexts but rather are "situation-free" personal characteristics which are, nevertheless, normatively governed, and communicable in the terms of ordinary discourse. "C" statements have the common characteristic that they support inference to an experience of self as a person interacting more or less directly with other persons with a minimum of institutional mediation, but within normative limits and generally toward consensually supported goals.

We use the letter "D" to designate our fourth category of self-identifying statements. The category subsumes statements which abstract social experience in terms which imply no particular context, act or attitude of interactive consequence, or which so remove the self from interactive commitment as to be ambiguous or non-differentiating, e.g., "I hope for the best for all," "I would like to try to be better." "D" statements support inference to experience of the self which transcends human social action or interaction, e.g., "I am one with God," "I am an intelligence;" or which negates personal commitment, e.g., "I am just one among billions," "I am nobody." The internalized *others* implicit in "D" statements about the self are transcendental ("the cosmos" or "mankind"), rather than "generalized" in the Meadian sense, and float beyond the possibility of consensual validation or even verifiable communication.

Although the "D" category is necessarily defined negatively, since it subsumes statements which by definition transcend consensual validation, it is worth noting that it is *not* a residual category in the sense that statements which do not fall in categories "A," "B," or "C" are collected by "D."

Viewed together, the "A," "B," "C" and "D" categories of self-identifying statements represent a spectrum which runs from conceptions of the self as a physical structure in time and space (category "A") through conceptions of the self as existing in social structures (category "B") and as a social interactor somewhat abstracted from social structures (category "C") to conceptions of the self abstracted from physical being, from social structure and from social interaction (category "D"). The letters used to designate the categories reflect the logical order of successive abstractions which is implicit in this conceptualization, and at the same time avoid any inferences about "goodness" or "badness" which more descriptive designations might invite.

In addition to the logical order of abstraction which the categories appear to have, they can be shown to have a "natural order" as well. To the extent that descending order on the page reflects successively "deeper" or "more defended" layers of the self-conception, these data also have relevance to interesting questions about the organization of self-conceptions which cannot be discussed here. Kuhn and McPartland (1) have reported that *consensual* self-identifications (nearly equivalent to the structural "A" and "B" categories of this analysis) are consistently listed first on the page, thus are more salient than sub-consensual self-identifications (generally equivalent to categories "C" and "D"). This ordering, among normal respondents, tends to place every consensual statement before any sub-consensual statement and is consistent enough to yield Guttman scales with coefficients of reproducibility above .90 in several different replications. Thus, categories "A" and "B" taken together are prior in order on the page to "C" and "D," in normal populations. This ordering does not appear with equal consistency in the responses of psychiatric patients, however, suggesting one kind of "disturbance" in the self-conceptions of patients.

Further, the relative ordering of the "A" and "B" categories on the page of responses to Twenty Statements Problems is such that "A" statements, if any are made, are consistently made early, followed by "B" statements, and then, as has been said, by "C" statements. "D" statements are rare in normal populations, but when they appear, they usually appear at or near the bottom of the list of responses.

It is obvious that this four-fold categorization of self-identifying statements does not exhaust the logical possibilities nor the empirically useful categorizations of this kind of content. Kuhn (2) has proposed to differentiate self-identifications on the basis of references to (a) social groups, (b) ideological beliefs, (c) interests, (d) ambitions, and (e) self-evaluations. Still other potentially useful schemes of analysis are discussed in the manual mentioned earlier.

We used these four categories to characterize respondents as well as responses. During the early work on the first of the two studies reported here we speculated that a respondent whose replies fell predominantly in the "A" (physicalistic) category might by hypothesized to exist in a "sub-social" state of being and, therefore, that his behavior would meet the expectations of social situations at a minimal level, or below. We speculated further that respondents whose replies fell modally in the "B" category of institutional memberships would behave in socially effective ways and be responsive to the role requirements under which they found themselves. Using the same line of reasoning, we speculated that persons whose responses fell modally in the "C" category of "situation-free" self-identifications would be freer and more variable in behavior than those whose responses fell in the "A" or "B" modes; and that persons whose responses fell in the "D" mode would be so free and variable in their behavior that they would frequently violate the norms of the situations in which they found themselves, behaving in bizarre and extravagant ways.

We treated these speculations about the self as hypotheses in the first study reported here. The replication, of course, took the findings of the first study as its hypotheses.

There are two important comments to be made about the use of modal categories of responses to characterize respondents. The first is a conceptual comment, the second is empirical.

Given the notion of the self-conception as an organization and internalization of past and current social experience, it follows that a marked shift in the social experiences of a person will exert a pressure toward reconceptualization of the self. This reconceptualization might deal only with the content of self-identifications, a change, for example, from "I am engaged" to "I am a married woman." In more radical experiential shifts, or with major changes in behavior of the kind involved in psychiatric hospitalization and treatment, one might look for more radical changes in conception of self, changes in organization and levels of abstraction as well as in content. Of course, one would expect that stable patterns of social experience would be accompanied by correlative stability of self-conception in both form and content. We have evidence, to be presented in another paper, which indicates that these propositions are essentially correct. The point is that the conception of self reported at a given time is probably more accurately interpreted as evidence about a state of being and a set of experiences of the self *at that time* than as an irreversible trend of personality. Thus, when we use modal categories of response to differentiate groups of patients we assume that these modes are influenced by the run of recent social experiences, as internalized and conceptualized by respondents, and that they will change as experiences and behavior change.

As to the empirical properties of modal categories of response, we have found that about nine patients in ten write responses which show a clear mode in some one category, that is, they made at least one more statement in some one category than in any other. The remaining ten per cent either tied in two categories or gave so few responses that the mode was obviously unreliable. These few respondents, nevertheless, were categorized by mode when there was one, or in the more "distinctive" category involved in a tie; in "A" or "D" if one of these was tied with "B" or "C" and in "D" if that category was tied with "A." The rationale is that more unusual responses should receive greater weight in analysis.

The reliability of categorization was high both in the original study and in the replication. For a sample of 60 respondents three independent coders agreed on more than 97 per cent of responses, and on the modal categorization of every respondent.

The operational meaning of the modal category as a characterization of respondents can be made clearer, perhaps, by a fairly simple line of statistical reasoning. The power of a mode to characterize a distribution increases as the modal category exceeds the next most frequent category by a greater number or proportion of items. For the 100 patients in the first of the two studies reported here, there were a total of 1146 responses written to the "Who am I?" question (a mean response total of 11.46 per respondent). Of these responses, 766 fell into the modal categories of the patients making them (.67 of the total) and 252 fell into the next most frequent category (.22 of the total). Thus, on the average, the modal category exceeded the next most frequent by 5.12 responses; the modal category was, on the average, three times as frequent as the next most frequent category of response. This degree of concentration of responses in modal categories appears to justify the use of modes of response to characterize respondents.

The characteristic level of ward behavior of patients was defined differently in the two studies because of differences in the ward procedures of the two hospitals. In the first study, we used accounts of ward behavior which were written by nurses and student nurses. These notes were routinely entered on the charts of every patient every four hours of the waking day. The notes reported instances of grossly disturbed behavior as well as reports of more conventional activities. The reports were made systematically, but were written by different persons at different times, so they may be supposed to vary somewhat while the behavior described remained the same. Again, behavioral reports of this kind may at times employ the same words for quite varied behaviors. Nevertheless, the reports used were written by persons familiar with the behavior of psychiatric patients and, therefore, provided a workable basis for generalized descriptions of patients' behavior.

Another problem in using these accounts of ward behavior as a criterion variable arose from the fact that patients in this hospital often receive drugs which are intended to have marked effects on behavior. Moreover, the ward setting is itself a source of variation in behavior, provoking more activity than usual from some patients, reducing the behavioral output of others. We made no attempt to control such factors in this study.

We took every note written about each patient in our sample of 100 for seven days immediately following completion of the Twenty Statements Problem. Since some patients left the hospital for short periods on passes, there was some variation in the number of entries available for different patients. The usual number of separate entries was 28; the smallest number was twelve. The notes were written in rather standard language, except when unusual events took place. In these cases, the notes gave a descriptive account of what happened.

These notes were readily and reliably categorized, so that we were able to identify the behavioral style which characterized each patient during the week in question. When a patient was described most of the time as "withdrawn" or "seclusive," as "not participating well" or the like, he was characterized as "withdrawn" in his ward behavior. Nine patients in our sample of 100 fell into this category. When a patient was modally described as "cooperative when asked," as "pleasant on approach but not initiating," or as "watching others (in recreation for example) but not participating," he was characterized as "pleasant." This level of interaction was reported for 37 patients.

Thirty patients were described in plurality of ward notes as "socializing well," as "taking an active part" in ward activities, or in other ways reported behaving within the limits of ordinary social expectations. These patients were characterized as "socializing well" in our analysis.

When the ward notes regularly reported that a patient was demanding, hostile, restless, or unruly, he was characterized as "restless." Nine patients fell into this group.

The most extreme forms of deviant behavior were described in some detail in ward notes. Since explosive or bizarre behavior is likely to receive extra weight in clinical thinking, extravagant behavior is also given great weight in the ward social system, by both patients and staff. In order to reflect these facts about ward society, however crudely, we gave double weight to instances of bizarre and "disturbed" behavior in making our characterizations of patients' behavior. With this adjustment, 15 patients fell into the class of extravagant behaviors.

In the replication study, the behavioral characterization of patients was made in the same terms used in the original research: patients were reported to be *withdrawn* (five patients), pleasant on approach (29 patients), socializing well (56 patients), restless (26 patients) and extravagant (four patients). Since no regular behavioral notes were available in this state hospital, it was necessary to characterize the behavior of patients by interviewing the ward personnel who had daily dealings with them. The interviews were focused on the behavior characterizing each patient in the study during the week immediately following the administration of the Twenty Statements Problem. Since each ward had at least two psychiatric technicians who worked with the patients every day, it was possible to take account of possible personal bias in the ward staff's assessment of patients' behavior.

These interviews resulted in complete agreement, as far as placement on the behavioral scale used here was concerned, among the technicians who worked with 106 of the 122 patients involved in the study. In five cases, three technicians agreed about a patient's behavior while another disagreed. In six cases, two agreed while a third disagreed. These cases were assigned to the behavioral level corresponding to the majority opinion. In five other cases, either two or four technicians divided equally on their assessment of a patient's behavioral level. In these cases, the tie was broken arbitrarily in favor of the more deviant behavioral characterization.

Findings

We derived four rather straightforward specific hypotheses from our speculations about the implications of our categories for social involvement and the normative government of behavior. Collectively, the hypotheses represent tests of the general proposition that the self conceptions of people give organization and guidance to their behavior; individually they provide tentative answers to the more specific questions: "What, if any, are the properties of the self-conception which are useful in understanding pathologically deviant behavior?"

We hypothesized: 1. *That persons whose responses to the Twenty Statements Problem fall modally into the "A" category (physicalistic) will have little to guide or motivate socially interactive behavior and thus will be "withdrawn" or under-active on the ward.*

We hypothesized: 2. *That persons whose self-conceptions are dominated by positions in socially defined situations ("B" modes) will behave in "socially acceptable" ways on the ward. Moreover, because of* the loss of role-connected behavior which hospitalization brings, we hypothesized that these persons would frequently show fairly low levels of interaction implied in the description, "pleasant on approach but not initiating," as well as of the socially more effective behavior described as "socializing well."

Closely related to hypothesis 2 is hypothesis 3: *That persons whose conceptions of self depend on styles of acting without reference to particular social situations ("C" modes) will be somewhat "freer" in behavior on the ward than either "A" or "B" categories.* Thus we hypothesized that this group would be described as "socializing well" or, because of rather loose involvement in the normative structure of the ward setting, would be "somewhat troublesome," "restless," "demanding," or "non-cooperating" in ward procedures.

Last in this series of hypotheses which relate ward behavior to different ways of conceiving of the self was the proposition that: 4. *Persons who make a modal number of statements in the "D" category will transcend the norms and behave on the ward in bizarre, unruly, extravagant or perhaps destructive ways.* But here again, as in other hypotheses, therapeutic effort and the pressure of the ward organization toward socially acceptable behavior led to modification of the hypothesis so that persons in the "D" category were expected to behave in "somewhat troublesome" or "restless" ways as well.

Table 1 shows the results of cross-tabulation of modes of self-conception and characteristic behavior on the wards of the small hospital, which emphasized intensive treatment. Small frequencies in some cells made it desirable to collapse the "withdrawn" and "pleasant" columns, yielding a class of "too little behavior" judged by the norms of the ward. Similarly, the "restless" and "extravagant" columns were collapsed into a class of "too much behavior" in the ward setting. The "socializing well" column was retained. The resulting table yields a chi-squared of 25.65 with six degrees of freedom, $P<.001$.

Table 1. The Association Between Modes of Self-Conception and Ward Behavior of Newly Admitted Patients in a Small, Active Treatment Psychiatric Hospital

	Model Ward Behavior					
Modes of Self-Conception	Withdrawn	Pleasant	Socializing Well	Restless	Extravagant	Total
A	6	11	3	1	0	21
B	0	9	5	1	0	15
C	2	9	14	2	4	31
D	1	8	8	5	11	33
Total	9	37	30	9	15	100

Table 2 shows data from the replication study, conducted in a state hospital with less pressure toward intensive treatment, with a longer average stay, and with different admission regulations, so that more deteriorated alcoholics, more patients with brain syndromes, and more long-term psychotics may be in the sample. With the same combination of columns as in Table 1, the table yields a chi-square of 35.59, $P<.001$.

Table 2. The Association of Modes of Self-Conception and Ward Behavior of Newly Admitted Patients in a State Mental Hospital

	Modal Ward Behavior					
Modes of Self-Conception	With-drawn	Pleasant	Socializing Well	Restless	Extravagant	Total
A	3	8	6	1	2	20
B	1	11	30	4	0	46
C	0	3	14	6	1	24
D	1	7	6	15	3	32
Total	5	29	56	26	[6]	122

Table 3 is a combination of Tables 1 and 2, and is presented to bring all available evidence to bear on the specific hypotheses about direction of deviation of patients in the four modes.

Hypotheses 1 and 2, relating "A" and "B" modes to deviation toward "too little behavior" in the ward situation, are strongly supported by the data; .87 of the "A" deviations are in the hypothesized direction, as are .81 of "B" deviations. Hypothesis 4, relating "D" modes to deviation toward "too much behavior," is sustained, although less strongly: .67 of deviations are in the hypothesized direction. Hypothesis 3, relating "C" modes to "too much behavior," fails to be confirmed; patients with this mode of response who deviate from ward behavioral norms are as likely to deviate toward too much behavior as toward too little. This result is due largely to the data from the small, municipally

Table 3. The Association Between Modes of Self-Conception and Deviant Ward Behavior Among Newly Admitted Patients in Two Psychiatric Hospitals

	Modal Ward Behavior		
Modes of Self-Conception	"To Little" Behavior	"Too Much" Behavior	Total
A	28	4	32
B	21	5	26
C	14	13	27
D	17	34	51
Total	80	56	136

Chi-square = 30.60 D.f. = 3 P<.001

supported hospital, as inspection of Tables 1 and 2 will show (11 contradicting cases out of 14). It should be pointed out that this hospital regularly uses tranquilizing drugs to control problematic behavior on the wards, and that there is considerable likelihood that the low levels of behavioral output observed in this group of patients may be due to the effects of these drugs, prescribed in generous amounts to patients who are serious management problems without them. The definitive decision on this line of speculation may come from research now under way.

It is worth noting that the distributions of modes of self-identification in the patient populations of the two hospitals confirm the conclusions of McPartland and Cumming's paper (3) on the relation of social class to self-conception and psychiatric illness. They report high incidence of "B" modes among middle-class adults, high proportions of "C" modes among lower-class respondents. The patient population of the small, acute-treatment center is drawn, by the eligibility rules of the hospital, from among the medically indigent, i.e., from lower socio-economic levels. The patient population of the state hospital is drawn, in the nature of the case, from a wider socio-economic range. The populations of the two hospitals differ in the proportion of "B" modes (.15 in the one, .38 in the other), in the direction which would have been predicted on the basis of the socio-economic origins of the respective populations. The difference in the proportion of "B" modes is significant beyond the .02 level (two-tailed test). The difference in the proportion of "C" modes in the two hospitals (.31 in the municipal hospital, .20 in the state hospital) confirms Cumming and McPartland's findings beyond the .05 level of significance.

Discussion and Implications

It seems desirable to warn against inference from our findings. We have no direct evidence that any kinds of self-conceptions, as we differentiate them, correspond to any proneness to psychiatric illness in persons outside a psychiatric hospital. We are inclined, on theoretical grounds and on the basis of fragmentary evidence, to think that the so-called "psychotic break" which results in hospitalization involves changes in both social participation and in conception of self. Therefore, we do not think that information about the self-conception alone will support predictions about the incidence of behavioral disturbance, but only about its character if disturbance occurs.

This research is addressed to a rather simple issue: "Can differences in people's reports of self-conception be used to predict behavior in realistic social situations?" The results of these two studies indicate that the self-conception, defined by the operations we use, can support predictions which are sufficiently precise for useful application to ward management in psychiatric hospitals. At the same time, the evidence presents features which indicate revision of our originally rather crude formulation of the relationship between different conceptions of self and behavioral differences.

Summary

This paper reports the results of a study of the relation of patients' reported conceptions of self to their behavioral characteristics in psychiatric treatment setting, and its replication in a markedly different hospital. Both studies find that self-conceptions, as reported in writing in response to the question, "Who am I?" are reliably related to different levels of ward behavior and to the occurrence of grossly disturbed actions as well. The studies use the analyses of different kinds of self-conceptions to bring these findings into relationship with the theoretical notions of symbolic interaction.

1. Kuhn, M.H., and T.S. McPartland, "An Empirical Investigation of Self-Attitudes," *American Sociological Review,* 1954, 19, 68-78.
2. Kuhn, M.H., "Self-Attitudes by Age, Sex, and Professional Training," *Sociological Quarterly,* 1960, 1, No. 1.
3. McPartland, T.S., and J.H. Cumming, "Self-Conception, Social Class and Mental Health," *Human Organization,* 1958, 17 (No. 3), 24-29.
4. Mead, G.H., *Mind, Self and Society,* Chicago: University of Chicago Press, 1934.

42. The Self in the Emotionally Disturbed[1]

William R. Rosengren

As George H. Mead has pointed out, human beings tend to act on the basis of their inferences about the probable behavior of others toward them.[2] Moreover, our feelings about ourselves are mediated by how we think others feel about us. This is to say that much of our behavior is guided by what we think others are thinking and by our confidence in what we judge to be the readiness of others to act upon what we think they impute to us. In brief, it is axiomatic in Mead's psychology that there are functional relationships between how we see ourselves, how we see others, and how we think others see us. Similarly, basic to Mead's theory is the idea that such relationships have important consequences in overt behavior and are also phenomena of interpersonal perception.

While it may be logically reasonable to set forth such principles, the occasion to validate them by means of operational procedures is less frequently at hand. For it seems implicit in Mead's theory that it is necessary to take temporal changes into account in order to demonstrate empirically functional relationships among the self processes. Ideally, changes in the self would occur over a relatively long period of time during which the individual moves sequentially through the stages of the play, the game, and the generalized other. Moreover, once having developed to that stage of socialization, most persons maintain a rather stable and continuing set of relationships among the functions of the self. In terms of the consequences in overt behavior, Sullivan has referred to such stability as "the repeated situations which characterize a human life."[3] Whatever the terminology, how-

From *The American Journal of Sociology,* LXVI (March, 1961), pp. 454-462, by permission of the University of Chicago Press.

[1] Part of a four-year project in social psychiatry under Grant OM-21 from the National Institute of Mental Health, United States Public Health Service.

[2] George Herbert Mead, *Mind, Self, and Society* (Chicago: University of Chicago Press, 1934).

[3] Harry Stack Sullivan, *Conceptions of Modern Psychiatry* (Washington, D. C.: William Alanson White Psychiatric Foundation, 1947), p. vi.

ever, the behavior of persons becomes relatively stable and predictable insofar as there is some convergence between how they see themselves, how they see others, and how they think others see them.

In the case of persons undergoing intensive psychiatric treatment, however, basic changes in interpersonal behavior frequently occur very rapidly. Therefore, the study of emotionally disturbed persons may offer opportunities to put to the test some aspects of Mead's theory which, under normal circumstances, would require either many years to do or could be done only by clinical or retrospective analysis.

With the exception of clinical descriptions of distorted self-concepts of individual psychiatric patients, little empirical evidence is available about the processes of self-definition, inference, and imputation among persons who have been institutionalized for emotional disturbance.[4] The purpose of this paper is to report the findings of a study of interpersonal inference and imputation among a group of institutionalized emotionally disturbed children whose chief reason for hospitalization was inadequate reciprocity with others. A major aim is to demonstrate empirically changes in the functional relationships of the processes of the self, before and after long-term residential treatment, and to report their relationships to other indexes of changed behavior.

The subjects were ten boys, ranging in age from ten to twelve years, who were receiving long-term residential treatment in a private psychiatric hospital for children. The total patient population numbered fifty-six, of which the subjects constituted one of six units. They had all received clinical diagnoses of "Passive-Aggressive Personality — Aggressive Type" and were the only patients in the institution who were homogeneously grouped on the basis of diagnosis and symptomatology. Such patients are more commonly referred to as "acting-out"; their overt behavior is generally typified by spontaneous verbal and physical aggression, short attention span, and inability to delay gratifications, and they tend to have histories of interpersonal difficulties with both adults and peers. At the time of the first testing, all of the boys had lived together twenty-four hours a day for at least one year, and some for as long as two years.

Procedures

Interpersonal Perceptions.

In September, 1958, an "inference-imputation" test was administered

[4] The most recent published attempt to put to test operational aspects of the social psychology of Mead is, perhaps, Carl J. Couch's "Self-attitudes and Degree of Agreement with Immediate Others," *American Journal of Sociology,* LXIII (1958), 491-96.

to the subjects along with tests of several other criteria. This "Self-definition Test" involved nineteen interpersonal qualities which were dichotomized into those which are "friendly-accepting" and those which are "hostile-rejecting" in nature; these are shown in Table 1.

Two days prior to the individual testing sessions, each boy was asked the following "near-sociometric" questions: (1) "Which of the boys (in the unit) do you like best of all?" (2) "Which do you dislike the most?" (3) "Which do you think likes you the most?" and (4) "Which do you think dislikes you the most?"

Table 1.

Interpersonal Qualities

Friendly-accepting	Hostile-rejecting
Generous	Selfish
Good	Bad
Nice	Mean
Smart	Dumb
Kind	Cruel
Brave	Afraid
Clean	Dirty
Well-liked	Ugly
Honest	
Strong	
Neat	

For ease in administration, each quality was printed in India ink on a 5 x 7-inch card. Each boy then sorted the cards at least five times: (1) a description of himself *(self-definition)*, (2) a description of the boy he had chosen as the one he liked best *(imputation)*, (3) a description of the boy he had chosen as the most disliked *(imputation)*, (4) a description of himself from the point of view of the boy whom he thought liked him *(inference)*, and (5) a description of himself from the point of view of the boy whom he thought disliked him *(inference)*. Those boys who had been chosen by others as either "I think he likes me" or "I think he dislikes me" were then asked to describe the individuals who had chosen them in those ways.

One year later, in September, 1959, the boys underwent the identical sociometric and inference-imputation procedures.

Observation

Over a six-month period—from October, 1958, to March, 1959, —the subjects were observed by a non-participant observer in a variety of situations for a total of sixty hours of direct observation. The overt behavior of the ten boys was rated on a "moreness-lessness" basis using the qualities of interaction listed in Table 2. Those on the left of the rating scale are symptomatic forms of behavior, while those on the right are non-symptomatic for this diagnostic category of patients. The methods, procedures, and findings of this part of the study are reported elsewhere.[5]

Table 2.
Scale for Behavior of Rating "Acting-out" Patients

Symptomatic Behaviors	*Non-symptomatic Behaviors*
Irrelevant: Diffuse and random activity	*Relevant:* Goal-directed activity
Active: Mobile, labile, expressive behavior	*Passive:* Restrained, inexpressive, inactive behavior
Rejecting: Disassociates from others; rejects interactions	*Affiliative:* Associates with others; responds to and initiates interactions
Narcissistic: "Exclusive" interest in self	*Other-oriented:* Shows interest in others, positively or negatively
Dominant: Attempts to dominate, control, and direct	*Submissive:* Submits to domination, control, and direction by others
Succorant: Seeks help, assistance, support, and affection	*Nurturant:* Gives help, assistance, support, and affection
Aggressive: Attempts to destroy, humiliate, and degrade	*Blamavoidance:* Withdraws from or otherwise avoids aggression-eliciting situations
Immediacy: Seeks for immediate gratification	*Endurance:* Foregoes immediate satisfactions for future gratifications
Impulsive: Spontaneous and unreflectful behavior	*Deliberation:* Hesitant, cautious, and reflectful behavior
Non-verbal: Little talking of affiliative or rejecting type	*Verbal:* Much talking either of affiliative or rejecting type

Control-eliciting behavior

The behavior of patients of this type occasionally becomes so dangerous either to themselves or to others that, if some means of restraint were not used, severe physical harm would result. In such instances the acting-out patient is placed alone in a locked room until his behavior becomes physically tolerable. Accurate records are maintained of

[5] See William R. Rosengren, "The Social Field in Relation to the Behavior of Emotionally Disturbed Children," *Sociometry* (in press).

the use of this means of restraint in the institution. These data were accumulated for each of the ten subjects at the end of one year.

Institutional expectations

In both 1958 and 1959 the subjects responded to a test of "institutional expectations."[6] This consisted of ten story completions in which a boy was depicted as engaging in some moderately acting-out form of behavior in an institutional setting. The boys responded to each story by describing events which they expected would follow the incident which was presented. One, for example, read as follows: "Bob is supposed to take pills in the morning and in the afternoon. But he doesn't swallow them — he throws them out the window. One day the nurse found out about it and then. . . ." The subjects' responses were classified as involving either hostile or benign institutional responses. An example of a hostile expectation is, "she (the nurse) drags him to the room and gives him needles and he gets sicker." An example of a benign expectation is, "She tells him that the pills help him so he takes them." Typically, the more severely disturbed the patient, the more hostile are his expectations and, presumably, his anticipatory responses to them.

Treatment of Data

Interpersonal perceptions

Sums of "friendly-accepting" and "hostile-rejecting" choices were computed on the first (1958) and second (1959) series of self-definition tests on each of the dimensions — inference-imputation, definition-inference, and definition imputation. The study was chiefly concerned with changes in the similarity and dissimilarity in choices of qualities in the one year. Because the total number of choices was not the same for all the subjects on either the first or the second series, changes were measured in terms of proportions rather than raw choice scores. Comparing, for example, the similarity of self-definitions and inferences, a "similar" choice was regarded as one in which the subject defined himself as generous and expected (inferred) that others (either the liked or disliked person) would also define him as generous. There were two possibilities for "dissimilar" choices: (1) the subject defined himself as generous but felt that the referent person would not so define him; or (2) the subject did not ascribe the quality of generosity to himself but felt that the referent person would define him as generous.

[6] This was an adaption of a similar set of story completions reported in W. and J. McCord, *Psychopathy and Delinquency* (New York: Grune & Stratton, Inc., 1957).

Proportions of each similar inference-imputation, definition-inference, and definition-imputation dimension were computed in that fashion for each subject on the first and then on the second testing.

The significance of proportional change was computed through the use of the Wilcoxon Matched-Pairs Signed-Ranks Test, with probability levels derived directly from the value of T.[7] In all cases the one-tailed test was used because the direction of change was predicted.

The following classification was used for comparing the boys' patterns of interpersonal definition with the other indexes of change: Frequency distributions were made for the total quantity of proportional change under each perceptual relationship for each subject. Those whose total proportion of change in self functions was one standard deviation or more above the mean for the ten subjects were classified as "high self-changers." Those whose extent of change was one standard deviation or more below the mean are referred to as "low self-changers." In these terms there were three high and three low self-changers.

Other indexes of change

At the end of the six-month period of observation, frequency distributions were made of the extent of change in overt behavior as indicated by the rating scale (Table 2). The extent of change was determined by the difference between the sums of scores on the left side of the scale during the first three months and the sum of scores on the left side during the second three months. Three of the boys had undergone significant changes from symptomatic to non-symptomatic behavior (one standard deviation or more above the mean), and three had experienced comparatively little change in behavior (one standard deviation or more below the mean).

Similar frequency distributions were made of the number of "isolations" which each boy had elicited by his physically intolerable behavior during the first six months as compared with the second. Finally, computations were made on both the first and second testings of the number of "benign" [and] the [number of] "hostile" expectations of the institution which each boy had expressed.

Some Expectations from Mead's Theory

Clinical knowledge concerning the disturbance syndrome of the patients as well as participant observation for a year and a half formed the chief basis of the general hypotheses; Mead's principle of the interrelated-

[7] This statistic is described and probability tables presented in S. Siegel, *Nonparametric Statistics for the Behavioral Sciences* (New York: McGraw-Hill Book Co., 1956).

ness of self-definition, inferences of others, and imputations by others underlay each expectation.

It was expected that on the first test the boys would define themselves quite differently from the ways in which they thought others would define them, as compared with the second test. Moreover, it was anticipated that the inferences they made of others on the first test would be different from others' actual imputations, as compared with the second test. More specifically in Mead's terms, it was expected that after one year the subjects would tend to "call out in themselves the responses which they think they call out in others" and that they would " call out in others responses similar to those which they think they call out in others. "

Furthermore, it was anticipated that inferences of others would be less contingent upon the "liked-disliked" distinction on the second test as compared with the first. More specifically, it was expected that the boys would infer *more* friendly-accepting qualities of disliked persons and *less* friendly-accepting qualities of liked persons on the second test as compared with the first. Both of these related hypotheses were intended to serve as a means of empirically demonstrating whether the boys would make inferences concerning the ways in which they thought others viewed them with regard to a generalized conception of others' points of view — what might be referred to as the "generalized others" — or would persist in making inferences with reference to specific others in the environment.

Table 3. Similar Self-Definitions and Inferences of Others' Imputations: Signed Ranks Proportions for First and Second Tests

Inference	*N**	*T*	Less Frequent Sign	p (One-tailed Test)
Liked and disliked persons	10	3	–	>.005
Disliked persons only	10	9	–	>.025
Liked persons only	10	8	–	>.025

*Refers to the elimination of tied proportions between pairs. Levels of significance for N's less than 25 are determined directly from the magnitude of T.

Third, it was expected that the boys would tend to make different inferences concerning liked and disliked persons on the first test and more similar inferences on the second. Specifically, it was anticipated that inferences concerning disliked persons' imputations would be less accurate on the first test as compared with the second. Moreover, it was expected that inferences concerning liked persons' imputations would also be less accurate on the first test than on the second, that is, that the boys would tend to "take the role of specific others" in regard to themselves in an inaccurate fashion on the first test and the "role of the generalized other" in a more accurate fashion on the second test.

Last, it was expected that the boys would tend to define themselves more similarly to the ways in which they thought others defined them on the second test as compared with the first. Specifically, the subjects would define themselves significantly more as they thought the disliked persons defined them. It was also anticipated that a similar change would take place with regard to the liked persons. These two propositions were designed to test the expectation that the subjects would tend to define themselves more in terms of a conception of a generalized other than in terms of a consideration of specific individuals about whom they had contrasting attitudes themselves.

In general, therefore, the data were analyzed with a view to determining the extent of convergence with some basic principles of Mead's social psychology.

First, it was expected that on the first test the subjects would tend to define themselves differently from the ways in which they thought others defined them, while on the second test self-definitions and inferences of others' imputations would be more similar. This expectation was borne out with respect to disliked as well as liked persons (Table 3). There was significantly more similarity between how the boys defined themselves and how they thought both liked and disliked persons would define them on the second test as compared with the first.

Second, it was expected that a comparison of the responses on the first and second tests would reveal an increased tendency for the boys to define themselves more as others actually defined them. This expectation was also borne out with regard both to liked and disliked persons, although with somewhat greater confidence in relation to the liked persons (Table 4). In general, the data suggested that on the second test the subjects defined themselves more like the ways in which they thought others would define them. Moreover, there was a tendency for the "others" actually to impute those qualities which the boys thought would be imputed to them.

Furthermore, it was predicted that the subjects would be less likely to infer hostile-rejecting qualities of the disliked persons and friendly-accepting qualities of the liked persons on the second test than they did a year earlier (Table 5). There was, in fact, a tendency for the boys to infer, proportionately, more friendly-accepting qualities of the persons whom they disliked and less hostile-rejecting qualities on the second test. Moreover, they also tended to expect proportionately less friendly-accepting imputations by liked persons on the second test. These findings may indicate that on the second test the subjects made inferences on the basis of a somewhat more generalized view of themselves rather than of a conception of specific persons' probable views of them.

Table 4.
Similar Inferences of Others and Imputations by Others: Signed-Ranks Proportions for First and Second Tests

Person Making Imputation by	*N**	*T*	Less Frequent Sign	p (One-tailed Test)
Liked and disliked	10	2	—	>.01
Disliked only	10	8	—	>.025
Liked only	10	0	—	>.005

*See n. to Table 3.

The fourth general expectation was related to the issue of the subjects' accuracy in making inferences about other persons' imputations to them. Was there, in other words, a tendency for the boys increasingly to "call out from others the responses which they thought they called out in others"? The findings with regard to person referent — liked and disliked — and type of qualities inferred — friendly or hostile — are reported in Table 6.

As Table 6 indicates, the most discriminating differentiation was that in which the referent person involved as well as the distinction between friendly and hostile qualities were controlled. The most significant change between the first and second test was with respect to the disliked rather than the liked persons. Specifically, the subjects

Table 5.
"Friendly-accepting" Qualities Inferred of Specific Others: Signed-Ranks Proportions for First and Second Tests

Referent	*N**	*T*	Less Frequent Sign	p (One-tailed Test)
Disliked person	10	1	—	>.005
Liked person	10	0	+	>.005

*See n. to Table 3.

tended to infer qualities of disliked persons more similar to those which were actually imputed to them by disliked persons on the second test, as compared with the first. Furthermore, while there was increased similarity concerning inferences of friendly imputations by liked persons which was not statistically significant, the changes which did appear were in the predicted direction. With this qualification, the data do suggest two tentative conclusions. First, the boys were more accurate in inferring those qualities which others actually imputed to them. Second, this might indicate that on the first test the boys attempted to define themselves from the point of view of specific others, and to do this in a comparatively inaccurate way. On the second test, however, they seemed to define themselves from the point of view of a more generalized frame of reference which resulted, in fact, in considerably greater accuracy in inferring imputations by specific others.

Table 6.
Similar Inferences and Implications: Signed-Ranks Proportions for First and Second Tests

Referent and Inference-Imputation	*N**	*T*	Less Frequent Sign	p (One-tailed Test)
All persons, all qualities	10	2	—	>.01
All persons, "friendly"	10	1	—	>.005
All persons, "hostile"	10	1	—	>.005
Liked persons, all qualities	10	0	—	>.005
Liked persons, "friendly"	10	6	—	>.025
Disliked persons, all qualities	10	8	—	>.025
Disliked persons, "friendly"	9	1	—	>.005
Disliked persons, "hostile"	9	0	—	>.005
Liked persons, "hostile"	6	3	—	<.025

*See n. to Table 3.

Finally, it was anticipated that on the second test the boys would be more likely to define themselves in the same terms as they thought both the liked and disliked persons would define them. That is, greater similarity between self-definitions and inferences was expected. As can be seen in Table 7, significant changes could best be identified when the referent person and the type of interpersonal quality were controlled. Specifically, the boys did tend to define themselves somewhat more as they thought the disliked persons would define them, but only with regard to the hostile-rejecting qualities. Moreover, while the increased similarity in this regard relative to the liked persons was not beyond what could have been expected by chance alone, it was in the predicted direction. It might be concluded, therefore, that on the first test the boys defined themselves as they thought both liked and disliked persons would do, but only with regard to friendly-accepting qualities. On the second test, however, they showed an increased inclination to include hostile-rejecting qualities in the similarities between how they defined themselves and how they thought significant others would define them.

Table 7.
Similar Self-definitions and Inferences: Signed-Ranks Proportions for First and Second Tests

Referent and Self-definition-Inference	*N**	*T*	Less Frequent Sign	p (One-tailed Test)
All persons, "hostile"	9	0	—	>.005
Disliked persons, all qualities	10	5	—	>.01
Disliked persons, "hostile"	10	0	—	>.005
All persons, all qualities	9	10	—	<.025
All persons, "friendly"	10	22	+=—	<.025
Liked persons, all qualities	10	14	—	<.025
Liked persons, "friendly"	10	10	—	<.025
Liked persons, "hostile"	9	8	—	<.025
Disliked persons, "friendly"	9	11	—	<.025

*See n. to Table 3.

When one contrasts the responses of the subjects on the first test with those on the second, several distinct patterns appear. On the *first* test they tended to define themselves dissimilar to the ways in which they thought others defined them. Second, both liked and disliked persons tended to impute to the subjects qualities dissimilar to those which the subjects expected would be imputed to them. Furthermore, the subjects tended to expect that liked persons would impute significantly more friendly-accepting qualities and that disliked persons would impute significantly more hostile-rejecting qualities. This is to say that their inferences about themselves appeared to be made with reference to particular persons in their immediate experience. Fourth, they were comparatively inaccurate in inferring what qualities others — both liked and disliked persons — would actually impute to them. Last, they tended to define themselves differently from the ways in which they thought both liked and disliked persons would define them with an accompanying tendency for them to be somewhat more sensitized to friendly-accepting than to hostile-rejecting attributes.

On the *second* test, on the other hand, they tended to define themselves more as they thought others defined them. Second, both the liked and the disliked persons tended to impute those qualities which the inferring subjects thought the others would. Third, the boys tended to expect that liked persons would impute significantly more hostile-rejecting qualities and that the disliked persons would impute more friendly-accepting qualities. Fourth, they were somewhat more accurate in inferring those qualities others actually imputed to them. Last, they tended to define themselves somewhat more as they thought both the liked and disliked persons would define them and were increasingly accurate in regard to hostile-rejecting qualities.

In terms of Mead's theory of the self, it would appear that on the first test the boys tended to (1) call out in themselves responses unlike those which they thought they called out in others, (2) call out in others responses unlike those which they thought they called out in others, (3) make inferences from the point of view of specific others rather than of a generalized other, and (4) define themselves in terms of specific other persons.

On the second test, on the other hand, they tended to (1) call out in themselves responses more like those which they thought they called out in others, (2) call out in others responses more like those which they thought they called out in others, (3) make inferences from the point of view of a generalized other rather than of specific others, and (4) define themselves in terms of a generalized other rather than of specific others.

Relationship to Other Indexes of Change

Although these findings may well suggest that both the functions and the content of the self changed significantly in the one year, it is of further interest to know to what extent and in what ways such patterns might be associated with other indexes of change.

First, the three "high self-changers" were also the three boys whose overt behavior changed most significantly from symptomatic to non-symptomatic during the six months in which observational ratings of behavior were made: the boys whose self functions more nearly approximated Mead's ideal were those who experienced increasingly fewer difficulties with both their peers and the adults working with them. Conversely, those whose self processes changed the least along lines of Mead's expectations were those who continued both to initiate symptomatic interactions and reacted to others in a significantly symptomatic fashion.

Second, with regard to highly disruptive behavior which necessitated isolation of the patient, the three high self-changers were also those who were significantly less often isolated in the one year than formerly. On the other hand, those boys whose self processes changed the least were also the ones who were isolated either significantly *more* often, or as often, in the one year.

Last, with regard to expectations of the institution, the three high self-changers were also the boys whose expectations of the institution's actions toward them changed most significantly from "hostile" at the beginning of the year to "benign" at the end. Conversely, the "low self-changers" continued comparatively often to expect hostile action and seldom to expect benign action in the one year.

On the basis of these findings it is concluded that, in the boys studied, changes in the functions and content of the self were associated with overt changes in behavior as well as with changes in a somewhat more basic orientation toward their immediate social environment.

Conclusions

This paper has reported an attempt to relate data from a test of interpersonal inferences, imputations, and self-definitions to some of the chief assertions of Mead's social psychology. The findings are tentative, and the conclusions and interpretations which have been made are best regarded as only suggestive. Because of the small number of subjects involved and the difficulties characteristic of studies of interpersonal perception,[8] both the findings and the conclusions are best regarded as a preliminary effort.

The concept of the self as used in the social psychology of Mead is one that continues to be an intriguing basis for much speculation and interpretation. It also continues, however, to present many difficulties for empirical investigation and validation. The limited field study reported in this paper is an attempt to put the concept of the self to empirical test with a view to further elaborating its importance in human behavior.

[8] See, e.g., L.J. Cronbach, "Proposal Leading to Analytic Treatment of Social Perception Scores," in R. Tagiuri and L. Petrullo (eds.), *Person, Perception and Interpersonal Behavior* (Stanford, Calif.: Stanford University Press, 1958), pp. 353-78.

43. Reference Group Influence on Political Party Preference*

Richard S. Brooks

A much-discussed topic in American politics is the hereditary character of political party affiliation. Numerous empirical studies demonstrate that there is a strong tendency for political party preference to be socially transmitted from parents to children, but many of these are exercises in naive empiricism. They establish an empirical fact while failing to offer a systematic explanation which will account for it. There are, however, a few very good studies of this subject. One of the best of these is the study conducted in Cambridge by Maccoby, Matthews, and Morton.[1] But the most important work in this area is that of Herbert Hyman, who summarizes and reports many of the studies of this problem in his recent inventory of research relating to political socialization.[2] In fact, Hyman offers much more than a mere summary of the research on this subject. His orientation to the study of politics not only provides a framework for explaining the tendency of children to adopt the political parties of their parents but also accounts for the deviants who do not follow in the political footsteps of their parents. The present study is an attempt to build upon the work begun by Hyman.

Politics is hereditary, according to Hyman, because the family is so important as an agency of socialization. Throughout the early years of life the child has little contact with any other group; hence the family is the primary agency in shaping and directing the attitudes of children. If a child deviates from the politics of his parents, it is because he has come into contact with new groups which hold norms different from the norms of his parents. "We might generally expect parental influence to wane somewhat

From *Papers of the Michigan Academy of Science, Arts and Letters,* XLVIII (1963), pp. 331-340, by permission of the journal.

*I am greatly indebted to Robert L. Stewart for his help in the preparation of this study.

[1] Eleanor E. Maccoby, Richard E. Matthews, and Alton S. Morton, "Youth and Political Change," *Public Opinion Quarterly,* 18, (Spring 1954), pp. 23-39. This study not only offers a systematic explanation for hereditary politics, but also attempts to account for deviants.

[2] Herbert Hyman, *Political Socialization: A Study in the Psychology of Political Behavior* (Glencoe, Ill.: The Free Press, 1959).

as the individual grows up. He is widening his experiences and may well confront other groups presenting different norms for political conduct."[3]

Although the present study is in fundamental agreement with Hyman's theoretical approach, there is one major point of difference. This difference is the method of determining the groups which present norms for political conduct. Hyman attempts to make this determination in an indirect fashion by using chronological age as an indicator of exposure to new groups and the adoption of new norms.[4] In contrast, this study attempts to ascertain directly the major groups and individuals which present norms for conduct to the individual.

The use of age as an instrument for measuring the emergence of new groups and the relative decline of parental influence presents several difficulties. It is true that as the child grows up he usually comes into contact with new groups, and frequently this results in a decline in parental influence. Hence it is possible to correlate age and political agreement or disagreement of parents and children and find that older children are more likely to be politically different from their parents than younger children. But correlation does not, of course, necessarily mean causal relationship. Many older persons who have had extensive contacts with other groups do not deviate from the norms of their parents. Hyman's approach takes account of those who deviate from their parents, but it does not explain those who, according to his theory, should deviate but do not do so.

Part of this difficulty arises from the implied assumption that mere exposure to new groups causes the parental influence over the child to decline. As the child grows up he is almost inevitably exposed to a larger number of groups, but this does not necessarily mean that these new groups will displace the family as the primary agency of socialization. The important consideration is not exposure, but the extent to which the individual comes to define the new groups as significant to him. For the parental influence to decline, the child not only must come into contact with new groups, but he must come to accept some of these new groups as important to him.

This research project attempts to do two things. First, and most

[3] *Ibid.*, p. 98.

[4] In addition to chronological age, Hyman uses several other items to indicate the extent to which children are exposed to the norms of groups other than the family. For example, he uses sex, social mobility, geographic mobility, strictness of parental control, and a changing social environment. For the most part, these are subject to the same limitations as age: they merely provide the opportunity for children to be exposed to a larger number of groups, while not indicating the extent of psychological identification with the new groups.

ambitiously, it is an attempt to set the problem of explaining party affiliation within the framework of Symbolic Interactional theory, an approach to human behavior which has received fairly wide acceptance in the fields of sociology and social psychology.[5] Secondly, it attempts to provide a more predictive and theoretically relevant instrument than age for measuring the displacement of parents by other groups or persons.

The Symbolic Interaction theory of human behavior has been developed by the Mead-Cooley school of social psychology.[6] Orientations closely related to it are also known as "self-theory,"[7] "reference group theory,"[8] or "role theory."[9]

A basic proposition in this orientation is that human beings derive their norms from the groups with which they identify, not simply from the groups to which they are exposed or of which they are a member. That is to say, individuals learn the appropriate norms of conduct from the groups they feel are significant to them. This general proposition, when applied to political behavior, means that an individual will have the same political affiliation as his "reference groups" or "significant others."[10]

[5] It should be noted that this theory is not limited to explaining political party affiliation, or even political behavior, but is applicable to human behavior in general.

[6] Important pioneer works are George Herbert Mead, *Mind, Self, and Society* (Chicago: The University of Chicago Press, 1934); and Charles H. Cooley, *Human Nature and the Social Order* (New York: Charles Scribner's Sons, 1902). A textbook in social psychology written from this point of view is Alfred R. Lindesmith and Anselm L. Strauss, *Social Psychology*, rev. ed. (New York: Henry Holt and Co., 1956). A brief summary is Bernard N. Meltzer, *The Social Psychology of George Herbert Mead* (Kalamazoo: Division of Field Services, Western Michigan University, 1959).

[7] C. Addison Hickman and Manford H. Kuhn, *Individuals, Groups and Economic Behavior* (New York: The Dryden Press, 1956).

[8] Muzafer Sherif, "The Concept of the Reference Group in Human Relations," in Muzafer Sherif and M.O. Wilson (eds.), *Group Relations at the Crossroads* (New York: Harper, 1953); Herbert Hyman, "The Psychology of Status," *Archives of Psychology*, 1942, No. 269; Tamotsu Shibutani, "Reference Groups as Perspectives," *The American Journal of Sociology*, 60 (May, 1955), pp. 562-569; Robert K. Merton and Alice S. Kitt, "Contributions to the Theory of Reference Group Behavior," in Guy E. Swanson, Theodore M. Newcomb, and Eugene L. Hartley (eds.), *Readings in Social Psychology*, rev. ed. (New York: Henry Holt, 1952); Harold H. Kelley, "Two Functions of Reference Groups," *ibid.*

[9] Theodore R. Sarbin, "Role Theory," Gardner Lindzey (ed.), *Handbook of Social Psychology* (Cambridge, Mass.: Addison-Wesley), 1954, 1, 223-258.

[10] In this paper the terms "significant other" and "reference group" will be used synonymously. They may be defined as a group or person "with

Consistent with this theoretical orientation it can be hypothesized, with respect to the political party affiliation of parents and children, that: (1) if the parents are relatively more significant than other reference groups, the party affiliation of the children will be the same as their parents, and (2) if other groups have displaced the parents as significant others, the party affiliation is more likely to be different from that of their parents.

Two instruments were used to test these hypotheses. One was a "Significant Others Test," and the other was a questionnaire which asked for several items of personal data including the political party preference or affiliation of the students and their parents.

The tests were given to a group of unmarried college students. After eliminating a few students whose parents were divided in their political party preference, 243 students were included in the study. The age distribution of the 243 students was from 16 to 29 years of age, but 203 (83%) were between the ages of 18 and 20. This sample is not representative of any larger population, but the nature of the hypotheses makes this unimportant.

The Significant Others Test (SOT) is of the "open-ended" variety. This type of test has the technical disadvantage of being more difficult to work with than the "check-list" type, but it has the theoretical advantage of not suggesting specific responses. The SOT consists of giving each student a sheet of paper with 20 numbered blank spaces on it. At the top of the page is this set of instructions: "In the spaces provided below please list those persons and groups of persons to whom you refer yourself, either directly or in your thinking, when confronted with a problem, or in order to support or justify your actions."[11]

On the basis of this test each student was placed in a category determined by the saliency of mention of parents or family. Those who mentioned parents or family in first or second position were assigned to the "high saliency group," and those who mentioned parents or family in third place or lower, or who did not mention parents or family anywhere on the test,

---

which an individual feels identified and to which he aspires to relate or maintain his identity." Manford H. Kuhn, unpublished manuscript (undated) Muzafer Sherif and Carolyn W. Sherif in *An Outline of Social Psychology*, rev. ed. (New York: Harper, 1956), pp. 175-177 also emphasize that the reference group is not primarily a matter of membership but a matter of "psychological relatedness."

[11] The Significant Others Test was given its first form by H. L. Mulford, "Toward an Instrument to Measure the Self, Significant Others, and Alcohol in the Symbolic Environ: An Empirical Study," State University of Iowa Library, Ph. D. thesis, 1955, microfilm. However, the form used in the present study was developed by Robert L. Stewart, "The Self and Other Objects: Their Measurement and Interrelationship," State University of Iowa Library, Ph. D. thesis, 1955, microfilm.

were assigned to the "low saliency group." This means that the high saliency students usually list parents or family ahead of all other reference groups, and in no instance did anyone in this group list more than one person or group before parents. All of the students in the low saliency group listed at least 2 persons or groups ahead of their parents or family. Of the 243 students in the survey, 201 mentioned parents or family in first or second place and 42 mentioned them in third place or lower.

When the political preferences of the students in each of these groups were compared to the preferences of their parents, the hypotheses were confirmed. Those students with a high saliency of mention of parents on the SOT tended to have the same party preference as their parents; the low saliency students tended to have a different party preference. Using the chi square test, this association was significant at .001% level. Table I shows that 70% of the high saliency students had the same political party preference or affiliation as their parents, while 57% of the low saliency students was different from their parents.

The SOT proves to be a much better instrument than either age or sex for predicting political party preference. Herbert Hyman reports several studies which show that the agreement between parent and child attitudes declines with age.[12] Table II shows that there is a slight association in this direction for the students in this survey, but it is not significant. A comparison of Tables I and II shows that there is a stronger association between the SOT and political agreement of parents and their children than there is between age and political agreement of parents and their children. It should be emphasized that the division into age groups in Table II is the most favorable possible; any other grouping would be even less significant. Older children are no more likely to be different from their parents than younger

Table I

A Comparison of the Political Preferences of a Sample of College Students and Their Parents, by Saliency of Mention of Parents on the SOT*

	Saliency of Parents					
	High		Low		Total	
Political Preference	No.	Per Cent	No.	Per Cent	No.	Per Cent
Same as parents	141	70.15	18	42.86	159	65.43
Different from parents	60	29.85	24	57.14	84	34.56
Total	201	100.00	42	100.00	243	100.00

*$X^2 = 11.49$; $p < .001$; Q = .52

[12] Herbert Hyman, *Political Socialization,* pp. 98-103.

Table II

A Comparison of the Political Preferences of a Sample of College Students and Their Parents, By Age*

	Years of Age					
	16-18		19-29		Total	
Political Preference	No.	Per Cent	No.	Per Cent	No.	Per Cent
Same as parents	81	69.23	78	61.90	159	65.43
Different from parents	36	30.77	48	38.10	84	34.56
Total	117	100.00	126	100.00	243	100.00

*X^2 = 1.41, not significant; Q = .16

children. However, it should be pointed out that the age range of the 243 students is very small; if the range were greater the results might be different. Table III compares the students to their parents by sex. There is a slight association in the direction of females being more like their parents than males, but again the association is not significant.

Although Table I supports the hypotheses beyond the level of chance, two groups which do not fit the hypotheses need to be explained: (1) the 18 students with the same political party affiliation as their parents who did not mention parents in first or second place on the SOT; (2) the 60 students whose politics was different from their parents but did mention parents in first or second place on the SOT.

For the group of 18 students one possible explanation, consistent with the orientation, is that they have acquired new reference groups with the

Table III

A Comparison of the Political Preferences of a Sample of College Students and Their Parents by Sex*

	Sex					
	Females		Males		Total	
Political Preference	No.	Per Cent	No.	Per Cent	No.	Per Cent
Same as parents	111	68.52	48	59.26	159	65.43
Different from parents	51	31.48	33	40.74	84	34.56
Total	162	100.00	81	100.00	243	100.00

*X^2 = 2.05, not significant; Q = .20

same political party preferences as their parents. New significant others mean new norms, but if the new groups have the same political norms as the parents there will be no change in the politics of the children. Therefore, even under ideal conditions, the instruments of measurement used here should not be expected to predict party affiliation with complete accuracy. A better test of the hypotheses would be possible if the questionnaire obtained not only the political party preferences of the students and their parents but also the political preferences of all persons and groups mentioned on the SOT. It is also possible to explain some of the 18 students in this group on the basis of the need for refinement of the SOT, 8 of these 18 students mentioned parents in third place, and this certainly does not indicate rejection of parents. Only 3 students in this group failed to mention parents at all.

The second group in Table I which does not conform to the hypotheses is the 60 students in the high saliency group whose politics is different from their parents. These are the students whose parents are significant to them but no longer hold, or have not acquired, the political norms of their parents. A possible explanation, consistent with the Symbolic Interactional orientation, is that these students came from homes which placed little emphasis on politics. Perhaps the parents were apathetic toward politics or else presented very weak political norms for the children to follow. Nominally Democratic or Republican parents who are largely disinterested in politics might well produce Independent children. Furthermore, the children of apathetic Independent parents might acquire their norms from partisan peers or other reference groups even though these groups are less significant than the parents. If this interpretation is correct, and since apathy is itself a norm which children can acquire from their parents, one would expect to find a high concentration of Independent students and Independent parents in this group of 60 students.

For the same reason, one would also expect the SOT to be more accurate in predicting the norms of partisan students than of Independent students. Tables IV, V, and VI support this explanation.

Table IV compares the party preference of this group of 60 students to the party preference of all other students in the survey. More than one-half of the group of 60 are Independents, while less than one-fourth of the other 183 students are Independents. Since 36 of this group of 60 students are Independents who have partisan parents, a better test of the hypothesis would be possible if information were obtained on the political involvement of the parents. But, in the meantime, a good hypothesis is that their parents presented weak political norms for the children to follow. Further support for the above explanation can be found by examining the 24 students in this group who identify themselves as partisan but are politically different from their parents. 19 of the 24 have Independent parents; only 5 are Republicans or Democrats with parents of the opposite party. Of the remaining 219 students in the survey, only 41 have Independent parents. This associ-

Table IV

A Comparison of the Political Preferences of the 60 High Saliency Students Who are Different from Their Parents, with All Other Students*

Political Preference	High Saliency Group, Different from Parents		All Other Students		Total	
	No.	Per Cent	No.	Per Cent	No.	Per Cent
Independents	36	60.00	40	21.86	76	31.28
Partisans	24	40.00	143	78.14	167	68.72
Total	60	100.00	183	100.00	243	100.00

*$X^2 = 30.44$; $p < .001$; $Q = .69$

ation in the direction of this group of 24 students being more likely to have Independent parents than the other students produces a chi square 42.77.[13]

Tables V and VI show that the SOT will predict the political norms of the students who express a party preference, but will not predict for the independents. Table V, which includes only partisan students, shows a strong, significant association in the direction of the high saliency students having the same party preference as their parents and the low saliency group being different from their parents. It should be noted that this association is somewhat stronger than in Table I, which includes independents as well as partisans. Since no significant association is present in Table VI, which includes only Independent students, one must conclude that the instruments used in this project will not predict the political affiliation of these students. To predict for this group it would be necessary to obtain

Table V

A Comparison of the Political Preferences of the Partisan Students and Their Parents, by Saliency of Mention of Parents on the SOT*

Political Preference	Saliency of Parents: High		Low		Total	
	No.	Per Cent	No.	Per Cent	No.	Per Cent
Same as parents	113	82.48	14	46.67	127	76.05
Different from parents	24	17.52	16	53.33	40	23.95
Total	[137]	100.00	30	100.00	167	100.00

*$X^2 = 17.25$; $p < .001$; $Q = .69$

[13] $P < .001$.

information on the degree of political involvement of the students and their parents, and information on the political preferences and involvements of all persons named in the SOT.

Table VI
A Comparison of the Political Preferences of the Independent Students and Their Parents, By Saliency of Mention of Parents on the SOT*

	Saliency of Parents					
	High		Low		Total	
Political Preference	No.	Per Cent	No.	Per Cent	No.	Per Cent
Same as Parents	28	43.75	4	33.33	32	42.10
Different from parents	36	56.25	8	66.67	44	57.89
Total	64	100.00	12	100.00	76	99.99

*X^2 = .49, not significant; Q = .22

Conclusions

The significance of this research lies in three areas—the theoretical, the empirical and the instrumental. Results of this investigation illustrate the utility of Symbolic Interactional theory in the explanation of political party preference. Furthermore, the study has produced a basis for making more accurate predictions of party preference than the demographic variables traditionally employed. Finally, a simple and theoretically valid instrument of observation has been employed with considerable success.

44. Role-Taking Accuracy and Adjustment[1]

Sheldon Stryker

The assumption that knowledge is necessarily adjustive and ignorance or lack of knowledge necessarily maladjustive may fairly be said to suffuse the thinking of current social science whether in its "pure" or "applied" forms (8, 19). This assumption is clearly, and perhaps especially, embedded in various therapeutic uses of role-playing techniques (2, 7, 20, 21, 27). It is present as well in the use of role-playing as a teaching aid (4, 15) and in the increased use of this technique in diverse business settings (3, 11, 17). In all these instances, it is assumed that role-playing will improve role-taking skills and that the increases in knowledge of others consequent to improved role-taking will mean more adjusted social relationships.

This line of thinking takes on wider interest with the observation that many who write in the tradition of George Herbert Mead argue the adjustment functions of accurate role-taking (5, 16, 22).[2] Here, it must be stressed that Mead's usage of the adjustment concept differs significantly from contemporary usage. For Mead, adjustment is synonymous with adaptation, both terms referring to a *process* whereby one alters the course of his behavior in terms of the demands of the social situation (18, pp. 155-

From *Sociometry,* XX (December, 1957), pp. 286-296, by permission of the American Sociological Association.

[1] This research was partially supported by a grant from the Graduate School, Indiana University.

[2] While our interest in the question being raised stems from Mead, and thus the paper is oriented to his work and interpretations of it, the fact that persons of somewhat different theoretical leanings present analogous arguments should not be overlooked. So, for example, Sullivan (26) discusses "selective inattention," describing this process as a "security operation" by which "we fail to recognize the actual import of a good many things we see, hear, think, do and say, not because there is anything the matter with our zones of interaction with others but because the process of inferential analysis is opposed by the self system." Sullivan clearly regards selective inattention in negative terms, a "powerful brake on personal and on human progress" and "more than any other of the inappropriate and inadequate performances of life, the classic means by which we do not profit from experience..." (26, pp. 374, 346).

159). Adjustment, as it is currently used, is a static concept, typically referring to an *end-state* of happiness, satisfaction, and the like (10, pp. 48–49). Again, however, the implication of adjustment in the sense of happiness and satisfaction as an end-product of accuracy in the role-taking process had been drawn by many.

Thus, on both practical and theoretical grounds, the answer to the question of the relationship between role-taking and adjustment (as end-state) becomes important. This question may be formulated as an hypothesis: the adjustment of the individual is a function of the accuracy with which he can take the role of the other(s) implicated with him in some social situation.

This hypothesis and the design of the study stem from an interest in testing implications drawn from Mead's theory. Given this interest, we have utilized a conception of role-taking as anticipation of the responses of others implicated with one in an ongoing social situation (18, pp. 151, 242-243, 253-254). Accurate role-taking has been operationally defined as the correct prediction of the responses of others. Role-taking, so conceived, is obviously related to such concepts as empathy, insight, social sensitivity, and so on, studies of which have used similar measurement procedures. These concepts are not, however, synonyms; and the similarity of measurement procedures should not be taken to imply identical conceptualization or theoretical concern.[3]

[3] There is considerable confusion in the literature with regard to the concepts role-taking, empathy, sympathy, identification, insight, social sensitivity, etc. These are sometimes seen as independent, sometimes as overlapping and sometimes as essentially identical. We cannot attempt, here, to distinguish systematically among these concepts: Dymond (9) provides an extensive review of this literature, offering necessary distinctions. Suffice it to say that, for us, role-taking is anticipatory behavior; and that the emotional unity, participation in emotional life of others, "feeling-with" quality, and fellow-feeling that sometimes (although not always) are incorporated into these other concepts are not seen as part of the role-taking concept.

It is true that there may be diverse sources of accuracy when role-taking scores are based on correctness in prediction. From the standpoint of Mead's theory, which postulates that one's behavior is predicated on the symbolic anticipation of responses of others, the "impurity" of our role-taking index is of little consequence. This theory, as it has thus far been developed, does not require distinguishing the various possible bases of accuracy. The problem of "impurities" in studies of empathy, insight, etc., has been attacked by Hastorf and Bender (13), Cronbach (6), and Gage and Cronbach (12). Hastorf and Bender suggest that "projection" can be screened out by subtracting from an accuracy score a second score based on the coincidence of ascriber's own responses and his predictions

The role-taking conception requires that predicter and other be mutually implicated in an ongoing social situation, and that predictions be made with reference to responses meaningfully related to that social situation. These, and consideration of desirable controls, led to the selection of the family as the most appropriate setting for the study. Data pertinent to the hypothesis were gathered in the summer of 1954 from 46 family units, residents of Bloomington, Indiana. Each family unit consisted of a married pair and the parents of one, but not both, of this pair.[4] Each subject responded to a 20-item Likert-type attitude scale dealing with traditionalism in family-related matters.[5] He was asked for his own attitudes, and to predict or ascribe the responses the two other-generation members of his family would make to the items of this scale. An index of role-taking accuracy, consisting of the number of correct predictions person A makes of person B's responses, expressed as a percentage of total predictions of B's responses, was computed for each subject.[6]

From the same set of responses, an index of agreement between parent and offspring was devised, consisting of the percentage of items on which a

---

for another. This technique is unable, however, to distinguish between correct ascriptions based on knowledge and correct ascriptions based on projection when, in fact, ascriber and other respond identically to an item. The technique has the same difficulty with correct predictions when ascriber and other disagree with respect to an item (12). Cronbach (6) develops a model which distinguishes four components of accuracy scores. The model is, however, premised on a research design which requires judges to predict responses of (the same) multiple others, rather than on a design strictly analogous to ours.

[4] In most instances, only the parents of one of the offspring pair resided in the community. When both sets of parents were available, the choice of one was determined by the desire to maintain a balance in the numbers within relationship categories. It should be stressed that "sampling" was not random. We have used statistical techniques based on random sampling, nonetheless, on the grounds that formal (objective) assessment of our data was preferable to nonformal (subjective).

[5] This instrument was adapted from a scale devised by P.E. Huffman (14) and entitled "Traditional Family Ideology Scale." There is evidence from this source that the instrument is reasonably reliable and valid.

[6] Subjects responded to the attitude items via a four-point continuum: Strongly Agree, Agree, Disagree, Strongly Disagree. The decision to use this set of response categories was reached after extensive pretesting designed to provide items which were relatively stable both when a subject responded for himself and when he predicted how another would respond. The requirement of item stability also dictated that the two agree, and the two disagree, responses be scored as identical for purposes of the role-taking index.

given parent's own responses to the items of the scale corresponded with his offspring's responses.

Subjects also responded to a 40-item instrument indexing their adjustment to each of the persons for whom they ascribed attitudinal responses, and to a 10-item instrument indexing their dependence upon these persons. Odd-even correlations of from .88 to .92, and a test-retest correlation of .87, deriving from various pretests of the adjustment index provide evidence that this index meets minimal reliability requirements. That the index is, to a degree, a valid instrument is indicated by its ability to distinguish between groups whose adjustment scores may be expected to differ: e.g., the scores of females with reference to their own relatives are higher than are those of males; scores with reference to own relatives are higher than those with reference to in-laws. We have no reliability data for the dependence index. Validity evidence includes the facts that, in accord with expectations, females indicate a greater degree of dependence upon their relatives than do males, and that there is greater "neutrality" on this index in relation to in-laws than in relation to own relatives. Further, unpublished data show that offspring scores indicating dependence on parent are associated with parent scores indicating dominance over offspring, and that offspring scores indicating dominance over parent are associated with parent scores indicating dependence on offspring.[7]

Table 1

Parent Adjustment by High or Low Role-taking Accuracy

	F-S	F-D	F-IS	F-ID	M-S	M-D	M-IS	M-ID	Row
High									
M	56.70	60.10	54.23	48.67	59.58	58.42	50.58	58.64	55.71
N	10	10	13	12	12	12	12	11	92
Low									
M	59.15	64.15	53.70	58.45	61.55	66.72	55.45	57.08	59.66
N	13	13	10	11	11	11	11	12	92

Completed Analysis of Variance

	Sums of Squares	d.f.	Mean Square	F
Columns	2372.58	7	338.94	2.24
Rows	616.95	1	616.95	4.07
Interaction	627.82	7	89.69	
Within groups	25470.82	168	151.61	

Weighted mean difference, rows: 3.68. F_{95} (1,168) = 3.90.

[7] For more complete accounts of these indices, and the data on the basis of which many of these remarks are made, see (24). The unpublished data will be made available to anyone interested in them.

The study has available, then, indices of role-taking accuracy, agreement, adjustment, dependence, and subjects' own attitudes on family traditionalism.

Each subject ascribed the attitudes of two others. There are, consequently, 16 categories of subjects —8 parent and 8 offspring—each containing the responses of 23 persons. The notations in subsequent tables follow the convention of placing the role-taker first, the person whose role is taken second, and use the following abbreviations: son—S; son-in-law—IS; daughter—D; daughter-in-law—ID; father—F; father-in-law—IF; mother—M; mother-in-law—IM. Thus, for example, the notation S-IF refers to the category comprised of male offspring who ascribed the attitudes of their fathers-in-law.

The expectation from the initial hypothesis is that high role-taking accuracy will be associated with high adjustment. To test this expectation, subjects in the various relationship categories were dichotomized, using median role-taking or ascription accuracy scores as the breaking point. The eight parent and eight offspring categories were grouped and analyzed separately, using analysis of variance.

Table 1 presents the test of the hypothesis for the parent categories. The cell entries are mean adjustment scores, with higher scores indicating better adjustment. There is, it will be noted, a statistically significant difference between the weighted row means. However, the direction of the difference is not in accord with that hypothesized. That is, parents who are comparatively *poor* role-takers are significantly *better* adjusted with reference to their offspring than are parents who are comparatively accurate role-takers. The row mean difference in Table 2, for the offspring categories, is in the expected direction. However, this difference is not statistically significant.

What might explain the inverse, statistically significant relationship between role-taking accuracy and adjustment for the parent category?[8] Clues are provided through speculation concerning the parent-adult offspring relationship and the cited findings, and through a consideration of thinking and research already in the literature.

[8] It has been pointed out to me by Dr. Nathan L. Gage that the inverse relationship between role-taking accuracy and adjustment appearing in Table 1 could occur if there is also an inverse relationship between parent adjustment to offspring and offspring scores on the family traditionalism scale; and that, under these circumstances, the inferences drawn from the table are not warranted. Similarly, the implications drawn from subsequent Tables 3-8 would not be warranted if a negative relationship between parent adjustment and offspring traditionalism existed for the subjects represented in Tables 3, 5, and 7, and if a positive relationship between parent adjustment and offspring traditionalism obtained for the subjects represented in Tables 4, 6, and 8. These possibilities have been checked,

Table 2
Offspring Adjustment by High or Low Role-taking Accuracy

	S-F	S-M	S-IF	S-IM	D-F	D-M	D-I F	D-I M	Row*
High									
M	42.90	57.50	51.89	47.00	58.67	63.46	47.09	52.18	52.91
N	10	10	9	12	12	13	11	11	88
Low									
M	55.62	48.08	48.79	49.73	61.18	60.10	37.75	42.25	50.13
N	13	13	14	11	11	10	12	12	96

*Preliminary analysis of variance indicated no statistically significant difference between row means appears in this table.

Theorizing about the parent-adult offspring relationship, the following assertions seem justified: (a) the self-identifications and respect of parents are bound up with the lives of their *adult* offspring to a greater degree than are those of such offspring with the lives of their parents. That is, (b) parents are psychologically more involved with their offspring than are offspring with their parents. Thus, (c) evidence of gaps between the attitudes and behaviors of parents and offspring are more likely to be resisted and distorted by parents; and (d) when such evidence becomes open and recognized by parents, its consequences for their adjustment to their offspring are likely to be accentuated.

More generally, Moore and Tumin argue that "... ignorance must be viewed not simply as a passive or dysfunctional condition, but as an active and often positive element in operating structures and relations" (19, p. 787). Robin Williams writes: "It is extremely important also that many of the implicit understandings that make society possible are not just *implicit* but are also resistant to statement: it is as if there is a tacit agreement not to express or become aware of what would be dysfunctional.... We suspect that a study of areas of blocked communication would often reveal conflicts that remain non-disabling only so long as they are kept from overt crystallization" (29, pp. 528-529). Pertinent are the researches of William F. Whyte (28) and Howard S. Becker (1). Whyte, describing the social structure of the restaurant, points out that, in a society in which males are expected to originate action for females, interposing a high counter as a physical barrier to free communication between waitresses and countermen filling their orders serves to protect the countermen. Becker suggests that platforms, pianos, chairs, and so on, perform the same function for the dance musician in relation to his audience.

---

using Pearsonian correlations and also using analysis of variance. The results of these analyses were negative; i.e., relationships between parent adjustment and offspring traditionalism which would call for an alternative interpretation of the findings did not occur.

Table 3

Parent Adjustment, High-tradition Parents Only, by High or Low Role-taking Accuracy

	F-S	F-D	F-IS	F-ID	M-S	M-D	M-IS	M-ID	Row
High									
M	53.50	57.20	51.00	42.50	57.80	61.57	48.86	60.20	53.80
N	4	5	7	6	5	7	7	5	46
Low									
M	67.83	62.50	59.83	60.25	65.00	65.40	60.60	60.83	62.87
N	6	8	6	4	6	5	5	6	46

Completed Analysis of Variance

	Sums of Squares	d. f.	Mean Square	F
Columns	1622.09	7	231.73	2.13
Rows	1588.41	1	1588.41	14.60
Interaction	586.78	7	83.83	
Within groups	8270.83	76	108.83	

Weighted mean difference, rows: 8.42. F_{99} (1,76) = 6.99.

The foregoing suggests an hypothesis which would serve to explain the finding that parents who are accurate in their role-taking are significantly less well adjusted to their offspring than are parents who are inaccurate

Table 4

Parent Adjustment, Low-tradition Parents Only, by High or Low Role-taking Accuracy

	F-S	F-D	F-IS	F-ID	M-S	M-D	M-IS	M-ID	Row
High									
M	58.00	66.60	60.50	54.83	63.50	64.60	61.50	61.20	60.98
N	7	5	4	6	4	5	4	5	40
Low									
M	51.50	63.20	48.33	57.43	57.13	59.00	46.57	51.14	54.12
N	6	5	6	7	8	6	7	7	52

Completed Analysis of Variance

	Sums of Squares	d. f.	Mean Square	F
Columns	1356.93	7	193.85	1.37
Rows	1012.96	1	1012.96	7.17
Interaction	587.69	7	83.96	
Within groups	10735.66	76	141.26	

Weighted mean difference, rows: 6.75. F_{99} (1,76) = 6.99.

role-takers, while the same finding does not hold for offspring role-takers. The hypothesis asserts that the greater one's vulnerability in a relationship, the greater the tendency to erect blocks to full knowledge of the other in that relationship.

Data are available to test this explanatory hypothesis. Earlier it was noted that the study provides scores on scales measuring traditional family attitudes, dependence, and agreement of parent and offspring with respect to familial attitudes. It may be expected that highly traditional parents will be more vulnerable in their relations to offspring than nontraditional parents; that parents who are dependent upon their children will be more vulnerable than independent parents; and that parents whose views do not agree with their offspring's will be more vulnerable than will parents whose views coincide with those of their offspring. Treating vulnerability as an intervening variable, from the hypothesis, then, it follows that the inverse relationship between role-taking and adjustment should be more marked for highly traditional parents than nontraditional, for dependent parents than independent, for low-agreement parents than high-agreement.

These expectations are examined in Tables 3-8. In each instance, analysis proceeded as follows: the parent sample was dichotomized, using median scores (on tradition, dependence, agreement). Then, each subsample was further broken down into two categories, accurate and inaccurate role-takers, on the basis of median scores within these subsamples. The cell entries in the tables are, as earlier, mean adjustment scores.

As the analyses of variance indicate, the expectations deriving from the vulnerability hypothesis are borne out. For highly traditional parents

Table 5

Parent Adjustment, Dependent Parents Only, by High or Low Role-taking Accuracy

	F-S	F-D	F-IS	F-ID	M-S	M-D	M-IS	M-ID	Row
High									
M	52.75	57.00	58.00	48.33	57.57	64.43	59.86	60.57	57.65
N	8	4	6	6	6	7	7	7	51
Low									
M	64.80	66.29	57.17	64.17	67.40	67.83	63.00	62.33	64.00
N	5	7	6	6	5	6	7	6	48

Completed Analysis of Variance

	Sums of Squares	d.f.	Mean Square	F
Columns	1099.01	7	157.00	1.12
Rows	1119.86	1	1119.86	8.01
Interaction	642.53	7	91.79	
Within groups	11603.41	83	139.80	

Weighted mean difference, rows: 6.58. F_{99} (1,83) = 6.95.

Table 6

Parent Adjustment, Independent Parents Only, by High or Low Role-taking Accuracy

	F-S	F-D	F-IS	F-ID	M-S	M-D	M-IS	M-ID	Row*
High									
M	54.00	62.17	51.83	52.40	59.75	58.14	40.67	55.25	55.13
N	5	6	6	5	4	7	3	4	40
Low									
M	64.00	61.67	49.20	48.33	57.25	55.33	39.17	51.83	53.24
N	5	6	5	6	8	3	6	6	45

*Preliminary analysis of variance indicated no statistically significant difference between row means appears in this table.

(Table 3), dependent parents (Table 5), and low-agreement parents (Table 7), accurate role-taking is accompanied by comparatively poor adjustment. In each of these cases, row differences are statistically significant. For nontraditional parents (Table 4), independent parents (Table 6), and high-agreement parents (Table 8) row differences are *reversed*—i.e., the mean adjustment scores for accurate role-takers are higher than they are for inaccurate role-takers, although only in the case of the nontraditional parents is the difference significant, and in one case (Table 8) the row difference is extremely slight. It should be noted, however, that in the independent parent table (Table 6), in seven of the eight relationship cate-

Table 7

Parent Adjustment, Low-agreement Parents Only, by High or Low Role-taking Accuracy

	F-S	F-D	F-IS	F-ID	M-S	M-D	M-IS	M-ID	Row
High									
M	56.40	53.60	52.33	41.50	60.80	61.43	49.00	51.86	53.37
N	5	5	6	6	5	7	5	7	46
Low									
M	60.00	63.33	49.87	57.40	64.00	65.40	51.80	63.60	59.32
N	7	6	7	5	7	5	5	5	47

Completed Analysis of Variance

	Sums of Squares	d.f.	Mean Square	F
Columns	2484.87	7	354.98	2.52
Rows	793.71	1	793.71	5.63
Interaction	710.24	7	101.46	
Within groups	10848.37	77	140.89	

Weighted mean difference, rows: 5.89. F_{95} (1,77) = 3.97.

Table 8

Parent Adjustment, High-agreement Parents Only, by High or Low Role-taking Accuracy

	F-S	F-D	F-IS	F-ID	M-S	M-D	M-IS	M-ID	Row*
High									
M	56.00	66.60	56.17	55.83	60.20	66.33	53.00	64.50	59.40
N	6	5	6	6	5	6	7	6	47
Low									
M	59.60	64.86	62.00	60.83	56.50	57.20	57.00	52.40	58.95
N	5	7	4	6	6	5	6	5	44

*Preliminary analysis of variance indicated no statistically significant differences between row means appears in this table.

gories there are higher mean adjustment scores in the accurate role-taker cells; one large "reversal" in the F-S category probably accounts for the absence of statistically significant results. There is, it may also be noted, no particular consistency in the direction of the row differences in the high-agreement parents table (Table 8).

In over-all terms, the evidence clearly supports the hypothesis that vulnerability increases the likelihood of blocks to communication.

To return to our point of departure, the presumed adjustive consequences of knowledge of others: our findings clearly call into question any easy assumption on this score. Rather, they point to the conclusion that, at least under certain circumstances, such knowledge is maladjustive. Further, these findings serve to emphasize the lack of clarity in interpretations of Mead's social psychological theory. It may still be true, as Mead held, that the process of adapting one's behavior to others with whom one is socially implicated is dependent on role-taking.[9] That one will always become better adjusted, in the sense of happier or more satisfied, through role-taking must, on the basis of these findings, be doubted.

The reverse side of this coin should be noted. The assertion that knowledge is necessarily adjustive cannot be defended; it is highly probable that the unqualified assertion that ignorance is adjustive is equally invalid.

[9] Recently, Steiner (23) has questioned the generality of this assertion, noting that empirical evidence with regard to the propositions that accurate social perceptions are responsible for interpersonal competence and for group efficiency is contradictory. His analysis of assumptions concerning collective activity leads him to conclude that these propositions will hold when "(a) group members are motivated to cooperate; (b) the accurately perceived qualities are relevant to the activities of the group; (c) members are free to alter their own behaviors in response to their perceptions of other members; and (d) the behavioral changes which are a consequence of accurate social perceptions are the kinds which produce a more thoroughly integrated dyadic system" (23, p. 273).

The problem, now, is to specify further the conditions under which knowledge or ignorance is adjustive or maladjustive.[10]

References

1. Becker, H.S., "The Professional Dance Musician and His Audience," *American Journal of Sociology,* 1951, 57, 136-144.
2. Borden, R., "The Use of Psychodrama in an Institution for Delinquent Girls," *Sociometry,* 1940, 3, 81-90.
3. Chapman, E.A., "Role-Playing in a Cooperative Retail Training Class," *Occupations,* 1951, 29, 358-359.
4. Coleman, W., "Role-Playing as an Instructional Aid," *Journal of Educational Psychology,* 1938, 39, 427-435.
5. Coutu, W., *Emergent Human Behavior: A Symbolic Field Interpretation,* New York: Knopf, 1949.
6. Cronbach, L.J., "Processes Affecting Scores on 'Understanding of Others' and 'Assumed Similarity,'" *Psychological Bulletin,* 1955, 52, 177-193.
7. Curran, F.J., "The Drama as a Therapeutic Measure in Adolescents," *American Journal of Orthopsychiatry,* 1939, 9, 215-232.
8. Davis, K., "The Application of Social Science to Personal Relations," *American Sociological Review,* 1936, 1, 236-247.
9. Dymond, R.F., *Empathic Ability: an Exploratory Study,* Ph.D. dissertation, Cornell University, 1949.
10. Foote, N.N., and L.S. Cottrell, Jr., *Identity and Interpersonal Competence,* Chicago: University of Chicago Press, 1955.
11. French, J.R.P., "Role-Playing as a Method of Training Foremen," *Group Psychotherapy,* New York: Beacon House, 1945.
12. Gage, N.L. and L.J. Cronbach, "Conceptual and Methodological Problems in Interpersonal Perception," *Psychological Review,* 1955, 62, 411-422.
13. Hastorf, A.H., and I.E. Bender, "A Caution Respecting Measurement of Empathic Ability," *Journal of Abnormal and Social Psychology,* 1952, 47, 574-576.
14. Huffman, P.E., "Authoritarian Personality and Family Ideology," M.A. thesis, Western Reserve University, 1950.
15. Kay, L.W. "Role-Playing as a Teaching Aid," *Sociometry,* 1946, 9, 263-274.
16. Lindesmith, A.R., and A.L. Strauss, *Social Psychology,* New York: Dryden, 1949.
17. Liveright, A.A., "Role-Playing in Leadership Training," *Personnel Journal,* 1951, 29, 412-416.
18. Mead, G.H., *Mind, Self, and Society,* Chicago: University of Chicago

[10] For materials suggestive of further conditions, see (25).

Press, 1934.

19. Moore, W.E., and M.M. Tumin, "Some Social Functions of Ignorance," *American Sociological Review,* 1949, 14, 787-795.
20. Moreno, J.L., "Psychodramatic Treatment of Marriage Problems," *Sociometry,* 1940, 3, 1-23.
21. Moreno, J.L., "Psychodramatic Treatment of Psychoses," *Sociometry,* 1940, 3, 115-132.
22. Newcomb, T.M., "Autistic Hostility and Social Reality," *Human Relations,* 1947, 1, 69-86.
23. Steiner, I.D., "Interpersonal Behavior as Influenced by Accuracy of Social Perception," *Psychological Review,* 1955, 62, 268-274.
24. Stryker, S., "The Adjustment of Married Offspring to Their Parents," *American Sociological Review,* 1955, 20, 149-154.
25. Stryker, S., "Relationships of Married Offspring and Parent: A Test of Mead's Theory," *American Journal of Sociology,* 1956, 62, 308-319.
26. Sullivan, H.S., *The Interpersonal Theory of Psychiatry,* New York: Norton, 1953.
27. Trendley, M.B., "Psychodrama and Social Case Work" *Sociometry,* 1944, 7, 169-177.
28. Whyte, W.F., "The Social Structure of a Restaurant," *American Journal of Sociology,* 1949, 54, 302-310.
29. Williams, R., *American Society: A Sociological Interpretation,* New York: Knopf, 1951.

Selected Bibliography
Part V, Research Implications and Applications

Becker, Howard S., *The Outsiders* (Glencoe: Free Press, 1963), pp. 1-18.
Shows how responses to deviation shape deviant behavior. This reference should be compared with the one by Lemert, below.

Brookover, Wilbur B., Thomas, Shailer, and Paterson, Ann, "Self-Concept of Ability and School Achievement," *Sociology of Education,* 37 (Spring, 1964), pp. 271-278.
Research relating self and role theory to classroom performance.

Cohen, Albert K., "The Sociology of the Deviant Act," *American Sociological Review,* 30 (February 1965), pp. 5-14.
An effort to integrate anomie theory with Meadian role theory.

Deutscher, Irwin, "Words and Deeds: Social Science and Social Policy," *Social Problems,* 13 (Winter 1966), pp. 235-254.
A careful consideration of the implications of research findings on inconsistencies between verbalized attitudes and overt behavior. Applies the perspective of symbolic interactionism in explaining the findings.

Dick, Harry R., "The Office Worker: Attitudes toward Self, Labor and Management," *Sociological Quarterly,* 3 (January 1962), pp. 45-56.
Study of 141 office girls, showing how white-collar workers see themselves in relationship to labor and management.

Elkin, Frederick, *The Child and Society* (New York: Random House, 1960), pp. 25-30.
Describes the role of significant others in early socialization.

Haskell, Martin R., "Toward a Reference Group Theory of Juvenile Delinquency," *Social Problems,* 8 (Winter 1960-61), pp. 220-230.
Exemplifies a growing tendency to incorporate symbolic interactionism into theories of delinquent and criminal behavior.

Lemert, Edwin M., *Social Pathology* (New York: McGraw-Hill, 1951), pp. 75-78.
Introduces the concept "secondary deviation" to describe how the reactions of others reinforce the individual's deviance.

McPartland, Thomas S., and Cumming, John H., "Self-Conception, Social Class, and Mental Health," *Human Organization,* 17 (Fall, 1958), pp. 24-29.
Compares the self-conceptions of 173 normal adults and 120 mental patients and finds that "self-conceptions provide a link which relates social class origin to behavior pathology."

Stewart, Robert L. and Vernon, Glenn M., "Four Correlates of Empathy in the Dating Situation," *Sociology and Social Research,* 43 (March-April 1959), pp. 279-285.

A processual conception of empathy is tested on 52 dating couples.

Turner, Ralph H., "Self and Other in Moral Judgment," *American Sociological Review,* 19 (June 1954), pp. 249-259.

Responses of 88 individuals and their friends toward the respondent's hypothetical involvement in a theft situation.

Vercors (pseudonym), *You Shall Know Them* (New York: Pocket Books, Inc., 1955).

A novel that raises the question, "What are the attributes which most clearly distinguish man from other living forms?"

Waisanen, Fred B., "Self-Attitudes and Performance Expectations," *Sociological Quarterly,* 3 (July 1962), pp. 208-219.

Replication of a study on the relationship between self-attitudes and aspirations.

Conclusion

A brief summary and assessment of symbolic interactionism may help to tie things together. Listed below are the basic theoretical propositions of the symbolic interactionist, which have been presented, both explicitly and implicitly, at various points in this book.

1. Mind, self, and society are most usefully viewed as processes of human and interhuman conduct.
2. Language is the mechanism for the rise of mind and self.
3. Mind is an importation of the social process, that is, of interaction within the individual.
4. Human beings construct their behavior in the course of its execution, rather than responding mechanically to either external stimuli or such internal "forces" as drives, needs, or motives.
5. Human conduct is carried on primarily by the defining of situations in which one acts.
6. The socialization of the human being both enmeshes him in society and frees him from society. The individual with a self is not passive but can employ his self in an interaction which may result in behavior divergent from group definitions.

Among the major adverse criticisms leveled at symbolic-interaction theory have been (1) the indeterminism of many of its exponents, (2) its presumed inapplicability to broad, societal phenomena, (3) its neglect of the emotional dimension in human conduct, (4) its failure to come to grips with the unconscious, and (5) the limited researchability of some of its concepts.

1. Viewing human behavior in terms of the interaction between the "I" and the "Me" aspects of self, Mead's closest followers build into such behavior an unpredictable, indeterminate dimension. For some, this interaction is the fundamental source of innovation in society. Exponents of the "Iowa School," however, reject the "I" (indeterminism in human conduct) and the explanation of social innovation on the basis of the emergent, creative element in "I" - "Me" interaction.

2. In the running debate between advocates of symbolic interactionism and those of structural-functionalism, each side refers to the putative shortcomings of the other relative to level or scope of

analysis. Thus the former perspective is held to be limited to such microsociological phenomena as intra-and interpersonal relations, while the latter is presumed to apply only to such macrosociological phenomena as institutional and societal patterns. At the same time, adherents of each theory reject the restrictions in scope placed upon their theory by their opposite numbers.[1] Like so many other controversies in sociology and social psychology, this one still awaits a crucial test and resolution.

3. Mead's presentation of his major ideas overlooked the role of emotional elements in human behavior and interaction. Modern symbolic interactionists have not significantly remedied this omission. The affective aspects of the self and of personal relationships are so thoroughly ignored, by all but a few writers, as to suggest an unacceptable image of man as purely rational.

4. Closely related to the preceding stricture is another that, similarly, concerns scanting of the irrational aspect in man. It is difficult to find a considered discussion of the idea of the "unconscious" in the writings of symbolic interactionists. The few references we do find tend to renounce the concept without substituting adequate explanatory principles.

5. It is with regard to its heuristic value that most critics of symbolic interactionism believe themselves to be on firmest ground.[2] The paucity of significant research generated by the theory is especially reflected in Part II, "Society," and Part IV, "Mind," in this book. Contributing to this deficiency is the vague, "intuitive" character of various concepts of Mead's, some of which have not yet been revised or discarded. "Impulse," "meaning," the "I," "objects," "images," and other ambiguous and inconsistently used concepts persist in substantially the same non-operationalized form in which Mead used them.

In the face of the criticisms of symbolic interactionism, why has this frame of reference commended itself to most sociologically-oriented social psychologists? The answer to this question probably lies in the fact that symbolic interactionism clearly represents the most *sociological* of social psychologies. Adopting a distinctly sociological perspective, it directs attention to the social derivation of man's unique attributes; presents mind and self as society in microcosm; describes how the members of any human group develop and form a common world; illuminates the character of human interaction by showing that human

[1] See Helmut R. Wagner, "Displacement of Scope: A Problem of the Relationships between Small-Scale and Large-Scale Sociological Theories," *The American Journal of Sociology,* LXIX (May 1964), pp. 571-584.

[2] For a recent example of such criticism, see Robert F. Bales, "Comment on Herbert Blumer's Paper," *The American Journal of Sociology,* LXXI (March 1966), pp. 545-547.

beings *share* one another's behavior instead of merely responding to each other's overt behavior; and, in numerous other ways, implicates the individual with society and society with the individual.

The perspective of symbolic interactionism is not a finished product. As is true of other current social-psychological theories, much further revision and testing is needed. Meanwhile, it is our hope that the present volume will provoke such revision and testing.

INDEX